The Paradox of Two Sudans

THE PARADOX OF TWO SUDANS

THE CPA AND THE ROAD TO PARTITION

Mansour Khalid

AFRICA WORLD PRESS
TRENTON | LONDON | NEW DELHI | CAPE TOWN | NAIROBI | ADDIS ABABA | ASMARA | IBADAN

AFRICA WORLD PRESS
541 West Ingham Avenue | Suite B
Trenton, New Jersey 08638

Book design: Lemlem Taddese
Cover design: Ramez Elias
Cover pictures: Courtesy of Issam Abdel Hafiez

Library of Congress Cataloging-in-Publication Data

Khalid, Mansur, 1931- author.
  The paradox of two Sudans : the CPA and the road to partition / Mansour Khalid.
      pages cm
  Includes bibliographical references and index.
  ISBN 978-1-56902-451-5 (pb : alk. paper)
  1. Sudan--History--Civil War, 1983-2005--Peace. 2. Sudan--Politics and government--1985- 3. South Sudan--Politics and government--2005-2011. 4. South Sudan--Politics and government--2011- 5. Partition, Territorial. I. Title.
  DT157.673.K485 2015
  962.4043--dc23

                          2015023233

THE INSTITUTE
FOR COMPARATIVE
MODERNITIES

Dedication

In memory of John Garang de Mabior:
the political leader who made our lives sublime,
the liberation fighter who struggled for the people's cause
with the courage of the damned, and
the starry-eyed political thinker whose vision left indelible
marks on the sands of time.

John Garang with a child (Courtesy of Issam Abdel Hafiez)

Table of Contents

■ ■ ■ ■ ■ ■ ■ ■ ■ ■ ■ ■ ■ ■ ❖ ■ ■ ■ ■ ■ ■ ■ ■ ■ ■ ■ ■ ■ ■ ■

List of Illustrations

Figures

Maps

Abbreviations

■■■■■■■■■■■■■■■❖■■■■■■■■■■■■■■

ABC	Abyei Boundary Commission
ADSC	All Darfur Stakeholders Conference
AMIS	African Union Mission in Sudan
AU	African Union
AUHIP	African Union High-Level Implementation Panel on Sudan
AUPSC	African Union Peace and Security Council
COMESA	Common Market for Eastern and Southern Africa
CPA	Comprehensive Peace Agreement
CPPCG	Convention on the Prevention and Punishments of Genocide (1948)
DLF	Darfur Liberation Front
DPA	Darfur Peace Agreement
DRA	Darfur Regional Authority
DUP	Democratic Unionists Party
ECOSOC	UN Economic and Social Council
FFAMC	Fiscal and Financial Allocation and Monitoring Commission
GOS	Government of Sudan
GOSS	Government of South Sudan
ICC	International Criminal Court
ICJ	International Court of Justice
ICTY	International Criminal Tribunal for Yugoslavia
IDP	Internally displaced persons
IGAD	Intergovernmental Authority on Development
IRIN	Integrated Regional Information Network (United Nations)
JAM	Joint Assessment Mission
JEM	Justice and Equality Movement
JIUs	Joint Integrated Units
LJM	Liberation and Justice Movement

LRA	Lord's Resistance Army
MDTF	Multi-Donor Trust Fund
NBI	Nile Basin Initiative
NCP	National Congress Party
NDA	National Democratic Alliance (umbrella opposition groups against the NCP 1995-2005)
NIF	National Islamic Front
OAG	Other armed group
OAU	Organization of African Unity
OLS	Operation Lifeline Sudan
PCP	Popular Congress Party
PDF	Popular Defense Force
RTC	Round Table Conference (1965)
SAF	Sudan Armed Forces
SCP	Sudan Communist Party
SLM/A	Sudan Liberation Movement/Army
SPLM/A	Sudan People's Liberation Movement/Army
SPLM/N	Sudan People's Liberation Movement, North
TMC	Transitional Military Council
UMMA	National Umma Party
UNAMIS	United Nations Mission in Sudan
UNICEF	United Nations International Children's Emergency Fund
UNSC	United Nations Security Council
USAID	United States Agency for International Development
WFP	World Food Program

Foreword

■■■■■■■■■■■■■■❖■■■■■■■■■■■■■■

President Thabo Mbeki

There is perhaps no better Sudanese than Mansour Khalid to present an objective assessment relating to the negotiation and implementation of the Sudan Comprehensive Peace Agreement (CPA) signed in January 2005.

One only has to look at the Contents page of this book, which lists twelve chapters, as well as a Preface, an Introduction and a Conclusion, to understand how comprehensive it is.

Mansour Khalid is eminently qualified to report and comment on the matters covered in this book because he has been at the centre of the protracted conflict in Sudan for many decades.

He has been involved in this conflict as an honest Sudanese and African patriot, at all times driven not by selfish and myopic interest but by the larger objective to serve the fundamental interests of the all the Sudanese people, both North and South.

In addition, he has brought into a reflection on all these matters his enormous intellect, and therefore his ability to serve as an objective commentator, even as he was also an activist in the protracted internal conflict which has afflicted Sudan even before its independence.

Personally I do not know of any better summary of the intentions and hopes that attended the signing of the CPA than what Mansour Khalid has written in this book.

I refer here to this particular statement by Mansour Khalid:

"The CPA, in addition to putting an end to the destructive fury of war in south Sudan, had also constructed a high way that was to lead Sudan to permanent peace, sustainable development and national unity in diversity. To achieve these ends, it envisioned the elimination of historical injustices, rationalization of the arthritic administration of the country and creation of public institutions and promulgation of national laws to ensure good governance. The interlocking dynamics of democracy, justice and equitable development were hoped to make the balance of probability in favour of faithful implementation of an agreement that would guarantee for Sudan a level of peace and political stability it had never enjoyed since independence. That proved not to be the case."

In this statement Mansour Khalid identifies in a very precise manner the challenges the Sudanese leadership and people had to address to end the protracted Sudanese crisis.

In this book he explains in a convincing manner how the CPA was so constructed that it would serve as a driving force to achieve the objectives he mentioned in the paragraph I have cited.

In reality, when he writes that "That proved not to be the case," he was making the statement that the CPA failed in its purposes and therefore that, tragically, Sudan would remain mired in its contradictions and conflicts.

The media published an article I wrote immediately after the independence of South Sudan on July 9, 2011. In this article I said:

> "(When the CPA was signed)…a difficult choice had to be made, either to continue the war to maintain the forced integrity of Sudan, or to divide it into two to achieve peace and create the possibility for a new beginning in terms of the relations between the peoples of North and South Sudan.
>
> "As they signed the Comprehensive Peace Agreement (CPA) in 2005, which ended the North-South civil war, and conscious of their historic responsibility, the Sudanese leaders gave themselves the task to use the period January 2005 to January 2011 to make the unity of Sudan attractive."
>
> "In the end, as the people of South Sudan voted overwhelmingly in January 2011 in favour of secession, the Sudanese leaders had to admit that they had failed 'to make unity attractive'."

My comments addressed the specific challenge of the danger of the fragmentation of the African state of Sudan, which would result from the failure to attend exactly to the various issues raised by Mansour Khalid.

In almost all respects Sudan, both as one and two countries, represents a concentrated microcosm of 'the African problem.'

As indicated by Mansour Khalid, the CPA provided the lodestar not only for the solution of the challenges of Sudan. Its faithful and successful implementation would also have positioned Sudan as an exemplar in terms of helping our Continent to address its urgent tasks, and therefore 'the African problem.'

It is for this reason that this book is both very timely and requires close study especially by all Africans who are genuinely interested not only in a sustained better life for the peoples of Sudan and South Sudan, but also in the renaissance of our Continent.

In this regard all of us as Africans must internalise this into our thinking and strategizing, that Sudan and South Sudan are destined to continue playing an important role in terms of helping to determine the future of our Continent.

The rigorous, passionate but objective analysis by Mansour Khalid contained in this book tells a story which, in a real sense, can and should serve as an important manual to help guide all of us as we continue to engage the struggle for the renewal of our dear Continent.

This is a book that we must not only read, but which we must study.

Thabo Mbeki,
January 2013

Preface

■■■■■■■■■■■■■■■■■■■❖■■■■■■■■■■■■■■■■■

Civil war in Sudan has a long history; its genesis goes back to the 1950s. That war has been more pervasive than what many commentators would have us believe, or what many Sudanese (in the north and south) have continued to assume. While southern Sudan had been the main theater of civil war, ominous flashpoints were evident all over the peripheral regions of the country. Those flashpoints were accidents waiting to occur as future developments in the Nuba Mountains, southern Blue Nile, Abyei, and most recently in Darfur, amply proved. Rather than objectively analyzing the root causes of the country's dawning problems and facing them head-on, the ruling class and the majority of political analysts in the north opted for concealment, double talk, and spin politics. None of these wiles had done these groups, or the Sudan, any good.

In the case of southern Sudan, war had spiraled to an infernal conflagration as a result of myriad political, economic, and social causes with deep cultural undercurrents. The failure of Khartoum rulers and public opinion formulators to make of the country's multiple diversities a source of strength rather than a begetter of discord, made conflict inevitable and turned Sudan into an illusory country. Countries can never be forced into being; they are born out of the coexistence of people on the basis of fellowship—universal compassion, tolerance, and mutual recognition.

That failure brought about a progressive escalation in the political demands of southern Sudanese, beginning with calls in 1955–1956 for a united federal Sudan made of two entities (north and south), to demands in 1965 for a federal system of rule for the whole country, to a settlement in 1972 based on regional autonomy for southern Sudan within a united country (which lasted up to 1985), and ultimately, to demands by southern Sudanese political elites of all stripes for the exercise by the people of that country of the right to self-determination, including an option to secede. During all this time national leaders at the center of power failed to see the interrelationship between their failure to respond positively to well-grounded demands by southern Sudanese and the build-up of anger and frustration in southern Sudan. Eventually, frustration and hopelessness led to an intensive war and calls for secession. Why was it then possible in 2005 for the government of Sudan and the Sudan People's Liberation Movement (SPLM) to adopt Sudan's Comprehensive Peace Agreement (CPA) in order to resolve problems that had tormented the country for almost 50 years?

Response to this question requires a historical contextualization of conflict in Sudan, and for that reason, the first chapter of the book shall be dedicated to political conditions that prevailed in the country since the declaration of its independence on January 1, 1956. As Sudan's history had a contorted context, it would be adequate to recount political developments that occurred, and conditions that ensued therefrom, in the course of the first decade of independence. During that decade it became increasingly obvious that the more those conditions prevailed, the worse the situation would become. Flashbacks to that era shall also be made as the book traces the evolution of peace negotiations from their inception in July 2001 until their denouement in January 2005, with a view to analyzing factors that had made possible an agreement that could have been achieved since Sudan's independence but was dodged by all Sudanese national governments, either as a result of political indecision or moral evasion. To be sure, there is abundant contemporary literature on this period to which the reader may wish to refer.[1]

At the personal level, the author was part of the Sudan government's delegation during the rule of President Gaafar Mohamed el-Nimeiri (1969– 1984), which had negotiated and concluded the first political agreement that had helped end Sudan's first civil war, which intermittently lasted for 17 years (1955–1972). The Addis Ababa Accord (as it was then called) was mediated by Emperor Haile Selassie of Ethiopia, the World Council of Churches in Geneva, and the Nairobi-based All Africa Conference of Churches.[2] It was ratified at Addis Ababa on February 27, 1972 by Colonel Joseph Lagu, on behalf of the South Sudan Liberation Movement (SSLM) and the Sudan government, and by the author, who ranked second to the leader of the delegation, Vice President Abel Alier. On March 12, Sudan's first civil war, for all intents and purposes, ceased, and the agreement lasted for 11 years (1972– 1983). In 1983, war flared up and was again led by a "rebel" hailing from Southern Sudan but espousing a national agenda for change. This leader, John Garang de Mabior, changed the character of Sudan's civil war as well as north/south politics like no other Sudanese politician. In effect, for the two decades that ensued after the emergence of the SPLM at the national political scene, Garang not only catalyzed change in the country, but also effectively became its prime mover. The veracity of this assumption shall be examined in the different chapters of the book.

By design, not circumstance, the author decided to band together with Garang and his party: Sudan People's Liberation Movement (SPLM). In time, the author became senior political advisor to Garang, the SPLM chairman, from 1987 to his death in 2005 and continued to play that role with Garang's successor, Salva Kiir Mayardit. To the chagrin of many of his friends in north Sudan, the author came to the conclusion that the political ills of the country would never be set to rights as long as Khartoum, the fulcrum of power in the country, remained the same. Nimeiri, the only northern ruler who succeeded in putting an end to the 17 year war, had no qualms about tearing to shreds the peace agreement he had concluded and was eulogised for doing so by the whole of Africa; this is enough testimony that the author's decision was not based solely on premonitions, but on personal experience and empirically confirmed evidence.

Garang's ideas, however, blazed their way across Sudan's political landscape. The novelty of his articulation of the Sudanese crisis drove many northern Sudanese intellectuals to his vision. Nevertheless, whether for lack of moral courage to challenge received wisdom, or because they estimated that affinities based on kinship were higher than commitment to universal values of justice, a large sector of this *avant-garde* class was not willing to suffer for its beliefs, and Sudan became the poorer for it. If those elite had fully understood Garang's ideals, things would have radically changed in Sudan. In the words of Bengali poet and thinker Rabindraneth Tagore, "It is my conviction that my countrymen will truly gain their India by fighting against the education which teaches them that a country is greater than the ideals of humanity."[3] For these reasons, while endeavoring to fully document the events narrated in this book, the author shall retrieve from past events and personal experiences causes, or historical origins, of the present agonies of Sudan. The author's aim is to illuminate the events through private information garnered either from his own peacemaking efforts or from his involvement in the CPA negotiations as advisor to the SPLM negotiating team and its leader.

Within this context, the author shall also essay to give the reader insight into the personality of Garang as an intellectual thinker, an intrepid warrior, and a compelling negotiator with a masterly grasp of his brief. Without such qualities, a peace agreement as comprehensive and far-reaching as the CPA would never have been achieved. The role Garang played in steering the negotiations, the analytical intelligence that enabled him to separate the chaff from the grain, as well as his ability to convincingly put forward his ideas, contributed immensely to results that could not have otherwise been attained. Hence, without verging into the anecdotal, references to remarks by Garang relating to events during the negotiations, or commentaries he made on major developments during that process, are interwoven into the author's account and analysis.

Equally, the manner in which the leaders of the government of Sudan and the SPLM reacted to each other during the negotiations is highlighted in the book. In any peace negotiations, the human chemistry of the interlocutors, especially in the way they relate to each other, inexorably plays a determinant role in the success or failure of negotiations. For the same reason, the author follows the rise of Garang's deputy, Salva Kiir Mayardit, to the SPLM leadership after the untimely demise of Garang, because responsibility for the CPA implementation had squarely fallen on his shoulders. John Garang, the multifaceted military, political, diplomatic, and academic man, and Salva Kiir, the soldier's soldier who kept away from the limelight even when he was thrust into it by high profile positions, were obviously not two peas in a pod. Still, they proved to be complementary during the struggle in more than one way, as the book will demonstrate. After Garang's death, the presumptive inadequacies of Kiir as Garang's deputy proved to be his greatest assets, in particular, his inclinations to continually seek to broaden the base of consultation and his deference to the views of others, including those whom Garang would not have touched with a 20-foot pole. Although some of the SPLM senior cadres were piqued by his style of management, Kiir was able, in a well-calculated manner, to keep the SPLM united and to ensure that the referendum on self-determination was reached peacefully.

This book, however, chiefly focuses on developments that led to the conclusion of the CPA in the period 1990–2005, including events that ensued after the National Islamic Front (NIF) usurped power on June 30, 1989. I have two reasons for singling out this period. First, the NIF brought Sudanese contradictions and polarization to their extreme. Second, it was this politically immoderate party that, to the surprise of many, was the first northern party in government to recognize the country's multiple diversities. Without that recognition, it would not have been able to properly analyze the root cause of Sudan's long-lasting crisis. As one analyst observed, "No other regime in Sudan's history has been able to come up with a political framework to match its practicality, maturity and vision."[4] Whether that "vision" and "maturity" had remained alive in the course of CPA implementation was answered by the National Congress Party's reluctance to, or complacency about, being faithful to the agreement it had taken pride in concluding.

In essence, the confluence of conditions that allowed for a negotiated settlement of the 21-year war between the government of Sudan and the SPLM/A arose, above all, *within* Sudan. Remarks by some commentators that the CPA could not have been reached without coaxing—or, indeed, as some contended, arm-twisting—by external mediators, was only a half-truth. At numerous times, remarks disparaging the peace agreement came from northern Sudanese political leaders who failed to put an end to Sudan's conflict when they were in power, as well as from a section of northern Sudan's media who never ceased to find justification for the political and intellectual ineptitude of those leaders. Thus, without underestimating the invaluable contribution of mediators and international partners in providing diplomatic, technical, and material support to the peace process as well as interventions at critical moments to mediate differences between the negotiating parties, the internal factors should never have been sold short. Those internal factors arose, on the one side, within the dynamics of the conflict inside and between the warring parties and in the country's broader polity. It was this range of critical internal conditions that enabled external engagement to support, facilitate, conciliate, and even exert pressure upon the negotiators to end the civil war. Hence, in the last phase of the peacemaking process, numerous mediators attempted to resolve Sudan's spun-out conflict, including the United States, the United Kingdom, Kenya, Nigeria, Norway, Uganda, South Africa, and Egypt, as well as the Vatican and the World Council of Churches, who were approached by Khartoum's Islamist regime to intervene between the warring parties.[5]

In effect, international interest in Sudan's conflict had no parallel in other conflict-resolution efforts. One reason for such interest might have been the conflict's long duration. Sudan's civil war had been the longest conflict in Africa, spasmodically flaring up between 1955 and 1972 and vigorously between 1983 and 2005. Moreover, the geographic space that became the theater of war comprised southern Sudan (an area as large as France) in addition to South Kordofan and Blue Nile, areas of 79.470 square kilometers and 45.844 square kilometres, respectively. That war also extended to eastern Sudan in the mid-1990s, not to mention the conflict in Darfur, which while not a direct adjunct to the civil war, was still inspired and supported by the SPLM/A. The extension of war to such a vast geographic space generated horrendous losses of life and displacement of people in a manner that heightened the world's concern for the plight of the Sudanese. Only in Sudan's second civil war (1983–2005) over two million people were reported to have perished directly or indirectly because of war; nearly one million people went into refuge in neighboring countries, and four to five million people were internally displaced. Furthermore, the humanitarian crisis engendered by that war reached such grisly levels that international and regional organizations, human rights groups, and humanitarian agencies could not turn a deaf ear.

War also affected, directly or indirectly, neighboring and distant countries. While the largest number of southern Sudanese refugees sought sanctuary in Ethiopia, Kenya, Egypt, and Uganda, Sudanese political and economic refugees inundated countries like Australia, Canada, and the United States seeking safe haven or a better livelihood. In addition, the flirtation of the NIF government with radical Islamist groups, especially those labelled by the United States as terrorist organizations, brought in their wake other anxieties, notably after the attacks on the United States on September 11, 2001 by one of those groups. Lastly, Sudan's new oil wealth had a great effect on the attitude of some European and Asian countries towards Sudan and its internal crisis. Nevertheless, efforts by neighboring states to bring peace to Sudan, especially intervention by the countries comprising the Intergovernmental Authority on Development (IGAD),[6] provided the peacemaking process with a much-needed stimulus. These countries played a decisive role in the acceleration of peacemaking and the harmonization of outside intercessions aimed at bringing the warring parties together. With thousands of Sudanese refugees and war-displaced persons drifting into their countries, IGAD leaders became increasingly alarmed by Sudan's unending conflict. Interestingly, the invitation to IGAD to be involved in the conflict came from President Bashir, during the IGAD summit held in 1993 at Addis Ababa.

Against this backdrop, attempts to resolve Sudan's conflict had never been linear. Direct negotiations between the parties in the last phase of the peacemaking process could not have happened without earlier, parallel, indirect talks; proximity talks; and seminars and workshops organized by peace institutes with a view to enabling the parties to get to the bottom of their disagreements. In a previous work on the last phase of Sudan's war, the author wrote: "What sort of peacemaking has Sudan tried not; mediation, direct negotiations between belligerents, indirect talks through the good offices of mutual friends...intellectual probing of conflictual issues in international fora."[7] Those efforts, despite worthy achievements in the humanitarian field, did not succeed in bringing war to its finale; only in the first decade of the third millennium (2002–2005) did negotiations give hope to a possible resolution of Sudan's protracted conflict.

Success in the last phase of negotiations, however, would not have been possible without the occurrence of two events: the stepping up of IGAD's peace efforts and a crucial decision taken by IGAD mediators. In their first two years of mediation, IGAD peacemaking efforts proceeded by fits and starts due to administrative inadequacies as well as maneuvers by some neighboring countries to derail the process because it conflicted with their interests in Sudan. Nonetheless, at the behest of the leaders of Eritrea and Ethiopia, IGAD mediators made a momentous decision on July 20, 1994, that radically changed the direction of the peacemaking process. President Isayas Afewerki of Eritrea and Prime Minister Meles Zinawi of Ethiopia decided that without operational goals for the negotiations, it would be well-nigh impossible to pin down the parties to unambiguous choices or give content and coherence to the negotiations. As a result, the two leaders penned what came to be known as the IGAD Declaration of Principles (DOP), which was eventually issued in the name of the IGAD Assembly of Heads of State and Government.

The Declaration of Principles was meant to establish clear points of reference that would guide the negotiations and methodologically identify goals, especially on the interrelated issues of the unity of Sudan, granting self-determination to the people of southern Sudan, and the relation between religion and state. The ultimate aim of the mediators was to put an end to the conflict and lay down conditions for the unity of Sudan in a way that was winsome to southern Sudanese and agreeable to NIF and the government of Sudan. To this end they proposed that: "Any comprehensive resolution of the Sudan conflict requires that all parties to the conflict fully accept and commit themselves to the position that:

1.1 The history and nature of the Sudan conflict demonstrate that a military solution cannot bring lasting peace and stability to the country.

1.2 A peaceful and just political solution must be the common objective of the parties to the conflict.

2. The right of self-determination of the people of south Sudan to determine their future status through a referendum must be affirmed.

3. Maintaining unity of the Sudan must be given priority by all parties provided that the following principles are established in the political, legal, economic, and social framework of the country:

3.1 Sudan is a multi-racial, multi-ethnic, multi-religious, and multi-cultural society. Full recognition and accommodation of these diversities must be affirmed.

3.2 Complete political and social equalities of all peoples in the Sudan must be guaranteed by law.

3.3 Extensive rights of self-determination on the basis of federation, autonomy, etc., to the various peoples of the Sudan must be affirmed.

3.4 A secular and democratic state must be established in the Sudan. Freedom of belief and worship and religious practice shall be guaranteed in full to all Sudanese citizens. State and religion shall be separated. The basis of personal and family laws can be religion and customs.

3.5 Appropriate and fair sharing of wealth among the various people of the Sudan must be realized.

3.6 Human rights as internationally recognized shall form part of this arrangement and shall be embodied in constitution.

3.7 The Independence of the Judiciary shall be enshrined in the constitution and laws of the Sudan.

4. In the absence of agreement on the above principles referred to in 3.1 to 3.7, the respective people will have the option of determining their future including independence through a referendum."[8]

Failing to accept those principles, the IGAD mediators concluded that the government of Sudan should defer to granting the people of southern Sudan the right to self-determination with no option barred, including secession.

In the manner it was proposed, the Declaration of Principles was a heavy dose for the NIF to swallow; neither could it as a self-styled Islamic regime recognize secularism, nor would it envisage a process of self-determination that might lead to the secession of southern Sudan. Needless to say, this formula was far from anything President Bashir had bargained for when he invited the IGAD in 1993 to mediate in the Sudan conflict. Having been manifestly unhappy with the Declaration of Principles, the NIF struggled to writhe free of it by going around the world on a shopping spree for mediators other than IGAD, even though it was President Bashir himself who willingly invited that organization to intervene in Sudan's conflict. That unrestrained bout took the government to South Africa, Egypt, Libya, Malaysia, Norway, and the World Council of Churches, among others. In all those endeavors, the NIF put at the top of its priorities the establishment of not only a temporary cessation of hostilities during the peace talks, but also a permanent cease-fire between the combatants. On its side, the SPLM fervently argued that any permanent cease-fire would only come as the culmination of, not a starting point to, peace talks. It also tenaciously pitched its tent on the IGAD and its Declaration of Principles.

To build up their efforts, IGAD mediators sought support for their initiative from the international community. That ultimately led to the creation of an IGAD Partners' Forum (IPF) comprising Italy, Norway, the Netherlands, the United Kingdom, and the United States at the beginning and eventually engulfing other countries from Europe and North America. The IPF provided the IGAD process with a greatly needed technical, material, and diplomatic support. To lend credence to its support of the IGAD process, U.S. President Bill Clinton appointed Harry Johnston (former chairman of the House Subcommittee for Africa) as his personal envoy to Sudan and charged him with following up, among other things, the IGAD peace process. Johnston was succeeded by three U.S. presidential envoys during the era of President George W. Bush.[9] Of the three envoys, John Danforth was the one who played the most determinant role in stimulating the peace process.

On coming to power in the closing years of the six-year interim period provided for in the CPA, U.S. President Barack Obama nominated former Air Force General Scott Gration as his presidential envoy to Sudan. Gration's mission, more than any of his predecessors, was the most controversial, both within the U.S. as well as in Sudan. While Danforth had played a central role in the extinction of Sudan's unabating war, Gration homed in on achieving faithful implementation of the CPA, particularly in the run-up to the referendum on the future of South Sudan. Gration, like his predecessors, was also entrusted with the intractable mission of bringing peace to Darfur. The Darfur conflict was concomitantly, though not directly, related to the CPA and of great consequence to comprehensive peace in Sudan. The crucial roles played by U.S. peace envoys, their government, and especially the U.S. Congress throughout the CPA negotiations and in the course of its implementation process shall be adequately reviewed in the book. Also reviewed are the factors that had propelled the U.S. with such intensity into Sudan's political quagmire and led to fierce infighting between Congress and the administration, and of late within the administration itself, on what constituted peace in Sudan.

Other countries that were ever present in peacemaking and humanitarian relief efforts in Sudan included Italy, the Netherlands, Norway, and the United Kingdom. Norway, in particular its former Minister for International Cooperation Hilde Johnson, proved to be an effective liaison at the highest level between the two parties given the open channels of communication she was able to establish between them. During the struggle, Norwegian People's Aid, a nongovernment organization of the Norwegian Confederation of Trade Unions, served as the rampart of humanitarian aid to areas under the SPLM/A control, while Norwegian Christian Aid provided humanitarian assistance to both north and south Sudan. On the other hand, the Norwegian government, building on its success in concluding the first peace accord between Israel and the Palestinians,[10] also tried behind-the-scenes to bring peace to Sudan. On the other side, Italy, the Netherlands, and the United Kingdom were deeply involved in both humanitarian and peacemaking efforts in Sudan. In this connection, Italian Deputy Foreign Minister Rino Serri, U.K. Ministers for International Cooperation Clare Short and Hilary Benn, and their Dutch counterpart Agnes Van Ardenne (following in the footsteps of her predecessor, Jan Pronk), became enwrapped in Sudan's conflict by supporting peace negotiations and later contributing to post-conflict rehabilitation efforts. To that end, Jan Pronk, Clare Short, and Hillary Benn made several visits to Khartoum and the SPLM headquarters in South Sudan to ensure free passage of humanitarian relief and explore avenues for peace. Furthermore, Italy, at the behest of Deputy Foreign Minister Rino Serri, unsuccessfully tried to bring the two conflicting parties together through the Community of St. Egidio, which scored resounding success in resolving the Mozambique conflict between Frelimo (government party) and Renamo (opposition rebel group) at Rome in October 1992.

The contributions made by the governments and people of Kenya and Uganda were as important, if not more, to the peace process. Presidents Daniel arap Moi and Mwai Kibaki of Kenya, Yoweri Museveni of Uganda, and Kenyan Vice President Stephen Kalonzo Musyoka were personally involved throughout the negotiations. Worthy of special note is the role played by the IGAD mediator, General Lazaro Sumbeiywo:[11] the mediator and his team set up the agenda for the meetings, framed issues for debate, established norms for dialogue, and provided alternative solutions to problems that had appeared to be intricate and insoluble. Sumbeiywo's optimistic approach to his mission was premised on his estimation that parties in conflict would not have resorted to mediation unless they were looking for solutions. With military firmness and diplomatic finesse, General Sumbeiywo was able to move the protagonists from entrenched positions to mutually acceptable conclusions, which satisfied both parties and provided a win-win conclusion. Sumbeiywo's win-win formula, far from being a cliché, was to package an agreement with which both parties could live. Those interventions encouraged various powerful players to support an African initiative, despite the initial scepticism by the IPF about the workability of that initiative.

Nevertheless, it would be stretching the truth to attribute regional and international efforts with the decisive role in the success of the negotiations. The two sides ultimately took control of the dialogue and drove the negotiation process toward its conclusion. It would be appropriate, then, to say that external actors and influences made the most of an opportunity provided by a changed internal landscape in Sudan. What, then, were the factors within Sudan, and especially within the conflict parameters, that allowed this attempt at a settlement to succeed on the heels of a score of failed peace negotiations? Probably, it was because all previous attempts to reach a negotiated settlement for Sudan's intricate conflict were targeting quick fixes, not a definitive resolution of the root cause of the conflict. As experience had confirmed, quick fixes would only provide a hiatus in war, not a final denouement of the conflict for which the SPLM had called and to which mediators agreed. All the same, that alone would not explain the reason behind this deferred peace accomplishment. Another factor that drove the warring parties to serious negotiations was the realization by both of them, after 10 years of pernicious fighting, that war was unwinnable by either. Furthermore, of all previous peace mediators, the IGAD was the first to underscore the relevance of Sudan's diversities to peace, a fact that the northern political class spurned and some external mediators often downplayed. The author discussed at length elsewhere the dangers inherent in the simplistic explanation of Sudan's multiple crises as a reflection of dichotomies such as north versus south, Muslim against non-Muslim, and Arab vis-à-vis African.[12] That reductionist interpretation, prevalent in Western media, did not help former mediators fully understand, let alone resolve, Sudan's multiple crises.

The CPA was also unique in that it had been both a peace agreement that established parameters for two former warring parties to govern together and a state-building blueprint, especially for southern Sudan and other areas directly affected by conflict. Consequently, any assessment of the bona fide implementation of CPA would require analysis of two separate but interrelated processes: the dynamics of the relationship between NCP and SPLM, on the one hand, and the role of regional and international guarantors of the agreement in ensuring its successful conclusion, on the other hand. It is to be noted that 14 countries and international and regional organizations countersigned the CPA, upon its conclusion, as guarantors to its implementation.[13] While it would be fair to assume that no legal obligation ensued from that commitment, states and organizations that co-signed the CPA were still politically and morally beholden to that obligation.

During the interim period, peace guarantors were deeply engrossed in peacemaking and peace-building in Sudan in different guises. For example, the United Nations Security Council established a peacekeeping special force and remained seized of the conflict throughout the interim period, while IGAD and other observer nations remained engaged in the process of evaluation and assessment of CPA implementation. Other peace partners held out to the last in providing technical and material support to institutional and human capacity-building programs, especially in southern Sudan. In the second half of the interim period, however, the African Union emerged as the most credible mediator in the peace process, particularly when it established a comprehensive framework for addressing the country's multiple crises. Indubitably, responsibility for consolidation of peace in Sudan fell primarily on the parties. Even so, the unremitting involvement of CPA guarantors in the process of peacemaking was indispensable, especially by remaining attentive to factors that had *ab initio* led to conflict. Inattention to these factors had, disconcertingly, led to two developments in the second half of the interim period that had serious repercussions on the peace process: the dead end reached by the two CPA partners in their numerous attempts to resolve differences over cardinal issues in the agreement, and the failure of efforts by the two CPA parties to end conflict in Darfur jointly.

As regards CPA implementation, the NCP held back on carrying out in a timely manner commitments that related to important issues such as border demarcation, census, final resolution of the Abyei question, popular consultation in Blue Nile and South Kordofan states, democratic transformation, and above all, organization of the South Sudan referendum. Underperformance in these areas led to a loss of faith between the two parties and, in part, drove southern Sudanese toward secession. So, when the results of the referendum came out, it was not only the NCP, but also close observers of the South Sudan political scene who were surprised to see 98.83 percent of the voters opting for secession. As to the Darfur conflict, which was not intrinsic to the civil war, John Garang believed from the outset that any north/south peace deal could easily be derailed if conflict in Darfur was allowed to seethe. Accordingly, he suggested during the CPA negotiations that the two parties work together toward achieving a peaceful resolution for that conflict. That offer was straightaway snubbed by the NCP, as were similar offers made by Garang's successor, Salva Kiir Mayardit. The Darfur conflict, nonetheless, went through a succession of stumbles and swerves and continued to do so throughout the interim period. Though it would be beyond the purposes of this book to analyze the causes of the Darfur conflict, the author broaches developments in the Darfur conflict for three reasons: (i) its impact on CPA implementation, (ii) merger by concerned international organizations and observers of peace-building efforts in areas covered by the CPA with peacemaking endeavors in Darfur, and (iii) the heavy shadow cast on CPA implementation by the indictment for genocide by the International Criminal Court (ICC) of senior Sudanese government officers, including the president.

The indictment of the president by the ICC brought an unanticipated result: political involvement of the African Union in Sudan's conflict. Since the early 1990s, Sudanese governments were reluctant to allow direct involvement by the Organization of African Unity, and later the African Union, in Sudan's conflict. In effect, the history of discouraging African institutions from being involved in Sudan's internal war went back to 1957--1958, when Foreign Minister Mohamed Ahmed Mahjoub conveyed to Kwame Nkrumah Sudan's rejection of any "foreign" intervention in the then-budding Sudanese conflict. Nkrumah was then pained to see Sudan, the first decolonized country in sub-Saharan Africa,[14] threatened with dismemberment. Mahjoub's rationale for rejecting Nkrumah's bid was that Article III (2) of the Organization of African Unity charter called for "non-interference in the internal affairs of states." However, reluctance to involve Africa in Sudan's conflict, then and later, was probably due to what Sudan governments had assumed, or perceived, as empathy of a large number of African countries with South Sudan. Even the offer made by Nigeria's Muslim president, Ibrahim Babangida, in May/June 1992 to intervene in the Sudan conflict in his capacity as Organization of African Unity chair was turned down by the NIF government. Babangida's offer was later accepted, but only in his capacity as president of Nigeria.

The ICC's issue came as a blessing in disguise to the government when the African Union turned out to be the only regional organization that challenged the ICC's indictment of a serving African head-of-state and volunteered to challenge the court's action within the bounds of international legality. The government consequently acquiesced for the first time to African involvement in Sudan's conflict. An African Union High-Level Implementation Panel on Darfur (AUHIPD) was formed to follow the matter through. The panel was to be headed by former South African president, Thabo Mbeki, and comprised two former African presidents as well as politicians and political activists.[15] The African Union, however, made it clear that it was not seeking impunity for anybody but envisaged applying African traditional justice, where punishment was tempered with avowal, penitence, and forgiveness. In its wisdom, the AUHIPD thought, and the African Union and the government consented, that the panel should address the two aspects of Sudan's crisis: CPA implementation and the Darfur conflict, including the aftermath of the ICC indictment. Whether Khartoum's ruling party was wholeheartedly committed to the African Union's position, as expounded by the AUHIPD, was doubtful given its vacillation on the panel's recommendations relating to transitional justice in Darfur. Albeit, without the African Union panel's focused attention on the twin issues of the CPA and

Darfur, things would not only have taken a turn for the worse in Sudan, but the country might have fallen apart.

While conflict in Darfur remained simmering and cardinal elements of the CPA hung in the air, the people of South Sudan decided on February 7, 2011, to secede. Predictably, that decision raised questions as to why unity of Sudan was not preserved despite all the guarantees enshrined in the CPA. To the author's mind, failure by the two signatories of the CPA to carry out obligations imposed on them by the agreement was neither due to structural deficiencies in the agreement, nor to time and logistical constraints; it was conclusively caused by human agents. With varying degrees of responsibility, the two parties did not take their contractual obligations seriously. For example, the NCP repeatedly and irreverently made a mockery of the transformative aspect of the CPA, while some influential members of the SPLM became increasingly convinced that the be-all and the end-all of the agreement was self-determination by the people of southern Sudan. For that to happen after having persuaded the people of Sudan that the struggle was to reform a system of rule, not dismember a country, those leaders would appear to many as back stabbers.

Notwithstanding, on July 9, 2011, the Republic of South Sudan was born and received a thunderous welcome by the world. That was reflected in the participation at its independence celebrations of 30 heads of state and government as well as an equal number of high-level delegations from Africa, Europe, Middle East, Asia, the Americas, the United Nations, the African Union, and the Arab League. To be sure, all those well-wishers set their eyes on how the 54th member state of the African Union and the 193rd member of the UN would do after the end of the fiesta. This expression of goodwill manifested the great expectations the world had in the new republic. These expectations shall only be realized under two conditions: first, the ability of the new republic's political elite to live up to the compassion toward the common man that prompted the SPLM struggle and the altruism that has guided it since 1983; and, second, awareness by the Republic of Sudan that the two components of the old Sudan shall not be viable unless they maintain live-and-let-live policies.

With the south gone, however, the north has also been left with a load of political, economic, and security problems. These problems are, to a large extent, an outgrowth of the NCP's politics of patronage and coercion. For over two decades, the NCP had continued to rule north Sudan with an iron rod. And whenever coercion failed to deter opponents, it had invariably turned to inducement through pecuniary gratifications or peddling of political positions. As a result, the government became top-heavy and unwieldy, while public expenditure on security surpassed that on services and employment-generating activities. This situation was aggravated by the separation of South Sudan, which deprived the north of two-thirds of the oil revenues it had been collecting since 2005. To get out of both political and economic predicaments, the NCP, first, has to open up and accommodate all shades of opinion in the country, thus realizing what it has avoided doing through the interim period: democratic transformation. Second, both the north and south Sudan states need to be fully aware of the multiple interdependencies between the two former parts of the country. Those interdependencies dictate cooperation, not rivalry, between the two states and support, not opposition, to each other.

As a result of a lack of genuine desire to resolve outstanding issues with the CPA, relations between the two states reached their lowest point less than one year after separation. That was characterized by border conflicts and proxy wars that had afterwards degenerated into engagements by the armies of both states. Moreover, those small wars were accompanied by the suspension by the Republic of South Sudan of oil production, which had a crippling effect on the economy of the two countries. In retaliation, the Sudan government closed all avenues for trade between the two states. This gamble by both states could have been tolerated, except the stakes they played for were extremely high: the livelihood of the people of both countries. That dangerous folly was finally restrained by the African Union Peace and Security Council at its meeting on April 24, 2012, and on May 2, 2012, the United Nations Security Council resolved that both parties should immediately cease hostilities, including inflammatory statements. The AU Council also demanded that the parties seriously address CPA outstanding issues, with a view to resolving them through the intermediation of the AUHIPD and the late prime minister of Ethiopia, Meles Zinawi, in his capacity as IGAD chairman. The UN Security Council resolution was adopted under Chapter VII of the charter, delineating what that would entail for the party who failed to abide by the resolution. The UN Security Council also ruled that the parties must reach a settlement on the issues within three months and requested the U.N. Secretary General to keep abreast of their compliance with the resolution in two-week intervals. On September 27, 2012, with skillful counseling from the AUHIP, the two parties obliged. Were they in need of the heavy stick of the United Nations Security Council in order to sign an agreement whose main objective was to ensure their viability? As the author shall try to expose in this book, the reticence to reach an agreement was due to two characteristics that became apparent after the separation of South Sudan: the first was excessive pride and prejudice; the second was a suicidal desire among the two brother enemies to destroy each other. Little did they know that if there was an enemy at all to destroy, "the last enemy that shall be destroyed is death."[16]

NOTES

1   Douglas H. Johnson, *The Root Causes of Sudan's Civil Wars*, James Currey, Oxford and Fountain Publishers Kampala, 2003, Deng, Francis M. (ed.), *New Sudan in the*

Making: Essays on a Nation in Painful Search for Itself (Trenton, N.J.: Red Sea Press, 2010);Mansour Khalid, *War and Peace in Sudan: A Tale of Two Countries* (London: Kegan Paul, 2003); Muddathir Abdel-Rahim, *Imperialism and Nationalism in the Sudan: A Study in Constitutional and Political Development, 1899–1956* (Oxford: Clarendon Press, 1969);. M.W. Daly and Ahmad Alawad Sikainga (eds.), *Civil War in the Sudan* (London: British Academic Press, 1993).

2 For details on the Addis Ababa negotiations see Abel Alier, *Southern Sudan: Too Many Agreements Dishonoured*, second edition (Ithaca, NY: Ithaca Press, 1992), 108–120.

3 Rabindranth Tagore, "Essay on Nationalism in India." Satish C. Aikant, Reading Tagore: Seductions and Perils of Nationalism, 55, Asiatic, Volume 4, Number 1, June 2010.

4 Edward Thomas, *Against the Gathering Storm: Securing Sudan's Comprehensive Peace Agreement* (London: Chatham House, 2009), 26.

5 In July 2000, Sudan's foreign minister visited the Vatican and met with Monsignor Jean-Louis Tauran to seek the Vatican's intervention to bring peace to Sudan. *Al Sharq al Awsat, London, 28 July* 2000+ Ghazi.

6 The Intergovernmental Authority for Development (IGAD) is a regional organization comprising Djibouti, Eritrea, Ethiopia, Kenya, Sudan, and Uganda that was formed in the mid-1980s after severe drought that had struck East Africa and the Horn. It was then conceived as an environmental protection outfit called the Intergovernmental Authority on Drought and Desertification (IGADD). In 1993, the organization was transformed into a subregional institution entrusted with the development of the subregion and establishment of peace and stability within it. Thus, the two Ds for drought and desertification were dropped from its name.

7 Khalid, Mansour. *War and Peace in Sudan.* (New York: Routledge, 2012), 479.

8 IGAD Secretariat, Nairobi, Declaration of Principles Relating to Resolution of Sudan Conflict, July 20, 1994.

9 Envoys included Richard Williamson, a diplomat and former assistant secretary of state for international organizations; Andrew Natsios, former administrator of USAID; and former Senator John Danforth, who later became as U.S. representative to the United Nations.

10 In the mid-1990s, Norwegian foreign minister Johan Jorgen Holst invited representatives of both parties for informal talks in Oslo to probe the possibility of identifying benchmarks for peace. Holst was probably encouraged by Norway's success in concluding the Oslo Accords on Arab-Israeli conflict in August 1993.

11 Lieutenant General Lazaro Kipkurui Sumbeiywo, the Kenyan army commander, was one of six Kenyan officers recruited in 1968 from among 43 candidates to join the Royal Military Academy at Sandhurst in the United Kingdom. His meteoric rise in the Kenyan army culminated in his appointment as commandant of the defence staff college in Kenya, in September 1999, and then army commander of the Kenyan army in December 2000.

12 Khalid, *War and Peace in Sudan*, 467-8..

13 African Union, European Union, Egypt, IGAD, IGAD Partners Forum, Italy, Kenya, League of Arab States, the Netherlands, Norway, United States, United Kingdom, United Nations, and Uganda.

14 On January 1, 1956, when Sudan won its independence, the only two independent countries in sub-Saharan Africa were Ethiopia and Liberia; all the other countries were either "colonial" or "mandated" properties.

15 The panel included, in addition to Mbeki, General Abdulsalami Abubakar, former head of state and commander in chief in Nigeria; Pierre Buyoya, former president of Burundi; Ahmed Maher, former foreign minister of Egypt; Judge Florence Ndepele Mumba of Zambia, a reserve judge in courts in Cambodia for the prosecution of crimes against humanity and before that judge of the appeals chamber for the United Nations international tribunals for Yugoslavia and Rwanda; Kabir Abdulfatah Mohammed, former executive secretary of the Nigerian Petroleum Technology Development Fund; and Rakiya Omar from Somali, lawyer and human rights activist.

16 Corinthians 15:26.

Introduction

■■■■■■■■■■■■■■■■❖■■■■■■■■■■■■■■■■

All I have is a voice
To undo the folded lie,
The romantic lie in the brain
Of the sensual man-in-the-street
And the lie of Authority
Whose buildings grope the sky:
There is no such thing as the State
And no one exists alone;
Hunger allows no choice
To the citizen or the police;
We must love one another or die.
—W.H. Auden
Excerpt from "September 1, 1939"

The book is divided into 12 chapters in which events that had stoked the flames of Sudan's second civil war, or enhanced the break of peace in Sudan on January 9, 2005, are chronicled and analyzed. In order to put these events within a proper perspective, the book shall focus in **Chapter One** on rooted political, economic, and cultural factors that accentuated the north/south aspect of the conflict. Yet, the materialization of a political force in southern Sudan committed to addressing war as a symptom of a national crisis produced a new set of dynamics that led to reconfiguring peacemaking in favor of an all-embracing negotiated compromise. As a result, peace negotiations ceased to be reaching settlement around the north/south axis of the conflict but rather toward a comprehensive deal that would resolve a composite of problems precipitated by the dysfunctional nature of the Sudanese state. Those factors shall be analyzed in the book within interrelated political, economic, cultural, and military dimensions.

Chapter Two throws light on how the watershed Machakos Protocol, agreed upon by the SPLM/A and the government of Sudan on July 20, 2002, had recognized the right to self-determination for the people of South Sudan without losing sight of the national dimensions of the Sudanese conflict. The salience of the internal factors that allowed for negotiated settlement at Machakos would best be understood by contrasting the Machakos process with peacemaking processes that prevailed in previous aborted attempts to reach such a settlement, notably the Abuja talks in 1992-1993;[1] earlier attempts under the IGAD framework in 1993 and 1997-2000;[2] and the Joint Egyptian-Libyan Initiative (JELI), which began in 1997 and rose to prominence between 1999 and 2001. The undeclared objective of JELI was to derail the IGAD process on the belief that it would not have achieved the result desired by the proponents of the initiative, namely, maintaining unity of Sudan at all costs. The key words are "at all costs" since the SPLM never wasted an opportunity to declare its determination to keep the country united, but only on a new basis. Indubitably, the unity the SPLM had yearned for presupposed radical changes in the political culture that had dominated Sudan since its independence. Notwithstanding, the agreement reached at Machakos after five weeks of tortuous negotiations could not have been achieved without three interlinked events that shall be analyzed in the chapter. These were the readiness of the two warring parties to retract their steps from entrenched positions; energization of the IGAD initiative through support from the IPF, mainly Norway, United Kingdom, and United States;[3] and the change in the parties' positions, not only as a result of cajolement by mediators, but, more important, because of a hurtful stalemate in the war.

Chapter Three deals with the Machakos agreement itself, which came to be known as the "Machakos Framework Protocol" and provided the politicolegal substructure for all agreements that followed. More consequential, it settled main South Sudan, in particular, issues such as granting its people the right to self-determination, recognizing administrative autonomy for southern Sudan, and guaranteeing its citizens a share in national governance during the interim period commensurate with their demographic weight. Of all those issues, granting southern Sudanese people the right to self-determination, including the right to secede, was the most significant but cumbersome to achieve. Opposition to that proposal came not only come from the government of Sudan, but surprisingly from U.S. Envoy Senator Danforth, who vehemently pleaded for unity of Sudan with extensive autonomous powers granted to South Sudan. The chapter shall shed light on the reasons behind that U.S. position as well as on the infighting that took place in the corridors of power in Washington on the issue.

To the dismay of many southern Sudan politicians, including some SPLM cadres, negotiations continued for another two years and a half after the signature of the Machakos Protocol before a final peace agreement was concluded by the end of 2004 and formally signed on January 9, 2005. In actuality, serious attempts were at play to persuade Garang to end the talks after Machakos, as long as the south had been granted the rights it was fighting for, especially conditions of self-determination and administrative autonomy that had not been conceded to it by any Khartoum government before. Those were, for sure, the rights for which the majority of southern Sudanese politicians had been struggling since independence, but they were not the ultimate goals for which the SPLM was fighting. Having made his case to his southern Sudanese detractors and leaving behind what he thought to be an unresolvable clash over what the negotiations were about, Garang immediately began to seriously look into robust guarantees that would make the agreement hold out.

Chapter Four concentrates on guarantees for the implementation of the Comprehensive Peace Agreement. Garang was of the opinion that agreements would only be viable if precautions were taken to forestall attempts by the other party to go back on their contractual obligations. These he described as "organic guarantees," that is, guarantees to be ingrained in, and to become an integral part of, the agreement. It is, however, reasonable to think that Garang's personal experience with Khartoum's betrayal of the Addis Ababa Agreement had been one of the reasons behind his distrustfulness in the government of Sudan. Yet, some of the organic guarantees Garang pleaded for were much higher than what even his closest aides had contemplated such as having two standing armies with different command and control structures in one and the same country. On the other side, from the commencement of the negotiations, government representatives persisted in demanding a comprehensive ceasefire before major political issues were addressed. Hence, the chapter shall deal with vital security fears and demands raised by the two parties, together with the resolution of two conundrums: having two separates armies in the same country, and determining what came ahead of the other— a comprehensive ceasefire or a political agreement coupled with organic guarantees.

Chapter Five shall expatiate on the first attempt by the chief mediator, General Sumbeiywo, to present an all-inclusive negotiating framework that addressed the political, economic, and security concerns of the two parties. A negotiation's framework document dubbed the Nakuru Document was presented by Sumbeiywo to the parties and was generally accepted by the SPLM but caused an uproar in Khartoum. The government's detailed rebuttal of the document, and the reasons behind its uproar against Sumbeiywo, shall be analyzed in the chapter.

Chapter Six seeks to throw in sharp relief the nub of SPLM's mission, announced during the negotiations with a flourish of trumpets. This included transformation of national politics through a multiplicity of measures, including decentralization of the system of rule all over Sudan, equitable

3

sharing of national wealth, democratic transformation (that is, transforming Sudan from one party rule to a multiparty democracy), recognition of Sudan's diverse cultures and languages, and defining a new foreign policy for Sudan that would first and foremost serve national interests. If negotiations on these issues took over two years, it was not only because of the intricate nature of the issues, but also due to a tiff between the parties resulting from the government's conjecture that the SPLM was intruding into matters that were beyond its mandate. In other words, only southern politicians (including those in the SPLM) were entitled to discuss matters that related to the south even though northern parties had, since independence, arrogated to themselves the right to debate and decide on the destiny of the whole country, including how South Sudan should be ruled. Eventually, those issues were resolved, but only after both principals—Sudan's vice president and the SPLM chairman— became personally involved in the process. The impact on the negotiations of that high-level intervention, as it will be explained in the chapter, could not have taken place without intensive coaxing, especially by Kenya.

Chapter Seven addresses grievances suffered by the people of the Nuba Mountains and Blue Nile, as well as the nettlesome problem of Abyei; these areas were denominated by the parties during the negotiations as the "Transitional" or "Three" Areas. Garang's accentuation of the problems of these areas in the course of the negotiation was a reflection of his unyielding commitment to the eradication of distortions in national politics that left peripheral areas painfully abandoned. The chapter shall also touch on developments that ensued in the Three Areas after the announcement of the results of the southern Sudan referendum and the impression it created among large groups within the people of Blue Nile and Southern Kordofan that they were both forsaken by Juba and jilted by Khartoum. In addition, the chapter shall also hint at the catalogue of disasters that befell Abyei and threatened turning it, as some observers hypothesized, into Sudan's Kashmir.

Chapter Eight shall, at the outset, delve into the greatest tragedy that befell southern Sudan, indeed the entire country: the untimely death of John Garang after a historic and resounding reception in Khartoum that was testimony to how the New Sudan idea had captured the imagination of Sudanese of all colors. More significant, the chapter shall probe the impact of Garang's departure from the political scene on CPA implementation and seek to explain why the NCP seized the occasion of Garang's premature death to virtually undo the CPA and reshape the SPLM from within, with the help of few prominent southern Sudanese politicians who had historically been wrapped up in themselves. In the same vein, it shall shed light on the ideological ambiguities that emerged within the SPLM after the founding father's death, partly as a result of the above-mentioned maneuvers by the NCP, but mainly for lack of moral courage among key SPLM leaders at the testing moment. To put all these issues within context, the chapter shall enumerate major implementation challenges faced by the NCP and SPLM and assess whether the two parties were on the same level with these challenges. In particular, the chapter will focus on cardinal issues, the realization of which peace and unity could have stood or fallen. It also will bring to light the quibbling of peace guarantors in relation to these issues.

Chapter Nine shall expose a hitherto unpublished document reflecting Garang's design for Sudan (not only southern Sudan) during his first 180 days in office both as president of the government of South Sudan (GOSS) as well as first vice president of Sudan. Garang's priorities, as they were reflected in his 180-days agenda, covered rural transformation with a view to realizing his prized project: *taking towns to rural areas*. For this reason Garang gave priority to rural development projects in the allocation of oil revenues. The 180 days plan also comprised modernization and professionalization of the SPLA, ensuring full integration of joint integrated units (JIU) as a nucleus for Sudan's future national army and shifting the balance of government expenditure from Juba and Khartoum in favor of states. Were that to happen neither Khartoum nor Juba would have been able to squander resources on ostentatious administrative spending. Moreover, the chapter shall analyze the manner in which Garang's successor, Salva Kiir Mayardit, managed, against all odds, to keep southern Sudan and the SPLM intact, and it will document his underachievements in areas that ranked high on Garang's agenda, particularly ensuring peace dividends to the people. Also highlighted here will be the emergence of a venal bureaucratic elite, which not only betrayed the SPLM's revolutionary ideals, but also robbed the people of southern Sudan of dividends of peace, and in the process, put the survival of the new state at risk.

Chapter Ten is divided into two parts. Part One shall analyze how the NCP bent over backwards to frustrate the referendum, leading to both a separatist backlash and an outrage by the international community, in particular, the United Nations and IGAD countries. The NCP, which proved to be a successful high-stake political gambler since 1990, appeared to have gotten it wrong this time. Unlike in past peace processes where national governments unilaterally abrogated, or perfunctorily retracted from, peace agreements, the NCP did not realize that the CPA was a qualitatively different document. So, when it commenced dilatory tactics to frustrate the referendum, the NCP did not ponder the high price Sudan would pay in terms of its unity and territorial integrity.

Part Two, on the other hand, will debate the successes and failures of the SPLM, and the Government of southern Sudan it had been leading, in the fields of policy articulation, governance, security, service delivery, economic transformation, and integrity in public life. Despite its success in preserving the territorial integrity of southern Sudan and the unity of its people the SPLM and Government of southern Sudan had notably underperformed in providing peace dividends to its people. Reasons for that underperformance shall be explained. The chapter also recapitulates post-referendum challenges that Sudan, especially South Sudan, would face and ventures to propose how these challenges may be addressed.

Chapter Eleven deliberates on the anxieties that have pervaded northern Sudan when south Sudanese secession appeared to be a fait accompli. While the demonstration of such sentiment by ordinary northern citizens was justified as either a sigh for the good old days or a curse for the policies of their leaders that had led to the dismemberment of the country, its exhibition by the NCP and its media acolytes was, to all ends and purposes, sheer dissembling, especially since the NCP had hardly expressed any contrition for its policies that have led to the country's breakup, while the northern media supporting it have remained speechless while that party has been tearing up the CPA. That may also explain the coldness with which the NCP has met the secession of the south.

Likewise, Chapter Eleven shall deal with the insensitivity shown by some SPLM leaders in southern Sudan towards their co-partisans in the north (including the Blue Nile and Nuba Mountains) when they decided to drift with the secession tide and jump onto the independence bandwagon. Doubtless, the wind of change in South Sudan was strong and irresistible. Even so, what had caused concern among SPLM constituencies outside South Sudan were disingenuous attempts by these leaders to present their political afterthought— however compelling the reasons for it were—as a ratification of a political position the SPLM had always maintained. In this regard, the chapter shall attempt to explain why leaders of a party that has raised the banners of national unity not only ended up opting for secession, but also pretending to be its standard-bearers throughout its struggle. If that pretence had an iota of truth, then the pretenders—especially those who were Garang's spokespersons—would effectively have condemned themselves as counterfeit dispatch riders. Furthermore, in addition to the plans thought out by Garang for managing the Sudanese state, referred to in Chapter Nine, this chapter will highlight his bold program for the de-ethnicization of the administration in southern Sudan, with a view to alleviating ethnic antipathies and averting state failure.

Chapter Twelve shall address the Darfur conflict, if only because peace in Sudan shall never be comprehensive without putting an end to that conflict, which generated in half a decade much more regional and international attention than was engendered during the two decades of war in South Sudan. The crisis in Darfur shall be discussed alongside the heightened involvement by the Africa Union and the international community in that conflict, especially the U.S. administration, Congress, and civil society organizations. The Darfur conflict, as will be explained, was prolonged not only by the government's misbelief that the conflict could be settled militarily, but also by two additional factors: tactics of Darfur rebels who were pulling in different ways and the conflicting agendas of external mediators and external champions of the Darfur cause. Without ascribing malice to mediators or external champions of the Darfur cause, the ardor and militancy with which some approached their mission had unwittingly harmed Darfur immensely. On the one hand, it increased the government's fear and intransigence, and on the other hand, it raised expectations among the more militant Darfuri rebels. Emboldened by rhetorical support from the outside, those rebels had set their hearts on no less than the removal of the regime in Khartoum. If that objective was at all what Darfur warriors and their external patrons wanted to achieve, then the least those patrons were to do was offer Darfur the wherewithal to neutralize the government that was prosecuting war. Since support by those patrons was neither obvious nor feasible, the only way out for them as well as for others who wished Darfur well was to support credible and even-handed intermediation to resolve the conflict. In this connection, the AUHIP, more than any other mediator, remained the only focused, single-minded, purposefully devoted mediator that was also free from external and internal influences. Regrettably, despite all these laudable attributes, the AUHIP's efforts were, time and again, frustrated by the small-mindedness of negotiators on all sides and nuisanced by tunnel-visioned outside supporters. Even so, all parties to Sudan's multiple conflicts remained with no alternative but to cleave to the AUHIP.

The **Conclusion** both recapitulates the main theses of the book and essays to explore the possibility of extrication of Sudan from the dire straits in which it presently is. Averting an approaching meltdown of the country requires a radical review of past policies; it can neither be achieved through a business-as-usual approach, nor cosmetic changes in the regime. In this regard the chapter shall evaluate attempts by NCP leadership to seek support from the country's traditional leaders, the very persons who have immutably been behind all the political disablements Sudan suffered from for half a century. Becoming increasingly aware of the tenuousness of its position, the NCP's resort to support from, and legitimization by, the erstwhile northern political leadership that had brought the country to its knees is not a foresightful decision.

NOTES

1   See especially Ann Mosely Lesch and Steven Wöndu, *Battle for Peace in Sudan: An Analysis of the Abuja Conferences, 1992-1993* (Lanham, MD: University Press of America, 2000).

2   See Abdelwahab El-Affendi, "The Impasse in the IGAD Peace Process for Sudan: The Limits of Regional Peacemaking?" *African Affairs* 100, no. 401 (2001): 581-599.

3   The three were nicknamed the "Troika." Italy later joined that group, which came to be known as "Troika +1."

Chapter One
Roots of Sudan Civil Wars
(1956–2000): Political Myopia
and Cultural Proclivities

■ ■ ■ ■ ■ ■ ■ ■ ■ ■ ■ ■ ■ ■ ■ ■ ❖ ■ ■ ■ ■ ■ ■ ■ ■ ■ ■ ■ ■ ■ ■ ■

> The truth which makes men free is for the most part the truth which men
> prefer not to hear.
> —**Herbert Agar**, *A Time for Greatness*

1. Introduction

Sudan's second civil war ignited in 1983 after a 10 year spell of peace. There were immediate reasons that made war erupt, but behind these reasons lurked fundamental causes that should not be ignored in any search for a lasting peace to Sudan's drawn-out civil wars. The collapse of the 10 years of peace enjoyed by southern Sudan following the 1972 Addis Ababa Peace Agreement corroborated this view. Although the demise of that agreement was the proximate cause of the second civil war that engulfed almost the entire country for over two decades (1983–2005), a long history of political myopia and cultural proclivities had debilitated the country and made war inescapable. While identifying the proximate cause of the second civil war, the author shall also dwell in this chapter on inveterate causes behind Sudan's civil wars.

Invariably, northern politicians, media, and a number of political analysts made of colonialism a *portmanteau* for all the woes that had befallen Sudan; seldom did they analyze their own role in the creation of these woes. Admittedly, colonialism had committed manifold sins against humanity, but "if we say that we have no sin, we deceive ourselves, and the truth is not in us."[1] In this chapter the author shall throw light on the extraordinary political myopia that characterized national (in effect, northern Sudanese) politics and on the innumerable opportunities Sudanese post-colonial governments missed to keep Sudan united in peace. Underneath this political myopia a surprising ethnocentricity rendered northern politician sightless of the virtues of other Sudanese cultures, indeed unaware of the existence of such cultures. Ethnocentricity, even if reserved to the private domain, is an affronting idiosyncrasy, let alone when it impinges on citizens' rights in the public domain. The chapter shall draw attention to how the Arabo-Islamic cultural identity of the ruling northern elite was not only assumed to be the solitary badge of national identification, but also a determinant for acquisition of paramount civil rights such as the right to be president. Verily, he who denies other people's cultural identities negates his own, for "a person is a person because he recognizes others as persons."[2]

2. The Writing on the Wall That Nobody Saw

At the initial signing of the Comprehensive Peace Agreement (CPA) at Naivasha, Kenya on December 31, 2004, (before its formal signing in Nairobi on January 9, 2005), leaders of the two signatory parties made two consequential statements. Sudanese President Omar al-Bashir, on behalf of the Government of Sudan and his ruling party, the National Congress Party (NCP), described the occasion as "Sudan's second declaration of independence." Dr. Garang, chairman and commander-in-chief of the Sudan People's Liberation Movement/Army (SPLM/A), in turn, called it the "birth of Sudan's Second Republic." The two statements were rich in innuendos and epitomized a telling critique of Sudan's *status quo ante*. Indeed, not a single issue that was debated and resolved at the negotiations in Machakos and Naivasha was unfamiliar to national Sudanese leaders. Just about all the issues that were under discussion in the CPA negotiations had been, in one way or the other, a subject of debate since the eve of Sudan's independence on January 1, 1956, between the ruling class in Khartoum and armed or non-armed southern Sudanese political leaders. As well, grumblings in the marginalized areas of Sudan had a long life story dating back to 1958, the year the Beja Congress emerged in eastern Sudan. If anything, failure by the northern ruling class between 1956–2005 to properly identify the underlying causes of the Sudanese crisis—at least insofar as nation building and equitable sharing of wealth were concerned—bespoke an endemic ineptitude suffered by the political class that ruled Sudan then to identify the root cause of their country's political malady.

As it were, as early as 1953 the political elite in Khartoum were informed, or were supposed to have been informed, of what it would have taken to keep Sudan united. Nevertheless, when all northern parties assembled in Cairo in 1952 under the auspices of the Egyptian government to reach agreement on the future of the Sudan as a **united country**, not a single south Sudanese party or politician were invited to that meeting, as if southern Sudanese had no say on the destiny of the country or, at least, of the part in which they were settled. Amazingly, that meeting was crucial for the conclusion of the Anglo-Egyptian Agreement, which was to usher Sudan into self-government. The Cairo meeting, as to be expected, prompted southern Sudanese politicians in January 1954 to form the first southern political party: the Liberal Party.[3] In October of the same year, the second Juba conference[4] was held to discuss several issues relating to "the future of Sudan as a whole and that of **south Sudan within a united country.**" The Congress authorized its chairman, Benjamin Lwoki, to convey its conclusions to the prime minister in Khartoum, as well as to the two colonial powers.[5] In that letter, Lwoki unequivocally said that Sudan could either be united on the basis of two autonomous regions under a federal status or divided "the way Pakistan was separated from India"[6]. If that was not enough to alert Khartoum politicians to the legitimate demands of south Sudan, then nothing else would.

Indeed, it was not only the political class that was impervious to those demands, but even the media treated southern Sudanese core demands with insouciant disregard. For example, on September 31, 1954, the highly-respected Khartoum daily *Al Ayaam* blasted the Juba meeting as "inordinately racist" because it was only limited to southern Sudanese. The newspaper also surmised that that meeting was expected to demand equalization of northern and southern Sudanese civil servants' salaries, a matter the newspaper thought would undermine the integrity of the civil service, as recruitment into that service should remain based on "competence and precedence." The surmise was unerring since one of the issues raised by the Juba Congress was equalization of civil service pay in the whole of Sudan. During the colonial era, southern Sudanese civil servants received disproportionally lower salaries than those earned by their northern colleagues. That article was flawed on two counts.

First, it would appear that it had never dawned on its author that the Cairo meeting from which southern Sudanese politicians were excluded could, by the same token, be reviled as racist. Regrettably, the term "racist" had a special meaning in the lexicon of northern Sudanese politics. For example, since Sudan's independence, three successful, and a score of unsuccessful, military coups had been staged by northern officers and non-commissioned officers, who, irrespective of how people received them, were never defined by the ethnic origin of the coup plotters. However, all attempted coups by officers and non-commissioned officers of Nuba provenance were invariably depicted as "racist" coups.

Second, the article's total heedlessness to the issue of equity in national civil service postings betrayed the fickleness with which northern governments and media treated historical injustices suffered by southern and other Sudanese citizens in the peripheries. In effect, this formalistic approach to recruitment in the national civil service was behind the allocation by the Sudanization Committee[7] of only six low-level posts to southern Sudanese out of 800 posts. Two hundred other officials voluntarily retired, and their posts were filled by northern civil servants.[8] Of the six southern Sudanese officials, two were appointed as assistant district commissioners and four as mamurs, a post that fell in the lowest rungs of the administration hierarchy. That added to the rancor of southern elites, as revealed in Judge Cotran's report.[9] Amazingly, by the time of self-government in Sudan, the Sudanese government could have drawn on sufficient experiences in the world, especially as regards putting an end to injustices suffered by sectors of society who were, for whatever reason, segregated from the social main stream of that society. The Indian Constitution, for example, did not only guarantee equality to all citizens (Articles 15, 16, and 29), but also included special provisions that ensured preferential treatment to weaker sections of the society (Articles 15 (4) and 16 (4)).

On December 15, 1955, in preparation for Sudan's declaration of independence, southern Sudanese parliamentarians called for a **united federal** Sudan made up of two entities: North and South Sudan. That was the same position conveyed by Lwoki to Prime Minister Ismail el Azhari and the foreign ministers of the condominium powers; therefore, only the unwary would have been surprised by the southern Sudanese demands. In the meantime, considerable evidence existed in the world to support federalism as the most appropriate system of rule in fairly large countries, or those pervaded by multiple diversities, such as the United States, the Union of Soviet Socialist Republics, India, Brazil, and Canada. Even smaller countries comprising multiple linguistic groups such as Switzerland opted for that system. To underline the gravity of the matter, southern Sudanese parliamentarians served notice on their northern colleagues that acceptance of their demand was a condition that must be met before they agreed to the declaration of independence of Sudan as a united country.

Eager to scurry the country's independence from Anglo-Egyptian co-dominion, northern political parties promised to give due consideration to the southern call for federalism, once Sudan's new constitution was drafted. But no sooner had that constitution been drafted than Khartoum's political class, both in government and opposition, walked over the promise. They declared that after giving due consideration to the issue, they found that the disadvantages of federalism outweighed its advantages. That was both a flawed and an uncharitable decision: flawed because the advantages of federalism in vast countries, or those with multiple diversities, were persuasively proved; and uncharitable because it was nowhere near the magnanimity shown by southern parliamentarians in consenting, on the basis of an unguaranteed promise, to the declaration of independence through parliament even when that decision contravened the procedures on self-determination set by the

Cairo agreement.[10] In effect, southern parliamentarians were cajoled by their northern counterparts to be accomplices in the unilateral annulment of a crucial part of the Cairo agreement, which gave the self-government process its legitimacy. However, the most hilarious contention made by the media of the day, including the organ of the ruling party, was that federalism was nothing but a contrivance by Sir William Luce to divide the country.[11]

This misanthropic vision by Khartoum political elite of the experiences of other countries, especially India, was reflected in its hypersensitivity towards such issues as affirmative action to end inequities in the civil service, decentralization of governance, and identification of an appropriate national capital in a federal state, as will be explained in Chapter Six. This insensitivity was all the more surprising, given claims by the advance guard of the northern political elite of the time, that the Congress Party of India was their exemplar in politics.[12] Why then did those elite, which comprised well-learned politicians, trained civil servants, and educationalists of renown, lose sight of the political experiences of a country that they claimed to be their guiding light in the national struggle as well as in managing post-independence politics? The truth is that those elite had a fixed idea about the peculiarity of their country; to them, Sudan was a country without equal and, therefore, had nothing to learn from others. That was pride and prejudice at their highest and eventually resulted in the downfall of successive regimes in Khartoum, for "pride goeth before destruction and a haughty spirit before a fall."[13] The writing was, therefore, legibly on the wall from the eve of Sudan's independence.

3. The Missed Opportunity

As a consequence of the above, the unity of Sudan, which was a matter of political debate in parliament on the morrow of independence, turned into a duel with swords until October 1964, when a new government assumed power in Khartoum following the overthrow of General Ibrahim Abboud's military rule. The new government was headed by Sir-el-Khatim el-Khalifa, an apolitical northern educationist who served in South Sudan and developed a feeling of fellowship with the southern Sudanese teacher and student community. His government organized the first ever north-south dialogue in what came to be known as the Roundtable Conference (RTC). For the first time since independence, a northern Sudanese government put Sudan's civil war within historical, political, and economic contexts. The working paper that el-Khalifa presented to the RTC maintained that the conflict:

- Was multifaceted and had its roots in history, including colonialist policies and slave trade in the nineteenth century;
- Had cultural and religious dimensions;
- Was mishandled by former Sudanese democratic and military regimes alike; both treated the "Southern Question" as solely an issue of law and order;

THE PARADOX OF TWO SUDANS

- Was aggravated by lopsided economic development plans, "even though that inequitable development applied to other regions in Sudan."

That was the first time the north-south conflict was addressed as a multifaceted problem plagued with issues such as the historical remnants of slavery and economic inequities in the regions that northern politicians and many academics consistently evaded in their research. Also for the first time, a Khartoum government involved African countries in the resolution of its unyielding civil wars; invitations were extended to a number of African governments: Egypt, Ghana, Nigeria, and Uganda to participate in the RTC.[14]

The RTC initiative failed due to two reasons: first, maneuvers by the same political forces that grudged southern Sudan a federal status on the declaration of independence, and second, disunity among southern leaders at the conference. In the first case, the northern political class showed once more its knack for missing no opportunity to miss an opportunity. The RTC had before it a feasible plan to put an end to war that provided the mainstream of southern politicians of the day with a fairly acceptable system of rule. That plan was prepared by the Twelve-Man Committee, on which the parties to the RTC had agreed. Even that modicum of success was not sustained in view of wrangling among northern political parties over power and failure of southern politicians to talk with one voice. To northern politicians, power struggle had every appearance of taking precedence over peacemaking and nation building, as if power was an end in itself.

As for southern Sudanese participants in the RTC, their inability to talk with one voice inhibited progress in the talks. One group, led by Aggrey Jaden, called for instant independence because, to his mind, north was north and south was south, and the two would never meet. A second group made up of southern Sudanese bureaucrats-turned-politicians (Clement Mboro, Abel Alier, Bona Malwal, and Hilary Paulo Lugali) formed a new party under the name "Southern Front." That party demanded a plebiscite by southern Sudanese in order to allow them to ascertain for themselves the future of their region. A third group, the Sudan African National Union (SANU), pleaded for a revamped federal status. As if that division among southern Sudanese politicians was not enough, northern parties manufactured another southern group and foisted it on the RTC. That group was led by the veteran southern Sudanese politician, Santino Deng Teng, who was known for his unionist tendencies and prominent in all the national governments from independence throughout the rule of Abboud's military regime (1958–1964). The problem with Teng, however, was not his unionist tendencies but his rejection of federalism, a watchword in southern politics since independence. Teng went to extremes when he maintained that even the discussion of the issue of federalism by northern with southern parties represented an undeserved concession by the north to those parties. As a result, lack of concord among southern politicians became a heaven-sent opportunity to northern parties who were not in a hurry to address the legitimate claims of south Sudan.

Nonetheless, a tragic event followed the RTC and completely befouled the political atmosphere: the fateful end of William Deng Nhial. Nhial was the only southern leader who was determined to play the game according to the rules. Subsequent to the inconclusive RTC, Nhial engaged in coalitions with northern parties, including the Umma Party led by Sadiq al Mahdi; regionally based political groups such as Beja, Nuba, and Fur; and the emerging Islamic Charter Front, led by Hassan Turabi. In 1968, he fought and won elections in his traditional constituency in Bahr el Ghazal but was not allowed to enjoy that electoral victory. He was assassinated by the Sudanese army, while the Khartoum government saw nothing, heard nothing, and said nothing. That alone led many southerners to the conclusion that Khartoum's political establishment, to say the least, was to be regarded with suspicion.

Those recurrent failures from 1955 to 1965 were slovenly expunged from memory by the majority of north Sudan politicians and the parade of their apologists in the Khartoum media. Equally, not a small number of northern political historians treated these duplicitous schemes as mere footnotes in the annals of history. As a result, Khartoum's political elite, time and time again, repeated the same mistake of relying on northern Sudanese amnesia about their own history. So long as that memory gap in the minds of northern politicians, academics, and media analysts is not plugged, a proper contextual understanding of the so-called southern question, as well as other lurking conflicts in the country, will never be reached.

The term 'Southern Question,' like the Eastern Question in European history, had been a volitional de-emphasis of Sudan's real problem: a country at war with itself. For example, in their scramble to the East during the eighteenth and nineteenth centuries to safeguard strategic advantage and commercial interests in the remnants of the decaying Ottoman Empire, European powers found no name for a problem generated by their own greed other than the Eastern Question. By the same token, Sudan's northern metropolitan elite, consciously or subconsciously, deflated Sudan's "national question" into a regional one in order to obviate the national character of the crisis and, thus, absolve themselves from responsibility for provoking it. By so doing, they probably comforted themselves that nothing was the matter with their hegemony over the country's peripheries. The term 'Southern Question,' therefore, became a euphemism minted by northern politicians and academics in order to avoid addressing the root causes of a national crisis. Euphemisms are much the same as lies, and predicating the destiny of any nation on lies is an untenable proposition. For all of the above reasons, civil war once more broke out, but this time with better organization and increased popular support. With the inflammation of war, Sudan's "democratic" governments, mainly for their inability to set their priorities straight, collapsed in May 1969 under the heels of the military, led by Gaafer Nimeiri.

4. Proximate Causes of the Second Civil War

In a speech delivered on March 22, 1985, John Garang de Mabior, the man who launched Sudan's second civil war, explained to the public the historical as well as the proximate causes of the second civil war. He said:

> "The regime in Khartoum [Nimeiri's] fought very hard to isolate the Movement [SPLM/A] from the Sudanese masses by depicting [it] as what they call Communist, and blaming all difficulties in the South on alleged foreign conspiracies emanating from Moscow, Addis Ababa or Tripoli. But the Sudanese people and the Sudanese army see the war in War Zone No. 1 [South Sudan], not as Communist inspired, but on the contrary as caused and kept alive by Nimeiri himself. The Sudanese people and the Sudanese army know that:
>
> 1. It was Nimeiri, not SPLM, who tore up the Addis Ababa Agreement in June 1983, in violation of his own constitution and laws.
> 2. It was Nimeiri, not SPLM, that started the unlawful policy of removing troops from the South to the North, again in contravention of the Addis Ababa Agreement.
> 3. It was Nimeiri, not the SPLM, that sabotaged the democratic process in the South by dissolving legally elected regional governments for the South in 1980, 1981 and 1983, again in violation of the Addis Ababa Agreement."[15]

Garang went on to explain that Nimeiri's actions were a replication of the wrongheaded policies of former "national" governments, and so long as those policies were not reversed, peace would never be achieved in Sudan. His prescription for change was premised on taking the country back to the drawing board. To Garang, the myopia of a self-absorbed political class at the center had rendered it blind to the root causes of the troubles Sudan had been going through since independence. It was with this in mind that the SPLM/A waged a sustained armed political and diplomatic struggle for over two decades (1983–2005) in order to change politics in Khartoum. Even though that struggle had not achieved its ultimate goal, namely the creation of a New Sudan, the conclusion of the CPA represented an important milestone on the road to that goal, or so believed Garang and unfeigned devotees to the New Sudan cause.

From the start, Garang made it clear to powers at the center that his was a struggle neither for power nor for the extinction of the flames of the civil war *per se*; his aim, he declared, was to unite Sudan on a new basis and put an end to the manifold social tremors in east, center, and west Sudan, as well as to the impoverishment of the extreme north. The political class of the day did not take pleasure in Garang's words, since their main political preoccupation had been to make and remake political coalitions that would ensconce them in power *ad infinitum*. In effect, *ad infinitum* is not a hyperbolic turn of phrase but a statement confirmed by the fact that the leaders of the two major northern parties (Umma and UDP) have been in the saddle of their parties for over 40 years and are still battling to stay on.

To console themselves, those leaders frequently maintained that they had not captured power through the barrel of a gun but were brought to it through popular will, that is, elections. That self-serving explanation misses a cardinal rule in party politics: parties, like human beings, need new blood, much as young party workers aspire for upward mobility. During these 40 years, party and government leadership all over the world had changed hands many times *through popular will.* That happened, not because leaders were under pressure to climb down, but because they had the decency to give way to rising generations, as well the foresight to know that there was life beyond politics. This had not only been the case in established Western democracies like the United Kingdom, Germany, the United States, France, the Scandinavian countries, and Italy, but also in African countries like Ghana, Botswana, Mozambique, Nigeria, Tanzania, Senegal, and South Africa. All those countries had witnessed changes through democratic processes in both party and government leadership. Even in countries such as China and Russia, where gerontocracy prevailed for over half a century, things had changed, but not in northern Sudan. Still, Sudanese political leaders—on the right and left—continued singing hymns of praise to the peaceful transfer of power, but they seemed to believe that this worthy principle applied to everybody other than themselves.

5. From War to Peace and Back to War

President Nimeiri's government, to its credit, gave priority in its plan of action to ending the war in the South. In 1972, that government signed with the SSLM the Addis Ababa peace accord. That accord was based on a declaration of principles announced by Nimeiri's regime in June 1969 and to which the Sudanese Communist Party had immensely contributed. Ironically, it was also founded on conclusions reached by the Twelve-Man Committee that had been formed by the RTC to study and recommend constitutional, administrative, and financial arrangements between the central government and South Sudan. The Twelve–Man Committee began its work in June 1965 and was initially led by Abdel Rahman Abdalla, a Sudanese administrator of international renown, and later by Yousif Mohamed Ali, an independent-minded lawyer. The committee comprised representatives of six northern and two southern

17

political parties.[16] However, two of the parties—the People's Democratic Party and the Sudanese Communist Party—had withdrawn from the committee, not because they had any quarrel with the committee's recommendations, but as a result of party realignments in preparation for the impending national elections. Thus, while the committee was deliberating on matters pertinent to peacemaking and nation building, northern political leaders were jockeying for positions in the government that would follow the national elections. It appeared that the scramble for power by the northern parties, especially Umma and DUP, consumed the parties' energies to the extent that capturing power, rather than consolidating peace in Sudan, became the most pressing political end in view.

The chair of the Twelve-Man Committee, however, handed over its report to Prime Minister Mohamed Ahmed Mahjoub on June 26, 1966, but for the above reasons, the report was disregarded. Rather than give precedence to the implementation of its report, Prime Minister Mahjoub side-tracked the committee into a distractive exercise. In effect, the prime minister, supported by the withdrawing parties, persuaded the committee to give prime attention to the denunciation of violence in southern Sudan, which the government attributed solely to southern Sudanese elites, while absolving the army, security forces, and extremist parties in northern Sudan of any responsibility. Southern members of the committee stood firm against that one-sided judgment, which if it were to be accepted by the committee, would have tarnished its image as an independent reconciliation committee and, consequently, undermined its effectiveness. Even the proposition, made by committee members from southern Sudan, that a statement be issued denouncing violence from whichever source it came was not satisfactory to the government. That was yet another proof of how off-center—not to say biased—the priorities were of Khartoum's political class. It was only in early 1971 that Nimeiri's government removed dust from that report and presented it to the southern armed group, South Sudan Liberation Movement (SSLM), as the basis for negotiations. That movement was led by Colonel Joseph Lagu, who mutinied against the Sudanese army late in the 1960s. The SSLM was not even in existence in 1966 when the committee finished its work and handed the government a road map to peace and reconstruction. One could assume that had the committee's report been implemented in time, southern politicians would not have been further alienated, and the warriors among them would not have been stimulated to prepare for a vicious armed struggle.

Notwithstanding, Nimeiri's government, in bidding for peace, made an offer to the SSLM based on the recommendations of the Twelve-Man Committee. That offer granted autonomy to southern Sudan as a united region made up of the three provinces of Bahr el Ghazal, Equatoria, and Upper Nile, each having its own legislative and executive arms of government. Under that arrangement Abel Alier became the first president of the interim executive council in Juba pending the forthcoming parliamentary elections provided for in the Addis Ababa agreement. The elected legislative assembly would, among other things, select a president. To boot, Alier became vice president of the republic. The appointment of Alier as vice president of the republic was the first time a citizen from South Sudan had occupied that post. Joseph Lagu, on the other hand, was reintegrated into the Sudanese army and promoted to the rank of brigadier general, the first time ever for an officer from southern Sudan to attain that rank in the army. The greatest boon of the agreement, however, was the 11 years of peace it brought in its wake (1972-1983), the longest period southern Sudan had enjoyed any tranquillity since independence. Paradoxically, the national parties who failed to implement a peace plan prepared by the committee in which they were the majority, shamelessly begrudged Nimeiri's triumph in putting an end to Sudan's civil war and boasted that the 1972 Addis Ababa accord was based on a scheme they had established in 1966. Apart from the pedantry exhibited in it, that reaction revealed how green with envy those parties were and how disrespectful they were to the intelligence of the common man. The Sudanese people knew very well who had frustrated the Round Table Conference process and, sadly, why.

Albeit, when the "secular" President Nimeiri metamorphosed into an Islamic Imam, the first casualty on his road to Damascus was the Addis Ababa peace agreement. To say that agreement was unilaterally abrogated and the unity of the southern region dismembered by Nimeiri would not be the whole truth, for Nimeiri was not the only villain of the piece. To all intents and purposes, Nimeiri had subordinate accomplices from South Sudan, including General Lagu, the cosignatory of the agreement, as well as three southern politicians: Othwan Dak, Philip Obang, and Oliver Albino. The four provided Nimeiri with the pretext he needed to meddle with the agreement, claiming that the government of the South was dominated by the Dinka people and, therefore, the southern region would best be divided (see Chapter Ten). Conveniently, President Nimeiri went ahead with dividing southern Sudan, purportedly in response to the "will of its people," regardless of the scores of political and social leaders from that region who challenged the decision taken by Nimeiri and others and were, accordingly, hurtled into prison for objecting to the presidential decision.[17]

As if the abrogation of the agreement was not enough, Nimeiri proceeded to undo its cultural underpinnings by issuing a republican order in which he specifically repealed Article 6 of the agreement. Article 6 of the 1972 Addis Ababa Accord provided that, "Arabic shall be the official language for Sudan and English the principal language for the southern Region without prejudice to the use of any other language or languages which may serve a practical necessity or the efficient and expeditious discharge of executive and administrative functions of the Region." That provision did not come easy, for in the course of the negotiations, one of the leading SSLM negotiators

19

(Mading de Garang) proposed that only English should be the official language in southern Sudan, because, in his words, Arabic was a "foreign language" to southern Sudanese. De Garang failed to remember that in southern Sudan the majority of citizens who did not share a common native tongue communicated in Arabic rather than English. A government negotiator, Gaafar Bakheit, told de Garang that he would have made more sense if he had proposed English as an official language because it would be a better medium for higher education or business; otherwise, English was more "foreign" to southern Sudanese than Arabic. Bakheit added that the government's delegation might have gone along with the SSLM negotiator had he suggested a widely spoken indigenous language such as Dinka as the official language for southern Sudan. Evidently, Arabic, assumed to be the language of northern "oppressors," was being punished by association.

Apparently, some southern Sudanese elites at the time, such as de Garang who wanted to see the Arabic language expunged from that region, took no account of the way in which that language had penetrated southern Sudan long before its diffusion in post-independence Sudan through education and media. Arabic, in reality, was not implanted in southern Sudan through coercion but as a result of an osmotic penetration generated by intergroup relations, commerce and trade, personal interactions and intermarriages, and movement of people in the two directions for engagement in gainful activities. That was why a sort of patois (pidgin Arabic) known as Juba Arabic became the *lingua franca* of the south. Even the colonialists who wanted to erase the use of Arabic in southern Sudan had second thoughts about it.[18]

The rationale behind Article 6 in the Addis Ababa agreement, however, was to facilitate the use of indigenous languages as media for basic education, public outreach through radio or television, and administration purposes at the local government levels. In the meantime, Arabic was to be recognized as the official language of the country and English as the principal language of the administration in southern Sudan. Here, again, it may be relevant to contrast Nimeiri's action with the way India addressed and resolved its linguistic conundrum. With its 415 living languages, compared to Sudan's 134 spoken and lived languages,[19] India refrained from recognizing its two main languages—Hindi and the subsidiary English language—as national languages. Moreover, Article 345 of the Indian Constitution empowered all states of the union to legislate their own official languages based on linguistic demographics.

By making all these misguided decisions, "peacemaker" Nimeiri was in reality hoping to gratify two of his staunchest opponents who eventually came to terms with him: Sadiq al-Mahdi, leader of the Umma party, and Hassan Turabi, leader of Sudan's Muslim Brothers, later known as the Islamic Charter Front.[20] Both leaders took umbrage against the agreement when it was signed and particularly challenged its cultural underpinnings, probably because they saw in them a dilution of the Arabo-Islamic character of Sudan. Indeed, the two leaders were also not happy with another article in Sudan's 1973 constitution relating to religion.[21] However, in Sudan's political theater of the absurd, that constitutional article became, without attribution, a permanent feature in almost all attempts by Sudan's constitutional architects to reconcile Islam with other belief systems in Sudan.

Nonetheless, on becoming Nimeiri's assistant after reconciliation between the two men, Turabi prepared a draft constitution for **Amir al Mu'mineen** (Prince of the Faithful), the new title bestowed upon the president of Sudan, and which entailed repeal of 100 articles of the 1973 Constitution, all penned by Hassan Turabi. Abel Alier stated that following Nimeiri's reconciliation with the Northern opposition in 1977, he was cajoled by that group to abrogate the Addis Ababa agreement including article 16 of the constitution so as "to go down as the greatest Sudanese leader in history and regain the following of the bulk of society in Northern Sudan"[22] Even so, the two leaders lived to regret their connivance with Nimeiri in his premeditated decision to abolish the Addis Ababa agreement. As it had later transpired, the two leaders were not so much ruffled by religious concerns as they were by Nimeiri's success in achieving what they had aspired, but failed, to achieve: bringing an end to the civil war. Immediately after Nimeiri's downfall, al-Mahdi welcomed the decision of the Transitional Military Council (TMC), which replaced Nimeiri's government, to resuscitate the Addis Ababa accord, while Turabi, soon afterwards, engaged in indirect talks with the SPLM, promising much more than what the Addis Ababa agreement had offered to southern Sudanese.[23] That behavior not only revealed a lack of creativity on the part of the two leaders to devise a better formula for ending war than the one designed by the "discredited" Nimeiri, but it also exhibited utter cynicism. Cynics "never see a good quality in a man, and never fail to see a bad one."[24]

Inescapably, war broke out anew in southern Sudan, but with a difference. Sudan's second civil war was led by a new breed of southern Sudanese who were more exposed to the world and who did not share the vision of their predecessors, whose political objectives were either secession from the north or autonomy for southern Sudan. The SPLM/A, a politico-military movement, was formed by this breed of leaders, of whom John Garang de Mabior was the head of the pack. By dropping one "S" from South Sudan Liberation Movement, the party that led the rebellion in southern Sudan up to the Addis Ababa agreement, Garang made his real intention obvious. To Garang, the "Southern Question" was a figment of the imagination of northern political elites; if anything, it was a subset of a national problem. Garang's unionist agendum was not to be achieved without a fratricidal war within the ranks of the movement between those who had espoused the idea of a new Sudan united in diversity and another group that was content with the separation of south Sudan. Garang, on the defeat of the "separatists,"

21

described the situation as such: "From June to November 1983 we engaged in an extensive and intensive debate concerning the direction of the newly formed Movement. Ardent separatists, reactionaries and opportunists gave us a very hard time….The principles proclaimed in our revolutionary Manifesto prevailed. The forces of reaction and separation were defeated."[25] To be fair to those "separatists, reactionaries and opportunists," as Garang had described them, that fratricidal war was not only about vision, it also had all the marks of a power struggle, especially as to who should lead the Movement (SPLM) and the Army (SPLA).[26] Two aspirants to the leadership, Samuel Gai Tut and Akowt Atem challenged Garang to those positions and lost in battle.

Having emerged victorious from that little war, Garang proceeded to restructure his originally South-focused movement into one with a national vocation and a vision to transform the "old Sudan" into a "New Sudan," not destroy it. His vision of the New Sudan was characterized by a secular constitutional order that embraced all Sudanese diversities: ethnic, cultural, religious, linguistic, and regional. Clearly, he was intent on making Sudanese in both north and south Sudan rearticulate their raison d'être. By so doing, he turned upside down what was considered received wisdom in northern, as well as in southern, Sudan. That was particularly the case where national identity was defined by exclusivist parameters—Islam and Arabism—and where not a small number of the northern political elite of the time refused to recognize southern Sudan as a country inhabited by people who had legitimate rights and genuine aspirations.

To the paternalistic fathers of independence, southern Sudanese were but wards to be protected and groomed by northern mentors. Understandably, southern Sudanese perceived attitude as demeaning, even if it was motivated by care, not scorn. On numerous occasions southern Sudanese leaders did not shy away from claiming that northern politicians were not so much concerned with the people of southern Sudan as they were with the South as a real estate and a resource base. The reverberation of fraternal terms like *Akhwana al Janoubieen* (our Southerner brothers), a term commonly used in northern Sudanese political utterances and media comments of the day, was often treated by southern elite as specious sentimentality. Thus, the obliviousness of Khartoum's political class to cultural, religious, and ethnic differentiations between the two parts of the country, together with their insusceptibility to what southern Sudanese considered their legitimate rights, led to belief among the latter that the northern political class saw them only as abstractions of racial stereotypes, not citizens with a cognitive ability to define by themselves the place they wish to occupy under the sun. The northern elite's mindlessness of the deleterious effects of their policies toward southern Sudan, in conjunction with their imperviousness to their co-citizens' resentment of these policies, could only be explained by the fact that within a closed system of prejudice, people rarely realize how prejudiced they are.

6. The Cultural Underpinnings of Conflict

Behind the haughty bearing of not a small sector of northern elites towards southerners existed an assumption of innate superiority characterized by disdain to all things African. That comportment was particularly prevalent within the northern intelligentsia of the first half of the twentieth century who set their sight firmly in one direction: Egypt in the north. Professor Muhammad al-Nuwayhi, an Egyptian academic who taught in the University of Khartoum in the 1960s, proffered an explanation for the way that group perceived its own identity. In a treatise he wrote on northern Sudanese literati of the time, al-Nuwayhi opined that northern Sudanese writers and poets attached greater value "to classical Arabic literature to the complete expulsion of their African heritage and environment."[27] He went on to argue that "the Sudanese having been defeated and humiliated by the Anglo-Egyptian forces, needed psychological reassurance which they could neither find in their African past or the realities of contemporary Africa. Instead of empowering them to regain self-confidence, Africa would have accentuated their feeling of inferiority to the British and Egyptians."[28] Muddathir Abdel-Rahim, an eminent Sudanese political historian, corroborated that judgment by saying that in the eyes of that generation of northern Sudanese, "their non-Islamic present, like their pre-Islamic past, was for them the *Jahilliya* (the age of ignorance), and they could not, therefore, identify themselves with either." [29]

That type of Arabo-Islamic identification conduced to two results. First, it set that intelligentsia intellectually and emotionally apart from Africans, including Africans who shared the land with them. Those Africans, the author observed earlier, were viewed as racial stereotypes believed to have no mental faculties for perception and cognition and, to boot, as ungodly pagans.[30] Second, this mind-set also provided that intelligentsia with a bulwark of self-reassurance. As Abdel-Rahim rightly averred, that attachment to the past of Islam and classical Arabic culture "provided them [the northern elite] with a necessary psychological prod."[31] Whatever explanation is given, that attitude elicits a psycho-pathology of racism. In reality, besmirching all things African reached such a level of idiocy that even African Nubia, which had made a seminal contribution to human civilization and was glorified by the world as one of the greatest cultural heritages of mankind, was derided by its northern heirs as worthless paganism.

This idiosyncrasy waned considerably in the second half of the last century as a result of three factors. The first was the exposure of the northern Arabized elite to the outside world (including some Arab countries). That exposure made them realize obvious indicators of an admixture in which the African element is unmistakable. On the face of it, it looked as if this category of Sudanese elites had never cared to regard their visages on a reflecting surface

23

before they were forced by the outside world to rediscover their chromosomal complexion. Second, as Abdel-Rahim pointed out, was the "emergence of southern Sudanese as active agents in national politics after the termination of the colonial Southern policy in 1946."[32] That policy, announced by the colonial authorities on January 1, 1930,[33] was meant to prepare administrative cadres in southern Sudan to use English, not Arabic, to conduct government business. The memorandum also ordered a reduction of the number of northern traders, replacing them with Greek and Syrian Christian merchants and encouraging education through Christian missionaries. The ridiculousness of that policy became absolute when southern Sudanese were restrained by the colonial administration from wearing so-called Arab attire. The third factor was the resurgence of Africa in the world and the rise of a new African generation of leaders who restored self-respect and *amour-propre* to the continent after centuries of humiliation by colonialism, slavery, and racial discrimination. That was the time when it had become almost bad manners not to be identified with the likes of Kwame Nkrumah, Ahmadou Sekou Toure, Julius Nyerere, Walter Sisulu, and Modibo Keita. Oddly enough, the intellectual retreat to Africa by that extremely Arabocentric elite was also influenced by President Gamal Abdel Nasser's position toward Africa. Nasser, from the early days of the Egyptian revolution, emphasized the pride of place in his global strategy to African liberation and unity.

That was also the time when northern intellectuals relished calling Sudan a microcosm of Africa, a term coined by British historian Arnold Toynbee. After a visit to a number of Arab and African countries, including Sudan, Toynbee wrote: "The problem of the two Sudans [north and south] is the problem of the two Africas on a miniature scale." He went on to say:

> "The Sudan holds Africa's destiny, as well as her own destiny, in her hands. If she can succeed in reconciling the two elements in her own population, she will have done a piece of constructive pioneer work for the continent as a whole. If the conflict in the Sudan becomes acute and chronic, this will heighten the tension between the two Africas everywhere; and, sooner or later, the Southern Sudan will become a focus for Negro Africa's latent resentment against Northern Africa. If things were to come to this pass, the fission of the African continent might become irremediable. The Northern Sudanese have been saddled by fate with a heavy load of responsibility. Let us hope that they will rise to the occasion."[34]

Toynbee's prophecy that Sudan would be the linchpin of African unity was hampered by the revulsion harbored by the Sudanese intelligentsia of the first half of the last century of any claim of Sudan's African belonging. Even those among them who reconciled themselves with, or resigned themselves to, the duality of Sudanese identity were still suspicious of calls for Pan-Africanism that was emanating from some Sudanese elites (both from the North and South). These calls seemed to have been viewed by ultra-Arabo-Islamists as attempts to adulterate the Arabo-Islamic characteristics of Sudan, as if African identity was not also part of Sudanese national identity. Surprisingly, even northern Sudanese intellectuals, who were fairly open to European progressive schools of thought such as the Fabians in England,[35] were never roused by the enthusiasm the Fabians had demonstrated towards Indian and African decolonization. And much as that group of Fabian devotees in Sudan were enthused by efforts of the Fabians to liberate India, they were never turned on by similar efforts toward Africa. For example, in the mid-1940s, Fenner Brockway, a Fabian and Labor Member of Parliament, visited Sudan with a view to interacting with the country's political class.[36] Brockway, who was very close to Pan-Africanists in Manchester and a sponsor of their cause,[37] was almost cold-shouldered during that visit by the political group that was presumed to be the closest to him intellectually.

The mystification of identity was further reinforced by a futile debate among Sudan's political elites on Arabism and Africanism as exclusivist defining characteristics of Sudanese identity, despite the fluidity in both characteristics. Arabism, as Iyoub and Khadigala remark, "can be defined as an ideology of ethno-cultural superiority that manifested itself in Sudan following the rule of the Ottomans in 1821. While Islamism provided the theological and economic justification for continued subjugation of unbelievers, Sudanism is a territorially centred nationalist formulation that rejects both the racialization of Arabism and sectarianism of Islamism."[38] One, therefore, wonders whether the constant whipping by northern elites of the colonial policy in southern Sudan is motivated by the humiliation that policy had inflicted on their southern brothers and sisters, or because that policy has not given the north a free hand in Arabicizing and Islamicizing the South. No matter what, southern Sudanese Africanists manufactured their own, equally racial counter agent to that racial definition of national identity, since they defined African identity primarily by race. Without openly claiming to be adherents to *negritude*, their approach to identity was akin to the quasi-ideological disquisition of the 1930s that was led in France, among others, by Martinican poet Aimé Césaire and the future president of Senegal, Léopold Sédar Senghor. However, neither Césaire nor Senghor had envisioned *negritude* as a racist concept in the way the soi–disant southern Sudanese Africanists appeared to have thought but saw it, rather, as an antivenin to French colonial racism and political and intellectual hegemony.[39] Though a literary intellectual movement, negritude ended by finding political and ideological sustenance in a European-conceived philosophy, Marxism, not in a "rediscovered" African cultural heritage. However, those approaches to African unity were overtaken by the creation of the Organization of African Unity (OAU), and its progressive evolution towards an African Union (AU), based not on geography and racial origin, but primarily on mutual economic interests, interactive cultural enrichment, and political solidarity in a world that was increasingly turning into a global village. Within this context, Pan-Africanism in Sudan shall only make sense when, and if, it realizes that Sudan is a country of two worlds. Thus, with what appeared to be a regressive vision of Pan-Africanism, that class of "Pan-Africanists" neither did justice to themselves, nor to the cause of African unity.

In a recent lecture the eminent academic, Mahmood Mamdani, came up with a refreshing analysis of the duality of Sudanese identity that challenged trite definitions of identity spouted by some elites in North and South Sudan.[40] For example, southern elites invariably claimed that Islam was foisted on them by the Arabs of the North, while not a few northern elites assumed that Southern Sudan had always been the land of Christianity. Mamdani recounted that not only did Nubian (northern) Sudan remain a Christian kingdom until the sixth century, it was also Nubian kings in the North who thwarted the Arabo-Islamic invasion of Sudan.[41] In effect, the first two kingdoms—the Funj, who established Islamic rule and abolished Christianity in north-central Sudan; and the Daju and their successors the Tunjur, who implanted Islam in Western Sudan (Darfur)—were led by kings of pure African genealogy, while the royal house of the Fung descended from the Shilluk tribe in southern Sudan, despite their claim of descent from the Umayyads. That claim has been neither conclusively established by historians, nor borne out by the physiognomy of the Funj. On the other hand, the Tunjur moved into Sudan (Darfur) from Borno and Wadai and reduced Daju chieftains to submission. One of their offspring, Suliman Solon, established in 1603 the first Islamic kingdom in Darfur. In running their new kingdoms, both Funj and Fur kings used to good advantage Islamic *fuqaha* (learned men), especially as clerks and legal advisors of the court. But despite their application of Koranic laws with the help of the *fuqaha*, pre-Islamic customary laws, such as Darfur's local penal code known as the Kitab Dali (Book of Dali), endured. Moreover, both Funj and Fur kings, in order to build up their armies, enticed able young men from neighboring southern Sudanese tribes to become military slaves.

It is thus evident that both northern and southern Sudanese elites were effectively perpetuating myths about their identities. On the one hand, northern elites claimed that Sudan had been Arabicized and Islamicized since time immemorial, without the least regard to the country's Nubian Christian history or the Nubians' resistance to the Islamic invasion from Egypt. As for the southern elite, they had gone along with the conventional Western understanding that equated Islam with Arabism,[42] notwithstanding that the first Sudanese kingdoms that comprehensively Islamicized the country were ruled by kings of a purely Africa pedigree. Seemingly, both the Muslims of North Sudan and the Christians of South Sudan are reluctant to reconcile themselves with the fact that the two religions were embedded in the country through a special process of indigenization. For while Islam was progressively indigenized in the North by non-Arab kingdoms (Funj and Darfur),

Christianity was "paganized" in the South ("paganism" being the derogatory term colonialists used to refer to African belief systems). According to the Federal Research Division of the Library of Congress, no more than 10 percent of southern Sudan's population is Christian.[43] This historical exposé would neither extenuate the sufferings that non-Muslims experienced as a result of forced Islamicization, nor should it serve as a justification for attempts by contemporary Islamists to do the same. It only serves to explode two myths: that Islam was imposed on the Sudanese by conquering Arabs, and that South Sudan was the wellspring of Christianity in Sudan.

The zenith of inanity was reached by a small sector of southern elites who maintained that Arabism and Islamism in Sudan should be erased before the two parts of the country could be united; otherwise said, the "Arabs" should go back to where they came from.[44] The idea of obliterating centuries of a sustained process of acculturation in any country, let alone the expatriation of whole peoples from a country where they and their ancestors were born, would be a reckless and impulsive idea. If universalized, that idea would undo the seams of all countries of the world. The proponents of that ill-considered notion appeared not to have considered the impact that process would have on the whole of Africa. This racist position—not so uncommon among separatists of the 1960s such as Aggrey Jaden—dwindled by the close of the century. That was why one of the first lessons Garang sought to impress on those exclusionists was about mobility and nation formation. Throughout history, he said, people have been in constant flux for whatever reason, and wherever they chose to settle became their home. In recent African history, narrow-minded black South Africans proposed expatriating whites from that country in punishment for their multitudinous sins against blacks, only to be told by Nelson Mandela in his Johannesburg speech on April 20, 1964, that South Africa belonged to all its people, irrespective of their original provenance. Mandela, after his release from prison 26 years later, quoted himself, saying: "I have fought against white domination, and I have fought against black domination. I have cherished the ideal of a democratic and free society in which all persons live together in harmony and with equal opportunities. It is an ideal which I hope to live for and to achieve. But if need be, it is an ideal for which I am prepared to die." That was not only an act of magnanimity, it was primarily a display of common sense.

Moreover, southern Sudanese, including some of the presumed pacesetters in the SPLM, developed their own conventional image of northerners; they almost always characterized them as *jalaba* (slave traders). There were surely reasons that had driven southern Sudanese to associate the north, in general, with the humiliation that their ancestors had suffered from slave raids originating in northern Sudan or carried out by northern slave traders. But, no matter how traumatized southern Sudanese were by that suffering in the nineteenth century, the perceptions of that experience spawned a different type of racial prejudice.

Those were the contradictions Garang hastened to cut through in order to position Sudan to occupy an esteemed historical and geographical place in the world. For example, though Garang was the first leader to propagate the recognition of Sudan's linguistic diversity, he also had the courage to tell a national congregation in 1986 that the "Arabic (though I'm poor in it – I should learn it fast) must be the national language in a new Sudan and therefore we must learn it. We are as frank and as sharp in everything. Arabic cannot be said to be the language of the Arabs. No, it is the language of the Sudan. English is the language of Americans, but that country is America, not England. Spanish is the language of Argentina, Bolivia, Cuba and they are those countries, not Spain."[45] There was a lesson in that statement to both northerners and southerners. To northerners Garang was saying that embracing Arabic culture and language would not make them Arabs; they would remain Sudanese. To southerners he was practically saying that since the Arabic language had been adopted as the *lingua franca* in northern Sudan and between northerners and the majority of southern Sudanese, it should be assumed to be the language of Sudan, not that of distant Arabs. That said, Garang sharply stated on numerous occasions that Islam and Arabism were often used as pretexts to deny southern Sudanese, who were neither Arabs nor Muslims, political space at the national level where Arabic language and culture permeated all public institutions.

While the above-mentioned dichotomies that had torn Sudan asunder for half a century were on their last leg by the end of the second half of the century, the emergence of the Islamists breathed new life into these disagreements, especially through calls for the Arabicization and Islamicization of the entire country. Sudanese Islamists, to be fair to them, had been the least ethnocentric group within Sudan's political elite, as their aspiration had always been the creation of *al-Umma al-Islamiya* (Nation of Islam) across all ethnic and cultural divides. However, to them the Arabic language was inseparable from Islam because it was the language of the Quran. With this mind-set, that group not only accentuated the schism between the two Sudans, but it also came close to making irremediable the fission of African countries Toynbee had predicted and warned against. That was when the Islamists ventured to forcibly Islamicize non-Muslims in Sudan and carry the banner of Islam into the heart of Africa, to what they probably assumed was "the heart of darkness."

7. A Country Looking for its Soul

Through the vision he had articulated, Garang put an end to the mumbo jumbo of contrived perceptions about the self and the other by directly addressing the roots of those perceptions. Sudan, he said, "is still looking for its soul, for its true identity. Failing to find it (because they do not look inside the Sudan, they look outside), some take refuge in Arabism, and failing in this, they find refuge in Islam as a uniting factor. Others get frustrated as they fail to discover how they can become Arabs when their creators thought otherwise. And they take refuge in separatism. In all of these [perceptions], there is a lot of mystification and distortion to suite the various sectarian interests."[46]

To dispel this mystification, Garang concluded that the Sudanese national identity could only be defined by historical realities. He was referring to the Nubian, Nubian Christian, and Islamic civilizations that had shaped Sudan's history, as well as contemporary realities reflected in the political and cultural experiences that had molded and eventually tormented Sudan since the Turkish rule (1881–1885). To him, predicating identity of a country on subjective particularities such as ethnic origin or religion would be a non sequitur. Assuredly, Garang never wished to assert that Sudan's history was a continuum from the Nubian era to the Anglo-Egyptian colonial rule; he only wished to pull together filaments from a multistranded history that had blended to produce a polymorphous country. In singling out the Turkish rule, Garang was patently aware of the role the Turks played in creating modern Sudan, because it was under Turkish rule that North and South Sudan were united and the latter mercilessly exploited by rulers in the center. The Turks, as observed by Iyoub and Khaldagala, also made Islam "the theological and economic justification for subjugation of unbelievers,"."[47] Still, Garang maintained that a Sudanese nation is yet to be born through metamorphosis from a country defined by subjective criteria to one where identity is determined by objective factors. One of Sudan's political analysts pertinently averred that "though nationalists in both north and south would claim that Sudan [had] existed for thousands of years, it only became recognizable as a colonial state in the late nineteenth and early twentieth centuries. Before then it was home to enclaves of small, relatively unhierarchical political communities, developing into Sultanates and as emerging merchant kingdoms along the Nile."[48]

Consequently, Garang moved forward with his political crusade to create a New Sudan where all Sudanese were equal rather than being divided into superior and subaltern identities, where church and mosque were separated from the state, where all religious beliefs were respected as a source of inspiration to those who adhered to them, and where all cultural singularities and native languages were given worth and treated as part and parcel of Sudan's cultural patrimony. By cutting across all divisive misconceptions of what makes Sudan one country and its people one people, he also hoped to put an end to the reductionist approach to Sudan's conflict which, as I alluded earlier, had been prevalent in academic and media circles in the Western world.

Garang also became a pioneer in elevating the issue of economic marginalization to the top of the national agenda. By so doing, he won over disparate groups throughout Sudan, especially areas in the geographic north that were coincidently populated by non-Arabs such as the Nuba Mountains, Blue Nile, Darfur, and Beja. It was not only Garang's charisma and gravitas that seduced those people to his call, but his articulation of their economic woes resonated most in their minds. Arabocentric Sudanese only saw in the inroads Garang made upon those areas an attempt to mobilize non-Arabs in the north against Arabs. Aside from the unseemliness of categorizing citizens of the same country as Arabs and non-Arabs, it was not Garang's fault that those areas represented the epicenter of economic deprivation in Sudan. Well versed in the sciences, Garang was aware of Archimedes' premise that the crushing power of a juggernaut can only be controlled from the peripheries, not from the center. His innovative analysis of, and groundbreaking ideas on, the *problematique* of national identity captured the imagination of large groups of citizens from within Sudan's geographic north as well as from his traditional base of support in southern Sudan. Support in the geographic north came from young men and women who were disenchanted with traditional national politics, while support from marginalized people in the peripheries emanated from societies whose bellies were stoked with anger at Khartoum's policies. That was a quantum leap in Sudan's hackneyed national politics; to both groups Garang became the antidote to old Sudanese politics.

That coup de théâtre did not endear Garang to historical political leaders both in the north or south because it had remorselessly cut the ground from under their feet. In the south, as Francis Deng observed, "John Garang raised the South and the Sudan as a whole to heights previously never conceived or considered possible, especially from a Southern Sudanese leader."[49] Rather than becoming a source of pride to southern politicians, Garang's political and intellectual ascent in the national scene was looked at with both suspicion and envy: suspicion because it was assumed to be a threat to the separation of the south; and envy because of the success of a political *parvenu* in achieving what they had been craving to achieve over the years. On the other side, northern traditional politicians saw in Garang's national agenda a source of destabilization of what was deemed self-evident truths, not only about national identity, but also about how to run and maintain Sudan as a viable and united country.

8. Neo-Islamist Counter Revolution

Following the fall of Nimeiri's regime, in April, 1985, political Islam emerged as a major force at the center of Sudan's politics in a way that radically changed the rules of the game. The National Islamic Front (NIF), the umbrella organization that encompassed Sudanese Islamist activists, usurped power through an effortless military coup on June 30, 1989. At the time, all of Sudan, including its armed forces, was geared up for the imminent collapse of an inept civilian government and an ill-fated multiparty democracy.[50] Even those who craved change were ready to welcome any change other the one that took place on June 30, 1989.

In the weeks that followed, the NIF had virtually butchered its way to power, but its most inauspicious *faux pas* was the decision to turn Sudan's civil war into a *jihad* (holy war), or more precisely, a war between faithful Muslims in the north and infidels in the south. As if they were drawing a leaf from General Francisco Franco's book, the Sudanese "soldiers of God" comforted themselves by repeating with the Spanish dictator: "our war is not a civil war... but a Crusade...Yes, our war is a religious war...we are not fighting against men but against atheism and materialism."[51] That decision brought Sudan's polarization to its highest point and made Sudan's civil war increasingly uncivil. That was not the first time the Islamists tried to mold Sudan into an Islamic state; they made the same attempt in the mid-1960s, in cahoots with northern traditional Islamic parties. That attempt failed to take off because it threatened the country's integrity. Notwithstanding, the neo-Islamists, with reckless audacity, took to the sword to impose their Islamic project, even though Islam in northern Sudan, as history has taught us, percolated into the hearts and minds of men through guidance, teaching, and role modeling. It is revealing to recall that the often ruthless attempts by the Mahdiyya to revive Islamic faith ultimately drove many northern Muslims into the laps of external supporters in order to shake off the Mahdists. Indeed, without tolerance of native habits, ways of life, and mores, early Islamic preachers and *fuqaha* (learned men) would have found it extremely difficult to implant Islam in northern Sudan.

Contrary to that tradition of bringing people to God through forbearance, the NIF's approach was dogmatic and intolerant. In their alleged preaching of Islam, they followed examples of freakish absolutist regimes. In essence, the NIF style of propagating Islam represented a counterrevolution to Sudan's traditional Islam. Their rallying cry from the start was pure and simple: *al Islam Hua al hal,* "Islam is the answer." Regardless of its vapidity, as it meant different things to different people, the slogan also prophesied trouble in a country beleaguered by a multitude of diversities, including religious diversity. This became even more problematic when the only solution the Islamists proposed for addressing the "Question of the South" was forcible Arabicization and Islamicization. Unity of any multireligious country can neither be realized through a process of moral homogenization based on values drawn from one religion, nor can it achieve national coherence in such a country.

Sudan's Islamists, however, claimed that the process of Islamicization should have been the natural course of history in Sudan were it not for its deliberate obstruction by colonialists who derided all cultures other than their own. That was an equally vapid statement since colonialism, by its very nature, represented the apotheosis of European cultural arrogance. Consequently,

31

derision of other cultures was a function of that haughty colonialist predisposition. But if colonialists had completely sealed off south Sudan from the north, it was not because of their desire to bring southern Sudanese to God or transform them into British citizens, much as they wanted to keep southern Sudan under control as a reserved property for future exploitation. Even among themselves, colonial administrators in Khartoum used to call their agents in south Sudan (district commissioners) "swamp barons." The south Sudan of these barons, to all ends and purposes, had become a human museum frozen in time. Save for small elite groups, the people of southern Sudan were neither Christianized nor Anglicized; they were left in a state of nature—unlettered, underdeveloped, and abandoned to listless somnolence. The only concern colonialists had in southern Sudan turned out to be security and delivery of basic services. British haughtiness towards the south was outrageously reflected in the way in which the Azande scheme, the first development project in southern Sudan, was launched as "an experiment for the social emergence of indigenous races in remote areas."[52] On the other side, the British established in north Sudan a viable civil service, worthy judicial institutions, well-disciplined army and police forces, and a reputable educational system up to tertiary level. In effect, the attitude of the British toward southern Sudanese was no less patronizing than that of the northern political class who took over the reins of power from them.

Countless Sudanese politicians and commentators still persist on blaming colonialists, half a century after their departure, for the protraction of the north-south conflict, even though whipping a dead horse is but a futile exercise. Without exonerating colonialists from responsibility for keeping southern Sudan in a state of woeful underdevelopment for a nigh 50 years, national Sudanese governments who succeeded the British had equally another half-century to put right what had gone wrong during the rule of their predecessors. From the eve of the declaration of independence, it was clear to anybody who was not stone-blind that there were religious, social, cultural, and economic factors that had sustained tensions between the two parts of the country. Nationalist leaders, including the Islamists, were either unable, or reluctant, to see those factors. Recognition of those factors in the CPA lent credence to the latter hypothesis. That the northern political class had to wait until war overwhelmed the whole of Sudan to realize the relevance of those factors to peace and unity says a lot about the political savvy of that class. Above and beyond, what dazes one is that the same class of politicians, together with the mainstream of northern academics and media commentators, had always been ready to deplore all manner of discrimination—religious, cultural, and political—in other countries, but never on their own home ground. Standing firm against cruelties and injustices inflicted by the strong against the weak in any part of the globe ennobles humanity, but imperviousness to similar inequities in your own backyard makes what is meant to be a noble act bogus indignation.

For all that, attempts to achieve a peaceful settlement of Sudan's conflict between the SPLM/A, a secularist movement that believed politics are rooted in the here and now, and the ruling Islamist party, who infused religion with politics and believed that Allah was on its side, became an exercise in futility. On the other hand, with unyielding dogmatism, NIF became obsessed with remodeling the multicultural and multireligious Sudan to its image. Their indoctrination was not solely restricted to south Sudanese "unbelievers" but also covered the north, where Islam had a long pedigree. Northerners who espoused Islam for centuries did not need to be reintroduced to that religion by anybody. Nonetheless, the NIF for over a decade remained firm in its attempt to propagate and enforce its own brand of Islam on those who did not share its religious orientation. That folly reached its acme when the NIF categorized citizens of the same country into believers and infidels. In so doing, they were mindless that in this day and age such religious proselytization was not only impolitic, it was also offensive to basic universal human rights and would not be tolerated at both regional and international levels. So, as a result of serious violations of religious rights and the brutal manner by which the NIF carried out its mission among Muslims and non-Muslims alike, pressures on the regime by international and regional nongovernmental organizations multiplied and intensified. Eventually, the NIF learned how to do business in the real world, but only after a decade-and-a-half of blood and tears.

NOTES

1   John 1:8
2   Desmond Tutu, on his enthronement as Anglican Archbishop of Cape Town.
3   The Liberal Party was led by Benjamin Lwoki (Equatoria) together with Stanislaus Payasama (Bahr el Ghazal) as deputy leader, Paulo Logali, (Equatoria) as treasurer, and Buth Diu (Upper Nile) as secretary general.
4   The first Juba Conference was held in 1946 under the guidance of the colonial administration. It brought together for the first time northern and southern politicians and government officials to discuss the future of the South and secure its place in the forthcoming self-government arrangements. For more details, see Faisal A.A. Taha: *Sudan at the Threshold of the Second independence, 1954–1956* (Sudan: Abdel Karim Mirghani Cultural Centre, 2010.
5   The letter was addressed by Benjamin Lwoki to Sudan's Prime Minster Azhari, governor general of Sudan, British foreign secretary, and Egyptian foreign minister. See British documents on Sudan, *16* November 1954, Fo371/108326.
6   Ibid.
7   The Sudanization Committee was formed in the run up to Sudan's self-government in order to replace British and Egyptian officials in the colonial

administration by Sudanese officials. The Committee comprised five members of whom three were Sudanese but none was from South Sudan.

8 In effect there were 1,111 British and 108 Egyptian who were in the employ of the colonial administration, but 300 of them opted for voluntary retirement.

9 Judge Tawfiq Cotran, a Palestinian of British nationality who served as Khartoum police magistrate, led the Investigation Committee into Incidents in South Sudan (1955). The committee comprised Khalifa Mahjoub, a senior police officer who was by then serving as general manager of Nzara Scheme, and Pacifico Lolik Lado, a southern tribal leader.

10 Article 12 of the "Agreement between the Government of the United Kingdom of Great Britain and Northern Ireland and the Egyptian Government concerning Self-Government And Self-Determination for the Sudan," signed in Cairo on February 12, 1953, provided for the creation of a Constituent Assembly whose duties shall be first to decide the future of the Sudan as one integral whole. The second will be to draw up a constitution for the Sudan compatible with the decision which shall have been taken in this respect, as well as an electoral law for a permanent Sudanese Parliament. The agreement also provided that the future of the Sudan shall be decided either

(a) by the Constituent Assembly choosing to link the Sudan with Egypt in any form, or

(b) by the Constituent Assembly choosing complete independence." The first option in that article was never put to the vote, because the Sudanese Parliament decided to abrogate it.

11 *Sawt al-Sudan*, the daily organ of the Khatmiyya sect, wrote on February 15, 1956, that the idea of federalism was planted in the minds of southern Sudanese by Sir William Luce. Luce, a colonial administrator who had wide relations with northern Sudan elite and almost none with southerners, ended his service in Sudan as advisor to the governor general in the run-up to independence.

12 The Sudanese political elite coalesced in the 1940s into an organization called the Graduates' Congress and promised to emulate India's modes of struggle for independence. As it turned out, that emulation was only in name. The congress did not follow in the footsteps of the leaders they claimed to be their *beau idéal*, neither on the decentralization of governance and the uplifting of marginalized groups, nor in recognition of cultural, religious, and linguistic diversity.

13 Proverbs, 16:18

14 Felix.K. Onama, Minister of Home Affairs, and E.Lakidi Member of Parliament (Uganda); The Hon. Al Haji Yusuf Maitama Sule, Minister of Mines and Power, and Richard Ainjudi, member of Federal Parliament (Nigeria); Sayed Fathi El Deeb, Minister of State and Director of Arab Affairs in the Arab Socialist Union, Egypt's ruling party (UAR); Nathaniel Welbeck, Minister of Information, and K. Edusei, Minister of Agriculture (Ghana); P.C. Walwa, Member of Parliament, and A.P. Leyki, assistant foreign minister, (Tanzania); and Sayed Abdel Rahman El Sherif, Cabinet Affairs Minister, and Tidjani Haddam, member of the Central Committee of the Algerian Liberation Front (Algeria).

15 John Garang, *The Call for Democracy in Sudan*, ed. Mansour Khalid (London: Kegan Paul International, 1992), 31.

16 Islamic Charter Front (led by Turabi), National Unionist Party, People's Democratic Party, Professional Front, Sudan African National Union, Sudanese Communist Party, Southern Front, and Umma Party.

17 Among the leaders incarcerated in Juba were speaker of the South Sudan Parliament Mathew Obur and vice president of the Executive Council Dhol Acuil. The two were accused of propagating unity of the South.

18 Sir John Maffey, British Governor-General of the Sudan, wrote in 1927: "Whenever I penetrated, whether to the top of the Imatong or to the Belgian Congo border, I found Arabic readily used by the local spokesman of the people. In the face of this *fait accompli* we shall have to consider very carefully how far it is worth effort and money to aim at the complete supersession of Arabic. Indeed, we shall have to consider whether Arabic, in spite of its risks, must be our instrument." Sudan Archives, "Note by the Governor General," 12 June 1927.

19 Languages in Sudan (Wikipedia), Ethologue: Languages of the World, 15th ed., Dallas, US

20 Both al-Mahdi and Turabi emerged as champions of the recognition of Sudan's multidiversities; al-Mahdi in the course of his negotiations with the SPLM in the mid-1990s, and Turabi in the 1998 constitution that he authored.

21 Article 16 of the 1983 Sudan constitution provided for the recognition of Islam, Christianity, and "noble spiritual beliefs." The latter term denoted African belief systems. The same article criminalized acts that foment hatred against any religion or noble spiritual belief.

22 Abel Alier, *Southern Sudan: Too Many Agreements Dishonoured*, 277.

23 Turabi, through the mediation of an eminent Sudanese businessman, George Haggar, sought to meet Garang in Nairobi to reach an agreement with him on the peaceful resolution of Sudan's conflict and, especially, an understanding on the worrisome issue of politics and religion.

24 H.W. Beecher, *Proverbs from Plymouth Pulpit* (New York: D. Appleton and Co., 1887), Quoted by Collins Thesaurus of the English Language, Harper Collins Publishers, 2008.

25 Speech by John Garang on the second anniversary of the Bor, Pibor, and Fochella resistance and the Ayoud revolution, 26/27 May 1985, cited in *The Call for Democracy in Sudan*, ed. Mansour Khalid, Kegan Paul, London 1990, 48.

26 Douglas Johnson, *The Root Causes of Sudan's Civil Wars*, 65.

27 Quoted by Muddathir Abdel Rahim in Sudan in Africa, ed. Yousif Fadl Hassan (Khartoum: University Press, 1957), 231.

28 Ibid.

29 Ibid., *Jahilliya* refers to pre-Islamic Arabia characterized by idolatry as opposed to the enlightenment brought by Islamic divine laws.

30 Supra note 27

31 Ibid., 234.

32 Supra note 27, 236

33 Memorandum issued by colonial civil secretary Harold Mac-Michael, Khartoum, Civil Secretary's Office, *Sudan Archives*, "Memorandum on Southern Policy, 1930," 25 January, 1930.

34 Arnold Toynbee, *Between Niger and Nile* (London, New York: Oxford University Press, 1965), 6.

35

35 Within the intelligentsia of that period, members of al Itihadiyeen (unionists) party were habitué to the socialist ideas of the Fabian Society and avid readers of their publications, especially the *New Statesman and Nation.*

36 Brockway visited Sudan in the company of Yacoub Osman, the only Sudanese intellectual in the diaspora who was actively engaged with the Pan-Africanist movement in London and Manchester. Osman later joined the Umma Party and became editor of that party's daily organ.

37 The leadership of the Pan-Africanist movement in England had by that time (1945) moved from Afro-American and West Indian to African pioneers such as Kwame Nkrumah (Ghana), Jomo Kenyatta (Kenya), and Peter Abrahams (South Africa).

38 Ruth Iyob and Gilbert M. Khadiagala, *Sudan: The Elusive Quest for Peace* (Boulder, CO: Lynne Rienner Publishers, 2006), 20.

39 Léopold Sédar Senghor, *Ce que je crois: nenghoremy Occasionaloneers such as Kwame Nkrumah* (Paris: B. Grasset, 1988)

40 Mahmoud Mamdani, "South Sudan and the African Experience: The Quest for a New Political Order," presented at Makerere University, Kampala, Uganda, May 20, 2011. http://www.independent.org/2011/05/20/south-sudan-and-african-experience-quest-new-political-order

41 Nubia had been Christianized by the Romans since 580 A.D., and its three states—Nobatia (lying between the first and third cataract on the Nile), Makuria (between the third and sixth cataracts), and Alwa (from the sixth cataract to Blue Nile)—remained Christian up to 1504 B.C. Several attempts by the Islamic caliphate in Cairo to subjugate Nubia by force failed, and eventually Egypt's Islamic rulers opted for a coexistence treaty that lasted for 600 years. It was during these six centuries that Islam trickled into Nubia through traders and learned men.

42 Mamdani, "South Sudan and the African Experience."

43 U.S. Library of Congress, Federal Research Division, "Sudan: A Country Study," ed. Helen Chapin Metz, ch. 2, Robert O. Collins, "Society and its Environment: Regionalism and Ethnicity," (1991).

44 During the Round Table Conference, Aggrey Jaden, then a member of the extremist faction of the Sudan African National Union, declared "there are in fact two Sudans, and the most important thing is that there can never be a basis for unity between the two. There is nothing in common between the various sections of the community: no body of shared beliefs, no identity of interests, no local signs of unity and, above all, the Sudan had failed to compose a single community." *The Vigilant* (Khartoum), 23 March 1965.

45 Address to the Koka Dam dialogue between the Sudan People's Liberation Movement and the National Alliance on 20 March 1986. Garang, *The Call for Democracy in Sudan,* 142.

46 Ibid.,127.

47 Supra note 38, 20.

48 Atta el-Batthani, "A complex web politics and conflict in Sudan," *Peace by Piece: Addressing Sudan's Conflicts.* Peter Dixon and Mark Simmons, (eds). (London: Conciliation Resources, 2006), 11.

49 Francis Deng, *New Sudan in the Making,* 51

50 Khalid, *War and Peace in Sudan,* 180–188.

51 General Francisco Franco: Speech during the Spanish Civil War, 1973.

52 Tothill, J. D., An experiment in the social emergence of indigenous races in remote places, Memorandum in Ministry of Agriculture, Khartoum, File 2-1, Vol.1,1943. The initiator of the project, Dr. J.D. Tothill, was at the time director of agriculture and forests in Uganda and thereafter became director of agriculture in Sudan (1939–1944), after which he moved to be the first principal of Sudan's Gordon Memorial College.

Chapter Two
Roadblocks on the Way to Machakos

■ ■ ■ ■ ■ ■ ■ ■ ■ ■ ■ ■ ■ ■ ❖ ■ ■ ■ ■ ■ ■ ■ ■ ■ ■ ■ ■ ■ ■

They make a wilderness and call it peace…it is part of human nature to hate
the man you have hurt.
—**Publius Cornelius Tacitus,**
On the destruction of Agricola

1. Introduction

Machakos, a town 64 kilometers southeast of Nairobi, earned its fame as the
first capital of colonial Kenya.[1] In the beginning of the third millennium,
however, it became widely known for another reason: being the cradle of the
agreement that paved the way for a definitive settlement of Africa's longest
civil war. While the previous chapter drew a political profile for the period that
stretched from the declaration of Sudan's independence to the time when the
National Islamic Front (NIF) wrested power from an infirm multiparty
government, this chapter shall put in relief political and military evolutions in
the country in the periods that followed Nimeiri's downfall and succeeded the
NIF's coup. It was within these two periods that issues like religion and
culture, though threateningly divisive, were fairly quiescent until the NIF
usurped power.

John Garang, who had no faith in the new regime let alone in its ability to
resolve Sudan's conflict in a comprehensive manner, appeared to be the most
improbable negotiator with that regime. Because of that distrust, Garang
sought political alliance with northern political opposition, including parties
who were, paradoxically, responsible for aggravating Sudan's conflict since
independence. That alliance was, however, mitigated by Garang's association

with a network of emerging political forces in the peripheries and within Sudanese urban centers, especially new social forces disenchanted with traditional politics. Those forces collectively provided a robust challenge to the NIF. In the meantime, having failed to attract Garang to negotiate with it on its terms, the NIF moved to its Plan B: causing fissures within the Sudan People's Liberation Movement (SPLM) as well as within northern political forces that chose to cooperate with it in order to dislodge the regime. That regime was described night and day by the SPLM leader John Garang as "too deformed to be reformed."

In addition, the chapter shall review, on the one hand, the blundering manner in which the new Islamist regime dealt with the outside world, and on the other hand, the ruthlessness it exhibited in treating real or perceived enemies inside the country. At that time political party activists, journalists, and trade unionists who took exception to the NIF policies or even refused cooperation with it were systematically intimidated and sometimes killed. Those actions generated external reactions that left an enduring mark on the country's political life. The NIF repeatedly described external reactions to its internal politics either as ideologically inspired plots against an Islamist regime or as conspiratorial intrigues against Islam itself. These, as the author shall explain, are only strained and self-serving justifications. If truth be told, external reactions to the Sudan government on many occasions were responses to unprovoked aggression by that government toward the outside world, including some of Sudan's closest neighbours such as Egypt, Saudi Arabia, and the Gulf states. By the same token, international human rights groups objected to the beastliness with which the regime treated its political opponents inside the country.

2. Downfall of Nimeiri Regime

On April 6, 1985, Nimeiri's government fell as a result of a popular revolt spearheaded by an unlikely alliance between the army led by Nimeiri's minister of defence, Abdel Rahman Siwar al-Dahab; opposition parties; and professional and workers' trades unions. The new regime was headed by a Transitional Military Council (TMC) that was to prepare for national elections within one year. However, the first decision taken by the TMC regarding South Sudan was the resurrection of the Addis Ababa agreement without the least regard to the critique made by the SPLM leader on March 24, 1986, of the structural defects of that agreement that had enabled Nimeiri to abrogate it. That was the reason why the SPLM categorically refused to negotiate with the generals, although it expressed readiness to discuss Sudan's crisis with all concerned political and social groups. In response to an invitation to the SPLM from northern political parties and trades unions the first formal meeting between SPLM and northern parties took place in an Ethiopian resort at Koka Dam in 1986.[2] The upshot of the meeting was a declaration of commitment to:

(i) Repeal the 1983 shari'a laws and all other laws that restrict freedoms and replace them with the 1974 Penal Code.
(ii) Lift the state of emergency.
(iii) Replace the 1985 Transitional Constitution of the Republic of Sudan with the 1965 constitution, as amended in 1964.

On the other side, the NIF came out with a national charter that reflected its analysis of, and conclusions on, conditions that would ensure peace and unity. The charter maintained that since the majority of the people of Sudan were Muslims, then it followed that they should have the right to apply Muslim laws, while guaranteeing to the "minority" the right to apply its own laws on personal matters. In other words, the so-called non-Muslim "minority" of whatever denomination had to suffer gladly shari'a-based civil and criminal laws.

Figure 1: John Garang and author with former U.S. President and Mrs. Jimmy Carter at Plains, GA (1987)

3. Duel between Two Rebels

On June 30, 1989, NIF decided to realize its divine mission through the bullet, not the ballot. That was surprising since the NIF had gained through the ballot a reasonably advanced position in Sudan's parliament in the 1986 elections,

41

which gave the Umma Party 101 seats, the Democratic Unionist Party (DUP) 63 and the NIF 51. However, upon coming to power on June 30, 1989, the NIF coup leaders claimed that they were constrained to stage a coup because the other two parties had "failed miserably" in ending the war in South Sudan or managing the economy. They also accused the two parties (Umma and DUP) of plotting to exclude Islamists from government. Ostensibly, the NIF viewed party coalitions—a regular exercise in multiparty democracies—as plots. The NIF, however, baptized its coup as *thawrat al Ingaz al watani* (revolution of national salvation). By dressing their coup in a national garb, the plotters wanted to hide the ideological disposition of the coup. They also naively declared that "John Garang is a soldier, and we are soldiers, thus we understand the problem of the South more than anybody else and shall be able to solve it together."[3] The fact that the new military rulers of Sudan led by Brigadier Omar Hassan Ahmad al-Bashir could not see in the Sudan People's Liberation Movement/Army (SPLM/A) leader anything other than his martial character and military accoutrements did not auger well for the negotiations. With this shallow understanding of, and approach to, Sudan's civil war, the new government moved quickly to commence dialogue with Garang, "the soldier." Two rounds of negotiations were conducted through outside facilitation or mediation, with a view to putting an end to Sudan's war. The first took place at Addis Ababa, Ethiopia, in mid-August 1989 on the invitation of former Ethiopian President Mengistu Haile Mariam; the second was held in Nairobi, Kenya, in December 1989, mediated by former U.S. President Jimmy Carter and hosted by Kenya's former president, Daniel arap Moi. The talks in both meetings did not lead to any concurrence of views.

Failure of the two meetings was unmistakably due to discordant perceptions of Sudan's conflict, for while the SPLM/A was seeking resolution of a national problem that was political in nature, including questions relating to religion and politics and the transformation of Sudan's system of rule, the NIF was only looking for an end to war between two armies that would lead to a coalition between the NIF and SPLM. Thus, cessation of hostilities and putting an end to media campaigns were at the top of the list of demands presented by the government's delegation in both the Addis Ababa and Nairobi meetings. On *shari'a*, the NIF delegation came forward with a jaw-dropping proposition: putting *shari'a* for a plebiscite throughout Sudan. They were probably counting on support of the application of *shari'a* by the overwhelming majority of Muslims in North Sudan. The SPLM never took seriously the pretence by the NIF to seek popular consultation on *shari'a*, particularly when it came from the very party that had overthrown an elected government for no reason other than its intention to freeze (not repeal) *shari'a* laws pending their consideration in a national constitutional conference in which the SPLM committed to participate. The SPLM/A also stuck to its agreement with DUP leader al-Mirghani in that regard.[4] That was the last thing the NIF delegation wanted to hear, as they proved by staging a coup on the same day the Mirghani-Garang agreement was to be enacted into law. Indeed, Garang later sarcastically described the NIF proposition as a sacrilege and sarcastically asked the author: "How can mortals decide in a plebiscite the fate of laws ordained by Allah, if those laws are really Allah's laws?"[5].

As a result of the failure in both instances on the part of the two armies who "knew each other well"[6] to negotiate a settlement, the NIF cobbled together in September 1989 a National Dialogue Conference (NDC), comprising a large number of its own cadres as well as a medley of nonpartisan academics and self-styled independent intellectuals. No other political party was invited, since by then all parties had been banned and their leaders incarcerated at the NIF's pleasure. In an utterly impertinent manner, the NIF invited the SPLM to the dialogue through Sudan Radio. In turn, the SPLM replied to that invitation in an equally disrespectful manner through its own radio service.

A month before the holding of the NDC Garang delivered on August 10, 1989 a major speech through Radio SPLM[7] in response to Omar al-Bashir's call for peace. In that speech Garang underlined three major demands: address the root causes of the conflict and not the so-called Southern Question, return to democracy, and separate religion from state. On the first demand, Garang said: "Bashir's perception and contention that he has come to solve the problem of southern Sudan misses the point by a wide margin; it is a step backwards, a retrogression, indeed a crude and reactionary position that can only bring disaster, not peace, to the country."[8] He also challenged Bashir's claim that he spoke on behalf of the whole Sudan: "Omar thinks that he is the Sudanese nationalist and we in the SPLA are his southerners, and according to him all that is required is for him to sit down with John Garang representing the South, and him representing the Sudan, and in his words talk soldier to soldier to solve the Southern problem." Garang further asked, probably with a glint of mockery: "Has Brigadier Omar al-Bashir bothered to ask the question as to what is it that makes him the Sudanese and makes Dr. John his southerner."[9] This was the type of simple, unadorned question that could only be asked by a politician of a southern provenance who was capable of shirking off any sense of inferiority and conceiving Sudan as a country belonging to all of its citizens.

Concerning democracy, Garang declared that the "junta [meaning by that the perpetrators of the coup] has come to establish a military dictatorship at a time when the wind of democracy is blowing all over the world and at a time when dictators are being toppled in popular uprisings....Can Sudan be an exception to democracy?"[10] he queried. As for religion, Garang asked: "What is the position of the junta on religion and the state?" Judging from the junta's statements, he said, "there is sufficient reason for concern that Brigadier Omar has a hidden agenda, with or without the NIF, to impose a theocratic state on the Sudan, or part of the Sudan. When Brigadier Omar took over, it was widely expected that his first act would be to abolish Nimeiri's September Laws."[11] Garang said, in the above cited radio statement, that "Al-Bashir outdid Siwar al-Dahab in his fundamentalism and started to talk the same language of Dr. Turabi." Al-Bashir, Garang went on saying, declared the constitution suspended, but curiously picked one item—Nimeiri's Shari'a Law—for discussion with the SPLM/A, thereby exposing his ideological colors. Garang proceeded in the same radio broadcast to say that if Bashir failed to reach an agreement with the SPLM/A on the question of Nimeiri's September (*shari'a*) Laws, these laws would be taken to the people for decision in a popular referendum. The SPLM leader thus wondered how a self-imposed military junta would have the audacity to talk about carrying out a popular referendum on *shari'a* laws when no referendum had been carried out by that junta on its assumption of power. Setting its lack of legitimacy aside, Garang added, "The junta's friends in the NIF will tell them that Allah's Laws [Laws of God], are not subject to human opinion! Indeed it is blasphemous for Bashir to say that God's laws shall be [subjected to] human judgment."

To rub salt into the wound, Garang added in his radio speech a derisive comment: "Omar Bashir is a rebel against a constitutionally formed government just like the SPLM, and it is not for the senior rebel to participate in a national dialogue in Khartoum organized by his junior in rebellion." Nevertheless, Garang conceded at the end of that speech, that "if Al-Ingaz [salvation government—the name chosen by the military rulers to designate their coup d'état] wants the SPLM to participate in the NDC, it has first to lift the ban on political parties, trade unions, and the print media before the SPLM ever considers participating in the conference." Perforce, the NDC met without the SPLM, and without rhyme or reason, issued a verbose document, which in sum called for a federal system of rule, equitable apportionment of wealth and power, and dialogue as a means for conflict resolution. Thereafter, in view of the SPLM/A's refusal to take its peace overture seriously, the NIF concentrated its energies on preparing for *jihad* against "the infidels" without ceasing to explore windows of opportunity for reaching a peace agreement with the very same "infidels." Additionally, the NIF, though weakened in the theater of war, believed that it could contrive a kind of peace "from within" that would force the SPLM/A to capitulate. That meant creating fissures within the SPLM.

4. Dividing the South

Realizing that its Achilles heel was its total monopolization of power, which drove all banned political forces in Sudan to line up against it, the NIF began to play with cosmetic changes to the way it governed the country. In the mid-1990s it began to bring into its orbit smaller opponents, one by one, without losing hold on its power or compromising its *thawabit* (immutable fundamental principles).[12] In 1996, the regime brought in a "civilian" government, with Hassan al-Turabi as speaker of parliament, and into the bargain it signed a peace charter that same year with Riek Machar Teny's faction of the SPLM. That faction was later called the South Sudan Independence Movement (SSIM) to distinguish itself as a separatist party as opposed to Garang's unionist SPLM. That marriage of convenience between a party (NIF) that was fighting a war in southern Sudan to keep the country united and a southern Sudanese party whose whoop of war was independence of the south revealed the scornful nature of the politics of both parties. Oddly enough, one article of the peace charter committed the signatory parties, including SSIM, to unity of Sudan. How a unionist party could coalesce with a separatist movement in order to keep Sudan united was a question that confuted the science of reasoning.

The parties also pledged, among other things, to implement *shari'a* and custom as sources of legislation in Sudan and to conduct a plebiscite to ascertain the "aspirations" of the people of southern Sudan after "*full establishment of peace and stability*" and "*a reasonable level of social and economic development in the South was achieved.*"[13] Recognizing the right of southern Sudanese to self-determination, which was one of the main causes of the SPLM split in 1991, was never featured in the charter. It was thus mind-boggling that while Machar made any agreement with Garang contingent on the endorsement by the latter of the right to self-determination, he was amenable to abjuring that condition in his negotiations with the NIF. Even the reference to ascertaining the "aspirations" of the people of southern Sudan was subject to woolly conditions such as full establishment of peace and a reasonable level of development in the South. These terms could only have been inserted in the charter in order to obfuscate, not clarify, the issue. In a former publication the author wrote: "It is this kind of defectively open-ended provision that, economically speaking, would apply with equal facility and legitimacy to any of Rostow's levels of economic development, and socially, to any of Marx's stages of human civilization. It is, therefore, worthless for all practical purposes."[14] Thus, alliance between Machar, the leader of the movement for the independence of southern Sudan, and the governing party in Khartoum from which he sought independence, looked bizarre and improbable in the eyes of sane observers. Horror and disbelief were thus the words that sprang to the lips of those who lived through the agonies of the split engineered by Riek Machar Teny for the sole reason of achieving instant self-determination that would lead to independence. The NIF government also formalized its arrangements with Kerubino Kuanyin Bol's militia; Kerubino, though a stalwart fighter of the SPLA, was known for his mercurial character. In effect, he was reported to have approached the Ethiopian government to arrest Garang and replace him with new leadership, but the Ethiopians did exactly the contrary by arresting Kerubino.[15]

On April 21, 1997, the NIF government sought to give momentum to the shaky charter signed with Machar by bringing in other armed opponents from southern Sudan who were apparently manufactured by the NIF under the name of the United Democratic Salvation Front (UDSF) and signing a peace "agreement" with them. The word "salvation" was the most intriguing since it matched the name given by Bashir to his military coup: *thawarat Al-Ingaz* (salvation revolution). The NIF also persuaded southern militias to merge into a South Sudan Defence Force (SSDF). In addition to Riek Machar Teny and Kerubino Kuanyin Bol, those who succumbed to the NIF enticements included Dr. Theopolous Ochang of the Equatoria Defence Force (EDF) and Mohammed Harun Kafi of (SPLM/A-Nuba), a fictitious movement that was only meant to create the impression that there was a split within the SPLM/A's ranks in the Nuba Mountains. Four months later (September 1997), the government signed the Fachoda Accord with Lam Akol Ajawin's pitiful remainder of SPLM-United. Akol, who was the brains behind the split, readily joined the increasingly farcical arrangement in Khartoum.

It may be recalled in this connection that back in 1993 (October 22) Riek Machar, on behalf of SPLM-United (the party he had established with Lam Akol after the split from SPLM/A), signed in Washington a very important document prepared by Congressman Harry Johnston, chairman of the African Subcommittee of the U.S. House of Representatives, and his congressional aide Ted Dagne. That document contained three provisions:

(i) The right to self-determination for people of southern Sudan (to which Garang added "*and marginalized areas of the Nuba Mountains and Southern Blue Nile.*"

(ii) Cessation of hostilities between the SPLM/A and those who had split from it (meaning by that SPLM-United).

(iii) Opposition to policies of the NIF, to which Machar added "*or any subsequent regime that denies southern Sudanese the right to self-determination.*"

The three-point document was accepted by the SPLM/A and Riek Machar's group, even though the SPLM leader refused to append his signature to it in Washington for a technical reason. Far from being "technical," the issue to Garang was one of substance. In a meeting to which the author was privy, Garang told Congressman Johnston that there was only one SPLM, so for a splinter group to call itself SPLM/A-United was inadmissible. As a result of the Congressman's persuasion, the agreement was signed between SPLM-Mainstream and SPLM-United.

But rather than opposing the NIF policies as they had promised to do in Washington, the two supposed southern Sudan separatists decided to put all their weight behind those policies. In effect, Machar cited his concern for "his people"—the Nuer, not those of southern Sudan for whom he was seeking secession—as justification for his alliance with the government against the

SPLM/A. He claimed that Garang posed a greater threat to the Nuer than the government.[16] As future experiences would show, the two leaders (Riek Machar and Lam Akol) became adept in the art of being separatists on odd days and unionist on even days. Surprisingly, in that same year the government also accepted the Intergovernmental Authority on Development (IGAD) Declaration of Principles (DoP) as one of many bases for negotiation. By so doing, the government reversed its acceptance-then-rejection of the IGAD framework in 1993–1994, probably as a stalling tactic and without full commitment to the DoP. The NIF's irresoluteness regarding the DoP would soon be evident in the 1998 negotiations at Addis Ababa under the IGAD auspices.

Meanwhile, the NIF continued with its artless designs to conceal the illiberal nature of its governance system. In June 1998, it promulgated a new constitution, drafted word-by-word by Hassan al-Turabi. That constitution omitted any reference to state and religion and posited the rights of citizens on *almwatana* (citizenship). Nonetheless, the NIF continued to sing hymns to its *mashru'a al Hadhari* (civilizational project), another code name for the Islamicization of Sudan. Put within its appropriate concomitant, the civilizational project comprised fragmented and disjointed initiatives that hardly added up to a project, let alone a civilizational one. If the word "civilization" signified enlightenment, cultivation, and refinement, then what the NIF had offered was a malapropism. To add insult to injury, Sudan's self-appointed civilizers encircled themselves with a potpourri of business groups and military security networks; that, by necessity, divested the *mashru'a* of any Islamic pretence or claim to propagate Islam as a system of belief, a cultural stimulus for change, or a fount of values that inspire men. If anything. Islam only became a tool for the mobilization of Muslims in the North behind a worldly project called power. In pursuance of that aim, the NIF established a "civilian" government and held tightly controlled elections. For that sham democratization, the NIF won cautious support from various quarters, including Egypt and some European countries. Before the promulgation of its new constitution, the NIF also succeeded in pulling in a minority faction of the northern opposition, the DUP, led by Sharif Zayn al-Abidin al-Hindi. For two decades Hindi's party had been making political capital of its opposition to Nimeiri's "dictatorial regime," but that crowing over democracy was completely forgotten when the DUP gladly joined a regime that had almost made an angel of Nimeiri. In a country where many political analysts and chroniclers were known for their perforated memories, that discordance went unnoticed and, thus, caused no embarrassment to the DUP.

5. National Democratic Alliance: Chaotic Aggregate

Between 1995 and 1999, while the NIF was endeavoring to gloss over its autocratic mien through implausible alliances, the SPLM/A *also* retained hope that it could deliver the greater promise of the New Sudan by removing the NIF from power in Khartoum. Future events showed that that promise was equally implausible. Notwithstanding, the SPLM pushed on with its New Sudan agenda after it had recovered from its internal splits of 1991. To actualize that dream, Garang estimated that Sudan's political space should first be recaptured from the NIF. Accordingly, the SPLM moved successfully to build a political coalition, coalescing exiled Northern opposition parties under the umbrella of the National Democratic Alliance (NDA). Though that alliance was formed in Cairo in April 1990 and subsequently held two meetings, one in London in February 1992 and the other in Addis Ababa between March 15–19, 1991, it only began to have coherence after the so-called conference on Sudan's fundamental issues, held in Asmara, Eritrea, in June 1995.

While being detained by the new government at Kober Prison (north of Khartoum), the northern opposition parties came up with a political charter that mirrored charters that had been improvised after the fall of General Abboud in 1964 and Nimeiri in 1985. The document was surreptitiously leaked out of Kober Prison on October 21, 1989, to symbolically mark the 25th anniversary of Abboud's fall (October 21, 1964). The authors of that charter didn't acknowledge that the situations in 1964 and 1985 were exceedingly different from that created by the NIF coup. They also seemed not to have taken into consideration the reconfiguration of Sudan's political scene after the emergence of the SPLM and the inroads it had made in central Sudan, especially in the Nuba Mountains and Blue Nile. To that alliance, however, was soon added a military arm made up of the remnants of the Sudan Armed Forces' high command who had been retired by the NIF regime. To highlight its nonrecognition of the NIF regime, that military faction was named "Legitimate Command of the Sudanese Armed Forces." As Douglas Johnson observed: "Neither the NDA nor the Legitimate Command had an active strategy for opposition. Both placed their hopes on risings inside the Sudan – another *intifada* in the streets of Khartoum, or a counter-coup within the army - to topple the regime and bring the old forces back to power."[17] The opposition parties' incomprehension of political developments that had ensued since 1983 reflected either an inappropriate analysis of the situation or utter belief in the immutability of their antiquated vision of Sudan. In effect, when Garang declared in his radio message to Bashir that the SPLM was the only national political party that the junta did not, and could not, ban, and consequently asked the banned parties to make use of that opportunity, it was these parties, not Bashir, who were enraged by the statement. Even if the SPLM leader was stating the realities on the ground at that point in time, the paralyzed parties were neither ready to recognize their incidental and circumstantial incapacitation, nor accept even temporarily a leading role at the national scene for the SPLM.

In June 1995, the NDA meeting in Asmara went into a thorough review of the fundamental causes of the Sudanese—not the southern Sudan—crisis. Garang not only repeated to that coalition his agenda on the New Sudan, but he also added the emerging issue of self-determination, which had taken prominence in the SPLM's and southern Sudanese political debate since 1994. Garang maintained that self-determination was part and parcel of the tenets of democracy to which the NDA was attached. As a consequence, the NDA agreed to a liberation agenda that included recognition of the right to self-determination to all people in Sudan who called for it. There was also reason to believe that Eritrean President Isaias Afwerki, one of the two authors of the IGAD DoP, had a hand in cajoling the NDA to espouse the principle of self-determination.

The Asmara resolutions, in addition, laid the foundation for a future political settlement with, or without, the NIF and sketched a military plan for dislodging it. However, if the NDA failed to deliver its part of the bargain, that was essentially because of structural distortions in its makeup. The NDA was as good as what system theorists called a chaotic aggregate; it encompassed the SPLM, a politico-military organization with a vision for the creation of a New Sudan and the capability to wage a sustained armed and unarmed struggle to achieve it; communists and left-leaning parties who had consistently been staunch fighters for people's causes but were encumbered by the damaged intellectual baggage they had carried since the 1940s; region-based political organizations who were basically preoccupied with regional problems; newly created armed groups and self-styled modern forces who, though well-meaning patriots, were shorn of a compass to aid them in navigating Sudan's turbulent political waters; and, finally, traditional political parties, who like the restored French Bourbon kings, had "learned nothing and forgotten nothing."[18]

On the military side, the SPLM/A's 1995–96 offensive was the first for numerous years. The offensive succeeded in rolling back the government's 1992 gains in Eastern Equatoria.[19] By late 1996, it was also on the offensive in the Nuba Mountains under Yousif Kuwa's leadership. Moreover, it took Kurmuk and Geissan in Blue Nile in early 1997 under the command of Malik Agar, with Ethiopia as a willing rear-base. In early 1998, the SPLM/A attacked and briefly took Wau, the capital of Bahr el Ghazal, with Kerubino Kuanyin Bol's support and pushed government army troops back in Aweil. The mercurial Kerubino had by then quit the SPLM renegades in Khartoum, not on principle, but because Khartoum had elevated Riek Machar over him in rank.

Victories in the SPLM/A traditional zones of war (south Sudan, Blue Nile, and the Nuba Mountains) were surely augmented by the political accord reached in the NDA's Asmara Declaration of 1995, regardless of the alliance's organizational frailties. SPLM/A also succeeded in convincing the NDA to take a more aggressive approach to the struggle to recapture from the NIF the political space within which it would enact the politicomilitary program it had sketched out. That led to the establishment of the fourth war zone in eastern Sudan under the overall command of John Garang and the direct command of Pagan Amum Okech and Abdel Aziz Adam al-Hilu. Northern NDA leaders, especially the populists among them, were by then still under the impression that the NIF could be dislodged through a popular *intifada* (uprising), the way the regimes of Generals Abboud in 1964 and Nimeiri in 1985 had been overthrown. To explain to his NDA allies how the ball game had changed with the coming of the NIF, Garang maintained that the success of the two popular uprisings in 1964 and 1985 was due to support from the armed forces, mobilization of workers and professional trades unions, and the people's insurrection. That, he said, could not be replicated today.

In explaining that thesis, Garang told the NDA leaders what they should have known by then but pretended not to admit. He stated that the Al-Ingaz regime had neutralized the army by removing from within it elements that were not, or suspected not to be, loyal to the regime. In addition, it had created a constellation of parallel armies: popular defence militias, armed security agencies, and paramilitary police contingents, all with a view to beating back popular insurrections and also neutralizing the army in case of munity. As for trades unions, Garang observed that the unions had been completely domesticated through expulsion from service of civil servants and workers who were not loyal to the NIF or to transforming trades unions into partisan vehicles of popular mobilization. Regarding popular insurrection, Garang maintained that the NIF was not Nimeiri's Sudanese Socialist Union (SSU), but a party with credible popular support. However limited that support was, Garang reasonably estimated that if the NIF only represented five percent of Sudan's population, there would be among every hundred demonstrators at least five NIF cadres, each with a Kalashnikov. That was enough, he said, to overawe a thousand, let alone a hundred, armless demonstrators.

Based on that assessment and reasoning, the NDA agreed to establish a new war zone in eastern Sudan with three objectives: first, to ease military pressure on the SPLM/A in other zones of war; second, to bring war closer to Khartoum; and third, to embolden popular forces of the *intifada*. As it were, forces in the new zone were primarily drawn from the SPLA, but they were also supported by the Sudan Allied Forces (SAF) and batches of combatants drawn from other NDA parties. Nonetheless, failure of these groups to provide the military forces in the Eastern Front with the resources they needed to carry out their job, devitalized these forces, indeed left the battlefield almost entirely to the Eritreans and the SPLM/A. Despite this failure, the SPLM/A's military and political resurgence after the signing of the Asmara Declaration in June 1995 took the shine off the superficial political gain the NIF experienced after the April 1997 Peace Charter signed with Riek Machar in April 1997. Nevertheless, that Peace Charter with Riek Machar and company had given the government a superficial political advantage.

6. Religion and Politics: Putting an End to Equivocation

Exasperated by the government's quibbling on the issue of religion and state, the SPLM/A decided to come out with a six-point plan, with a view to calling a halt to that quibbling. In a watershed meeting held in Addis Ababa, Ethiopia, in 1997, the SPLM/A presented to IGAD that plan, in which it demanded from the government of Sudan:

(i)   To make an unqualified acceptance of the DoP, especially on separation of religion and politics during the interim period;
(ii) to recognize the right to self-determination for the people of southern Kordofan and southern Blue Nile at the end of the interim period;
(iii) to install governance of Sudan on confederal basis during that period;
(iv) to implement a pluralistic democracy as a basis of governance;
(v)   to ensure participation by the NDA in the interim arrangements;
(vi) to commit to a comprehensive cease-fire once the above conditions were met.

On the issue of religion and politics, the SPLM/A went all out to explain what it meant by secularism, a term that had become open to all interpretations, including equating it with profanity. In order to confute this false interpretation of secularism, the SPLM/A, in a statement delivered to IGAD mediators, called for the separation of religion from politics during the interim period, save in the sphere of personal laws and also demanded that no policies shall be promulgated by government or decisions taken by courts that stem from the tenets of *any* religion.

When the government of Sudan received the six-point plan it became livid; its response was "No" to the separation of religion from politics, "No" to multiparty democracy, and a big "No" to the incorporation of the NDA in government. On the latter issue, the government delegation told the mediators that it sought negotiation in order to end the war and resolve the problem of southern Sudan, not to dismantle the Khartoum regime. Obviously, the remark on "dismantling the regime" was provoked by the SPLM's call for multiparty democracy and the inclusion of the NDA in the interim period's

51

arrangements. The government waited for over three years before it started knocking at many doors (Egypt, Libya, and Eritrea) in order to bring on board the very NDA it had tried to firmly shut out of the peace negotiations.

Another IGAD meeting was held a year later on August 4–6, 1998, in Addis Ababa on the invitation of the Ethiopian foreign minister. The meeting was chaired by Kenya's foreign minister, Bonaya Godana, and attended by Uganda's minister in the Office of the President, Ruhakana Rugunda, while the parties to the conflict were represented by foreign minister Mustafa Ismail, on behalf of the government of Sudan, and Commander Salva Kiir Mayardit, the then deputy chair of the SPLM and chief of general staff of the SPLA, on behalf of the SPLM/A. Secretary General Salim Ahmed Salim, of the Organization of African Unity (OAU), was also invited to the meeting to add the OAU's weight to the peace negotiation process. Other than congratulating themselves on the maintenance of a limited four-month cease-fire to facilitate humanitarian assistance to areas affected by famine, both the parties to the conflict and the mediators had nothing else to put on display. They were neither able to make headway on the issue of religion and state nor that of self-determination. In sum, the conflict was not yet ready for a negotiated settlement because both sides thought that they could still prevail outside of the peace talks.[20] Although war had intensified in the years between 1998 and 2002, the prospects for decisive military or political victory by one side over the other diminished, and this came to be better understood by both the government of Sudan and the SPLM/A. At the same time, the value of accepting some measure of compromise, as well as the risks for not doing so, rose greatly for both of them. This was especially so because of the long-awaited bounty of oil revenues on which I shall elaborate later in this chapter.

7. Split within the NIF

Any hope by the NIF to achieve a monopolistic "peace from within" was severely eroded when that party split in late 1999, following a power struggle between the speaker of the Sudanese parliament and NIF's secretary general, Hassan al-Turabi, on the one side, and President Bashir, on the other.[21] The struggle for power within that party evidenced the ruthless nature of its internal politics, as well as its deft capacity for survival. Turabi had sought progressively to take the reins of power during a transition to civilian government. In this regard he shrewdly fended off challenges to his roles as secretary general of the party and as speaker of parliament. In the meantime, the NIF was refashioned in political terms, but only in name; the National Islamic Front was renamed the National Congress Party (NCP). By removing the word "Islamic" and conferring on their party a national character only, the Islamists attempted to delude the world, as well as their non-Islamic constituency (including southern Sudanese and Egyptian Copts), that the party was not the dogmatic party it was assumed to be. That gambit, at its most farcical, allowed non-Muslims in the NCP to chant "Hallelujah" (praise to the lord) at public rallies, while Muslims bellowed "Allahu Akbar" (Allah is great). But at the level of substance (policies and decision-making processes) nothing changed; power was kept in tight control by the party's oligarchy. Neither the chanting non-Muslim cadres nor the bellowing Muslims had any contribution in that regard, save for straining their voices in public rallies.

Turabi, however, went on with endeavors to curtail Bashir's power, which culminated in a motion in parliament in November 1999 to amend the constitution with a view to creating a position of prime minister, who would be responsible to parliament, and making all state governors electable rather than appointed by the president. On the face of it, Turabi's revolution came across as an attempt to democratize the system, but Bashir saw it as a ploy to clip off his wings. He also feared that Turabi might not stop at what was purported to be a limited change. As a result, he went on to thwart Turabi's scheme by dissolving Parliament on December 12, 1999, declaring a state of emergency and ousting Turabi from any position of power he was holding. That led to an intraparty crisis followed by a party split. Turabi and his group parted ways with the NCP and formed their own party, the Popular National Congress (PNC), again with the brand name "Islamic" removed from the title.

The split weakened the NCP considerably, as Turabi left with a fair slice of its regional popular support base as well as its Islamist credentials. That support was soon to erode, either through coercion or patronage by the party that held the purse and wielded official power. Nonetheless, Turabi sought to reinvent himself ideologically by retreating from many of the politicoreligious pronouncements that were anathema to the majority of Sudanese Muslims and non-Muslims alike. One such pronouncement related to the holy rewards of *jihad.* Before the split, Turabi had often been seen over Sudan television officiating apocryphal weddings of martyrs to virgins in heaven—70 of them to each martyr. Laugh much as you like, but that TV program was proudly and emphatically called "The Wedding of the Martyr."[22] How easy it had been in the NIF's political show business for the Pope to turn into a Luther?

Withal, Turabi went on a rampage to wash the NIF's dirty linen in public so as to discredit his "disloyal" disciples. In a fit of rage, Turabi opened hitherto well-sealed tins of worms that included revelations of who was responsible for the attempted assassination of Egypt's President Mubarak in Addis Ababa in 1995. He also gloated over his contribution to the regime, both in equipping Sudan's armed forces with weaponry and securing funding to development projects, especially in the oil sector. Turabi, understandably, saw not only scorn in the action taken toward him by his disciples, but more important, betrayal. In effect, Turabi's intellectual arrogance was such that he assumed that the deference showed to him by his "disciples" was not a sign of respect, but a mark of servility. To the chagrin of Turabi, the oligarchy around President Bashir represented by a range of heavyweights and hardliners with a grip over the country's military and security apparatus and economic assets, held tightly all reins of power.

In launching his campaign against Turabi, Bashir appeared on TV fully clad in his military uniform as commander-in-chief of the Sudanese army, as if to proclaim what his real power base was. Even so, he desperately sought to publicly reassure Islamic followers of his legitimacy by emphasizing his Islamist credentials. In that respect, he stressed that *jihad* would continue (irrespective of Turabi's new *fatwa*) and that the army would never let the South go. He also added that the "civilizational project" would be accelerated, with every primary school turned into a *khalwa* (Quranic school) teaching religion.[23] One would have expected Bashir, who was eager to enact his civilizational project, to declare that he was also going to establish a technical or vocational training institute beside every *khalwa*, but obviously the civilization NIF envisaged was not akin to that which made Muslim countries like Malaysia what they had become. To those Muslim countries, civilizational projects were not about creedal matters but about spreading literacy and numeracy, diffusing professional knowledge, and expanding saviour faire. Bashir's performance showed in a single act the duplicitous nature of his politics; on the one hand, he wanted to dupe the general public that he was only a national leader owing allegiance to a national institution (the army) while, on the other hand, he endeavored to ensure the Islamist rank and file of his commitment to the core values of that party. Bashir should have known that neither were the values to which he was committed embraced by the whole nation, nor was the national army undividedly dedicated to them. Even so, that was a pardonable fib by Bashir compared to earlier statements he made when he assumed power. In one such statement Bashir denied any connection between the coup officers and the Islamists, claiming that Al-Ingaz was a national salvation movement triggered by the army and had no partisan affinity.[24] To give credence to that fib, Turabi, the Islamist leader, was sent to prison alongside all the leaders of the banned parties. With that history of audacious mendacity, Bashir's statement that he was *only* the army's man did not surprise his listeners.

Despite all that bravado, Bashir's fears of Turabi's revenge rose significantly, especially with the publication and distribution in May 2000 of the anonymously authored Black Book.[25] That book created an upheaval in Khartoum as a result of its detailed account of the marginalization of peripheral regions (especially Darfur and Kordofan) by successive Sudanese governments, including the NIF. The book's critique of Sudan's failure to be a "just" Islamic State was clearly a jibe at the NCP. With abundant statistical data, the Black Book claimed that Sudan was controlled by only one region (northern) whose population represented just over five percent of the country. The report also claimed that power in Sudan was monopolized by three ethnic northern groups, whose coethnics controlled major ministerial posts as well as high-level positions in the army, police, and banks. Though weakened by the split, the NCP nonetheless exploited the situation to feign expulsion of fundamentalist elements in the party and jettison foreign Islamic radicals who were harbored by the NIF as fellows in faith. Before the split, those radicals were gladly embraced by Bashir, but after Turabi's political downfall, they became hazardous goods. The NIF made some short-term political gains domestically in the region as non-despairing Sudanese hoped that relieving Turabi from all his positions was the forerunner of better things to come. But the big prize to the NCP had to wait, as we shall see later, until after the September 11 events in the United States.

8. Machiavellian Alliances

In late 1999, Bashir succeeded in convincing the ever Machiavellian and politically flawed Umma leader Sadiq al-Mahdi to sign a "Call of the Homeland" pact in Djibouti on November 7 and a promise to return to Khartoum.[26] By doing so, Bashir outwitted Turabi's efforts to stealthily reach a pact with al-Mahdi in Geneva earlier that year. The meeting between Sadig al Mahdi and Turabi was arranged by the Sudanese director general of the World Intellectual Property Organization (WIPO). Al-Mahdi, who never discussed his move with his colleagues in the NDA, was given a roasting by the alliance for his unilateral decision to meet with Turabi. Incredibly, the only leader within the NDA who came to al-Mahdi's rescue was Garang, probably because he was equally engaged in "extracurricular" negotiations outside the portals of the NDA. But Garang's reaction to the Djibouti pact differed from his reaction to the Geneva meeting; he accused al-Mahdi of treachery and called for his expulsion from the NDA. Yet, to avoid suffering the humiliation of being expelled from the NDA, the Umma party took the pre-emptive measure of resigning from the alliance in March 2000, after facing a howl of protests from the NDA's leadership meeting in Kampala in December 1999.

It did not take al-Mahdi long to realize that the only role the NCP wanted him to play was that of second fiddle. Come what may, the NCP never wished to bring the Umma leader into government as prime minister, as he had believed, but only wanted to smother him to death in its embrace. In the meantime, al-Mahdi rightly never envisaged his role as that of a finger puppet who would provide the NCP with much-needed legitimacy; consequently, he began to distance himself from the Khartoum regime. Rather than being humbled by the way the NCP treated him, al-Mahdi wrote to the NDA chairman that he was willing to join the NDA Congress that was scheduled to be held at Massawa, Eritrea, on June 13, 2006, on two conditions: adoption of *his* plans for peace and restructuring the NDA.[27] The NDA leadership never expected an apology from al-Mahadi, as the Umma leader was never known to have admitted, let alone apologized for, a mistake. But making conditions for his readmission into the alliance after having been taken down a peg by the NIF was a bit too much.

On its side, the NCP went on to hold an ersatz election in late 2000, in which President Bashir was reported to have won 85 percent of the votes. Bashir's enthusiasm for that sham election verged on self-ridicule when he praised the event as one "which allowed every citizen to make his choice in complete freedom and fairness."[28]

9. Brother Enemies, Back to the Fold

During the "peace from within" period and as the Khartoum Peace Agreement began to unravel, Bashir, on Sudan Independence Day in January 2001, vowed to be a "leader for all Sudanese,"[29] yet that was even less plausible than ever. Disquiet from Riek Machar and Lam Akol became visible by late 2000, as the date for the promised plebiscite drew near (April 2001). The Khartoum Charter was finally seen by Machar and Akol as the charade it always had been. The date of the agreed plebiscite to ascertain the wishes of southern Sudanese came and passed quietly. Machar, who was then settled in his post as assistant to the president, resigned from that position in February 2001 to avoid the humiliation he was about to face. The then minister for peace, Mekki Ali Balayel, explained that the Khartoum Agreement was not implementable because the SPLM/A was outside it,[30] a reason that could only have riled Machar and Akol. Both SPLM defectors thought that by joining the government, the SPLM/A became as good as dead. The United Democratic Salvation Front (UDSF) complained that the government had lost all credibility.

That situation signaled the time of return to the fold. In May 2001, senior figures in Machar's party, led by Taban Deng Gai, signed an agreement to merge with the SPLM/A.[31] Machar, the South Independence leader, was left companionless and had to swallow his pride and make his way back to the SPLM. As for Lam Akol, he resigned from the NCP in July 2002 and together with Mekki Ali Balayel and Amin Benani Neo—both longtime members of the Islamist movement—formed the Justice Party on August 22, 2002. At the time of resignation, Lam Akol adopted without attribution John Garang's words, saying that the NCP was "so deformed that it is incapable of effecting reforms for change towards peace in Sudan."[32]

By all accounts Lam Akol, who engineered the SPLM/A split on August 28, 1991, thought that this time he would be able to rig up a party comprising the south, represented by himself; the Nuba people, represented by Balayel; and Darfur, represented by Benani. That party, in the language of Westerners, turned out to be an army of chiefs without Indians. Fractures within the UDSF and among southern signatories to the 1997 Khartoum Peace Agreement benefited the SPLM/A, with various defectors going back to their ranks, and culminated in the 2002 consolidation of the SPLM/A-SPDF merger agreed to a year before. With Riek Machar back on board and Lam Akol in clear opposition to the NCP in 2002, some of the wounds of the 1991 SPLM/A split had almost been healed, or so thought the unsuspecting. Both Garang and Salva Kiir were not enthusiastic about the reintegration of Riek Machar and Lam Akol to their former positions in the leadership structures before the split. Others pleaded for meeting the two leaders' demands and argued that both Machar and Akol should adorn the SPLM Leadership Council, given their former ascendancy in the party as well as their academic attainments: Machar as a doctor in mechanical engineering and Lam as a doctor in chemical engineering. With his mordant wit, Garang told these colleagues that the problems of Sudan are neither chemical, nor mechanical. Eventually, as a result of some of Garang's trusted aides (Nhial Deng Nhial and Deng Alor) beseeching the SPLM chairman and his deputy, Salva Kiir, the SPLM Leadership Council yielded to pressure to install Machar in his former position, but not Akol.

Most alarming for the NCP, however, was the meeting between the SPLM/A and al-Turabi's PNC held in February 2001 in Geneva. Delegations from the two parties signed a Memorandum of Understanding (MoU) in which they agreed that "peaceful popular resistance [to the NCP] through all means must be stepped up."[33] The reaction of the government to the MoU was to promptly place Turabi under house arrest. Equally, the MoU was not gladly received by a large number of Sudanese in the north and south because, to them, Turabi was the architect of all the troubles they were in.

10. Return to a Sterile War

Encouraged by their military and political success, the SPLM/A moved to extend the war theater to areas in southern Sudan, closer to areas in northern Sudan that were considered by Khartoum military strategists as unassailable targets. In early June 2002, the SPLM/A boldly captured Raja in northern Bahr el Ghazal. Some strategists thought that the capture of Raja might have been helpful to Turabi's game plan by providing Fur and Zaghawa fighters an entry point into Darfur,[34] but those fighters never materialized. At the same time, President Bashir, who was on his way to Nairobi for another IGAD summit on Sudan, found himself embarrassed and on the defensive.[35]

For the SPLM, the period between 1998 and 2001 was one of mixed success regarding its overall strategy. Before and after the Raja offensive, numerous advances had been achieved. For example, the SPLM/A had pursued successful offensives in Equatoria upon its revival between 1995 and early 1998; reintegrated Kerubino's forces into the SPLM/A later that year, and advanced in 1999 within shelling distance of the Khor Adar oil wells in north-eastern Upper Nile. In August 2001, the SPLM/A captured the oil-producing area of Heglig and continued to threaten oil production into 2002. In addition, other NDA-allied forces made advances throughout eastern

Sudan.[36] It is to be noted here that the NDA-allied forces included the newly formed New Sudan Brigade (NSB).[37] The NSB was a brainchild of John Garang; in a policy document entitled "The New Sudan Brigade Working Programme," Garang maintained that the concepts of New Sudan and Sudanism must be operationalized and nurtured to become an ideological weapon of struggle for nation formation, national renaissance, and unity of the Sudanese people. He also went on to advise that the story of the SPLM's historical mission had to be taught in all our schools and reflected in our public attitudes. These offensives of the combined NSB and its allied forces culminated in the capture of the government garrison of Hameshkoreb in March 2000, an attack on the town of Kassala in November 2000, and successful attacks on the new oil pipeline.

In March 2002, the SPLM/A absorbed the small but predominantly northern Sudan Alliance Forces (SAF) led by General Abdel Aziz Khalid.[38] Were that absorption to happen five years earlier, the fate of war and peace in Sudan, indeed of the new Sudan vision, would have been different. During those five years, the SAF leader, animated by the support he was receiving from Eritrea and the inflation of his ego by the credulous elites around him, struggled to persuade Garang's deputy, Salva Kiir Mayardit, to put the NCB forces under his (Khalid's) control. Salva Kiir, who was at that point overseeing the NSB's 7,000-strong force in the Eastern Front, retorted that the brigade was not made of mercenaries, but of warriors with their own military doctrine, line of command, and system of control. That altercation left a sour taste in Salva's mouth and probably recalled to his mind perceptions by not a small number of southern Sudanese that the only place northerners envisioned for southern Sudanese in any organization was in the second row. Sadly, perceptions are often more indelible than actualities.

In this particular case, the issue was not only one of perception, but also of immodesty and fraudulence. The NSB forces in that front, whose overwhelming majority came from Southern Sudan and the Nuba Mountains, numbered over 7,000 battle-ready and hardened men, while those of the SAF counted to less than one third of that number. Khalid's design was to lead that force to Khartoum with the ungrudging help of Eritrea so as to emerge in Sudan's national capital as the Garang of the north. In effect, were Khalid to have joined the SPLM/A, Garang would have appointed him commander of that force, since he had always maintained that the role of the SPLM/A was not to fight the wars of others but only to help organize their anger.[39]

Still, another set of dynamics diminished the viability of an armed struggle aimed at forcibly ejecting the NCP from Khartoum. On the one hand, there were limits to the military successes of the SPLA, since in terms of sheer military capacity it was "out-gunned" by the government's army. Ultimately, this meant a failure of the SPLA to push forward its northern front or to capture and hold onto strategic locations in southern Sudan. In addition, with the death of Yousif Kuwa Mekki in London on March 31, 2001, the SPLM/A lost an inspirational leader who was a galvanizing force for the movement around the New Sudan vision. Kuwa was succeeded by the senior SPLM/A commander Abdel Aziz Adam el-Hilu.[40] Other setbacks included the defections to the government in 2002 of SPLA commanders Tito Biel and Peter Gadet. Though the two commanders were nonentities in political terms, their ability to cause mischief at the authority of Khartoum was incalculable. There was also the failure of NDA to consolidate, popularly and militarily, its social base. Neither were the parties, who were assumed to have, or claimed to have had, a wide popular base in the north, able to motivate their supporters to action inside Sudan against the government, nor were they able to provide sufficient hardware or software for the battle front, as intimated earlier. Even repeated attempts by the Eritrean hosts of the NDA to urge that leadership into doing more to support the struggle in which the SPLM/A had invested tremendous manpower and Eritrea had provided requisite resources, came to naught. That failure was further aggravated by the withdrawal of the Umma Party from the alliance. As far as one knew, therefore, armed and non-armed northern opposition seemed to have believed that the struggle would continue until the last SPLA soldier fell.

Outside of the SPLM, the NDA relied heavily on the presence and leadership of the Umma Party's old rival, the Democratic Unionist Party (DUP). Its leader, Mohamed Osman al-Mirghani, had close ties with Egypt and was under increasing pressure to return to Khartoum following Sadiq al-Mahdi's example. By early 2002, the International Crisis Group assessed that pressure on al-Mirghani to get back into Sudan to compete directly with the Umma Party was eating away at DUP's resolve and further weakening the NDA.[41] Al-Mirghani, though very tight-fisted on expenditures related to armed struggle or diplomatic action that might have made of him president of Sudan, nonetheless provided a much-needed political cover for struggle in the Eastern front.

In addition, a wider set of shifts dimmed the prospect of military victory by the SPLM/A. First, factions that had parted company with the SPLM, especially Riek Machar, helped the NIF government identify new partners from Asia (China, India, and Malaysia) who could develop oil resources that had remained unexploited since the withdrawal of U.S. companies in the mid-1980s. Success in commencing oil production and generating oil revenues enabled the government, from 1999 onwards, to build up its war machine.[42] Although recruitment was difficult, the army became better able to invest in heavy weaponry and, reportedly, weapons of mass destruction. On the other side, thanks to the oil bounty, the NCP was given the means to buy itself a domestic constituency that it had failed to secure through coercion or political inducement. In effect, despite instability in the peripheries, the regime was able, as one observer noted, to maintain its hold on power through a "commercial-security nexus at the centre that is flexible enough to create incentives and niches for former adversaries."[43] Still, generating revenues from oil required some modicum of peace to allow for oil exploitation in many areas of southern Sudan and to attract a wider range of investors on better terms. As the NCP pretended to be willing to reach a peace agreement, various outsiders willingly swallowed the story, and it became more difficult for the SPLM/A to maintain its long argument that the regime in Khartoum was "too deformed to be reformed." Deformed it might have been, but the machine of reform was now greased with oil.

Consequently, the NCP began, with some success, to repair ties with various neighbors after the Bashir-Turabi split; the split provided the former with the pretext to attribute to Turabi all foreign exploits that brought the regime notoriety. That, on the back of its newfound status as an oil producer, enabled the NCP to engage a host of new partners. This included dialogues and pacts with Ethiopia as well as support from Egypt, Algeria, Libya, and Qatar. Though hesitant in some cases, that support undermined the NDA's strategy to isolate the regime and also opened the way for rapprochements between the NCP and the world. Though the international dimension of the conflict shall be discussed further below and in the next chapter, suffice it to note here that between 1998 and 2000 some European governments, in particular, bought into the "reform" *ignis fatuus* that Khartoum was peddling. The NDA and opposition groups inside Sudan vigorously argued that Khartoum's political reforms were merely a ruse to entrench its power, achieve legitimacy, and improve its image abroad, "especially in the United States and Europe."[44] Peace notwithstanding, the NCP maneuvers achieved some success.

11. War Weariness: An Impulse to Negotiated Settlement

Given the above factors, the prospect of military victory became unfavorable for both sides. Hence, a situation of military stalemate and war fatigue began to set in on both of them. For the NCP, the mobilization of young men to war was dealt a blow after Turabi's exit and the retraction of his earlier *fatwas* on *jihad*, as well as from the increasing migration of young men from northern Sudan to Egypt and, thereafter, to Europe, Canada, the United States, and distant Australia. This stampede for exit from Sudan intensified in the mid-1990s when the NIF decided to make *jihad* an obligation for all Sudanese, not only its adherents. Thus young Sudanese were being forcibly dragged from their homes and schools and compulsorily enlisted as warriors. The worst blow to the NIF's war mobilization efforts came from Darfurians, the majority of whom were groomed by Turabi. Darfur's disaffection with the NIF dated back to 1991 when one of their stalwarts, Yahia Dawood Bolad, broke ranks with the NIF and sought support from the SPLM/A. The NIF's assumption of Bolad's action as a betrayal of Turabi, in addition to the brutality with which he was killed, brought the estrangement between the two groups to its extreme, as evidenced by the emergence of the Justice and Equality Movement (JEM) led by Khalil Ibrahim, who turned out to be Khartoum's archenemy. Ibrahim was among those who were enticed by Turabi's indoctrination to serve as a jihadist in southern Sudan before he turned his bayonet in the other direction.

In late 2001 and early 2002, the International Crisis Group (ICG) captured some of the perspectives of both sides. For the government, it said, "unease [over troop losses] is compounded by the sense that little has changed on the battlefield in the last half decade. Neither side has gained or lost much real estate. The war has been high in cost and low in outcome since 1996." It also reported that one leading Sudanese government official had acknowledged that "the status quo is unacceptable,"[45] and that "the army is fed up with the war." One senior government official who served in the armed forces for two decades was reported by the ICG as saying that "The army want it to end."[46] It is doubtful whether this assessment was shared by all army officers, for a civilian peace would have threatened the army's position of power and hold on resources. War, to some officers on both sides, had by that time become a predatory industry.

In considering the position of the SPLM/A, the ICG aptly noted that "the SPLA also is uncertain about the direction the wind will blow. It faces an unfavourable long-term battlefield scenario in which continued aggressive acquisition of highly destructive weaponry may give the Government considerably increased capability to pulverize the south."[47] However, the ICG added that "this does not obviate the likelihood that the SPLA could survive indefinitely as a guerrilla force, but if trends continue and the SPLA is not able to disrupt significantly the government's ability to extract oil, the insurgency's prospects are bleak."[48] Analyzing the situation in 2001, Peter Woodward concluded, using the phrase coined by I. William Zartman, that the conflict between the SPLM/A and the NCP was "ripe for resolution."[49] Peter Woodward, a political historian well versed in Sudan's politics, maintained that "despite the customary ebb and flow of conflict, generally with government advances in the dry season and SPLA counter moves with the onset of rains, the overall picture was one of military deadlock."[50] And, indeed, that was the situation at the beginning of the third millennium.

12. Outside Factors Pushing toward Negotiated Settlement

As we have argued earlier, international factors played upon these internal dimensions to increase the viability of negotiated settlement. The details of the actual efforts of various actors to mediate a settlement based on the IGAD initiative shall be dealt with in the next chapter, yet it may be beneficial to the reader to indicate, at this stage, the main dynamics that have been at play around the IGAD effort.

12.1 Regional Factors

Within the region, renewed concern arose to find an end to a war that had caused burden and destabilization beyond Sudan's borders. Thus, President Moi of Kenya took it upon himself to bring Garang and Bashir closer to the negotiating table and away from the battlefield.[51] As the pivotal force behind the Intergovernmental Authority on Development (IGAD) mediation efforts, Moi sought to build upon the DoP, as well as the NDA's achievement with the Asmara Declaration, to deliver a final settlement through an IGAD initiative. Under Kenyan leadership, and with support from Friends of the IGAD,[52] a permanent secretariat for the peace talks was established in Nairobi, first led by Ambassador Tom Mboya and then by General Lazaro Kipkurui Sumbeiywo. Sumbeiywo, a man of great integrity, had always taken his missions in a humorless and grave manner. He was also a God-fearing man; by way of illustration, he reported that before he accepted President Moi's request to take up the Sudan mission, he and his wife fasted and prayed for three days.[53]

IGAD's efforts to achieve a negotiated settlement, however, were, compromised by the actions of other neighbors in the region (Egypt and Libya), who aimed at political changes within Sudan that were more suited to their own agenda—namely, averting secession of the South and maintaining unity of the Sudan at any cost. Greatly anxious about the possible separation of southern Sudan, Egypt first attempted to join the IGAD initiative to influence the process from within. That was not to happen since Egypt was not, and could not have been assumed to be, a member of IGAD, the subregional organization comprising countries from East Africa and the Horn. Egypt then endeavored to be included in the open-ended IGAD Partners Forum (IPF), which at that time only comprised Western countries in addition to Japan. The Friends of the IGAD gratified Egypt's wish, but only as an observer.

Also that year, Libya proposed its own peace plan—the Tripoli Declaration—which Egypt supported. By all appearances, Egypt did not want Libya to go it alone, fearing that it might run the peace process off course. Fundamental to this effort was a push by Egypt for reconciliation among northern Sudanese political groups, including the NCP; through this gimmick, Egypt hoped to avoid the DoP's principles on separation of religion and state and self-determination for southern Sudan. In a previous publication, the author analyzed the shortcomings of what had become the "Joint Egyptian-Libyan Initiative" (JELI).[54] It is important, however, to emphasize that different regional points of view on what kind of peace Sudan should have altered the overall strategic landscape and left a negotiated compromise, as ever, less probable. Unqualified support from northern Sudanese parties in the NDA to the Tripoli Declaration contradicted their acceptance in the Asmara resolutions of the right to self-determination for the people of southern Sudan and revealed internal disaccords within the alliance. As a result, the SPLM declared its strong reservations about the JELI, particularly that it had skirted around the two issues of self-determination and separation between state and religions.

Al-Mahdi who was obviously on the lookout for a straw to hold on to, cited the SPLM/A's rejection of the JELI as one reason for leaving the NDA. He also claimed that SPLM/A's rejection showed the movement's "lack of commitment to peace."[55] Having returned to Khartoum, he then sought to make himself central to peace initiatives as one way to compensate for his disempowered position vis-à-vis the NCP and estrangement with the NDA. Al-Mahdi, a tireless politician who was always on the move, never missed an opportunity to launch himself into the fray. So when he saw a possible opening thousands of miles away from Khartoum, he seized the occasion to involve himself in a peacemaking effort, set in motion by President Olusegun Obasanjo of Nigeria.

The interest of Nigeria in Sudan's conflict went back to 1991, when its president at that time, Ibrahim Babangida, made strenuous efforts in an Organization of African Unity (OAU) meeting at Abuja to bring the parties together. Though Babangida was then chairman of the OAU, Sudan only acceded to his request in his capacity as president of Nigeria. Babangida's efforts expectedly collapsed because of the failure of the parties to come to terms on the two issues of religion and state and self-determination. Even when the SPLM proposed the creation of confederal arrangements as a solution to the impasse, it was told point-blank by the government's lead negotiator, Mohamed al-Amin Khalifa, that *a confederal system could only be realized through the barrel of gun*. A few years later, Nigerian President Olusegun Obasanjo interceded in Sudan's conflict by organizing a meeting between Garang and al-Mahdi at the instigation of the latter. That meeting ended in failure, with Garang noting that while he welcomed any call for peace talks with the government, he did not see a need for an opposition group to mediate.[56] In effect, Garang called al-Mahdi a *samsar* (peddler) for the government. Moreover, Garang reasserted the precedence of the IGAD over the JELI, the latter of which al-Mahdi wanted to market and persuade Obasanjo to help him in that effort. Garang, instead, stressed that "what was needed was negotiations between the warring sides, not a reconciliation conference."[57] In turn, al-Mahdi criticized the "narrowness" of IGAD for "overlooking the issue of governance in Sudan."[58] Many of those who heard al-Mahdi's critique of the IGAD initiative wondered if he had read the DoP at all. If issues like decentralization of the system of rule, equitable distribution of wealth, and upholding rule of law and human rights principles did not address the issue of governance, then what else would? Seemingly, governance to al-Mahdi was not about systems, norms, and political ethics, but only about the sharing of power, irrespective of the normative rules that govern the exercise of that power. Thus, the tireless Umma leader gave credence to the impression that his movements were akin to those of a walker on a treadmill: constantly on the move but toward no destination.

The NCP, in turn, latched onto the JELI both as a way to undermine the IGAD talks and create fissures within the NDA. The JELI, to both the NCP and al-Mahdi, provided a golden opportunity for them to reinforce relations with Egypt and ensure that Qaddafi was kept in good humor so that he could continue to distribute largess on the leadership of the NDA. So, in January 2001, Sudan's foreign minister Mustafa Ismail met with Egyptian and Libyan ministers in Tripoli to follow up on JELI. An official statement afterwards reported that "the parties underlined that this initiative was the **best means**" (emphasis added) for ending Sudan's civil war.[59] The IGAD effort, in this context, was doomed to fail during this period.[60]

12.2 International Factors

In addition to regional attempts to rejuvenate, or frustrate, peacemaking efforts, as the case might have been, international factors also assumed increasing importance. Four factors are to be underlined:

(i) **Oil:** As already mentioned, the NCP's ability to profit from oil contributed to the "ripeness" of the conflict for negotiated settlement. Indeed, the NCP's ability to develop oil production, notwithstanding the ongoing war, was one of its successes. Oil production allowed the NCP to raise its status in external relations and also puff up its self-importance. Thus, Khartoum succeeded in courting outside investors, beginning in the mid-1990s. The Greater Nile Petroleum Operating Company (GNPOC) was established in 1997 to develop oil-field blocks 1, 2, and 4, which straddled the north-south frontline of the war in Bahr-el-Ghazal, South Kordofan, and South Darfur. GNPOC began producing oil in 1999, while Sudan's emergence as an oil producer corresponded with increased international interest in both its oil production and its oil industry. Khartoum, notwithstanding its wobbly international relations, was able to woo investors from Europe (Lundin of Sweden and OMV of Austria) and the United Kingdom (Rolls Royce). The former two companies were engaged in oil production, while the latter provided pumps to oil industry. From North America, Talisman Energy (Canada) grabbed a contract for oil production in one of the most promising wells in Unity State in southern Sudan but was soon forced to abandon it to Asian operators under pressure from its government, the U.S. Congress, and civil society activists. Rolls Royce withdrew from Sudan after being named and shamed by Christian Aid in March 2011. Nonetheless, the impatience of outsiders to see an end to the war grew as they fixed one eye squarely on profiting from Sudan's new wealth. According to one report, the growing threat posed by the SPLM/A to the oil fields had also left investors jittery, as "they want peace to secure their investments."[61] Moreover, potentially larger oil fields in southern Sudan remained out of reach so long as the war continued. This applied to the very promising Block B in Jonglei State, an area that was completely under SPLM/A control. Block B was reserved to a consortium, bringing together Total of France, Marathon of the United States, and the Kuwait National Petroleum Company.

(ii) **European Rapprochement**: Having window-dressed political reforms and with a lucrative oil industry in the offing, Khartoum succeeded in getting some of its strongest critics to engage "constructively," a vacuous adverb that was too thin to see through. As things stood then, such engagement was tantamount to discussing business with Khartoum while closing both eyes to the carnage in southern Sudan and the repression in other parts of the country. In November 1999, the European Union wrote to the government of Sudan to begin a "critical dialogue," with a view to opening the way for the resumption of official aid. The term "critical," as much as "constructive," was a hoax, particularly when the European Union countries proceeded to support the government of Sudan in the meeting of the U.N. Commission on Human Rights in 2000.[62] In that respect they joined China, which consistently defended the Sudan government's human rights records even when numerous U.N. Human Rights observers had reported, with evidence at hand, cases of glaring human rights abuses.

(iii) **Counter-terrorism**: Khartoum's ability to court the United States was more complex. The Clinton administration had effectively entrenched its policy of Sudan isolation during the 1990s, but even this began to thaw in the final years. One important dimension of the change of direction was the vexed issue of counter terrorism. Having been flirting with Islamist radical groups for a number of years, Sudan's Islamist government came to its senses and recognized the dangerous dance it had been playing. Thus, it offered cooperation as one way to keep further U.S. hostility at bay.[63] Engagement on counter-terrorism slowly eroded the cogency of an isolationist stance, whatever the other shortcomings were of such an approach to ending the war.

(iv) **Donor Fatigue and Aid Quandary:** If the two parties were suffering some measure of war fatigue, most Western countries were also beginning to tire of the high expense burden that became attached to the humanitarian crisis inflicted by the war. "Operation Lifeline Sudan" (OLS) became less of a "lifeline" and more of an entrenched social services structure with no end in sight. OLS was a groundbreaking negotiated access accord reached between the government of Sudan, the SPLM/A, and the United Nations in 1989 to facilitate lifesaving aid to southern Sudan. That achievement should never be recalled without paying tribute to the late James Grant and the U.N. organization he had been heading: the United Nations International Children's Emergency Fund (UNICEF). Though it developed into the world's largest humanitarian effort of its kind, OLS was criticized for having inadvertently become part of the war's economy and, thus, prolonging the conflict.[64] The longstanding high cost of humanitarian assistance, together with the controversies over the way in which aid was interacting with the dynamics of conflict, put pressure on the donor community to find an end to the war. In fact, in its meeting at Oslo in March 1999, the Technical Committee on Humanitarian Assistance of the IGAD Partners Forum (IPF) observed, in the course of a review of humanitarian support plans, that "it would be difficult for the international community to continue offering humanitarian aid without an accelerated and strengthened political process towards peace."[65]

(v) **Changes in U.S. Policy Toward Sudan:** A strategy of containment and isolation was the cornerstone of the Clinton administration's policy toward Sudan during the 1990s.[66] U.S. antagonism to the NIF peaked between 1995–1998, following the attempted assassination of Egyptian President Mubarak in Addis Ababa, which was hatched in and facilitated by Khartoum. President Mubarak should have been the last target for a murderous attack by the NIF, given the decisive support he had given to the coup makers from the beginning. Egypt was not only the first country to recognize the new regime, it also became its salesman to the world, including the United States and Saudi Arabia. Mubarak first persuaded Saudi King Fahad to recognize the new regime, issuing for a "military coup" that he described to the king as engineered by nationalist officers. On the other hand, having been disturbed by the issuance by the U.S. Department of State of a standard statement in which it criticized the military overthrow of an elected government, Mubarak proceeded to reverse the decision of the U.S. administration on Sudan. Two weeks after the coup, Mubarak met with President Bush in Paris on the occasion of the second centenary of the French Revolution. One of the main issues the two presidents discussed was Sudan. Mubarak prevailed on Bush not to discount the new regime in Sudan, because in Mubarak's estimation, that regime was led by young nationalist officers who were capable of putting an end to war in Sudan and restoring stability to the country. Probably because of his disenchantment with the convoluted manner in which Prime Minister al- Mahdi dealt with Egypt when he assumed power in 1986, Mubarak had an axe to grind with the leader of the government deposed by Bashir.

After November 1997, President Bill Clinton issued Executive Order 13067, which declared that the Sudan government's actions represented an "unusual and extraordinary threat" and enumerated the Sudan government's support of international terrorism, the prevalence of human rights abuses, and the destabilization of neighboring countries. With the intensification of war, including aerial bombardment of civilian targets, the assassination attempt on President Mubarak, and embrace of Osama Bin Laden in Khartoum, Clinton had enough evidence to justify that order. Penalties that were meted on the Sudan government included blocking Sudanese government assets in the US and banning trade in goods, technology, or services with Sudan.[67] The Clinton administration, on the other side, decided to step up support to the NDA, excluding arms.

Surprisingly, since March 1996 and during Clinton's presidency, the NCP wanted to jettison Bin Laden, who was living in Sudan and increasingly becoming an embarrassment to its rulers. The embarrassment and fear heightened after the attacks on the U.S. embassies in Nairobi and Dar es Salaam, Tanzania, in which Bin Laden was reported to have been involved. Through a special emissary, ambassador Al Fatih Irwa, who was a senior officer in Nimeiri's security agency with close relations to his counterparts in Washington, the government of Sudan proposed to hand over Bin Laden to either the U.S. or Saudi Arabia.[68] The Saudis refused to embrace their countryman, ten to one, out of fear of a backlash from his "sleeping" agents within the kingdom. The United States, raven by conflict on whether to engage Sudan's government or isolate it, opted for the latter, particularly since it had never believed in the sincerity of its offer.[69]

In August 1998, the United States bombed the Al-Shifa pharmaceutical factory in Khartoum based on shady information.[70] In addition, a formidable team under Secretary of State Madeleine Albright that included White House appointees Susan Rice, Gayle Smith, and John Prendergast—all with strong Sudan experience—advocated a tough stance toward the NIF. Afterwards, Rice was promoted to Assistant Secretary of State for African Affairs, a position that gave her more leverage in the U.S. administration's decision-making centers. Furthermore, a group of longstanding congressmen and senators from both sides of the aisle (Senator Bill Frist [R], Congressmen Frank Wolf [R], Congressman Donald Payne [D], and Congressman Tom Tancredo [R], as well as Congressional aide Theodros Dagne) abhorred the Khartoum regime's record of human rights abuses. Nevertheless, they were also very critical of SPLM/A excesses and never shied away from drawing the attention of its leadership to those excesses. The U.S. administration and Congress, therefore, resisted European willingness to engage with Khartoum.[71] Instead, they supported engagement with the SPLM/A and the NDA because, in the estimation of U.S. institutions, these were the only viable alternative to the NIF regime. Although this view was held by Albright and Rice, it was not shared by the Bureau of African Affairs in the State Department, which was distrustful of the politics of traditional leaders in Sudan and, thus, not convinced of their ability to be viable alternatives to the Islamists. These misgivings were not entirely unwarrantable. Nonetheless, U.S. policy makers in the administration and legislative branches were also sympathetic to neighbors, especially Eritrea, Uganda, and Ethiopia, who wanted to isolate and confront the NCP after the failed attempt on the life of President Mubarak.

The United States' disavowal of the legitimacy of the NIF regime was so pervasive that some U.S. senior officials and legislators ignored diplomatic decorum in their dealings with Sudan. For example, Senator Frist, a medical doctor by profession, visited South Sudan without the knowledge, let alone the authorization, of Khartoum and carried out surgical interventions in the Lui hospital (Equatoria), a medical outfit operated by the Samaritan's Purse.[72] Susan Rice, in her capacity as assistant secretary of state, also visited the same sight to denounce its air bombardment by the Sudanese army. Khartoum, uncharacteristically, kept silent on the issue save for a cursory statement from the foreign minister. Also, Secretary of State Madeleine Albright held a meeting at the U.S. Embassy in Kampala in October 1997 with an NDA team led by John Garang to discuss modes of delivering assistance to the NDA, other than providing offensive weapons.[73] Washington, in addition to humanitarian assistance, provided NDA with funds to cover diplomatic activities and communication equipment, in addition to 20 million dollars' worth of surplus nonlethal military equipment, the latter through Eritrea, Ethiopia, and Uganda. In her meeting with the NDA leadership, Albright declared her government's support of the NDA's 1995 resolutions and requested the alliance to deepen democracy and respect for human rights, especially in areas under its control. In the meantime, the Clinton administration received for the first time Sudan's foreign minister, Mustafa Osman Ismail, who delivered a plea from his government for the United States to lift sanctions and normalize relations. The minister was received in Washington by Susan Rice, who identified three conditions that needed to be met before relations between the two countries were improved and sanctions removed. Those were: stop providing support to terrorist groups and allow U.S. antiterrorism officials to be stationed in Sudan, cease gross human rights violations in Sudan, and expedite the peace process to end the civil war.

Congressional politics towards Sudan, in general, and the NIF regime, in particular, did not change after the departure of President Clinton. There were two reasons for this: first, the Khartoum government policies that galvanized the U.S. Congress against the regime did not change, except on the surface; and second, these policies enjoyed bipartisan support in Congress and within the wider nongovernmental organization (NGO) community. Nevertheless, in the early months of the Bush administration, the new assistant secretary of state for African affairs, Walter H. Kansteiner, considered cutting any support that was coming to SPLM and NDA through Eritrea, Kenya, or Uganda. Eritrea was then host to, and an open supporter of, the Sudanese opposition, while Uganda and Kenya were providing the SPLM with a platform for diplomatic, media, and political activities. According to a brief by John Garang to the author, the assistant secretary conveyed the message to the leaders of the three countries through diplomatic channels. Of the three, President Isaias of Eritrea was curt in his response; in his report to Garang, Isaias said he told the diplomat relating the US message to him that Eritrea would not discuss its bilateral relations with any third party, nor would it allow being questioned about that.[74]

No sooner had Congressman Frank Wolf got wind of the assistant secretary's contacts than he called Secretary of State Colin Powell to inquire on whose authority the assistant secretary was acting, especially in the face of a clearly defined policy by Congress toward the Sudan government. Powell promised to look seriously into the matter, especially after Wolf threatened to withhold part of the State Department's budget appropriation for building a new U.S. embassy in Sudan. Wolf was then chairman of the powerful House Appropriations Committee. The congressman refused to receive Kansteiner to explain his position, and as a result, Deputy Secretary of State Richard Armitage entreated the congressman to do so. When the meeting between Wolf and the diplomat took place, Kansteiner effectively walked into a trap. The assistant secretary denied that he was trying to modify U.S. standing policy on Sudan, claiming he might have been misunderstood. While Kansteiner was assuring the congressman of his support to the NDA and his good relations with whom he called "my friend Garang," a telephone conference was already being prepared. On the one side was the congressman, the assistant secretary, and Congressional aide Ted Dagne; on the other was John Garang, the assistant secretary's "good friend." Garang confirmed the episode as it was conveyed to him by the Eritrean leader and Kenyan and Ugandan diplomats. In an effort not to embarrass the disconcerted diplomat any further, Wolf told Kansteiner to go and fix it. Ted Dagne, who was nicknamed "the emperor" (probably after Emperor Tewodros of Ethiopia), teamed up with two middle-level administration officials in Washington and dedicated themselves to promoting Garang's cause in Washington.[75] The role the three played in influencing U.S. policy toward John Garang should not be minimized.

Albeit, the confrontation between Wolf and the resistant secretary of state revealed how Garang's supporters had wormed their way through the U.S. corridors of powers. It also reveals how staunch Congress's position was toward conflict in Sudan and how ambivalent it was toward the stance on Sudan that the Bureau of African Affairs took. As future events would prove, the Bureau of African Affairs consistently maintained that a change of regime in Khartoum was not an option, let alone a priority, to the administration. Owing to its low regard for the "restored Bourbon kings" of Sudan, the Bureau of African Affairs never believed that these relics from the past would be a viable substitute for the NCP government, much as they had no love for that party. Consequently, the Bureau of African Affairs seemed to have been happy with incremental changes in Khartoum politics. Unfortunately for Washington's diplomats, their initiatives were often stymied by NCP politicians who had obviously no time for diplomatic nuances. Within their ranks, campus politics and megaphone diplomacy continued to reign supreme.

Despite all his diplomatic successes in Washington, Garang received an unpleasant shock from his own home base in the course of his efforts to promote the NDA as a viable alternative to the NIF regime. Inspirited by the wide bipartisan support he had received in the U.S. Congress and administration, Garang wished to meet Colin Powell to brief him on the Sudan situation and also to organize a meeting between al-Mirghani, chairman of the NDA, and the new secretary of state. Although Powell's diplomatic advisors welcomed the idea of receiving Garang at a high level in Washington, they were not sure the meeting should be with the assistant secretary or the deputy secretary, ruling out any meeting with Powell. Garang, who had by that time became well versed in walking his way through the labyrinth of Washington's power corridors, managed to secure a meeting for himself with Powell through Congressman Wolf and the new speaker of the House, who seemed to have been enthralled with Garang's presentation. Obviously, the diplomats were not sure of what surprise Garang would drop before the secretary. Notwithstanding, the meeting between Garang and Powell, which was scheduled for 20 minutes, took one hour, without any bombshells.

In the course of that meeting Garang raised the issue of al-Mirghani's visit and the importance of his meeting with Powell. To that request the secretary told the SPLM leader that he had won him over, so why did he want the Secretary to meet the NDA chairman?[76] Garang answered that al-Mirghani, as the leader of the largest Islamic sect in Sudan would surely have something to add to his (Garang's) claim about the viability of the NDA as an alternative to Khartoum's Islamists. A date was set for al-Mirghani to meet with U.S. authorities, to which al-Mirghani agreed. To the surprise of everybody, however, al-Mirghani backed out of the visit at the eleventh hour, after all the energy that had been put into organizing it. When al-Mirghani asked for an adjournment of the meeting for health reasons, no one in Washington took him seriously, especially since there were plausible conjectures that he was shying away from the Washington visit for fear of enraging Qaddafi and displeasing Egyptian authorities. Both Egypt and Libya at that point in time believed that Sudan's peace could only be attained through the JELI and not through the IGAD imitative that was embraced by the SPLM and supported by the United States. Whatever the reasons were for al-Mirghani's vacillation about that meeting, Washington diplomats became doubly sure that the NDA chairman, who was not even able to independently decide on his own travels, could never be counted on to fearlessly and independently decide on serious national matters. If only for that reason, Washington diplomats deemed al-Mirghani as an unsuitable alternative to the strong-minded NCP, no matter what Garang had said about "his chairman."

In view of all the above, NCP was not off track when it blamed the United States for giving support to the SPLM/A and, through that, to an "undeserving" northern leadership. Sudan presidential peace advisor Ghazi

Salahuddin Atabani reflected late in 2001 that the [U.S.] administration (and some of its associates in the U.S. public) had, in different ways, been the mainstay of the SPLM/A. This, according to Salahuddin, had caused the movement to believe in the certainty of its ultimate victory over the central government, and encouraged and emboldened it [to the extent of] blocking any progress towards peace.[77] The peace advisor had unquestionably gone a bit overboard in calling U.S. support the mainstay of the SPLM, as he had obviously held cheap the contributions of thousands of southern and northern Sudanese professionals who abandoned their jobs to join the movement. He also underestimated the alliances the SPLM/A was able to make with the totality of northern Sudanese opposition, enfeebled as it had become, as well as the support it continued to receive from neighboring African countries, indeed from the whole of Africa.[78] Moreover, Salahuddin conveniently discounted the NIF's reckless adventures against Egypt, including the assassination attempt on its president in 1995, which brought the SPLM and its leader much closer to the Egyptian leadership as well as to Egypt's intellectual circles. What the NCP politicians had also stopped thinking about was the reason why an array of U.S. policy makers and NGOs became so emotionally involved in Sudan's affairs. If the NCP politicians had given a thought to that probability, they would have discovered that "angry Americans" were not driven by hatred toward Islam but by humanitarian reasons, namely, famines and population displacements, grave human rights abuses such as alleged religious persecution, or war crimes that were totally prohibited under the international laws of war such as the bombardment of civilians. However lofty the ends it was fighting for, the NIF seemed not to have ever questioned the means by which it sought to realize those supposedly grand goals. Noble ends could never be achieved by iniquitous means. Consequently, the way out of the international isolation in which the NCP had found itself was to mend its ways, a matter that was entirely in its own hands.

Nevertheless, toward the end of the Clinton administration, momentum was growing to reappraise U.S. policies regarding Sudan, especially after the outcome of the January 1999 consultations led by the United States Institute of Peace (USIP).[79] Participants in that debate included representatives of the NDA and SPLM; ambassadors of Kenya and Egypt to the US, and representatives of the Norwegian government, the U.S. National Security Council, the Council on Foreign Relations, the U.S. State Department, and other experts on Sudan.[80] An invitation was made to the NCP to participate, but bureaucratic delays in visa clearance impeded their participation. The consultations concluded:

- "The IGAD process needs to remain the vehicle for mediation and negotiation, with Kenya continuing to take the lead.
- The process must be strengthened through international assistance to permit more effective and sustained negotiations.

- The countries of the IPF, including the United States along with the United Nations and the Organization of African Unity, need to give financial and technical support to make the IGAD process more effective.
- The Declaration of Principles (DoP) agreed to by both parties needs to be the framework of the negotiations.
- By giving particular attention to the principle of self-determination for the South, the process shall make more significant progress."[81]

Despite that impetus, relations had not materially improved between the government of Sudan and the United States when George W. Bush took office in January 2001. The arrival of the Bush administration, needless to say, meant a change in key policy makers on Sudan at senior levels and an opportunity for domestic lobby groups concerned with Sudan to avail themselves of that opportunity to advance their agenda. Those included the Christian right, which enjoyed an enhanced position of influence with the new administration. As well, the Congressional Black Caucus, human rights groups, and commercial actors jostled to have their concerns heard in a period of policy reformulation. The coalition of the American Christian right and the left (represented by the Black Caucus) was described by a media commentator as a "coalition that any politician would be proud to step out and get in front of."[82] However, President Bashir had a different reaction to the change of administration in Washington; he told Reuters that his government would not blame Bush for the "sins" of the Clinton administration toward Sudan and that he was ready to discuss U.S. concerns with him.[83] Sudanese diplomats, if the president had ever sought counsel from them on what the U.S. concerns were, would have certainly told him that all issues that irked the United States, as well as African and Western countries, were home grown.

Yet, the most important debate on U.S. policy toward Sudan occurred early in 2001. The Center for Strategic and International Studies (CSIS) held an extensive consultative process led jointly by J. Stephen Morrison and Francis Deng.[84] The deliberations of that meeting, attended by representatives of both parties to the conflict, had an everlasting impact on the peace process. The CSIS report of February 2001 emphasised ending the war "in the south" as the priority strategic concern.[85] For this reason, it contemplated that a "one country, two systems" formulation might allow the impasse on the issue of religion and state to be resolved during an interim period before the exercise of self-determination through referendum in South Sudan. Essentially, the CSIS report argued for a north-south approach to defining the problem and the solution. It considered that other problems within the country (such as governance in the north or conflicts in other marginalized areas) should not be an equal priority focus of the United States. It further argued that the resolution of these problems depended upon ending the war with the SPLM/A first.

In March 2001, the Subcommittee on Africa of the U.S. House Committee on Foreign Relations debated a new direction in U.S. policy on Sudan. While a hard-line position on the NCP was still advocated by some, a consensus grew toward a redoubled approach on achieving a negotiated end to the war. Sudan quickly became a priority concern in Washington, with new Secretary of State Colin Powell quoted as saying that "there [was] **no greater tragedy on the face of the Earth than the one unfolding in Sudan**" (emphasis added).[86] The context within which that statement was made should not have been flattering to the Khartoum regime, which was described as "one of the world's most brutal regimes."[87] In May of the same year, Powell intimated that the United States was "going to work hard to bring a cease-fire into effect" and would appoint an envoy to reinvigorate the IGAD.[88]

Appointment of a high-powered presidential envoy on Sudan has been consistently challenged by the State Department, probably for fear of competition over turf. Since the appointment of Congressman Harry Johnston by President Clinton, the Bureau of African Affairs in the Department of State saw to it that envoys to Sudan were drawn from medium-ranking officials amenable to influence by diplomats in the State Department. All the same, Congress and the anti-NIF group within the National Security Council continued to put pressure on the administration to appoint high-level envoys. In a very revealing letter to Congress members (December 6, 1993), the State Department maintained in the letter that the appointment of a high-power envoy would send the erroneous impression that the United States is becoming directly involved, since Khartoum has made it clear that it rejects a role by the United States in the peace process. That overindulgent and velvety approach to the NIF did not amuse Congress, so it persevered in calling on the administration to be proactively and visibly engaged in Sudan. Thus, on January 2, 2001, Congressman Frank Wolf wrote to the incoming President Bush, requesting the appointment of "a full-time high-profile envoy of national stature such as former Secretary of State James Baker or US Ambassador to the UN Richard Holbrooke." The envoy, Wolf said, must "have the President's ear."[89] Subsequently, on September 6, 2001, prior to the events of September 11 in the United States, President Bush appointed Senator John Danforth as his special envoy on Sudan.[90]

In launching his new envoy to Sudan, President Bush declared in a White House ceremony that "for nearly two decades, the government of Sudan has waged a brutal and shameful war against its own people. And this isn't right, and this must stop."[91] Danforth, in a more measured response to the president's words said: "…the effectiveness of America's efforts for peace in Sudan will depend on our communication and cooperation with other interested countries, including the European Union and countries neighboring Sudan, especially Egypt."[92] Evidently, the senator had his own estimation of

73

the Sudanese crisis and of how to solve it. With resolve, Danforth embarked on his mission, guided by his own interpretation of the presidential mandate.

Danforth's mission was initially to help address issues that were of concern to two unimaginable allies in the United States: The Christian right and the Congressional Black Caucus. The former were troubled by the Sudan government's reported intimidation of Christians; the latter was agitated by alleged enslavement of southern Sudanese in some war zones. Furthermore, Danforth and his government were also preoccupied with two occurrences: first, the worst humanitarian crisis southern Sudan had ever faced in recent times (the famine in Bahr el Ghazal), and second, the terrorist attack on the New York World Trade Center and the Pentagon in Washington. The famine, on the one hand, caused an international uproar and put the SPLM in an embarrassing situation by adding to the crises with which it was already grappling such as raids by government-sponsored militias and clashes between SPLM factions. As for the terrorist attack on New York and Washington, it virtually became the determinant factor in the formulation of U.S. policy toward Sudan, a country that had been included by the United States since August 1993 in the list of countries supporting terrorism. On the issue of peacemaking, Danforth, while underlining the humanitarian character of his mission, added that the United States would play a role in peacemaking in Sudan. He added, however, that his government had no peace initiative but would support any existing one. With this in mind, Danforth established contacts with the two parties to the conflict as well as with other Sudanese political forces and regional mediators. In his report to President Bush in April 2002, he stated that "The participation of the United States in the search for peace, while being collaborative and catalytic, must also be energetic and effective."[93]

NOTES

1   Machakos was the administrative capital of Kenya up to 1887. In 2002, it hosted for a year the peace talks that led to a historic breakthrough in the negotiations to resolve the Sudanese conflict that had defied all attempts for a pacific settlement since 1983.

2   The meeting took place in an Ethiopian resort outside Addis Ababa in March 1986 and was attended by representatives of northern as well as southern Sudan-based parties, alongside representatives of trades unions and civil society organizations.

3   Statement by the spokesman of the Ingaz coup, SUNA *Sudan News Agency* (Khartoum), 1 July 1989.

4   In November 1988, Mohamed Osman al-Mirghani, leader of the Democratic Unionist Party, and John Garang, on behalf of the Sudan People's Liberation Movement, signed in Addis Ababa, Ethiopia, an agreement called the Sudan Peace Initiative. In that agreement, both parties settled on freezing *shari'a* laws pending the convocation of a constitutional conference in which the SPLM promised to

participate. The NIF, who were then part of the coalition government in Khartoum, withdrew from the government in protest against what they called the abolition of Allah's laws.

5   Personal recollections

6   Supra note 3

7   Policy statement by John Garang to the people of Sudan, 10 August 1988, in Khalid, *The Call for Democracy*, 237.

8   Ibid., 240.

9   Ibid., 241.

10 Ibid., 245.

11 Islamic laws promulgated by President Nimeiri in September 1983 and by which he ushered in the Islamist phase of his rule.

12 The term is one of the code names of the NIF's Islamicization project. It signifies rules governing public and private life to which all other rules are secondary. Those rules were allegedly derived from the *Quran* and the *Sunna* (the practice and pronouncements of the prophet Muhammad).

13 For details see Johnson, *The Root Causes of Sudan's Civil Wars*, 92.

14 Khalid, *War and Peace in Sudan*, 339. See also discussion in Johnson, *The Root Causes of Sudan's Civil Wars*, section 8.5.

15 Johnson, *The Root Causes of Sudan's Civil Wars*, 92.

16 Ibid., section 8.5.

17 Ibid., 103

18 http://www.hoover.org/publications/policy-review/article/5646

19 Supra note 15, 103

20 See Iyob and Khadiagala, *Sudan: The Elusive Quest for Peace*, 107–12.

21 See Khalid, *War and Peace in Sudan*, 244–50.

22 Ibid., 233.

23 See analysis in "Falling out, Falling in," *Africa Confidential*, 4 February 2000, vol. 41, issue 3.

24 Turabi told the Arabic service of the BBC (29 June 2000) that he had engineered the NIF coup, recruited Bashir, and camouflaged his action in order to "hoodwink the Americans and the communists." In a pointed threat to Bashir, he told the BBC that he was capable of doing the same thing again.

25 Anonymous, *The Black Book: Imbalance of Power and Wealth in Sudan* (Khartoum: "Seekers of Truth and Justice," 2000). An English translation of the Arabic is available on the Internet, translated by Abdullahi Osman El-Tom.

26 See discussion in "Pointers: Niger, Algeria and Sudan," *Africa Confidential*, 3 December 1999, vol. 40, no. 24.

27 See analysis of the event in Khalid, *War and Peace in Sudan*, 415–16.

28 Sudan TV, Omdurman, "Sudan: President Bashir vows to nation he will be a 'leader for all,'" 1 January 2001, translated by BBC Monitoring.

29 Ibid.

30 *Al Hayat*, London, 23 April 2001.

31 The agreement was signed in Nairobi by Justin Yac Arop on behalf of the SPLM/A. It is discussed further in Khalid, *War and Peace in Sudan*, 343.

32 Rebecca Oloo, "Sudan: Too Deformed to Effect Reforms," *African Church Information Service*, 1 July 2002.

33 See Sudan People's Liberation Movement (SPLM) and Popular National Congress (PNC), *Memorandum of Understanding between the Sudan People's Liberation Movement and the Popular National Congress* (2001).; in Khalid, *War and Peace in Sudan*, 401–03.

34 Johnson, *The Root Causes of Sudan's Civil Wars*

35 See Wainaina Kiganya, "If IGAD Has Failed on Sudan, How About UN?" *The Nation*, 18 June 2001. The paper noted: "Virtually every day now, the rebels of the Sudan People's Liberation Army claim battlefield successes, which, if true, constitute a major setback for the government in Khartoum."

36 See, especially, Appendix in Johnson, *The Root Causes of Sudan's Civil Wars*.

37 NSB was the code name for SPLA contingents operating in the new war zone in eastern Sudan. It also included groups from northern Sudan, who responded to appeals from the SPLM leadership to disparate political factions to join the brigade.

38 Sudan Alliance Forces, Political Department press release, "The Historic Unification of the Sudan People's Liberation Movement (SPLM) and the Sudan Alliance Forces (SAF)," 28 February 2002 .

39 Garang was asked at one time whether he genuinely believed that the SPLM/A would conquer the North forcibly. He answered, "categorically not," adding that when the SPLA reaches the north/south borders, it would not be commanded by Colonel Garang, but by Colonel Mohamed Ahmed. By that time there was a score of Mohamed Ahmed's within the top ranks of the SPLA, of whom not a few were defectors from the Sudanese army.

40 See Julie Flint, "Rebel Leader Says Nuba Have the Will to Fight Khartoum," *The Guardian*, 16 April 2001.

41 Gareth Evans, *God, Oil and Country: Changing the Logic of War in Sudan*, International Crisis Group, 28 January 2002, 48. The International Crisis Group is an independent, nonprofit, nongovernmental organization committed to preventing and resolving deadly conflict.

42 See discussion in Jemera Rone and Human Rights Watch, *Sudan, Oil, and Human Rights* (New York: Human Rights Watch, 2003); Daniel Large, *Arms, Oil, and Darfur: The Evolution of Relations between China and Sudan* (Geneva: Small Arms Survey, 2007), 7; and Johnson, *The Root Causes of Sudan's Civil Wars*.

43 Edward Thomas, *Against the Gathering Storm: Securing Sudan's Comprehensive Peace Agreement* (London: Chatham House, 2009), 33.

44 Warburg, *Islam, Sectarianism and Politics in Sudan since the Mahdiyya*, 216.

45 Evans, *God, Oil and Country*.

46 Ibid., 27.

47 Ibid., 28.

48 Ibid.

49 I. William Zartman, "The Timing of Peace Initiatives: Hurting Stalemates and Ripe Moments," *The Global Review of Ethnopolitics* vol. 1, no. 2 (2001).

50 Peter Woodward, "Peacemaking in Sudan," in *Ending Africa's Wars: Progressing to Peace*, (eds. Oliver Furley and Roy May (Aldershot, ENG: Ashgate, 2006), 169.

51 See especially the reflections of General Lazaro Sumbeiywo, Moi's chosen mediator for the IGAD talks, in Waithaka Waihenya, *The Mediator: General Lazaro Sumbeiywo and the Southern Sudan Peace Process* (Nairobi: Kenway Publications, 2006), 4.

52 The group comprised the US, Canada together with western European countries, and Japan, who volunteered to push forward the IGAD peace process.

53 Supra note 46, 49

54 Khalid, *War and Peace in Sudan*, 379–401 and 411–417.

55 Johnson, *The Root Causes of Sudan's Civil* Wars, 176.

56 "Al-Mahdi Blames Garang for Talks Breakdown," U.N. Integrated Regional Information Network (IRIN), 15 May 2001.

57 Ibid.

58 BBC Worldwide Monitoring, "Opposition Leader Calls on State to Respect Religious Freedom (in Arabic)," *Al-Ra'y al-Amm*, 18 April 2001.

59 Agence France-Presse, "Egyptian, Libyan, Sudanese Ministers Meet on Sudan Peace Plan," 20 January 2001.

60 See Abdelwahab El-Affendi, "The Impasse in the IGAD Process for Sudan: The Limits of Regional Peacemaking?" African Affairs 100, no. 401 (2001): 581–99.

61 See Evans, *God, Oil and Country,* 25.

62 See Rone and Human Rights Watch, *Sudan, Oil, and Human Rights,* 673–87.

63 See discussion in J. Stephen Morrison, "Somalia's and Sudan's Race to the Fore in Africa," *The Washington Quarterly* 25, no. 2 (2002): 191-205.

64 See, for example, discussion in Larry Minear, *Humanitarianism under Siege: A Critical Review of Operation Lifeline Sudan* (Trenton, NJ: Red Sea Press, 1991); Mark R. Duffield, *Global Governance and the New Wars: The Merging of Development and Security* (London: Zed Books, 2001); Johnson, *The Root Causes of Sudan's Civil Wars.*

65 The Committee, which was formed in Rome in 1998, endorsed a plan for humanitarian assistance, especially to famine stricken areas of Southern Sudan. The plan was sponsored by Italian deputy foreign minister, Rino Serri.

66 Discussed in Center for Strategic and International Studies (CSIS), *U.S. Policy to End Sudan's War: Report of the CSIS Task Force on U.S.-Sudan Policy* (Washington D.C. 2001).

67 Willam J.Clinton, Message to the Congress on the National Emergency with with Respect to Sudan November 3, 1997 http://www.presidency.ucsb.edu/ws/index.php?pid=53506

68 Barton Gellman, "In '96, Sudan Offered to Arrest bin Laden; Saudis Balked at Accepting U.S. Plan," *Washington Post,* 4 October 2001.

69 See Africa Confidential, "Washington's Military Option," Africa Confidential 39, no. 17 (28 August 1998), 39, no. 17 (1998).

70 See "Washington's Military Option," *Africa Confidential* 39, no. 17 (28 August 1998).

71 For example, in mid-1998, shortly before the bombing of the Al-Shifa pharmaceutical factory, the United States resisted the Friends of IGAD position that the time was ripe to seek a compromise peace agreement that would recognize the NCP in the North in exchange for self-determination for the South: "Long War, Quick Fix," *Africa Confidential* 39, no. 14 (10 July 1998).

72 Samaritan's Purse is a Christian aid group, established and sponsored by Franklin Graham, which engaged in humanitarian activities in both northern and southern Sudan.

73 The meeting was attended by Dr. Garang (SPLM/A), Mubarak al-Mahdi (Umma Party), General Abdel Aziz Khalid (SAF), Farouq Ahmed Adam (DUP), and the author, who accompanied Garang.

74 Personal recollection.

75 Brian D'Silva's relationship with Garang went back to university days when both were enrolled at Iowa State University. Roger Winter initially came close to South Sudan and Garang through the organization he was leading: U.S. Committee for Refugees. However, Dagne's role was crucial in mobilizing support to Garang in Congress. See special report to Reuters by Rebecca Hamilton, "The Wonks who Sold Washington on South Sudan," July 11, 2012.

76 Personal recollection.

77 Evans, *God, Oil and Country*, 173.

78 Throughout the struggle, and particularly when the NIF usurped power and engaged in its policy of forcible Islamicization and Arabicization of the country, regardless of its cultural and religious diversity, African countries began to lend their ears to the SPLM. Among the countries that did not hesitate to give material support to the SPLM were Ethiopia, Eritrea, Ghana, Namibia, Nigeria, South Africa's African Nationalist Congress party, Zambia, and Zimbabwe.

79 David R. Smock, "A New Approach to Peace in Sudan: Report on a USIP Consultation," Special Report 45 (February 1999).

80 Among those were Bona Malwal, Francis Deng, Abdul Mohamed, Abdelwahab El-Affendi, British expert on Sudan Alex de Waal, Roger Winter, Ted Dange, and the author.

81 Supra 76

82 Mary McGrory, "Suddenly, Sudan," *Washington Post,* March 11, 2001.

83 Alistair Lyon, Reuters, January 16, 2001.

84 Morrison is senior vice president of the CSIS and a frequent contributor in major media on U.S. foreign policy. Deng, a former ambassador and foreign minister of Sudan, is known and respected for the many sober and thought-provoking books he authored on Sudan's conflict.

85 See "U.S. Policy to End Sudan's War," Report of the CSIS Task Force on U.S.-Sudan Policy (Washington D.C.: Center for Strategic and International Studies, February 2001).

86 See Elliot Abrams, "What to Do about Sudan: Steps the Bush Administration Can Take against One of the World's Most Brutal Regimes," *The Weekly Standard,* May 7, 2001.

87 Ibid.

88 BBC Worldwide Monitoring, "Powell Says USA Will Engage in Efforts to End Wars in D.R. Congo, Sudan," *The New Vision, Kampala,* 28 May 2001.

89 *Frank Wolf in the Newsroom,* newsletter released on January 25, 2001

90 Danforth was U.S. Senator from Missouri, and after his mission in Sudan he became U.S. Ambassador to the United Nation (2004–2005). He was also an ordained Episcopal priest. In addition, Danforth was known for his moderate Christianity as reflected in an op-ed piece he published in the *New York Times* on March 30, 2005, in which he wrote: "by a series of recent initiatives, Republicans have transformed our party into a political arm of conservative Christians."

91 The president appoints Danforth envoy to the Sudan, The White House, September 6, 2001. http://georgewbush-whitehouse.archives.gov/news/releases/2001/09/20010906-3.html

92 Ibid.

93 Danforth, John C., Report to the President of the United States on the Outlook for Peace in Sudan, April 26th, 2002.

Chapter Three
Machakos Protocol:
Breakthrough in Peace
Negotiations

■■■■■■■■■■■■■❖■■■■■■■■■■■■■

> It always seems impossible until it happens.
> —**Nelson Mandela**
> Inaugural Speech, 1994

1. Introduction

Up until late 2001, the rejuvenated Intergovernmental Authority on Development (IGAD) talks failed to make any headway.[1] External assessments in late 2000 and early 2001 were sceptical that these talks could ever succeed, especially if the Joint Egyptian-Libyan Initiative (JELI) undermined them.[2] In February 2001, for example, the Center for Strategic and International Studies (CSIS) published a report condemning the IGAD process as "increasingly ineffectual and fragmented," claiming it "could not be relied upon to persuade Sudan's warring principals to enter into serious negotiations."[3] That condemnation extended, in an overhasty judgment, to the host country, Kenya, when the CSIS claimed "infrequent Sudan peace talks chaired by Kenya show no evidence of progress."[4] Other commentators characterized the period from January 2000 to November 2001 as "IGAD under siege."[5] Lack of faith in the IGAD process became contagious, affecting even the Friends of IGAD. At a meeting in London in October 2000, the IGAD Partners Forum (IPF) concluded that the process was failing badly, as a result of which they suspended their financial support for the process in early 2001.[6]

This chapter shall deal with how victory was virtually snatched from the hands of defeat through a concerted effort of the IGAD mediators, IPF, and the United States, especially Senator John Danforth. In some cases the protagonists were brought to the negotiating table practically kicking and screaming. Those were the cases in which negotiations, according to the IGAD chief mediator, turned into shouting matches. Eventually, the shouting subsided and the parties, with firm and adept steering by the chief mediator, made their first breakthrough in the negotiations.

2. Old Problems Loom out of the Past

Despite setbacks and excessively pessimistic assessments, President Moi in 2001 adjudged that it was time to resuscitate the IGAD process. In March 2001, the Kenyan leader visited Khartoum and persuaded Bashir to call for an emergency IGAD summit to push forward the talks.[7] As discussed in the previous chapter, the Sudan People's Liberation Army (SPLA) captured Raja in early June 2002, when President Bashir was on his way to Kenya to attend the IGAD summit initiated by President Moi. That did not augur well for the impending summit meeting. In the meantime, disagreement between the Sudan People's Liberation Movement (SPLM) and the government of Sudan on the fundamental issue of religion and state still remained a major stumbling block. A report from March 2001 captured the problem: "SPLM insists on a secular constitution, or alternatively, that southern Sudan should either secede or be part of a confederation with the Muslim-dominated north. The Khartoum government for its part is suggesting a federation, where each region shall be allowed to choose a legal system of its own choice. In addition, the government proposed a general referendum for southern Sudanese to choose between federal rule and an independent state of their own."[8] Apart from cliché expressions like "Muslim-dominated north," this report conveyed a true picture of the situation.

In response to Khartoum's suggestions, the SPLM contended that having separate legal systems for small federal regions would be a divisive and disempowering arrangement. In reality, dividing the Sudan into small units, each with its own legal system, would not have been disempowering; it would have been a desirable thing to do in a country as vast as Sudan. However, decentralization of legal systems as a ploy to evade an overarching Bill of Rights that would apply to all states and citizens of the federation irrespective of their religious, cultural, ethnic, or regional provenance would be a perversion of these rights. In no existing democratic federal system are states of the federation empowered to legislate laws that are repugnant to federal enactments, nor are state citizens immunized against application of the federal constitution or international law.

Another stumbling block was the government's request for a cease-fire *before* talks on political settlement commenced. As the SPLA took control of Raja and Deim Zubeir in Bahr el Ghazal, Mustafa Ismail, Sudan's foreign minister, argued the governments' case as follows: "Our aim for calling for cease-fire is to smooth the way for talks, and we have even accepted international observers to monitor the cease-fire."[9] The idea of "smoothing the way for talks" had always been rejected by the SPLM/A, who interpreted it to mean allowing the government to continue with business-as-usual under no real pressure. A cease-fire, the SPLM argued, had to be the outcome of an agreement on a final political solution.

Regardless of the controversies on cease-fire, two positive outcomes came out of the Nairobi IGAD summit: the establishment of permanent negotiating teams from both sides, and renewed international support to the IGAD secretariat based in Nairobi. In effect, as early as July 21, 1999, a year before the Nairobi Summit, the IGAD ministerial committee on Sudan, also meeting in Nairobi, recognized that there was a need to institutionalize the IGAD initiative and the peace process. To that end the ministerial committee decided on:

(i) Appointment by the president of Kenya of a special envoy to "mount concentrated, coordinated, and continuous mediation efforts on a full-time basis."

(ii) Appointment by each IGAD member state of an envoy on Sudan peace. The envoys' meetings would be chaired by the special envoy, and their decisions would be consensual.

(iii) Establishment of a permanent secretariat in Nairobi.

The call by the summit for support to the IGAD secretariat indicated that the institutionalization of the IGAD initiative, as demanded by the ministerial committee, was not fully attained. Vacillation of the IPF on support to the process, as referred to earlier, was one reason for the secretariat's under-achievement. However, after the Nairobi Summit, the IPF made a U-turn on its position regarding the IGAD peace process and its host, Kenya. In the meantime, the IGAD process received a great boost when U.S. Secretary of State Madeleine Albright told the press in Nairobi, "We believe the IGAD process is the best way to go forward and do not support other processes that some are suggesting, the Egyptians or the Libyans."[10]

3. Choosing between Two Competing Peace Initiatives

Despite the shortcomings of the Nairobi Summit, notably President Bashir's refusal to meet with John Garang,[11] the SPLM seized the opportunity to ensure that IGAD was the main focus for negotiations, with JELI either merged into it or dropped. In June 2001, Garang said that the IGAD initiative must be seen "as the only credible forum for resolving the Sudan conflict." Talking to *Newsweek*, he stated, "We have as a movement decided that we will negotiate one initiative at a time, not parallel initiatives. And so we are calling for a unified forum with IGAD as its core, because that's the primary initiative, and that has a declaration of principles."[12] Garang couched things slightly differently when talking to the Khartoum newspaper, *Al-Ra'y al-Amm*: "Unfortunately, the current impression is that the IGAD initiative favors the south while JELI is for the north. Consequently, we have appealed for the unification of the two initiatives so that we can be assured of a comprehensive solution to the Sudanese problem,"[13] said Garang.

Following the failure of the IGAD talks, the government turned once again to JELI, exploiting the SPLM/A's refusal to accept a cease-fire as a basis for asserting its bonafide peace intentions. In June 2001, the *Khartoum Monitor* reported Mustafa Ismail as saying, "the government is now looking forward to the Joint Egyptian-Libyan Initiative after the IGAD has not shown any positive step toward a solution". Nevertheless, the last gasp of JELI was yet to come. In late September 2001, the government of Sudan justified its delays and blockages of the IGAD process, citing the need to consult with IGAD first "'to review the whole peace process and propose ways and means for tackling the difficulties which arrested any progress since 1997.'"[14] In October 2001, presidential peace advisor Ghazi Salahuddin Atabani said that the government was giving IGAD "a final chance to advance the peace process."[15]

Still, in January 2001, Egyptian Foreign Minister Amr Musa declared that IGAD should merge with the JELI because "'IGAD's partners in European and world capitals will not solve the Sudanese problem via the IGAD initiative alone." He added that if Egypt were not to be involved in the peace process through the JELI, then the IGAD initiative shall "remain as deadwood unfit for burning."[16] That was the measure of Egypt's revulsion of the IGAD process and the presumptuousness of its minister. Patently, the JELI once again raised its head after the failure of the June 2001 IGAD summit to advance the peace process. In July 2001, Egyptian and Libyan governments presented the government of Sudan, the SPLM/A, and the National Democratic Alliance (NDA) with a Nine-Point Plan to resolve the conflict. The plan included basic and uncontroversial provisions: the unity of Sudan; recognition of ethnic, religious, and cultural diversity; plural democracy; guarantee of basic freedoms and human rights; citizenship as a basis for assigning rights and duties to citizen; decentralized system of rule; rule of law; the urgent need for a cessation of violence; and a Sudan foreign policy that guaranteed national interests and fostered good neighborly relations. The insertion of a clause on foreign policy would appear apposite to peace negotiations regarding domestic political, economic, and cultural issues. In effect, the SPLM had reckoned that Sudan's foreign policy in the past was invariably off-center and often ideologized by Khartoum's rulers without regard to the country's politicocultural diversity. For that reason it urged the NDA to incorporate into any future peace agreement a nonaxial foreign policy program that would first and foremost serve Sudan's highest national interests.

As for the modalities envisaged for achieving peace, the Nine-Point Plan proposed the creation of an interim national government made up of all Sudanese political groups. That government was to organize a national conference to review the constitution and prepare for, and hold, elections.[17] Regardless, SPLM/A seized an opportunity at the Cairo meeting of July 2001 to reiterate that unity of Sudan could only be maintained on a "new basis," not on archetypical patterns of the past. On the other hand, the government accepted the Nine-Point Plan unconditionally, although it did so tactically, knowing full well that the plan fell short of the SPLM/A's long-standing demands concerning separation of religion and state and self-determination for the South. As for the NDA, it embraced the nine points in their totality, since the plan opened a window of opportunity for those of its members who wanted to share in, if not recapture, the power they had claimed in Asmara. Expediently, they overlooked the absence from the Nine-Point Plan of any reference to the right to self-determination by any people in Sudan who so desired it, which had been enshrined in the 1995 Asmara Resolutions.

4. National Constitutional Conference

One of the nine points in the Egyptian proposal reflected a long-standing position by the SPLM/A on how to end the conflict: by convening a national constitutional conference to review, among other things, the structures of power and the equitable sharing of wealth in the country. The idea of a constitutional conference had never been contemplated by northern political leaders up to the 1980s, since they seemed to believe that the only source of destabilization in Sudan was the Southern Question. The closest thing to an all-embracing national conference was the Round Table Conference (RTC) organized by Sir al-Khatim al-Khalifa's regime in 1965. That exercise was not only frustrated, but also undermined by northern political forces. However, since the early 1980s, the SPLM/A had maintained that Sudan was in need of constitutional restructuring through a national conference. When Dr. Jizouli Dafa'a Allah, prime minister of Sudan in the interim government that replaced Nimeiri, proposed to the SPLM a plan for peace in Sudan, Garang promptly answered that any peace arrangement should be discussed and adopted by a peace conference. In his communication to Garang, the prime minister suggested the following:

(i) Resolution of the **Southern Problem** according to the *National Charter*[18] agreed upon by the trade unions, political parties, and army (all those bodies were predominantly northern);

(ii) Revival of Addis Ababa Accord (which was recurrently denounced by the SPLM/A);

(iii) Joining the government of a united Sudan based in Khartoum.[19]

In his response to the prime minister, Garang welcomed dialogue on certain conditions, the foremost of which was what he called the self-delusion of considering the crisis as the "problem of Southern Sudan" instead, of seriously addressing the germane issue: namely, the problem of Sudan. That, he said, would require convening a national constitutional conference to discuss fundamental issues such as the system of government in Khartoum and the regions. Garang had made the same proposal to emissaries of President Nimeiri, before his fall, in response to Nimeiri's first and only serious attempt to sue for peace with the SPLM. In his peace deal, carried by British business tycoon Roland "Tiny" Rowland, Nimeiri offered Garang a vice presidential post and one-third of the cabinet posts. Garang, in a mordant tone, told the president's emissaries that Nimeiri had had several vice presidents since he came to power, and he (Garang) would like to know what had happened to each one of them. He also asked Nimeiri what would be left for the people of the West and the East if he allocated one-third of his cabinet to the South. Nevertheless, in a more serious tone, Garang conveyed another message to Nimeiri over SPLM Radio on March 2, 1985, in which he called for direct talks to take place between the SPLA and the Sudanese Army in south Sudan, and at the national level, a *national congress* to be convened to which all political forces in the country would be invited to discuss the formation a *New Sudan*. [20]

Obviously, the term New Sudan and national conference were no music to Nimeiri's ears or to his military successors. It had, thus, taken the northern parties a decade and a half to realize that the destiny of the country would only be decided to the satisfaction of all stakeholders through a collective effort, not by fiats from Khartoum. It is interesting to note here that since the RTC, which was bungled by northern political parties, the only time those parties collectively met with leaders from the South and other regions in Sudan[21] to map out a plan for peace, unity, and development was on the occasion of the launching of the National Democratic Alliance (NDA) at Asmara in June 1995. By that time all those parties were out of power, and as likely as not, they jointly wanted to rectify the mistakes they had committed severally since independence.

5. Garang and Qaddafi

The relationship between Garang and Qaddafi went back to the early 1980s, when Ethiopia (which was hosting Garang), Libya, and South Yemen banded together to form the Addis Ababa-Aden-Tripoli triangle. That alliance was at the time the most radical political association in the region. Through the intervention of Ethiopian President Mengistu Haile Mariam and South Yemeni President Ali Nasir Muhammad, the Libyan leader was persuaded to provide the new rebel movement in Sudan with the assets it needed for sustaining the struggle it had just launched. But, irrespective of the Ethiopian-Yemeni intervention, Qaddafi was already predisposed to support any opposition against Nimeiri. In fact, at the very time his emissaries, led by Abdel Salam Jalloud, were negotiating with Garang, Gaddafi was also maintaining, arming, and training Sudanese northern opposition forces in Kofra (Libya), intending to infiltrate Sudan and overthrow Nimeiri's regime. That force was drawn from the main opposition groups against the Sudanese regime: National Unionists, Umma, and Islamists. Astoundingly, following Qaddafi's death and the demise of his regime, National Congress Party (NCP) leaders, supported by a chorus of castigators of the Libyan leader, engaged in rewriting the history of Sudan-Libyan relations. Taking advantage of what they assumed to be a lapse of memory among Sudanese, they accused the late Libyan leader of conspiring with John Garang to divide Sudan. Much as one understood the NCP's bile at Qaddafi for supporting the newly formed Darfur armed opposition movement Justice and Equality Movement (JEM), especially in its audacious attack on Omdurman (see Chapter Twelve), their attempt to adulterate history was both thankless and fraudulent. For example, the Islamists were the avant-garde of the forces maintained, trained, and logistically supported by Qaddafi to invade Sudan in 1976. On the other hand, Qaddafi's support to the SPLM was part and parcel of his grand strategy to dislodge Nimeiri. Over and above, the issue of self-determination by the people of southern Sudan was not in the cards at the time Qaddafi volunteered to support Garang; it only emerged at the first convention of the SPLM at Chukdum in 1994, and later adopted by all northern Sudanese political parties in Asmara (Asmara Declaration of June 1995).

After the fall of Nimeiri, Qaddafi made a relentless effort to persuade Garang to stop the war and join the Transitional Military Council (TMC) which had replaced Nimeri in Khartoum, an offer Garang refused, arguing that comprehensive resolution of Sudan's conflict could only be realized through dialogue with all political forces. At that point Qaddafi shifted ground; he stopped all military assistance to the SPLA and began to support the TMC with the wherewithal it needed (including air fighters) to continue war in southern Sudan. As had been the case in all Qaddafi's dealings, the TMC was made to pay a heavy price for that support; namely, authorizing Libyan forces to be stationed in Darfur, first in El Fashir and then in Sagal Niaam, 15 kilometers southeast of El Fashir. That force was to be a component part of Qaddafi's Islamic Legion (Chapter Twelve). Nevertheless, Qaddafi's diplomatic contacts with Garang did not cease. During the JELI negotiations in 2001, the Libyan leader insisted that Garang visit Tripoli for a face-to-face dialogue. The SPLM leader politely eschewed the invitations. Qaddafi, who never took no for an answer to his invitations, decided to send a special plane to carry the SPLM leader from Asmara to Tripoli, which added to Garang's disquiet. It was at this point that President Isaias of Eritrea informed the Libyan leader that Garang would travel to Tripoli in the Eritrean president's plane. To the surprise of Libyans, the presidential plane landed in Tripoli with two passengers, President Isaias and Garang; the former was probably Garang's human shield, albeit an odd human shield.

On July 17, 2001, before the presentation of the Nine-Point Plan, Garang met with the Libyan leader in Kampala, Uganda (with Uganda's President Museveni present). The Libyan leader told Garang that the JELI dealt sufficiently with the SPLM/A's concerns, as well as with those of the NDA. Museveni disagreed and went directly to the root cause of Sudan's conflict as he saw it. He told Qaddafi that Africa admired him for his relentless effort to unite the continent. . But if unity meant making a Qaddafi out of Museveni, then Museveni would opt out of that unity. By the same token, if the unity at which Bashir aimed meant that John should be traduced into an Omar, then John equally would have the right to turn his back on that unity.[22] Museveni, unmistakably, was aware of the politicocultural dimension of Sudan's predicament. Later, he embellished on his abstraction of that predicament when he said in his address during the signature ceremony of the Comprehensive Peace Agreement (CPA) at Nairobi stadium (January 9, 2005): "That he had seen in that gathering the reality of Sudan when [the Sudanese] were dancing the people of the turban, the people of the ostrich feather. How did they live together respecting each other's culture. This has been the problem of Sudan."[23] Mussevini was effectively referring to varied Sudanese tribal groups from the north and south who were singing and dancing at the Nairobi stadium while the CPA was signed.

In order to convince Garang to talk with Khartoum, Qaddafi told the SPLM leader that that regime had changed after the "expulsion" of Turabi. The SPLM leader explained to Qaddafi how that was not the case and passed to him a copy of Sudan's 1998 constitution, with a number of articles highlighted. After running his eyes over those articles the Libyan leader made an intriguing remark: "This is a Quran, not a constitution," he said. With or without Museveni, Garang won the day.

6. JELI in the Throes of Death

In a statement subsequent to the meeting with Qaddafi, the SPLM/A leadership declared that the movement resolved to call upon all mediators to recognize the IGAD Declaration of Principles (DoP) as the basis for arriving at a peaceful solution to the Sudanese issue. In this regard, it asked Egypt and Libya to adopt two points of the 1995 NDA resolution on separation of religion from state and recognizing the right to self-determination for the people of southern Sudan.[24] The SPLM resolution also added that an agreement should be reached on a new transitional constitution that would form the foundation for a transitional government, and the unification of the fora of negotiation by merging, or JELI and the IGAD initiatives.[25]

The government's reaction was unsurprising; it accused the SPLM/A of not earnestly pursuing peace. Ghazi Salahuddin Atabani said that the SPLM/A's statement regarding the JELI "clearly indicates that the movement, contrary to its previous declarations, does not want peace to be achieved under the joint initiative."[26] Mustafa Ismail, in turn, told the *Mideast Mirror* that "the SPLM does not have a clear strategy for peace; in fact, it does not even have the most basic idea of what peace requires." Regarding the SPLM/A's (not to mention the NDA's) preconditions for the JELI, Ismail was quoted as saying: "As the late Mohamed Ahmed Mahgoub [Sudan's foreign minister in the 1960s] used to say, 'it is no use arguing about the cut of the clothes before we get the material itself.'"[27] Rather than educating the SPLM/A, who "did not have a strategy on peace" or how to make peace, the minister turned to sartorial craft to evade the issue in question. The subsequent failure of Egypt and Libya to secure a collaborative approach with IGAD, or to address SPLM concerns regarding the key issues missing in their plan, ultimately became JELI`s undoing. It was left to other external powers to hang their hat on either the IGAD or the JELI, or both, or neither.

7. Obasanjo Picks up the Gauntlets

As the IGAD negotiations in October and November 2001 made little headway, Nigeria called on the then Organization of African Unity (OAU) to back an initiative put forward by President Olusegun Obasanjo, who was no newcomer to Sudanese peacemaking. Long before his assumption of power in May 1999 as Nigeria's elected president, Obasanjo was immersed in Sudan affairs and made peacemaking in that country one of his central concerns.[28] To that end, he had established contacts since the 1980s with both the government of Sudan and the SPLM. In his first meeting with Garang, Obasanjo made three memorable comments about why he was concerned with conflict in Sudan. The first, he said, was his belief that Sudan was one of three countries in Africa that represented linchpins of continental unity: Angola in southern Africa, the Congo (Democratic Republic) in central Africa,

89

and Sudan in east and northeast Africa. The second point was the pain he had felt on seeing an African sisterly country torn from within because of home-grown historical injustices, especially inclusions and exclusions in public life of citizens of the same country on the basis of race, religion, or culture. Third was his admiration of Garang for his desire to keep the country intact while fearlessly struggling to erase historical injustices. He then told Garang not to expect the commander of the Nigerian Third Marine Commando Division, who fought against Biafran separatists, to be overjoyed by the dismemberment of Sudan. Obasanjo rightly saw in Garang what many Sudanese in the north or south of the country did not, or never wished to, see: an African hero who was determined to make a united Sudan the backbone of African unity. As a result, Obasanjo not only became one of Garang's most trusted friends, he also evolved into the SPLM's ambassador at large. In March 1988, in his capacity as chair of the InterAction Council,[29] Obasanjo presided over a meeting by that body in Harare, Zimbabwe. That meeting, which was dedicated to the Sudanese conflict, developed resolutions that could have put an end to the war.[30] Regrettably, both sides to the conflict were not yet ready to budge from their unshakable positions.

By the time Sudan reached another deadlock in 2001, 13 years after his intervention in the InterAction Council, Obasanjo once again entered the fray and sought to bring Sudan's case before the OAU. As observed earlier, the Nigerian leader had unsuccessfully tried to reconcile John Garang and Sadiq al-Mahdi in order to move the IGAD-JELI peace initiative forward. This time, Obasanjo dispatched a special envoy, Usman Bugaje, to formally request the OAU to support his call for an "inter-Sudanese peace conference."[31] Despite Obasanjo's credentials and his ardent desire to bring the Sudanese warring parties together, his efforts came to grief. Behind the failure of these efforts by such a dedicated African leader were irrational, sometimes irresponsible, attitudes by his northern Sudanese interlocutors towards grave national issues.[32]

8. The National Islamic Front: Taking on the World

From the beginning, Sudan's ruling Islamist party appeared to have had a blind view of the outside world and a puerile attitude toward international politics. This attitude had surprised friend and foe alike, since that party was led by a group of educated Sudanese who were schooled in some of the best institutions within and outside Sudan. Nevertheless, when they assumed power in June 1989, their rallying cry was neither for rebuilding the country and devising a new formula for the unity of Sudan, nor for improving the human condition in the country in the way governments throughout the world would do. Their supreme aim was to take on *dwal al istikbar* (arrogant states), that is, the big powers. Accordingly, their watchword became: "America, Russia *ghad dana azabuha, alia in laghituha dhirabuha,*" meaning "the day of reckoning for America and Russia has come, and we shall triumph over them." By taking on the toughest two guys on the block and fantasizing that they would get the better of them, Sudanese Islamists were evidently not aware of their frailties and cared less about the might of the powers they were matching themselves against. Why then did Sudanese Islamists exhibit such a level of immaturity? Contemporary political Islamists, far from being a lunatic ideological fringe, comprised a group of intellectuals who sincerely believed that Islam was not only a religion, but also a mass culture and a way of life. As such, they reckoned that Islam would serve them well both as a popular mobilization vehicle and a liberation theology superior to all other systems of ideas, including those that helped make them the cultivated persons they had become. Consequently, the Islamists hypothesized that their mission was not only national, but also universal, if not cosmic. If that was the case, then their slogans against "arrogant states" were nothing more than pretentious twaddle by an immature group.

What filled one with wonder was the overly high regard with which this group viewed the experimental Islamist system they had installed while undervaluing other systems that had stood the test of time, despite their foibles. Regardless of this intellectual vanity, it also boggled the mind to see an elitist group in a country besieged by all manner of problems giving such free rein to their imagination. Probably, at that point in time, Sudan's Islamists were still under the sway of the campus politics that had shaped their thinking and attitudes in the formative stage of their political development. Sudan's secondary and higher schools were incubators of contemporary political Islam. Because the majority of those who graduated from these schools were hardly exposed to the real world in and outside Sudan, they probably believed that government politics was a continuation of campus politics. With that mind-set to propel them, they began dauntlessly to bully Sudan's neighbors such as Egypt, Saudi Arabia, Ethiopia, and Eritrea. Gradually, they began to realize that states were governed by international norms and conventions and, alas, not by realpolitik. They also came to understand, although they never admitted it, that when it came to political brutality, bigger thugs existed in the world who could harm Sudan and its government badly. Grudgingly, the Sudan Islamists recognized that there was a price to pay for political adventurism. The day of reckoning (for the Sudan crusaders, not America and Russia) was near; the measures taken by President Clinton, to which reference was made in the previous chapter, were just starters. That development, however, made the wise among them (and there were still a few) conclude that rather than change the world, the Islamists had to learn how to adapt to it.

9. United States: Carrots and Sticks

With Clinton's administration gone in 2001, Sudan's foreign minister, Mustafa Ismail, tried to ingratiate his government with the incoming administration. In a statement to the *Mideast Mirror* he said: "There is no doubt that a country with the political, economic, and cultural influence of the United States can—should it so wish–force the rebels to lay down their arms and sit down to talk peace...The most important quality any peace sponsor must have is neutrality." He also added, "It is inconceivable that a country which supports the rebels and receives all its information about Sudan from them—without listening to the Government's opinion—can be anxious about peace in the country."[33] The foreign minister concluded by expressing hope "that the new U.S. administration shall adopt a more neutral and objective stance vis-à-vis Sudan."[34]

Evidently, the issue was not about talking to, and exchanging information with, the government of Sudan concerning peacemaking, since the United States had on several occasions engaged Khartoum on questions relating to peace, humanitarian relief, and terrorism. As likely as not, the foreign minister was hoping to inveigle the new U.S. administration into distancing itself from the SPLM/A and the northern opposition or, at least, treating the government of Sudan on a par with them. To all appearances, Khartoum policy makers, as we mentioned earlier, never took notice of issues that riled a large sector of the American public and its government such as the alleged persecution of non-Muslims, aerial bombardment of civilians, and offering support and solace to terrorists. Over the years those issues, which some assumed to be transcendent to American internal politics, became of great concern to strong lobby groups in America and, thus, ended up becoming matters of local politics. However, the foreign minister's statement revealed that either the Sudan government was not ready to reconcile itself with the realities of the world or, simplemindedly, that it wanted the United States to take what the Sudan government said at face value while business continued as usual in Khartoum. That was guileless advice to a government that had been known to see through walls.

Ismail's statement, however, came just three days before President Bush appointed John Danforth as his special envoy on peace in Sudan, and only eight days before the terrorist attacks of September 11. The U.S. Department of State indicated three fundamental objectives for Senator Danforth: "one is to end the killing by reaching a just and lasting peace; two, to ensure that needy Sudanese who are affected by the war and drought are assisted; and third, to bring an end to Sudanese support for international terrorism."[35] Predictably, the terrorist attacks of September 11 on New York's twin towers of the World Trade Center and the Pentagon in Washington turned the attention of the

United States to a single issue: pursuing the fight against international terrorism. President Bush warned that any country that helped, provided facilities to, or gave sanctuary to Osama bin Laden would be equally responsible for the attacks. On the other hand, Bush promised a reward to countries that shared intelligence about bin Laden and his network. Wary of the consequences of the U.S. president's threats, and eager to be in good standing with the new U.S. administration, the Sudan government wisely opted for cooperation.

As a result, the National Islamic Front (NIF), despite all its simulated loathing of the United States, set its heart on doing commerce with it. So, for reasons of fear of American retaliation and a burning desire to improve relations with the new U.S. administration, the NIF moved fast to rebut reports that insinuated it had any relations with bin Laden. Sudan's foreign minister referred to "Khartoum's **now** clean record regarding harboring or protecting terrorists" (emphasis added).[36] The word "now" was telling. "Now," to the utter satisfaction of Americans, U.S. security operatives were allowed into Sudan to interrogate persons and investigate places, including having access to bank accounts. In consequence, the United States rewarded Sudan's government through a symbolic and backhanded gesture. On September 29, 2001, the U.N. Security Council resolved (with the United States abstaining) to remove the largely symbolic sanctions that had been imposed on the NIF regime in 1996 in order to pressure it to hand over Islamist militants who were accused of attempting to assassinate Egyptian President Hosni Mubarak in Addis Ababa.[37]

10. Senator Danforth's Odyssey

Two weeks following that symbolic gesture, Charles Snyder, of the U.S. Department of State, and Ambassador Robert Oakley visited Sudan in preparation for Danforth's forthcoming visit. Of the two, Oakley was the more conversant with the Sudan and had many friends in the country from the years he and his wife had served as young diplomats. Snyder and Oakley, however, argued against creating a new U.S. peace initiative but also expressed reluctance to "pick among the initiatives."[38]

In November, Danforth visited Khartoum and then Nairobi, where he laid out four demands to test the climate for peace: improved humanitarian access in conflict areas, the creation of zones and periods of tranquillity in which immunization efforts and other humanitarian activities could proceed in peace, an end to aerial bombings and other military attacks on civilians, and an end to the abduction of civilians. The latter pertained to claims about the forcible abduction and enslavement of southern Sudanese in Bahr el Ghazal by "Arab" tribal militias reported to be directly or indirectly supported by the government. However, if truth be told, the ethnicization of war in Sudan predated the NIF rule; it was initiated by Prime Minister Sadiq al-Mahdi in the mid-1980s when he created tribal militias to shore up military efforts in southern Kordofan[39] despite objections by parliament and dissatisfaction by the Sudanese army. In a memorandum sent to the prime minister, the army command demanded, among other things, the dissolution of those militias. Yet, the NIF government that replaced al-Mahdi's not only maintained the militias, but also made them a major tool of destabilization in the southern Sudan areas shared by "Arab" nomads and southern Sudan pastoralists. Notwithstanding, after his meetings with the government in Khartoum, Danforth traveled to Nairobi where he lent support to President Moi's efforts.[40] In late November 2001, upon prompting by Danforth, the government of Sudan and the SPLM/A agreed to a four-week period of tranquillity for humanitarian access in the Nuba Mountains. Doubtless, Khartoum's readiness to respond favorably to Danforth's requests was largely due to its anxiety to restore bilateral relations with the United States, especially due to its increased leverage in the wake of the September 11 attacks.

By mid-January 2002, the Khartoum regime was upbeat about its experiences with the Bush administration. Information Minister Mahdi Ibrahim Mohammed told the *Christian Science Monitor*, "There is a new perspective in Washington. A new policy of engagement."[41] Ghazi Salahuddin Atabani told the same newspaper: "The new administration is *less* ideological, more pragmatic, and we welcome that [despite continuous bias towards the south]."[42] That was simply playacting; both the minister and advisor knew that if there was ever an American administration that was suborned by ideological influences, it was that of President George W. Bush. On the U.S. side, one commentator surmised that the motive that drove Khartoum to mend fences with Washington was that it no longer needed to rely on Islamist organizations for funds, thanks to newfound oil wealth.[43] There was, undoubtedly, a grain of truth in that estimation since bin Laden and his ilk were providing generous financial support to the NIF at a time when that party was in dire need of funding. Turabi, as alluded to earlier, was instrumental in mobilizing funds from wealthy Islamist groups and individuals in support of a common cause. Nonetheless, the NIF's desire to win over the United States (whose day of reckoning had come) should not be minimized.

As a matter of fact, the government of Sudan went to great lengths to appease Danforth. For example, on the issue of forcible abduction and slavery, it acquiesced to field investigations of allegations related to slavery through an International Eminent Persons Commission. That commission included experts on Sudan designated by their governments from among their nationals: two each from Norway, the United Kingdom, and the United States and one each from Italy and France and Holland. The nine commissioners were supported by a technical team of researchers from Canada, the United Kingdom, and the United States. Senator Danforth was happily surprised when the government of Sudan accepted the nomination of Penn Kemble of

Freedom House as chair of the group. Freedom House, a nongovernmental organization (NGO) close to the Bush administration, was probed by Sudan, China, Cuba, and Russia at the U.N. General Assembly; the four countries demanded in May 2001 the expulsion of Freedom House from the United Nations, where it had been recognized as an NGO under Article 71 of the UN charter. This article which entitles the UN Economic and Social Council (ECOSOC) to make arrangements governing cooperation between NGO`s and the UN. While China, Cuba, and Russia were on the warpath against Freedom House for its investigation of human rights abuses in their countries, Khartoum was upset by a high-level seminar organized by that NGO on religious persecution in Sudan.[44] Thanks to Danforth, the government of Sudan chose to close an eye on the presence of a Freedom House "eminent consultant" as chair of the International Eminent Persons Group investigating slavery in Sudan. The committee's report did not make the government feel good; nonetheless, the government let it pass.[45]

The most difficult of Danforth's four tests was putting an end to air raids targeting civilians and the international monitoring of the same. Khartoum refused international monitoring, with Dr Ghazi Salahuddin calling the idea "embarrassing."[46] Indeed it was, and moreover, it would have been shameful. When Danforth informed John Garang of Bashir's acceptance to voluntarily suspend the bombings for four weeks, Garang sarcastically said: "'In the first place, nobody should bomb civilian targets; it's an insult to human rights. For a member of the United Nations and Organization of African Unity to present [cessation of bombing civilian targets] as a concession from the bottom of their hearts is laughable."[47]

On January 19, 2002, the government and the SPLM/A reached a humanitarian cease-fire agreement after one week of negotiations in Bürgenstock, Switzerland, led jointly by Switzerland and the United States. The partied agreed on a truce covering the Nuba Mountains region in south central Sudan that was to be renewed on a six-month basis. Attempts by the SPLM to extend that agreement to southern Blue Nile were met by stiff resistance from the government of Sudan. The two sides consented to the establishment of a Joint Monitoring Committee (JMC), made up of 10 to 15 foreign observers, as well as a local bipartisan monitoring committee overseen by a neutral chairman. Brigadier General Jan Erik Wilhemsen of Norway was agreed upon by the parties as the neutral chairman. The agreement called for the free movement of people and aid supplies in the Nuba region, a ban on the laying of landmines in the mountain area, and recovery and rehabilitation in due course. It was signed by Dr. Mutrif Siddiq Ali for the government and Commander Abdul Aziz Adam el Hilu for the SPLM/A-Nuba.[48] Though we shall further elaborate on the Nuba Mountains cease-fire in the next chapter, it is important to note here an intriguing event that took place following the signature of the Bürgenstock agreement. Some elements within the northern

95

opposition (NDA) conveyed to the SPLM/A leader their concerns about that agreement, especially the presence of foreign forces in central Sudan. Ostensibly, in the minds of those leaders, northern and southern Sudan were two separate countries; otherwise, they would not have been stigmatized by the presence of peacekeeping forces in central Sudan while tolerating them in the southern part of the country. That was yet more proof of how reality in Sudan's political theater was sometimes stranger than fiction.

While the Danforth initiative was under way, the situation tended toward negotiated settlement. In November 2001, presidential peace advisor Ghazi Salahuddin told the International Crisis Group that "conditions [had] changed in favor of a settlement."[49] The kind of settlement, however, remained confused, especially given the conclusions reached by Danforth in his report as well as the continued wrangling about the JELI and IGAD initiatives up to the beginning of 2002. Despite its prevarication regarding the DoP, the government decided to go back to the IGAD negotiations after all the alternative roads to peace it had tried led to a *huis clos*. That decision was confirmed in the seventh IGAD Summit (November 7, 1999, in Djibouti), which was attended by President Bashir. In that meeting it was resolved, with Bashir's agreement, that the IGAD initiative was the **sole peace forum for negotiating Sudan's conflict**. Yet, it took over a year and half for any progress to be made.

11. IGAD's Mother of all Summits

At the beginning of January 2002, a decisive shift in favor of the IGAD and away from the JELI came during the ninth IGAD Summit in Khartoum. That summit was attended not only by heads of state from the IGAD countries, but also by the Egyptian foreign minister and chief of intelligence as well as Libya's minister for African unity, Ali Abd al-Salam al-Turayki. The London Arabic daily, *Asharq al-Awsat*, wrote on that occasion: "Sudan has a rare chance these day—a chance that it has not had since Bashir's coup in 1989—to emerge from its wars and its governmental crisis."[50] In addition, at the time of the summit, the three main backers of the IGAD—the United States, the United Kingdom, and Norway—descended upon Khartoum. The British secretary for international development, Clare Short, arrived stating that her concern was "war and peace in Sudan."[51] Her counterpart from Norway, Hilde Johnson, arrived on January 8, promising that her country would "push forward the peace process."[52] Senator Danforth arrived to assess the latest situation with respect to his four tests. A week later on February 14, U.K. Foreign Secretary Jack Straw announced the appointment of Alan Goulty as U.K. special representative for Sudan. Goulty was the British ambassador to Sudan from 1995 to 1999 and had previously served in the country from 1972 to 1975.[53] Also, a week later on January 6, ahead of the summit, U.S. Assistant Secretary of State for African Affairs Walter Kansteiner wrote to President

Bashir urging him to "continue the momentum all the parties have established" under the renewed efforts of the IGAD secretariat and suggested that Bashir should now meet Garang under the auspices of President Moi.[54]

The communiqué issued by the summit called on its chairman to "rejuvenate the IGAD Peace Process and invite other initiatives with a view to coordinate the efforts."[55] That revealed that there was still concern to involve Egypt. Around January 10, Danforth was reported as saying that he hoped President Moi would lead the renewed peace process, but with Egypt included in the process. "Our hope is [that] a core of support for peace, led by Egypt and Kenya and joined in by the Europeans, Canadians, and ourselves, is going to have an effect," said Danforth.[56] However, by mid-February, it was increasingly clear that Egypt's real wish was to be involved in the IGAD with or without Libya. Desperately, the Libyan minister talked of reviving the JELI and claimed that he had discussed with Egyptian President Mubarak[57] the reactivation of JELI in order "to achieve unity in Sudan."

12. Meeting in an Open Prison

Following closely on the heels of Danforth's report to the U.S. President on April 26, 2002,[58] General Lazaro Sumbeiywo organized a round of talks in May at the Kenya Commercial Bank's training center in Karen, near Nairobi, to set a work plan for the negotiations. According to General Sumbeiywo, the two sides considered the site of the talks an "open prison or army garrison," and the mood was tense.[59] Far from being an open prison, Karen is a verdant and serene suburb of Nairobi named after the Danish writer, Karen Blixen, who lived there between 1915 and 1931 and described it as a dreamland.[60] Apart from that glib complaint, negotiators didn't have a problem with the program of work or the modalities, as the mediator reported. But they could not agree on two words: the government insisted on the phrasing, "interim" period; the SPLM wanted to call it a "transitional" period.[61] What is there in a word, one may ask? Indeed, by insisting on the word "transition," the SPLM negotiators wanted to underscore transformation from one system of rule to another, from a one-party regime to a multiparty system, while government negotiators envisaged continuity of an ongoing process. So it was not just semantics. Eventually, the government negotiators, led by Idris Mohammed Abdel Gadir, refused to sign the document laying out the program of work. Frustrated with the government delegation's position, Sumbeiywo threatened to tell the international community that the government of Sudan was reneging on the process. The government, well experienced with the petty tactics of peace talks, simply walked out and went back to Khartoum. According to one government negotiator: "[Sumbeiywo] learned to do things differently after this."[62] Sumbeiywo saw the episode differently, recalling that the government wrote him a "stinking letter" saying he was "insolent and disrespectful" to its delegation and appeared to be a partial mediator. The letter stated that the government had adopted a policy of "constructive engagement and cooperation with the chair" but that Sumbeiywo's threat to report the government of Sudan as a "renegade" hurt the process. Sumbeiywo responded to the letter with a "curiously toned-down communication" that invited both sides to Machakos on June 19.[63] Obviously, the mediator sought to make amends with the government to enable the process to continue.

On June 9, the SPLA took over Kapoeta in eastern Equatoria in a lightning attack. The reoccupation of Kapoeta was followed by a warning from peace advisor Ghazi Salahuddin Atabani that the government "may pull out" of the upcoming Machakos talks. He also threatened that it would "complain to the United States" because the SPLA's actions contravened the truce agreed to as part of Danforth's plans.[64] The SPLA claimed it had killed some 200 soldiers in that attack and seized vehicles, arms, and food supplies. It suggested to the media that its victory emboldened it to capture Torit and Juba. "'Of course, we are committed to peace talks, but this will not stop us from continuing military operations,'" SPLA commander Oyai Deng Ajak told the BBC in Kapoeta.[65] Ajak was one of the outstanding heroes in the war of liberation, but his jingoism at that point in time was not in line with the equanimity of peace talks.

13. Shouting at Each Other

The government of Sudan's delegation to the talks, which began on June 19, was headed by Atabani, although up until 2002 that delegation had been headed variously by Nafie Ali Nafie or Atabani, assisted by Minister of State Idris Mohamed Abdel-Gadir. Ghazi, a cerebral and engaging debater, also turned out to be a vigorous protagonist. The SPLM negotiating delegation was headed by Salva Kiir Mayardit, though the chief negotiator was Nhial Deng Nhial, an equally refined and deferential debater at the negotiations. Both were unfailingly in control of their brief. Nevertheless, for 29 days, according to Sumbeiywo, the delegations led by two refined negotiators were mostly shouting at each other.[66]

Shouting at each other seemed to have been a hallmark of negotiations between Sudanese protagonists; the same remark was made six years earlier by another mediator. In May 1996, Professor Roger Fisher of Harvard University was moderating a dialogue between the NCP and SPLM/A organized by the United Nations Educational, Scientific, and Cultural Organization (UNESCO) under its Culture of Peace program. The purpose of the meeting was to explore the intellectual underpinnings of questions at which the parties were at variance. Fisher was stunned, not only by the shouting at a meeting that was assumed to have been a forum for intellectual probe, but also by the fraternal manner in which the parties interacted with each other outside the meeting. Fisher told the author, who was attending the forum as a UNESCO resource person, that in similar meetings he had moderated the parties never shook hands during, or talked to each other outside, the meetings. He also recounted that in one of the intermediation efforts he had undertaken between protagonists from Central America, guns were drawn. So, while the irascibility of those protagonists was comprehensible to Fisher, the discrepant attitude of Sudanese negotiators was not. He found the incessant ill temper of Sudanese interlocutors during meetings and their congeniality to each other outside the meeting room confusing and beyond comprehension. "Are the Sudanese so cynical, or what is it exactly?" Professor Fisher asked. Whether it was a desire by brother/enemies to mitigate their rancor during the meetings by being cordial and decent to each other outside them, one wouldn't know. But cynicism, in the manner of British novelist George Meredith, should not be excluded.[67]

Notwithstanding what Sumbeiywo called shouting, what was actually happening at Karen was argumentation on issues that the SPLM considered cardinal but which the other side at the table treated as immaterial to the negotiations. Those issues included the creation of a *shari'a*-free capital other than Khartoum, a new model for the presidency of the republic during the interim/transitional period, and the core elements of Sudan's new constitution. For example, the SPLM/A called for the alternation of the presidency between Garang and Bashir during a six-year interim period (three years for each). On the national capital, the SPLM proposed that in the event the government of Sudan refused the SPLM/A's proposal for the creation of a new capital for Sudan free of *shari'a*, the SPLM would not settle for less than having an enclave within Khartoum. That enclave should not be subject to any religious laws. As for Sudan's new constitution, the government wanted that constitution to be based on the NIF's 1998 constitution, while the SPLM refused to be tied to any constitutional framework. Disagreement on all of those issues made the debate a dialogue of the deaf, and that perhaps was what the mediator viewed as shouting.

14. U.S. Prevarication over Self-Determination

While the so-called shouting was going on, the mediators proceeded to prepare a single negotiating text.[68] On this matter, Sumbeiywo recalled receiving valuable advice from former U.S. President Jimmy Carter, who visited Nairobi in June and met Sumbeiywo.[69] That text caused a furor within the SPLM ranks. According to Sumbeiywo, the draft was prepared in one night between the IGAD mediators and some observers, and it did not mention self-determination or the right to secede. Small wonder the SPLM/A went "ballistic"[70] and the U.S. "hit the roof."[71] The proposal, to the eyes of the SPLM/A, gave southern Sudanese less than what they had received in the Addis Ababa agreement. More infuriating to the SPLM/A was the replacement of self-determination by self-rule, and separation of religion and politics by religious tolerance. According to one IGAD staff member, the U.S. envoy to the process "just snapped. He swore, went red in the face, and walked out."[72] On the other hand, the US envoy said that: "the United States had been promising the SPLM/A certain things that, because it was not in charge of the process, was simply not in a position to guarantee."[73] Sumbeiywo, though ever cognizant of the help the United States was giving to the process, was not ready to cede the driving seat to its representative at the process. Douglas Johnson put it differently; he said that the United States had drafted a contentious text, which southerners vigorously opposed. Kenya backed a redraft in line with the DoP, and a rift opened between the State Department and the White House, the latter supporting self-determination.[74]

In the author's estimation, there had always been nuances in the U.S. position on self-determination. For example, as early as the mid 1990s, Congress (103rd) passed a resolution in which it urged the government of Sudan to recognize the right to self-determination to the people of southern Sudan. Equally, the State Department had consistently supported self-determination for the people of southern Sudan based on its regular contacts with the SPLM/A and its awareness of the position taken by the NDA in favor of that matter. Nevertheless, presidential envoy Danforth had a different view on self-determination. In his report to the president on April 26, 2002,[75] the senator made the following conclusions:

- "Southern Sudanese have consistently experienced mistreatment at the hands of governments in the north, including racial, cultural and religious intolerance and restricted access to the nation's resources. Any peace agreement must address the injustices suffered by the southern Sudanese people.
- Southern Sudanese have claimed the right of self-determination as a means of protecting themselves against persecution; however, there are different views of what self-determination means in Sudan's future.
- The view that self-determination includes the guaranteed option of secession is contained in the IGAD Declaration of Principles, and is supported by many Sudanese. However, secession would be strongly resisted by the Government of Sudan, and would be exceedingly difficult to achieve.
- A more feasible, and, I think, preferable view of self-determination would ensure the right of the people of southern Sudan to live under a government that respects their religion and culture. Such a system would require robust internal and external guarantees so that any promises made by the Government in peace negotiations could not be ignored in practice."

Danforth's interpretation of self-determination caused agitation within the SPLM/A ranks in view of the qualifications he attached to the process. In particular, Garang's team thought that the qualifications would divest self-determination of its real meaning. In response to later developments, some southern Sudan elites, including a few SPLM leaders, believed that self-determination and secession were one and the same thing. Nevertheless, as two eminent Sudanese scholars observed, "While emphasizing that secession and separate statehood are not the only way for realizing a people's right to self-determination…this option must be considered seriously when a people is denied their right to self-determination within the country."[76] Secession is viewed here as a weapon of last resort to which a certain group within a country—ethnic, cultural, religious, or linguistic—shall resort if and when its fundamental rights are not fully guaranteed. According to the same scholars, if these rights are satisfied within an existing state, it is extremely unlikely that a minority shall opt for the high political, economic, and security risks of separate statehood.

Danforth, however, made his views on self-determination clear to Garang when they first met in in 1991. The senator recommended that the SPLM leader drop the demand for self-determination leading to secession because, in his estimation, it would neither be accepted by Khartoum nor welcomed by Egypt. Garang tried hard to convince the senator that all Sudanese political forces, including the NCP,[77] had reconciled themselves to the inevitability of self-determination, even if it would lead to secession. Garang was beyond doubt a unionist, and for good reasons; but no matter how committed to unity he was, he could not compromise on the issue of self-determination, particularly when it had become cast in stone in the SPLM and NDA resolutions since 1994 and 1995. Besides, the last thing he would have liked to do was offer a pretext to the Nasir separatists who parted ways with the SPLM to point an accusatory finger against him, even at a time when it was abundantly clear that that group had become political pawns to the NCP.[78]

Consequently, discussions between Garang and Danforth became impassioned, according to a brief submitted to the author by Ambassador Robert Oakley, the senator's diplomatic advisor who attended the meeting. During that meeting, Danforth explained the "tests" he was putting to both Bashir and Garang and how Bashir reacted negatively to them. Garang, Ambassador Oakley recounted, said that he did not like them either. On the issue of self-determination, Danforth suggested that it was essential to get the Egyptians on board before putting the matter on the table. Danforth's belief in the cardinality of Egypt's role in the resolution of the Sudanese conflict was almost religious; he made it clear at the ceremony of his appointment before the president and repeated it later in his report to the president in April 2002. What he did not declare, however, were his fears that the secession of South Sudan might also have a domino effect on other regions in Sudan and, thus, become a source of destabilization in East Africa. Danforth seemed to also believe that were Sudan to be divided, it would stir up latent desires for secession in a number of states in east Africa. As a result, the Rumbek meeting ended inconclusively, with the senator telling Garang and his entourage that his mission and the efforts of President Bush had to end, and that he would immediately return to Washington to tell this to the President.[79] Probably, what angered the senator most was not the animated discussion he had had with Garang as much as the seemingly discourteous remark made by one of Garang's senior advisors and a grandee of the SPLM, Elijah Malok. Malok told Danforth that if that was all what he was offering to the SPLM then he might as well pack up and go to Khartoum and Cairo.[80]

Putting its global strategic concerns ahead of Sudanese domestic worries was not new in U.S. policy. Historically, the United States had scoffed at Sudan's national interests whenever such interests appeared to put Egypt's back up. For example, during the Anglo-Egyptian negotiations over the future of Sudan in the early 1950s, British officials in Sudan were entreating the British Foreign Office not to accede to Egypt's demand that Sudan be united with it rather than become independent. Jefferson Caffery, the U.S. ambassador to Egypt at the time, surprised his British counterpart, Sir Ralph Stevenson, by saying, "I don't understand why anybody should be bothered about the fate of a few million niggers."[81] Caffery's "few million niggers" represented all Sudanese, including those who never ceased to claim a pure Arab genealogy, a matter that would have made the blood of these "Arabs" boil. Caffery's personal remark was unsurprising, as he was predisposed to make such an inelegant utterance at a time when racist sentiments were rampant in the United States. However, the attitude toward Sudan of the government that Caffery represented was perplexing. On the declaration of Sudan's independence on January 1, 1956, the State Department was among the first to recognize the new state in a statement that gave a different identity and a new mission to the country of "few million niggers." The statement said, among other things, "Sudan will be deeply involved in the future cause of Africa, and as a **Middle East** nation too, it will be a bridge to Africa, importing into it ideas, philosophies, and forces which may have great influence on African future" (emphasis added).[82] There was every reason for the State Department to expect a country that had behind it an ancient history of edifying achievements in industry, linguistics, and architecture bequeathed by the Nubian kingdoms, as well as an enduring tradition of learning and value systems bestowed by Islam, to have a role to play in Africa. However, the description of Sudan as a "Middle East nation" contravened both the facts of history and geography and made U.S. confusion of Sudanese politics more confounding. Even at the organizational level, the State Department until recently did not know whether to place Sudan in its African or Middle East bureau. This alone proves that the muddle in U.S. policy toward Sudan had a long history.

Furthermore, Senator Danforth's concern over Egypt's anticipated reaction to a possible secession of southern Sudan was a far cry from his fears of Egypt's reactions despite his genuine commitment to the well-being of the Sudanese people and justice to all of its people. Indeed the Senator might have had other thoughts on the matter if he had researched the history of Sudano-Egyptian relations in the run up to independence. Back in 1952, the Anglo-Egyptian agreement on self-government to Sudan offered the Sudanese the right to self-determination based on two options: independence or unity with Egypt. Nonetheless, the National Unionist Party (NUP), Sudan's foremost unionist party led by Ismail al-Azhari, decided to wheel round that provision in the Anglo-Egyptian agreement and declare independence instead of unity with Egypt, the cause which he and his party were fighting for with Egypt's support. Azhari and the majority of northern Sudanese parties in parliament tore the agreement to shreds and declared independence. By so doing they circumvented the exercise of the right to self-determination by Sudanese in the manner prescribed by the Anglo-Egyptian agreement. In effect, Sudan's constituent assembly resolved to repeal the articles in that agreement relating to self-determination before proceeding to declare independence. So, no matter how politically advantageous it was to the Sudanese people, the declaration of independence, in strict legal terms, was fraudulent. Egypt, after some murmuring, reconciled itself with the breach of the very agreement to which she was a signatory as well as a direct beneficiary. Why, therefore, should Egypt not be able to live with independence of southern Sudan, which was ordained by the Comprehensive Peace Agreement and achieved through the internationally guaranteed self-determination process that comprised Egypt and the Arab League?

15. Sumbeiywo Firmly on the Saddle

Despite all those happenings, Sumbeiywo continued with his efforts unperturbed. His style in guiding the talks was, at the beginning, a cause of consternation to one party and outrage to the other. Being a soldier's solider, Sumbeiywo never minced his words nor cared for diplomatic niceties. But with admirable dexterity he managed to balance pressure and dialogue. Without dialogue, the talks could not have progressed, and too much pressure would have alienated one or the other of the parties. The General, as the parties used to call him, was indubitably impartial even though his refusal to yield to impossible demands from one party or the other was wrongly interpreted as partiality to the party on whose side he stood. What made the General's job burdensome, however, was the lack of trust between the two parties and the implicit prejudice each one had toward the veracity of the contentions of the other. Such an attitude, inevitably, impaired negotiations and made mediation critical. The prime role of the mediator in such circumstances is to remove parties from rigid positions and help them deepen their knowledge of the issues on both sides. The General, therefore, pulled out all the stops in order to enable both parties to reach an agreement with which both sides could live, even if they were not utterly satisfied with it. Sumbeiywo was convinced that in order for a deal to be palatable to the two protagonists, it should be a win-win settlement. As matters progressed, the General won both appreciation and respect. A member of the government delegation described his style as "more proactive and military than that of his predecessors." According to that delegate, Sumbeiywo was "to get agreement paragraph by paragraph and to put every agreed paragraph into a new document that would become the agreement, rather than to try to agree every detail before finalizing an agreement."[83] In achieving the success he had achieved, Sumbeiywo was supported by a secretariat and advisors, including the U.S. State Department lawyer Dr. Susan Page (who was recently named as the first U.S. ambassador to South Sudan); Dr Nicholas "Fink" Haysom, a lawyer from South Africa who was part of the African National Congress's (ANC) negotiating team in the early 1990s and legal counsel to Nelson Mandela; and Dr. Julian Hottinger, a constitutional expert from Switzerland who played a role in the conclusion of the Nuba Mountains' cease-fire. Haysom and Hottinger had experience offering mediation advice to peace processes in many countries, including, between them, South Africa, Viet Nam, Somalia, Burundi, Rwanda, Nepal, Sri Lanka, and Nigeria.[84] In addition, the IGAD envoys from Eritrea, Ethiopia, and Uganda played important roles. This team of competent advisors contributed immensely to the drafting of documents that eventually became the Machakos Protocol. According to Haysom, an effective approach to negotiations at Machakos was to "workshop" the key issues: the state and religion problem was work-shopped and alternatives were developed and ranked by the negotiating teams. From these documents, a single text was prepared and used as the basis for a model of asymmetrical federalism.[85] Regrettably, since the publication of the CPA, more than a few dabblers in the local media reporting on the genesis and evolution of the CPA reduced the agreement to a document penned by the Americans and handed to the parties to sign on the dotted line. The painstaking and assiduity of experienced men and women who had put their minds, hearts, and souls into that endeavor was utterly ignored.

Out of the debates and workshops, texts were drawn up on self-determination, state and religion, and a Bill of Rights. "There were intense debates over every line of the text, and sometimes over each word."[86] A basic document was then developed by the parties, which they called a "Negotiating Framework Document."[87] According to Sumbeiywo, on July 19, three days before the talks were due to end, he delivered an ultimatum to the negotiating teams. The mediators and envoys created a single negotiating text, which provided that for the people of south Sudan, state and religion would be separated and they would decide their destiny in a referendum.[88] Again, in Sumbeiywo's account, the government reportedly agreed to this but insisted that a referendum could only be held in 10 years. The SPLM/A retorted that they would accept only two years. Sumbeiywo suggested a compromise six years, and "both sides emphatically said, 'No.'"[89] The General was irritated, and according to him, "I decided that enough was enough, consulted with the observers and envoys, and gave the text to the parties at about 10 p.m." He added that he told the parties that he needed the answer that night. In his words: the General said, "I gave them an hour, but they wanted two weeks. They started using their mobile phones to talk to their bosses. So the decisions were not being made in Machakos, but somewhere else. By midnight they were not through. At one o'clock they called me and said, 'Yes we have agreed on the two issues.' The two parties then asked: 'Can we write them tomorrow?' the General's answer was curt, 'No you must write them tonight.'"[90] In another account, Sumbeiywo recalls: "'We have an answer,' they said, 'but we want you to modify the documents on the two issues.'" Sumbeiywo agreed but only if any changes entered were agreed upon by both parties.[91] According to Nicholas Haysom, one of the lead advisors to General Sumbeiywo, "While we had expected the parties to engage with each other we noted that each, instead, sought to call their principals."[92] That was to be expected since there were agents on both sides who wanted to achieve peace without a price. There was, evidently, a lot of persuasion to be done at home base.

At this juncture, the American interests reportedly nearly jeopardized the talks. The U.S. envoy asked whether Washington had been informed that the document was to be announced before the actual signatures were appended. Apparently, the Americans were afraid that if that were to happen, one party or the other might renege on the agreement. In his response to that American concern, General Sumbeiywo was blunt: "My friend, I'm not answerable to Washington."[93] His biographer recorded: "This was the beginning of problems between Sumbeiywo and the Americans." The General, as we shall see in Chapter Five, was cruder with the U.S. observer. Later, the United States would laud his role.[94] Thus, the Machakos Protocol was written that night and initialled, but Ghazi Salahuddin Atabani and Salva Kiir Mayardit were not available to sign it until the next day. The signing took place at the State House in Nairobi in a ceremony presided over by the new Kenyan President Mwai Kibaki.

16. Elusive Meetings between Bashir and Garang

To no avail, a score of attempts were made to bring Bashir and Garang together since the former's seizure of government in June 1989. Kenya's Daniel arap Moi and Mwai Kibaki, Libya's Muammar al-Qaddafi, Nigeria's Olusegun Obasanjo, and South Africa's Nelson Mandela all pressured Garang to do so. Of those interventions, Mandela's is worthy of special note, not only because the African National Congress, Mandela's party, was one of the major supporters of the SPLM/A in the struggle, but also because the African leader was to the whole world an exemplar of rationality and judiciousness to whom no right-minded African would say no. Garang and Mandela met twice in the decade of the 1990s: one, in order to ensure ANC's continued support to the SPLM/A; and, second, to discuss an offer by Malaysian Prime Minister Mahathir Mohamad to mediate between the government of Sudan and the SPLM. Garang accepted Mohamad's offer and dispatched a delegation to Kuala Lumpur, Malaysia, which met with both the prime minister Mohamed and his deputy, Anwar Ibrahim. However, the SPLM leader had a hunch that this third attempt had been set up to bring him together with Bashir; that meeting eventually took place in Cape Town in the late 1990s. However, when the issue of Garang's meeting with Bashir was aired, the SPLM leader, a master of walking on tight ropes, briefed Mandela about the nature of the Khartoum regime, particularly concerning religious persecution, human rights abuses, and disrespect to international humanitarian law reflected in indiscriminate bombing of civilians. Garang added that South Sudan had been suffering this agony for twelve years, and in Mandela's case, he opted to stay for twenty-seven years in prisons until the apartheid regime learned how to do things decently. "Your victory," he told Mandela, "would not have come without internal struggle and international pressure. I, therefore still have fifteen years more to remain in the trenches, unless pressure is brought to bear on Khartoum to change course sooner."[95] Mandela smiled and said, "Brother John, now I understand you."[96] The SPLM leader was still under the impression that the NIF regime was "too deformed to be reformed" and, thus, hoped that with cumulative external pressures on Khartoum and concerted efforts by the NDA, the "deformed regime" would either be reformed or eliminated, root and branch.

Garang, however, did not have to wait for another 15 years. On July 27, 2002, after the signing of the Machakos Protocol, a meeting between Garang and President Bashir took place in Kampala, Uganda. That third attempt at a meeting between Garang and Bashir was arranged by Ugandan President Yoweri Museveni and was the second meeting between the two leaders. The first which took place in Nairobi in July 1997 at the IGAD summit was the first ever between the two Sudanese leaders. It had taken the conclusion of a framework agreement on peace for the meeting between Garang and Bashir to materialize. President Bashir arrived with his peace advisor, Ghazi Salahuddin Atabani, only to be told by Museveni that the meeting was to be one-on-one between Garang and Bashir, and Museveni would only be a moderator. When Bashir informed his host that he needed his advisor to translate for him, Garang volunteered to be the translator. That was the beginning of the thaw in the icy relationship between Bashir and Garang. During that meeting, the two leaders engaged in a mundane conversation on their experiences in the Sudanese army and the common friends and comrades-in-arms they shared. On the subject at issue, they assured their host of their commitment to abide by the terms of the agreement reached at Machakos. The meeting ended with the two Sudanese leaders emerging smiling but, unexpectedly, Garang had to face an embarrassing question by a BBC correspondent: "Dr Garang, have you been fighting Bashir for fifteen years only to end up joining his government as his deputy?" Garang, who was known to be a good communicator with a silver tongue, paused for a while before saying: "I shall not be joining **his** government, but a new government that both of us shall establish." Later, in relating to the author the story of his meeting with Omar Bashir, Garang said: "I don't care for what Omer says, but I shall closely watch what President Bashir does." And watch he did with an eagle's eye.

17. Reactions to Machakos Protocol

The Machakos success was acclaimed by mediators and observers. It also made sub-Saharan Africa sigh with relief because it offered an opportunity for breaking Sudan's cycle of violence and promised an end to the longest civil war on the continent. Nonetheless, the agreement also caused trepidations among other groups. Various requests subsequently came from groups who wished to be included in the IGAD talks: the Egyptians, the NDA, and other northern political parties. France, who was not part of the observers' team (Troika + 1), expressed its desire to join the process as an observer. We recall that originally the three states facilitating the IGAD negotiations (Norway, the United Kingdom, and the United States) were dubbed the troika and when Italy expressed desire to be involved in the peace process the group became known as Troika+1. The request was presented by an envoy carrying a donation of $100,000 to the IGAD secretariat.[97] The visit to the secretariat was followed by the dispatch of a high-level political delegation led by former French Prime Minister Édouard Balladur, who met with Garang at Naivasha, Kenya, to express France's interest in peace in the Sudan and its desire to partake in the consolidation of that peace. Also, South Africa, as chair of the African Union, the Arab League, and the United Nations, wanted to be part of the process. Sumbeiywo invited only the African Union and the United Nations as institutions to be observers.

Reactions to the Machakos Protocol varied. The prophets of doom saw in it a backhanded reward by American and British peacemakers to the NIF because it gave that party a new lease in life. According to *Africa Confidential,* the "arch manipulation of American and British peacemakers bought Bashir 'another six-and-a-half years' time." The main message of the Machakos Protocol, according to that publication, was "divide to rule," since that agreement departed from the DoP on religion and state and also from the

Asmara Declaration of the NDA.[98] Other Sudan observers took a different view. *Justice Africa,* for example, maintained that "the Protocol contains little that is new or surprising, but is a distillation of various points of agreement reached over recent years."[99] That assessment was not off the mark. The agreement delivered the major points demanded by the SPLM/A—self-determination and a peace agreement before a cease-fire—while recognizing a regime that was, in Garang's words, too deformed to be reformed. Nevertheless, some grey areas still remained such as the status of the national capital, democratic transformation beyond the generalities of the Bill of Rights agreed upon at Machakos, and the future of the transitional areas.[100] Regarding self-determination, *Justice Africa* also recounted that the government had already agreed to it in Constitutional Decree 14 of 1998, though in a very convoluted manner. Nevertheless, secession as an option became clearer in the Machakos Protocol.

The restatement of the principle of self-determination in the protocol was immediately undermined by clashing interpretations as Egypt announced its opposition to independence for the South; a spokesmen for Khartoum denied that the protocol allowed the partition of the Sudan; and U.S. Assistant Secretary of State for Africa Walter Kansteiner reiterated what he claimed to be the State Department's position that "only autonomy, not independence, was on offer."[101] Kansteiner's position was in line with that of Senator Danforth and reflective of the messy position on the conflict in Sudan taken by the Bureau of African Affairs in the State Department. Could the reason be that Washington at Capitol Hill was often influenced by local constituencies, without losing sight of the United States' vital interests, while the State Department had been looking to mend fences, or put to right the differences, with Sudanese governments?

The issue of religion and state was also ambiguous, leading to contradictory interpretations. Recognizing secularism for the South and leaving the North to the wiles of the NIF only led to exasperation among northerners, including the NDA. The NDA was hoping that the SPLM/A would reach a comprehensive agreement with the NIF that included putting an end to religious laws that had nettled northern secularists and Muslims who did not share the Islamists' intemperate approach to *shari'a* since the latter captured power in 1989. One observer assessed that "'the issue will remain a live one until an agreement is reached on a constitution for the central government that is neutral on religion."[102] That still remains the case.

In effect, the SPLM found itself in a double bind. On the one hand, its southern constituency, whose major demands of autonomy for South Sudan—self-determination and secularization of state in the South—were achieved, was not ready to relinquish these gains and continue war in order to de-Islamize the Sudanese state. On the other hand, mediators were not persuaded by the cogency of Garang's argument that the secularization of the

Sudanese state was crucial for the consolidation of peace in the whole of Sudan. Much to the discomfiture of southern separatists and some observers, Garang maintained that the movement he led was a wide-based national movement that was struggling for the creation of a New Sudan united in diversity.

When Garang persisted in his arguments in favor of the abolition of *shari'a* in the whole of Sudan, one observer (U.K. ambassador Alan Goulty) retorted: "If the abolition of *shari'a* is what northerners want, why don't they demonstrate in the streets of Khartoum against Islamic laws?" The statement was made by the ambassador to a group of SPLM negotiators in the presence of the author. Goulty had actually hit home; both traditional and modern forces in northern Sudan had a period of three years between Nimeiri's fall and the NIF coup to abolish those laws, which were initially promulgated by President Nimeiri in September 1983. In actual fact, neither the interim government headed by General Abdel Rahman Swar al-Dahab (1985–1986), which was dominated by the "modern forces," nor Sadiq al-Mahdi's coalition government, in which northern Sudanese political parties on the right and left participated, had the daring to remove the laws from the books. As I observed earlier, even when the leader of one of the major parties in that coalition, Mohamed Osman al-Mirghani, reached an agreement with Garang to freeze *shari'a* laws until a constitutional conference was convened to debate their fate, it took Prime Minister al-Mahdi eight months to get that agreement adopted by the cabinet and endorsed by parliament. That was enough time for the NIF to move against al-Mahdi's government. It seems clear that the Sudanese prime minister had never encountered the words of wisdom attributed to the British labour leader and former prime minster at a lobby briefing in 1964: "A week is a long time in politics."[103] Consequently, hinging the removal of *shari'a* in the north *only* on external pressures and the military might of the SPLM/A was, putting it mildly, an ill-judged proposition.

If Sudanese Muslims flared up at the Machakos arrangement relating to religion and state, Christians also had their qualms about the arrangement. Paulino Lukudu Loro, the archbishop of Juba, issued a press statement on August 27, 2002, on behalf of the Sudan Catholic Bishops. In that press release, the archbishop applauded the agreement but maintained that it should be clearly understood that the recognition of religious rights was "based on the human dignity possessed by every human person and not merely based on constitutional law." The Bishop wanted to underline that it should not be assumed that those rights were emanating from any political agreement or constitutional arrangement but were inalienable rights entrenched in human rights covenants. The aforementioned press statement also added four observations about what the archbishop called matters of concern:

109

    (i)   Role of *shari'a* in relation to Christians living in areas under that system of law.

    (ii)   Making *shari'a* a source of legislation puts the unity of Sudan in jeopardy.

   (iii) A need exists for firm guarantees for the implementation of the agreement, especially since "the history of past agreements has made our people hesitant to embrace wholeheartedly the framework of the Machakos Protocol."

   (iv) The protocol must be subject to "open and responsible discussion by all Sudanese people regarding content, development, and implementation."

In addition, the NDA, SPLM constituencies in the Three Areas, and Sudanese civil society organizations at large voiced their concern about being excluded from the Machakos talks. An NDA meeting was convened in Asmara, which began on August 6, 2002, and ended August 14 with a proclamation from the NDA of reserved support for the agreement. However, in his brief to the NDA on the protocol, Garang told that body that the Machakos Protocol had reinforced the SPLM/A position on "voluntary" unity of Sudan. He also recommitted the SPLM to the NDA Charter and affirmed that it would continue advocacy for the participation of all political forces in the implementation of the accord reached at Machakos. The NDA's final statement emanating from that meeting noted that the Machakos Protocol presented "a *partial* solution of the Sudanese problem" and that "for any final and proper solution to the conflict, the Alliance has to be included in the peace process."[104]

Egypt, on the other side, was understandably nervous with the decisions reached in Machakos. In a joint press conference held on August 1, 2002, with Sudanese Minister of Information and Communication Mahdi Ibrahim, Egyptian Foreign Minister Ahmad Mahir said, "Egypt stands firmly behind **Sudan's unity**" (emphasis added).[105] On August 8, the Egyptian newspaper *Al-Wafd* published an interview with Minister Mahir in which he revealed that the Machakos agreement had taken his government by surprise and that it felt excluded from the talks. He added: "I want to stress that Egypt's relationship with Sudan is vital. Consequently, Egypt cannot forsake Sudan under any circumstances. If the south secedes from the north after six years, it would mean that we have failed." On August 15, Mahir stressed that the JELI was still "not out-of-date."[106] It might have been, but it certainly became irrelevant after the acceptance of the protocol by the two parties to the conflict. Nevertheless, Mahir's statement was much more measured than that of his predecessor, Amr Musa.[107]

With the two issues of self-determination and religion and politics behind its back, the SPLM/A was now purposefully set to continue dealing with issues such as the decentralization of the system of rule throughout Sudan, democratic transformation with a view to enabling Sudan to graduate from a one-party regime to a multi-party democracy, equitable distribution of wealth, uplifting the lives of the economically marginalized areas in the country, and addressing problems relating to the Transitional Areas. In addition, considerable time and energy would be spent on deliberating guarantees to ensure full implementation of the agreement. To Garang, agreements would never be viable if they were not enforced with incentives for compliance and disincentives for noncompliance. Bearing in mind the history of broken promises in past peace agreements, the adamance of the SPLM to obtain such guarantees should not be a matter of surprise to anyone.

NOTES

1   See Abdelwahab El-Affendi, "The Impasse in the IGAD Process for Sudan."
2   See, for example, "As IGAD Unravels at the Helm, What Are the Prospects for Peace in Sudan?" *Sudan Democratic Gazette*, December 2000.; Francis M. Deng and J. Stephen Morrison, *U.S. Policy to End Sudan's War: Report of the CSIS Task Force on U.S.-Sudan Policy* (Washington DC: Center for Strategic and International Studies, 2001).
3   Deng and Morrison, *U.S. Policy to End Sudan's War*, CSIS Report. 5-8.
4   Ibid., 8
5   Iyob and Khadiagala, *Sudan: The Elusive Quest for Peace*, 116.
6   See "As IGAD Unravels at the Helm, What Are the Prospects for Peace in Sudan?". Bona Malwal Supra note 2.
7   "Kenyan President Promotes Sudan's Peace Process," Xinhua (Nairobi), March 18, 2001.
8   Yahya El Hassan, "Moi, El-Bashir Push for IGAD Summit on Sudan," Pan-African News Agency (Khartoum), March 30, 2001.
9   "Foreign Minister Says Rebels in Control of Two Towns in South," *Khartoum Monitor*, 7 June 2001.
10 Statement by Secretary of State Albright to the press, *Agence France-Press* 22/10/1999.
11 "Sudan's President Bashir Declines Meeting Garang," Pan-African News Agency Daily Newswire, June 2, 2001. Bashir, enraged by the capture of Raja, would not meet with the SPLM leader until he recaptured Raja.
12 Roy Gutman, "Sudan: 'Let Us Have Two Constitutions,'" *Newsweek (website)*, 1 June 2001.
13 BBC Monitoring, "Garang Denies Southern Rebels Favour Secession, Quoting Khartoum daily " *Al-Ra'y al-Amm (web site)*, 23 June 2001.
14 "Khartoum Denies Obstructing Peace Talks," UN Integrated Regional Information Networks October 1, 2001.
15 "Sudan: Peace Adviser Says Khartoum 'Fed up' with Peace Talks," *UN Integrated Regional Information Network*, 8 October 2001.
16 Iyob and Khadiagala, "Sudan: The Elusive Quest for Peace," 119.
17 "Egypt, Libya Hand Government, Opposition Peace Bid Proposals," Agence France-Presse, June 26, 2001.
18 Soon after the collapse of Nimeiri's government in April 1985, northern political parties and trade unions hastily agreed on a political charter, dubbed the national

charter. That charter was thought to have encapsulated the essentials of Sudan's conflict and provided a road map that would lead to a final solution for Sudan's perennial problems. The haste with which the charter was drafted, as well as the complete obliviousness of its authors to the alternative plan for change proposed by the SPLM, inevitably rendered that charter irrelevant to any future dialogue with the SPLM/A.

19 John Garang, *John Garang Speaks*, ed. Mansour Khalid (London, New York: Kegan Paul International), 86.

20 Ibid., 87

21 The NDA, in addition to traditional parties and the SPLM, incorporated the United Sudan African Party (USAP) from southern Sudan; the National Party from Nuba Mountains; Beja Congress from eastern Sudan; and Darfur, represented by veteran Darfurian politician, Ahmed Ibrahim Direig.

22 Personal recollection.

23 Personal recollection.

24 The NDA Resolutions on Fundamental issues provided on the matter of religion and state the following: "(i) All laws shall guarantee full equality of citizens on the basis of citizenship and respect of religious beliefs and traditions without discrimination on grounds of religion, race, gender, or culture. Any law contrary to this requirement shall be unconstitutional; (ii) Prohibition of the formation of any political party on the basis of religion; (iii) The state shall be under obligation to acknowledge and respect religious pluralism in Sudan; promote and bring about peaceful interaction, coexistence, equality, and tolerance among all religious and noble spiritual beliefs; permit peaceful religious proselytization; and prohibit coercion in religion or the perpetration, in any place, forum, or location in the Sudan, of any act or measure intended to arouse religious sedition or racial hatred."

25 See BBC Monitoring, "Rebel SPLM Gives Conditions for Participating in Dialogue," *Al-Ra'y al-Amm (web site)*, 9 August 2001.,"SPLA Wants Opposition Demands Included in Sudan Peace Plan," Agence France-Presse (Cairo), July 17, 2001.

26 "Sudan Government Accuses SPLA Rebels of Rejecting Peace," Agence France-Presse, August 13, 2001.

27 *Mideast Mirror,* September 3, 2001.

28 General Obasanjo was catapulted to power in 1976 after the assassination of Murtala Mohamed, the then military ruler of the most populous African country. To that position he ascended by virtue of being the second in command in the Nigerian Army. The general never gave up saying that he had come to power against his will. On that account, he spent only three years in office to prepare Nigeria for an elected government. After handing power over to President Shagari, he dedicated himself to African causes.

29 The InterAction Council brought together former heads of state and government, including among others, Pierre Trudeau of Canada, Helmut Schmidt of Germany, Prince Talal bin Abdul Aziz of Saudi Arabia, Giulio Andreotti of Italy, and Lord Peter Carrington of the United Kingdom.

30 In that meeting the council decided to form two groups of eminent persons: one to engage the two parties in the conflict with a view to reaching a negotiated settlement, and the other to mobilize resources for post-conflict reconstruction.

31 "Sudan: Confusion over Abuja Peace Efforts," UN Integrated Regional Information Networks, November 9, 2001.

32 Khalid, *War and Peace in Sudan*, 559.

33 Ibid.

34 "Sudan's FM: The U.S. Has a Role to Play," *Mideast Mirror*, September 3, 2001.

35 "Sudan: Washington Sets Three Key Tasks for Danforth," UN Integrated Regional Information Networks, September 10, 2001.

36 "Sudan: Foreign Minister Says 'Government Does Not Expect Any U.S. Attack.'" Pan-African News Agency, September 21, 2001.

37 In 1996, the U.N. Security Council passed three resolutions condemning the government of Sudan, following the attempted assassination of the Egyptian president. The first resolution demanded the government to extradite the suspected assassins (believed to be hiding Sudan) to the Ethiopian government, since Addis Ababa was the locus of the crime. The second called on the government of Sudan to "desist from engaging in activities of assisting, supporting, and facilitating terrorist activities and from giving shelter and sanctuaries to terrorists." The third imposed sanctions under Chapter VII of the UN Charter, including reducing member country embassy staff in Sudan and banning officials of the government of Sudan entry into U member countries. A subsequent resolution also threatened to impose a ban on flights by Sudan Airways, the carrier that was alleged to have transported the assassins.

38 "U.S. Pushing No New Peace Initiative for Sudan: Official," Agence France-Presse, October 31, 2001.

39 This issue is discussed at length in Khalid, *War and Peace in Sudan*, 185.

40 "Sudan: US Envoy Makes Four-Point Peace Proposal," UN Integrated Regional Information Networks (Nairobi), November 15, 2001.

41 Danna Harman, "Sudan Leads Antiterrorist Push," *Christian Science Monitor* (Khartoum), January 14, 2002.

42 Ibid.

43 Ibid.

44 That seminar was attended by five members of the U.S. Congress, including Senator Sam Brownback and Congressman Frank Wolf.

45 The International Eminent Persons Group (IEMP) concluded in its report that "in significant number of cases, abduction is the first stage in a pattern of abuse that falls under the definition of slavery in the International Slavery Convention of 1926 and the Supplementary Convention of 1956." The IEMP also affirmed that the government of Sudan provided direct support to armed groups engaging in abduction and slavery.

46 "Sudan: Danforth Leaves without Deal on Government Bombings," UN Integrated Regional Information Networks, January 17, 2002.

47 Ibid.

48 Government of the Republic of Sudan and the Sudan People's Liberation Movement/Nuba, *The Nuba Mountains Cease-Fire Agreement*, January 19, 2002.

49 Evans, *God, Oil and Country*, 24.

50 Quoted in "Making a Move in Sudan," *Mideast Mirror*, January 9, 2002.

51 Ibid.

52 "Norwegian Minister Says Norway Committed to Support Peace Process," British Monitoring/Sudan News Agency SUNA (Khartoum), January 10, 2002.
53 "Sudan: British Envoy to Join Wider Push for Peace," UN Integrated Regional Information Networks, February 14, 2002.
54 UN Integrated Regional Information Network, January 10, 2002.
55 Mark Simmons and Peter M, "An Interview with General Lazaro Sumbeiywo," in *Peace by Piece: Addressing Sudan's Conflicts*, eds. Mark Simmons and Peter Dixon (London: Conciliation Resources, 2006).
56 "Danforth in Peace Bid in Sudan," United Press International, January 13, 2002.
57 "Sudan: Revival of Cairo-Tripoli Peace Initiative," UN Integrated Regional Information Networks, February 18, 2002.
58 John C. Danforth, "Report to the President of the United States on the Outlook for Peace in Sudan, April 26, 2002," (Washington, D.C.: The White House, 2002).
59 Waithaka Waihenya, *The Mediator: General Lazaro Sumbeiywo and the Southern Sudan Peace Process* (Nairobi: Kenway Publications, 2006), 81.
60 Karen Blixen wrote on the place that was deemed a desolate prison: "Here at long last one was in a position **not** to give a damn for all conventions; here was a new kind of freedom which until then one had only found in dreams." Karen Blixen, wikipedia, http://en.wikipedia.org/wiki/Karen_Blixen
61 Harriet Martin, *Kings of Peace, Pawns of War: The Untold Story of Peace-Making* (London: Continuum, 2006), 140.
62 Ibid.
63 Waithaka Waihenya, *The Mediator*, 82–83.
64 "Sudan: IGAD Talks Threatened by Kapoeta Seizure," UN Integrated Regional Information Networks, June 14, 2002.
65 Ibid.
66 *Peace by Piece, Addressing Sudan's Conflict*, Mark Simmons and Peter Dixon (eds): An interview with General Lazaro Sumbeiywo, 23.
67 "Cynicism is intellectual dandyism without the coxcomb's feathers." George Meredith, *The Egoist: A Comedy in Narrative*, Collins Thesaurus of the English Language, Collins 2008. Quoted by Collins Treasures, Harper and Collins Publishers, 2008.
68 Simmons and Dixon, "An Interview with General Lazaro Sumbeiywo," 23.
69 Waithaka Waihenya, *The Mediator*, 85
70 Martin, *Kings of Peace, Pawns of War*, 140.
71 Ibid.
72 Ibid.
73 Ibid.
74 Johnson, *The Root Causes of Sudan's Civil Wars*, 179.
75 John C. Danforth, *Report to the President of the United States on the Outlook for Peace in Sudan, April 26, 2002* (Washington, DC: The White House, 2002), 25–26.
76 Abdullahi A. An – Naim in *Sudan at the Brink* (Francis Deng ed) Red Sea Press Inc., Trenton, NJ 2010. P Francis M. Deng, *Sudan at the Brink: Self-Determination and National Unity* (New York: Fordham University Press and The Center for International Health and Cooperation, 2010).

77 Garang was referring to the Asmara Resolution of 1995 as well as to the agreement signed in Frankfurt, Germany, in January 1992 between Dr. Ali al-Haj (NIF) and Dr. Lam Akol Ajawin (SPLM-United).

78 The separatists were led by Riek Machar Teny and Lam Akol Ajawin, both from Upper Nile. They parted company with the SPLM/A and formed in August 1991 their own faction under the name SPLM United. Douglas Johnson, *The Root Causes of Sudan's Civil War*, 97.

79 Personal recollection.

80 Personal recollection.

81 Jack Mavrogordato, *Behind the Scenes: An Autobiography* (Tisbury, Wiltshire: Element Books: 1982), 106. Mavrogordato participated in the Cairo talks in his capacity as the legal advisor to the Sudan government at the time.

82 Francis M. Deng, *Dynamics of Identification: A Basis for National Integration in the Sudan* (Khartoum: *Khartoum University Press*, 1973), 8.

83 Mohamed el-Muktar Hussein, "Negotiating Peace: The Road to Naivasha," in *Peace by Piece: Addressing Sudan's Conflicts*, eds. Mark Simmons and Peter Dixon (London: Conciliation Resources, 2006), 19.

84 Waihenya, *The Mediator*, 86.

85 Simmons and Dixon, "An Interview with General Lazaro Sumbeiywo."

86 Martin, *Kings of Peace, Pawns of War*, 143.

87 Waihenya, *The Mediator*, 87.

88 Ibid., 87.

89 Ibid.

90 Simmons and Dixon, "An Interview with General Lazaro Sumbeiywo," 23–24.

91 Waihenya, *The Mediator*, 88.

92 Simmons and Dixon, "An Interview with General Lazaro Sumbeiywo," 28–29.

93 Waihenya, *The Mediator*, 90.

94 Ibid., 90–91.

95 Personal recollection.

96 Ibid.

97 Waihenya, *The Mediator*, 92–93.

98 "Calling the Shots at Machakos," *Africa Confidential* 43, no. 15 (July 26, 2002)

99 "Prospects for Peace in Sudan: June–July 2002," *Justice Africa* (2002)

100 That term transitional areas refers to the three areas contiguous to the South: Abyei, Nuba Mountains, and southern Blue Nile, sometimes called the Three Areas. Though those areas lie in the geographic north, they became part of the theater of war after joining the SPLM/A in 1991.

101 Johnson, *The Root Causes of Sudan's Civil Wars*, 179.

102 "Sudan Peace Talks in Kenya: A Shaky Chance for Peace," International Crisis Group (Nairobi/Brussels), August 12, 2002.

103 Ualden on politics, January 12, 2006 the Westminister Hour, http://news.bbc.co.uk/2/h/programes/the_westminister_hour/4603210.stm

104 "Sudanese Opposition NDA Supports Machakos Protocol," BBC Monitoring (of the Eritrean news agency Hadas Eritrea), August 17, 2002.

105 "Sudan: Focus on Egyptian Role in Peace Process," UN Integrated Regional Information Networks, August 20, 2002.

106 Ibid.

107 Musa was reported to have said: "The Egyptian role in the issue [conclusion of
peace in Sudan] is important to Egypt, and there can be no solution without it."
"Has Egypt Derailed IGAD Peace Process," Bona Malwal *Sudan Democratic
Gazette*, February 2001.

Chapter Four
Security Arrangements: Of Worries and Obsessive Phobia

■■■■■■■■■■■■■❖■■■■■■■■■■■■■

> There never was a good war or a bad peace.
> **Benjamin Franklin**

1. Introduction

The Machakos negotiations successfully closed on July 20, 2002, with the signature of the framework protocol and the announcement of another round of talks that was to commence on August 12, 2002. That round was to discuss wealth and power sharing, but before embarking on that discussion, a more urgent task awaited the parties: attending to the issue of a comprehensive cease-fire, which the government placed topmost on its negotiations agenda. The Sudan People's Liberation Movement (SPLM), on the other side, consistently maintained that permanent cease-fires between warring parties were normally declared either as part of a formal peace agreement, or as a pro-tempore arrangement for humanitarian considerations. Despite its cognizance of the international principles governing the prosecution of war, the SPLM was also aware of contrivances by warriors to exploit lulls in war for scoring a gain for themselves or disadvantaging the other side. For instance, a warring party under pressure may call for a cease-fire feigning compassionate reasons, while it is actually on the lookout for breathing space to reequip itself, restore vitality to its forces, or rethink its tactics. Conscious of the fact that one man's loss is another man's gain, Garang considered calls by the government of Sudan, even for a temporary cessation of hostilities, in this light. Those were not just inklings he had but certainties based on evidence gathered on the battlefield. This chapter shall disclose how numerous attempts by the government of Sudan to conclude cease-fire agreements with the Sudan People's Liberation Movement/Army (SPLM/A) were almost made when the Sudan government army was under pressure.

Furthermore, the chapter shall trace the tortuous history of negotiations between the parties—often with external help—on the cessation of hostilities, temporary cease-fires, or brief respites to facilitate vital humanitarian work. Those negotiations had repeatedly led to circuitous talks between the parties as the SPLM/A uncompromisingly maintained that a peace agreement without solid guarantees for implementation and international monitoring and verification would be worthless. Far from being a reflection of combative bellicosity on its part, the SPLM/A's position on security arrangements had its genesis in the first civil war, when the first betrayal of the Addis Ababa agreement concerned the security protocol. But even though the SPLM disposition was driven by a survivalist instinct, it had on occasions developed into irrational fears that bordered on phobia, as the chapter shall reveal.

2. Comprehensive Cease-Fire Initiatives

Since the 1990s, the two parties had declared nearly a score of cease-fires, while other attempts fell by the wayside. Almost all these cease-fires were initiated or facilitated by the United States: the 1990 initiative by U.S. Assistant Secretary of State Herman Cohen; the 1995 proposal by President Jimmy Carter for ending hostilities in order to enable the Carter Center to carry out its campaign for the eradication of *dracunculiasis* (guinea worm disease); and Senator Danforth's effort to introduce a temporary cease-fire in the Nuba Mountains in cooperation with the Swiss government. Few others were either initiated by concerned Western countries, including the three-month cease-fire brokered by Derek Fatchett, minister at the British Foreign Office to ensure delivery of food to areas affected by famine in Bahr el Ghazal, or the cease-fire unilaterally declared by the SPLM/A on religious occasions such as Christmas or Muslim holy feasts. The latter, however, were rarely recognized by the other party.

Albeit, the SPLM had frequently expressed misgivings about calls for cease-fire coming forth from foreign intermediaries; they had both strategic and tactical reasons for these misgivings. Strategically, Garang could not comprehend why would a regime that had been extremely reticent about discussing the root causes of conflict should always be ready to call for, or give the nod to, calls for comprehensive cease-fires. At the tactical level, Garang evaluated in each offer the advantages to the other party against disadvantages to the SPLM/A, a mind-set that evinced deep mistrust between the two parties. The perpetual insistence by the government of Sudan that agreements on a comprehensive cease-fire should precede peace negotiations only heightened SPLM/A suspicions.

The first time the SPLM became susceptible to calls for a comprehensive cease-fire by the government of Sudan was when Herman Cohen, U.S. Assistant Secretary of State for African Affairs, presented a proposal for a cease-fire in 1990. That proposal came at a time when the SPLM/A had captured a series of garrisons in Equatoria and brought Juba, the capital of southern Sudan, within firing range. The town was then bombarded on a daily basis by the SPLA. Two emissaries, General Olusegun Obasanjo of Nigeria and Dr. Francis Deng of Sudan, conveyed to the government of Sudan a U.S. package deal that included cease-fire and withdrawal of government forces to the 11th parallel under international supervision, while the SPLA ceased pressure on Juba. These actions, according to Cohen's deal, should immediately be followed by a constitutional conference to deliberate the causes of Sudan's crisis with a view to reaching a final peace agreement. Cohen evidently wanted to seize this occasion when the southern Sudan capital city was under pressure to goad the parties into a pacific settlement of conflict. The SPLM, seeing the advantages of the withdrawal of government forces to the 11th parallel and the convocation of a peace conference for which it had always been calling, agreed to Cohen's deal. On the other side, the National Islamic Front (NIF) was divided; some elements within the party were hesitant to embrace the offer Cohen proposed, even though they were eager to see military pressure on Juba eased and its fall into the hands of the SPLA averted. However, the hawks within the National Islamic Front (NIF) were loath to the idea of international supervision, while the military only saw in the acceptance of Cohen's proposal a humiliating surrender. So, by March 1990, Cohen's initiative was killed by both the Sudan Armed Forces (SAF) and hawks in the NIF.

As for the Carter initiative, it came after a 1994 report by the World Health Organization (WHO), which revealed that Sudan was afflicted with the third highest global total of cases of dracunculiasis, a disease caused by guinea worms affecting humans and animals. According to that report the disease was endemic in 780 localities in southern Sudan, with 53,721 cases observed. The areas that had suffered most were in Upper Nile, Bahr el-Ghazal, and Eastern Equatoria. Both parties agreed to Carter's proposal for the eradication of guinea worm but the SPLM/A rejected his call for a *comprehensive* cease-fire. A comprehensive cease-fire, Garang told Carter, could only come as a result of political agreement guaranteed by independent observers with the capacity to provide and enforce such guarantees, powers that the Carter Center did not have. Garang also guessed that by calling for a comprehensive cease-fire, Carter was not acting on his own volition, but had been prevailed upon by the government of Sudan to do so. In effect, Garang asked Carter, why he would need a *comprehensive* cease-fire all over southern Sudan in order to fight guinea worms in identified areas in Upper Nile, Bahr el-Ghazal, and Eastern Equatoria? Eventually, a two-month cease-fire was agreed upon to ensure the eradication of the guinea worm in the affected areas. That cease-fire was to be extended, if need arose. For that reason, the arrangements agreed upon with Carter were derisively called "the guinea worm cease-fire."

On the other side, Fatchett's efforts to ensure the delivery of food support to famine stricken areas in southern Sudan were readily welcomed by the SPLM/A on July 14, 1999, because they targeted areas under their control in Bahr el-Ghazal and Upper Nile that were severely hit by famine. The SPLM/A declared a three-month cease-fire in those areas and opened "corridors of peace" to enable delivery of relief (food and medicine) to those who were most in need. As for the Nuba Mountains cease-fire, though supported by the United States, it was a Swiss brainchild. Switzerland strove to play a role in the resolution of Sudan's conflict within the constitutional parameters that allowed it to intervene in outside conflicts. The Swiss ambassador to Libya, Josef Bucher, was coincidentally charged with the task. Before the idea of the cease-fire had come up, Bucher was encouraged by his Sudanese counterpart in Tripoli, Abbas Ibrahim al-Nour, to induce his government to contribute to peacemaking in Sudan. After consulting his government, Bucher was authorized to make contacts with Khartoum. His knowledge of the other party to the conflict (SPLM/A) was meagre; he only began to have a better knowledge of the movement after he was later transferred to Nairobi as the Swiss ambassador to Kenya. The SPLM's reaction to Bucher was glacial at the beginning, probably because his confidentiality with Khartoum discomforted the SPLM. Nonetheless, Bucher was able to sponsor seminars in Kenya that brought together southern leaders and civil society activists to discuss issues relating to women's development and the role of traditional leadership in southern Sudan. On the latter activity, Bucher was aided by a Swiss scholar, Conradin "Kwacakworo" Perner, a Swiss anthropologist who had studied the Anyuak tribe of eastern Africa. Because of its initial misgivings, the SPLM leadership was neither charmed by Bucher's idea of engaging southern Sudanese women groups in peace making, nor won over by the scholarship of his advisor.

On leaving Kenya, Bucher was appointed by his government as special representative on conflict, with a focus on Sudan. It was in his new capacity that he came up with a more relevant proposition: cease-fire in the Nuba Mountains. That area was then under a severe humanitarian crisis, which was made worse by its inaccessibility from southern Sudan and the difficulties of getting assistance to the region through Operation Lifeline Sudan (OLS). That operation was initiated by the UN, with the agreement of both sides to the conflict, with a view to ensure delivery of food and services to citizens in the war zones in South Sudan, but not in the Nuba Mountains because the area was not of prime strategic significance to the warring parties in the overall war scene, both the government of Sudan and the SPLM/A found the call for a cease-fire there more palatable. At this juncture, the Swiss government invited the United States to join the process, especially since the issue of ensuring unimpeded humanitarian assistance to civilians within war zones was at the top of Senator Danforth's priorities. Without a doubt, it was the U.S. persuasion, if not pressure, that brought the government of Sudan to the negotiation table on the Nuba Mountains cease-fire. The Swiss-U.S. negotiations took place at Bürgenstock, Switzerland, a mountain resort above Lake Lucern.

Against this background, it was predictable that the government would, once again, underline the priority it gave to cease-fire on the eve of the opening of the second Machakos negotiations (Machakos II). Chol Deng Alak, junior minister in Sudan's Ministry of Foreign Affairs, told reporters in Khartoum on July 20, 2002, that he expected the two sides to agree to a "cessation of hostilities as a step towards a comprehensive cease-fire." Such a step, he added, "is a government strategy and an important stage that softens bitterness, builds up confidence, and steps up the chances of peace."[1] The SPLM, as to be expected, thought otherwise. It remained steadfast in its position that "a ceasefire will be the last item to cement the political agreement that we are working on now," as SPLM spokesperson Samson Kwaje told a press conference in Nairobi the same day.[2] General Sumbeiywo later intimated to friends that with Machakos I he had acquiesced in the SPLM/A seduction of negotiating without an agreed cease-fire. Sumbeiywo and observers gave the SPLM/A limited backing for its position on that issue, but then none of them was suffering from Garang's "musophobia;" Garang invariably detected the smell of dead rat in any call by the NIF for a comprehensive cease-fire.

Although a new round of talks began in mid-August, by September 1, 2002, the two sides had not had face-to-face talks; any communication between them was conducted through intermediaries. The situation was complicated on September 1, when the SPLA attacked and took the key government garrison town of Torit in eastern Equatoria, as mentioned earlier. Torit had both historical and contemporary significance to the SPLM. Historically, it was the site of the first rebellion in southern Sudan on August 18, 1955; later, it became the hub of SPLM activities for a number of years. Aside from those symbolic considerations, the SPLM might have thought that the occupation of Torit would strengthen its hand in the negotiations, while arguing that the occupation was in response to government provocation. As a result, on September 2 the government suspended participation in the Machakos II talks to protest the SPLM/A's military offensive and ordered its army to mobilize. The "occupation of Torit is unacceptable," said Foreign Minister Mustafa Ismail. "All the capacity of the state and the people will be used in military operations [to take back the land seized by the SPLM/A]."[3]

121

3. Failure of Cease-Fire Talks Irks Mediator

In its written memorandum to the Intergovernmental Authority on Development (IGAD), the government gave a different explanation for the suspension of talks. It referred to what it called SPLM/A "backtracking on the commitments" made in the Machakos Protocol and complained that it was introducing new issues that were not on the negotiating table at Machakos II, namely, redrawing the boundaries of southern Sudan to include the Three Areas, calling for a shari'a-free national capital, and seeking a confederal solution to north-south governance. Admittedly, the SPLM leadership was badgered by its constituencies in the Nuba Mountains and southern Blue Nile who thought that they had been left out of the Machakos Protocol. As well, the SPLM was under fire from its core members who championed the idea of creating a new shari'a-free capital for Sudan. The government of Sudan considered these proposals "completely incompatible" with the Machakos Protocol.[4] The government also accused the IGAD mediation team of giving in too much to the SPLM/A—actually, of indulging in "active advocacy" on the SPLM/A's behalf.[5] Rather than considering the Machakos Protocol as a framework for resolving outstanding issues between the parties, the government had clearly assumed the agreement was the end of the novel. The situation became so tense that the U.N. secretary general had to step in and call on the two parties to resume talks.[6]

In reality, issues regarding the Three Areas and the north-south border demarcation were not new. At the 1998 IGAD ministerial meeting at Addis Ababa, both parties agreed that southern Sudan constituted the area so defined at Sudan's independence on January 1, 1956. In that meeting, the SPLM agreed that the delineation of the north-south border on that date definitively defined the contours of southern Sudan. The SPLM also persevered in calling for the incorporation of the area of Abyei in southern Sudan, contending that, for administrative reasons, the colonial administration had transferred this area from the Province of Bahr al Ghazal in south Sudan to that of Kordofan in northern Sudan. Interestingly, the government did not deny the special status of Abyei at the Addis Ababa meeting but declared that it was not prepared "at this stage" to include it within the boundaries of southern Sudan for the purposes of the referendum. The way it expressed its position on Abyei revealed that the government of Sudan was still at two minds about the issue. Regarding southern Blue Nile and the Nuba Mountains, the SPLM/A agreed at the Addis Ababa meeting to exclude them from the definition of southern Sudan without prejudice to the right of the people of the said areas to self-determination. In response, the government of Sudan made it clear that self-determination was only agreed upon for the people of southern Sudan as defined on January 1, 1956.

To allow negotiations to proceed at Machakos II, the SPLM/A softened its position by claiming that the points it raised on borders, governance, the Three Areas, and the national capital were mere proposals on matters that were already on the table. It also accused the government of fidgeting about issues that had been repeatedly on the negotiating table as a pretext for walking out of the talks. The SPLM was of the opinion that the government believed that it had already given away too much in the Machakos Protocol. It also reckoned that the government representatives were under pressure from military hardliners in Khartoum. A member of the SPLM delegation to the talks, Justin Yaac Arop, observed on this matter that "this time round when they [government of Sudan] came, they definitely had this agenda of the military: that the Sudanese army must wipe out the SPLA throughout all theaters of war. And, therefore, they became militant representatives of a militant military institution."[7]

Sumbeiywo, considering that the capture of Torit had deeply angered the government, later recalled that Khartoum "did not have the guts to tell us that they were withdrawing because the SPLM/A was fighting."[8] The government did, however, return to its demand for an end to hostilities with a view to "creating an atmosphere more conducive [sic] to a successful conclusion of the peace talks."[9] Fearful of an international backlash against their withdrawal from the talks, the government chose to go on a diplomatic offensive. Officials from Khartoum were immediately sent to Kenya, Syria, Libya, Ethiopia, Chad, Nigeria, Uganda, South Africa, Qatar, Oman, United Arab Emirates, Kuwait, and Saudi Arabia[10] to explain the reasons for suspending the talks. Meanwhile, the army prepared its offensive. "The return of Torit will be the first step toward the return of all areas currently under rebel control," said Sudanese Defence Minister Major General Bakri Hassan Salih. Salih was quoted as saying to a battalion of paramilitary troops preparing to leave Khartoum for Juba, "We will teach the rebels a lesson in sacrifice and jihad."[11] On September 9, 2002, reports came in of heavy bombardment of Torit by the Sudanese army. The recapture of Torit by the Sudanese army was soon to come.

The SPLA, in retaliation to the government's attacks on Torit, announced that it was "on the march" to Juba. On September 10, the SPLM/A's Commander Oyay Deng Ajak told the BBC's Network Africa radio that he was speaking from a position between Torit and Juba where government forces were trying to halt them. "We are actually moving to Juba as I speak to you now. We are moving to Juba from multiple directions," Ajak said.[12] That statement enraged the government considerably and precipitated a lash out at the international community for its alleged softness towards the SPLM/A. Sudan's chargé d'affaires at the embassy in Nairobi, Muhammad Ahmad Dirdeiry, said that the government held the SPLM/A responsible for the collapse of the talks. He criticized the international community for putting pressure on Khartoum and not the SPLM/A. "'No real effort is being made to bring back the parties back [sic] to the table," he said. He also added that "'if there is any pressure, then it should be directed at the rebels, who have violated the Machakos Protocol. We cannot be expected to negotiate when fighting is going on.'"[13] But contrary to what the chargé d'affaires said, pressure was being brought to bear on the SPLM/A behind the scenes. On September 12, Kenyan President Moi met with Garang, along with Sumbeiywo and Kenyan foreign minister Kalonzo Musyoka. The three urged Garang to cease the SPLM/A offensive. According to the account in Sumbeiywo's biography, Garang told President Moi that the occupation of Torit was "not important" to the SPLM/A but was only meant to show the government that "it was not out of weakness that [the SPLM/A] was negotiating."[14] Moi offered to assist with a return to the negotiations. Resumption of talks between the two parties was soon to occur as a result of Moi's pressure and intermediation by southern Sudanese dignitaries led by former vice president Abel Alier.[15]

4. Cessation of Hostilities at Long Last

The occupation of Torit had apparently driven the government up the wall to the point that the issue of cease-fire became a precondition to resuming talks in Machakos. "'Without a cease-fire there is no need to return to Nairobi,'" Foreign Minister Mustafa Ismail told reporters on September 20, 2002, during a visit to Washington.[16] The government's chief negotiator, Ghazi Salahuddin Atabani, added that the government was ready to resume talks if the SPLM/A showed commitment to end hostilities and did not introduce new issues. He reasoned that the two parties "had made great progress toward a just and lasting peace in the Machakos Protocol that laid solid groundwork for resolving our problems. We could have by now reached a peace deal if it were not for those interruptions."[17]

On September 28, the SPLM/A began to yield to pressure and offered to resume negotiations if a temporary cease-fire was agreed to. "'The SPLA units will be instructed to maintain defensive posture and not go into offensive military operations," spokesman Samson Kwaje told reporters.[18] In order to profit from this opening, Sumbeiywo visited Khartoum on October 3 to discuss the issue with President Bashir. In that meeting, Bashir "insisted that he would not discuss anything with Garang unless there was total cessation of hostilities first."[19] Sumbeiywo gave President Bashir a draft of a cessation of hostilities proposal to review.[20]

On October 4, the opposition National Democratic Alliance (NDA), of which the SPLM/A was one of the larger components, announced that they had taken the garrison towns of Hamashkoreib and Shallob on the Sudanese-Eritrean border and were marching on Kassala. The government, instead, blamed the Eritreans, and on October 5, Sudanese Foreign Minister Mustafa Osman Ismail told a press conference that they would file complaints against Eritrea's "aggression" before the U.N. Security Council, the Arab League, and the Organization of African Unity (OAU).[21] For certain, the government was more preoccupied with Torit than with the eastern front, and reports differed as to the change of hands in Torit. On October 8, the government announced that it had recaptured Torit.[22] Sudan's chargé d'affaires in Nairobi told reporters that Khartoum had decided to retake Torit to quell rumors that the government was "'unable to control the situation in the south, and had its back against the wall.'"[23] The SPLM/A, on the other side, declared that it had made a strategic withdrawal from the town.[24] However, recapture of Torit by government forces did not end incursions by the SPLA and its allies on the eastern front. The NDA announced that it had captured the government's garrison of Rissai and was blocking the strategically important Kassala-Port Sudan road.

In view of this military jumble, General Sumbeiywo doubled his efforts to organize a cessation of hostilities on the lines he had presented to Bashir as a prelude to the continuation of peace talks. On October 4, after his meeting with President Bashir the day before, the general announced to reporters that both sides had agreed to a cessation of hostilities and the resumption of peace talks on October 14.[25] However, this was premature, as the recapture of Torit by the government and events in eastern Sudan had demonstrated; agreement on a resumption of negotiation by the two parties was reached on October 15. On that date, a Memorandum of Understanding on Resumption of Negotiations on Peace in Sudan between the Government of the Sudan and the Sudan People's Liberation Movement/Army (MoU) was signed and went into effect on October 17,[26] following an IGAD ministerial intervention led by Kenya's foreign minister Kalonzo Musyoka.[27] On that occasion, General Sumbeiywo declared that "'both parties have signed the cessation of hostilities, which will take effect on 17 October at noon...it will last for as long as the talks are on, which could be until the end of the year."[28]

In that MoU, the Sudan government and the SPLM/A first agreed to resume negotiations from where they had stopped when the government withdrew its delegation on September 2, 2002. They then agreed to create and maintain a conducive atmosphere [sic] throughout the negotiations until all the outstanding issues in the conflict are resolved. This entailed an agreement between the two parties to maintain a period of tranquillity during negotiations by ceasing hostilities *in all areas of the Sudan*" (emphasis added) and ensuring a military stand-down for their own forces, including allied forces and affiliated militia. The MoU preserved for the two sides the right to "take any legitimate measures in self-defence against any hostile act from a party or force other than those referred to above."[29] This self-defence provision allowed the government to retain options in the east.

The requirements of the cessation of hostilities were defined as follows: to retain current military positions; refrain from any offensive military action by all forces; cease laying of land mines; refrain from occupation of new areas; cease supplying all areas with weapons and ammunition; refrain from any act of violence or other abuse on civilian population, and freeze media wars and propaganda against one another.[30] The parties also agreed to allow "unimpeded humanitarian access to all areas and for all people in need." That clause called on the government to end its refusal to allow lifesaving drugs to be supplied to crisis areas such as western Upper Nile. And while the MoU was to last throughout the round of talks, that is, up to December 31, 2002, at the latest, provision was made for it "to be renewed by mutual consent of the parties to continue negotiations on any outstanding issues."[31]

5. Violations of Cessation of Hostilities Agreement

Peace talks resumed on October 15, 2002, but only two days later (on October 17), the SPLM/A accused the government of violating the MoU by attacking its forces in eastern Sudan. The government's position was confused in the beginning, though ultimately it claimed that it was responding to "Eritrean aggression," adding that IGAD's mandate, and any IGAD-brokered agreement, only covered "southern Sudan."[32] Probably in retaliation, the SPLA captured the southern town of Akobo in Jonglei State a week later. Serenely, Khartoum said that it would make an official complaint to IGAD over the matter.

The cessation of hostilities soon appeared to be fragile; accusations and counter-accusations of violations were made galore. On October 25, the government of Sudan released a statement through its embassy in Nairobi claiming that the day before at around 8:00 a.m., the militia of Peter Gadet, who was then an ally of the SPLM/A, attacked Koch and Thorken in western Upper Nile; both sites were held by the government's loyal militia of Paulino Matip Nhial. The SPLM/A countered that the situation was the other way around; SPLM/A spokesman Samson Kwaje claimed that government forces based in the garrison town of Mankien had attacked the SPLM/A-held village of Rier and three other adjacent villages but were repulsed.[33] These accusations and counter-accusations immediately exposed a deficiency in the MoU: scant power to monitor and verify the cessation of hostilities. The IGAD secretariat and General Sumbeiywo were consequently swamped by missives from the two parties accusing one another of breaches of the MoU. Although the government had acknowledged that there were no longer Eritrean troops in the east, reports indicated by November 6 that it was preparing an offensive to recapture lost territory in that region. Observers noted this could plainly be in violation of the MoU.[34]

126

The actual round of peace talks at which the MoU was signed made only limited progress despite overly optimistic claims that a deal had been all but clinched. The only substantive outcome in that round of talks, beside agreement on cessation of hostilities, was another Memorandum of Understanding on Aspects of Structures of Government, dated November 18, 2002. Notwithstanding, the United States considered the talks "very successful." Its observer at the talks, Jeff Millington observed that the MoU worked significantly well: "The fighting, killings, will remain stopped. There have been no significant military engagements. Relief is going unimpeded throughout the south and other areas. This is important,"[35] Millington said.

On the back of this assessment, Secretary of State Colin Powell phoned President Bashir and John Garang on December 2 to "congratulate them on progress on the peace front."[36] The call to General Bashir by the U.S. Secretary of State was a long awaited one by the head of a regime that had often been depicted by Washington as a "sponsor of terrorism." Indeed, the National Congress Party (NCP) leadership, to the displeasure of its dyed-in-the-wool hardliners, was delighted to bask in a diplomatic glow it was scarcely habituated to. The United States then arranged for unofficial talks between the government and the SPLM/A to be held in Washington in December. That meeting did not take place due to resistance from Congress, which thought the time was not yet ripe for such a meeting.

Ironically, Powell's call to Bashir came shortly after President Bush signed into law the Sudan Peace Act.[37] That act threatened to impose sanctions on any of the two parties—the government of Sudan and the SPLM/A—that did not negotiate in good faith, while at the same time laid the foundation for substantial development assistance for the South. The reference in the act to "sanctions against parties to the negotiations who acted 'in bad faith'" appeared to have been an afterthought, since the act was initially drafted with a view to tightening the noose around the neck of the NIF. In effect, the two prime movers of the act, together with 21 other members of Congress, had initiated three years earlier Resolution 73, which was adopted by the House on March 24, 1999. That resolution condemned the NIF government for its *genocidal* (emphasis added) war in south Sudan, support for terrorism, and continued human rights abuses. The resolution also called on the U.S. president to (i) implement Security Council resolution 1070 relating to air embargo[38] on Sudan, (ii) make a determination that the NIF war policy in south Sudan and Nuba Mountains constitutes genocide, and (iii) create no-fly zones in southern Sudan, Nuba Mountains, and Ingessana Hills (Blue Nile) "to protect civilians from aerial bombardments." Over and above, Section 5 of the act authorized the U.S. president to provide increased assistance to the areas of Sudan that were not controlled by the government of Sudan in order to prepare the population for peace and democratic governance, including support for civil administration, communications, infrastructure, education, health, and agriculture.

The MoU on Cessation of Hostilities was renewed on November 18, 2002, to operate until March 31, 2003, in order to maintain temporary peace during a recess necessitated by Kenya's landmark national elections in December 2002.[39] The renewal of the MoU did not prevent various instances of military activity in breach of its terms. Most important of these was the government's offensives in western Upper Nile, especially attacks on Leer in January 2003. In addition, the government's plans to construct the Bentiu-Adok oil road angered the SPLM/A immensely and led to protest letters addressed to the IGAD secretariat as well as to the U.S.-led Civilian Protection Monitoring Team (CPMT), established under the Danforth initiative. The cessation of hostilities was, therefore, in danger of being a poorly monitored agreement that existed largely on paper.

6. Cessation of Hostilities Verification and Monitoring Mechanisms

Although the two parties agreed in November 2002 to return to talks on January 15, 2003, the government did not show up, citing as its reason that it was not formally invited. But, according to the IGAD secretariat, that was a flimsy excuse; it was simply untrue. The government finally showed up in Karen, on January 23.[40] As the talks commenced, the leader of the SPLM/A delegation, Nhial Deng Nhial, complained of the government's heavy fighting, especially in the western Upper Nile region, despite the extension of the MoU. The SPLM/A had already written to Sumbeiywo to this effect on January 21. Nhial Deng Nhial also noted that "the lack of a credible mechanism of verification of compliance (with the terms of truce) by the parties...has not helped matters."[41] For days after the commencement of talks on January 27, the SPLM/A requested to have the talks suspended for a day after the government captured Leer in western Upper Nile. SPLM/A spokesman Samson Kwaje told reporters in Nairobi, "We asked for the suspension because the government of Sudan has continued to break the [MoU] we have both signed...by violating the ceasefire and capturing further territory." Kwaje added: "They have captured the town of Leer and this afternoon, after we asked for the suspension, they also seized the town of Dut Lual."[42] Nevertheless, peace talks resumed on January 29 with the issue of cease-fire violations addressed separately, alongside the substantive negotiations. For that reason, the CPMT was instructed to travel to southern Sudan to verify mutual claims of cease-fire violations.[43] However, it was arguable whether this was properly within the mandate of the CPMT, since its team was essentially established to protect civilians, not to investigate violations.

On February 4, 2003, the parties agreed to the Addendum to the Memorandum of Understanding on Cessation of Hostilities between the Government of Sudan and the Sudan People's Liberation Movement/Army on Resumption of Negotiations on Peace in Sudan. This important addendum paved the way for much-needed verification and monitoring of the cessation of hostilities. The addendum included the following important provisions to which both parties were obligated:

(i) To notify in advance the MoU Channel of Communications Committee (MoU Committee) of all troop movements, including rotations, and the supply and resupply of noncombat items.

(ii) To provide to the MoU Committee with the identity and location of their own forces as well as all allied forces and affiliated militia.

(iii) To allow a Verification and Monitoring Team (VMT), which may include, in addition to the two parties, personnel and aircraft from an expanded CPMT, IGAD, African Union, observer nations (namely, Italy, Norway, United Kingdom, and the United States), and any other nation that may be agreed to by the parties. Members of both parties shall have the right to participate in verification and monitoring missions.

(iv) To permit free access to VMTs to travel in and around areas where a complaint has been filed by any of the parties. The team shall notify the MoU Committee of the results of such missions. All reports of the VMTs and monitoring teams shall be made public by the MoU Committee without delay or alteration.

(v) To take immediate steps to ensure that any location/s taken over by any party in violation to the MoU since that MoU came into effect (17th October 2002) are immediately restored to the party that had control over such location/s prior to the violation.

(vi) To suspend work on the Bentiu-Adok road until the final Comprehensive Peace Agreement is signed.

(vii) To take further measures to ensure compliance with the requirement to freeze media wars and propaganda against one another in accordance with Article 3 of the MoU.

The addendum was applauded by all sides and injected optimism into the negotiations. Sumbeiywo noted, "'We didn't have a mechanism of implementing [the MoU on cessation of hostilities]. Now we have a mechanism to check when there is violation, we go there and check. We are able now to point fingers at who started the firing.'"[44] Sumbeiywo, in particular, considered this as one of the mediation team's most important achievements.[45] The two parties to the negotiations also expressed satisfaction with the new arrangement. On behalf of the government, Muhammad Ahmad Dirdeiry remarked: "This is the first time for us to talk about stopping war since we started fighting 19 years back. It's a very big achievement."[46] On the other hand, the SPLM's spokesman, Samson Kwaje, was more precise in his praise for the addendum: "'This is important because we wasted a lot of time the last session talking about violations of the Memorandum of Understanding and fighting in western Upper Nile, eastern Upper Nile.'"[47]

While the Addendum did indeed secure cessation of hostilities, it didn't stop the government from breaching the MoU. For example, the SPLM/A wrote to General Sumbeiywo on March 9, 2003, raising concerns about a series of attacks by the Sudanese army and the militia sponsored by it on Tam, Lingera and Wanglieth, Keriel, Loth, Ruothnyia, and Nyibol and Gol in western Upper Nile, in addition to efforts to build an oil and military road between Khor Adar in eastern Upper Nile and Ulu in southern Blue Nile. Also in March, the SPLM/A notified the IGAD of the government's attacks on Jekou, Pagak, Maiwut, and Abaldugu in southern Blue Nile. Other communications in March related to movements of government troops on barges from Malakal to Bor and Juba without prior notification. The VMT also investigated an alleged breach of the MoU in the Mading area in eastern Upper Nile on June 3, 2003.

Creation of the CPMT and VMT, nonetheless, was a breakthrough, particularly insofar as the protection of non-combatant civilians was concerned. Despite tardiness in implementation, the logistical capacity with which both bodies were endowed contributed immensely to their relative success. For example, it took seven months between the date on which the CPMT was created (March 2002) and when it commenced operations (October 2002) for the verification process to start. Given the gravity of the situation, a seven-month delay was inexcusable. In addition to delays, there was also serious concern by the SPLM/A that Khartoum-based U.S. diplomats appeared to have been reluctant to allow any evidence damning to the government of Sudan to be revealed for fear of jeopardizing the peace talks. That would not have been a wild guess given the hesitation on the part of the Bureau of African Affairs in the U.S. State Department to reveal any information concerning government breaches of the MoU for fear of agitating Khartoum. One such case was the report of a team led by U.S. Colonel Paul Davenport on offensives led by government forces against civilians in oil-producing areas in western Upper Nile. Davenport provided a list of significant breaches of the MoU and delivered them to the IGAD during the period of January 26 to 30, 2003. Khartoum's response to Davenport's reports was to punish the team by denying it flight access and effectively grounding CPTM from March 7 to April 11, 2003. This action was not covered in the report prepared by the State Department to Congress, as required by the Sudan Peace Act. By omitting that incident in its report to Congress, the State Department likely did not want to inflame Congress against the government of Sudan on that account and jeopardize the ongoing peace negotiations. The SPLM made some noises but decided not to make a big issue of that violation of the CPMT mandate, especially when it was assured by the government that there would be no more obstacles to visits by the CPMT to any site.

Meanwhile, complaints by the SPLM/A continued into 2004, with some particularly linked to Lam Akol's return to the SPLM/A in October 2003. Akol, the celebrated political nomad, had now moved back to the SPLM leadership after a period of cohabitation with the NCP and then the formation of his own party, as explained in Chapter Two. With his return, operations intensified in Upper Nile, leading to reprisal by the Sudan Armed Forces. The SPLM/A complained of an attack on Nimna in western Upper Nile in February 2004. Letters from the secretariat of the SPLM/A to the IGAD in March 2004 raised SPLM's concerns regarding Renk-Malakal and Malakal-Nasir road construction; the government army force's assembly in Nasir, Alali, and Pibor in Upper Nile; road construction from Rubkona to the east in western Upper Nile; an attack from Kwach; an attack on Obai village in Upper Nile; and the shelling of the Nyilwak relief center. On April 19, 2004, the IGAD VMT confirmed that it had evidence of a campaign of violence led by forces allied to the government of Sudan against civilians in the Shilluk Kingdom (Upper Nile).

As if all those violations of the MoU were not enough, the government also planted some of its elements as VMT members in Lokichoggio, on the Kenyan-Sudan border. Those poseurs were, to be sure, placed in that border town to eavesdrop on activities in an area that represented the nerve center of SPLM/A movements into, and out of, Sudan. Be that as it may, without the CPMT and VMT interventions, despite all their frailties, peace negotiations would have been derailed, if not totally undermined. Most of the fears, apprehensions, and suspicions by one party against the other concerned military movements. None of the parties was willing, at that crucial moment in the negotiations, to provide the other with better leverage, especially on the battlefield.

7. Causes of SPLM Anxieties on Security Arrangements

Jostling between the parties on the issue of cease-fire portended more trouble regarding the knotty issue of final security arrangements at the conclusion of the peace agreement. Consequently, that issue became a critical topic in the talks, especially assurance that these arrangements would include guarantees that the SPLM/A could rely upon in the implementation period and in safeguarding the integrity and autonomy of southern Sudan. For that reason the SPLM/A demanded firm **organic guarantees**[48] in addition to any constitutional and legal guarantees that would be embedded in the agreement, and regardless of pledges made by regional and international observers to secure implementation of the agreement. In other words Garang was seeking peace guarantees which would give SPLM/A leverage. That position was mostly influenced by John Garang's long-held position, which originated from his personal experiences with the Addis Ababa agreement. Throwing some light on these experiences may, therefore, help explain Garang's adamance regarding the inclusion of organic guarantees in the agreement.

In January 1972, John Garang, then a young captain in the South Sudan Liberation Movement (SSLM), wrote to his leader, Colonel Joseph Lagu, opposing the imminent signature of a peace agreement with Nimeiri's government unless certain conditions were satisfied. Garang was concerned with a number of issues, top of which was the security arrangements envisaged in that agreement. The other issues related to the necessity for allowing a trial period for the agreement; that is, an interim period by the end of which the agreement would either be endorsed, modified, or rejected by the people of southern Sudan through plebiscite. Garang's criticism of the imminent agreement did not endear him to Colonel Lagu. Indeed, Lagu was so infuriated by the young officer's remarks that he struck his name from the list of SSLM delegates who were to attend the peace negotiations. Nevertheless, Lagu later seemed to have espoused Garang's idea for a moment during the Addis Ababa negotiations. No sooner had the SSLM finalized a draft agreement with the government covering all areas under discussion, including security arrangements, than Lagu made exception to some major issues resolved by the two negotiating teams. One issue related to allowing the South to have its own independent army.

Abel Alier, vice president of Sudan under Nimeiri who led the government delegation to the Addis Ababa negotiations, recounted the issue: "Garang proposed three distinct armies for Sudan: one to be recruited from citizens of Southern Sudan and be stationed there; a second recruited from the citizens in Northern Sudan and to be stationed there and a third to be recruited in equal numbers from both the South and the North."[49] Clearly, what Garang was aiming at was the creation of two separate armies: one for the North, the other for the South, and a national army that would bring together elements from both regions. That was precisely what he asked for and achieved in the CPA. Garang firmly believed that the only credible guarantee for any agreement would be one that would afford him leverage in the process of implementation, or what he called organic guarantees. While aspects of Garang's ideas were debated during the course of the Addis Ababa negotiations, the negotiators ultimately agreed that the SSLM forces should be absorbed into one national army. A range of shortcomings in the policy and process of absorption cumulatively led to the failure of that peace agreement.[50]

8. The Making of Colonel John Garang

At this juncture it may be relevant to briefly relate the course of action Garang had taken after his confrontation with Lagu, as well as the path he had charted for himself. That path had a great bearing on future developments. Following the signature of the Addis Ababa Accord, Garang approached Lagu (who was by then elevated to the rank of general) with a request to be absorbed into the Sudanese army, even though absorption of men and officers of the Anya Nya (rebel force led by Lagu) in Sudan's army was a matter Garang priorly objected to. The general was stunned and asked the disobliging captain, "Why now?" The young captain answered his general that he wanted to give the agreement a try and history would tell. In what appeared to be a calculated plan, Garang masterfully took advantage of his stint in the army to improve his academic credentials, acquaint himself with the social milieu of northern Sudan, and upgrade his military proficiency.

Before joining the South Sudan Liberation Army (SSLA), Garang was known for his studious nature. During the first civil war he was encouraged by elders in his community to complete his secondary education in Tanzania. After completing that level of education, Garang sought and obtained a scholarship for further studies at Grinnell College in Iowa, from which he graduated with a Bachelor of Arts degree in economics in 1969. Thereafter, he was offered another scholarship to pursue studies at University of California, Berkeley, but instead opted for a Thomas J. Watson fellowship to study East African agricultural economics at University of Dar es Salaam, Tanzania. Dar was then the shrine of African liberation to which academics, researchers, and freedom fighters made pilgrimage. Like many Africans of his generation, Garang had been mesmerized by Julius Nyerere's village-based socialism, Ujamaa. It was at that time that Garang decided to return to Sudan and join SSLM. A fellow warrior, Frederick Magot, introduced Garang to Lagu, who received the young man with open arms due to his academic attainments. Lagu also badly needed Garang to replace Aquila Manyoun, a war hero from Bor, Garang's native land, who had died in combat. However, Garang's enlistment did not occur without argumentation with Lagu. The would-be Anya Nya recruit who was influenced by the pan-African milieu of Dar es Salaam told Lagu point blank: "Your movement is reactionary because it seeks separation." Nonetheless, as a result of explanations by Lagu and persuasion by Magot, Garang agreed to join the SSLM, though he never stopped challenging Lagu's political approach and military modus operandi. Lagu, who seemed to have liked Garang for his intelligence and courage, disliked his lack of military discipline. He told Magot, *"dhabit da askriyaa ma khasa fi rassu"* (this officer is yet to learn military discipline). Evidently, Garang, for his own ulterior motives, endured Lagu's merciless castigations.

In his short term of duty in the Sudan Army, Garang proved to be an atypical soldier. For example, when SSLM officers were integrated into the Sudan Armed Forces and given the opportunity to import tax-free vehicles, Garang told his direct superior, Brigadier Mirghani Suleiman Khalil, that he planned to import a tractor. Sarcastically, the brigadier asked Garang if he needed that tractor for his transportation. Garang answered, "No. I am taking it to my village to introduce my people to modern agriculture." Evidently, Garang was entertaining the idea of creating his own ujamaa at Bor. After a short stint in the Sudan army's military intelligence, Garang enrolled in an infantry advanced course at Fort Benning, Georgia, where he studied counter-insurgency. There is reason to believe that Lagu made sure that Garang was dispatched outside Sudan, as the general appeared to have been wary of attempts by the young officer to "contaminate" the minds of the rank and file with his subversive ideas. After his return to Khartoum, Garang was integrated in the Sudan army's research department. Lagu was still concerned with Garang's destabilizing effect on soldiers stationed in south Sudan. Ergo, when Captain Garang secured scholarship for higher studies at Iowa State University, Lagu was happy to see him leave for a few years. With help from the then director of military operations, General Abdel Magid Hamid Khalil, and the army commander in Upper Nile, Yousif Ahmed Yousif, Lagu saw to it that the study leave was granted. In effect, both Khalil and Yousif had great regard for the young officer on account of his performance in the army, his studiousness, and the sheer daring with which he always expressed his views. That was why Garang, even during the war, remembered those two officers with affection. In actual fact, Garang offered in 1985 to step down from the SPLM leadership and invited General Yousif to take the lead.[51] Whether he was serious about handing over SPLM/A leadership to the General or trying to emphasize the national character of the Movement was another matter.

Upon return to Sudan from the United States with a doctoral degree in agricultural economics, Garang served as senior instructor at Sudan's Military College at Wadi Sayidna for four years while teaching agricultural economics at the Khartoum University Faculty of Agriculture in Shambat. When he decided after the collapse of the Addis Ababa agreement to quit the army and mount his own insurgency, Garang already had enough knowledge on how and why peace agreements fail as well as sufficient theoretical knowledge and practical experience on how to be a successful insurgent. His ability to navigate his way through the upper reaches of Sudanese politics, as well as his genius in warfare, testified to that.

9. Security Arrangements Dominate Post-Machakos Talks

When the Machakos breakthrough was achieved, security arrangements rose quickly as a likely thorny issue that could arrest further progress in negotiations. In effect, before the government withdrew from the Machakos II round of talks in early September 2002, an official from the IGAD secretariat said that the toughest remaining issue was security arrangements.[52] At the same time, the *Indian Ocean Newsletter* explained the impasse as follows: "The question of the national army brings up another sensitive point. At this point in the discussions, the southern rebellion refuses to discuss the integration of its men in the national army because, in its opinion, that would water down its hand in the South's struggle for self-determination. The SPLA also demanded that Khartoum pledge to reorganize its various security services that it estimates to number *as many as fourteen,* a figure the authorities reject."[53] Whether or not that figure was correct, it was common knowledge that the NIF had established a network of civil and military security apparatus, each spying on the other. It also established a Gestapo-type apparatus that spread dread and fear among Sudanese, especially those opposing, or suspected of opposing, the NIF government.

To the surprise of the majority of Sudanese, the NIF had made its way to power at a time when totalitarianism was collapsing all over the world. It endeavored to erect its own brand of totalitarian system through the device of *al tamkeen* (consolidation of power). As a result of that policy, emergency laws became a permanent feature of governance rather than an exception to be resorted to sparingly. Incarceration of opponents was also carried out with casual cruelty, and security agents were allowed unimpeded freedom to harass and persecute their victims. That situation, in essence, revealed the contempt of the regime to the people of Sudan, nay to the very Islam on whose values the new system of rule was purportedly built. In every respect, the NIF's multiple security apparatus were to ensconce the regime in power forever, as future experiences had validated. The ardor with which the NIF government strove to remain in power brought to mind Wole Soyinka's adept query: "What is this craving for power that arms the human psyche with such murderous proclivity?"[54] However, having presented its case against the regime's security agencies, the SPLM left the fight for restructuring those agencies to a later date and focused on the armed forces. That was a faux pas the SPLM/A lived to regret.

As to the armed forces, the SPLM was uncompromising on one issue: withdrawal of government troops from the South after an agreement was reached. It argued, as rightly reported by one observer, that the best way to insure the materialization of the referendum on self-determination and respect for its results would be a strong and autonomous SPLA military presence in

135

control of the South. Conversely, said that observer, "the government is extremely hesitant to withdraw from its positions in the south, where it controls most of the large towns and several small garrisons, in case the agreement breaks down during the implementation stage and the parties return to the battlefield."[55] Indeed, the issue of having its own armed forces was a red line for the SPLM/A, as the government slowly came to realize. But until that point in time, the proposal was met with stiff resistance from the government of Sudan, while observer nations at the negotiations, including the United States, were disinclined to seriously entertain a view they considered incompatible with prevailing state practice. Garang's dexterity in modulating brinkmanship with discernment of the fears of the other party was best reflected in his ability to win over both the government of Sudan and the hesitant observers.

10. President Kibaki Pushes for a Cease-Fire

Security arrangements, therefore, topped the agenda of substantive issues for negotiations in the fifth round of talks in April 2003. That round was incorrectly referred to as the fourth round of talks by the IGAD secretariat, since it omitted the one from which the government withdrew in September 2002. Albeit, the April round of talks devoted to security issues was supposed to begin on March 19,[56] but the government once again delayed them. As a result, fears arose that momentum was being lost.

On April 2, 2003, Kenya's President Mwai Kibaki, who took over the reins of government from Moi after the first multiparty elections were concluded, presided over a meeting he organized between President Bashir and Garang. Having never met face-to-face until 2002 (when they met in Kampala),[57] this was now their second meeting in less than one year. General Sumbeiywo recalled soon after: "This was one of the pressure points by the Kenyan government. They were asked when they expected to sign the final ceasefire. Both of them said they were hopeful to get an agreement by the end of June [2003]."[58] In the joint communiqué released after the meeting, the two adversaries "reiterated their confidence in the mediators" and "agreed on the need to maintain the momentum toward reaching a comprehensive peace agreement."[59]

Against this shaky backdrop of need for reassurances at the highest level, the fifth round of talks addressing security arrangements took place between April 7–16, 2003. The talks achieved very little. Nhial Deng Nhial, the SPLM/A's lead negotiator, reported after the talks that the government sought in vain to convince the SPLM/A to integrate their forces into the national army during the transition period. Nhial also said that failure to make progress in the security arrangements was a major setback in the talks because it would have been a safety valve of the whole talks. On the other hand, General Sumbeiywo admitted: "'We can say there was a deadlock, I would like to sincerely express the regret that we have not been able to make the progress expected during this phase of talks.'"[60]

One reason why that round of talks failed was that the government sought to undermine the SPLM/A position by allowing a range of pro-government militia leaders to descend upon Nairobi. Reports at the time indicated that a total of 17 militia groups were represented.[61] Though they were not allowed to participate in the talks, the presence of militia leaders around these talks had, nonetheless, enabled their spokesperson, Commander Martin Kenyi of the Equatoria Defence Force (EDF), to make an unhelpful commotion. Kenyi, speaking to reporters, said, "We are warning that if we are excluded, this agreement will not succeed."[62] That was hardly the type of pressure that would build confidence between the parties. By presenting a divided South to mediators and observers, the government-allied militias sought to sow seeds of doubt regarding the SPLM/A's position, indeed about the viability of the talks. Another militia leader, Chief General Ismael Konyi, militia leader and NCP-appointed governor of Jonglei State, told reporters, "'We came here to seek peace, especially among southern Sudanese...The church is divided, SPLM/A is divided, and the tribes in the south are divided, especially the Nuer and the Dinka.'"[63]

The failure of the April 2003 round of talks affected the IGAD negotiations significantly. In addition, as shall be discussed later in Chapter Seven, talks on the Three Areas that were being held under the government of Kenya auspices, were also making little progress. A new round was thus scheduled for May to address wealth and power sharing, as well as the status of the national capital. Those dilatory tactics gave the impression that both parties were not yet ready for the day of reckoning. Unsurprisingly, the May round of talks, like its predecessors, ended having achieved little. The government's lead negotiator, Ghazi Salahuddin stated that the session ended having "'made very little progress toward peace in the Sudan.'"[64]

The IGAD secretariat, however, sought to sound more optimistic in its communiqué: "The parties engaged constructively in the talks through consultations on all the agenda items. We have jointly set out to develop an all-inclusive negotiating framework on all the outstanding issues in power sharing, wealth sharing, and security arrangements."[65] Security arrangements, then, would now be dealt concurrently with outstanding disagreements over power and wealth sharing. The moderator and observers had rightly thought fit to disaggregate soft and hard issues. But as future events proved, security arrangements remained the one issue that had, time and again, put the peace negotiations in jeopardy. Even after the conclusion of the CPA, security arrangements remained a boiling point. Up to the close of the interim period it still represented a flashpoint in the implementation of the Comprehensive Peace Agreement.

NOTES

1   "Sudan Says Deal Is 'Turning Point' in Peace Talks with Rebels," *Agence France-Presse*, July 20, 2002.
2   "Sudan Rebels Say Ceasefire Will Be Last Item on Peace Agenda," *Agence France-Presse*, July 20, 2002.
3   "Khartoum 'Suspends' Peace Talks with Rebels, Orders Army Mobilisation," Agence France-Presse (Khartoum), September 2, 2002.
4   Waihenya, *The Mediator*, 95.
5   Ibid.
6   "Annan Urges Sides to Resume Talks," UN Integrated Regional Information Networks, September 5, 2002.
7   Katy Salmon, "Politics: Sudan Mediators Cautiously Optimistic on Peace," Inter Press Service (Nairobi), September 4, 2002.
8   Waihenya, *The Mediator*, 96.
9   Ibid.
10 "Sudan Sends Emissaries to Explain Suspension of Peace Talks with Rebels," Associated Press, September 9, 2002.
11 Ibid.
12 "Sudan Rebels 'on the March,'" *BBC News*, September 10, 2002.
13 "Sudan: Government Aircraft Bomb Torit," UN Integrated Regional Information Networks (Nairobi), September 10, 2002.
14 Waihenya, *The Mediator*, 97.
15 "Kenyan President Reportedly Holds Talks with Sudanese Rebel Leader Garang," BBC Monitoring, *Al-Ra'y al-Amm*, September 12, 2002.
16 Charles Cobb Jr., "Sudan: Ceasefire Will Bring Us Back to Talks, Says Foreign Minister," *all Africa.com* (Washington, DC), September 20, 2002, http://allafrica.com/stories/200209200828.html.
17 "Khartoum Gives Conditions for Resumption of Peace Talks," PanAfrican News Agency Daily Newswire, September 21, 2002.
18 "Sudan: Rebels Offer Temporary Ceasefire," UN Integrated Regional Information Network (Nairobi), September 30, 2002.
19 Waihenya, *The Mediator*, 98.
20 Ibid.
21 "Sudan to Complain to UN Security Council against Eritrean 'Attacks'", BBC Monitoring, Middle East News Agency (Khartoum), October 5, 2002.
22 "Sudan Recaptures Key Town," BBC News, October 8, 2002.
23 "Sudan: Government Claims Recapture of Torit," UN Integrated Regional Information Networks, October 8, 2002.
24 See "Sudanese Army Recaptures Stronghold from Southern Rebels," Agence France-Presse, October 8, 2002. For the view of General Sumbeiywo, see Waihenya, *The Mediator*, 98.
25 "Sudan Peace Talks to Resume," BBC News, October 4, 2002.

26 Government of the Sudan and Sudan People's Liberation Movement/Army (SPLM/A), *Memorandum of Understanding between the Government of the Sudan and the Sudan People's Liberation Movement/Army (SPLM/a) on Resumption of Negotiations on Peace in Sudan. Signed 15 October 2002* (Nairobi: Intergovernmental Authority for Development, 2002).

27 Waihenya, *The Mediator*, 99.

28 "Sudan Truce Deal Signed," BBC News, October 15, 2002.

29 Supra 26, Clause 3

30 Clause 3, Ceasefire Memorandum of Understanding between the Government of Sudan and Sudan People's Liberation Movement/Army (SPLM/A) and *Memorandum of Understanding* 2001.

31 Ibid., Clause 8.

32 "Sudan Denies Violating Cease-Fire, Says It Is Fighting Eritrea's Aggression," Associated Press, October 18, 2002.

33 "Sudan's Govt, Rebels Accused Each Other of Truce Violations," Agence France-Presse, October 25, 2002.

34 Mohamed Ali Saeed, "Sudanese Troops Prepare to Recapture Territory in East," Agence France-Presse (Khartoum), November 6, 2002.

35 "US Envoy Says Last Round of Talks 'Very Successful,'" *Khartoum Monitor*, November 22, 2002.

36 "US Steps up Contacts in Sudan Peace Process," *Agence France-Presse*, December 2, 2002.

37 "Sudan: Bush Signs 'Peace Act,'" UN Integrated Regional Information Networks (Nairobi), October 22, 2002.

38 On August 16, 1996, the U.N. Security Council adopted yet another resolution to tighten measures imposed on the government of Sudan for "the terrorist assassination attempt on the life of President Mubarak of Egypt." The resolution called on "all states' members to deny aircraft permission to take off from, land in, or overfly their territories if the aircraft is registered in Sudan or owned, leased, or operated by, or on behalf of, Sudan Airways or by any undertaking wherever located or organized, which is substantially owned or controlled by Sudan Airways."

39 For an account of this period and the impact the change of government and president in Kenya had on the IGAD mediation, especially General Sumbeiywo, see Waihenya, *The Mediator*, 103-110.

40 "Third Round of Sudanese Peace Talks Open in Kenya," Agence France-Presse (Nairobi), January 23, 2003.

41 Ibid.

42 "Southern Sudanese Rebels Request Suspension of Talks for a Day," Agence France-Presse (Nairobi), January 27, 2003.

43 "Sudan Peace Talks Resume after Setback over Truce Violations," Agence France-Presse (Nairobi), January 29, 2003.

44 Salmon, Katy, "Politics-Sudan: The End of War within Reach—Mediator," Inter Press Service (Nairobi), February 6, 2003.

45 See Waihenya, *The Mediator*, 101–02.

46 Salmon, "Politics-Sudan: The End of War within Reach—Mediator.

47 Ibid.

48 Garang was seeking iron-clad guarantees for the implementation of the CPA which he described as "organic" i.e entrenched within the terms of the agreement.

49 Abel Alier, *Southern Sudan: Too Many Agreements Dishonoured* (Ithaca, NY: Ithaca Press, 1992), 261.

50 Ibid., 281–87. See also Johnson, *The Root Causes of Sudan's Civil Wars*, 60–62.

51 General Yousif visited Garang in Addis Ababa in 1986 to convey to him a message from the Transitional Military Council with a view to engaging him in peace talks. In response to that message, Garang told the general that he had no trust in the Khartoum generals, but he had full confidence in Yousif. He added that since he knew that political circles in Khartoum would not trust his motives, Garang was ready to cede his leadership in the SPLM/A to the general. Khalid, *War and Peace in Sudan*, 170

52 "Sudanese Peace Talks Likely to End Earlier: Official," *Xinhua*, 30 August 2002.

53 "During Talks, the War Continues," *The Indian Ocean Newsletter*, 30 August 2002.

54 "The Deceptive Silence of Stolen Voices: Lecture Honouring the 70th birthday of Chief Emeka Anyaoku, former secretary general of the Commonwealth." Lecture delivered in Abuja, July 2004. http://www.dawodu.com/soyinka3.htm

55 Dave Mozersky, "Reinforcing Peace in the Sudan," *Peace Magazine*, October–December 2002, 25.

56 "Sudan Peace Talks to Resume on March 19," Agence France-Presse (Nairobi), February 20, 2003.

57 "Sudan President, Rebel Head Meet in Nairobi," Agence France-Presse, April 2, 2003.

58 "Interview with Lazarus Sumbeiywo, Chief Mediator in the Peace Talks," UN Integrated Regional Information Networks (Nairobi), May 30, 2003.

59 "Sudan Foes End Peace Talk Round without Agreeing on Security Issue," Agence France-Presse, April 16, 2003.

60 Makur Kot Dhuor, "Sudan: Militias Solicit for 'Inclusive and Comprehensive' Pact," African Church Information Service (Nairobi), May 26, 2003.

61 Ibid.

62 Ibid.

63 "Sudan Peace Talks Adjourn after Little Progress," PanAfrican News Agency, May 21, 2003.

64 Ibid.

65 Ibid.

Chapter Five
The Nakuru Document: Crisis and Opportunity

■ ■ ■ ■ ■ ■ ■ ■ ■ ■ ■ ■ ■ ■ ❖ ■ ■ ■ ■ ■ ■ ■ ■ ■ ■ ■ ■ ■

> Peace is indivisible.
> —**Maxim Litvinov**
> *Note to the Allies*, 1920

1. Introduction

It is reported that in the Chinese language the word "crisis" is depicted in two characters: one symbolizing trouble, the other opportunity. And so was the crisis generated by the Nakuru document, encapsulating the "all-inclusive negotiating framework" hinted at by the Intergovernmental Authority on Development (IGAD) secretariat at the close of the sixth round of talks. The document was meant by the secretariat to constitute a point of departure for the talks. Sumbeiywo characterized it as a "holistic approach." In his words, it was "about looking at everything in totality. There are many areas in which the parties have not agreed on and we have bracketed some of these issues which might be used by the parties to trade off one thing for another. But they cannot agree to trade off without knowing what is in it for them in this context."[1] With the two most contentious issues—self-determination for southern Sudan and religion and state—resolved in Machakos, no less troublesome issues remained. Those substantially included power and wealth sharing, democratic transformation, contextualization of cultural diversity, and the status of the national capital. In addition, a need existed to embellish on the broad lines agreed upon in Machakos on security arrangements, autonomy of southern Sudan, and protection of the rights of non-Muslims in the national capital.

Those were the issues on which the mediator and his team elaborated at a meeting in Nakuru, Kenya, and eventually presented to the parties.

But before any discussion commenced within the framework of that document, the two parties had to come to terms on the document itself. The Sudan People's Liberation Movement/Army (SPLM/A) accepted it as proposed, though spuriously claimed that it did not respond to all of its demands. In its response to the document dated July 11, 2003, the SPLM/A said that though "the draft Framework neither addresses all the concerns nor satisfies the perspectives of the SPLM/SPLA on some important and critical issues of the conflict, but nevertheless we recognize that the document contains most of the important elements for a just and lasting peace." It also added that "Given the time, effort and resources invested by the international community into this process, the SPLM/SPLA affirms its unwavering commitment to the IGAD mediation as the only forum that has taken us much nearer to achieving peace for our country."[2] On the other hand, President Bashir, in his first public response to the document on July 15, considered it unreasonable and demanded that the mediators "'come up with a reasonable alternative, otherwise they have to dissolve the document in water and drink it.'" And if they insisted on their draft, Bashir added, "'let IGAD and those behind it go to hell.'"[3] President Bashir, known for temper tantrums, had patently over-excelled himself on that occasion. But what he did not ponder was that if the peace negotiators and "those behind them"—the six IGAD countries and observers—went to hell, then they would inevitably drag others with them to the abode of the damned. The IGAD peace talks, according to observers, entered a moment of grave crisis after the president's message;[4] however, empirical evidence had proved that words in Sudanese politics, much too often, did not mean what they said. Consequently, one had every reason to assume that the document was not totally blackballed.

Realizing that things were at a very critical stage, the mediator decided to consult more widely and at much higher levels within the two parties. This, he said, necessitated "visiting the country [Sudan]" in order to "be able to detect the best way to proceed" and "enable me to complete the draft agreement."[5] Sumbeiywo and members of his team traveled to areas held by the SPLM/A in southern Sudan (Rumbek, Yambio, Yei, Malualkon, Ikotos, and Agok. The latter was the area where the Ngok Dinka from Abyei had settled). The mediator also visited the Blue Nile (Kurmuk and Damazin), and the Nuba Mountains (Kauda and Kadugli) as well as Khartoum and government-held garrisons in southern Sudan (Malakal, Heglig, Rubkona, Bentiu, Wau, and Juba).[6]

That excursion enabled the mediator to have a sounder feel of the place and a better grasp of the issues. According to Sumbeiywo's biography: "In almost all the places he went to under SPLM/A control, at stake was not the oil or the natural resources. The people did not mind dividing the oil or living under sharia law. This was not an immediate concern. All they wanted was to have their own Army. 'Stop the war,' a group of people shouted, 'Let's remain with our army, let the Arabs remain with their capital.'" No doubt this was a grave oversimplification of the situation, but the people the general met in southern Sudan, Nuba Mountains, and Blue Nile had one thing on their mind: security of person and an end to the spoilage and destruction of war.[7] To that end they had every reason to pin their hopes on their army: the SPLA. Notwithstanding, the general's understanding of the gravity and significance of security arrangements was certainly made clearer.

2. Squabble over Nakuru Document

In summary, the Nakuru document offered the south the vice presidency position at the national level, while the SPLM's requested for the alternation of the presidency during the interim period between the current president of Sudan and the chairman of the SPLM. Additionally, the document proposed a 50 percent share of oil revenues to each side; a national capital free for all religions; a separate army for southern Sudan; and 35 percent of the political and civil service positions in the central government. The IGAD secretariat also presented another document relating to the Three Areas, which focused on a strong decentralized governance and a referendum during the first half of the interim period on the status of Abyei (whether to be part of Bahr el Ghazal or Western Kordofan).[8] Sumbeiywo recalled in his biography that the Nakuru document raised what he "could not have known at that time." The document, he said, stirred the hornet's nest and had almost "become the bane of the talks."[9] Nevertheless, Sumbeiywo and Kenya's foreign affairs minister, Kalonzo Musyoka, "rallied the entire region to support the document."[10] According to the general, his strategy was not meant to present the document as a take-it-or-leave-it text but rather one that could be changed as long as both parties agreed. The government, however, refused to negotiate on the text at all.

At the same time as an African Union summit was being held in Maputo, Mozambique (July 8-11, 2013), Sudan's foreign minister presented a paper to the Council of Ministers preceding the summit in which he requested that South Africa take over the role of mediator. South Africa initially agreed, but Kenya's Musyoka dissuaded it from doing so.[11] The government of Sudan then approached the Egyptians and the League of Arab States through Riak Gai, a southern Sudanese politician aligned to the National Congress Party (NCP). Gai told Amr Musa, secretary general of the Arab League, that "the Sudanese people and government's desire [is] to see Egypt play an important role in any mediation between the parties to the conflict in order **to maintain the unity of Sudan** and protect its stability" (emphasis added).[12] Separately, the government requested that Kenyan president Mwai Kibaki replace General Sumbeiywo as mediator.[13] When Kibaki succeeded Daniel arap Moi as president of Kenya, Kibaki was about to replace Sumbeiywo as mediator, not for the general's failure to carry out the mediation mission entrusted to him, but because he was considered a leftover from Moi's government. Fortunately for the sake of Sudan's peace, Kalonzo Musyoka, who retained his post as foreign minister in Kibaki's government, dissuaded the new president from that decision. Notwithstanding, by making an issue of the impartiality of the mediator, the government went back to its old tactics of playing one country against the other and one peace envoy against another. When the SPLM/A learned of the government's tactics in Maputo, it assessed the situation with the cynicism of long experience. Samson Kwaje told reporters that this was "'typical of Khartoum's policy of "forum shopping" whenever it is confronted with truth.'" He warned, "The SPLM/A will not leave the IGAD process and will not follow the Sudan government wherever it goes on its mission of forum shopping."[14]

The parties returned to negotiations in Nakuru in early July 2003, but ahead of the negotiations Sumbeiywo presented them with the essence of what would be the "Draft Framework for Resolution of Outstanding Issues Arising out of the Elaborations of the Machakos Protocol" (the Nakuru document).[15] The document aspired to give substance to Sumbeiywo's holistic approach, presenting a starting point for negotiations on the outstanding issues of security arrangements, wealth sharing, and power sharing. On the issue of security arrangements, the document called for the creation of two armies: Sudan's national army and a southern Sudan army.[16] The proposition provoked the government of Sudan immensely. In a written submission to the IGAD mediators dated July 11, 2003, the government took exception to nearly all the negotiating points in the Document.[17] Regarding security arrangements, the government claimed that Sumbeiywo's proposition undermined the country's unity by calling for "a completely separate army for southern Sudan." Instead, it proposed as a "middle ground subject to further negotiations" that "there shall be a single united National Armed Force (NAF)" and that "all armed forces shall be integrated in the National Armed Force (NAF) before the end of the interim period according to agreed arrangements."[18] The government should have known that its proposition would be nothing less than a Hobson's choice to the SPLM/A, especially given the experience of its leader with similar arrangements under the Addis Ababa agreement. On other outstanding issues, the government's position is hereunder detailed and analyzed.

2.1 Power and Wealth Sharing

The Nakuru document's suggestions on power and wealth sharing were clearly aimed at a middle ground between the positions of the parties. It is useful to examine these proposals in detail, especially since the government had hit the proverbial roof on the release of the Nakuru document. Yet, in many respects, the document would bear close resemblance to the final protocols on wealth and power sharing agreed upon by the government of Sudan and the SPLM/A. Evidently, it was not the "mediators and those behind them" who eventually "soaked the document and drank its water." The Nakuru document proposed as follows:[19]

2.1.1 Power Sharing

On the issue of power sharing, the main points of concentration in the document related to the national presidency, governance of southern Sudan, national legislature, executive and civil service, and the national capital. The mediator's proposal on these issues were as follows:

i. **National Presidency**

With respect to the presidency, the Nakuru document sought to pivot the issue on national elections, leaving it to the parties to decide when those elections should first be held during the interim period. Elections were thus envisaged as the culmination of a democratic transformation process. During the interim period, however, the document proposed:

- Until such time as elections are held, the current incumbent President (or his successor or nominee) shall be President and Commander-in-Chief of the Sudan People's Armed Forces (SPAF). The Vice President shall be the current SPLM/A Chairman (or his successor or nominee) who shall at the same time hold the post of Chairman/Head of the Government of Southern Sudan and Commander-in-Chief of the Sudan People's Liberation Armed Forces (SPLAF), the armed force previously referred to as the Sudan People's Liberation Army (SPLA).
- The President shall be elected in national elections; the position of Vice President shall be filled by the person who has been elected to the post of Chairman/Head of the Government of Southern Sudan. However, in the eventuality that a person from the South wins the Presidential elections, the non-southerner with the most votes from the Northern States in the Presidential elections shall become the Vice President.

ii. **Government of Southern Sudan Executive**

Until such time as elections are held, the current SPLM/A Chairman (or his successor or nominee) shall be Chairman/Head of the Government of Southern Sudan (GOSS). He shall at the same time hold the post of Vice-President of the Sudan and Commander-in-Chief of the Sudan People's Liberation Armed Forces [Sudan People's Liberation Army]...The Vice-Chairman of the [government of Southern Sudan] shall be appointed by the chairman.

iii.   National Legislature

As regards the National Parliament, the NCP was awarded an absolute majority until elections, while southern representation was set at one-third. Specifically, the Nakuru document suggested the following:

> Sixty-six and two thirds percent (66.6%) being members representing the North of whom fifty one (51%) of the total number of Assembly members shall be from the current National Assembly [dominated by NCP] and fifteen and two-thirds percent (15.6%) shall be from otherwise unrepresented forces or parties so as to promote inclusiveness and stability; and thirty-three and one-third percent (33.3%) being members from the South of whom twenty-six percent (26%) of the total number of Assembly members shall be appointed by the SPLM/A and seven and one-third percent (7.3%) shall be from other forces, parties or sitting members from the South.

iv.   National Executive and Civil Service

Relating to national ministries, the Nakuri document classified cabinet portfolios in clusters—sovereignty, economic, and services—and proposed in clause 4.7.2 that SPLM/A representation in each of the clusters should be "at least twenty-five percent," and that "such representation means both twenty-five percent (25%) of the Ministers and Deputy Ministers." It suggested the NCP proportion be at least fifty percent.

To address imbalances and inequities in the national civil service, the Nakuru document proposed that between 25 to 35 percent of newly recruited national civil servants would be drawn from southern Sudanese who qualified, though the exact proportion shall be based on the outcome of the proposed census. In this respect, the document put forward that no less than 20 percent of middle and upper level positions in the National Civil Service (**including the positions of Undersecretaries**) [be filled] with qualified persons from the South **within the first three years** [emphasis added]. It is to be recalled that up until the time when the IGAD mediators proposed ending disparities in the national civil service, no single department undersecretary, chairperson of a public corporation, army chief of staff, or commissioner general of police hailed from southern Sudan. The Nakuru document also suggested the establishment of a border commission (clause 7) and made some rudimentary suggestions regarding matters of "Amnesty, Reparations, Truth, Justice, and Reconciliation" (clause 8).

v.   National Capital

Concerning the status of the national capital, the Nakuru document treaded cautiously. In part, this reflected the government-supported protests that greeted General Sumbeiywo when he visited Khartoum the previous month. The public demonstrations were meant to show the general the support shari'a had in that city. Thus, instead of being specific on the status of shari'a in Khartoum, the document suggested the designation of an area within that city that should fall under national administration. Clause 3.1 suggested: "The National Capital shall be a symbol of unity that should reflect the diversity of the Nation. Khartoum city shall be the Capital of the Republic of the Sudan. A district within the city of Khartoum, within which the buildings and offices of the national government are situated, as well as the site of the National Parliament, shall be known as the Capital District of the Sudan." It further suggested in clause 3.4: "The National Assembly shall be responsible for the administration of the Capital District and in enacting laws, and bylaws, shall take into account the religious and cultural diversity of the Sudanese people."

2.2 Wealth Sharing—Land and Oil

On wealth sharing, the document focused attention on subterranean natural resources, oil being the most contentious issue in the negotiations. In addition, the document was on the lookout for a common ground on land ownership, oil revenue sharing, as well as modalities for wealth sharing in general. It also emphasised priorities that needed to be met with regard to reconstruction and capacity building of southern Sudan and other war-affected areas, and dipped into the issue of currency.

2.2.1 Land

Concerning land, the document called on the parties to "reaffirm the principle that Sudanese law pertaining to land, including in Southern Sudan, is based on, among other things, local customary laws and traditional communal rights to land" (clause 11.6). In order to address grievances and uncertainties arising from such recognition, it proposed in clause 12 that the parties set up a National Land Commission in the interim period, which would, inter alia, focus upon:

- The content of customary/communal land rights;
- The relationship between customary/communal land rights and other rights in land;
- The criteria for recognizing customary/communal land rights;
- The principles for deciding whether, and to whom, compensation should be paid as a result of recognition of customary/communal land rights.

The SPLM's assertion of communal ownership of land was intended to guard against government land grabbing and to give primacy to customary law relating to land disputes. Also in the back of the SPLM negotiators' minds were national legislations that were promulgated in the recent past with a view to attracting investors, but which resulted in divesting local communities of traditional land holdings. One such law was the Unregistered Lands Act

(1970), which was promulgated during the early years of Nimeiri's rule and made all nonregistered land automatically government owned, as if that land was terra nullius. Equally, that law did not pay regard to traditional community ownership, or *usufruct*, of that land by those communities. The expropriated land was invariably allocated to northern investors, mainly businessmen and retired army officers and civil servants. These so-called investors, except few established businessmen, were funded by government-owned banks, with the land used as collateral for the loans. Coincidentally, all expropriated lands, except those in Gedaref in eastern Sudan, were either situated in south Sudan (northern Upper Nile), Blue Nile (Aggady), or the Nuba Mountains (Habila).

The 1970 Act was repealed in 1990 and replaced by the Civil Transactions Act, which was adopted by the National Islamic Front (NIF) as an integral part of its policy to Islamicize laws. That act expressly prohibited recognition of customary land rights and gave a legal definition to land ownership that could hardly be applied by worldly justices: It provided that "land belongs to Allah and the state is His successor." With this legal surrealism there was every reason for the SPLM negotiators, or indeed any temporal jurist, to be sceptical about the laws. The SPLM/A's call for recognition of community rights to land was, therefore, defensible both in light of the prevailing law and practice. Notwithstanding, when the chicken came home to roost, the government of Southern Sudan, before anybody else, suffered from the legal contrivance it fought to introduce into the agreement in the course of negotiating the land issue at Naivasha. As a result, up to this day the government of Southern Sudan is unable to persuade the government of the State of Central Equatoria, which houses southern Sudan's capital town, Juba, or convince the Bari community, who are the predominant traditional owners of the land, to allocate land within that city to be capital of South Sudan under the tutelage of its government. The justification for that intransigence had always been: "Dr. John said land belongs to the people." That is one example of how misread, or misunderstood, provisions in the Comprehensive Peace Agreement can become counterproductive.

2.2.2 Oil

On the subject of oil, the Nakuru document suggested establishing a National Petroleum Commission with bipartisan representation to oversee oil production policy and implementation (clause 14). Clause 14.2 provided that: "The approval of development and exploitation of all petroleum resources shall only be carried out through the Petroleum Commission." The Petroleum Commission was to comprise permanent or representative members, depending upon the specific decisions under examination. The document proposed that "any contracts approved by the Petroleum Commission *must* be signed by the Minister of Energy on behalf of the government of the Sudan" (clause 14.9). Conversely, "if a member, of the Petroleum Commission, whether permanent or representing a petroleum producing state, disagrees with a decision of the Commission to approve a contract relating to his or her state, the Minister of Energy must not sign the contract and must refer the matter to the Council of States" (clause 14.10). And since the mediator rightly guessed that the government of Sudan would not be well disposed to open a Pandora's box by subjecting existing oil contracts to examination, that is, contracts signed by it before the conclusion of the peace agreement, the Nakuru document suggested in clause 15 that the SPLM/A "shall appoint a limited number of representatives to have access to all existing oil contracts." The SPLM/A had always suspected that those contracts had given very generous terms to companies, especially Chinese, in return to providing it with armament.

As for oil revenues, the mediators (clause 16) departed from their early position of urging the SPLM to take the government's skimpy offer on revenue sharing (10%) by claiming that "something is better than nothing." A new formula was set out for oil revenue sharing, namely that from the first day of the interim period forward, two percent (2%) of the net revenue from oil contracts (existing and new) should be transferred to the oil-producing state, and where the oil was extracted from a state in southern Sudan, 48 percent (48%) of the balance should be paid to the government of Southern Sudan and the remainder of the proceeds to the government of Sudan. The document also suggested, somewhat optimistically for the interim period, that the parties set up a Future Generations Fund "once national oil production reaches two (2) million barrels per day" (clause 16.6).

2.3 Reconstruction and Development

Furthermore, the document proposed detailed fiscal redistribution figures aimed at reconstruction of the south and war-affected areas as well as general budgetary requirements (clause 18). Specifically, it propounded that the national government transfer annually 35 billion Sudanese dinar to southern Sudan (approximately 140 million U.S. dollars in 2003) for general budgetary expenditures (clause 18.4). It also put forward that an increasing range of amounts be allocated through the interim period based on gross domestic product (GDP) percentages for reconstruction, development, and reintegration, ranging from 0.3 percent of GDP, or 12.5 billion Sudanese dinar (approximately 50 million U.S. dollars in 2003) in year one, to 1.2 percent of GDP in years three through six (clause 18.5). In clause 18.6, the document proposed that the southern states and the government of Southern Sudan "shall retain and dispose of such other incomes raised and collected under their own taxing powers." This is what later became known as nonoil revenues.

149

2.4 Currency

The other economic proposal to note in the Nakuru document concerned currency and banking arrangements. In clause 25.2, the Nakuru document provided, "There shall be a single currency for the whole of the Sudan. The Central Bank of Sudan shall adopt a programme to issue a new currency." Also in clause 25, the document advanced that a Bank of Southern Sudan be established as a branch of the Central Bank of Sudan (clause 25.4), and the Bank of Southern Sudan would be tasked and supported to establish "the central banking facilities that are necessary for the working of conventional and Islamic financial institutions located in southern Sudan" (clause 25.11). The Bank of Southern Sudan was also empowered to charter conventional banks in southern Sudan.

3. Government Rails against Nakuru Document

The government was furiously incensed by the Nakuru document, specially its provisions on power- and wealth-sharing. But rather than settling for President Bashir's censorious statement, "soak it and drink its water," the NCP decided to refute the document point by point. With the unmistakable imprint of Ghazi Salahuddin's painstaking style, its detailed written response of July 11, 2003, raised a range of objections. However, in an untiringly combative manner, the objections were primarily oriented around the contention that the Nakuru document was "anti-unity" and many of its proposals were described by the government as illogical, flawed, or failed to see the bigger picture as many of the issues raised were matters *to be negotiated* and not yet decided. In other words, the government concluded that the mediator was precipitate and ahead of himself. The points raised by the government in its rebuttal of the Nakuru document were as follows:

(i) Power Sharing

On this issue the government argued that the Nakuru document was one-sided, favoring the SPLM/A's priorities, and that it strengthened the south at the expense of the center and the north, thus "shifting the balance towards southern secession." In further details, the government's response enumerated what it considered lacunae, or flaws, in the Nakuru document

- Giving the president and the national government a limited role in the South, even where the role is called for by the document itself such as the appointment of the deputy chairman of the regional government of the South (2.1.2.2)
- Failing to emphasize, or even mention, the decentralization of the South (2.1.2.5)

- Suggesting the creation of a Ministry for Defense in the regional government of the South (2.1.2.8)
- While it appropriately called for national presidential elections, the document left the post of the vice president [in southern Sudan] to be filled as a result of regional elections in which only the voters of southern Sudan participate (2.1.2.7).
- Complete failure to recognize that the principle of power sharing should apply to both the national government and the regional government of southern Sudan and the states in southern Sudan, and paying attention only to demands of the SPLM as regards its (and not the South's) share in the national government, to the complete elimination of any accommodation of the National Congress Party in the government of the southern region (3.1)
- Employing an appeasement approach that ignored the totality approach when it came to qualitative representation in the national cabinet, as it said nothing about the incompatibility of the constitutionalization of a defense ministry for the South while opening up of all cabinet posts at the national level for the SPLM (3.4)
- Being "hopelessly oblivious" of the danger [inherent in] lack of recognition of the non-SPLM southerners [and the dangers that this] could pose to the sustainability of the peace (3.5)
- Neglecting the elections, one of the outstanding issues to them. This could have been a benign omission were it not for the fact that the framework pushed the timing of the census [Nakuru document clause 4.3.3] to the end of the first half of the interim period, which automatically pushes the election to the second half of the interim period. This decision of the drafter favors one side's early position, without any justification (4.1).
- Removing the option of having a presidency comprised of a president and one or more vice president(s) (4.5).

Three things emerged from that criticism. First, the government was clear that the government of Sudan and the NCP at that point were not contemplating the creation of a full-fledged autonomous regime in the south; thus the Sudan government sought to assign a role for the national president in appointing the vice president of southern Sudan. Second, what transpired from the rebuttal was the desire of the government of Sudan to create distorted, asymmetrical relations between the national government ruling the whole Sudan and the government of the north overseeing the northern state. The perception by the SPLM of the national government becoming a government of the north became a reality when the final peace agreement was concluded, and both north and south Sudan suffered greatly from the anomaly. Third, while decrying the failure of the Nakuru document to accommodate the North in the government of the South, it only referred to representation by the NCP, not other northern parties, in the proposed southern Sudan government.

(ii) Wealth Sharing

The government argued in unconvincing and vague terms that the Nakuru document drafters had disrupted the "technical" progress both parties were making on the different issues, benefiting from inputs by various experts. It also argued that the drafters had oversimplified the complex principles discussed in previous talks and arrived at a range of figures that suited the SPLM/A. If the government's tactic at the time was to stall and prolong the negotiations, its spurious objections on these points were good evidence for this. The government said of the Nakuru document:[20]

- "As regards budgetary allocations and equalization, the government's rebuttal claimed that the parties had agreed in the last round of talks to "convene a technical group meeting supported by the World Bank and IMF consultants to agree with the parties to work out the allocation based on an agreed upon framework. Instead of doing that, [the government has] been presented with a set of figures which is far removed from what had already been projected, and which in our opinion defeats the principles referred to earlier" (5.3).

- "The issue of land and rights was extensively thrashed out in the last round with the valuable assistance of an Australian expert and it was decided that a land commission shall be set up to address land claims, with consideration to the need for progressive legal review that keeps abreast of modernization requirements, and a means for compensating lawful claimants. Yet the land issue appeared again in such a way that complicates the problem and takes it out of the context in which it has been dealt with in draft (8)" of the wealth-sharing protocol (5.4).

- "The approach to subterranean natural resources as envisaged by the consultants in the last round was a very positive one. It stressed the need for focusing on the revenues emanating from subterranean resources rather than who owns them. On that basis, the suggested framework for allocation was developed. We now see in the proposed document a departure from this if read with what is suggested in the land ownership part" (5.5).

- "To have a unified fiscal and monetary policy, it was technically agreed that there should be one Central Bank with a branch in the South with a very clear mandate and boundary. Reference to the bank in the document as the Bank of Southern Sudan clouds the issue and makes it look like an independent entity" (5.6).

- Concerning membership of the Petroleum Commission, "it was agreed that the Regional Government in the South will have one representative as the producing states will have their representatives as well. What appears in the document is unlimited membership" (5.7).

- "The document states **'persons enjoying rights in land shall be consulted and their consent shall be sought in respect of decisions to develop subterranean natural resources'** [Nakuru document] item 13.1.3. The underlined phrase is an addition which has never been entertained before in the discussions" (5.8). (emphasis added)

The SPLM/A, it may be recalled, accepted the Nakuru document as a basis for negotiations, notwithstanding the fact that it "neither [addressed] all the concerns, nor [satisfied] the perspectives of the SPLM/SPLA on some important and critical issues of the conflict."[21] Indeed, the subsequent positions of the SPLM/A on wealth and power sharing indicated that it had substantive concerns with the Nakuru document. These are discussed further in later sections.

Later, in August 2003, foreign minister Mustafa Osman Ismail made out the government to be a bastion of political pluralism and castigated the SPLM/A and Nakuru document drafters. "One of the reasons the government rejects the Nakuru document," he stated, "is that it calls for political pluralism in the North and does not do so in the South; rather, it makes the South the monopoly of the SPLM." Ismail went on to say that "political pluralism is a preventive measure, a means of salvation, and a national necessity," adding that the president of the republic "had made it a priority in his second term to abide by political pluralism and affirmed in his recent meeting at the Republican Palace with the leaders of the different political forces that there is no going back on this path."[22] This discursive statement was simply self-serving and hollow to the core. Without adornments, political pluralism is political dispensation that entails multiplicity of parties who compete with each other on level ground for votes from enfranchised constituencies. It is, therefore, not through presidential announcements that such a system shall be established.

The government, in its strong and drawn-out rebuttal, was conspicuously silent on the Nakuru document's rather vague provisions for the status of shari'a in the capital. Such silence suggested that it was quite satisfied with the failure of the mediators to achieve any clarity on this thorny issue. Indeed, the issue of the capital would remain the elephant in the room until 2004, looming over the talks as the big symbolic issue that spoke, as we had suggested, to what appeared to be the paltry commitment of the government to protecting the unity of the country. The president admitted as much in early 2004, when the outstanding issues for agreement were power sharing and the Three Areas. He told reporters that the government's negotiating team in Kenya was under orders to "observe three areas: no relinquishing of Islamic shari'a laws, no dismantling of north Sudan, and, last, unity as a *preferable* option" (italics added).[23] Nevertheless, after much diplomatic maneuvering and persuasion, the government reluctantly returned to the IGAD negotiations in August 2003. That reluctance presaged little prospect for constructive negotiations. On August 9, ahead of the talks scheduled between August 11 and 23 in Nanyuki, Kenya, President Bashir was reported to have said on national television that the Nakuru document "was aimed at dismantling not only the present regime but the whole of Sudan."[24] Unsurprisingly, therefore, the August round of talks in Nanyuki focused on power and wealth sharing and achieved little.

4. New Alignments

Meanwhile, the failure of the April and May talks led the SPLM to re-engage with the northern opposition and the National Democratic Alliance (NDA) to reassure them and gain their support. On May 21, 2003, just as the fifth round of talks ended, the exiled leader of the Democratic Unionist Party (DUP), Mohamed Osman al-Mirghani, had warned that the IGAD would fail as long as the northern opposition in the eastern front remained sidelined. He dismissed the "partial" peace talks as serving no purpose.[25] In that assessment, al-Mirghani did not factor in the underachievement of the northern political parties in providing forces in eastern Sudan with the appropriate wherewithal that would have enabled them to prosecute the struggle more effectively and thus ward off pressures by outside powers on the SPLM/A to sue for peace at any cost.

A meeting in Cairo held on May 25 brought together Garang, the Umma Party's Sadiq al-Mahdi, and Mohamed Osman al-Mirghani. The face-to-face meeting between the leaders of the SPLM/A and Umma was the first since the Umma left the NDA and sought to conciliate with the NCP. After the talks, the three leaders issued a joint statement promising to "make all efforts to support the current negotiations and to forge a national consensus through the participation of all political forces."[26] Al-Mahdi, needless to say, was seeking once more to be part of the opposition after having been cold-shouldered by the NIF.

On June 3, Nhial Deng Nhial and the Popular National Congress (PNC) party's Ali al-Hajj met in London and agreed on some common points regarding peace and democratic transition. The joint working paper produced from that meeting called for "democratic transition that allows for complete freedom, through a direct practical approach accommodating all including those of the regime."[27] The London meeting was followed by a meeting of the NDA in Asmara, Eritrea, that concluded on June 18, 2003, during which Garang updated his partners in the alliance on the IGAD talks and the joint working paper with the PNC. There were murmurings from some NDA members about the SPLM's deal with Turabi's party, the PNC. Garang explained that Turabi and his party were no longer the government but an opposition force against Bashir. Not only were his NDA colleagues flummoxed by Garang's deal with Turabi, but the Egyptians also were. In an interview by Egyptian journalist Hamdi Rizg, writing for the Cairo weekly *Al Mussawar*, Garang was asked: "Why would you agree with Turabi who was the ideologue of the Ingaz?" Garang answered: "Do you want me to talk to the bishop rather than to the Pope?" In politics, Garang said, there were neither permanent friends nor permanent enemies. Regarding the peace process, however, the final communiqué of the NDA meeting reported that Garang believed that "the IGAD initiative had not realized meaningful progress after the signing of the Machakos Protocol, adding that the SPLM/A was striving to realize a national consensus by involving all political parties.

5. The Principals Step In

As the Nakuru document became "hellish" since President Bashir called its authors to "go to hell with it," the peace talks once again reached a major impasse. Under great external pressure, the government delayed and then agreed in mid-August 2003 to resume talks in Nanyuki, near Mount Kenya. Again, little progress was made in the first meeting. The SPLM/A affirmed in that meeting that it would only negotiate on the basis of the Nakuru document, and the government was categorical that it would not. A way out was broached, which involved raising the level of negotiations to the principals on both sides. It was then thought by the mediators that it was time for Garang himself to lead his team, while persuading Bashir to assign Vice President Ali Osman Mohamed Taha to head the government's delegation. The International Crisis Group, in a report from December 2003, reflected: "Vice President Taha remained ominously quiet during July and August. Yet, by sending positive messages to the mediators and observers on the process, he positioned himself to transform his international image from extremist to peacemaker."[28]

At General Sumbeiywo's instigation, Kenya's Kalonzo Musyoka once again stepped in to push the process forward. Musyoka traveled to Khartoum to meet Bashir and beseech him to agree to a head-to-head meeting between Taha and Garang.[29] The idea had been mooted and attempted before, but with the impasse reached at Nakuru, Taha, as some observers estimated, pounced on the opportunity for "a political victory and international redemption if he could reach an agreement with Garang."[30] Taha's position also displeased those within the NCP ranks who were not desperate about any compromise with the SPLM. Moreover, presidential peace advisor Ghazi Salahuddin, hitherto central to the peace talks, was not amused by the idea as he would have predictably wanted to be the midwife of the peace agreement, if there was to be one. After all, he was the one who established the framework for the eventual peace agreement.

No matter what conflict had been going on within the higher echelons of the NCP, Musyoka formally wrote to Garang and Taha suggesting that a meeting take place on September 2 in Naivasha, Kenya. Garang had long been wary of such high-level meetings, for any failure that occurred at such a high level could threaten gains achieved and might push the situation toward a resumption of war. This view was also shared by one of the advisors at the peace negotiations. Drawing from his personal experience in the South African negotiations, Nicholas Haysom told an interviewer that "bringing the leaders of the parties to the table is a weapon of last resort."[31] It is the author's belief, however, that Garang's reticence to attend the meeting in Kenya was not because he wanted to ride the issues out by evading them but because he believed that high-level meetings would be counterproductive when issues were not ripe for resolution. Also, previous experiences deepened Garang's scepticism about being trapped in situations for which he was not prepared. In actuality, before the Kenyan intervention to bring the SPLM leader together with Vice President Taha, General Obasanjo of Nigeria invited Garang with his wife to spend the Christmas holiday at his farm in Abeokuta, the capital city of Ogun State, Nigeria. Without informing the SPLM leader, Obasanjo also invited the vice president to the same venue. Whether Obasanjo was setting a trap for Garang or only wished to surprise him with the presence of Taha and his team, who were already negotiating with the SPLM, one wouldn't know. But irrespective of Obasanjo's motives, Garang, who received the news about Taha's presence at the airport, threatened to fly back because he felt that he had been ambushed. In so doing, he did not mind causing immense embarrassment both to the host and his high-ranking visitor.

In addition, before receiving the Kenyan invitation, Garang decided in late August to convene at Rumbek an SPLA senior officers' conference, which brought together approximately 2,000 officers. That was the second such meeting for SPLA officers after the one held in Chukudum on April 2, 1994. Garang briefed the meeting about progress (or lack of it) in the negotiations, especially as they related to the future of the army and security arrangements. Out of that meeting a strong message emerged that the SPLM/A should remain on the qui vive and stay the New Sudan course. With no tangible diplomatic progress since the Machakos Protocol, and increasing signs that the government was not serious about a comprehensive peace agreement, some observers reported that there was a vocal lobby urging Garang to return to the battlefield.[32]

In view of the above situation, Garang wrote to Musyoka on August 31, apologizing that he would not be able to keep the date with Taha. He also gave as an excuse the difficulties of traveling to Kenya on short notice. In his letter to Musyoka, Garang requested that the meeting be postponed for one week until he finished the conference with his officers. According to General Sumbeiywo, the letter did not reach Musyoka because senior SPLA commanders had allegedly intercepted it.[33] Not only was there no evidence to substantiate that claim, but also those who were aware of the command and control structures of the SPLA would never make such a divination. Albeit, on September 2, 2003, Taha arrived in Naivasha and awaited Garang. In the meantime, news emanating from Khartoum did not divulge the purpose of Taha's trip to Kenya; indeed, the trip was passed off by the Khartoum media as a mission for the government of Sudan to offer condolences to the Kenyan president on the death of Kenyan Vice President Kijana Wamalwa, whose burial was to take place around that time. If anything, that proved how Taha was equally circumspect and watchful.

General Sumbeiywo recorded in his biography, however, that after a couple of tense days with Ali Osman Taha, and fearing that the whole exercise would backfire badly, he learned that "Garang had been informally held hostage by his own soldiers who had learnt of the intended meeting in Naivasha."[34] That was an even more inconceivable allegation, but in uncertain situations like the one prevailing in Nairobi at that time, it was not surprising that rumormongers had a field day. Notwithstanding, Sumbeiywo, according to his account, confronted SPLM/A representatives in Nairobi and "made it clear that if [Garang] failed to keep the appointment, he would no longer receive the kind of warm hospitality he had received in Kenya throughout the years."[35] In particular, Sumbeiywo told Dr. Justin Yac Arop, the SPLM/A's Nairobi representative, "'If we do not have Garang here today, we will kick you out of the country.'"[36] The general rightly assessed that his honor and credibility were at stake, especially after persuading Bashir and Taha about the momentous nature of the meeting between the two principals. The general had always balanced pressure and dialogue and was ever conscious that exceeding pressure might alienate the parties; but without pressure, parties would not budge from entrenched positions. This time around the general almost went beyond the pale.

Fortunately, senior SPLM/A members in Kenya, together with the international community, sought to ensure that Garang would not miss the meeting. The imminent tension in the relationship between the SPLM/A and Kenya government was eased by SPLM/A friends in the country, especially Bethuel Kiplagat, the former permanent secretary of Kenya's foreign ministry and a highly respected statesman in his country and beyond. Justin Yac Arop, however, sent an urgent message to Garang saying: "'If you do not come…you won't find us here and the Kenya Government won't allow you in.'"[37] On

September 3, SPLM/A spokesperson Yassir Arman told Qatar-based Al Jazeera television by satellite telephone that Garang was on his way to Naivasha. "It's the first time in twenty years that Garang heads the delegation to peace talks," reported the media.[38]

Garang arrived in Nairobi on September 4, 2003, accompanied by Riek Machar. The break between the two men had been repaired in January 2002 through the intermediation of Senator Danforth. Garang and Machar agreed to work hand-in-hand to achieve the SPLM/A agenda. However, on his arrival, Garang addressed reporters saying, "It is now time for the process to show some tangible results...the [SPLM/A] has accepted the Nakuru Framework document as the basis to negotiate a final agreement. The rejection by the GOS...is threatening the whole IGAD peace process with collapse. We are going to Naivasha...to resolve the deadlock." Garang went on to say: "I and my team are going to Naivasha ready and prepared to make tough decisions to bring a just peace to Sudan...[and] to bring the war to an end through a just and fair political settlement...Peace has a price that must be paid, as it has a dividend that will be enjoyed by the whole Sudanese people."[39]

On the evening of September 4, Ali Osman Taha and Dr. John Garang met for the first time. General Sumbeiywo delighted in recounting that the success or failure of the meeting, in Taha's view, rested on a single bottle of water placed on a side table between the two seated adversaries. He later facetiously said: "What the Sudanese might never know to this day is that the fate of peace in their country hung on this bottle of water whetting the two men's tongues."[40] According to Sumbeiywo, Taha, "the more superstitious of the two" (as he described him), considered that if he opened the bottle of water first, the meeting would not be successful, and if the bottle was not opened at all, the talks would not bear fruits. After some tense moments, the general reported, Garang opened the bottle, took Taha's glass and poured in some water, then poured some water for himself. "The talks, Taha now believed, would be successful," wrote the general.[41] On September 5, General Sumbeiywo told reporters, "'This is the determining point for the peace talks...Both leaders are under tremendous pressure to go back home with a deal.'"[42]

The United States was soon to warmly welcome the meeting. On September 8, the U.S. envoy to the talks, Jeff Millington, arrived in Naivasha and held separate discussions with Taha, Garang, and General Sumbeiywo. "Washington is closely watching this peace process, and I came along to see developments in the talks," said Millington.[43] As the talks progressed beyond the first days, Garang presented Taha with the SPLM/A's proposals to address the outstanding issues of security arrangements, wealth and power sharing, the Three Areas, and the status of the national capital. Another visitor to the scene was Hilde Johnson, the Norwegian international development minister. Norway, as we had intimated in Chapter Three, was deeply engaged in attempts to bring peace to Sudan, but more than any of her predecessors, Ms. Johnson became personally involved in the peace process, and her engagement was highly appreciated by the two parties.

6. Understanding Your Adversary

The meeting of the principals was meant to put an end to the stalemate, but rather than going into the nitty-gritty of negotiations, Garang and Taha spent considerable time trying to understand each other by debating issues relating to religion, cultural diversity, and experiences of other countries beset by problems similar to those of Sudan. At one point Garang told Taha that Sudan had been bleeding for decades and it would be the duty of both parties to save it. Indeed, that question opened the door for lengthy and relaxed head-to-head conversations, which often unnerved Garang's (and possibly Taha's) teams who were, evidently, concerned with the nuts and bolts of the process. However, knowing your opponent well is part of the art of negotiation. Indeed, in order to achieve mutual understanding, a negotiator may have to empathize with his interlocutor, even if he does not sympathize with his ideas. Interpersonal chemistry, as behavioral psychologists say, may be determinant in the creation of favorable human bondings. The negotiating teams on both sides were at sixes and sevens as to why their leaders were wasting time on issues of little account, while (to them) the clock continued to tick. Clearly they had missed the point, for without deep understanding of the bottom line to each party and deciphering the concerns that prey on each of their minds, there would be no purposeful dialogue on the issues that separate them.

Furthermore, the two leaders had to remove the unfavorable perceptions each had of the other, created by the media during the war. Garang, with his caustic sense of humor, tried to persuade Taha that he was not the vampire Khartoum portrayed without break on Sudan television. Taha, on the other hand, managed to convince Garang that he was not the fire-breathing Islamist crusader who wished to eradicate "infidels" from the face of the Earth. Even if he wanted in the bottom of his heart to carry out that "godly" mission, Taha was still able to bring Garang around to realize that he was sophisticated enough to know what was possible and what was impossible in the real world. Those dialogues also revealed to each of the two parties hitherto undisclosed concerns. Nevertheless, Taha, more than Garang, had another important concern, which the SPLM leader could not ignore: how to make any agreement he reached with the SPLM/A marketable to his wider public back home.

7. Proposals and Counterproposals on Security Arrangements

Aware of the high-level international concern with the peace process, both sides decided to focus first on the all-critical issue of security arrangements during the interim period. In this connection, the SPLM/A proposed that both the SPLM and government would retain their forces during that period and proposed joint/integrated units would be established while the government's army was redeployed out of the south and the SPLA out of the north. That was the first time the term joint/integrated units (JIUs) surfaced, though Garang, as alluded to earlier, suggested a similar arrangement in his proposal to General Lagu. Regardless of how, the SPLM/A proposed the creation of units with up to 21,000 soldiers. Half of that force was to come from the SPLA and the other half from government forces. The units were to be deployed in sensitive areas (up to two brigades of 3,000 soldiers in the South, one brigade each in the Nuba Mountains and southern Blue Nile, up to two brigades in Khartoum, and up to one brigade in other parts of northern Sudan). In its second position paper of September 9, the SPLM/A noted that the deployment of JIUs in the Nuba Mountains and southern Blue Nile "will resolve the issue of security arrangements in these areas. No military forces other than the JIUs will be deployed in these two areas."[44]

On September 10, as a sign of the seriousness of the negotiations on security arrangements, Sudan's defense minister, Major General Bakri Hassan Salih, and other senior military personnel arrived in Naivasha to reinforce the government delegation. At first, General Bakri's team rejected the concept of integrated units as well as the redeployment of government forces out of the South. Redeployment was a euphemism for "withdrawal," a term used in Herman Cohen's plan, referred to in Chapter Four. Proposals went back and forth, and the government instead sought a larger joint/integrated force in the south, SPLA redeployment out of eastern Sudan, and a phased approach to redeployment. The SPLM/A's third position paper of September 16 responded to these demands, proposing a force of 12,000 soldiers in the south and 75 percent redeployment within the first one-and-a-half years from the beginning of the pre-interim period.[45] By that stage, an internationally monitored cease-fire was also to be created as part of the deal. The parties agreed that the two of them, together with the IGAD mediators and international experts, would work out the details of the cease-fire. The term joint/integrated revealed one aspect of the trivialities of negotiations. While the SPLM/A maintained that those forces be called integrated units, since they were meant to be the nucleus of Sudan's future army were the south to opt for unity after the referendum, the military on the government side preferred to call them joint units as long as the SPLM refused to integrate its army, the SPLA, into the SAF. An agreement was also reached on the coordination between two standing armies in one country and also on the recognition of both armies, though separate, by the new Sudan constitution. Thus, both armies were constitutionally recognized and treated equally as the Sudan National Armed Forces (SNAF). As we shall see, that recognition was only theoretical.

160

Stories of possible deals on security arrangements were now reaching the public domain. On September 15, John Prendergast of the International Crisis Group maintained that the key issue for moving the peace process forward was solving problems relating to security arrangements: "If you unlock this, you will definitely lock down a peace deal. The SPLA will walk away from a deal that doesn't nail down security arrangements that are satisfactory to them."[46] To another analyst those were "two armed groups ultimately—a military junta and an armed opposition group—and you need to get the bread and butter issues nailed down first with groups like this before you can move on to anything else."[47]

On September 21, the parties agreed to extend the cessation of hostilities for two more months, a sign that confidence was beginning to be restored to the negotiations. Three days later, on September 24, the parties reached agreement on security arrangements. The Framework Agreement on Security Arrangements During the Interim Period was signed by Idris Mohamed Abdelgadir for the government and Pagan Amum Okech for the SPLM/A on September 25.[48] Agreement on the principle of having two standing armies in Sudan, however, did not come easy. As mentioned earlier, neither the government negotiators nor military advisors were persuaded by Garang's argument in favor of two armies in the same country. Those advisors included General Abdel Magid Khalil, Sudan's former minister of defense and a man who was highly respected by Garang, as alluded to in the former chapter. In addition, the military advisors included General Sumbeiywo, who served as former chief of staff of the Kenyan army, and a U.S. officer brought by Senator Danforth to convince the reluctant SPLA commander-in-chief of the untenability of his proposition. Senator Danforth and the above-mentioned military cognoscenti argued against what they thought to be an anomalous arrangement. The idea of one country having two armies with different command and control structures was surely repugnant to classical constitutional theory on sovereignty over national territory, as the protection of a country's territorial integrity is a fundamental attribute of that sovereignty. To that contention, Garang, known for his acerbic tongue, retorted that Sudan itself was an anomaly. To the mediators he said: "Where else in the modern world would you find a country that has remained at war with itself for half a century?"[49] In no uncertain terms, he made clear to the peace mediator and observers that the fate of any agreement depended precisely on guarantees on defense and security.

In a bid to resolve the riddle posed by having two standing armies in one country, it was agreed, as hinted earlier, that both forces, together with the JIUs, form Sudan's National Armed Forces (SNAF) during the interim period. As a result, Sudan's Interim National Constitution (INC) 2005, which encompassed the Comprehensive Peace Agreement, stipulated that "the Sudan Armed Forces and the Sudan People's Liberation Army shall remain

161

separate, regular, professional and non-partisan armed forces and shall be treated equally as the Sudan National Armed Forces" (Art. 144.1). The INC further provided that "the mission of the Sudan National Armed Forces is to defend the sovereignty and secure the territorial integrity of the country" (Art. 144.2). The INC went on to add that "the Sudan National Armed Forces and the Joint/Integrated Units shall defend the constitutional order, respect the rule of law, the civilian government, democracy, basic human rights and the will of the people; they shall undertake the responsibility of the defence of the country against external and internal threats in their respective areas of deployment" (Art. 144.3). Though separate, the two armies were constitutionally empowered to carry out national duties within their areas of deployment, without excluding joint action in other areas.

It is interesting to draw a comparison between Sudan's and Iraq's experiences. At about the same time the Sudan peace agreement was being negotiated, the Iraqis were also grappling with the issue of Kurdistan and specifically with that of the future of the Peshmerga army. The Peshmerga operated in the Kurdish region throughout the war years and was the only standing army in that area. However, when the new Iraqi constitution was drafted and finally adopted, it was agreed that the defense of the country shall be solely the responsibility of the Iraqi army. Nevertheless, the Iraqi constitution also entrusted to the Peshmerga powers normally exercised by the army.[50] By giving the SPLA a role in defending Sudan's territorial integrity, the national government was making mileage of the SPLA's strategic advantages. Three of Sudan's eight neighbors share borders only with southern Sudan—namely, the Democratic Republic of the Congo, Kenya, and Uganda—while the longest portion of the borders with one of Sudan's neighbors to the east (Ethiopia) lies in southern Sudan.

To ensure coordination among those disparate armies, the two parties created a Joint Defense Board (JDB). That body was to harmonize the work of the two armies and provide command and control for the JIUs. The JDB would be directly under the presidency of the republic (not the national ministry of defense). The JIUs were described as a symbol of national unity and sovereignty and the nucleus of Sudan's future army, if unity were confirmed. In addition, the JIUs would have a new military doctrine other than that of the SAF, which had become religiously inspired since 1983 when Nimeiri Islamicized the SAF. Furthermore, SAF and SPLA components of the JIUs would be treated equally and trained, armed, attired, supplied, and paid uniformly. In this connection, the final protocol on the JIUs provided that there shall be uniformity in welfare, salaries, emoluments, pension rights, supplies, armament, and equipment.

The test of the equality of treatment to the two armies soon came up when Garang requested Taha to ensure government funding to the SPLA since it was recognized as part of the Sudan National Armed Forces. Taha categorically rejected the request and almost considered the proposition outré. Only the government of southern Sudan should shoulder that responsibility, Taha told Garang. The negotiations almost reached a point of collapse on this point were it not for the intervention of U.S. Secretary of State Colin Powell. The secretary contacted Garang to urge him to sign the JIUs protocol after the success he had scored, against all odds, in having his own separate army. As a sweetener, he promised Garang that the United States and "other friends" would help in the "professionalization" of the SPLA; the term "professionalization" was an understatement of "funding." Garang, adept in creative ambiguity and double entendre, told the secretary of state that he would give thought to the idea.

While rejecting government funding to the SPLA and restricting it only to the JIUs, Taha also proposed that during the interim period the elected National Legislative Assembly shall review and resolve the issue of funding Sudan's National Armed Forces, which comprised both SAF and SPLA, in order to make unity an attractive choice in the referendum and to create a sound basis for the formation of the future army of Sudan. That, to Garang, was too tentative an offer on which to base the funding of the SPLA. Accordingly, he proceeded to merge Taha's counterproposal that SPLA funding should only come from the government of southern Sudan with Powell's promise for assistance to rebuild the SPLA. The final provision in the protocol relating to funding [paragraph 21(1)] thus came as follows: "During the interim period, SAF forces and JIUs shall be funded by the National Government, whereas the SPLA forces shall be funded by the Government of Southern Sudan, subject to the principle of proportional downsizing as per Security Arrangements Protocol and the approval of the Southern Sudan Legislature." To meet this obligation, the protocol provided, "the Government of Southern Sudan shall raise financial resources from both local and foreign sources and seek international assistance. The financial resources shall be channeled through the Bank of Southern Sudan and managed according to the principles of Wealth Sharing Protocol."

The final agreement showed that the SPLM/A, in order to maintain an independent force for the south during the interim period, also had to make a range of concessions to the government. The size of the JIUs in southern Sudan would be 24,000 soldiers, whereas in Khartoum it would only be 3,000. That meant that there would still be a 12,000-man force of SAF in southern Sudan, though operating as a component of the JIUs led and controlled by the Joint Defense Board (JDB) referred to above. Also, the SPLM/A agreed to redeploy out of eastern Sudan within one year after the beginning of the pre-interim period and out of the Nuba Mountains and southern Blue Nile "as soon as the JIUs are formed and deployed." The protocol, on top of that, allowed the government up to two-and-one-half years after the beginning of the pre-interim period to redeploy out of the south to north/south of the

163

borders as they were defined on January 1, 1956. The parties lastly agreed to an internationally monitored cease-fire, effective from the date of signature of a Comprehensive Peace Agreement. Details of that arrangement would to be worked out by the parties, together with international experts and the IGAD.

Figure 2: Presidents Bashir of Sudan and Kibaki of Kenya together with Ali Osman Taha and John Garang holding a copy of the CPA (January 9, 2005)

One crucial issue that was almost left to the will of the two parties was the downsizing of forces. In the protocol, the parties agreed to the "principle of proportional downsizing of the forces on both sides, at a suitable time following the conclusion of the cease-fire agreement." Clearly, at that moment, neither party was anticipating an immediate downsizing of the forces. Nevertheless, both parties agreed (clause 19) that "after completion of SAF redeployment to the North, the parties shall begin negotiations on proportional downsizing." They also agreed to allow voluntary downsizing and demobilization of nonessential soldiers and elderly and disabled persons, meaning by that elements that were hors de combat.

After exchanging the signed agreements, Taha and Garang expressed their excitement about the breakthrough. "This is an historic occasion....It has paved the way for a comprehensive peace agreement," Taha said.[51] Garang looked ahead: "We will go into this agreement with resolve, energy and focus so that we resolve the remaining issues. With this agreement, the direction and orientation for peace in Sudan is irreversible."[52] In the week that followed, leaders from both sides expressed optimism that a full agreement was very close.[53] The protocol on security, together with five other protocols—wealth

164

sharing, power sharing, Abyei, Nuba Mountains, and Blue Nile—as well as that on Comprehensive Cease-fire were signed in Nairobi on June 5, 2004, in the presence of Kenya's President Kibaki. However, the final touches were to be made in annexes on which the parties continued working.

8. U.N. Security Council Supports the Agreement

The "Agreement on Permanent Cease-Fire and Security Arrangements Implementation Modalities," signed by both parties on 31 December 31, 2004, would be the final substantive agreement on security arrangements before the signing of the Comprehensive Peace Agreement on January 9, 2005.[54] That agreement, however, only came after an important event: the meeting by the U.N. Security Council in Nairobi on November 19, 2004, which was solely dedicated to discussing Sudan's peace efforts. The parties had previously agreed "to request the United Nations to constitute a lean, effective, sustainable, and affordable U.N. Peace-Support Mission to monitor and verify the agreement and bolster its implementation as provided under Chapter VI of the charter" (clause 15.1). Anticipating a role in helping maintain Sudan's peace, the Security Council endorsed in Resolution 1547 (2004) the secretary general's recommendation that the United Nations should undertake preparatory work through the United Nations Advance Mission in Sudan. The upshot of the council's meeting in Nairobi was attestation of the Declaration on the Conclusion of IGAD Negotiations on Peace in the Sudan. That declaration, which was signed by Yahia Hussein Babiker, on behalf of the government of Sudan, and Nhial Deng Nhial, on behalf of the SPLM/A, provided in its substantive paragraphs that: "The parties affirm that the six protocols referred to in the Nairobi Declaration of 5th June, 2004,[55] constitute and form the core Peace Agreement and, therefore invite the UN Security Council in this its Nairobi sitting to pass a resolution endorsing the six Protocols." Further the parties declared "their commitment to expeditiously complete Negotiations on the two annexes on Ceasefire Agreement and Implementation Modalities so as to conclude and sign the Comprehensive Peace Agreement no later than 31 December 2004." The declaration was witnessed by General Sumbeiywo on behalf of the IGAD and Jan Pronk, the special representative of the secretary general in Sudan, on behalf of the United Nations. The signing ceremony was witnessed by the 15 members of the council who also appended their signatures to the document.[56]

Four months after its Nairobi meeting, the Security Council devoted another sitting to Sudan (March 24, 2005), in the course of which it passed another major resolution: Resolution 1590 on peacekeeping in Sudan. The resolution stated that the Security Council, "**considering that 'the situation in Sudan continues to constitute a threat to international peace and** security,'" (emphasis added) decided to establish a United Nations Mission in Sudan (UNMIS) for an initial period of six months. It further decided that UNMIS would consist of up to 100,000 military personnel and an appropriate civilian component, including up to 715 civilian police personnel. The mandate of UNMIS was to undertake the following tasks:

(a) "To support implementation of the Comprehensive Peace Agreement by performing the following tasks:

    i. To monitor and verify the implementation of the Ceasefire Agreement and investigate violations;

    ii. To liaise with bilateral donors on the formation of Joint Integrated Units;

    iii. To observe and monitor movement of armed groups and redeployment of forces in the areas of UNMIS deployment in accordance with the Ceasefire Agreement;

    iv. To assist in the establishment of the disarmament, demobilization, and reintegration program as called for in the Comprehensive Peace Agreement, with particular attention to the special needs of women and child combatants, and its implementation through voluntary disarmament and weapons collection and destruction;

    v. To assist the parties to the Comprehensive Peace Agreement in promoting understanding of the peace process and the role of UNMIS by means of an effective public information campaign, targeted at all sectors of society, in coordination with the African Union;

    vi. To assist the parties to the Comprehensive Peace Agreement in addressing the need for a national inclusive approach, including the role of women, towards reconciliation and peace building;

    vii. To assist the parties to the Comprehensive Peace Agreement, in coordination with bilateral and multilateral assistance programs, in restructuring the police service in Sudan, consistent with democratic policing, to develop a police training and evaluation program, and to otherwise assist in the training of police;

    viii. To assist the parties to the Comprehensive Peace Agreement in promoting the rule of law, including an independent judiciary, and the protection of human rights of all people of Sudan through a comprehensive and coordinated strategy with the aim of combating impunity and contributing to long-term peace and stability and to assist the parties to the

Comprehensive Peace Agreement to develop and consolidate the national legal framework;

ix. To ensure an adequate human rights presence, capacity, and expertise within UNMIS to carry out human rights promotion, protection, and monitoring activities;

x. To provide guidance and technical assistance to the parties to the Comprehensive Peace Agreement, in cooperation with other international actors, to support the preparations for and conduct of elections and referenda provided for by the Comprehensive Peace Agreement;

(b) To facilitate and coordinate, within its capabilities and in its areas of deployment, the voluntary return of refugees and internally displaced persons, and humanitarian assistance, inter alia, by helping to establish the necessary security conditions;

(c) To assist the parties to the Comprehensive Peace Agreement, in cooperation with other international partners in the mine action sector, by providing humanitarian demining assistance, technical advice, and coordination;

(d) To contribute toward international efforts to protect and promote human rights in Sudan, as well as to co-ordinate international efforts toward the protection of civilians, with particular attention to vulnerable groups including internally displaced persons, returning refugees, and women and children, within UNMIS's capabilities and in close cooperation with other United Nations agencies, related organizations, and non-governmental organizations."

With such an inclusive mandate to the United Nations, which was voluntarily accepted by the two parties and endorsed by the totality of the Security Council, one would have expected that the implementation of the Protocol on Security Arrangements would have been plain sailing. As we shall see in Chapter Twelve, that was, regrettably, not to be the case. In effect, the levity with which the government of Sudan had taken these obligations was such that even the special representative of the secretary general was not saved from the embarrassment of being chased out of the country as a persona non grata by one of the signatories of the Comprehensive Peace Agreement.

NOTES

1 Mark Simmon and Peter Dixon, *Peace by Piece*, "Interview with Lazarus Sumbeiywo," 22-27.

2 Sudan People's Liberation Movement/Army (SPLM/A), "SPLM/A Response to the Draft Framework for Resolution of Outstanding Issues Arising out of the Elaboration of the Machakos Protocol," July 11, 2003, Points 4, 5.

3   "Bashir Tells Mediators to 'Go to Hell,'" PanAfrican News Agency, July 15, 2003.
    See also Sumbeiywo's accounts in Waihenya, *The Mediator*, 114 and Martin, *Kings of Peace, Pawns of War*, 146.

4   For a commentary on the situation at that time, see John Prendergast and David Mozersky, "Going to Hell?" *The Observer*, August 24, 2003.

5   Supra note 1

6   See Waihenya, *The Mediator*, 111–13.

7   Ibid., 111.

8   Intergovernmental Authority for Development, "Draft Framework for Resolution of the Three Conflict Areas," (Nairobi, Sudan Peace Secretariat, July 2003).

9   Waihenya, *The Mediator*, 114.

10 Ibid., 114.

11 Ibid., 115–16.

12 "Sudan Calls on Arab League to Help End Deadlock in Peace Process," BBC Monitoring (Al Khartoum), July 15, 2002.

13 *Sudan: Towards an Incomplete Peace* (Nairobi, Brussels: International Crisis Group, Africa Report 73, 2003), 3.

14 "Rebels Urge AU Summit to Support Regional Grouping's Peace Efforts for Sudan," Agence France-Presse (Nairobi), July 9, 2003.

15 Intergovernmental Authority for Development, "Draft Framework for Resolution of Outstanding Issues Arising out of the Elaborations of the Machakos Protocol," Sudan Peace Secretariat, Nairobi, July 2003.

16 Ibid.

17 Government of the Republic of Sudan, "Comments and Remarks of the Government of the Republic of Sudan Delegation on Draft Framework for Resolution of Outstanding Issues Arising out of the Elaborations of the Machakos Protocol and Other Important Issues," July 11, 2003.

18 Ibid., sections 2, 6.

19 All numbers cited refer to clauses in "Comments and Remarks of the Government of the Republic of Sudan Delegation on Draft Framework for Resolution of Outstanding Issues Arising out of the Elaborations of the Machakos Protocol and Other Important Issues.", IGAD Secretariat, Sudan Peace Negotiation, Nairobi

20 Ibid.

21 "SPLM/A Response to the Draft Framework for Resolution of Outstanding Issues Arising out of the Elaborations of the Machakos Protocol," point 4.

22 Muhammad Sa'id Muhammad Al-Hasan, "Sudanese Foreign Minister: Khartoum Not Bound by 'Nakuru Document' Because It Is Unfair," translated from Arabic, *Asharq Alawsat* (London), August 24, 2003.

23 Kate Luxford, "President Refuses Sudanese Boundary Changes, Lifting of Islamic Law for Sake of Peace," World Markets Research Centre, 2004.

24 "Sudanese President Criticizes Draft Peace Agreement, Opens National Dialogue," Agence France-Presse, August 9, 2003.

25 "Opposition Leader Dismisses Sudanese Peace Talks," PanAfrican News Agency (Khartoum), May 22, 2003.

26 "Sudan's Opposition Ends Cairo Talks on Note of Unity," PanAfrican News Agency, May 25, 2003.

27 Sudan People's Liberation Movement and Popular National Congress, *Working Paper between the Sudan People's Liberation Movement and the Popular National Congress on the Issues of Peace and Democratic Transition* (2003).

28 *Sudan: Towards an Incomplete Peace*, International Crisis Group, 4.

29 See Waihenya, *The Mediator*, 119–20.

30 *Sudan: Towards an Incomplete Peace*, 4.

31 Simmons and Dixon, "Interview with Nicholas Haysom," *Peace by Piece*, 28-31.

32 Waihenya, *The Mediator,* 122–23.

33 Ibid.

34 Ibid.

35 Ibid.

36 Ibid.

37 Ibid.

38 "Garang Reportedly Heads for Sudanese Peace Talks," PanAfrican News Agency (Khartoum), September 3, 2003.

39 "Sudan Rebel Leader Garang Arrives Here for Peace Talks," PanAfrican News Agency, September 4, 2003.

40 Waihenya, *The Mediator*, 124.

41 Ibid., 125.

42 Bogonko Bosire, "Sudan VP, Rebel Chief Hold Talks in Kenya to End Africa's Longest War," Agence France-Presse (Naivasha, Kenya), September 5, 2003.

43 "US Envoy Joins Khartoum, Rebel Leader Talks," PanAfrican News Agency, September 8, 2003.

44 Sudan People's Liberation Movement, "Security Arrangements During the Interim Period," (Naivasha, Kenya: SPLM Paper 2, September 9, 2003).

45 Sudan People's Liberation Movement, "Security Arrangements During the Interim Period," (Naivasha, Kenya: SPLM Paper 3, September 16, 2003).

46 *Sudan: Towards an Incomplete Peace*, 5.

47 Andrew England, "Analyst: Sudan Peace Process Reaches Crucial Stage as Sudanese Vice President Continues Unprecedented Talks with Rebel Leader," Associated Press (Nairobi), September 16, 2003.

48 Government of the Sudan and Sudan People's Liberation Movement/Army, *Framework Agreement on Security Arrangements During the Interim Period between the Government of the Sudan (GOS) and the Sudan People's Liberation Movement/ Sudan People's Liberation Army (SPLM/SPLA),* signed September 25, 2003 (Nairobi: Intergovernmental Authority for Development, 2003).

49 Personal recollection.

50 Chapter V of the Iraqi constitution relating to regional powers provided that the constitution, on application, recognizes Kurdistan as a federal region with all the powers it currently enjoys (article 113). It further added that "the region's government shall be empowered to carry out all functions required for the administration of the region, *especially the formation and organization of the region's internal security and regional protection*" (article 117). Since the Peshmerga is the only force in the region it was made to effectively assume the responsibility of protecting the borders of Iraq with Turkey and parts of Iran.

51 "Khartoum, Sudan Rebels Sign Deal on Security Arrangements," Agence France-Presse (Naivasha, Kenya) September 25, 2003.

52 Ibid.

53 "Sudan's Vice President Says a Final Peace Accord Could Be Reached in Weeks," Associated Press, October 1, 2003. Also, Andrew England, "Rebel Leader: Road to Peace in Sudan's 20-Year Conflict 'Irreversible,'" Associated Press (Rumbek, Sudan), September 30, 2003.

54 Government of the Sudan and Sudan People's Liberation Movement/Army (SPLM/A), *Agreement on Permanent Ceasefire and Security Arrangements Implementation Modalities During the Pre-Interim and the Interim Periods between the Government of the Sudan (GOS) and the Sudan People's Liberation Movement/ Sudan People's Liberation Army (SPLM/SPLA), signed December 31, 2004* (Nairobi: Intergovernmental Authority for Development, 2004).

55 The declaration was signed by the two parties in the State House, Nairobi, in presence of the President of Kenya, IGAD mediators, and representatives of observer countries.

56 The signatory countries were Algeria, Angola, Benin, Brazil, Chile, China, France, Germany, Pakistan, Philippines, Romania, Russia Federation, Spain, the United Kingdom, and the United States. The United States was represented by Senator Danforth, who was by that time also a U.S. representative to the United Nations.

Chapter Six
Reconstruction of the Sudanese State

■■■■■■■■■■■■■❖■■■■■■■■■■■■■

Politics makes strange bedfellows.
—**Proverb**

1. Introduction

Another Kenyan town, Naivasha, became the birthplace of the five protocols that had put flesh into the framework agreement signed at Machakos. Unlike Machakos, Naivasha is a tranquil locality off the beaten track in the northwest of Nairobi. That alone qualified it to be an appropriate venue for undisturbed negotiations of Sudan's backbreaking problems, especially those that the National Congress Party (NCP) wished to avert discussing, claiming that they were not directly related to Southern Sudan. The NCP, like other northern political parties in office, had since 1986 rejected any claim made by the Sudan People's Liberation Movement (SPLM) to speak on behalf of any non-southern community, even though that movement had unceasingly characterized itself as a national movement organized around a national liberation agenda.

Through these agenda, the SPLM aimed at fashioning a new political dispensation, in the interest of all Sudanese peoples, to replace Sudan's unavailing system of rule. John Garang had not only fought resolutely for that vision, but also succeeded in building broad national support for it. In this respect, he weathered assaults from all corners, including from within the south. One of the greatest challenges Garang faced during the peace talks was how to raise and address national failures that had cumulatively triggered conflicts across the country. This did not sit well with his interlocutors, who were never willing to recognize the movement as a champion of the causes of aggrieved Sudanese, other than southerners. If anything, that alone proved who the real separatists were.

This chapter shall address the phenomena of economic disempowerment, political disenfranchisement, and cultural alienation at the heart of the Sudanese multiple crises for which the SPLM strove to place at center stage of national politics. Garang took pains to emphasize that at the heart of Sudan's conflict lay manifold inequities that related to the manner in which the country was governed, to the way its resources were exploited by a narrow set of ruling interest groups, and to the marginalization of all Sudanese cultures other than that of the dominant majority. At the political level, by way of example, Sudan—the largest country in Africa—continued to be run from Khartoum, the way it had been run by Wingate Pasha,[1] with the sole objective of establishing governmental authority and providing minimum development and services. That model of governance gave rise to pervasive economic inequities characterized by levels of poverty in Sudan's rural areas in the east, south, west, and extreme north way above those in the riverain north i.e areas of northern Sudan lying on, and between, the river Nile and tributaries. The lightheartedness with which the ruling elite of Khartoum treated these inequities since Sudan's independence in 1956 led to a buildup of anger in all marginalized areas. Even though Arabic had evolved as the language spoken by 70 percent of the people of northern Sudan, those whose mother tongue was not Arabic hardly abandoned their indigenous languages and cultures. So, wherever there were social tremblings or protestations in the peripheries,[2] behind them had always been political, social, cultural, and above all, economic causes.

Those grievances were aggravated when Islamists came to power, especially when they sought to obliterate indigenous cultures and religions. On the other hand, the socioeconomic and cultural underpinnings of protestations in the marginalized areas of Sudan were either deliberately concealed by the Khartoum political elite or, sadly, not obvious to the majority of them. Whatever the causes of this inattention were, the situation went out of hand, as wars in southern, eastern, central (Nuba Mountains), and western (Dar Fur) Sudan had borne out. With the emergence of the Sudan People's Liberation Movement/Army (SPLM/A) as a central player in national politics, those in the peripheries, who had kept their heads down and quietly endured their suffering, became emboldened by the SPLM's trumpet call to awaken Sudan's marginalized peoples.

2. Ending Political and Economic Disempowerment

Beyond the breakthrough of the Machakos Protocol (see Chapter Three) and dealing with the brute military aspects of the war (see Chapter Four), Garang became determined to pin down the NCP government on exact details as to how the country would be governed, how its wealth would be equitably shared, and how its diverse cultures would be given worth. He maintained that if unity was ever to be made attractive to southern Sudanese, or for that matter, if peace were be enjoyed by ordinary folk across the country, that would entirely depend upon the benefits they accrued from peace and the justness of the state and society to which they would have to pledge enduring allegiance.

The Machakos Protocol laid out some broad thrusts for the direction of the Intergovernmental Authority on Development (IGAD) peace talks on matters of power sharing and governance. In a section titled "Part C (Structures of Government)," the Machakos Protocol provided for inclusive processes to review the country's controversial 1998 constitution.[3] Clause 3.1.2 of the protocol stipulated that "a representative National Constitutional Review Commission (NCRC) shall be established during the Pre-Transition Period which shall have as its first task the drafting of a Legal and Constitutional Framework to govern the Interim Period and which incorporates the Peace Agreement." The SPLM/A and government of Sudan would adopt such an agreed framework for the interim period and agree that during that period a more comprehensive and inclusive "constitutional review process" would be undertaken. The latter clause, cardinal to both democratic transformation and voluntary unity, was never put into effect. As we shall see in Chapter Ten, the timely operationalization of that clause could have saved the two parties, especially the SPLM, the embarrassment of trying hard to make up for lost time when the issue of post-referendum measures came to the fore.

In addition, the Machakos Protocol stipulated that the people of Sudan agree to work together to "establish a democratic system of governance **taking account of the cultural, ethnic, racial, religious, and linguistic diversity and gender equality of the people of the Sudan**"[4] (emphasis added). In past Sudanese constitutions, the country was either identified on the basis of exclusivist parameters, such as the description of Sudan as an Arabo-Islamic country in the draft Islamic constitution of the mid-1960s, or meaninglessly denominated as an Arab, African, or Arabo-African country. The religion of the state or the ethnocultural origins of its citizen were never an issue in Sudan's past constitutions of 1956 and 1964. Both constitutions were based on the self-government constitution prepared during the colonial rule, and many of its parts were copied verbatim into the independent Sudan's constitutions. To its credit, the Machakos Protocol characterized Sudan as a "multi-cultural, multi-racial, multi-ethnic, multi-religious, and multi-lingual country." This characterization, belabored as it might seem, would only be understood in light of what Francis Deng called attempts by dominant groups "to impose their self-perception as the framework for national identity" while eliminating cultures of other groups.[5] Deng appropriately called those attempts "culturocide," explaining that "if genocide is the physical elimination 'in whole or part' of a particular identity group, then eliminating the culture of a group is tantamount to 'culturocide,' which is arguably just as objectionable."[6]

The protocol went further to say that such diversities "shall be mutually enriching and, therefore, they shall "coexist and be sources of strength, harmony, and not used for causing division."[7] Founding constitutional rights and duties on this definition of national identity, unwieldy as its wording is, may be the only way to put an end to self-interested mystifications of that identity. As two observers of the Sudanese crisis wrote: "the Sudanese of the twenty-first century are being asked to face the truth about the ties that bind them to each other and to seek reconciliation in order to equitably share decisions regarding the allocation and distribution of resources in ways that benefit *all* citizens."[8] That was precisely what the Comprehensive Peace Agreement (CPA) sought to achieve.

On the issue of religion, the protocol provided the following in clause 6:

- "Religions, customs and beliefs are a source of moral strength and inspiration for the Sudanese people."
- "There shall be freedom of belief, worship and conscience for followers of all religions or beliefs or customs and no one shall be discriminated against on such grounds."
- "All personal and family matters including marriage, divorce, inheritance, succession, and affiliation may be governed by personal laws (including Shari'a or other religious laws, customs, or traditions) of those concerned."

In order to put an end to deliberate attempts to make of any religious or cultural particularity a prerequisite for enjoying constitutional rights, duties, or roles, the protocol provided that "eligibility for public office, *including the presidency,* public service and the enjoyment of all rights and duties **shall be based on citizenship and not on religion, beliefs, or customs**" (emphasis added).

To protect the rights of groups in the north who wished to maintain their customary laws, part C, clause 3.2.1 required that the "National Government in all its laws shall take into account the religious and cultural diversity of the Sudanese people." In clause 3.2.2 it provided: "Nationally enacted legislation having effect only in respect of the states outside Southern Sudan shall have as its source of legislation Shari'a and the consensus of the people."

Consequent to protests by SPLM members in the Nuba Mountains and Blue Nile who belonged to the geographic north and were, thus, discontent with being left under shari'a law, the parties agreed that "where national legislation is currently in operation or is enacted and its source is religious or customary law, then a state or region, the majority of whose residents do not practice such religion or customs may:

(i) Either introduce legislation so as to allow or provide for institutions or practices in that region consistent with their religion or customs, or

(ii) Refer the law to the Council of States for it to approve by two-thirds (2/3) majority or initiate national legislation which will provide for such necessary alternative institutions as is appropriate."

This stipulation was particularly relevant to the Nuba Mountains, a region that had been struggling since the 1960s against economic deprivation and social marginalization, but had become incensed since the 1990s by the National Islamic Front (NIF) policy of forcible Islamization, coupled with suppression of indigenous cultures and traditional belief systems.

3. Sharing Power and Wealth: General Principles?

Since the resumption of negotiations in the ill-fated Machakos II round of talks in August 2002, the issue of power sharing became more specific and, in turn, more disputatious. One thorny issue was the presidency of the republic during the interim period. The government, as observed earlier, offered a simple bilateral formula: Bashir would remain president of the republic throughout the interim period and Garang would be the vice president. The SPLM/A opposed this formula unless the interim national government was one of national unity, including adequate representation of the National Democratic Alliance (NDA). It also rightly demanded that the powers of the vice president be real and specified in detail. If the government chose to reject this offer, the SPLM/A maintained that it would then go back to its initial proposition of a rotating presidency—three years for Bashir and three for Garang.[9] The SPLM/A also made it clear that the Machakos Protocol did not imply their agreement to the application of shari'a in northern Sudan, especially not in the capital city shared with the SPLM. In an interview reported on August 21, 2002, Garang railed, "We did not agree to apply shari'a in the North. However, that is the situation now. I wish to stress that the SPLM/A did not agree with the government on that. If Khartoum remains the capital in the new arrangement, then shari'a will not be applied there, since the agreement stipulates that central government will be exempt from shari'a law."[10] As for the government of Sudan, Garang's interpretation flew in the face of their understanding of Machakos as a deal for the South that, by implication, left the North under the tight control of the NIF ruling party. It may be recalled that in September 2002, following the SPLM/A's capture of Torit, the government argued that the SPLM/A had "backtracked" on Machakos by reopening the issue of religion and state, and in particular, by demanding a shari'a-free capital.

Some reports coming out of Machakos in late August 2002 were incautiously optimistic that the two sides had "already agreed on power sharing and distribution of wealth."[11] To be precise, these issues would divide the parties for nearly another two years. Following the crisis in the talks in September and October 2002, negotiations on substantive matters made very little progress. The mediators sought to achieve some momentum and on November 18, 2002, the same day the parties agreed to extend the Memorandum of Understanding on Cessation of Hostilities to March 2003, the government and the SPLM/A signed a Memorandum of Understanding on Aspects of Structures of Government.[12] That memorandum was vague and lacked precise details, but it served to affirm that some progress was being made and that talks would resume in January 2003. Noteworthy principles contained in the memorandum were the agreement between the parties:

- To hold free and fair general elections during the interim period;
- To establish a bicameral national legislature with equitable representation of the people of Southern Sudan in both legislative chambers;
- To ensure that the national civil service and cabinet ministries be representative of the people of Sudan and that specifically the people of Southern Sudan shall be equitably represented at the senior and middle levels of the national civil service;
- To hold a census during the interim period;
- To have collegial decision making within the presidency; and
- To establish a government of National Unity during the interim period.[13]

When negotiations resumed in January 2003, power-sharing debates continued to show slow but steady progress. With the government offering little reassurance that a true government of National Unity was in the offing, the SPLM/A, by way of pressure, again proposed a rotating presidency during the interim period. That proposal was rejected by the government as too destabilizing. Regarding the alternative offer by the SPLM/A of a vice presidency for its leader guaranteed to have real executive powers, the government refused to countenance a situation whereby the vice president would have veto powers over decisions made by the president and, more important, that the vice president from the south would automatically become head of state were the post of president to fall vacant. The discussion turned to a first vice president with real powers and a provision for another vice president (from the NCP).[14] Garang was likely persuaded to accept the idea of a second vice president in order to accommodate the man who made agreement possible, Ali Osman Mohamed Taha, whom the SPLM chairman was to replace. But owing to other outstanding concerns, including allocation of seats in the bicameral national assembly and the distribution of civil service posts and government ministries, together with deadlocks on contentious issues such as the status of the national capital and the Three Areas, a firm commitment to any arrangement on power sharing had to wait some time.

Nevertheless, the mediators were upbeat after the January 2003 round of talks. An IGAD statement claimed that the two sides "reached agreement on many elements within the framework of a broad-based Government of National Unity," while Sumbeiywo, in closing the session, went so far to say "this was possibly the end of the war."[15] Areas of agreement, according to the IGAD statement, covered "the constitutional review process, including modalities of drafting and adopting an interim constitution," and filling in some gaps left from the November 2002 session. Sumbeiywo added that "a measure of understanding had been reached on structures of government in power and wealth sharing,"[16] including "significant progress on the structure of the national legislature, executive, and judiciary [and on] the government of National Unity."[17]

Expectations were thus high for the resumption of negotiations in March 2003, notwithstanding the tricky issues that still remained on the agenda, including the percentage of southern Sudanese to be integrated into the national service civil service. However, the issue of the Three Areas, which had continued to foment since Machakos, arrested this optimism. In this regard, the government had agreed to talks outside the IGAD auspices, to be hosted by Kenya and chaired by Sumbeiywo in his capacity as a Kenyan officer, not as the IGAD mediator. It was hoped that once progress was made with these side talks, Sumbeiywo and the two parties could quickly return to the IGAD peace talks. These preliminary "consultations" on the Three Areas, as Sumbeiywo would later concede, made only "limited progress."[18] As the IGAD peace talks stumbled with the Three Areas proving to be a major source of disagreement, and talks within the IGAD process making little headway, the prospects for the May 2003 round of talks became dim.

At the sixth round of talks, which commenced in early May, the SPLM/A's chief negotiator, Nhial Deng Nhial, told the Abu Dhabi daily *Al-Ittihad* that the key issues for power sharing were the powers of the vice president and the status of the national capital. He added that "the main principle for distributing sovereignty and civil service positions in the state organs between the North and South had been agreed upon, and it dealt with distribution according to demographic weights in the South and the North."[19] However, as subsequent debates exposed, even this issue would require further negotiations between the two sides. Moreover, the allocation of seats

177

in parliament and the federal ministries were issues in which disagreement was still significant. Those issues were of particular importance to the SPLM/A and to southern Sudanese, for whom national governments, including the NCP, had traditionally reserved minor ministries.[20] With regard to the civil service, not a single southern Sudanese was elevated to the post of permanent secretary by any government in Khartoum since independence in 1956.

4. Side Shows or Consolidation of Positions

With the talks failing, both sides sought to bolster their positions regarding the future political orientation of the country, especially regarding the status of the national capital, a matter on which the SPLM/A had more friends than the NCP. Most important, Garang met and successfully concluded an agreement with the leaders of the Democratic Unionist (DUP) and Umma Parties in Cairo in May 2003, resulting in the Cairo Declaration. That declaration reaffirmed the NDA's resolution on religion and politics passed in June 1995 and its declaration of 1993 issued in Nairobi. Both resolutions aimed at preserving Sudan's unity by guaranteeing equal constitutional rights and duties to all citizens, "irrespective of religion, gender, or ethnic origin." Accordingly, the three leaders deemed that any agreement on a national capital city should be based on equal treatment of all religions and beliefs in order to preserve the country's unity on a new basis.[21] The government was deeply worried by the Cairo Declaration, to which the two paramount religious leaders in northern Sudan had affixed their signatures. Sayed al-Khatib, a member of the government's delegation to the peace talks, considered that the declaration "represented [a] violation to the principles of the negotiations and the letter and spirit of Machakos Protocol."[22]

At the time, the author, in his capacity as advisor to the SPLM leader, presented the situation starkly in an interview with the London Arabic daily *Al-sharq al-Awsat*: "There is no alternative. The SPLM wants Khartoum to be the national capital 'under secular laws.' During the negotiations the regime has proposed the idea of two capitals—Khartoum and Juba. The SPLM says that this shall not work because there is no country with two political capitals." The important thing, the author added, "is that the prevailing laws in Khartoum be reviewed. The maintenance of those laws represents a call for separation, and the regime has to decide whether it wants a unified Sudan or a Sudan where Islamic shari'a is implemented and in such case the South is encouraged to secede."[23]

5. Why Wealth Sharing?

In the matter of wealth sharing, the SPLM called for nothing less than a shift in the development paradigm bequeathed on Sudan by the colonial

178

administration. The British concentrated development on the riverain parts of northern Sudan, especially Khartoum and Gezira, because these areas were endowed with fertile land, abundant water resources, relatively trained manpower, and proximity to seaports. That urban-biased development, which served colonial interests well, created serious distortions in the national economy, least of which was the marginalization of all areas in the outer edge of northern Sudan's riverain central areas. For example, gross domestic product (GDP) variations in Sudan at the time of independence (January 1, 1956) revealed that Khartoum ran away with 119 (in thousands of Sudanese pounds) of the GDP, Gezira with 71, all other parts of northern Sudan (Dar Fur, Kordofan, northern and eastern Sudan) with 28, while the south, which covered one-third of the total surface area of the country, was left with a miserly 12 percent.[24] Equally revealing were the figures on regional distribution of investment (both public and private) reported in the first years of independence by Sudan's department of statistics. According to that report, 60 percent of the total public and private investment in the country went to Khartoum, Northern Sudan, and Kassala (the latter probably related to investment in Port Sudan), while 23 percent went cumulatively to Equatoria, Blue Nile, and Kordofan; 12 percent to Upper Nile; and 2 percent to Bahr el Ghazal. The investment in Equatoria in all likelihood went to the Zande scheme in Western Equatoria.[25]

This pattern of marginalization was fortuitous, as the colonialists did not deliberately seek to marginalize those areas but selfishly wanted to maximize benefits and minimize costs. However, the perpetuation of that economic paradigm by successive national regimes was a different matter. Whether it was for self-serving purposes or the result of a lack of serious meditation into the root causes of misery in the rural areas, the ruling class could hardly steer clear of blame. Notwithstanding, the perpetuation of the colonial economic model after independence had two noticeable impacts. First, it made the marginalization structural and the disparities magnified, if only because concentrating wealth in Khartoum and Gezira boosted their tax base and, therefore, facilitated more expenditure on infrastructure and services. Second, it created intuitions within marginalized groups that Khartoum was not willing to change an economic situation from which it was reaping benefits. At the intellectual level, therefore, Garang fearlessly argued that Sudan's socioeconomic problems lay in the disparity and horizontal inequalities that pervaded Sudan's political and geographic landscape. Tactically, he argued, since the cost of rebellion in the marginalized regions of Sudan became very small, zero, or negative, it paid to rebel. As a consequence, he had success mobilizing large sectors of disempowered regional groups from the Nuba Mountains, eastern Sudan, Blue Nile, and Dar Fur to join or work in unison with the SPLM/A.

Two issues relating to wealth sharing and financial management added to the economic problems under negotiation. In late 2002, the SPLM/A issued a new currency, the New Sudan pound, in the areas under its control, and this angered the government considerably. The SPLM/A was making an important point: that the existing national banking system based on Islamic law could not apply in the south. It was, again, a wake-up call to the government that a wide range of things needed to change before the SPLM/A could believe they were serious about peace. In addition, there was also the combustible issue of oil. In early 2003, a yawning gulf existed between the two sides on this issue, with the SPLM/A demanding 60 percent of oil revenues, and the government offering only 10 percent.[26] To the SPLM/A, the offer was outrageous, since it only pertained to revenues from oil produced in southern Sudan. Yet, the offer represented a move forward compared to an earlier offer of 5 percent, which the government had made in response to the SPLM/A's demand of a 90 percent share.[27]

Although the Machakos Protocol did not elaborate details on wealth sharing, the two sides did agree in principle to "find a comprehensive solution that addresses the economic and social deterioration of the Sudan and replaces war **not just with peace, but also with social, political and economic justice** which respects the fundamental human and political rights of all the Sudanese people"[28] (emphasis added). By recognizing historical economic injustice as an issue germane to peacemaking in Sudan, the government proved it had taken successive northern Sudanese governments nigh 50 years (1956–2002) to realize the root causes of their country's tragedy. In this respect, the preamble to the Machakos Framework Protocol provided:

- **"Whereas** the Parties are desirous of resolving the Sudan Conflict in a just and sustainable manner by **addressing the root causes of the conflict** and by establishing a framework for governance through which **power and wealth shall be equitably shared and human rights guaranteed;** and
- **Mindful** that the conflict in the Sudan is the longest running conflict in Africa, that it has caused horrendous loss of life and **destroyed the infrastructure of the country, wasted economic resources,** and has caused untold suffering, particularly with regard to the people of South Sudan; and
- **Sensitive** to historical **injustices and inequalities in development between the different regions of the Sudan** that need to be redressed" (emphasis added).

Despite this declared awareness of the root causes of the problem, the sixth round of talks (the fifth round according to the IGAD) made little progress. Nonetheless, that impasse led the two parties to resort (reluctantly in the case of the government) to supporting Sumbeiywo's idea of a "holistic approach" as explained in Chapter Four. An IGAD communiqué in late May explained the way forward as follows: "We have jointly set out to develop an all-inclusive negotiating framework on all the outstanding issues in power sharing, wealth sharing and security arrangements."[29]

6. Conflicting Conceptual Approaches

6.1 Power

By the close of the Machakos rounds, the two parties were strikingly at odds with regard to power and wealth sharing. That was the time the IGAD secretariat tabled the Nakuru Framework Draft, aware of the fact the parties' positions, particularly on power sharing, were significantly different. However, as it was proved later, that difference did not present an insurmountable gulf. For example, regarding the presidency, the government proposed that the SPLM/A would have the position of first vice president but not with the authority to succeed the current president in case of his removal from, or abdication of, office in the course of the interim period. That would necessarily ensure a permanent northern (or indeed NCP) presidency during that period. On account of this proposal, the SPLM/A fell back on the confederate option, demanding a rotating presidency that would entail three years each for the north and the south during the interim period. Eventually, the two parties agreed on the following compromise:

- The National Executive shall consist of the presidency and a Council of Ministers.
- There shall be established the institution of the presidency consisting of the president and two vice presidents.
- The functions of the two vice presidents shall be clearly defined by the parties to this agreement.
- There shall be a partnership and collegial decision-making process within the institution of the presidency in order to safeguard the peace agreement.[30]

With regard to representation in the national parliament, the SPLM/A proposed that it be guaranteed 40 percent of the seats in the lower house and 50 percent in the upper. Those percentages were not only based on the demographic weight of the south, but also calculated to insure that the NCP would not use its absolute majority in the lower house to torpedo proposals with which it disagreed or to sabotage the agreement. The government retorted that southerners were a minority in Sudan, and the demand was accordingly unjust. The SPLM/A countered that its membership consisted not only of southerners, but also citizens from the Three Areas. It also added that the NCP's actual popular constituency represented a much smaller minority.

181

As to the apportionment of cabinet positions, the SPLM/A was very apprehensive about being denigrated with marginal ministries. Accordingly, it demanded 40 percent of each of three categories of ministries: sovereignty (interior, foreign affairs, security, and justice); economic (including finance, energy, industry, and agriculture); and service (such as education, health, transport, and culture). It also demanded 40 percent of the positions in the executive and judicial arms of the proposed government of National Unity. While the SPLM/A claimed that 30 percent of positions in the national civil service should be allocated to southerners (not the SPLM), the government offered a meagre 10 percent on the economic issues.

On the other side, there was a tiff between the two parties regarding land, behind which lay different conceptual and normative approaches to issues of land ownership, financial equalization, and exploitation of subterranean resources. As John Ashworth noted in early July 2003: "Southerners believe in communal ownership of land unless there is a clear title, whereas government believes that all land is owned by the state unless there is a clear title."[31] As for oil revenues, the government had nothing to offer the south but a miserly 10 percent. Strangely enough, the mediator pressured the SPLM/A to take that offer, maintaining his early assertions that "something is better than nothing." But Garang would have nothing of that; he told his aides that the government was both arrogant and greedy.

7. The Wealth Sharing Protocol of January 2004

Recalling the government's refusal at the Nanyuki talks to continue negotiations on wealth sharing on the basis of the Nakuru document and the SPLM/A's holding fast to its position that south Sudan should receive no less than 60 percent of net oil proceeds,[32] it appeared that there was no solution in sight. No matter how, when the talks shifted to the level of the principals in early September, the SPLM/A produced a substantive proposal detailing its stance on land, apportionment of oil revenues, and currency.[33] In that proposal, the SPLM/A put forward its position across key dimensions, which may be summarized as follows:

(i) Land ownership is communal and rests with the people;
(ii) Land commissions shall be established to deal with land claims;
(iii) Subterranean natural resources are *owned* by land owners and *regulated* by governments;
(iv) The National Petroleum Commission should have 50:50 north-south representation. There should be a separate petroleum commission for Southern Sudan;
(v) There must exist the option of renegotiating existing oil contracts if they are deemed to have fundamental environmental or social problems;

(vi) As regards oil revenue sharing, five percent, after deductions, shall go to the oil-producing state, 60 percent of revenues generated from oil wells in southern Sudan to the government of Southern Sudan, and the rest to the Government of National Unity;

(vii) Ten percent of national revenues shall be allocated to the government of Southern Sudan as general budgetary support and 33.4 percent of the balance specifically to the government of Southern Sudan for reconstruction, rehabilitation, repatriation, and development;

(viii) As regards monetary policy, until a new currency is in circulation, the Sudanese dinar and New Sudan pound shall be deemed legal tender throughout Sudan, and a Bank of Southern Sudan shall be established as a branch of the Bank of Sudan, with foreign assistance for the south to be channelled directly through the Bank of Southern Sudan.

The initial reaction by the government to the SPLM/A proposals on wealth and power sharing, the Three Areas, and security arrangements was total rejection. In doing so, the government reiterated its claim that the proposals directly contradicted what was previously agreed upon, or proposed by the SPLM/A. Nevertheless, on September 11, 2003, coinciding with the arrival of Sudan's minister for defense, Major General Bakri Hassan Salih, and his team, the government's Sudanese chargé d'affaires in Nairobi, Dirdeiry Mohamed Ahmed, announced that "more delegates from Khartoum, who are experts on wealth-sharing, had arrived in Naivasha on Thursday to reinforce the government side."[34] Apparently, the government's initial reaction was meant to put things on hold until its economic experts arrived.

Negotiations on wealth sharing took a step back and were left to technical teams, while Taha and Garang focused upon security arrangements. After their success in signing the Framework Agreement on Security Arrangements on September 25, the two sides took a short break before resuming negotiations in October. Once more, they decided to focus first on the Three Areas, which again meant that negotiations on wealth sharing (as well as power sharing) were put on a back burner, at least at the level of the principals. By the time he visited Naivasha and met with both sides on October 22, 2003, U.S. Secretary of State Colin Powell considered that wealth sharing was "making excellent progress," and although there were a few remaining issues to be resolved, he could "see the end in sight on the wealth sharing discussions."[35] At the meeting with Powell, Taha and Garang reportedly committed to reaching a final agreement by the end of the year.

Following a hiatus in the talks during the fasting month of Ramadan, negotiations on wealth sharing picked up in earnest in late November and early December 2003. The SPLM/A's proposals were now more specific regarding the distribution of oil wealth and paying special concern to the plight of marginalized regions in northern Sudan. All the while the parties were debating the issue of oil revenues, it may be recalled that the government negotiators

183

were *only* discussing oil produced in the south. And even though nearly 80 percent of the oil produced in the country at that point in time was delivered from wells in southern Sudan, there was still oil produced in the north. On receiving the government proposal on oil revenues, Garang asked, "What about oil produced in other parts of Sudan?" In a conversation with his team, he argued that "those people (meaning the NCP), are both greedy and contradictory. On the one hand, they claim that Sudan is and has to remain one, but when it comes to oil, they want to separate oil produced in the North from that produced in the South."

Thus, in its second position on oil revenues, dated December 15[36] and presented to Taha, the SPLM/A came up with allocations of revenues derived from oil produced all over Sudan as follows: two percent for the Nuba Mountains, one percent for southern Blue Nile, six percent for greater Darfur (two percent for each of three Dar Furian states), and three percent for the greater eastern Sudan region (two percent each for Kassala, Red Sea, and Gedarif). The same paper demanded that 60 percent net oil revenues be channeled to the south but specified that 15 percent would be allocated to the government of Southern Sudan, 40 percent to the regions (states) of Southern Sudan, and 5 percent to the relevant oil producing state. Garang believed that the percentages proposed by the government's delegation for the north and south would not be dedicated to development and social welfare but rather to maintaining the bureaucracies in Khartoum and Juba. Hence, his proposals on oil revenue sharing were intended to push forward three envelopes simultaneously: decentralization, regional development, and economic empowerment of marginalized areas. That position took the government by surprise since its proposal neither envisaged a process by which the oil bounty would be shared equitably by all parts of Sudan nor contemplated radical reductions of expenditure on national government's bureaucracy, let alone defense and security. Garang's proposal was accompanied by a schedule for the distribution of revenues, which allocated administrative costs for running the two governments (national and Southern Sudan) but gave prominence to the development needs of all hitherto marginalized areas in Sudan, as well as to the reconstruction of the south after decades of war ruination. That was why he allocated only 15 percent to the government of Southern Sudan while proposing that 40 percent of the south's would go to the states.

That proposal should not have been surprising to the government delegation since they had been briefed on experiences in other countries as to equity in, and equalization of, the apportionment of national revenues. A number of seminars were held during the negotiations to apprise the parties on issues pertaining to fiscal federalism. Those seminars and workshops, among others, were organized by the World Bank, International Monetary Fund, USAID, and Norwegian experts. One of the documents presented to the negotiators contained a detailed review of the experiences of a number of countries on the sharing of oil and gas revenues between national and subnational levels of government. In Indonesia, for example, 70 percent of royalties from the sale of oil and natural gas goes to the autonomous provinces of Aceh and Irian Jay. In Bolivia, 10 percent of taxes on oil goes to provinces below the national average per capita, and in the Russian Federation, oil revenues are also shared between the federation and oil producing oblasts and republics for purposes of equalization.[37] The government's lopsided policy was not caused by a lack of awareness of the real needs of the marginalized areas in Sudan or of the experiences of countries akin to Sudan in the equitable sharing of national resources. Basically, it was due to the paternalistic mindset and acquisitive nature of the central governments in power in Sudan since independence. Those governments are yet to be weaned from the excessive concentration of power or the inveterate habit of taking the peripheries for granted. Another cause of the lop-sidedness of policies was the belief, or make-belief, by those governments that the highest priority was maintaining a self-perpetuating bureaucracy at the center rather than sustaining peace through administrative decentralization and equitable development. Garang also had inklings that Juba bureaucrats would find it easy, and certainly self-serving, to follow in the footsteps of their brothers in the north in ruling the south.

The government, in its (undated) position paper two,[38] moved a bit from its long-held position of granting the south only 10 percent of oil revenues, but still it did not countenance Garang's call for a decentralized approach to revenue sharing. It proposed to grant the south 20 percent of net revenues between 2004 and 2006 (the first three years of the interim period) and 25 percent between 2007 and 2009 (the final three years of the interim period). It would also grant two percent for the oil-producing states. In its position paper three[39] (also undated), it proposed 25 percent for the government of Southern Sudan in year one of the interim period, and then 30 percent for the remaining five years; it maintained the two percent allocation proposal for oil-producing states. No rationale was given for this erratic change of numbers, nor was there an enlightened reaction to Garang's reasoned allocation of revenues. In the same position paper three, the government also claimed that the government of Southern Sudan's entitlement to revenue from the center (budgetary support and reconstruction funding) would raise the effective total from revenues to 32 percent in year one and 37 percent for years two to six. Of course, these were separate matters, and the conflation of the two rightful demands of the SPLM/A revealed failure by the government's delegation to appreciate the inherent matters of justice and equity to which these issues related.

The SPLM/A also demanded that Khartoum reveal full details on oil production and revenues, broken down by region and state, which had long been kept out of the purview of everyone except the NCP's narrow coterie.

More than merely a matter of government transparency, the SPLM/A explained rightly that this information was necessary to determine which percentages of the oil resources should revert to the central power and how much should go to the region from which it was extracted. The government refused to budge on all counts. However, on December 20, 2003, Kenya's foreign minister Kalonzo Musyoka announced that the two sides had reached an agreement on wealth-sharing, assisted by a compromise proposal presented to them by the IGAD mediation team.[40] According to government spokesman Sayed al-Khatib, during the six-year interim period to follow a final peace deal, "50 percent of revenues from the oil produced in south Sudan will go to the SPLA."[41] The government's reference to the people and future government of Southern Sudan as "the SPLA" revealed an enduring, and in this case, mischievous bias. Musyoka's announcement, while true, referred only to the agreement on broad contours for a deal on wealth sharing. It took another two weeks, with breaks for Christmas and New Year's Day, before the agreement on wealth sharing was signed on January 7, 2004, in Naivasha, Kenya.

In addition, the two parties agreed to establish an Oil Revenue Stabilization Account from government oil net revenues to allow for fluctuations in oil prices and the allocation of two percent of oil revenues to the oil-producing states. After deduction of the above allocations, 50 percent of the revenues generated from oil in southern Sudan would go to the government of Southern Sudan and 50 percent to the Government of National Unity from the beginning of the pre-interim period (clause 5). The protocol also drew guiding principles for the management and development of the oil sector that would ensure "sustainable utilization of oil as a nonrenewable natural resource which would be exploited with due regard to public good, national environmental politics, and biodiversity conservation requirements." Furthermore, it was agreed (clause 3) that a National Petroleum Commission (NPC) be established and empowered to make consensus decisions on oil policies and contracting. The NPC was to be composed of equal number of members from the government of Southern Sudan and the Government of National Unity and co-chaired by the national president and president of the government of Southern Sudan, while oil-producing states were given the right to contest contracts presented to the NPC for approval if these contracts negatively affected their interests. If the NPC failed to decide collectively on the contested contract, then the matter would be referred to the Council of States for adjudication. In clause 4 the SPLM was given the right to pore over existing oil contracts with a view to identifying, if any, oil operations that were detrimental to the environment or well-being of societies in oil-producing areas. That clause was implemented on February 2007 when the president of the government of Southern Sudan, Salva Kiir Mayardit, formed an *ad hoc* petroleum committee in order to identify contracts "that are deemed to have fundamental social and environmental problems" (clause 4.3 of protocol). The government, as provided for in the protocol, "will implement remedial measures" in the eventuality that such problems were found. It was later discovered that the damage wrought by some oil operations on the natural environment, especially in Unity State, was nothing short of environmental hooliganism.[42] Up to this point in time, no follow-up to the experts' report has taken place.

With reference to non-oil revenues, clause 6 authorized the government of Southern Sudan to access particular national funds as agreed to by the national government, as well as to raise tax revenues from a selected range of categories, including excises and levies on small and medium business and personal income taxes. The parties agree that those non-oil national revenues should be allocated by the national government as follows: 50 percent of such revenues collected in southern Sudan would go to the government of Southern Sudan, with an upwards review midway through the interim period. Moreover, the Protocol on Wealth Sharing[43] recognized as a principle that the war-affected states of Southern Sudan, the Three Areas, and other parts of the country that lagged far behind in development should be the focus of special wealth-sharing and fiscal arrangements during that period. According to the "Guiding Principles in Respect of an Equitable Sharing of Common Wealth," those areas "shall be brought up to the same average level of socioeconomic and public services standards as northern states." The Government of National Unity was required to ensure disbursement of revenues, as per the agreement, to Southern Sudan and the states. On the other hand, the negotiators failed to reach a definitive agreement on land resources. Instead, they established normative rules and adjudication processes on land disputes, beginning with the establishment of a National Land Commission (clause 2.6); a Southern Sudan Land Commission (clause 2.7); and recognition that customary laws, local heritage, and international trends and practices should be reflected in national land laws (clause 2.5). While the Southern Sudan Land Commission was formed in 2006, the National Land Commission and those agreed to for southern Kordofan and Blue Nile were never established.

In order to insure equalization of financial appropriations, the parties agreed to establish an all-embracing Fiscal and Financial Allocation and Monitoring Commission (FFAMC) whose role was "to ensure transparency and fairness in regard to the allocation of nationally collected funds to the states." The FFAMC was to comprise three representatives of the Government of National Unity, three of the government of Southern Sudan, and all finance ministers in all states of Sudan from both the north and the south. The specific functions of the FFAMC comprised allocating, monitoring, and ensuring that equalization grants from national revenue funds were promptly transferred to the states and that appropriate utilization of those funds and their prompt transfer to war-affected areas were assured. A renowned economist and statesman was appointed to head the commission,[44] but he was relieved of that post after less than a couple of years. Having seriously taken up his job and the oath of allegiance he had given to the constitution, he rejected all interference by the central government on the manner in which allocations were to be made to states.

In addition, clause 15 established a Southern Sudan Reconstruction and Development Fund (SSRDF) for the south and a National Reconstruction and Development Fund (NRDF) for the rest of the country. Both funds were charged with mobilizing domestic and external resources to develop war-affected and other less-developed areas. According to the protocol, the two commissions were to realize the strategy for "equitable sharing of common wealth," referred to above. The fact that the NRDF was not formed until the end of the interim period shed doubt on the seriousness of the intentions of those who signed the protocol. As for the SSRDF, despite its establishment, it turned out to be a development fund in name only. Shorn of resources, political guidance, and resource mobilization mechanisms, the ineptitude of the SSADF did not surprise anybody.

Another notable clause (14) dealt with the establishment of a dual-banking system during the interim period, with Islamic banking operating in northern Sudan and conventional banking in southern Sudan. In lieu of a dual-banking system, however, the SPLM/A proposed that there should be one system in both the north and the south that permitted both Islamic and conventional banking in the two parts of the country. The government welcomed the readiness of the SPLM/A to accommodate Islamic banking in southern Sudan but was not ready to upset the shari'a-based banking system in the North. As a result of the NCP's rejection of a dual-banking system in the whole country, the SPLM/A decided that banking in southern Sudan would only be conventional. That resulted in the gradual closure of all shari'a-based banks operating in the South.

As for currency, the parties eventually agreed that a new Sudanese currency would be issued in pounds, as it used to be before the dinar was introduced by the NIF. Some SPLM negotiators mistakenly claimed that the dinar was an Islamic currency introduced by the NIF as part of its Islamization policy. Arguments to the contrary did not convince the doubting Thomases within SPLM. In reality, neither was the dinar Islamic nor the pound (jinaih in Arabic) indigenous. While the dinar was historically borrowed by Islamic caliphates from the Roman dinaro, the pound or jinaih that was used in Sudan since the colonial era, as well as in Egypt, was but a corruption of the English guinea. This was but one example of the level of ungenerous pettifogging born of gratuitous scepticism, or more likely, the desire to erase all symbols of the NIF era.

Another outstanding innovation in the field of post-conflict construction was the mapping out by the two parties of a development and reconstruction plan for the interim period. On March 18, 2005, nearly two months after the signing of the Comprehensive Peace Agreement, Vice President Taha and Dr. John Garang launched a document that was meant to be Sudan's road map toward the consolidation of peace through development. In the foreword to the document the two leaders wrote:

"Building on the peace agreement, we are proud to jointly present this [Framework for Sustained Peace, Development, and Poverty Eradication]. It is an ambitious but realistic plan that has been developed jointly with development partners and civil society to address the urgent task of meeting the basic aspiration of our people and accelerating progress towards meeting the Millennium Development Goals. It is founded on a clear recognition of the very different needs in different parts of the country, and especially the massive needs of the people of the South, and the Three Areas, while not neglecting other disadvantaged parts of the country. Despite the differences, there are common themes which include the focus on broad and inclusive economic growth and empowerment of the people through a decentralized system of governance and service delivery. It is also a strategy and vision that will give the unity of Sudan a chance during the Interim Period by making it attractive and through a reformed and fully developed system of governance in which all Sudanese are equal stakeholders."[45]

The leaders called on development partners and civil society to join hands with the people of Sudan in "a *partnership that supports the recovery, reconciliation, prosperity and restoration of the Sudanese dignity as well as upholding fundamental and basic human rights and good governance*" (emphasis added).[46] Clearly, the two parties realized that economic development, good governance, and the upholding of basic rights were inseparable themes.

That report was compiled by a Joint Assessment Mission (JAM) created by the two parties to identify economic needs and formulate economic recovery programs for southern Sudan and other areas of the country that were under economic stress. Alongside a group of competent economists and development experts from Sudan, the JAM brought in the World Bank and United Nations. The World Bank, under its program for Low-Income Countries under Stress (LICUS), funded the JAM, which produced a detailed three-pronged program for the reconstruction of southern Sudan, the Three Areas, and northern Sudan. It also defined macroeconomic coordinates and benchmarks without which no meaningful development could be achieved. Budget estimates to the tune of U.S. $7.9 billion were proposed for the implementation of the initial recovery phase (2005–2008) of the program.

Soon after the release of the mission's report, the Norwegian minister for international development convened a donors' conference in Oslo (April 11-12, 2005) to mobilize funding for the implementation of that ambitious program; 60 countries and organizations attended the conference. The results of the Oslo conference were thunderous; the donor community pledged U.S. $4.1 billion for the period 2005-2007. The two parties and donors agreed to channel the funds through a Multi-Donor Trust Fund (MDTF) to be managed by the World Bank. The high hopes raised by the Oslo conference were later dampened for various reasons, which we shall discuss in the chapter on CPA implementation (Chapter Eight).

8. The Power Sharing Protocol of May 2004

As wealth sharing was conceived during the Naivasha talks as a process to end historical inequities and structural distortions in the economy, power sharing was envisioned as a systemic reformation that would end political disempowerment, widen the margins of democracy, and set the stage for the emergence of good and just governance. With this in mind, negotiations between Taha and Garang since their first meeting in early September 2003 made incremental progress. The point of departure in these negotiations was the SPLM/A's position paper handed to the government in that month.[47] The paper represented the SPLM/A's post-Nakuru document negotiating position and responded, in part, to the government's July 11, 2003, reaction to the Nakuru text. The most important aspects of that position paper may be summarized as follows:

- **The Presidency**: There shall be only one president and one vice president.
- **Elections**: Elections are not necessary throughout the interim period, but acknowledging that the government and the mediators think otherwise, the SPLM/A suggested phased elections, with presidential elections unlikely until after the Southern Sudan referendum.
- **Government of Southern Sudan**: Inclusiveness is important, but the SPLM/A rejects the NCP's claim for having a say in the selection of the vice president of the government of Southern Sudan, and if this is to happen, then the SPLM/A will reopen Machakos and call for the formation of Northern Sudan (government of Northern Sudan), in which it will demand the post of vice president.
- **Governors**: Before elections, the national legislatures shall draw up a short list, from which a consensus of the presidency (president and vice president) shall decide. If this proves impossible, the president shall decide for northern Sudan and the vice president for Southern Sudan.
- **National Capital**: The whole of the present Khartoum State shall be the national capital area, and it shall not therefore be governed by religious laws or one single religion. Furthermore, there shall be a National Police Force and National Security Organ reflecting the diversity of Sudan to operate in Khartoum State.

- **Southern Sudanese and SPLM representation in the Government of National Unity and the National Assembly**: The SPLM shall be granted 40 percent of ministries (cf. Nakuru document: 25 percent); 40 percent of civil service (cf. Nakuru document: 25–35 percent); 40 percent of national judiciary posts (Nakuru document silent on this issue); Southern Sudanese (not only SPLM) shall be guaranteed 40 percent of lower house seats in the National Assembly and 50 percent of upper house seats. All political forces and civil society shall be involved in the interim national constitution review process.

Again the government's response to the SPLM/A's proposals was unhelpful, especially since it had not responded directly to the SPLM/A's September 2003 paper on power sharing. It was, nonetheless, clear from its response to the Nakuru document that the government had major problems with four issues: the structure and division of powers of the presidency; allocation to southerners and the SPLM of ministries in the Government of National Unity and seats in the national parliament; the timing of elections; and the status of the national capital. While it bleated out the argument of a lack of inclusiveness in the south, this only served to expose the government's real vulnerability to the SPLM/A's insistence on broad representation of other political interests and forces in the center, Khartoum.

During his visit to Naivasha in late October 2003, U.S. Secretary of State Colin Powell seemed to have wished to give confidence to both sides. On wealth-sharing discussions, he noted that they were "making excellent progress" and that he could "'see the end was in sight,'" adding: "'This is a moment of opportunity that must not be lost [and] the way is now open for a final and comprehensive solution.'"[48] Powell urged the parties to complete "'the final stage of this marathon'" so that Sudan could "'experience a new way of life unclouded by the suffering of war.'"[49] As to power sharing, Powell said that differences could be "dealt with in the near future."[50] However, matters of power sharing were closely tied up with what would arguably prove to be the most challenging disagreements of the whole peace negotiations: the status of the national capital and the Three Areas. Even though progress was made on many other issues of power sharing, final agreement would depend on resolving these other matters as well. As we had seen, security arrangements and wealth sharing were the main focus of talks during the last quarter of 2003, and it was only in January that the talks returned with greater vigor and in more earnest to power sharing, the status of the capital, and the Three Areas.

In his address on New Year's Day 2004, on the anniversary of Sudan's independence, President Bashir was a champion of peace. He exulted: "Honorable citizens, honorable members of parliament, the peace process is expected to undergo a great and deep transformation in its form and institutions, and this will put our country on the threshold of a bright new future based on new relations, confidence, mutual consent, and joint work so as to implement and complete the peace accord. **This means national**

participation is open to all, without any exclusion or predominance."[51] That being said, a different picture was painted by the tenor of the government's negotiating positions on issues of power sharing, the national capital, and the Three Areas over the subsequent five months. The president's assertion that the door was open wide "for all without any exclusion or predominance" was belied by the NCP's persistence at the negotiations to hold on to absolute power.

Indeed, the government's mood rapidly changed after the euphoria surrounding the signing of the agreement on wealth sharing on January 6. The turnaround was precipitated in part by the government's indefatigable position on the Three Areas and the national capital, but also by its increasing vulnerability with regard to the nearly one-year armed struggle in Darfur (see Chapters Nine and Twelve). In this context, negotiations were rather abruptly suspended in mid-January 2004 when Vice President Taha returned to Khartoum and proceeded to go to Mecca on *haj* (pilgrimage). He returned to the negotiating table in late February 2004, at which time the IGAD negotiations were increasingly vying for the spotlight with the humanitarian catastrophe unfolding in Darfur. Under the specter of this crisis, the negotiations pushed on, and deals on power sharing, Abyei, and the two states of southern Kordofan and Blue Nile were negotiated concurrently.

The power sharing protocol was finally agreed upon by the parties on May 26, 2004,[52] making it clear that the government had dragged its feet for two years since the talks began in Karen without destroying the will of the SPLM to achieve a decentralized, inclusive, and reformed system of government vastly different from that which the Sudanese had labored under since independence. The distortions in Sudan's system of rule did not start with the assumption of power by the NIF, though that party had the dubious distinction of aggravating these distortions by adding a heavy dose of religion to them.

The power sharing protocol, first, reaffirmed the asymmetric federal structure of government suggested by the Nakuru Draft Framework, with four levels of government consisting of national, Southern Sudan, state, and local. It then established (clauses 1.5 and 1.6) principles of good governance, upholding the rule of law, and universal human rights as enshrined in international covenants. The reluctance by government negotiators to embrace all universal human rights covenants was too funny for words. That reluctance was based on the claim that some of the covenants were contrary to Sudanese culture. SPLM negotiators, observers, and advisors agreed that the covenants, by their very universal nature, could not be indigenized. However, guarantees for those rights were extensive and well expounded in the protocol. In particular, the protocol affirmed the rights of Sudanese to protections relating to life; liberty; freedom from slavery; torture; fair trial; privacy; freedom of thought, conscience, and religion; freedom of expression;

freedom of assembly and association; family and marriage; the right to vote; equality before the law; freedom from discrimination; freedom of movement; and equal rights of men and women. A Human Rights Commission was mandated to monitor these freedoms and rights (clause 2.10.1.2), but, shamefully, those rights continued to be trampled upon with impunity, and the commission was not established until the end of the interim period. This issue shall be discussed in Chapter Nine within the framework of the implementation of the Comprehensive Peace Agreement.

One thing the SPLM/A failed to impress on the government's negotiators was the need for a process of truth, reconciliation, and healing similar to that adopted by the South Africans in the Truth and Reconciliation Process. Probably, with too many corpses in their closets, the sinners within the government did not want to open a Pandora's box they would rather keep closed. In order to argue the SPLM out of that proposition, one of the government negotiators warned his counterpart in the SPLM delegation that the SPLM/A had also committed grievous crimes in war, so they should better be careful. Rather than jumping to the defense of their party, SPLM negotiators publicly admitted that they had committed serious crimes in war against civilians, but now they wished to cleanse their souls. Even that contrition was not sufficient enough to make the government's reluctant negotiators give way. As a result, the protocol said little on the issue of national reconciliation, and even that was left to the Government of National Unity to elaborate and implement. Clause 1.7 of the protocol provided that "the Parties agree to initiate a comprehensive process of national reconciliation and healing throughout the country as part of the peace building process. **Its mechanisms and forms shall be worked out by the Government of National Unity**" (emphasis added). The absence of a clear provision on transitional justice became one area of disappointment to Sudanese civil society and analysts, particularly when the Government of National Unity made light of that crucial matter.

On census and elections (clause 1.8), the protocol affirmed that a national census be completed before the end of the second year of the interim period and elections held before the end of the third year of that period. Both issues became bones of contention when it came to implementation. However, an agreement was reached (clause 1.8.6) that "whoever runs in any election must respect, abide by, and enforce the Peace Agreement." That clause was meant to guarantee that those who might want to contest elections would have to commit first to the peace agreement. In effect, that requirement was also made a condition for the registration of political parties. This at last put to rest SPLM's fears that elections might result in bringing to power parties unfriendly to the CPA.

Concerning national institutions, Part II of the protocol detailed provisions for a bicameral national legislature (2.2); the executive, especially the institution of the presidency (2.3); the status of the national capital (2.4); the Government of National Unity (2.5); the civil service (2.6); and key national institutions such as national security (2.7), the judiciary (2.11), and the constitutional review process (2.12). The creation of a bicameral national legislature was not a novelty in Sudan; it had had a bicameral parliament, comprising a house of representatives and a senate, since 1953. By 1965, after the demise of General Abboud, the Senate was abolished. As it was constituted in 1953, the Senate allowed for the representation of traditional leaders, retired civil servants, and armed officers and businessmen. The presence of those elements was meant to enrich parliamentary deliberations, especially since many of them, for practical reasons, were not electable. However, the political class of 1965, mimicking President Nassir's abolition of the Egyptian Senate (*Majlis al Shioukh*) as a relic of the past, abolished the Senate. Sudan's political copycats never took notice of their country's sociocultural realities, which were far from being akin to those of Egypt. Thus, the recreation of a Council of States filled in the lacunae caused by the abolition of Sudan's old Senate. However, the Council of States was modeled on the U.S. Senate to ensure that each state in the north and south would have two representatives, irrespective of its size. But unlike the United States, members of the Council were to be indirectly chosen by state parliaments. The Council, as an upper house, was also expected to provide a degree of restraint on the lower house and to adjudicate on matters relating to oil contracts and equalization of revenue allocations to states. As for the allocation of seats in the National Assembly, the parties agreed that prior to national elections 52 percent of the seats would go to the NCP, 28 percent to SPLM, 14 percent to other northern political forces, and six percent to other southern political forces.

An agreement was also concluded on the institution of the presidency. That institution would be governed by the principle of collegiate decision making and shall consist of the president, a first vice president, and a vice president. Garang desisted from the SPLM's original position of having only a president and one vice president, because he realized that the loser in the arrangement initially proposed by the SPLM would be Ali Osman Taha, with whom he had developed a feeling of fellowship and a mutually beneficial rapport. However, the first vice president was guaranteed extensive powers during the interim period. Those included acting on behalf of the president when the president was absent and being a member of the Council of Ministers and National Security Council. More important, the first vice president's prior consent was required on four major decisions: declaration and termination of states of emergency; declaration of war; appointments that the president was required by the CPA to make; and summoning, adjourning, or proroguing the national legislature. The first vice president's consent was also required for the appointment of 27 positions.[53]

In addition, it was agreed that the president (also commander in chief of the Sudan Armed Forces) and vice president were to be members of the NCP, while the first vice president would be the chairman of the SPLM, president of Southern Sudan, and commander in chief of the SPLA. Should a "person from the South" win the elections, then he/she would be required to appoint the first vice president from the north (from the majority party in the elections). In the event that the presidency fell vacant during the interim period, a presidential council comprising the two vice presidents and the speaker of the National Assembly would jointly hold presidential responsibilities until a new appointment was made by the NCP (before the elections) or otherwise decided by elections held within 60 days.

On the subject of the National Executive, the parties acceded that prior to national elections the Executive was to have the same representation formula as the National Assembly. However, they failed to elaborate modalities to determine exactly which ministerial portfolios would be held by which party. That, as we shall see in Chapter Nine, led to the first crisis in the relations between the two partners in the Government of National Unity. The protocol also detailed how a National Constitutional Review Commission, referred to earlier, would take responsibility for developing a constitutional framework text that the National Assembly and the SPLM National Liberation Council (NLC) could adopt as the interim constitution for the country. The Sudan Interim National Constitution (INC) and the Interim Constitution for Southern Sudan (ICSS) were adopted on this basis in 2005. The same commission would then develop an "inclusive national constitutional review process" during the course of the six-year interim period in order to ensure wider participation in government. As we shall explain in the chapter on CPA implementation, that clause was just about neglected by the two parties.

Part III of the power sharing protocol dealt with the government of Southern Sudan, which was to administer that territory according to the administrative borders of Sudan's provinces established on January 1, 1956. Since Nakuru, the NCP had sought to achieve some counterbalance to what it believed to be concessions it had made to the SPLM on Government of National Unity power sharing. In the final result, the parties agreed that before the elections the SPLM would hold 70 percent of relevant posts in that government and seats in the Southern Sudan Legislative Assembly, the NCP would hold 15 percent, and other southern parties would hold 15 percent. The allocation of seats to the NCP in Southern Sudanese institutions was proposed by Vice President Taha. Garang asked Taha: "Why?" To that question Taha replied: "Because as partners we need to work for making unity attractive."[54] Garang did not answer promptly but asked for time to muse over the request. The next morning Garang returned with an affirmative response, coupled with his own request: "We also want to have the same percentage of executive positions and parliamentary seats in the executives and legislatures of all northern Sudan states." When Taha asked about the reasons for his demand, Garang reacted: "The SPLM, too, has a national mission in the North: the creation of New Sudan." [55]

Part IV of the protocol dealt with power sharing at the state government level. The parties agreed that before state elections the NCP and the SPLM would hold seven percent of state legislative and executive posts in northern and southern states, respectively, with the other parties holding 10 percent, and the remaining 20 percent for other northern and southern political forces, as appropriate. In clause 4.5.2, the parties agreed that prior to elections one governor of a southern state shall be from the NCP as well as one deputy governor of another southern state. The SPLM, having run with 15 percent of the seats in the executive of each of the 13 northern states did not vie for a governorship in those states. On the National Civil Service (NCS), the parties aimed at allocating 20 to 25 percent of the posts to eligible candidates from Southern Sudan. Clause 2.6 of the power sharing protocol was explicit about redressing imbalances in Sudan's public service, which was virtually privatized by the NCP, especially at higher and middle echelons. That clause provided, among other things, the following:

- "Imbalances and disadvantages which exist must be redressed."
- "There must be fair competition for jobs in the National Civil Service."
- "No level of government shall discriminate against any qualified Sudanese citizen on the basis of religion, ethnicity, region, gender, or political beliefs."
- The National Civil Service will fairly represent all the people of the Sudan and will **utilize affirmative action and job training** to achieve equitable targets for representation within an agreed time frame" (emphasis added).

None of those objectives or targets were achieved up to the close of the interim period.

The government was also piqued by the Nakuru proposal regarding the issue of the national capital. That proposal called for the establishment of a district within Khartoum under the administration of the National Assembly and in which equality of religions and respect for human rights and fundamental freedoms were guaranteed. That proposal was not out of the ordinary, as has been proved by the experience of many countries that were apprehensive of the encroachment of administrative powers in the hinterland. For example, the U.S. Constitution (article 1, section 8) provided for the creation of a federal capital district, distinct from the states, to serve as the permanent national capital. In Calcutta, India, the national capital under the British Raj was transferred in 1911 to Delhi, and after independence the Indian government conferred a degree of autonomy on New Delhi in 1956. In 1991,

New Delhi was rebaptized as the national capital territory of Delhi. Furthermore, Australia selected Canberra in 1908 as its capital in order to avoid the embarrassment of choosing between the rival cities, Sydney and Melbourne, as capitals. In Africa, Nigeria decided to choose Abuja in the center of the country as its capital, replacing Lagos. In 1976, Abuja was carved out of three states (Niger, Nasarawa, and Kogi), and unlike the states, it was to be run by a federal capital territory administration headed by a minister chosen by the president of Nigeria. All those experiences indicated that the SPLM's request for the creation of a new capital in Sudan was based on objective political, geographic, or administrative considerations. As usual, Khartoum rulers behaved as if Sudan was sui generis. In previous chapters, we amply demonstrated how northern regimes had consistently rejected the experiences of other countries with problems analogous to those of Sudan such as decentralization (federalism), linguistic plurality, and affirmative action in public employment as a mechanism for ending historical injustices. In all these cases, the northern political elite appeared to have assumed that Sudan was nonpareil.

Regardless, the SPLM conceded its core position on the national capital and accepted numerous compromises with a view to protecting diversity and respecting individual and cultural rights in the national capital. As for shari'a, clause 2.4.5.4 provided, somewhat opaquely, that courts imposing penalties on non-Muslims should observe the principle that remitted penalties—not shari'a-prescribed penalties—should only apply. That steep descent from the SPLM's original position hardly pleased its constituency in the north. However, were the SPLM to throw all its other gains—self-determination, participation in the national government at the political and civil service levels, full autonomy in Southern Sudan, a separate and independent army, assured financial entitlement—it would have neither been understood by its constituency in the south, nor by mediators. After all, the whole purpose of the negotiations was to achieve a win-win result. Were the SPLM to seek the ceiling of its agenda, it could only have done so by continuing the war until the NCP was vanquished. That would have been a tough and tall agenda, taking into account the fact that this objective was not achieved by the SPLM even when it was in alliance with NDA forces during the struggle.

9. Play Within the Play

In a play within the play, the United States was preparing the ground for enacting improbable political theatrics. Realizing that the peace agreement had but reached its conclusion, and desiring to reap the fruits of its efforts to reach that conclusion, the United States decided to call the main players—Bashir, Taha, and Garang—to Washington to sign the agreement in the U.S. capital. President Bush was by then depicted as a man of war, so advertising him as the man who had brought peace to the largest country in Africa and put an end to the longest conflict in that continent would help erase that image. The *mise-en-scène* included the presentation of the peace signatories on Capitol Hill during the State of the Union address, in the course of which the president would ask Congress to approve a special budget for consolidating peace in Sudan. Garang, with issues of the Three Areas and tightening the loose ends of security arrangements still hanging, declined the offer while thanking the United States for its continued support to the SPLM and its vital backing to the peacemaking process. Taha also thought that the time was not yet ripe to declare that peace was achieved.

After conveying their positions to the U.S. emissaries, Garang, with his caustic, sometimes self-deprecating sense of humor, told Taha: "I don't know what punishment shall be meted out on me by my friends, the Americans, but I know very well what awaits you: a one-way ticket to Guantanamo."[56] The United States' offer drove General Sumbeiywo round the bend and prompted him to say that he would not let the proposed signature of the agreement in Washington happen. It was after all, "a Kenyan-led process, and any signing ceremony would only take place in Nairobi."[57] In that fit of anger, the general locked out Jeffrey Millington, the U.S. observer to the talks, from a session during which the two parties were to deliberate on the remaining crucial issues in the negotiation.

10. Fighting Armed Robbers

Having established good relations with Taha, John Garang, in good faith, offered to bail the government out of the Darfur predicament.[58] He forecasted that, if it went unresolved, the Darfur conflict might jeopardize the peace agreement and detract national and international attention from it. With the SPLM/A's long relations with the new leaders of the Darfur rebellion (Suliman Arcua Minnawi and Abdel Wahid Mohamed Nour), Garang was desirous to capitalize on that relationship so as to make Sudan's peace comprehensive. The government at that time was overwhelmed by pressures from within and outside calling for an immediate resolution of the Darfur conflict, which the government persisted in describing as *al nahb al musalah* (armed robbery). That trivialization of the conflict reflected both political irresponsibility and sheer make-belief, particularly since the Darfur rebels were making embarrassing military victories. In the meantime, pressures were increasing from outside Sudan for a U.N. intervention to put an end to the fighting and facilitate delivery of humanitarian aid. Garang proposed to intervene with a view to persuading the two Darfurian leaders to sit with the government to negotiate a peaceful end to the conflict. He also suggested the establishment of a 20,000-man national peace force to be equally drawn from the SPLA and SAF. The force was to maintain order while peace negotiations were going on. That, he thought, would save Sudan from the embarrassment of international military intervention and enable the would-be Government of

National Unity to give unalloyed attention to the CPA. The government, as it seemed, did not yet have enough faith in the SPLA and its commander-in-chief, given the support he was offering to the two Darfurian leaders. It was also most likely that the NCP feared that any success that Garang might score in bringing peace to Darfur would give him an edge in national politics and set the stage for an alliance between the south and the west against the center. For all these reasons, Garang's offer was passed over, and the government was soon to rove around the world looking for mediators to assist with the western Sudanese "armed robbers."

11. Parameters for New Foreign Policy

In Chapter Three we pointed out that the SPLM was concerned with the way Sudan foreign policy was conducted and, therefore, prevailed on the NDA to agree to a foreign policy platform aimed, in the main, at serving the supreme interests of Sudan. That position was reiterated during the CPA negotiations, especially in view of the excessive ideologizing of foreign policy by the NIF during the first phase of its rule. That was the time when Khartoum's Islamist regime had gone on a warpath against Western countries and African and Arab neighboring states (Egypt, Eritrea, and Ethiopia) and threatened the rest of Africa with its declared policy of taking Islam to the rest of continent. Since the SPLM was to be a partner in government with the NCP, it arguably thought not to leave any door open for a relapse into foreign adventurism. Politics, not infrequently, makes strange bedfellows, but the SPLM, as it appeared, did not want to be part of an adventurous foreign policy that might superfluously take on the whole world. Consequently, the parties agreed in the power sharing protocol (clause 2.9) that "during the Interim Period, as a matter of principle, Sudan's foreign policy shall serve **first and foremost** Sudan's national interests" (emphasis added). The major objectives to be achieved by foreign policy, according to that clause, included "promotion of international cooperation, especially within the UN and other International and Regional Organizations for the consolidation of universal peace, respect of international law and treaty obligations and the promotion of a just world economic order… achiev[ing] African and Arab integration, each within the ongoing regional plans and forums…; non-interference in the affairs of other states…and mutual cooperation with all of Sudan's neighbors; combating international terrorism and transnational organized crimes and terrorism."

12. Giving Worth to All Cultures

A landmark agreement was also reached between the parties apropos cultural diversity with a view to giving meaning and substance to provisions on diversity in the Machakos Protocol. Hence, clause 2.8 of the power sharing protocol recognized "all indigenous languages as national languages which shall be **respected, developed and promoted**" (emphasis added). The clause further provided that "Arabic language is the widely spoken national language in the Sudan." By stopping at that, the parties might have wished to state the obvious without going further in characterizing it as the only national language of Sudan. That was the position taken by the Indian constitution regarding Hindu. The constitution also provided that "Arabic, as a major language at the national level, and English shall be the official working languages of the **National Government business** and languages of instruction for higher education" (emphasis added). There are three things worth of note in this provision: first, defining Sudan in the CPA and INC as a "multi-cultural, multi-racial, multi-ethnic, multi-religious, and multi-lingual country" was the first time any national (northern government) accepted this denomination of Sudanese identity. In Chapter One we alluded to mystifications of national identity by the dominant religious or cultural group in the center. This provision, added to the recognition at Machakos of making citizenship as the basis of rights (**including the right to be president**), had put an end to the addled and futile debate about what being Sudanese meant. More important, for this change to come from the northern party to which Arabization and Islamization became articles of faith, gave credit to that party, despite all its political misdeeds. By taking this position, especially on the use of English language as a medium for instruction in Sudanese schools in the north, the NCP was, in effect, changing course from the haphazard and unprepared Arabization of education in public universities in the north that it had adopted in the 1990s. During the interim period, the government of Southern Sudan adopted verbatim in the Interim Constitution of Southern Sudan (ICSS) the INC clause on languages. Article 6 of that constitution provided:

(1) "All indigenous languages of Southern Sudan are national languages and shall be respected, developed, and prompted.

(2) English and Arabic shall be the official working languages at the level of the governments of Southern Sudan and the states, as well as the languages of instruction for higher education.

(3) There shall be no discrimination against the use of either English or Arabic at any level of government or stage of education.

(4) English, as a major language in Southern Sudan, and Arabic, shall be the official working languages of the governments of Southern Sudan, and the states.

(5) In addition to English and Arabic, the legislature of any sublevel of government in Southern Sudan may adopt any other national language as an additional official working language or medium of instruction in schools at its level.

(6) The government of Southern Sudan shall promote the development of a sign language for the benefit of people with special needs.

(8) The State shall promote the development of a sign language for the benefit of people with special needs."

Sudan's national governments in the past, without exception, sang praises to Sudan's cultural diversity but never came as close to defining as did the CPA. Lip service was constantly given to multiple diversity, but the concept remained a slogan, an empty shell. Neither was it translated into constitutional edicts nor put into effect in educational and cultural policies and programs. Instead, those regimes, wherever faced by questions regarding Sudanese cultural diversity, took shelter behind abstractions.

NOTES

1   Sir Francis Reginald Wingate, governor-general of Sudan (1899–1916), and the founder of the modern state in the country.
2   Protest movements in the peripheries were registered since the early year of independence: Beja Congress in eastern Sudan in 1958, General Union of the Nuba Mountains in 1965, and Dar Fur *Nahda* (Revival), also in 1965.
3   Government of the Sudan and Sudan People's Liberation Movement/Army, *Agreed Text on the Preamble, Principles, and the Transition Process between the Government of the Republic of the Sudan and the Sudan People's Liberation Movement/Sudan People's Liberation Army (Machakos Protocol)*, signed July 20, 2002 (Nairobi: Intergovernmental Authority for Development, 2002).
4   Ibid., Part A (Agreed Principles), CPA.
5   Francis M. Deng, ed., *New Sudan in the Making?: Essays on a Nation in Painful Search of Itself* (Trenton, NJ: Red Sea Press, 2010), 39.
6   Ibid.
7   Draft of Machakos Protocol, Part 8: State and Religion.
8   Ruth Iyob and Gilbert M. Khadiagala, "The Elusive Quest for Peace," International Peace Academy Occasional Papers, 21.
9   "During Talks, the War Continues," *The Indian Ocean Newsletter*, Paris, August 30, 2002.
10 "The SPLA's Garang: 'Self-Determination Does Not Mean a Desire to Secede,'" *Mideast Mirror*, 21 August 21, 2002.
11 "Sudanese Peace Talks Likely to End Earlier: Official," *Xinhua*, August 30, 2002.
12 Government of the Sudan and Sudan People's Liberation Movement/Army, *Memorandum of Understanding between the Government of the Sudan and the Sudan People's Liberation Movement/Sudan People's Liberation Army on Aspect of Structures of Government*, signed *November 18, 2002* (Nairobi: Intergovernmental Authority for Development, 2002).
13 Ibid.
14 See Paul Nantulya, "The Machakos Protocol and Prospects of Peace in Sudan," *Conflict Trends* 4 (2003): 8–14.
15 "Sudanese Foes Make Headway on Power Sharing Arrangements," Agence France-Presse, February 6, 2003.

16 Ibid.

17 Ibid.

18 "Talks on Sudan's Disputed Territories Make Little Headway," Agence France-Presse (Nairobi), March 20, 2003.

19 BBC Monitoring, "Observers Consider Final Round of Sudanese Peace Talks 'Crucial,'" translated from Arabic," *Akhir Lahzah, Khartoum,* May 8, 2003. Khartoum Arabic daily.

20 The only exception was in 1965 when the all-powerful Ministry of Interior was allocated by the post-Abboud interim government to an able southern administrator, Clement Kutiya Mboro, and that of Transport to an Equatorian politician, Ozboni Mundiri.

21 Democratic Unionist Party, Umma Party, and Sudan Peoples Liberation Movement, *Sudanese Opposition Cairo Declaration,* Cairo May 26, 2003.

22 "Government Spokesman Attacks Cairo Declaration," Sudanese News Agency, June 8, 2003.

23 Sawsan Abu-Husayn, "Interview with SPLM Political Adviser on Southern Sudan Issues," translated from Arabic, *Al-Sharq al-Awsat* (London), June 15, 2003.

24 B. Yongo-Bure, "The Underdevelopment of Southern Sudan since Independence," in *Civil War in the Sudan,* ed. M.W. Daly and Ahmad Alawad Sikainaga, (London: British Academic Press, 1993), 51-77.

25 The Zande district in Western Equatoria province was chosen by the colonial administration for the establishment of an agricultural project to produce food for local consumption as well as cash crops (cotton and palm oil) for the market, Conrad C.Reining. The Zande Scheme, 142-147.

26 Paul Nantulya, "The Machakos Protocol and Prospects for Peace in Sudan," 11-12, Accord, Issue 4, 2003.

27 John Ashworth, "The Last Thing We Need Is Another 'Dodgy Dossier,'" *Parliamentary Brief,* July 2003.

28 Machakos Protocol, Part A, Clause 1.5.2.

29 "Sudan Peace Talks Adjourn after Little Progress," PanAfrican News Agency (Nairobi) May 21, 2003.

30 Supra note 28

31 See John Ashworth, "The Last Thing We Need is Another Dodgy Dossier," *Parliamentary Brief,* July 2003, 11–13.

32 "Sudan Rebels Demands 60 Percent of Oil Revenue," *Xinhua,* August 21, 2003.

33 "SPLM Position Paper on Wealth Sharing," SPLM HQ (undated, September 2003).

34 "Sudanese Wealth-Sharing Experts Arrive in Kenya to Help Peace Talks," Agence France-Presse, September 11, 2003.

35 U.S. Department of State, *Remarks with Kenyan Foreign Minister Kalonzo Musyoka and IGAD Special Envoy General Lazaro Sumbeiywo after Multilateral Meeting with Sudanese Peace Process Coordinators* (2003).

36 "SPLM Position Paper # 2 on Wealth Sharing," December 15, 2003.

37 Giorgio Brosio, "Report on Oil Revenues and Fiscal Federalism," (presented at the International Monetary Fund Conference on Fiscal Policy, University of Toronto, June 5, 2003).

38 "Government of Sudan Position Paper #2 on Wealth Sharing," undated.

39 "Government of Sudan Position Paper #3 on Wealth Sharing," undated.
40 Kate Luxford, "Wealth-Sharing Agreement Concluded, Final Sudanese Peace Deal Due in January 2004," World Markets Research Centre, 2004.
41 Ibid.
42 The committee, which was chaired by the author, submitted its report to the president of the government of Southern Sudan after a two-year deliberation to which Norwegian experts funded by the Norwegian Agency for Development (NORAD) had immensely contributed. The report especially dealt with the negative environmental impacts of petroleum activities in oil-producing areas. The committee also benefited from the counsel of Dr. Dennis Stickley, a New Zealand petroleum lawyer recruited by USAID, who gave advice on the legal aspects of oil contracts. Stickley concluded that the oil contracts were inadequate by international standards, since they were silent on indemnities or sanctions in case of damages caused in the course of operations. The Norwegian team identified over 30 defects or shortcomings in, or relating to, existing oil contracts.
43 See Government of the Republic of the Sudan and Sudan People's Liberation Movement/Sudan People's Liberation Army, "Comprehensive Peace Agreement between the Government of the Republic of the Sudan and the Sudan People's Liberation Movement/Sudan People's Liberation Army," January 9, 2005 (Peace Agreement, Chapter III), 45–62.
44 Ibrahim Moneim Mansour, former minister of finance in the Nimeiri era, was appointed to that position. Mansour was known for his integrity and serious approach to jobs entrusted to him.
45 Joint Assessment Mission Report, Volume 1, Khartoum, March 18, 2005.
46 Ibid.
47 "SPLM Position Paper on Power Sharing," SPLM HQ (undated, September 2003).
48 "Sudan Downplays Deadline," BBC News, October 23, 2003. http://news.bbc.-co.uk/2/hi/africa/3207225.stm
49 Ibid.
50 Ibid.
51 "Sudanese President Promises Far-Reaching Political Changes after Peace Treaty," Sudan Tribune (Khartoum), January 1, 2004. http://www.sudan-tribune.com/spip.php?article1337
52 See Government of the Republic of the Sudan and Sudan People's Liberation Movement/Sudan People's Liberation Army, "Comprehensive Peace Agreement between the Government of the Republic of the Sudan and the Sudan People's Liberation Movement/Sudan People's Liberation Army," January 9, 2005, (Chapter II) 9–44.
53 Appendix A of the protocol included, inter alia, all national commission, president, and justices of the national supreme and constitutional courts
54 Personal recollection
55 Ibid.
56 Personal recollection
57 Martin, Kings of Peace, Pawns of War, 153
58 The rebellion in Darfur (November 1991) was ignited by Dawood Yahia Bolad, a Darfuri politician of Islamist sympathies. Having lost faith in the desire or ability

of the Islamist regime in Khartoum to address the historical grievances of his people in Darfur, Bolad turned to Garang for support. In December 1991, Garang armed and trained Bolad and his team. With Abdel Aziz Adam El Helu as second in command, Bolad and his forces infiltrated Darfur. The SPLA-aided invasion became a fiasco when Bolad was arrested and eventually executed. Douglas Johnson, *Root Causes of Sudan's Civil War*, 140.

Chapter Seven
The Three Areas

■■■■■■■■■■■■■■❖■■■■■■■■■■■■■■

> Injustice anywhere is a threat to justice everywhere.
> —**Martin Luther King Jr.**
> "Letter from a Birmingham Jail,"
> April 16, 1963

1. Introduction

The term "Transitional" or "Three Areas" was the denomination given by the negotiators to the areas of Abyei, Blue Nile, and the Nuba Mountains. Though part of the geographic north, those areas were engulfed in Sudan's second civil war when large numbers of their sons and daughters joined the Sudan People's Liberation Movement/Army (SPLM/A). Given the inclination of the SPLM to highlight in its political program the peripheralization of rural Sudan by an overbearing center, it was not surprising that it decided to put the issue at the top of its negotiation agenda. To do so the SPLM did not need to look far beyond the areas neighboring south Sudan for allies in its struggle against marginalization. Those areas straddling the north-south border had been home to the diverse Nuba peoples of South Kordofan and the Funj of Blue Nile. Both peoples understood southern Sudanese grievances through their own experience. Living on the frontline of the conflict, these people became subject to various types of repression from Khartoum, which made them amenable to persuasion by the SPLM.

Ironically, in Sudan's first civil war, Nuba soldiers represented the backbone of the Sudanese army fighting in south Sudan. Because the first civil war was fought for a specifically southern cause with no national purpose it was difficult for south Sudan warriors to win over the Nuba to their side. Thus, when the second civil war started, not only was solidarity lacking between

Nuba and their southern neighbors, but there was also bad blood between them. Nonetheless, from the mid-1960s onward political activists within the Nuba began to assert their rights against Khartoum and advocated decentralization and regional equity. That brought them closer to southern Sudanese in the political arena, especially in various Sudanese parliaments where the two groups, alongside the Beja (eastern Sudan), and the Fur (western Sudan) formed coalitions clamoring for decentralization of the system of rule and equitable allocation of national resources.

Map 1: Sudan – Areas of conflict in Blue Nile, South Kordofan, and Darfur provinces

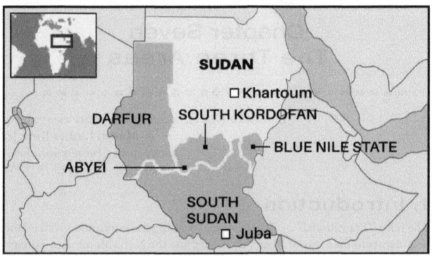

On the other hand, Dinka residents in Abyei, following the Addis Ababa Agreement (1972), began crying out for reintegration into southern Sudan of the area in which they and their ancestors historically lived. That area, with the willing consent of the Dinka tribal leadership, was sliced by the colonial administration from Bahr el Ghazal (south Sudan) and attached to Kordofan (northern Sudan). As for the Blue Nile area, which had been host to about 40 ethnic groups and was the cradle of the first Islamic kingdom in central Sudan (Funj Kingdom), it became completely cut off from Sudan's mainstream politics in modern times. This chapter shall address the underlying causes of conflict in the Nuba Mountains and Blue Nile, symptomized by historical neglect since colonial days and perpetuated by Sudanese post-independence governments. It shall also elaborate on the peculiar nature of the Abyei conflict, which has only come out in the open after the Addis Ababa agreement. The chapter shall also explore the relative importance of those areas to the two parties to the Comprehensive Peace Agreement (CPA), the reasons why negotiations to put an end to the conflict proved to be more cumbersome than those regarding north-south disputation, and the serious developments that have ensued after the referendum, which almost foreshadowed a return to war.

2. Strategic and Political Importance of the Three Areas

The importance of the Three Areas to the two parties stemmed from multiple causes. Chief among those were that the areas (i) straddled the north-south border, (ii) incorporated grazing lands used by pastoralists on both sides of the north-south divide, (iii) was known to be rich in agricultural land and mining (Nuba Mountains and Blue Nile) as well as oil (Abyei), and (iv) represented the dividing line between two standing armies: Sudan Armed Forces (SAF) and the SPLA. Given these reasons and the incorporation of tens of thousands of their young men in its ranks, the SPLM/A took it upon itself from the outset to speak on their behalf and represent their interests in all peace negotiations with the government. Nevertheless, as explained in previous chapters, the government eschewed any discussion of issues relating to the Three Areas, claiming that they were part and parcel of the North. Thus, both the SPLM and government had an ambivalent attitude toward Abyei. All the same, to the SPLM, Abyei was a self-evident case given the road it had traveled to reach the 1972 Addis Ababa agreement,[1] even though the Three Areas as a whole spoke to the core philosophy of the movement in seeking a new political dispensation for Sudan's marginalized peoples.

For example, during the Abuja II negotiations in 1993, the SPLM/A offered four alternative solutions to the problems of the Three Areas, namely: to be included in a secular democratic New Sudan, given the right to vote with southern Sudanese at the referendum, become part of an autonomous southern confederal region, or opt for secession.[2] Northern opposition parties also shared that ambivalence. For example, in its negotiations with the National Democratic Alliance (NDA) leading to the Asmara Declaration of 1995, the SPLM/A succeeded in ensuring the NDA's espousal of the exercise of the right to self-determination for the Three Areas, but only within the context of affirming a united Sudan on **a new basis**. That conditional acceptance of the right to self-determination by those areas was, effectively, contradictory to the NDA's own resolution, which recognized that right as a universal human right that should be granted to any Sudanese people who demanded it.

3. Wars of Attrition

Core grievances repeatedly professed by the Nuba people and those of Blue Nile related to security, respect of cultural identity, and economic marginalization, the latter mainly symbolized by dispossession of land. In the case of the Nuba, the announcement of these grievances predated the 1987 war enkindled by the SPLA's Volcano Battalion,[3] led by Yousif Kuwa Mekki and Abdel Aziz Adam al-Hilu. Back in 1965, the Nuba people surprised the slumbering political elite in Khartoum by forming the Nuba Mountains General Union under the leadership of Father Philip Abbas Ghaboush, a man of the cloth who turned politician. Expectedly, the agenda of the union revolved around social and economic marginalization. However, with the coming of the National Islamic Front (NIF) in 1989, the pattern of marginalization took a turn for the worse by adding to it a religious element reflected in the NIF's policy of forcible Islamization.

Nuba is a collective name for almost a hundred ethnic groups, each with its own language. These ethnic groups include, inter alia, Heiban, Kadru, Katla, Koalib, Krongo, Moro, Nyimang, Tegele, Talodi, and Tira. While some Nuba were converted to Islam and others professed Christianity, to which they were attracted through proselytization, a large number continued practicing traditional African religions. Even among the Nuba who converted to Islam or Christianity, only a few abandoned traditional rites. Nonetheless, the NIF's politics to destroy the Nuba cultural fabric made Nuba youth increasingly gravitate toward the SPLM/A. In reality, accounts of alleged genocide committed against the Nuba[4] prefigure much of the violence seen during the conflict in Darfur. The *jihad* waged against the Nuba peoples was the more surprising, since it did not even spare Nuba Muslims. Khartoum mobilized ethnic militias from the Arab Hawazma and Misseriya tribes to attack Nuba men who opposed the NIF, espoused SPLM views, or were even suspected to be sympathetic to the SPLM. In April 1992, NIF scholars issued a *fatwa* (religious edict), declaring that Muslims who joined the SPLM were deemed apostates. With two Muslim Nuba leaders (Yousif Kuwa and Abdel Aziz Adam el Hilou) the NIF had no way to declare them enemies of Islam, so it chose to demonize them.

On this account, the economic deprivation suffered by the Nuba people under previous Khartoum regimes was envenomed by the NIF's inhumane policies in a manner that they did not experience before. Human rights organizations chronicled alarming stories about Nuba repression by the Khartoum regime. For example, Africa Watch reported in December 1991 that the regime targeted educated Nuba in a policy of "elimination by attrition." Thirty-seven Nuba educated men (all of them Muslims) were kidnapped and disappeared without a trace.[5] In that orgy of killing, the SAF and the Popular Defense Forces (PDF) were also reported to have killed at least six and detained and beaten to death seventy.[6] That report equally charged the SPLM/A of crimes against humanity, of which one example was the cruel punishment SPLM/A commanders had allegedly meted on chiefs who obstructed the recruitment of youth into its ranks. Those included Chiefs Hussein Karbus and Ismail Ali Jiger of South Dalami who were reported killed, and Mek Hamid Nira and Imam Ali Abdalla Abri who were reported kidnapped.[7] The most damning report against the regime came from the South Kordofan head of security who later sought refuge in Switzerland. The deserting official confessed that orders were given to him "to kill anything that is alive; to destroy everything, to burn the area so that nothing can exist."[8] However, the SPLM organized in December 1994 an interfaith conference, bringing together leaders of the main faiths in the region—Islam, Christianity, and traditional belief systems—to encourage them to preach religious tolerance among their devotees.

On the other hand, the peoples of southern Blue Nile have a complex history with regard to both their ethnic composition and attachment to Islam. However, the majority of them are assumed to be Muslims since their land is the cradle of the first Muslim kingdom in northeastern Sudan (Funj Kingdom). Though a number of indigenous groups share Blue Nile State, the largest and most dominant among them is the Ingassana group. Other ethnic groups include Barta, Burun, Hamaj, Gumuz, Jamjam, and Uduk, among others. The Ingassana was only brought under full control of the colonial administration in 1926 after several rebellions, mainly against the tax regimes established by that administration. In their short-sighted and narrow vision of Sudan, colonialists attached southern Blue Nile, with its predominate Muslim population, to south Sudan under the Closed District Ordinances (1914-1946), which virtually cut off the North from the South. That policy backfired because it condemned the area to increasing underdevelopment, for neither was it allowed to benefit from the opportunities offered by the relatively advanced services in education and health available in the North, nor to avail itself of the limited opportunities in health and education offered by missionaries in southern Sudan. It is to be noted that while the colonial administration gave a long leash to Christian missionaries in southern Sudan, it was reluctant to allow them unimpeded proselytization in the Nuba Mountains and southern Blue Nile, as it was likely fearful of infuriating northern Muslims. Nevertheless, the Sudan Interior Mission[9] established a missionary center in the Uduk area at Chali that continued operating until 1964, when they were expelled by Abboud's military regime. That region was administratively attached to Upper Nile province but reintegrated into the Kurmuk district, northern Sudan, in 1953.

In the first decades after Sudan's independence, the people of southern Blue Nile, unlike the Beja, Nuba, or Fur, remained quiet and proved to be extremely docile. Their compliance with, and amenability to, political influences from Khartoum made them regularly embrace parliamentary candidates from central Sudan for election in successive Sudanese parliaments. Those candidates were either drawn from a northern trader community residing in the region or party candidates nominated by national party headquarters in Khartoum, even if some of them had never set foot on the land. That was why parliamentary representatives of the Blue Nile region were conspicuous by their absence from the alliances that brought together southern Sudanese, Nuba, Beja, and Darfurians in Sudanese parliaments in the decade of the 1960s. Only after the emergence of the SPLM, and the mobilization of the Nuba Mountains behind it, did political activists from the southern Blue Nile region, led by Malik Agar, become engrossed in the struggle.

The high watermark in the struggle was the fall of Kurmuk and Geissan in November 1987. Kurmuk, a strategically valuable town bordering Ethiopia, became the site of a violent contest between the SPLM/A and the Sudanese army, particularly since occupation of the two towns posed an imminent danger to the strategically vital Roseires Dam and hydroelectric power station close to the state's capital of Ad-Damazin. It was the NIF government's brutal counter-insurgency against the civilian population, charged with racial and religious propaganda, which motivated the peoples of southern Blue Nile to turn increasingly to the SPLM/A and the struggle it was leading.[10]

The Ngok Dinka of Abyei, whose habitual ancestral land was adjoined to Kordofan in 1905 by their paramount chief Kwol Arop, lived in Sudan's North but remained patently aware of ethnic, religious, and historical bonds to their brethren in the South. In the days of the Anglo-Egyptian Condominium[11] they had risen to the challenge of being a bridge between Sudan's North and South, which also allowed them to manage complex neighborly relations with the Misseriya, a nomadic Arab tribe. However, having acquiesced to remain within the North for decades, Ngok Dinkas began to yearn to return to south Sudan, probably because of the failure of successive northern regimes to forge a truly national identity for the people of that area. As a result, leading Ngok Dinkas increasingly identified themselves with the struggle of south Sudan. And though they were not actively involved in the first civil war, they still endeavored to state their case in the 1972 Addis Ababa agreement. The Addis Ababa agreement, however, did not directly accede to the demands of Ngok Dinka, but obliquely referred to their right to self-determination through referendum to decide whether to remain part of the North or join the South. The reference to Abyei, among other areas, came in article 3 of that agreement, which read: "Southern Provinces of the Sudan means the Provinces of Bahr el Gahzal, Equatoria, and Upper Nile in accordance of their boundaries as they stood on January 1, 1956, and **any other areas that were culturally and geographically a part of the Southern Complex as may be decided by a referendum**" (emphasis added).

In his last years in power, President Nimeiri charged Chief Justice Khalfallah al-Rasheed to review the legal situation of the two areas of Abyei and Heglig, taking into consideration, inter alia, the provisions of the Addis Ababa Agreement on north-south administrative borders. Al-Rasheed adjudicated, on the strength of article 3 of the agreement, that Heglig fell south of north-south borders as they stood on January 1, 1956 while Abyei, though situated north of the border line (that is, within the North), was deemed to be one of the areas that fell within what the Addis Ababa agreement described as "culturally part of the Southern Complex and whose future should be determined through referendum." Notwithstanding the chief justice's ruling, Nimeiri carved out the part of Upper Nile province where Heglig was situated and incorporated it into the adjoining northern province to create a so-called unity province. In effect, Heglig is a two-hour drive from Bentiu, southern Sudan, while it is five hours from Kadugli, South Kordofan. Aware of all these facts, Nimeiri, rather than appointing a governor for the new province from north or south Sudan, appointed himself as governor of the "The Unity Province." By adopting that anomalous measure, Nimeiri wished to virtually square the circle by not recognizing the oil-rich Heglig as part of the North, as some of his ministers advised, and ensuring northern control over it through the national government, which he headed. As for Abyei, its situation had to remain in abeyance until the minister for regional government in the NIF regime, Dr. Ali al-Haj, decided to firmly incorporate it in the North. Those clear violations of solemnly signed agreements and furtive ploys by President Nimeiri made Abyei citizens join the SPLM/A in droves and become part of the second civil war. Numerous members of Ngok Dinka from Abyei rose to senior positions in the SPLM/A. Their rise to those positions was not only due to the grievances they shared with southern Sudanese, but also to their academic and professional attainments, ironically because of the educational opportunities they had enjoyed by virtue of living in the North. Nonetheless, their elevation to senior positions within the SPLM/A and their being closely related to its leader, John Garang, evoked jealousy within not a few other ethnic groups in south Sudan. Francis Deng, who has for many years eloquently told the story of his people as a microcosm of Sudan's crisis, warned in 1995: "the problem of Abyei will almost certainly be one of the issues that the resolution of the North-South conflict will have to address. Unless the issue of Abyei is resolved, it will always be a source of conflict between the North and the South."[12] As Koul Deng Abot, one of the two deputy paramount chiefs of the Ngok Dinka, was quoted to have said, "Abyei is like an eye, which is so small, yet sees so much."[13] Deng Abot's words became a myth believed by all Dinka Ngok, including their elite.

By late 1990s a decade of NIF brutality had taken its toll on the Three Areas, especially among the Nuba. Although the local peoples had their grouses with each other, they still sought their own way out of that legion of conflicts to face a common enemy. As the Misseriya came to see themselves as pawns of the NIF's failed militant ideological expansionism to the south, local peace initiatives involving Ngok Dinka and Misseriya leaders were initiated by SPLM through the elders from both tribes. These negotiations culminated in accords between the tribes on key local issues such as seasonal migrations, water resource sharing, and carrying of small arms. One significant agreement was the peace agreement between Dinka (Abyei, Twic, and Gogrial) and the Misseriya, concluded April 12, 2000, which guaranteed grazing rights for the Misseriya cattle under SPLA protection, while that tribe assured citizens in the adjacent areas in southern Sudan the commodities they needed for subsistence.

4. IGAD and the Three Areas

The Intergovernmental Authority on Development (IGAD) Declaration of Principles (DoP) was not specific about the status of the Three Areas, though it had explicitly affirmed the right to self-determination by the people of south Sudan to decide their future status through a referendum. The DoP also did not specify what constituted the "South," although the SPLM had persistently treated areas of Blue Nile and Nuba Mountains as if they were under its control as part and parcel of the New Sudan. That interpretation, though valid to Garang because he had a mind to it, was not validated by the facts of history or geography. Nevertheless, the DoP had laid down preconditions for national unity of great importance to SPLM/A supporters in the Three Areas such as the decentralization of the system of rule, equitable sharing of resources, upholding human rights and the rule of law, and more important, recognizing "extensive rights of self-determination on the basis of federation, autonomy, etc., to the various people of the Sudan" (para 3.3). It also provided that "in the absence of agreement on the [principles enunciated in the DoP] the respective people will have the option to determine their future including independence through a referendum" (para 4).

In 1997 and 1998, when the government returned to negotiations, it made it clear that its acceptance of self-determination for the "South" was based on the borders identified on January 1, 1956, (independence). By adopting such a definition of borders (which was technically correct), the government wished to undermine the solidarity between southern Sudanese and the people of these areas. For instance, at the Addis Ababa IGAD ministerial round in August 1998, SPLM/A leaders from the Nuba Mountains and southern Blue Nile made it clear that their areas were part of the South, but if Khartoum would not accept this, then they would not stand in the way of self-determination for the "rest of the South." However, they also declared that their struggle to attain the right to self-determination would continue.

Subsequent rounds of IGAD talks prior to 2002, such as the round in Lake Bogorio in Kenya in September–October 2000, did little to advance a political settlement on the problem the Three Areas. The IGAD mediators suggested separate mediation efforts, but the government returned to its hackneyed argument that the areas were part of the North and, thus, did not fall within the IGAD mandate. Meanwhile, oil production from 1999 in and around Abyei, including the rich Heglig oil fields,[14] ensured that Sudan's "Kashmir" would be an even greater bone of contention in any future peace process. The area of Abyei, situated in the Muglad basin, was claimed to be rich in hydrocarbon accumulations, but excessive drilling of oil was reported to be depleting the yet identified reserves.

5. Selective Cease-Fire in the Three Areas

By the turn of the new century, the Nuba Mountains had suffered some of the greatest horrors of war. Not only was the government's campaign against the Nuba particularly brutal, even the United Nation's humanitarian response, Operation Lifeline Sudan (OLS), consistently failed to gain authority from Khartoum to access affected populations in the mountains, save for a limited intervention by the United Nations Children's Fund (UNICEF) in 1999, as the government continued to maintain that the Nuba area did not fall within the mandate of that program. Also, from the late 1990s, the United Nations tried and failed to achieve humanitarian cease-fires to reach Nuba civilians.

As noted in Chapter Two, the SPLM/A suffered a setback in March 2001 with the death of its leader in the Nuba Mountains, Yousif Kuwa Mekki. Before his death, Kuwa wisely called an advisory Nuba council in 1992 to decide whether the Nuba wished to continue fighting despite the human sufferings war had wreaked upon them. The council unanimously voted in favor of continuing the struggle. Kuwa's successor, as to be expected, was Abdel Aziz Adam al-Hilu who, though highly capable, was not able to give undivided attention to the Nuba cause since he was also shouldering responsibility for the New Sudan Brigade (NSB) operating in eastern Sudan.[15] With the government benefiting from new weaponry bought with oil money, this was a difficult period for the Nuba peoples and the SPLM/A. The brutality with which the government carried out war in the Nuba Mountains prompted Garang in mid-2001 to describe the government's dry-season offensive in no uncertain terms: "'Our commander in the Nuba Mountains [says that on May 26] alone they [the government] burned 14 villages in the mountains; more than 5,000 huts. And the [victims] are not Christians or southerners, they are Muslims. Because they are opposed to the regime, they are considered infidels. In the oil region, the civilian population is evicted, literally. There are gross human-rights violations and, really, genocide. There is really no country with power and will that has engaged in Sudan.'"[16]

Garang's was a timely appeal because it coincided with the appointment of Senator John Danforth as President Bush's special envoy to Sudan. Danforth, as mentioned in Chapter Three, took the lead from his advisors that pursuing humanitarian breakthroughs, especially in the Nuba Mountains, would be both highly beneficial to civilian populations who were in dire need of relief, as well as a dam-breaker in pursuing broader peace efforts. We may also recall that during his first visit to Sudan in November 2001, Danforth set

213

Khartoum and the SPLM/A four readily verifiable tasks to test the "climate for peace": a humanitarian cease-fire in the Nuba Mountains, zones of "tranquility" to facilitate humanitarian activities in southern Sudan, an end to military targeting of civilians, and discontinuation of the abduction of civilians (more contentiously described as "slavery").[17] Upon returning to the United States in late November 2001, Danforth revealed the priority given by the United States to the Nuba Mountains. In briefings at the State Department, Danforth said: "Nuba Mountains has been a beleaguered part of Sudan. It was an area that we visited. I think we were the first official group to go in from the United States into the Nuba Mountains."[18] Danforth added in his briefing that though both sides had given their informal support to a cease-fire, much remained to be decided with regard to an extended cease-fire that included verification and monitoring.

In mid-December 2001, talks were held in Sudan to extend the tranquility agreement into a more concrete arrangement. In the second week of January 2002, U.S. and Swiss diplomats succeeded in bringing negotiating delegations to Bürgenstock, Switzerland, to agree on formalizing a lasting cease-fire in the Nuba Mountains. The SPLM delegation was led by Commander Abdel Aziz Adam al-Hilu and the government's by Dr. Mutrif Siddiq from the Ministry of Foreign Affairs. On January 19, after seven days of negotiations, the two sides concluded "The Nuba Mountains Cease-Fire Agreement."[19] The agreement provided for an internationally monitored cease-fire, renewable on a six-month basis. The parties agreed that the Nuba Mountains constituted "the whole of South Kordofan and the province of Lagawa in West Kordofan" [article II (4)]. They also detailed the military requirements of disengagement, stand-down, and cessation of a range of hostile military actions, including laying of land mines. Moreover, the two sides committed themselves to a process of recovery and reconstruction, and agreed to allow unhindered movement of people and access for humanitarian aid. Meanwhile, cease-fire monitoring was entrusted to joint committees of the two parties. The Joint Military Commission (JMC), supported by a verification committee comprising 10 to 15 international monitors, was chaired and co-chaired by representatives of the Swiss and U.S. governments, chosen in consultation with the parties. They both headed the JMC and were part of the international monitoring unit. Under the central commission, the parties were to establish JMCs at the sector and local levels to enable ongoing monitoring, patrols, and peace-support activities.

The agreement's rigorous and detailed modalities allowed the cease-fire to take effect and a major humanitarian and recovery effort to be initiated with considerable efficiency. The underlying problem with the agreement was that although it was a limited cease-fire for humanitarian purposes, the government saw it as a palliative for not addressing problems that had driven the war in the region and in the wider country. In late January 2002, Dirdiery Mohamed

Ahmed, Sudan's chargé d'affaires in the Nairobi Embassy, said, "If that test of the Nuba Mountains is going to succeed definitely it will encourage everybody to see it replicated elsewhere in any other part of the country."[20] Evidently, the chargé d'affaires, known for his political discernment, was mindless of his government's intransigence in extending the cease-fire to southern Blue Nile. The SPLM/A was quick to rebuke Khartoum for holding cheap the causes of conflict in the two areas. Indeed, the government's jubilation about that selective cease-fire only reinforced the SPLM/A's conviction that a permanent cease-fire must only come after political agreement is reached.

6. Negotiations on the Three Areas

At the time of Machakos, Khartoum and the international community were largely satisfied with what had been achieved with the Nuba Mountains cease-fire, albeit for different reasons. Khartoum, for reasons already stated, was happy to have secured a cease-fire at little political cost. The international community was roused by having achieved a needed humanitarian and security outcome, as well as a bridgehead for wider peace negotiations regarding the South. Danforth's report, while praising the cease-fire agreement as "extraordinary"[21] made scant reference to a wider political solution for the Nuba Mountains. His report did not mention Abyei or Blue Nile and, thus, overlooked the challenges on the way to achieving substantive peace in these areas. Subsequently, during the Machakos negotiations that followed, the SPLM/A faced an uphill battle to ensure their inclusion within the talks.

The Machakos Protocol indeed made no reference to these Three Areas. By consistently maintaining that the Three Areas were part of Sudan's North, the government implicitly denied these areas the right to self-determination. Also, the provision in clause 3.2.2—that "nationally enacted legislation having effect only in respect of the states outside Southern Sudan shall have as its source of legislation shari'a and the consensus of the people"—boded badly for religious freedom in these areas. That clause was neither tantamount to the right to self-determination acknowledged by the NDA to all people of Sudan, nor was the mechanism for its implementation tight enough to enable the Nuba people, who wished to opt out of shari'a law, to do so. If anything, with the predominance of National Congress Party (NCP) members in the Council of States, and the dilution of Nuba presence within the newly crafted South Kordofan state, that mechanism would surely consolidate, not repeal, shari'a as the Nuba had wished.

A breakthrough though it had been, the Machakos Protocol raised great concern amongst senior SPLM/A figures from the Three Areas, especially Abdel Aziz Adam al-Hilu and Malik Agar. Accordingly, the issue of the Three Areas loomed ominously over future negotiations at Machakos. In one account from that time, Justice Africa observed that "these are profoundly

215

controversial issues, pitting Khartoum's conception of the territorial integrity of 'Northern' Sudan against the SPLA's contention that the majority of the people of these areas would prefer to be part of a future 'Southern' confederal entity. Some mechanism for consulting the people of these areas and ascertaining their demands is [therefore] required."[22] As a result Khartoum's adamant resistance to any discussion of the Three Areas when talks resumed in August surprised no one. The SPLM/A delegation at that round included leaders from the Three Areas, and in one standoff between the mediator and Malik Agar, the latter was reported to have said: "'General, if you do not include the Funj people of Southern Blue Nile, we shall finish you.'"[23] Such a remark from a corpulent and thickset person as Agar would have chilled the general to the bone had he taken the remark literally. Nevertheless, that remark made the mediator realize that the issue should not be played down. The rage by representatives of the Three Areas did not stop at the fracas between Agar and the mediator. Following the conclusion of the Machakos Protocol, about 300 officers from the Three Areas met with Garang at his headquarters in New Site (southern Sudan) to express their anger at being "sold down the river" at Machakos. Some harsh words were uttered by Malik Agar and, surprisingly, by some SPLA officers from Abyei who were close to the SPLM leaders. Garang reassured the angry officers that Machakos was just a framework protocol and there would be no comprehensive peace agreement without addressing the concerns of the Three Areas in separate protocols.

These were the nuances southern "nationalists," who wanted Garang to close the page after Machakos, failed to see. What did not linger in their memory was the contribution of Nuba fighters within the SPLA ranks, first to maintain their stronghold on Nuba land and, second, to stymie joint assault by SAF and SPLA renegades in the mid-1990s. The aim of that assault was to dislodge the SPLA from strategic positions in south Sudan. Garang was, therefore, on target when he told his southern critics, especially southern Sudanese leaders from outside the SPLM, that no one had the right to assume that the SPLM/A was fighting a war, or conducting a struggle, to achieve the strategies of "others." In effect, every so often the "others" were politicians and pseudo-politicians who had been skulking around during the two decades of a struggle that made peace and self-determination possible. From then on, Garang went into his national mission with the fervor of a crusader.

As alluded to, the mediator began to have second thoughts on the relevance of talks on the Three Areas to the overall peace objectives. Consequently, he revived his earlier proposals on the subject and suggested that they be discussed outside of the formal IGAD framework. However, the hostilities in September, referred to in previous chapters, meant that little progress was made. As a result of a slack in the Machakos negotiations following the capture of Torit by the SPLM/A in early September 2002, and the shift by the peacemakers toward the government's position to give priority to the cessation of hostilities, the SPLM/A decided to use the time available to it to highlight issues of the Three Areas. In an effort to make the government and the negotiators deal seriously with these issues, it resolved to mobilize the people of the two areas (Nuba Mountains and Blue Nile) in order to substantiate the legitimacy of its claim to talk on their behalf as well as the justice of their cause.

Garang therefore decided to go on a political offensive in the Three Areas in order to allay fears and calm the situation. Between December 2–5, 2002, a momentous event occurred in the Nuba Mountains: the holding of the historic first All Nuba Conference in Kauda (the Nuba provincial capital under SPLM/A control). The conference was organized by the Nuba themselves and brought together 380 representatives of Nuba civil society from across its political spectrum. In total, over 160 of the participants traveled from areas under government control, and 15 others came from the diaspora in Europe and North America. The presence of John Garang in that meeting added to the significance of the occasion, especially since that was the first time he had traveled to the Nuba Mountains in the history of the conflict. In addition, Malik Agar, SPLM/A's leader from southern Blue Nile; Yassir Saeed Arman from northern Sudan; and other senior SPLM/A figures attended.

The outcome of the conference was unambiguous on two fundamental points. First, the SPLM/A committed itself to negotiate for the full rights of the Nuba at the IGAD talks. The conference communiqué reported "unequivocal commitment of the SPLM/A leadership to the centrality of the Nuba Mountains Region (and South Blue Nile and Abyei) in all on-going peace process negotiations under IGAD."[24] The second key outcome of the conference was the endorsement of the IGAD process by all the Nuba representatives "as the means to negotiate a just and secure peace for the Regions of Nuba Mountains, Southern Blue Nile and Abyei, but only as part of a comprehensive settlement for the whole of Sudan." Also, a "clear mandate [was] given by the Conference to the SPLM/A to negotiate on behalf of the Nuba people in the IGAD peace process and for the new [United Sudan National Party] [25] also to play an active role in all such negotiations." Finally, the conference gave a strong recommendation for the unambiguous alignment of the Nuba people with the SPLM/A during the interim period. In December, a similar but smaller meeting was held in southern Blue Nile, and it also mandated the SPLM/A to negotiate on its behalf.

In December 2002, the IGAD secretariat, having recognized the gravity of the Three Areas problem, sought once again to place it foremost on the agenda at the round of talks due to begin on the January 15. The government refused to enter negotiations at all, replaying its position that the issue did not fall within the IGAD mandate. Finally, it was agreed that talks on the Three Areas would go ahead, but under Kenyan rather than IGAD mediation, the same proposition made by General Sumbeiywo. This trick only satisfied the vanity of the government, for the mediator remained General Sumbeiywo and the host remained Kenya. Not to ruffle the government's feathers, the general made it clear that the capacity in which he acted was different. The general also avoided diplomatic embarrassment for the rest of the IGAD member states by inviting them only as resource persons, not observers, to the adjunct talks.

After a false start in mid-January 2003, where the government again refused to send a proper delegation, the Kenyan-led talks on the Three Areas began in earnest in March 2003 in Karen, near Nairobi. The talks proved difficult from the outset. Sumbeiywo described them as achieving only "limited progress," and chose to emphasize "earnest and frank discussion" as a positive attainment.[26] In reality, the government thought that it had effectively diminished the importance of these talks in the wider IGAD negotiations by making them a sideshow. Progress continued to be elusive through late May, and when at the fifth round of IGAD talks was held that month the parties were still not ready for open consultations on the Three Areas.

In early June 2003, Khartoum showed its true colors when it obstructed a people-to-people peace conference in Abyei to which it had earlier agreed. Without warning, the NCP revoked its prior consent to allow local, national, and international participants from government-administered areas to attend the conference.[27] Those prohibited from attending included Roger Winter of the United States Agency for International Development (USAID), together with Dr. Francis Mading Deng, assistant to the U.N. secretary general on internally displaced persons; Misseriya Arab delegates; and over 100 other invited participants. It was clear that Khartoum did not want a repeat of the All Nuba Conference and the legitimization of the SPLM/A's role in its "northern" playground. It was during this time that Sumbeiywo made his visit to Sudan in preparation for the Nakuru Framework Document (see Chapters Four and Five). He was especially interested in visiting the Three Areas, and in June he traveled to Agok in the Abyei area, Kurmuk and Ad-Damazin in Blue Nile, and Kauda and Kadugli in the Nuba Mountains.[28] In Khartoum, Sumbeiywo consulted with representatives from these areas, many of whom were installed by the NCP for this purpose. When preparing his document on the Three Areas, Sumbeiywo was careful to print it on Kenyan, not IGAD, letterhead.

As regards Abyei, the Nakuru Document provided that its status (whether to be administered as part of Bahr el Ghazal state in the South or remain in West Kordofan state in the North) should be subject to a referendum to be held before the elections at the end of the first half of the interim period, and as determined by an Abyei Referendum Commission made up of representatives of the parties and international observers. It suggested that the referendum be open only to the residents in Abyei in 1972 (when the

Addis Ababa Agreement was signed) and their descendants, wherever they might have at that time been located. It also defined Abyei as the area agreed to in the 1972 agreement. Such an agreement did not exist, nor was the area defined in the Addis Ababa Agreement in 1972, save for the oblique reference to it among other areas that were "culturally and geographically part of the Southern Complex." For all intents and purposes, the suggestions in clauses 2 and 3 of the Nakuru Document on the Three Areas—respectively, the "Nuba Mountains (South Kordofan)" and "Southern Blue Nile (Blue Nile state)"— were identical to each other, with the odd exception of clause 2.6, which applied to the Nuba Mountains but not Blue Nile. That clause provided: "The Executive and Legislature shall accommodate and respect the Council of Elders and acknowledge an appropriate role for the Council." The Council, mistakenly called a council of elders, was established before the 1994 SPLM Convention by the late Yousif Kuwa Mekki as an advisory body to the SPLM, the first of its kind in the "liberated areas."

The Nakuru Document also focused on decentralization in these two states (Southern Kordofan and Blue Nile), granting them autonomy and a fiscal revenue base as well as authority over specific contentious issues such as education and land management. It made no mention of self-determination and, instead, included a vague provision linked to contestation of state elections at the end of the first half of the interim period. The provision read: "The Parties contesting this election may, notwithstanding other provisions of the Peace Agreement, seek a mandate regarding the state's constitutional status. In line with any such mandate, such elected state legislature may resolve, through consultations with its people, to engage directly with the National Government in regard to the variation or elaboration of its constitutional status or power, save that any such variation must conform with all relevant constitutional provisions" (clauses 2.11 and 3.10). This would be the basic formula later agreed to by the parties in providing for "popular consultation" in the two states (discussed below). The Nakuru Document, in actuality, brought the Three Areas to prominence as key negotiating issues, the successful resolution of which would have broader implications for governance throughout the country. In its June 2003 report, the International Crisis Group noted, "The negotiations on the Three Areas provide an opportunity to create an important peace template by dealing with the core issues of how the country has been governed from the center."[29] Yet the government's vehement rejection of the Nakuru Document extended to the Three Areas. When talks were raised to the level of "principals"—Taha and SPLM/A Chairman Garang—the Three Areas remained a critical stumbling block.

In its September 9, 2003, position paper on the Three Areas, the SPLM/A argued that during the interim period the Nuba Mountains and southern Blue Nile should be under its control and accorded autonomy within a

219

decentralized southern Sudan. The two states were to be granted their own constitutions, legislatures, security services, police, and judiciary. The SPLM/A also proposed a land commission, as was suggested in the Nakuru Document. Finally, it gave special attention to the reconstruction needs of these areas. Regarding Abyei, the SPLM/A argued that the government should restore the area to Bahr el Ghazal by presidential decree or, failing this, grant Abyei citizens the right to participate in the referendum to be held by the people of south Sudan. Khartoum refused all propositions and contended, as always, that all three areas be seen to be wholly within the North; the only concession the government of Sudan made was to provide additional support for reconstruction and development.[30]

For the remainder of 2003, Vice President Taha and Dr. John Garang turned the greater part of their efforts to security arrangements and the wealth sharing agreement, as described earlier (Chapter Five). Even in 2004, as the thorny power-sharing issues were progressively addressed and being resolved, the Three Areas remained on the "pending" tray. Meanwhile, the conflict in Darfur raged, casting a long shadow on CPA negotiations, particularly as the government's brutal counter-insurgency steamed ahead. Though the closeness of Darfur to the Nuba Mountains should have been a subject of concern to it, the government appeared to have decided that the resolution of a problem bristling with thorns had to wait.

7. The Three Areas Protocols

7.1 The Abyei Protocol

Chapter IV of the CPA, entitled "Resolution of the Abyei Conflict," incorporated the Abyei Protocol, signed by the two parties on May 26, 2004. Assigning in the peace agreement a separate protocol for an area of 10,460 square kilometers that hosted a population of 3,000 was testament to how vexed the issues of Abyei were that divided the parties. In early 2004, President Bashir had declared that the borders of southern Sudan were a "red line" issue; thus, the NCP was intransigent in facing up to the historical, cultural, and political realities in Abyei. Of course, the profits from Abyei oil wells almost literally added fuel to the flames. Hence, without heavy U.S. intervention, the Abyei deadlock could not have been resolved. The key to the resolution of all the Three Areas issues was to separate the political solution for Abyei from that of South Kordofan and Blue Nile. This allowed unique arrangements to be made relative to the administrative status of the area in the interim period; oil production and revenue-sharing; and, most important, its future constitutional status based on the right to self-determination by its people. Although the Abyei Protocol and the protocol on South Kordofan and Blue Nile were agreed upon together with the power sharing protocol in Naivasha on May 26, 2004, the text relating to Abyei was exactly what Senator Danforth had proposed to the two sides two months earlier.[31]

On March 19, 2004, Senator John Danforth presented Vice President Taha and Chairman John Garang with a U.S. proposal entitled "Principles for Agreement on Abyei." The U.S. State Department had carefully worked out a plan for Abyei that was to be considered by the parties as a *process* for resolution rather than a definitive settlement. Some key principles and definitions guided the U.S. proposal for Abyei. The protocol described Abyei as a "bridge between the North and South linking the people of Sudan" (clause 1.1). It also defined the territory of Abyei as "the nine Ngok Dinka chiefdoms transferred to Kordofan in 1905" (clause 1.1.2). In clause 1.1.3, the parties were to agree that "the Misseriya and other nomadic peoples retain their traditional rights to graze cattle and move across the territory of Abyei." Furthermore, during the interim period, Abyei's special status would mean that its residents were deemed citizens of both West Kordofan and Bahr El Ghazal, and governance would be administered by an executive council appointed by the presidency until such time as elections were held. Oil revenues during the interim period would be divided as follows: 50 percent to the national government, 42 percent to the government of South Sudan, two percent to West Kordofan, two percent to Bahr el Ghazal, two percent to the Ngok Dinka people, and two percent to the Misseriya people. The allocation of shares of oil revenues to the Dinka and Misseriya was, by all accounts, meant to tranquilize the two hostile tribes, but in an area shared by other groups, it was an inadvisable suggestion.

Most important, the protocol provided in clause 1.3 that at the end of the interim period, prior to the referendum vote exercised by the citizens of southern Sudan, the residents of Abyei would have their own referendum vote to decide whether to retain their special administrative status as part of the North or to become citizens of Southern Sudan. Residents of the Abyei area were defined, in clause 6, to include all Ngok Dinka **and other Sudanese** residing in the area. The criteria of residence, according to that clause, shall be determined by the Abyei Referendum Commission, which shall be established by the presidency.

One critical issue remained, namely, the definition of the exact territory of the nine Ngok Dinka chiefdoms transferred to Kordofan in 1905. The U.S. proposed and the parties agreed in clause 5 that an Abyei Boundaries Commission (ABC) be established by the presidency, composed of fifteen members, five appointed by the government, five by the SPLM, three experts by IGAD, and one expert each appointed by the United Kingdom and the United States.[32] The five impartial experts were entrusted with preparing the commission's report. The work of the commission was to be completed within the first two years of the interim period. Though the ABC had two years to prepare its report, with urgency it finalized and submitted that report during the pre-interim period. That confronted the presidency in the first week of its formation with what developed into the most rankling problem, particularly when the Misseriya and the NCP rejected the report *in toto* even though the Abyei Protocol stated that the ABC report "shall be final and binding." The spillover of the discord between the NCP and the SPLM/A on the issue of Abyei led to bloody conflicts in the area. The subsequent crisis and the armed confrontation between the two sides in 2008 shall be discussed in Chapter Eight. However, the haste of the ABC in submitting its report gave rise to three conjectures: the matter was not subjected to the full deliberation it deserved, the mind of the commissioners had been made up prior to the report, or the issue was so clear and simple that it did not deserve further investigation. Thus, NCP leadership chastised the commission for treating the Abyei question with such haste. Claims also abounded in the Khartoum media, always ready to rush to conspiracy theories, that the report was the brainchild of the U.K. and U.S. commissioners, irrespective of the fact that there were also three African members on that commission. The wrangle between the two parties over the ABC report, however, continued up to the time when it was theoretically resolved through international arbitration, as we will explain in the following chapters. Apart from the Khartoum media, there were also unwitting accomplices. In a feature published by the *New York Times*, Douglas Johnson wrote: "Bashir believes that transferring Abyei to the South would set a dangerous precedent for other disaffected areas, including Darfur...American officials have unwittingly encouraged the Bashir regime to take a hard line by supporting successive compromise proposals rather than insisting that Khartoum adhere to the peace agreement and abide by the court ruling."[33]

7.2 The South Kordofan/Nuba Mountains and Blue Nile Protocol

Though the resolution of the Abyei conflict, for better or worse, involved a significant success for the Ngok Dinka, the prospects for South Kordofan and Blue Nile were less optimistic. The protocol entitled The Resolution of the Conflict in Southern Kordofan and Blue Nile States was also signed on May 26, 2004, which reflected the close relationship the negotiations over this protocol had with the negotiations over power sharing. Were the SPLM to conclude a power sharing agreement without resolving issues pertaining to the Three Areas, it would only have done so at the cost of losing its honor in the eyes of those who sacrificed everything to realize SPLM/A's supreme objective: creating a New Sudan.

The protocol on the Two Areas finally appeared as Chapter V of the CPA. In that protocol the parties expressly recognized that a comprehensive peace agreement must resolve the conflicts in these states, and with one eye on Darfur, they also recognized that the agreement on the resolution of the problems of the two states could "serve as a model for solving problems throughout the country." However, the reference to Nuba Mountains in the protocol as "Southern Kordofan/Nuba Mountains" indicated disaccord between the parties over the name of the state. Subsequently, the NCP persuaded the SPLM to accept the name South Kordofan, whose boundaries were defined as those of the former southern Kordofan province when Greater Kordofan was divided into two provinces (clause 2). As such, South Kordofan encompassed what had remained of West Kordofan, including Abyei, until its final status was decided. That made the state the eighth largest in Sudan. It also meant that the Misseriya areas in old West Kordofan were now part and parcel of South Kordofan, thus changing its demographics to the benefit of the NCP and its allies. In effect, though it was host to Hawzma pastoralists, the Nuba Mountains were not home to the Misseriya before their merger with parts of West Kordofan, even though it provided corridors for northern pastoralists and their cattle who were trekking to southern Sudan in the dry season. The proposal came from Vice President Taha, and its acceptance by Garang represented a compromise on the part of the SPLM as it entailed departure from what was agreed upon by the parties in the Nuba Mountains cease-fire agreement and in the Kauda conference. SPLM Nuba were, understandably, not happy with this compromise, as they recognized its implications for their constituency in the elections that were to be held.

Elections were made critically important by the mechanisms agreed to in the protocol, which provided that whatever agreement was reached between the parties on the Nuba Mountains and Blue Nile areas should be subject to "popular consultation." The term is a parenthetical explication of direct democracy (through popular voting) or indirect representative democracy (through elected bodies). In choosing the latter, the protocol described that process as "a democratic right and a mechanism to ascertain the views of the people of South Kordofan/Nuba Mountains and Blue Nile states on the comprehensive agreements reached by the parties (clause 3.1). It also stipulated that "an independent Commission shall be established by the Presidency to assess and evaluate the implementation of the CPA in each [state]" (clause 3.4). This consultation would be carried out through the states' "respective democratically elected legislatures" (clause 3.2). Only after being "endorsed by the people through the legislature" would the agreement constitute a "final settlement" of the conflict (clause 3.5). Any changes would be subject to negotiation with the national government (clause 3.6).

Popular consultation was patently below Nuba expectations as it represented a toning down of their claim to the right to self-determination. Not only was popular consultation below the expectations of the people of the two states, but the procedure proposed for conducting it was ill-defined and undetermined. For example, the protocol stipulated that in case of disagreement between the central government and the legislature on the results of the consultation, the matter was to be referred to the Council of States. And if the aggrieved state failed to receive satisfaction from the council, the parties should seek arbitration by an "agreed upon body," without identifying standards for choosing the arbitrator. At Naivasha, a few Nuba leaders refused to accept this process, declaring that they would settle for nothing short of self-determination. One of those leaders was Daniel Kodi, who threatened to wreck the negotiations unless—and until—the self-determination demand was satisfied. Kodi calmed down at last and later became a docile ally of NCP.[34] That was yet another example of Sudan's tragicomedies, if not farcical political theatrics.

However, the fact that popular consultation in the two states did not take place before the southern Sudan referendum did not augur well for the two states. As it seemed, the NCP had persuaded itself that southern Sudan, after secession, should have nothing to do with the two states and would thus leave them under the mercy of the NCP. Khartoum was, thus, surprised by the turn of events in the two states. Rather than addressing the outstanding issues in the CPA relating to the two states and involving the SPLA (directly) and the SPLM (indirectly) in the matter, it went into a fit of pique, accompanied by fear of the emergence of a new South in the two areas. All the issues in question derived from the CPA and, therefore, could better be resolved within its framework. Among these issues were the completion of popular consultation, demobilization of the SPLA forces in the two areas, and the regularization of the status of the Sudan People's Liberation Movement/North (SPLM/N). Those were not insurmountable problems since SPLM leaders in the two areas were only seeking, after separation from south Sudan, a greater degree of autonomy from Khartoum, not separation. This should not have been a cause of uneasiness to Khartoum, especially since the government at that time was negotiating identical issues with Darfur rebels. In effect, the mismanagement of popular consultation, according to a political analyst who followed developments in the area, could have destabilized not only South Kordofan and Blue Nile, but all of Sudan.[35] In reality, the government's tactics to retard the process were very much ill-thought, for were popular consultation to take place as envisaged in the CPA, the serious escalation of violence in the two areas could have been averted, especially during the second half of 2011.

Other issues relating to the two states were underserved by the protocols. These included power sharing, wealth sharing, and security. For example, the gerrymandering of the borders of the Nuba Mountains made it impossible for the Nuba people to secure the plurality needed in what the CPA called a "democratically elected legislature that would reflect the genuine desire of the Nuba." Regarding structures of government at the state level, a detailed clause of the protocol embodied a decentralized system with considerable state powers for the two states. Most important, until state elections, the NCP was assured 55 percent of positions in the executive and legislature of each state and the SPLM 45 percent, both to be chosen by the presidency. That allocation of seats, unlike the case of the national legislature, did not include other political forces. There was also to be rotation of governorships and deputy governorships with no party holding the governorship of both states at the same time (clause 11). The short-lived honeymoon between NCP governor Ahmed Haroun and his SPLM deputy Abdel Aziz al-Hilu provided a model for how the two parties could leave the past behind and attend to the development of the state and the welfare of its people.

Regarding wealth sharing, South Kordofan, as an oil-producing state, was to be granted two percent of national oil revenues. As mentioned earlier, it was agreed by the two parties that a National Reconstruction and Development Fund (NRDF) would be established, with seven percent of the funds to go to "war-affected areas," which included the two states (clause 8). However, that fund was never established. State Land Commissions, which were supposed to be established to review existing land leases and contracts and recommend to the state legislatures (clause 9) proposals for restitution of, or compensation for, land, were also never established despite the portentous problems relating to land, especially in the Nuba Mountains.

As to security arrangements, the SAF were not required to redeploy outside of the two states, because both states were situated north of the 11th parallel, though allowance was made for the presence of JIUs (clause 10). Discretion as to the size of SAF troops in the two states during the interim period was left to the presidency. Ostensibly, this was meant to enable the SPLM to have a say in the deployment of those forces through "collegiate" decision making involving the first vice president's consent. Nonetheless, no provision was made for a monitored dematerialized zone between the two armies, probably because the euphoria created by agreement on army redeployment made the question redundant. For example, although the SPLA in southern Blue Nile had withdrawn south of the 11th parallel, the headquarters for their forces and heavy equipment were stationed at Guffa, seven kilometers away from the borders. Of the SPLA forces on the borders of South Kordofan, 3,000 were incorporated into the JIUs; 1,000 into the police; 8,500 were stationed in Bentiu and 8,000 in Lake Abyad; and 2,000 elderly and disabled men were demobilized. This area continued to be one of the contested areas in the north-south border dispute.

The two protocols were received with mixed emotions by the peoples of the Nuba Mountains and southern Blue Nile. After a long and brutal conflict, the vindication of their political rights was half-born, and final settlement was again deferred. The last word on the struggle of the peoples of the two areas is yet to come, with or without support from the SPLM. Even so, the power-sharing arrangements agreed upon between the parties provided a mechanism for national healing and peace enhancement among the people of these areas, especially in the Nuba Mountains where people were subjected to harrowing experiences for over two decades.

8. Failure to Address Core Grievances

It was earlier intimated that denial of cultural identity, insecurity, and dispossession of customary land represented core grievances by the people of Blue Nile and the Nuba Mountains. No significant progress was made on these three points, not even putting into operation the limited achievements scored in the CPA. With regard to the issue of recognition of cultural identity, even though the policies of forcible Islamization had ended, frenzied Islamists persisted in issuing *fatwas*, denouncing membership of the SPLM as apostasy, while the NCP and government of National Unity turned a blind eye. At the same time, the Government of National Unity had yet to ratify international conventions it had signed, as required by article 1.6.1 of the power sharing protocol. One convention of direct relevance to the indigenous people of the two areas was the International Labor Organization (ILO) Convention (169) concerning indigenous and tribal peoples in independent states.[36] However, the most serious dereliction of responsibility by the Government of National Unity was in the area of law reform; none of the arrangements called for by the CPA and incorporated in the national constitution and the constitutions of each of the two states was implemented. The protocols on the two areas had laid down detailed arrangements for dealing with land leases and contracts and reviewing the criteria currently being followed for the allocation of land rights, including making recommendations for changes as necessary.[37] These responsibilities were entrusted to a National Land Commission as well as to the State Land Commissions, none of which saw the light of day up to the time when the interim period came to close. The remissness of the Government of National Unity to the issue of land was such that even well-studied reports on land use prepared on the request of the negotiators at Naivasha were left to gather dust in government offices. One such study was the USAID-funded research,[38] which was presented to the two states by an independent land specialist. That well-researched and documented report was taken seriously by neither authorities at the center, nor at the state levels. Failure to carry out the CPA obligations relating to the two areas, while due largely to the NCP's hedging and dodging over implementing the agreement, was also encouraged by the SPLM's lack of focus on issues pertaining to the two areas, unlike the way it had focused, for example, on Abyei.

9. The Three Areas after the Referendum

9.1 Developments in the Two States

The CPA provided that popular consultation in Blue Nile and South Kordofan would take place by the end of the fourth year of the interim period. That, like other time lined provisions in the agreement, was not to take place as envisaged. The law regulating popular consultation was promulgated in December 2009, one year after the date provided in the protocol for the completion of the process. According to the CPA, the process of popular consultation was to commence in the beginning of the fourth year of the signing of the agreement (January 2009). Furthermore, while state elections in Blue Nile took place in April 2010, alongside national elections, those in South Kordofan were delayed until May 2011, after the referendum in southern Sudan. Wisely the governor of South Kordofan (NCP) and his deputy (SPLM) agreed to postpone state elections until a new population count and voter registration were conducted due to flaws that were believed to have marred the census process, constituency demarcation, and voter registration. In a November 2010 meeting the state government and National Elections Commission (NEC) agreed to hold gubernatorial and legislative elections in May 2011, six months after the conclusion of the national elections.

The South Kordofan election was heavily monitored by the United Nations, the Carter Center, the African Union, and international and regional nongovernmental organizations. However, after the completion of the polling, the SPLM contender for the governorship, Abdel Aziz al-Hilu, challenged the count and threatened to withdraw from the race. That position invited a joint message on May 10 from the Troika (Norway, United Kingdom, and United States) asking for restraint.[39] In their message, the three countries stated: "We welcome the peaceful completion of the polling for South Kordofan's elections but are concerned about rising tensions in the state due to a delay in the announcement of preliminary results. We call on local and national leaders to take immediate steps to improve the security situation and exercise control over all armed security elements." The Troika advised that "it is critical that the elections pave the way for the start of Southern Kordofan's popular consultations, which remain an important outstanding element of the CPA." That was an oversimplification of underlying Nuba concerns. Aly Verjee, a Canadian academic who was closely observing the situation, wrote: "If they fail, South Kordofan's elections may yield localized violence, derail the popular consultation, and destabilize the state, historically the site of the fiercest conflict of the north/south civil war."[40]

The elections in South Kordofan were, by a long shot, an improvement on the April 2011 national elections, despite misgivings the SPLM had about

227

the way they had been conducted. This conclusion was corroborated by the Carter Center, whose election observation mission reported that "despite a **climate of heightened insecurity and instances of procedural irregularities** that removed an important safeguard of the process, South Kordofan's elections were generally peaceful and credible"[41] (emphasis added). That conclusion seemed to have been validated in the eyes of some observers by the fact that the two contenders in the gubernatorial race, Abdel Aziz al-Hilu (SPLM) and Ahmed Haroun (NCP), came in neck-to-neck with the NCP candidate with 201,455 votes, while the SPLM candidate collected 194,955 votes, and General Telephone Kuku, an independent Nuba candidate who was sponsored by the NCP, received 9,130 votes. Kuku's sponsorship by the NCP was an unsporting act meant to reduce al-Hilu's plurality in the elections. Taken in isolation of the problems that lay on the crooked path ahead, the conclusion the Carter Center made about the elections was roughhewn. That report had unjustifiably downplayed irregularities in the parliamentary elections, especially incidents that had preceded the polls such as the non-application of a unified standard for demarcating geographic constituencies. In this respect, NEC had divided the constituencies in a manner that was unfavorable to the Nuba and led to extreme anomalies. As a result of that awkward demarcation of constituencies, the Nuba, with a plurality of 191,528 votes (47.16 percent of those registered and voting), ended up with 10 parliamentary seats, while the NCP, with a plurality of 182,751 voters (44.99 percent of votes), won 22 seats. Fears by the Nuba of election fraud were justified in another instance; prior to elections the Nuba challenged the results of the 2009 national census, which calculated their numbers at 1.4 million, but as a result of a recount in 2010, that number jumped to 2.5 million. Neither the NCP nor NEC seemed to have been embarrassed by those discrepancies in numbers. Small wonder the SPLM challenged the aggregation process and rejected the elections results.

The atmosphere, however, was envenomed long before the declaration of the elections results. In an electioneering speech at Muglad on April 27 in favor of the NCP candidate, President Bashir announced that if his party did not make it through ballot boxes, then his government had another alternative: "ammunition boxes." The president might have been enraged by the SPLM's campaign slogan: "al najma" (the star) or "al hajma" (the assault). Al Najma was the election symbol of the SPLM, and al hajma would have been less menacing if it had not been associated with a political party supported by a full-blown army. Nevertheless, the president's statement was hardly what one would have expected from the head of state in a combustible political situation. The Nuba were further put into a temper by President Bashir's speech at Gadaref in which he declared that after the secession of southern Sudan, he was not going to tolerate remarks about cultural or religious diversity.[42] Despite his formal acceptance of the results of the southern Sudan referendum, the president seemed to have forgotten that upholding Sudan's multiple diversities was a principle enshrined in Sudan's constitution to which he had pledged allegiance. In response to Bashir's statement, Najwa Musa, head of the Nuba Relief, Rehabilitation, and Development Organization, told the BBC that "if they will impose shari'a law, Islamic religion, and Arabic language on the Nuba people, then you will see a new Darfur coming,"[43] This eventuality had been predicted by the International Crisis Group three years earlier.[44]

Clearly, Blue Nile and the Nuba Mountains—especially the latter—were in a collision course with the NCP long before the elections. In May 2011 and prior to elections in South Kordofan, SAF demanded that SPLA forces stationed in northern Sudan, that is, in the two areas, either disarm or redeploy south of the north-south border or they "would be forcibly disarmed" by SAF. The SPLA in Juba responded that the bulk of its forces were already stationed in Bentiu (southern Sudan) and Jau Jau (Lake Abyad), a contested border area. As for the forces stationed in the two states inside Sudan, the SPLA maintained that they were made of sons and daughters of the two areas, and their future status was governed by the terms of the CPA. Since the future of these forces had not been agreed upon by the two parties by July 9, 2011, any unilateral decision on the forces might be as good as a breach of the CPA. After all, the future of the SPLA forces in the north was not the only issue in the security arrangements protocol that the NCP passed over while the SPLA shut its eyes. Another neglected issue related to the cardinal principle in the protocol, which demanded that SAF forces in the Nuba Mountains during the interim period should not exceed the peacetime level of military presence in the state. Nevertheless, the size of SAF forces in that state, according to a reliable source, was far above that level.[45] That situation was further complicated by the heavy presence of the Popular Defense Forces (PDF) units in both Blue Nile and South Kordofan.[46] It may be recalled that those forces were described by government negotiators at the peace talks as regular forces that fell under the command of SAF, not a militia force. In reality, the PDF remained "a military and civilian network to mobilize milita auxiliaries throughout Sudan in contravention of the CPA."[47]

Furthermore, according to a recent report, "unexplained movements of SAF tanks and troops in recent months and an increase in the number of civilians carrying guns, even in Kadugli, [led to] a growing conviction that the Nuba will remain marginalized—and physically at risk—without further armed struggle."[48] Accusations and counteraccusations continued to be traded between the NCP and SPLM and between SAF and SPLA regarding the objective of these movements. Those led to suspicions that the main reason for the SAF movement was either to prepare for an onslaught on the oil-producing areas in southern Sudan if the parties failed to reach an agreement on post-referendum arrangements relating to oil sharing before separation, or to subdue the Nuba area if and when southern Sudan decided to go its own way. With the absence of independent monitoring by the United Nations Missions in Sudan (UNMIS), the situation remained tense, especially since 40 percent of South Kordofan was off limits to the international force as a result of unceasing claims by the government of Sudan that UNMIS had no mandate in areas under SAF control. It may be recalled that UNMIS was established by the UN Security Council following the signature of the CPA to support implementation of the CPA, provide humanitarian assistance, and promote human rights.

Within this environment inflamed by mutual fears, intimidation, and heavy arms in the hands of regular and irregular armed groups, conflict became unavoidable. Fighting started in Kadugli with a house-to-house search for Nuba activists and SPLM cadres. According to UN reports during the period June 5-30, 2011, heavy fighting, summary executions, and gross humanitarian law abuses occurred.[49] Al-Hilu retreated with his forces to their strongholds in the mountains, especially when UNMIS was overwhelmed by SAF forces and, therefore, incapable of providing protection to the Nuba.[50] Attempts by the United States to negotiate a cease-fire between the warring parties failed, as the government appeared to have convinced itself that it was capable of resolving the issue militarily, while al-Hilu remained firm in his position that he would only negotiate a lasting political solution that included issues of power sharing and arrangements for the integration of his forces as provided by the CPA.[51] A group of researchers from Martin Luther University of Halle-Wittenberg, Germany, summed up the situation by stating that "a significant part of the problem lies in the fact that both main parties to the conflict, the NCP and the SPLM/A, are born out of a military confrontation, and their raison d'être was and remains military power."[52] It is well-nigh impossible to resolve a conflict that is political in essence either through military action or pre-set conditions for dialogue. The Halle researchers were on target when they observed that "the last election in South Kordofan was bound to fail not because of technical flaws, but because it was treated as a zero-sum game between two parties."[53]

Meanwhile, both security and humanitarian situations deteriorated immensely as a result of reported carpet aerial bombings by SAF and denial by both parties of access by land to those in need of humanitarian relief. The United States castigated both parties for what it claimed to be irresponsible behavior.[54] As a result, the untiring African Union peace mediators stepped in to persuade the parties to reach a cease-fire agreement. To that end the mediators met with NCP leadership and SAF command and undertook a mission to the Nuba Mountains to meet with al-Hilu. Their effort bore fruit when an agreement was signed between the government of Sudan and the Sudan People's Liberation Movement/North (SPLM/N) in Addis Ababa on June 28, 2011. That agreement, denominated a framework agreement, was signed by Nafie Ali Nafie on behalf of the government of Sudan and the NCP, and by Malik Agar on behalf of SPLM/N.

On the issue of security, the signatories agreed to immediately form a Joint Security Committee, facilitated by the African Union High-Level Implementation Panel on Sudan (AUHIP),[55] to address relevant security issues pertaining to the two states. The signatories also agreed on the principles that would govern the committee's work. Those included respect for the sovereignty and territorial integrity of Sudan, inviolability of its borders, ensuring safety and security to communities in both states, recognizing one national army into which SPLA forces from the two states would be integrated, as well as agreed-upon plans to achieve the above objectives prior to the declaration of Southern Sudan independence on July 9. The framework agreement was happily received by the people of the two states, peace-loving Sudanese and Africans, but that happiness did not last. President Bashir, on return from a state visit to China, distanced himself from the agreement, even though there were reports that the agreement was rejected by the NCP leadership even before Bashir's return to Khartoum from China. Nevertheless, Bashir was palpably angry with the continuation of the war in the Nuba Mountains and described al-Hilu as a war criminal who should be chased and brought to justice.

Rather than allow efforts by credible mediators to reach their expected denouement, the SPLM/N issued a declaration from Kauda, Nuba Mountains, which was virtually the same as a declaration of war. In a statement dated August 9, 2011 signed by Malik Agar, Abdel Aziz al-Hilu, and Yassir Arman, respectively, chair, vice chair, and secretary general of SPLM/N, a new politicomilitary alliance was announced. The alliance brought together the SPLM/N and two Darfuri rebel groups: the Sudan Liberation Movement (SLM) factions of Mini Menawi and Abdel Wahid M. Nour. The alliance was later joined by Khalil Ibrahim's Justice and Equality Movement (JEM) and baptized as the Sudan Revolutionary Front. The front declared as an objective the overthrow of the Khartoum regime "through all available means" and pledged itself to consolidate all Sudanese opposition forces with a view to establishing a new government in place of the NCP. Small wonder, Khartoum was up in arms to the point of freezing all negotiations with the SPLM/N, closing its offices in the North, and declaring that all further talks with its leaders would only be inside Sudan with no external mediators.

Aware of the dangers this escalation could pose both to the stability of the Republic of Sudan and good neighborly relations between the North and South, South African President Thabo Mbeki and Ethiopian Prime Minister Meles Zenawi once again interceded to wind down the escalation. To that end President Mbeki and former Burundi President Pierre Buyoya met with Malik Agar and Yasir Arman in Juba to persuade Agar to meet with President Bashir in Khartoum and restart negotiations between the SPLM/N and the NCP on the basis of the principles established in the Addis Ababa framework agreement. The response of the two SPLM/N leaders puzzled the two African leaders and perplexed the author, who was present at the meeting. Agar, after parlaying with Arman, said that they had taken note of the request and would give their answer after consultation with the leadership of the party. The author, who at the time was nominally a member of the party leadership, was taken aback by the statement since that leadership was neither consulted by Agar, al-Hilu, and Arman when they signed the Addis Ababa framework agreement, nor when war was declared against Khartoum. A week later, Prime Minister Zenawi prevailed upon Agar to meet with President Bashir in Khartoum. Agar, the elected governor for Blue Nile state, could neither spurn an invitation by the president, nor reject an intervention by the prime minister of the only country that would ensure him an exit from Sudan, in case of need. Most likely it was the latter reason that enabled Zenawi to persuade the governor to meet with Bashir, but again, little progress was made. While Agar was amenable to a process of negotiations that would achieve incremental results, his other two colleagues (al-Hilu and Arman) wanted to maximize profit with minimal output. In the art of negotiations, that would be the shortest route to a breakdown in any talks.

The three SPLM/N leaders had never cared to educate, let alone involve, their rank and file in the North about the endgame they were aiming at and the wherewithal in their possession to achieve it. Whoever was masterminding the game was clearly counting on support outside their main social base. That support was seemingly expected from SPLA forces in the two areas, Darfurian rebels, South Sudan, and the international community. The latter was expected to grill Khartoum the way it had been doing on behalf of the SPLM and Darfuri rebels. Trusting that this politicomilitary strategy would work, the leadership of the SPLM/N announced the merger of the two armies (SPLA in South Kordofan and Blue Nile) without realizing that those armies, according to the CPA, were no longer party armies but professional armies under the command and control of the government to which they owed allegiance.

Predictably, without waiting for the impending merger of the two armies to happen, the SAF intensified war in the Nuba Mountains and waged war against the SPLA in Blue Nile state. The last thing one would have expected the government to do was to sit passively awaiting war to extend from Sudan's borders with Chad in the west to Ethiopia in the east.

Hence, in addition to the ongoing fighting in the Nuba Mountains, war erupted in Blue Nile state in the beginning of September 2011 and soon engulfed the whole state. According to an observer, "it's not clear who exactly fired the first shot in the new Blue Nile conflict. But both the SPLM in Blue Nile and the government in Khartoum had been preparing for this scenario for weeks."[56] The eruption of war in Blue Nile on September 1 was followed by a declaration of a state of emergency in the state and the dismissal of the elected governor, Malik Agar. It is very doubtful, however, whether the president had the constitutional right to dismiss an elected governor. Of course, that did not exclude a vote of no confidence on the governor taken by the state legislature under article 179 (2) of the Interim National Constitution (INC), but apparently the president had no time for such legal niceties even though the legislature was dominated by the NCP. All the same, a sense of alarm ensued, and fears erupted that the conflict would not only spread to northern Sudan but might also encompass southern Sudan and flood out into Ethiopia. As a result the African Union, the IGAD countries, the United Nations, and the United States called for a cessation of hostilities and a return to negotiations. In calling for an end to hostilities, the U.S. State Department was more specific about what should be done. Victoria Nuland, the department's spokesperson, said: "We are particularly disappointed that there has been no follow-through after the meeting between President Bashir and SPLM/N Chairman Malik Agar in Khartoum on August 21."[57] That was the meeting brokered by Prime Minister Meles Zenawi.

As for counting on open support from the South Sudan government to former SPLA comrades-at-arm, that would have been a callous and irresponsible proposition, if it ever crossed the minds of the SPLM/N leaders. For one, it would have given those in the North who were ready to wage war against the South the pretext to ignite such a war. Moreover, with the multitude of problems it was facing, the new republic in south Sudan had enough concerns on its hands to grabble with. Regarding support from Darfurian rebels, the leadership of the SPLM/N seemed not to have factored in the regional and international reconfiguration of alliances after the Doha agreement (Chapter Twelve), let alone the logistical constraints on Darfuri rebel movements. On December 26, 2011, the alliance was deeply aggrieved by the demise of JEM's leader, Khalil Ibrahim, who was reportedly slain by an SAF rocket attack, although President Bashir described Khalil's killing as a divine intervention.

Finally, the assumption that the international community, especially the United States, was ever ready to respond to any call for the overthrow of Bashir's government—as desirable as that might be to the Sudanese opposition—was not fully substantiated by realities on the ground. Apart from the fickleness by which such a serious eventuality had been anticipated, the United States was on record that it was about to open a new page in its relations with Khartoum. In a statement to the media, U.S. Presidential Envoy Princeton Lyman said: "We don't believe the overthrow of the [Khartoum] regime is a reasonable proposition."[58] In another statement, Lyman declared that imposing a no-fly zone on Sudan would create more problems.[59] That response was specifically addressing a request by the emerging "liberation front" for the imposition of a no-fly zone in the Nuba Mountains. Regardless of the low threshold of boredom the United States has with distractive foreign stunts, and no matter how avid some American policy makers are for seeing the Islamists in Khartoum thrown out of office, the glibness with which some Sudanese politicians deal with serious matters of state can easily wear down even their most ardent supporters in the United States.

Nevertheless, the saga of the two states could have been avoided long before the independence of South Sudan. Before July 9, 2011, Salva Kiir drew Bashir's attention to the need for a definitive resolution of issues pertaining to the SPLA forces in the North. His proposition was to emulate the 1972 Addis Ababa agreement when former Anya Nya warriors were integrated into SAF, police, prisons and game warden forces. Bashir, who was not enthusiastic about the proposition, told Kiir that the last thing he would like to do was to enlist the kernel of a new rebel group into the Sudanese army. Bashir's apprehensions might have been justified, since it was from the bosom of former Anya Nya soldiers and officers integrated in the SAF in 1972–73 that John Garang and Salva Kiir emerged. However, these officers would not have rebeled against Nimeiri (and for that matter, Joseph Lagu) if the two leaders had respected the agreement they had signed. But to the utter surprise of those who were aware of the offer made by Salva Kiir to Bashir, the Sudanese president told an Arabic London daily after the eruption of war in Blue Nile that he had formed a committee to consider ways and means of integrating SPLA forces in northern Sudan into the SAF, Sudan police force, and the national civil service.[60] The contradiction between Bashir's refusal to heed Salva Kiir's advice on the integration of the forces long before separation and his statement to the media six months later was, to say the least, perplexing. More perplexing was his statement to the London daily that what had been happening in the Nuba Mountains was "a foreign plot."

Nevertheless, Salva Kiir's genuine desire to remove all factors that might cause conflict between the two armies was evidenced by his dispatch to Khartoum on October 18, 2011, of a high-level delegation to normalize the situation on the north-south border.[61] That meeting ended with an agreement to open up 10 entry points on the border to control and regulate the flow of persons, goods, and services, as well as to form of a tripartite observation force made of SAF, SPLA, and Ethiopian military observers. While that initiative may have only been a symbolic gesture, even the symbolic value of such high-level meeting in Khartoum was significant, given the strained atmosphere that dominated the political scene.

9.2 Developments in Abyei

Tension in Abyei had heightened considerably after the conclusion of the southern Sudan referendum, when no similar exercise was held in Abyei as provided for by the CPA. The Abyei referendum could not have been achieved without agreement on the criteria of residence in the area and the establishment of the Abyei Referendum Commission provided for in the

234

Abyei Protocol. Both processes were frustrated by Khartoum's reluctance to acknowledge the International Court of Arbitration (ICA) award. Nonetheless, Khartoum became almost neurotic when elements within the SPLM proposed the incorporation of Abyei as part and parcel of South Sudan in its new constitution. Aware of the sensitivity of the issue to Khartoum, and mindful of the legitimate demands of Abyei citizens, the drafters of the new constitution wisely made the incorporation of Abyei into the Republic of South Sudan subject to the process provided for in the CPA. Thus article 2 (b) read: (2) "The territory of the Republic of South Sudan comprises (a) all lands and air space that constituted the three former southern provinces of Bahr el Ghazal, Equatoria, and Upper Nile in their boundaries as they stood on January 1, 1956," and (b) "The Abyei Area, the territory of the nine Ngok Dinka chiefdoms transferred from Bahr el Ghazal Province to Kordofan Province in 1905 as defined by the Abyei Arbitration Tribunal Award of July 2009 in the event that the resolution of the final status of the Abyei Area results in the Area becoming part of the Republic of South Sudan."

Nevertheless, on May 2011, forces claiming to be part of the South Sudan police force moved into Abyei area and came in close quarters with a retreating SAF force. In the skirmishes that ensued between the two forces, SAF lost some men. As a result, President Bashir ordered a massive attack with the intent to occupy the area and dismissed its administration, a matter that he was not empowered to do, according to the CPA, which reserved the power to appoint and remove that administration to the institution of the presidency, subject to the consent of the first vice president. Once again, the AUHIP intervened to stop the deterioration of the situation and escalation of the conflict into a large-scale war. To that end, the AUHIP organized negotiations at Addis Ababa between the government of Sudan and the SPLM, which culminated on June 20, 2011, in an agreement that was signed by Idris Mohamed Abdel-Gadir on behalf of the government of Sudan, and by SPLM Secretary General Pagan Amum Okech on behalf of the SPLM. The agreement provided for the establishment of a new administration of the area consisting of a chief administrator to be nominated by the SPLM and a deputy to be nominated by the government of Sudan. In each case the nominating party was required to name three candidates from whom the other party would make a choice. The administration was to be composed of 20 members and their decisions made by consensus. In addition, the agreement provided for the creation of an Abyei Joint Oversight Committee consisting of four members, two representing each party, plus a nonvoting facilitator to be appointed by the African Union chairperson.

Regarding security arrangements, the area was to be demilitarized except for a United Nations Interim Security Force for Abyei composed of an Ethiopian force of 4,200 men and women. A special unit of the Abyei Police Service was established to deal with issues arising from nomadic migration, including the accompaniment of nomads within the Abyei area on their annual treks, monitoring and verification, protection of monitoring teams, security of the area, protection of borders from unauthorized incursions, building capacity of the police, protection of humanitarian assistance activities, and protection of civilians under imminent threat. The agreement brokered by the AUHIP was endorsed by the U.N. Security Council on June 20, particularly in-so-far as the Interim Security Force for Abyei (ISAF) was concerned. On September 9, however, the two parties, guided by the AUHIP, agreed that SAF forces were to leave the area between September 11–30. In September, it was reported that the government dropped its precondition that it would only leave the area after a new administration was established,[62] but that proved not to be true. On reviewing the situation a month later (October 7), the U.N. Security Council was told by Hervé Ladsous, the U.N. under-secretary-general for peacekeeping operations, that "neither Sudan, nor South Sudan has withdrawn their forces from Abyei as promised."[63]

As a result, the U.N. Security Council revisited the issue in November. In a statement issued on November 4, 2011, the Security Council "deplored the failure of the Sudan Armed Forces and the Sudan People's Liberation Army to redeploy their forces in accordance with the 20 June agreement on Temporary Arrangements for the administration and Security of the Abyei Area." The council underscored that there were no preconditions for the implementation of the agreement signed by the parties.[64]

10. Fallout of Unilateral Revocation of Framework Agreement

The unilateral revocation of the Addis Ababa Framework Agreement, however, shocked the nation as well as Sudan's neighbours and peace mediators. In addition to the president's anger at the escalation of war in the Nuba Mountains, other factors were at play within the leadership of the NCP and higher echelons of the SAF that led to the revocation of the agreement. For example, evidence suggested that an NCP clique was incommoded by the rise of Nafie Ali Nafie in the party hierarchy and were, therefore, happy to see him cut to size by the revocation of the Addis Ababa Framework Agreement he concluded with SPLM/N. There were also NCP leaders who perceived the recognition of, and partnership with, the SPLM as a sell out; their intention was to see that party sink into oblivion. It was this latter group who engineered a campaign of intimidation and denigration against the SPLM/N. That included closure of the SPLM daily organ and suspension of its activities in Gezira state, in the beginning, and later in other parts of the country, including headquarter offices in Khartoum. Much as the NCP's fury over the sabre rattling displayed by the SPLM/N leadership, which was about to drag the country back to war, could have served as a pretext for the NCP's hidden intention to ban the SPLM/N, it did not hold water in the eyes of many Sudanese. The claim that the SPLM/N had lost its legitimacy because it had an army was an alleged reason, since that army existed by authority of the CPA and was to be disbanded in accordance with the terms of that agreement. That was probably why the SPLM/N was neither deregistered by the Sudan Political Parties Commission[65] nor by the National Election Commission. Nonetheless, on November 7, 2011, when the SAF reported seizure of Kurmuk in Blue Nile, President Bashir was so overcome by a paroxysm of anger that he described the SPLM/N as a bug that had to be removed from Sudan's body politic,[66] notwithstanding the fact that that "bug" had by then members in the national legislature and national and state governments.

In his speeches regarding CPA conflicts, President Bashir, time and again, reacted in a rhetorical manner that was meant either to distract his audience from the regime's woes or pander to his party diehards. Among the diehards were groups who had never believed in the CPA. Nevertheless, those within the NCP who cared for the agreement and establishing good relations with South Sudan were expected to discourage the rhetoric of hate. The NCP could never achieve the goals President Bashir was aiming at through this kind of rhetoric of hate or military exploits. Hate only begets hate, and military victory, as the experience of the civil war in South Sudan and the rebellion in Darfur had taught us, would never translate into political victory. By the same token, the SPLM/N leaders who decided to engage in a miscalculated military adventure might by now have realized the perils attending the ill-starred route they had taken. Any future success that the SPLM/N might achieve will depend entirely on opting for a pacific settlement through AUHIP mediation, given the trust that the panel had enjoyed from all parties. This shall be the best route available for the SPLM/N to take in order to save the government of South Sudan the embarrassment of choosing between its own interests and those of its erstwhile "comrades," spare the president of Sudan the awkwardness of swallowing his words, and enable the SPLM/N to lawfully expand its political catchment area within the broader north Sudan.

Nonetheless, despite the NCP's reticence to recognize the SPLM/N, let alone engage in negotiations with it on the basis of the Addis Ababa Framework Agreement, the NCP yielded to persuasion by the AUHIP. Thus, on April 24, 2013 talks commenced in Addis Ababa between SPLM/N and NCP through facilitation by the AUHIP with support of the prime minister of Ethiopia in his capacity as current chairperson of IGAD. The aim of the talks was to reach a comprehensive solution for the conflict in the Nuba Mountains and Blue Nile.[67] After two days of negotiations the talks were adjourned *sine die*. According to Ibrahim Ghandour, NCP chief negotiator at the Addis Ababa talks, the U.S. administration had invited NCP to Washington to discuss outstanding issues between that party and the U.S. administration.[68] Ghandour added that his party did not envisage talks with

SPLM/N in the Washington meeting. The collapse of the talks in Addis Ababa led to a violent retaliation by the SPLM/N.

One day after the collapse of the talks (April 27, 2013) a contingent from SPLM/N in collaboration with JEM, under the label of Sudan Revolutionary Front (SRF), attacked Um Ruwaba town in Northern Kordofan State. The attack which was reportedly launched by the SRF, took the government by surprise. It was also an embarrassment to the Sudanese army as it was directed at a town that was close to el Obied, the capital of North Kordofan where a large military base was situated. As if that attack was not enough, the SRF mounted another attack, and occupied Abu Karshola, a location in the Nuba Mountains abutting the Teqali massif.

The Sudan government's embarrassment by the two incursions which moved the war front closer to Khartoum were such that it could not put up with the idea that they were mounted solely by the SRF. As a result government accusations came galore against the governments of South Sudan, Uganda, and even Israel. Consequently, President Bashir stated in a public rally on June 9, 2013 that cross border flow of oil from South Sudan would stop. He also called on Sudanese youth to join the Sudanese army and paramilitaries.[69] South Sudan president Salva Kiir described Bashir's announced decision as tantamount to an indirect declaration of war. Salva Kiir challenged insinuations by Bashir about the involvement of South Sudan in the two attacks and advised Khartoum to seek a solution for the alleged grievances by the Nuba Mountains and Darfur through negotiations.[70]

This return to hostilities between Sudan and South Sudan after the series of agreements reached between the two countries in September 2012 through the mediation of AUHIP and under the auspices of the United Nations Security Council, the African Union, and the IGAD was a cause of disenchantment for those organizations as well as by all Sudan well-wishers in Africa and abroad, especially since the agreements had created different mechanisms for the resolution on conflict on issues resolved to the September 2013 agreements.

On June 9, 2013, President Thabo Mbeki, chairperson of AUHIP intervened. In a twelve page letter to both Presidents Bashir and Salva Kiir, he called on the two presidents to desist from actions that would escalate the conflict. To diffuse the situation he advised that three immediate measures should be taken:

i. Completion of the demilitarization of the shared borders.
ii. Cessation of support to rebels in either / both countries.
iii. Withholding hostile propaganda against each other.

Both parties agreed to commence negotiations through the mediation of the AUHIP on the basis of Mbeki's above letter. Consequently, delegations representing the two governments met in Khartoum (June 30- July 2, 2013) "to diffuse the tensions between the two countries after Bashir's decision to stop the exportation of the South Sudanese oil over accusations of support to rebel groups."[71] The South Sudan delegation led by Vice President Riek Machar met with President Bashir and then proceeded for negotiations with its Sudanese counterparts led by first Vice President Ali Osman Taha. Before the commencement of negotiations, the leaders of the two delegations recommitted themselves to the implementation of the nine cooperation agreements of September 2012.[72] After intensive talks over the course of two days a joint statement dated July 1, 2013, was issued on behalf of the two negotiating teams. The statement summarised areas of agreement by the two parties as follows:

1. To refer the complaints to the agreed relevant bilateral mechanisms.
2. To reiterate their acceptance of the proposals of the AUHIP on the current stalemate, and call on the African Union and the Chairperson of IGAD, the Prime Minister of Ethiopia, to expedite the immediate implementation of the AUHIP proposals.
3. To commit themselves to bilateral dialogue and discussions without prejudice to the ongoing facilitation of the AUHIP.
4. To respect sovereignty and territorial integrity of each state.
5. To refrain completely from support and harbouring of one another's dissidents and in accordance with the Security Arrangements Agreement.
6. To normalize and promote the bilateral relations between the two states.
7. To operationalize the mechanism for implementation, monitoring, evaluation, and dispute resolution relating to the Cooperation Agreements signed in Addis Ababa on April 23rd, 2013.
8. To support any peace initiatives that will bring peace and stability in the two states.
9. To finalize the outstanding comprehensive peace agreement issues: namely, borders and the final status of Abyei.[73]

No matter how sincere the two parties are in their determination to live up to the obligations enshrined in the September 2012 and April 2013 agreements, that shall not be realized without the removal of the root causes of conflict between them, especially alleged support by one government to rebels in the other and final resolution of the Abyei conflict. While the Abyei issue is now in the hands of the UN Security and AU Peace and Security councils, non-recognition by Sudan government of the SPLM/N and conflict in Southern Kordofan and Blue Nile states are presently up in the air after the collapse of peace talks in Addis Ababa in April 2013 and the aggravation of the situation after attacks on Um Rwaba and Abu Karshola. The Sudan government continued to claim that these conflicts are internal and, thus, are not amenable to external mediation even by South Sudan. Nevertheless, para 8 of the statement of July 1, 2013, is probably meant to cautiously open a window of opportunity for the SPLM/ South Sudan republic to mediate between the Sudan government and SPLM/N with a view to resolving these conflicts.

NOTES

1   Article 3 of the Addis Ababa agreement (1972) defined South Sudan as the three provinces of Bahr el Ghazal, Equatoria, and Upper Nile and any other areas geographically contiguous to Southern Sudan or culturally part of the Southern complex which choose through plebiscite to join the Southern region.
2   See Lesch and Wöndu, *Battle for Peace in Sudan.*
3   Garang used to give nicknames to the different SPLA battalions such as *timsah* (Crocodile), Volcanto, etc.
4   See, for example, *Sudan: Destroying Ethnic Identity: The Secret War against the Nuba*, vol. 3, issue 15, prepared by African Watch (Washington, DC, 1991); Yusuf Kasumba, *Facing Genocide: The Nuba of Sudan* (London: African Rights, 1995); *A Desolate "Peace": Human Rights in the Nuba Mountains, Sudan 1997* (London: African Rights, 1997).
5   International Crisis Group, *Sudan: Destroying Ethnic Identity*, Vol III, Issue XV, December 10, 1991.
6   Ibid.
7   Ibid.
8   BBC news report from Sudan, July 22, 1995. Also Supra note 5.
9   Sudan Interior Mission (SIM), an independent faith mission that was one of the first missionary groups to penetrate the Sudan region of West Africa. In the 1980s its name was changed to Serving in Mission but still kept the acronym (SIM). http://protestantism.inacademic.com/581/Sudan-Interior-Mission
10 For a detailed account of the history of this area, its peoples, and the brutal experience of war, see Wendy James, *War and Survival in Sudan's Frontierlands: Voices from the Blue Nile* (Oxford: Oxford University Press, 2007).
11 When the offensive by the joint Egyptian-British forces (1896-1898) to topple the Mahdist regime conquered Omdurman, the Mahdist capital, the invaders decided to rule Sudan jointly. A governor general was to be appointed by Britain with the consent of Egypt.
12 Francis Mading Deng, *War of Visions: Conflict of Identities in the Sudan* (Washington, DC: Brookings Institution, 1995).
13 See Francis Mading Deng, "Abyei: The Ambivalent North-South Border" (unpublished paper, Sudan Open Archive, 1999, www.sudanarchive.net).
14 Detailed information on the early years of oil production and its relation to the infernal war machine built by Khartoum can be found in Rone, *Sudan, Oil, and Human Rights* and Evans, *God, Oil and Country.*
15 See Julie Flint, "Rebel Leader Says Nuba Have the Will to Fight Khartoum," *The Guardian* (Nuba Mountains), April 16, 2001.
16 Roy Gutman, "Sudan: 'Let Us Have Two Constitutions,'" *Newsweek*, June 1, 2001.
17 "Sudan: U.S. Envoy Makes Four-Point Peace Proposal.", The European Sudanese Public Affairs Council, The Peace Process, http://www.espac.org/peace_process/search_for_peace28.asp

18 Senator John Danforth, "Briefing on Trip to Sudan" (remarks made by the special envoy for peace in Sudan at a briefing at the U.S. Department of State, Washington, DC, November 27, 2001).
19 Nuba Mountains Cease-Fire Agreement, Government of the Republic of Sudan and the Sudan People's Liberation Movement/Nuba, January 19, 2002.
20 Katy Salmon, "Politics-Sudan: Cease-Fire Whets Hopes for Peace," Inter Press Service (Nairobi), January 31, 2002.
21 John C. Danforth, *Report to the President of the United States on the Outlook for Peace in Sudan*, (Washington, DC: The White House, April 26, 2002).
22 "Prospects for Peace in Sudan, June–July 2002," Justice Africa (London), July 1, 2002.
23 Waihenya, *The Mediator*, 93.
24 "Historic Political Developments in Nuba Mountains Region" (a communiqué from the All Nuba Conference, Kauda, Nuba Mountains, December 2–5, 2002).
25 When the SPLM/A invited the leadership of other Nuba parties to attend the Kauda conference, they came divided in four groups: Free Sudan National Party under Bishop Philip Abbas Ghaboush, Sudan National Party (Opposition) led by Professor Elamin Hamouda Dabib, Sudan National Party–Collective Leadership under Mohamed Hamad Kuwa, and the General Union of Nuba under Yussif Abdalla Jibril. The SPLM encouraged the four groups to unite under the name of United Sudan National Party led by Bishop Philip Abbas Ghaboush, with the three other leaders as deputies. That unity did not last long.
26 Waihenya, *The Mediator*, 110.
27 Makur Dot Dhuor, "Sudan: Government Censured for Attempting to Interrupt Abyei Conference," African Church Information Service (Abyei), June 30, 2003.
28 See Waihenya, *The Mediator*, 111–13.
29 *Sudan's Other Wars*, prepared by International Crisis Group (Khartoum/Brussels, June 25, 2003).
30 See also Paul Nantulya, "The Machakos Protocol and Prospects for Peace in Sudan," *Conflict Trends* 2003/4.
31 See Comprehensive Peace Agreement between the Government of the Republic of the Sudan and the Sudan People's Liberation Movement/Sudan People's Liberation Army, Government of Sudan and Sudan People's Liberation Movement, January 9, 2005, 65.
32 The United Kingdom and the United States appointed, respectively, Douglas Johnson, a university professor and author of several works on Sudan, and Donald Peterson, former U.S. ambassador to Sudan, while the IGAD nominated Professors Kassahun Berhanu of Addis Ababa University, Shadrack Gutto of the University of South Africa, and Godfrey Muriuki of the University of Nairobi.
33 Douglas H. Johnson, "Sudan's Peaceful Partition, at Risk," *New York Times*, May 30, 2011, Op-Ed.
34 Kodi served as a Nuba representative at the state and national levels in the Government of National Unity. After the secession of the South and clashes in the Nuba Mountains between al-Hilu (SPLM/N) and the NCP, he joined the ranks of the Islamists.
35 Jason Gluck, *Why Sudan's Popular Consultation Matters*, Special Report No. 260 prepared for the United States Institute for Peace, November 2010.

36 Convention 169 was adopted by the ILO as a legally binding instrument open to ratification by member states. A country that ratifies the conventional shall be bound to respect all provisions relating to non-discrimination of its citizens on the basis of ethnic origin, cultural way of life different than that of predominant segment of the population, traditional laws and customs, etc.

37 The Comprehensive Peace Agreement 2005, Article 9.7: The resolution of Conflict in Southern Kordofan and Blue Nile States.

38 Liz Alden Wily, *Making Peace Impossible? Failure to Honour the Land Obligations of the Comprehensive Peace Agreement in Central Sudan*, a resource paper by independent land specialist, September 2010.

39 Alex Thurston, "South Kordofan Elections Increase NCP-SPLM Enmity," Sahel Blog, posted May 17, 2011, http://sahel blog.worldpress.com.

40 Aly Verjee, "Unfinished Business: The May 2011 State Elections in Southern Kordofan," a briefing prepared for the Rift Valley Institute, March 31, 2011.

41 *Vote in South Kordofan is Peaceful and Credible, Despite Climate of Insecurity and Some Irregularities*, prepared by the Carter Center Elections Observation Mission in Sudan (Atlanta, May 18, 2011).

42 "Sudan's Bashir Endorses Lashing of YouTube Woman, Says North Will Transfer into Islamic State, *Sudan Tribune* (Khartoum), *December 19, 2010*.

43 James Capnalk, BBC, 10 May 2011.

44 *Sudan's South Kordofan Problem: The Next Darfur?* Africa Report no. 145 prepared by the International Crisis Group (Khartoum, Nairobi, Brussels, October 21, 2008.

45 *Armed Entities in South Kordofan*, prepared by the Small Arms Survey, Graduate Institute of International and Development Studies, for the Human Security Baseline Assessment for Sudan and South Sudan project (Geneva, Switzerland, June 4, 2011).

46 Ibid.

47 Ibid.

48 Julie Flint, *The Nuba Mountains: Central to Sudan's Stability*, CPA Alert No. 3, a report prepared by the IKV Pax Christi Sudan Programme, (Utrecht, The Netherlands, January 2011), 13.

49 *Preliminary Report on Violations of International Humanitarian Law in Southern Kordofan from 5 to 30 June 2011*, report from the U.N. Office of the High Commissioner for Human Rights (Geneva, Switzerland, August 15, 2011).

50 "Sudan: Southern Kordofan Briefing," Integrated Regional Information Networks (Juba), June 23, 2011.

51 Alan Boswell, "Inside Sudan's Nuba Mountains: Tales of Terror Bleed Out," *Time*, June 20, 2011

52 Richard Rottenburg, Guma Kunda Komey, and Enrico Ille, *The Genesis of Recurring Wars in Sudan: Rethinking the Violent Conflicts in the Nuba Mountains/South Kordofan* (Germany: University of Halle, October 2011).

53 Ibid.

54 Mark C. Toner, *Security and Humanitarian Situation in Southern Kordofan, Sudan*, statement made by the deputy spokesperson, U.S. Department of State (Washington DC, June 14, 2011).

55 The High-Level Panel was established by the African Union to help the Government of Sudan and SPLM in the consummation of the CPA as well as the resolution of the Darfur Conflict (see Chapter Twelve).

56 Alan Boswell, "Sudan's Conflict Spreads: Is This the Start of a New Civil War?" *Time,* September 2, 2011.

57 Victoria Nuland, "Escalating Violence in Blue Nile State of Sudan," press statement made by department spokesperson on behalf of the U.S. Department of State (Washington, DC, September 2, 2011).

58 "Removal of the regime is not an appropriate option," *Al Ahdath 14, September 2011*

59 Ibid.

60 What is taking place in the South Kordofan and the Blue Nile is a foreign plot, interview of president Bashir by Imam Mohamed Imam, *Sharq al Awsat,* September 25, 2011.

61 The delegation was led by General John Kong Nyuon, South Sudan minister of defense; James Hoth Mai, SPLA chief of staff; and Salva Mathok, South Sudan deputy minister of interior.

62 Tesfa-Alem Tekle, "North, South Sudan Agree to Complete Abyei Pullout This Month," *Sudan Tribune* (Addis Ababa), September 9, 2011.

63 Edith M. Lederer, "Sudan Will Leave Abyei When UN Fully Deploys," Associated Press, October 6, 2011.

64 José Felipe Moraes Cabral, *Security Council Press Statement on Situation in Abyei,* SC/10436/AFR/2276, issued by the president of the U.N. Security Council, November 4, 2011.

65 The commission is a regulatory body formed by the Sudan government to oversee the registeration and operation of political parties within the bounds of the law.

66 "Al-Bashir Warns South Sudan in Meddling over Sudan's Affairs," Sudan Radio Service (Kurmuk/Juba), November 7, 2011, http://www.eyeradio.org/drupal/al-bashir-warns-south-sudan-meddling-over-sudans-affairs

67 African Union Peace and Security. http://www.peaceau.org/en/article/direct-talks-in-addis-ababa-between-thegovernemnt-of-Sudan-and-the-splm-north.

68 Sudan rules out negotiations with SPLM-N outside Africa, Sudan Tribune. http://www.sudantribune.com/spip.php?article=46455

69 "Sudan's Bashir orders the stoppage of South Sudan's oil," Reuters, Sunday 9 June 2013.

70 Ngor, Mading and Michael Gunn."South Sudan leader labels Sudan oil threat a declaration of war," Bloomberg, June 10, 2013.

71 Machar meets Bashir and Taha over row between Juba and Khartoum , Sudan Tribune, July 1, 2013: http://www.sudantribune.com/spip.php?iframe&page=imprimable&id_article=47141

72 Ibid.

73 Joint Statement on the talks between the Government of Sudan and South Sudan between 30th June and July 2, 2013 in Khartoum on the issue of implementation of the Cooperation Agreements, Friendship Palace, Khartoum, July 1, 2013.

Chapter Eight
CPA Implementation
Challenges

■ ■ ■ ■ ■ ■ ■ ■ ■ ■ ■ ■ ❖ ■ ■ ■ ■ ■ ■ ■ ■ ■ ■ ■ ■ ■

Nothing doth more hurt in a state than that cunning men pass for wise.
—Francis Bacon

1. Introduction

It was hinted in the introduction that the Comprehensive Peace Agreement
(CPA) was unique in more than one way. First, it had undergone a long period
of gestation: three years before it was brought into the world. Second,
regardless of the local factors that conspired to make the agreement
achievable, its final delivery could not have been possible without the help of
a host of midwives in the form of observers, advisors, mediators, and
researchers, in addition to interventions by world statesmen at critical
moments. Third, unlike comparable peace agreements, the CPA negotiators
had gone into a painstaking process of establishing matrixes for
implementation with definitive time lines, sources of funding for different
activities, and clear identification of who should do what and when. The
meticulousness with which negotiators on the Sudan People's Liberation
Movement/Army (SPLM/A) side sought to have the CPA drafted in that way
revealed both the level of mistrust it had in the other party, as well as its desire
not to leave any loophole regarding implementation. That meticulousness was
understandable in light of episodes since the declaration of independence on
January 1, 1956, which demonstrated the predisposition of northern rulers to
take agreements with South Sudan lightly. From the shameful backpedaling
on the issue of federalism in 1956 to the abrogation of the Addis Ababa
agreement in 1983, keeping political promises had never been a strong suit of

the Khartoum ruling class. This was the case at least insofar as agreements with southern Sudanese were concerned. Fourth, the CPA had been designed to be both an agreement to conclusively put an end to war in southern Sudan as well as a prototype for resolving similar conflicts in other parts of Sudan. Fifth, the CPA established ground rules and parameters that would enable two former warring parties to govern together and achieve common goals. Six, the agreement also provided state-building plans as well as a blueprint for the reconstruction of South Sudan. Into the bargain, the CPA offered a road map for the transformation of the country from one party governance to multiparty democracy.

That was a giant plan whose implementation required commitment to the agreement in letter and spirit, not to mention faithfulness in implementation, with no malice afore or afterthought. However, no matter how well designed an agreement is, it would be worthless without faithful implementation. This would be even more so in the case of an agreement like the CPA that did not allow for exit options; a minor breach of the terms of such an agreement might, if tolerated, make the whole agreement unravel. In this chapter the author shall review achievements and underachievements in the implementation of cardinal obligations stipulated by the CPA, particularly those whose timely and satisfactory implementation would have provided a firm foundation for unity.

But before engaging in that review, the author shall evaluate the impact of a single unanticipated accident that had never been envisaged by the negotiators: the disappearance from the scene of one of the two principal signatories of the CPA. Garang's sudden death in July 2005 sparked off different reactions in Sudan, ranging from fear of nonimplementation of the CPA to total obliteration of the New Sudan vision. Those fears were to be expected as Garang had been the intellectual powerhouse behind the New Sudan vision and the originator of many of the novel concepts that found their way into the CPA. He was also the persuasive salesman of that agreement to both the North and the South. To the North, he had convincingly built a model for unity of Sudan on a new basis that only bigots could reject, while to southern Sudanese he compellingly presented a constitutional framework that would allow them, if they so wished, to secede peacefully from the North after giving unity a last chance during the interim period.

Garang's disappearance from the political theater also gave pleasure to a cabal within the National Congress Party (NCP) who seemed not to believe a jot in the CPA, even though that agreement was designed word by word by negotiators from both the NCP and the SPLM, and was finally signed by no less than President Bashir, on behalf of the government of Sudan. This group tore the mask off its face and revealed its real intentions the moment Garang was entombed. To them the CPA was welcome only as a permanent cease-fire agreement and an instrument of containment and accommodation, never as a

246

tool of political, cultural, and economic transformation of the country as it was envisaged. John Garang's death offered this group a golden opportunity to revoke the commitments that had been solemnly made under the glare of international cameras and witnessed by 15 observers representing governments and regional and international organizations.

As a result, any assessment of progress in the implementation of the CPA requires analyzing five separate, but interrelated, processes and events. The first is the impact of Garang's death on the SPLM/A and, at the same time, as a pretext for the NCP's changed perceptions of their "supposed" partner in government. Second is the dynamics of relations between the two parties after Garang's demise, especially on the implementation of various elements of the agreement. Those elements included issues that were about to derail negotiations at Naivasha such as Abyei and security arrangements, along with others issues that did not raise much debate during the negotiations but turned out to be nettlesome in the course of implementation such as census, border demarcation, Abyei, and elections. The third point requiring analysis is assessing the security situation in southern Sudan after the conclusion of the agreement. The fourth is highlighting the critical role the agreement envisaged for conducting an international assessment and evaluation of the implementation of the CPA through an independent body. The fifth is the responsibility the agreement placed on guarantors and development partners to ensure full implementation of the CPA and sustenance of peace through reconstruction plans in war ravaged areas, particularly South Sudan.

2. Facing the Unanticipated

One thing the negotiators did not envision and, therefore, never factored into the agreement, was the likelihood of the disappearance from the scene of the negotiation's prime mover. That happened when the dramatis personae of the play fatefully made a tryst with death on July 30, 2005. On that sad day SPLM leader, John Garang de Mabior, breathed his last following a tragic air crash over the hills of the Imatongs, south of Lotukei in South Sudan. Garang's tragic death was one of the ironies of history; for 21 years he had been preparing himself to play a central role in Sudan's national politics, only to enjoy that role for 21 days. The fatal air crash in which Garang perished took place only three weeks after he was sworn in as first vice president of Sudan, a position occupied for the first time by a southern Sudanese.

On his arrival in Khartoum on July 8, 2005, Garang was rapturously received by millions of Sudanese from all parts of the country. Some came on foot, others on bicycles, and others were transported from distant areas in the country via all available means of conveyance. They were men and women, young and old. Some were carrying their toddlers, seemingly to introduce them to John Garang whom they had justifiably thought to be the man of the hour. Enigmatic as the man of the hour had been to many of those who thronged around him in Khartoum, that enigma deepened when Garang died three weeks after a thunderous reception in the national capital that proved false the claims that northern Sudan was not yet ready to be led by a southern Sudanese. On his side, Garang was exhilarated by the reception, if only because it clearly showed that the New Sudan, his grand design, was not a castle in the sky but a feasible plan.

There were lessons to be learned by both northern and southern Sudanese from that event. To southerners who saw one of their own received in Khartoum with such rapture, the reception was ennobling and provided incontrovertible evidence that northern Sudanese were not loath to be led by a southern Sudanese. Still, Garang's departure seemed to have been a cause of mute jubilation by some southern Sudanese politicians who were enraged by his domination of the political arena in the South and envious of his emergence at the national, regional, and international levels as the undisputed spokesman for the people of South Sudan. As for the northern political class who had always assumed, though not declared, that south Sudanese were "a regional fossilized sub-specie,"[1] they were stunned by the sight of millions of ordinary northern Sudanese citizens coming out to welcome a national "savior" who hailed from Bor in the distant South.

3. Tensions between the Two Partners

The implementation of the CPA had been hampered from the start by potentially serious tensions between the two partners that led to widespread concerns. The overwhelming cause of that tension was the absence of a mutually agreed upon program for the Government of National Unity in the power sharing protocol. As a result, the SPLM practically ended implementing NCP policies. However, it soon became obvious that, if ignored, these tensions could lead to renewed conflict and might undermine the peace process. The worst-case scenario would have been a return to large-scale war in South Sudan, despite clear declarations by Salva Kiir that there would be *no return to war*. One would assume that enlightened self-interest, if not common sense, dictated that war should never be an option for either party. Also, with conflict in Darfur unresolved and outside pressures on the Sudan government unabating, return by the NCP to full-scale war in the South would have been a reckless enterprise. As for the SPLM, no leader who had gone through two decades of a deadly war would look forward to even one more day of war. But if that was what common sense ordained, countless experiences in Sudanese politics demonstrated that common sense had often been uncommon.

As soon as Garang was no longer in the picture, anti-CPA forces within the NCP engaged in incautious maneuvers that were prone to envenom relations between the partners. Instead of continuing to transact business with the party it had signed an agreement with, the NCP decided to deal with a fictitious SPLM: the SPLM as they would have wanted, or assumed it to be. As we endeavored to show in previous chapters, a long history existed behind that make believe. Traditional parties in the North, including Islamists, never accepted the idea that southerners were mature enough to define where their place under the sun should be, let alone capable to lead the nation. With this mind-set, the anti-CPA elements within the NCP who found Garang's vision of the New Sudan unsavory, decided to create their own South in the form of individual politicians or political groupings from South Sudan, the way they had tried before in the peace-from-within attempt in 1995. The terrible failure of that attempt did not dissuade them from trying it again. In all probability, the exclusion from the new government of NCP negotiators[2] who played a cardinal role with their SPLM counterparts in concluding the CPA paved the way for that misguided venture. If anything, NCP elements who actively participated in the negotiations fully understood that the viability of the agreement depended entirely on good faith between the parties. In the meantime, outside players whose contribution to the conclusion of the CPA was critical not only began to disengage from the process, but also treated the scheming by that NCP faction against its partner as small accidents on the road, rather than serious infractions of the agreement

The stratagem of the anti-CPA group was simple: isolate Salva Kiir from his power base, particularly from SPLM leaders who were dedicated to Garang's, indeed SPLM's, vision. Those were scornfully called *awlad Garang* (Garang's boys). In place of Garang's boys, the anti-CPA group within the NCP recruited south Sudanese politicians who were either known to have always looked askance at Garang's vision, or were disgruntled as a result of the way he had kept them at bay. Whether those backsliders were driven by their own belief as to what was good for the SPLM, were in a huff about the way the late leader treated them, or lured by rewards lavished on them by the NCP, none of them seemed to have been embarrassed by that behavior or discomfited by the damage caused to their own party, the SPLM.

To justify its misdeeds, that group claimed that the success of the CPA hinged on total cooperation between the SPLM and the NCP throughout the interim period, a cause to which they thought the Garang boys were not fully dedicated. To besmirch the reputation of the Garang boys they claimed that the main objective of the "boys" was to collaborate with northern opposition parties, particularly those on the left fringe, in order to subvert the national government. Those who purveyed such censorious remarks about their colleagues never queried themselves why any leader of a vibrant party like the SPLM would become a cat's paw for parties that were increasingly fading into irrelevance. In reality, whenever there were alliances between Garang boys and opposition parties in the North, these had invariably taken place in order to push certain CPA dossiers that the NCP had decided to put on ice, chiefly those related to democratic transformation.[3] Evidently, the SPLM cadres who maligned their party's national agenda seemed to have perceived partnership with the NCP as an end in itself, not a means to ensure the faithful implementation of the agreement. And although the NCP and its SPLM allies had never come out openly against democratic transformation—indeed, they continued to pay lip service to it—together they forged ahead furtively with intrigues to frustrate that transformation. As the referendum became imminent, those SPLM leaders, save for issuing supportive pro forma statements in favor of democratic transformation, almost eschewed its cardinality to comprehensive peace. Incredibly, the SPLM leaders who directly, or indirectly, held cheap the democratization process ushered in by the CPA for the whole Sudan, emerged later as champions of the democratization of South Sudan in the run up to independence and after.

While that was happening, Salva Kiir, a man who was known to be very economical with his words, observed those maneuvers in sphinxian silence. His silence on those issues, especially in his high-level meetings with the NCP, was more eloquent than his utterances. Both NCP schemers and their SPLM helpers either failed to decipher Salva Kiir's taciturnity or couldn't care less. Even the historical pronouncement made by Salva Kiir at Garang's burial in Juba on August 8, 2005, was not enough to convince them where the new leader stood. In that pronouncement, Salva Kiir affirmed that he was staying Garang's course and that "the SPLM/A [was] a vehicle without a reverse gear." Having been incensed by the NCP's tedious maneuvers to divide the SPLM into two imagined factions, Salva Kiir decided to state the obvious without any adornment on the occasion of the second anniversary of the signing of the CPA (January 9, 2007). On that occasion he said: "there are certain elements who wish to divide us into what they call *Awlad Garang* [Garang boys] and *Awlad who?*, I do not know. May I, therefore, unequivocally say that our Late Leader, may his soul rest in eternal peace, has bequeathed on us, alongside the CPA, a vision and a message. This vision and that message have indelibly impressed themselves on our minds, and to them we remain committed. *Those words, I call on those who wish to see us divided to abandon their illusions or delusions on what the SPLM stands for."* Principled as Salva Kiir's words were, Garang's grand vision for a New Sudan was mainly undermined by NCP prevarications on the CPA implementation as well as by attempts by some SPLM cadres to demote the transformative aspect of the agreement on somebody else's bidding.

4. Salva Kiir's Undervalued Magnanimity

Irrespective of the wrangling between SPLM renegades and a committed SPLM cadre, as well as among some of his aides, Salva Kiir was determined to maintain partnership with the NCP in order to ensure the faithful implementation of the agreement. He likely chose to do this in order to deny those in the NCP who wished to walk out of their obligations a pretext to do so. Even before the formation of the Government of National Unity, he resisted pressures from within the SPLM requesting him to stand firm on an equitable division of national ministries, especially in the economic sector. That position was based on an agreement in principle reached with the NCP during the Naivasha negotiations to ensure the equitable division of government departments (see Chapter Five). Although the Ministries of Energy and Finance were paired off in the economic cluster, the NCP persisted on maintaining both during the discussions on the formation of the Government of National Unity. The SPLM leader told the NCP from the start that his party did not lay claim on the Ministry of Finance, but it was demanding the Ministry of Energy for two reasons. The first was to abide by the principle of equitable sharing prescribed in the implementation modalities of the CPA, and the second was that more than 80 percent of Sudan's current oil production came from South Sudan. Regardless of this cogent argument and pressures on him from his own party not to yield to the NCP's demand, Salva Kiir decided to relinquish both ministries in deference to a personal appeal President Bashir made to him. One ministry was not as important as allowing CPA implementation to commence, he told his party aides. To his party leaders, he explained that the commencement of that process was contingent on the formation of the Government of National Unity and that of South Sudan. The veteran South Sudan politician who was by then advisor to President Bashir prevailed upon Salva Kiir to relinquish the Ministry of Energy and instead accept the Ministry of Industry. President Kiir, despite objections from his party advisors, went along with Malwal's suggestion only to learn later that President Bashir was not ready to allocate to the SPLM the Ministry of Industry as he had already promised to grant the portfolio to the chair of a minor party in the government: Jalal Digeir of the National Democratic Party. The only portfolio Bashir was ready to allocate to the SPLM was the Ministry of External Trace. That was the measure of Bashir's commitment to making unity attractive. Indeed Salva Kiir's magnanimity from the start proved to be a miscalculation, as it was never reciprocated by the NCP. In reality, the NCP progressively rolled back essential reforms provided for in the agreement.

Whether that concession had whetted its appetite to make more impingements on SPLM turf, or whether SPLM accomplices persuaded it that the new leader was amenable to pressure, the NCP went on to commit a series of violations of the CPA. Those violations collectively led the SPLM to suspend its participation in the government of National Unity on October 11, 2007, and recall its ministers, state ministers, and presidential advisers from that government citing "inexplicable" delays in CPA implementation. Those delays included completion of Abyei, border demarcation, redeployment of SAF units out of oil-producing areas in South Sudan, lack of transparency in figures relating to oil revenues, resolution of technical issues concerning the national census, and commencement of the process of national reconciliation and healing. Two things should be pointed out regarding why the SPLM decided to take the extreme position of withdrawing from government. At the top of the list were issues of national character, not southern Sudan-specific. These included democratic transformation and national reconciliation. Despite the prominence the SPLM had given these issues during its first confrontation with the NCP, the issues were soon relegated to the bottom of priorities. The second point is that issues that directly or indirectly pertained to southern Sudan were all matters on which the parties were at loggerheads during the three years of negotiations, but on which they eventually reached agreement and established specific time frames for their implementation. Any going back on positions agreed upon by any of the parties would be an act of bad faith and a breach of trust. Among these were deployment of SAF forces out of South Sudan, integration of other armed groups into two regular armies, border demarcation, census, and Abyei.

For faith to erode so quickly between two parties, who succeeded in concluding an epochal agreement which had been beyond Khartoum rulers for almost half a century, gave the impression that the CPA was not wholeheartedly welcome by all NCP constituencies, even though the eventuality that a group within either party might seek to renege on the CPA did not escape the minds of the SPLM/A negotiators. Indeed, awareness of this possibility impelled the SPLM to insist on the inclusion in the agreement of a clause that provided: "Upon signature, the Parties shall be bound by the Agreement and shall assume the obligations arising therefrom, more especially the obligations to implement the Agreement and give legal and constitutional effect to the arrangements agreed therein" (2.12.2 Power Sharing Protocol). That clause went on to say: **"Upon signature the Parties commit themselves to ensure that all the organs, committees and structures under their control, including their members, shall observe the terms of the Agreement"** (emphasis added) (2.12.3 Power Sharing Protocol). With such iron-clad provisions, the two parties were under obligation to ensure full compliance with the agreement by all their party instances as well as members, however high their positions were.

Map 2: Oil and gas production sites in Sudan

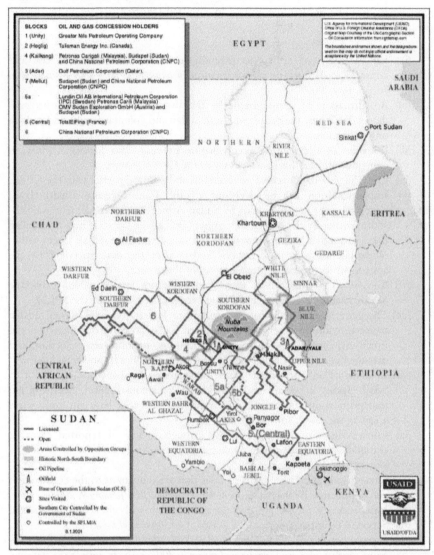

The withdrawal of the SPLM from the Government of National Unity in October 2007 in protest against the nonimplementation of preeminent parts of the CPA turned out to be a wake-up call, as the NCP moved fast to put together a plan to resolve all issues raised by the SPLM. In late December 2007, the SPLM returned to the Government of National Unity as a result of an agreement reached between the two parties that was formally incorporated in presidential decree (341/2007). That decree was accompanied by yet another matrix of implementation, which was prefaced by a recommitment by the two parties to the CPA as well as to *reinforcing confidence-building measures* (emphasis added) between them. On the substantive issues, the decree stipulated:

(i) Enhancement of efforts to promulgate the national elections law and consolidate democratic transformation *in consultation with other political forces* before July 2009.

(ii) Reaffirmation of commitment by the two parties to the right to self-determination by the people of South Sudan and voluntary unity, and making unity attractive.

(iii) Initiation of the national reconciliation process *before January 9, 2008,* to coincide with the third anniversary of the CPA signature.

(iv) Compliance of all levels of government and political parties with the CPA.

(v) Implementation of the decisions of the Joint Defense Board (JDB) concerning the redeployment by Sudan Armed Forces (SAF) to the north-south border by the end of December 2007 at the latest. It may be recalled that a major SPLM concern was the continued presence of SAF forces within oil-production sites in southern Sudan after the date specified by the agreement for their redeployment out of those sites.[4]

(vi) Review of national census forms, on or before January 2008, to include details relating to religion and ethnic origin, as requested by the SPLM.

(vii) The government of South Sudan, before January 9, 2008, would enable national institutions serving in southern Sudan to carry out their national functions, especially with regard to customs, national tax collection, and management of the Civil Aviation Authority activities in South Sudan.

(viii) Creation of an instrument by the presidency to enhance development of South Sudan, especially in the fields of road construction, river and rail transport, communications, and improving linkages between contiguous areas on the north-south border.

(ix) Consolidation of the rule of law through review of reported cases of extrajudicial measures such as illegal detention or frustration of justice by law-enforcement agencies.

(x) Review and repeal of all existing laws that are repugnant to the constitution and completion of that mission *within six months from January 9, 2008.*

(xi) Independence of the judiciary in consultation with the National Judicial Service Commission *within three months of the signature of the decree.*

(xii) Twenty percent of the national civil service would be composed of recruits from south Sudanese citizens *by January 9, 2008,* so as to reflect the national character of the service.

The majority of the undertakings provided for in the republican decree were not realized on the dates agreed upon by the parties. In fact, some remained unfulfilled by the time the interim period came to its end. While, one could accept that some of the dates stipulated in the decree were overly optimistic, nonimplementation of cardinal issues that led to the withdrawal of the SPLM from the Government of National Unity and whose implementation was within reach, reflected either a lack of seriousness toward solemnly made undertakings or want of political will. Either way, this was not the way to consolidate peace in Sudan or persuade southern Sudanese that unity was attractive.

Clearly, the issues that were most misprized by the NCP in the SPLM list of demands that were presented to, and acted upon by, the presidency were those relating to democratic transformation: repeal of laws that contravened the Interim National Constitution (Bill of Rights), independence of the judiciary, and failure to keep security and law-enforcement agencies within the bounds of the constitution. That stand gave rise to a plausible impression that the NCP was not yet ready to allow Sudan's graduation from one-party hegemony to multi-party democratic rule, nor was it ready to open up and allow other political forces to meaningfully participate in transition politics as the CPA had indicated. In its preamble, the CPA recognized "that the smooth and successful implementation of this Agreement shall, to a large measure, hinge on *rallying the majority of the Sudanese people behind it*" (emphasis added). The fact that the SPLM had accepted the NCP's debasement of cardinal issues relating to democratic transformation in exchange for unfulfilled promises relative to southern Sudan demands made a mockery of Garang's two-and-a-half years of negotiations at Naivasha precisely on these issues. That also explains why the Government of National Unity never cared for directives the Security Council made at its meeting in Nairobi that the CPA be propagated "through national media and schools," that national reconciliation be achieved, that "Sudan's Police Services be consistent with international democratic practices," and "that the Rule of Law including an independent judiciary be observed and that impunity be combated."[5]

5. CPA: Achievements, Under-achievements, and Missed Opportunities

In spite of the foregoing, significant achievements did occur in CPA implementation during the first half of the interim period. First, the presence of the SPLM in Khartoum was a major achievement, since it opened lines of communication between former foes, a matter that appeared to have boded well for the development and improvement of relations between them into the future. Second, as a result of that presence. the SPLM was able to regularly interact with other political forces, consolidate its support base in the North, and recruit more supporters. Third, participation of the SPLM in the Government of National Unity enabled the SPLM to present itself as a credible political party capable, whenever it was allowed, to govern at the national level and represent Sudan in regional and international arenas. Fourth, an ambitious state-building process in southern Sudan had progressed, although very slowly in view of a host of forbidding reasons such as lack of institutional and human capacity, zero-level of development from which South Sudan had started, and insecurity due to internal and external reasons. Over and above, for the first time in its 14 years of rule, the NCP had at long last enjoyed a large measure of national legitimacy and international acceptability; its main military challenger became its partner in government, and the combined northern opposition represented by the National Democratic Alliance (NDA) signed a peace agreement with it in Cairo in July 2005, before the formation of the Government of National Unity. The NDA, with its armed wings, later became a partner in government.

While the delinquency of the NCP in CPA implantation was flagrant, as the SPLM had exposed in the violations it catalogued when it suspended participation in the Government of National Unity in October 2007, the SPLM itself was not totally free of blame. For example, encroachments by Government of South Sudan officials on powers reserved by the CPA to the national government were often reported by that party, particularly in areas such as collection of customs and national taxes in South Sudan, civil aviation, communications, passport and immigration, and external relations. One aspect of the agreement that proved to be time-consuming in the negotiations was the apportionment of powers between the Government of National Unity and the Government of South Sudan, and between both of them and the states. Whatever agreement had been reached in this regard should have been keenly observed, especially since both the CPA and the INC established clear principles of "administration and inter-governmental linkages."[6] Understandably, some contraventions such as noncollection of national taxes in South Sudan or misuse of tax revenues collected was due to institutional inadequacy from which even internal revenue collection in South Sudan suffered. The government of South Sudan was equally a loser as a result of that administrative inadequacy since 50 percent of the national tax revenues collected in South Sudan were to be spent on development and services in that region. To add insult to injury, thugs in uniform stationed at tax collection points on the borders with Kenya and Uganda were allowed, with apparent impunity, to appropriate part of the revenues collected for their own account.

Be that as it may, what made the Government of National Unity's hackles rise was the meddling by some Government of South Sudan representatives abroad as if they were representing another country. It is to be noted that the Power Sharing Protocol had reserved foreign relations as the domain of the Government of National Unity.[7] However, the protocol also stated that "without prejudice to national regulations," subnational levels of government were empowered to "initiate, negotiate, and conclude international and regional agreements on culture, sports, trade, investment, credit, loans, grants, and technical assistance with foreign governments and foreign non-governmental organizations." Save for the government of South Sudan, no other subnational level in Sudan exercised this power. The rationale behind this exception was that the SPLM had virtually been a semi-independent government in southern Sudan, and for two decades it had established extensive relations with governmental and nongovernmental institutions abroad. This was taken by the SPLM to be an implicit endorsement by the Government of National Unity of the status quo, especially since it did not object to the government of South Sudan's decision to create regional representation offices abroad. In effect, a memorandum of understanding (MoU) was signed between the Ministry of Foreign Affairs in Khartoum (then superintended by an SPLM minister) and the Ministry of Regional Cooperation in Juba on the rules of engagement in the field of foreign representation during the interim period. Undeterred by that MoU, some Government of South Sudan representatives abroad did not mind violating some of these rules and were seldom called to attention by their direct superiors.

In all those cases, the president of the government of South Sudan, on numerous occasions, drew the attention of officials under him to the fact that southern Sudan was not yet an independent country. That was why, even at the level of symbols, he was very attentive to protocol. By way of illustration, Salva Kiir was often visibly annoyed by the absence of the national flag in official functions he attended, or by omitting his title as first vice president of the republic during foreign visits organized for him by the government of South Sudan. The sensitivity of the first vice president to the duality of his position was certainly engendered by his keenness not to allow even a small infraction of the CPA to become a pretext for more serious violations by the partner. Salva Kiir's political sensitivity to those matters was not shared by some of his aides, who often saw the speck in the NCP's eye but seldom the log that was in their own eyes.

Beyond the political dynamic between the SPLM and the NCP, and the ever-present threat of renewed conflict, several observers thought that the CPA was premised on overly optimistic assumptions and time frames, and that was why many of its deadlines proved unattainable or passed without achieving the desired results. But underachievement by the parties, in reality, was not necessarily because the set targets were overambitious or the timelines for implementation inadequate. The truth of the matter is that the aforementioned conflicting agenda of the two parties, and within each of them, have frustrated implementation. That is not to deny that the post-conflict transformation of Sudan has been an enormous undertaking that involved multiple and intersecting social, political, cultural, and economic processes that were never anticipated in any peace agreement similar to the CPA. For this reason, the CPA should have been viewed as a living document and a framework within which two former warring parties would meaningfully collaborate. That was not the case for the many reasons stated above. So, the process of continually building upon the terms of the agreement in order to make them relevant to the fast-changing political realities of Sudan was hardly done. Also, the flexibility and pragmatism that were essential to keep the spirit of the CPA alive were obviated by the small-mindedness of elements within the SPLM, and the greed of others within the NCP, who either did not realize that peace had a price or wanted peace without any price.

Two landmark events, however, awaited the parties: national elections and the referendum on self-determination scheduled for January 9, 2011. To be exact, the national elections were not conceived by the CPA as a procedural exercise, but rather as a process whereby trust in the government was obtained through the free will of the people and the exclusivity created by the CPA was toned down. The elections were also expected to determine the relative powers of the NCP and the SPLM during the second half of the interim period. Elections were also linked to other aspects of CPA implementation such as border demarcation, national census, and repatriation of internally displaced people to southern Sudan. Even so, there had always been ambivalence about elections on both sides. For the NCP, free, fair, and transparent elections posed the greatest threat to its power. Within the SPLM were two clashing schools of thought: one that viewed elections as the acme of the national democratic transformation process promised by the CPA, and the other that wished to give its back to the course of democratic transformation in order to concentrate on consolidation of southern Sudan's autonomy and eventual secession. Surely, the latter standpoint reflected a misinterpretation of what the CPA meant by making unity attractive. Part A of the Machakos Protocol (Agreed Principles) stated that the unity of Sudan, based on the free will of its people, democratic governances, accountability, equality, respect, and justice for **all citizens of Sudan is and shall be** the priority of the parties, and that it is possible to redress the grievances of the people of southern Sudan and to meet their aspirations within such a framework (clause 1.1). The Agreed Principles also provided that the two parties shall "design and implement the Peace Agreement so as to make unity of the Sudan an attractive option, **especially to peoples of Southern Sudan**" (emphasis added) (1.5.5). The CPA, therefore, did not aspire to make unity attractive only to southern Sudanese, but to all Sudanese, **especially southerners**. So, while the NCP is duty bound to carry out all obligations under the agreement that would make unity attractive, especially to the people of South Sudan, the SPLM was also under obligation to live up to, and concentrate its energies on, achieving all the principles enshrined in the CPA that would make unity and governance attractive to **all** Sudanese.

6. SPLM Ambiguities

Within the northern opposition, disbelief increased regarding the genuineness of the SPLM's commitment toward any national agenda after Garang's demise.

So were fears augmented about the SPLM's stamina to come in full force behind the CPA's transformation agenda. This sentiment appeared to have been heightened by the SPLM's trading off the repeal of all laws restrictive of freedoms (press and national security laws) for the promulgation of the referendum act. That enactment should never have been assumed to be a reward to the SPLM by the NCP as it was a right enshrined in both the CPA and the INC. Much as those fears might have had some justification, the SPLM critics should not have underrated the principled stand taken by the SPLM's chairman on issues of democratic transformation when he temporarily withdrew his ministers from the Government of National Unity in October 2007 and the valiant efforts exerted by SPLM's caucus in the Sudanese Parliament to take on the Government of National Unity on issues relating to human rights abuses and matters of concern to the common man. Nevertheless, misgivings remained about the SPLM's ultimate national goals, particularly in view of sustained efforts by the NCP and its helpers within the SPLM to create confusion in the minds of SPLM cadres as well as among SPLM allies nationwide.

In May 2008, the SPLM Second National Convention met to draw a new manifesto for the party and rearticulate its position on issues of policy relating to Sudan in general and South Sudan in particular. National unity headed the convention's agenda. While many of the resolutions adopted by the convention remained ink on paper, those on national unity, reconciliation, and healing would merit attention, if only because they deepened SPLM's ambiguities. In that resolution the convention reaffirmed its commitment to the vision of New Sudan, including *"unity of Sudan on a new basis"* (emphasis added). Without elaboration on what "new basis" meant, the convention went on to urge the Government of National Unity "to take all measures envisioned in the CPA and the Constitution to [ensure] unity and reconciliation among the people of the Sudan in order to promote respect for political diversity, racial harmony, religious tolerance, and fraternal relations among all people of Sudan." These were indeed measures that the Government of National Unity—a government dominated by NCP and SPLM—was obligated to realize by the CPA and the INC. Even so, that government could have only been constrained to carry those obligations if the SPLM had placed the questions at issue at the top of its agenda and brought pressure to bear on that government so that it took its constitutional obligations seriously. What was also missing in the resolution was the mapping out of SPLM's own plan for rebuilding Sudan on new basis. Regarding promoting "unity, reconciliation, and security in South Sudan," the convention rightly asserted that unity of the people of southern Sudan was critical as the South approached 2011, when the people were expected to choose in a referendum one of the two options provided for in the CPA and the INC. The convention went on to urge the SPLM leadership to double its efforts to consolidate unity and promote reconciliation among the people of southern Sudan.

Two things drew attention in those resolutions. First, by placing the responsibility for making Sudan's unity attractive entirely on the shoulders of the NCP while limiting the role of the government of South Sudan to consolidating the unity of the people of South Sudan, SPLM neither did justice to itself nor to the cause for which it had been struggling for two decades. Besides, the SPLM was equally obligated under the CPA to work toward making unity attractive, as the unity of Sudan could only be achieved by the two parties working in unison. Second, even though making unity of Sudan attractive became the duty of the Government of National Unity and the role of uniting the people of South Sudan fell to the government of South Sudan, it was still incumbent on the SPLM, as the pacesetter for the two governments, to define what these governments were to do, assess what its members within the two governments had jointly and severally achieved or failed to achieve, and establish mechanisms that would guarantee that members within both governments were abiding by party lines. Above all, SPLM adherents outside southern Sudan were dismayed by the failure of the convention to articulate a coherent political message that addressed, not only the future of South Sudan after the referendum, but also that of the whole country beyond the referendum and the interim period. Even if one gave the benefit of doubt to the SPLM convention since it had instructed its National Liberation Council (NLC) to elaborate on these issues, it would be extremely difficult to find an excuse for the party secretariat who failed to hold a single meeting of the NLC after the convention and up to the referendum. This matter shall be expanded upon in Chapter Nine.

7. Major Challenges in CPA Implementation

Pursuant to the above analysis, challenges that had faced the two parties to the agreement might be grouped into two categories: the first related to those issuing from nonimplementation of the agreement; the second was either brought about by, or during the course of, implementation. The first category includes the Abyei conflict, security arrangements, democratic transformation, elections, population census, resettlement of returnees, and north-south borders. In addition, this category shall include the very important process of assessment and evaluation of the CPA implementation, a matter that the SPLM had set great store by at Machakos but since then had played it down. The other set of challenges that the parties faced, jointly or severally, shall be addressed in Chapters Nine and Ten.

7.1 Abyei: Two Alternative Solutions

The problem of the Abyei area remained a thorn in the sides of both partners and an impediment to a long-term political solution to the north-south conflict. Abyei, an area with no strategic value to either the North or the South, had of late gainedf importance as a result of the claimed oil reserves that lay within, or around, it. Douglas Johnson had aptly remarked that "'if the issue was only to protect the rights of the Misseriya to access water and grazing, there would be nothing to hold up implementation of the [Abyei Boundary Commission] report. Their rights are guaranteed. The real issue is oil.'"[8] The disinclination of the NCP to proceed with the area's border demarcation as determined by the Abyei Boundary Commission (ABC) led to tensions on various axes: between local communities, between the SAF and the SPLA, between the NCP and the Misseriya, between the Misseriya and the SPLM, and within southern Sudan between SPLM elements who espoused the cause of the Ngok Dinkas of Abyei and other politicians who thought that the problem of Abyei was not worth losing all gains scored for South Sudan in the CPA.

In Chapter Five, it was explained how the issue of Abyei boundaries was resolved in a manner that appeared then to have been acceptable to both parties to the agreement and to the Abyei people. That solution entrusted the responsibility for delineating the boundaries of Abyei to an independent commission, the ABC, whose decision was to be final and binding. The ABC's report became neither final nor binding, as it was rejected by the NCP for reasons referred to in Chapter Seven. As a result, the people of Abyei began to think that they were forsaken and left in the lurch. The local administration provided for in the protocol was not set up, and the timely delivery of social services to the area was severely hindered. The two percent of oil revenue allocated to the people of Abyei from oil extracted in their area also remained unavailable to local communities. In addition, nondemarcation of boundaries was to have a direct impact on the determination of who would take part in the referendum.

Two schools of thought emerged as to how to address CPA implementation regarding Abyei. One considered the targets set in that agreement as cut in stone and, therefore, immutable. The second viewed the CPA as an agreement amenable to review to meet compelling circumstances without conceding the basics. The Abyei situation, however, ceased to be an issue relating to the area occupied by sheikhdoms of the Ngok Dinka and, instead, subsumed complex national, regional, and local dynamics that created a volatile political climate in the area. The increasing competition over natural resources at a time when those resources were dwindling as a result of war and climatic changes only exasperated the situation. Apart from oil, which had never been a factor in Abyei politics in the past, grazing rights were for centuries essential to Misseriya livelihood as they were to Ngok Dinka and

261

other pastoralists in the region. Thus, border delineation impinged directly on ethnic identities as well as on relationships between the Misseriya and Dinka and between these two populations and other communities that had continued to share the land with them. In reality, during their seasonal migration, the Misseriya were often in conflict with the Dinka in northern Bahr el Ghazal, the Ngok Dinka of Abyei, and the Lek Nuer of Unity State. Even beyond the Abyei area, conflicts were often reported for the same reason between the Rizeigat and the Misseriya even after the conclusion of the CPA. These local conflicts had long been woven into the fabric of broader Sudanese civil wars.

The Misseriya, who had aligned themselves with the NCP in the second civil war, had, in all likelihood, opposed the ABC report out of fear that Ngok Dinka might decide in the referendum to join the South. That decision, they might have thought, would jeopardize their grazing rights and endanger the integrity of their community. The clause in the Abyei Protocol guaranteeing grazing rights to them and to other communities had not been assuring enough. The Misseriya's line of thinking seemingly failed to notice that not only would they suffer if the new border demarcation became a hard dividing line, but pastoralists in South Darfur, Blue Nile, and White Nile would also be cut off from traditional grazing areas in southern Sudan. The over-politicization of the Dinka-Misseriya conflict curtailed rational thinking about the issue. Nevertheless, it would be oversimplistic to dismiss the Misseriya fears as only reactions by an irascible tribe. That tribe needed to be assured on what it considered a matter of life and death. Similar intertribal conflicts that had occurred in the past over grazing rights were resolved by the communities themselves through their elders. The way the Abyei Protocol had come into being gave the Misseriya the opportunity to claim that the agreement was forced on them by the SPLM, which had the support of foreigners (members of the ABC), and, therefore, they assumed they were victims of an external agenda. This fatuous accusation seemed to ignore that the Abyei Protocol was neither drafted by the SPLM nor the NCP, but presented to both of them by U.S. envoy, Senator John Danforth, in an effort to break an impasse in negotiations between them. According to the Abyei Protocol and its Implementation Modalities, which were also agreed to by the two parties, the ABC report was to be accepted as **final and binding**. No matter how thorough and academic the work of the international experts had been, the Misseriya were still able, once international pressure subsided, to take advantage of their presumed exclusion to resort to anti-Western and anti-imperialist rhetoric against the authors of the protocol and the ABC report.

Two observers who regularly followed the evolution of the CPA implementation argued that "if the NCP ultimately decides to abort the CPA, the Abyei issue is the most likely justification it will use. Its strategy appears to be to blame the Americans for the Abyei Protocol, blame the British and Americans for the ABC, and bait the SPLM into firing first by doing nothing on Abyei until the fighting starts."[9] That was what actually happened in Abyei. However, if there was one lesson to be learned from that saga it would be that knowledge of the local dynamics of Abyei was as important as the politics of CPA implementation. The Misseriya grew aware that their local political interests were distinct from those of the NCP. Not only were they angry about being excluded (as a community) from the CPA negotiations[10] on issues that had impinged on the future of Abyei, but they had also become increasingly conscious of how the NCP was exploiting them in a war that had not been their own. They became wary of the negative environmental impact of oil development in the area because of the damage it had visited on grazing lands. These facts, together with the lack of palpable community benefits from oil exploration as a result of the nonresolution of border demarcation, resulted in a shift of attitude within the Misseriya community against the NCP. The International Crisis Group reported that the Chinese National Petroleum Company was carrying out new exploration and developments through Abyei, including south of River Kiir (Bahr el Arab), which was causing environmental damage such as flooding and drastic changes in the irrigation of agricultural land.[11]

By 2006, the Misseriya allegiance to Khartoum had become significantly diluted, with some groups joining the Darfur-based rebel group, National Redemption Front, and large numbers seeking to join the SPLA in 2007 and early 2008. These developments were significant both in how they affected border demarcation as well as the conflict in Darfur. Within the SPLM most saw the Misseriya defection to their ranks as a positive sign, but there were still sceptics among them who feared that the shift in allegiance might have been an attempt by the Misseriya to increase their bargaining power with Khartoum.[12] In addition, ongoing political disputes over implementation of the Abyei Protocol had not only highlighted tensions between the NCP and the SPLM, and between the NCP and the Misseriya, but also pointed to internal tensions within each party. The Abyei issue, for example, had accentuated divisions in the South between those who continued to promote Garang's vision of a united New Sudan and those who favored South Sudan's independence. International Crisis Group argued that "some in the South see Abyei as a 'Ngok Dinka issue,' important because there are many Ngok Dinka in senior SPLM leadership positions but not worth risking the rest of the CPA over."[13] This view had been argued by senior southern Sudanese politicians and, in particular, Bona Malwal.[14] Resentment grew after the secession of South Sudan, and relations between Sudan and South Sudan deteriorated as a result of nonresolution of CPA outstanding issues. Even though some of these issues related to the very survival of the new state, Abyei advocates did not shy away during negotiations between the two states from demanding that agreement with Khartoum on these issues should be contingent on the resolution of the Abyei question. In effect, by so doing, these advocates made Abyei hostage to them.

Against this background, two approaches to addressing the Abyei problem. The first sought to expose the NCP as a party that did not respect solemnly made commitments, namely, refusing to stick to the letter of the Abyei Protocol. Those who held this view argued that tolerating any breach by the NCP of the protocol on Abyei would jeopardize the integrity of the entire CPA. This perspective was prevalent in writings by political activists who remained unanimous in their condemnation of the NCP for failure to implement the ABC's report. The second perspective favored easing away from focusing on implementing the ABC report and working toward finding a solution that was more feasible, if possible, within the framework of the CPA. Each of these perspectives involved different ways of understanding the CPA. The former viewed the CPA as a rigorous legal document upon whose full implementation Sudan's peace rested; the latter perceived it as a living document that should be adapted, if need arose, to changing realities in Sudan. Douglas Johnson viewed the deadlock on the status of Abyei borders as a potential "breaking point of the CPA"[15] and, therefore, called for exerting more pressure on the NCP and exposing its intransigence. Johnson also pointed out that there was overlapping territory to which both the Misseriya and Ngok Dinka could claim rights of use, and he suggested that this territory be divided in the middle, seeing in this process a space for cohabitation between the two groups.[16] Other exponents of this point of view also maintained that in order to protect peace, the international community should re-engage the parties concerned on the implementation of the Abyei Protocol as part of a broader re-engagement on outstanding CPA issues

Although agreements, including internationally mediated ones, are invariably signed to be implemented, obligations that are incurred under such agreements are liable to be violated. This often happens when the party who wishes to back away from the agreement becomes assured that the international guarantors of the agreement are either unable, or not ready, to bring pressure to bear on the erring party. In effect, pressure was neither exerted on the government of Sudan to agree to the ABC report nor to implement the International Court of Arbitration (ICA) award. Both were obligations accepted by the two parties as final and binding, and both were brushed off by the NCP. The international community also failed, in the case of Abyei, to show consistent resolve in its day-to-day follow-up of the implementation of the protocol. Radical changes in the U.S. foreign policy outlook under President Obama (See Chapter Twelve) resulted in a lot of dithering about U.S. policy toward Sudan, even though the United States had been the author of the protocol. As South Sudan came close to the referendum, the United States started a process of high-level mediation. Senator John Kerry, chair of the U.S. Senate Committee on Foreign Relations, and General Scott Gration, the presidential envoy to Sudan, intervened on behalf of their government, not to push for implementation of the ABC report or the ICA award, but to find a solution outside the protocol.

The second perspective on the resolution of the Abyei problem involved moving away from focus on the ABC report and concentrating energies on finding a solution that would be acceptable to both parties. The design of such a solution required ascertaining the real apprehensions of the Misseriya as well as understanding the causes for legitimate disquietude within the NCP with regard to Abyei. The NCP devised numerable false pretences, but it also had genuine concerns. Depicting the NCP's concerns simply as intransigence or lack of good faith would not help the peace process. Although there were reasons to see in the NCP's attitude toward the ABC report an unwillingness to implement the CPA faithfully, there were also real economic and political issues that underlined that unwillingness, especially if Abyei was to secede with its presumed oil reserves. For example, while 78 percent of Sudan's discovered oil reserves were situated in southern Sudan before secession, 60 percent of the portion that was produced outside southern Sudan came from the Abyei area. Addressing these concerns would have gone a long way toward finding solutions to the deadlock. Thus, a border demarcation that would have been economically favorable and thus politically sellable to both parties was critical to the political survival of the NCP.[17] Also, since the CPA was conceived as a win-win agreement, viewing it as a contraption for precipitating NCP's political demise would not have been the right thing to do, much as its opponents had wished. After repeated hemming and hawing, this understanding of the Abyei problem was what had seemingly informed U.S. policy in the second half of the interim period.

Wisely, the SPLM decided to seek a solution outside the ABC report when it agreed with its partner to refer the issue to adjudication by the ICA through a panel of five judges drawn from different nationalities.[18] The ICA reached its conclusions on the strength of its own legal analysis of the conclusions published in the ABC report and the position papers presented to it by the parties. Apart from its deliberations, which were held privately, the panel undertook only one trip to Nairobi to gather testimony concerning disagreements on the ABC findings from a number of concerned persons. After 90 days of investigation the panel disclosed its award on July 22, 2009.[19] In that award the panel redrew the Abyei borders in a way that corresponded with what the Ngok Dinka had consistently claimed, although it attached the richest oil fields to a yet disputed area: Heglig. The award, therefore, affirmed that the area of Abyei represented the heartland of the Ngok Dinka, with most of the Misseriya outside it. The award was accepted by both parties.

With the ICA award settling the burdensome problem of Abyei boundaries and allowing for the creation of the Abyei administration and the exclusion of competition over oil resources from the conflict,[20] one would have thought that the Abyei problem was behind the parties. That was not to be the case as two other issues remained: the referendum wherein the people of Abyei would determine the future of Abyei as it was defined in the CPA, and the identification of Abyei residents who would be entitled to vote in the referendum. Residency *per se* should not have been a problem since the Abyei Protocol provided that "simultaneously with the referendum for Southern Sudan, the **residents** of Abyei will cast a separate ballot" (emphasis added). The term "resident" certainly incorporates Ngok Dinka but is not limited to them; non-Ngok Dinkas who have habitually resided in the Abyei area shall also be entitled to vote. The question that remained was to define habitual residency. Though there are scant precedents in national and international law to go by, it is generally agreed that the right to participate in such referendums is governed by two factors: habitual residence and appropriate connection with the area. The former is commonly measured by cumulative periods of residence over several years.[21] In a recent case relating to the eligibility of newcomers to New Caledonia, France, to vote in the referendum on the independence of that territory from France, the U.N. Human Rights Council ruled that "ten years period of residence to qualify for voting is not unreasonable."[22] Thus the birth of a citizen in an area or his or her habitual residence in that area may qualify a person to vote in a referendum. However, in the case of Abyei, the situation is complicated by the incessant cross-border movement of inhabitants. It is interesting to note, however, that the Sudan government has been ever reluctant to recognize Mbororo pastoralists as citizens, despite the settlement of some of them in the Sudan for countless years.

Several propositions were forwarded by the SPLM based on Sudan's electoral laws and the experiences of other countries, but none of the propositions was convincing to the Misseriya. Those included a proposition that was meant to grant the right to vote to Misseriya who habitually lived in the Abyei area in a continuous and uninterrupted manner but excluded pastoralists who would only pass through the area on their way to South Sudan. In this regard, the SPLM maintained that granting voting rights to Misseriya who did not stay uninterruptedly for a reasonable length of time should entitle those of them who stayed for similar periods in southern Sudan to enjoy voting rights in that area. That would also apply to Dinkas and Nuers who spent similar periods in the North.

Despite the resolution of what was thought to be the major problem concerning the definition of borders, the Abyei question continued to embitter relations between the two parties, which made mediators lose patience. Even attempts by the United States to offer a deal that included an economic development package was not welcomed by the Misseriya. Eventually, the referendum of Abyei residents that was to take place with that of southern Sudan was postponed *sine die*. It is ironic that the Abyei question, which was assumed after the conclusion of the CPA to be the most manageable problem, turned out to be the most vexatious as a result of the constant shifting of goal poles by the NCP and Misseriya spokesman. Elements within that group also appeared to be blatantly acquisitive: the more they got, the more they wanted. Twice did the parties agree on a final and binding agreement—the ABC report and the ICA award—and twice did they renege on their undertakings. In this regard, the position taken by international observers, especially the United States who authored the Abyei Protocol, was defeatist.

7.2 Security Threats and Perils

During the second civil war there was pervasive insecurity throughout southern Sudan as a result of armed conflict, militia activities, incursions by rebels from outside Sudan,[23] and fighting between various factions of the SPLM, especially during the split of the 1990s. Though it officially marked the end of Sudan's second civil war, the CPA did not put an end to violence. Wartime attitudes and states of mind prevailed, and the parties failed to move beyond the dichotomy of war and peace. Even though war was declared over by the signature of the Protocol on Security Arrangements, there was no peace yet. In the first three years of the interim period, persistent insecurity continued to afflict various parts of South Sudan, the Nuba Mountains, and Abyei. The prevalence of arms in the hands of unauthorized persons within local communities continued militia activities in some pockets in southern Sudan in spite of commitment by the parties to disarm other armed groups (OAGs).[24] Clashes between the SPLA and SAF-aligned forces inhibited the full implementation of the Protocol on Security Arrangements and constituted a threat to economic and political reconstruction of the South. Moreover, violence persisted among pastoralist groups competing over natural resources, even though that violence was frequently ignited by intertribal rivalries and aggravated by the breakdown of traditional conflict resolution mechanisms or inadequate policing.[25] Insecurity inevitably diminished the ability of government of South Sudan to establish unchallenged authority over the area under its control and distracted it from giving total attention to state-building and economic development. Violence was also made more lethal by the proliferation of small arms in the hands of pastoralists who traditionally used sticks and spears to defend themselves.

By the end of 2009, the level of violence reached such an insufferable level that in Jonglei state alone 150,000 persons were displaced, according to United Nations estimates,[26] as a result of cattle raids and interethnic competition over power and resources.[27] In that year southern Sudan went through the most harrowing phase of conflict: 2,500 persons were reported killed and 350,000 displaced.[28.] Conflict in Jonglei state was predominately between Dinka and Murle pastoralists and Dinka and Lou. Disarming civilians, as demanded by the Security Arrangements Protocol, turned out to be a major challenge for the government of South Sudan and the SPLA, as the experience with Lou had attested. Furthermore, intraethnic conflicts often flared up within sections of the same community, for example, between the Lou and Jikany Nuer. Despite all efforts by the SPLM leader to urge all ethnic groups to consider bygones as bygones, memories of past tragedies continued to cast a shadow on the present. One such example was the memory of the 1992 onslaught by the Jiech Boor (Nuer White Army)[29] on Dinka Bor. The White Army was a loose army of youth gathered and armed by Riek Machar during the SPLM split from cattle camps assembled to fight the SPLA in Bor, the birthplace of John Garang and the SPLM/A. That raid, which mainly targeted civilians, left 2,000 dead, according to Amnesty International, and dealt a great blow to Riek's claim to being a human-rights champion as opposed to the 'nondemocratic' John Garang. Even after the peace agreement and reinstatement of Riek Machar in the SPLM, and later his appointment as vice president of the government of South Sudan, the White Army continued marauding around Nuerland, which led to serious engagement with the SPLA.

Besides this, small militias, roving bandits, and more organized groups such as the Equatorian Defense Force (EDF) continued to resist the authority of the government of South Sudan for no reason other than creating an atmosphere of instability in the region. Eastern Equatoria, alone, was caught in conflicts involving the Lord's Resistance Army (LRA), forces of Uganda People's Defense Forces, SPLA, SAF, and EDF. Even the United Nations was not spared from being a victim to this banditry; one of its peacekeepers was caught in crossfire in that area.[30] The LRA, or groups posing as the LRA, continued to raid and terrorize South Sudan communities throughout 2006 and 2007. Another group called LRA Sudan, likely an Acholi militia supported by Khartoum and possibly working closely with EDF, appeared in 2007.[31] The continuation of this violence made the government of South Sudan appear incapable of providing security, even in the capital, because its security forces were spread thin. In addition to the LRA and LRA Sudan, there were various OAGs in the South, as well as traders and bandits, who "sabotaged transportation routes in order to control prices of market goods."[32] Although it was not easy to assign responsibility for each attack, there was incontrovertible evidence that arms and funding to OAGs emanated from some power centers in Khartoum whose intention was to create instability in the South.

Low-level conflict between the North and South also continued in oil-rich border areas. The CPA laid the framework for ending the presence of OAGs and integrating them into the SAF and the SPLA. Elements of SAF, nonetheless, were reportedly active in supporting some OAGs that were resisting the authority of the government of South Sudan. The president of the government of South Sudan pointed an accusatory finger at SAF's military intelligence and blamed it for being the mastermind behind the OAG's attacks.

Thus, throughout 2006 and 2007, SAF-aligned groups, including remnants of the South Sudan Defense Force (SSDF) and OAGs who refused to disband in accordance with the CPA, engaged the SPLA in Upper Nile and Unity states.[33] On November 28, 2006, heavy fighting broke out between the SPLA and Gabriel Tang-Ginye's SSDF forces in the oil-rich region of Upper Nile.[34] After three days of fighting, many casualties were reported, and the United Nations was forced to evacuate 240 civilian personnel from the town.[35] Repeated clashes were also reported between SPLA forces and the SAF, the Popular Defense Force, and Misseriya in border areas throughout 2007 and early 2008. While most incidents were quickly contained, they still had the potential to conflagrate into larger conflicts.

In order to build authority in South Sudan, safeguard the integrity of the CPA, and above all, ensure human security, it was crucial to disband (or integrate) irregular armies as well as demobilize surplus forces. The CPA had established a fairly detailed program for formal disarmament, demobilization, and reintegration (DDR) precisely to neutralize organized militias operating in South Sudan, protect the civilian population, and enable the government of South Sudan to establish authority over the area it was to govern. However, without the "R" the "DD" would be futile. Armed persons and battle-hardened warriors should never be expected to lay down their arms unless they were ensured adequate living conditions and income-generating employment. In the first half of the interim period, the two parties made some progress toward an interim DDR program funded by donors. Regional DDR program offices were established throughout northern and southern Sudan, surveys and registration of ex-combatants were carried out, and the removal of child and disabled soldiers commenced in January 2006.[36] Even so, the DDR process had been a learning process for the SPLA. The disarming of the Nuer White Army, referred to above, was an example of a poorly planned and implemented approach. That campaign was perceived by the Lou Nuer as a political crackdown. Cattle keepers objected to giving up their weapons, arguing that they needed them to protect their herds from Murle.[37] Accordingly, they demanded that the SPLA first, or simultaneously, disarm that tribe. When their demands were ignored, the White Army attacked the SPLA, killing hundreds of soldiers. That conflict rapidly escalated as hardliners within the SPLA demanded a strong response. Estimates varied, but according to the United Nations and other sources, somewhere around 400 SPLA soldiers and 1,200 White Army fighters were killed during the Jonglei disarmament campaign.[38] This figure represents one death for every two weapons seized, a poor record for DDR. According to one observer, the failure of that disarmament campaign was the result of poor planning, communication, implementation, and lack of participation of local authorities.[39]

269

Reflecting on the experience of disarmament in Jonglei, it would be fair to assume that the Lou Nuer had genuine concerns about the security of their community and protection of their livelihood. Despite their past misdeeds, indeed the misdeeds they were herded into by their political leaders, it was also obvious that Lou Nuer were needed to protect grazing lands and watering points. Based on data collected in the Jonglei Household Survey conducted by the Human Security Baseline Assessment (Small Arms Survey, Geneva 2008), Garfield argued that residents were willing to disarm, but they were not ready to remain defenseless in the face of attacks by others who had not yet undergone disarmament, or who were not inclined to fully participate in the campaigns.[40] Thus, in the absence of a robust state security apparatus, as Garfield maintained, the acquisition and use of small arms became necessary for both community defense and maintenance of the pastoralist livelihood systems.[41]

DDR activities, in reality, should have gone hand-in-hand with reconciliation, diffusion of a culture of peace, assurance of community safety, and economic development. As Garfield observed, for disarmament to be effective, it should take place in the context of a comprehensive, holistic approach to community safety supported by strategies that address the root causes of conflict through participatory information campaigns.[42] Given the above, it came as no surprise when the vice president of the government of South Sudan, Riek Machar, declared on the occasion of opening the new DDR building at Juba in 2009 that of the 84,000 combatants to be demobilized, only 6,000 (or 6 percent of the total) were relieved by 2010. Machar rightly remarked that without training and resources that would ensure their integration in civilian life, it would be difficult to persuade a warrior to abandon the SPLA.[43] Were proper integration of former warriors into civilian life not to happen, then the rule of the gun would prevail, and abandoned former combatants would end up as marauding armed gangsters.

Beyond such obvious failures, serious questions regarding the potential for success of disarmament campaigns remained. Evidence showed that gains from the DDR campaigns in Sudan were short-lived. For example, Garfield gathered evidence on disarmament revealing that disarmed elements were soon rearmed either because communities stored weapons during the campaigns, or because they simply bought new weapons from what had become a relatively accessible arms market.[44] Another observer cautioned that growing enthusiasm for DDR within defense and development circles should not be taken as evidence that such interventions strengthen human security. He argued that "there is a surprising lack of evidence as to whether or not [DDR] works. With the exception of a smattering of assessments, post-mortems and superficial indicators relating to the number of weapons collected and the number of ex-combatants demobilised, there is virtually no proof that such interventions strengthen 'human security.'"[45] Human security, thus defined, is the essence of good governance and sane economic management. According to Ashraf Ghani, an international consultant on governance who is *au fait* with South Sudan, "the rule of the gun cannot be transformed into the rule of law without real economic incentives for young men."[46]

DDR, it was observed, seldom moved forward in the "sequenced and linear fashion anticipated by donors and project planners. Instead, a host of problems frequently emerge, ranging from competing objectives amongst donors and parties to the DDR; the poor articulation of benchmarks; flawed selection criteria; limited assessed funding for reintegration; and the mishandling of expectations."[47] It was also pointed out that the preparation, planning, and design of conventional DDR reflected conflicting objectives of military specialists, development practitioners, and donors. While DDR technical specialists favored "process" indicators such as the number of weapons collected and cantonment sites established, tangible measurement of the outcomes of DDR in terms of durable impact on lives, sustained development, restored livelihoods, and income generating opportunities were ignored.[48] This approach, according to Robert Muggah, reflected "a profound crisis of accountability at the heart of the DDR enterprise. With hundreds of millions of dollars currently being dispensed on these programmes—up to $69 million in Sudan alone—a more robust determination of success and failure is urgently required."[49] Rather than taking a formalistic approach to the problem, successful DDR policy should be based on "sound diagnosis of the 'post-conflict' environment, along with flexible and proactive implementation, monitoring and evaluation."[50]

Addressing such multifaceted security threats required concurrent processes outside law enforcement and defense measures, important as those measures were. High on the list of these processes was political action by the SPLM within communities and through traditional leadership structures to realize communal peace. In this respect, despite the numerous resolutions it had passed on security in South Sudan, the SPLM secretariat was hopelessly wanting in carrying out its own resolutions. President Salva Kiir had personally led important campaigns in this regard to which reference will be made in Chapter Nine. However, in no way or manner should interventions by the president absolve the party that leads the people and government from undertaking grassroots work with a view to enlightening people about CPA security requirements, reconciling conflicting groups, conducting fact-finding missions in conflict areas in order to ascertain facts, and creating party organs at state and county levels to ensure that communal peacemaking had become an unceasing political process. Megaphone politics reflected in ever flowing declarations about party achievements made to local and international media would never supplant planned, programmed, and monitored political operations.

Concomitant with the DDR process, the Security Arrangements Protocol included an agreement by the two parties to undertake a proportional downsizing of forces on both sides at a suitable time following the completion of SAF redeployment to the North. It was also agreed that "the parties shall allow voluntary demobilization, [and] demobilization of nonessentials (child soldiers and elderly, disabled)" (clause 19). Apart from the demobilization of a number of children and elderly and disabled persons referred to above, the reduction of the forces to peace-time levels had hardly begun. In the case of SAF, the continuation of conflict in Darfur and failure by the government of Sudan to reach a pacific settlement to that conflict led to the bolstering, not downsizing, of that army. With or without Darfur, the NCP's determination to make Sudan a police state made downsizing of military and paramilitary forces impossible. As for South Sudan, the prevalent insecurity in that region and fears of destabilization led to an expansion of, not a cutback in, the number of the SPLA forces. Legitimate as that expansion had been, its exorbitant cost to government of South Sudan's budget at the expense of other important social demands could have been mitigated through a number of measures. For example, it took five years for the SPLA to initiate its own farms to produce, and canteens to distribute, food to its men and women. Acting earlier on that would have saved the government budget the very high cost of feeding the army through dubious tendering processes. The SPLA could have also established vocational training centers to train men and women in trades such as masonry, carpentry, auto mechanics, and basic electronics, which would not only have served the army's needs, but also enabled it to thin out the forces. Surely, such trained artisans would have either established their own private businesses or made their services available to the marketplace.

An area in which peacekeeping went fairly smoothly with few hiccups was that of maintaining a comprehensive cease-fire. A Cease-Fire Joint Military Committee (CJMC), as mentioned in Chapter Four, was formed to observe cease-fire in six sectors: Equatoria, Bahr el Ghazal, Upper Nile, the Nuba Mountains, Blue Nile, Abyei, and Kassala. Subordinate bodies were also created. The CJMC was established to ensure compliance by the two parties to CPA provisions relating to cease-fire, coordinated joint activities, monitoring and verification of violations, decommissioning of unexploded ordinance, receiving and investigating complaints, and disarming and reintegrating former combatants. The CJMC emerged as one of the most effective national military institutions created under the CPA. Its meetings had been regular, coordination at all levels faithful, and follow-up exemplary.

7.3 Joint Integrated Units

The Joint Integrated Units (JIUs) represented an important component of the security arrangements, not only because of the role they were destined to play during the interim period, but also for their future role as a nucleus for the national army if and when southern Sudan opted for unity. Given the strained and arduous negotiations through which the parties had gone to reach an agreement on the creation of the JIUs, failure by any party to carry out obligations pertaining to the units would have not only been a breach of a contractual obligation, but also an act of heedlessness towards the country's unity. At the formal level, the National Assembly passed the Joint Integrated Units Act on January 17, 2006, which outlined their mandate and defined areas of deployment and common military doctrine. The act also provided for the formation and mandate of the Joint Defense Board (JDB).[51] The JDB was composed and structured on a parity basis and was to take decisions by consensus. It was made up of SAF and SPLA chiefs of staff and their deputies (clause 17 of the Security Arrangements Protocol). It is to be called to mind that the protocol and the INC stipulated that the JIUs shall represent national unity, uphold the rule of law, and undertake, alongside the SAF and the SPLA, defense of Sudan and its sovereignty against internal and external threats. In addition, by their very composition, JIUs were meant to achieve social cohesion and peace in Sudan. If the JIUs had been established as envisaged by the CPA and the INC, they could have served political and strategic objectives for both parties such as providing a forum for facilitating compromises between the two armies, reducing the likelihood of renewed conflict between the two regular forces (SAF and SPLA), and allowing both sides to maintain some forces on either side of the border, particularly in sensitive disputed areas.[52]

Nevertheless, several incidents occurred in 2007–2008 that did not bode well for the integration of the units. Those included the strike in December 2007 by SPLA JIU units in Juba and the behavior of the SAF JIUs in Equatoria.[53] The strike by the JIUs in Juba as a result of delays in salary payment was particularly alarming since it was the responsibility of the presidency, not the government of South Sudan, to ensure payment of the units' salaries. Although the total targeted size of the JIUs was estimated at 39,600 men, to be divided equally between SPLA and SAF,[54] only 33,698 JIUs were deployed as of January 8, 2008. The deployment time frames were renegotiated repeatedly and subsequently ignored. The problems were not confined to deployment; the JIUs also faced ambiguities over force composition and command and control problems. In addition, up to the referendum, the JIUs had never undergone systematic and coordinated training.[55] According to the Security Arrangements Protocol, the JDB was entrusted with working out "a comprehensive framework for confidence building" through such measures as "exchanging visits, organizing cultural and sport events, convening of joint training courses, and participating in national and religious celebrations." Those, too, never took place.

By 2008, the SPLA and SAF contingents within many of the JIUs were not integrated or operating under a common leadership and military doctrine.

The SPLA also accused SAF of contributing ex-militia (such as Gabriel Tang-Ginye's SSDF forces) to the JIUs before they were integrated into the SAF. That was not only a violation of the CPA, it was also an act that posed serious problems to security and army discipline. Allowing OAGs to be directly incorporated into JIUs without being disciplined as a regular force within an army (SAF or SPLA) had actually reduced their professional competence and orderliness and detracted from their ability to function cohesively within existing forces. It may also be recalled that the CPA provided that oil-producing areas south of the 11th parallel would be protected by JIUs when the SAF moved north (30 months after D-Day);[56] however, it took the withdrawal of the SPLM from the Government of National Unity in 2007 to make the NCP move towards implementing that CPA clause. During this period, the SAF wasted time arguing that the presence of the SAF in those areas was necessary for the protection of oil wells.

As for the JIUs in the Nuba Mountains, the situation was less problematic. A 6,000-man force divided between the SPLA and the SAF was established and stationed in different parts of that region: Kadogli, Heiban, Talodi, Buran, Julud, Um Sirdiba, Dilling, and Arid. Although those units were placed under a joint command, until the approach of the southern Sudan referendum, they were not properly integrated in the sense envisioned in the CPA, which stipulated that they would receive common training, identical equipment, and similar perks and emoluments. On the other hand, the Security Arrangements Protocol provided that SAF units in the Nuba Mountains be reduced to peacetime levels. That provision, as we recall, was totally forgotten, even though the SPLA had deployed its forces south of the north-south border identified on January 1, 1956, as required by the protocol. Were it not for urgings by the SPLA commander-in-chief that the terms of the CPA be rigorously respected, SPLA forces would not have withdrawn from the Nuba Mountains until the CPA provision relating to the reduction of SAF units to the peacetime level was implemented. Despite appeals they made to the SPLA commander-in-chief to link their withdrawal southward to the downsizing of SAF units in the Nuba Mountains as provided for in the CPA, the Nuba forces yielded to the instructions of their commander-in-chief, who argued that he would rather occupy the high moral ground by respecting the security protocol to the letter.

Regarding the demobilization of OAGs, not only did the Popular Defense Force (PDF) continue to exist, but it had been revamped. The existence of the PDF as a partisan military force flew in the face of the CPA and the INC. It is even more surprising that the NCP continued to claim that the PDF, far from belonging to OAGs, was a regular force that fell within the SAF's direct hierarchical command and was, thus, governed by the code of conduct established for the SAF in both the CPA and INC. Nonetheless, the PDF continued to operate as a partisan militia with unconcealed allegiance to the

NCP, including engagement in party rallies. That behavior was blatantly antithetical to all constitutional edicts and norms that govern performance of national armed forces, including the SAF.

The international community should have viewed the JIUs as an instrument for encouraging cooperation between the parties in building the capacity of Sudan's National Armed Forces, as observed by Matthew Arnold and Matthew LeRiche, two commentators who closely followed the post-CPA security scene in Sudan.[57] Nevertheless, external support to the JIUs was hardly forthcoming despite promises mediators, including Secretary of State Powell, made during the negotiations. Despite the fact that delays in the organization, deployment, and functioning of JIUs had serious implications to CPA implementation, international observers who watched the birth of the protocol and argued fiercely against having two standing armies in one country never raised the alarm bells on the NCP's actions, which were clearly frustrating the transformation of the JIUs into a nucleus of Sudan's future united army. Those observers, including the United Nations Missions in Sudan (UNMIS) and the Assessment and Evaluation Commission (AEC), were never perplexed by the fact that the SAF, in assigning men and officers to the JIUs, drew almost all their recruits for these units from southern Sudanese OAGs. No person in his or her right mind would believe that the NCP wished to have the future army of Sudan composed only of south Sudanese. A different reading of this incongruity led to one of two conclusions: either the NCP never believed in any restructuring of the Sudanese army, even if the South opted for unity; or it had persuaded itself that unity was an impossible dream and, therefore, cared less for the JIUs composition. In effect, the Sudanese army under the NIF/NCP had increasingly been indoctrinated to the point that even its military doctrine was impregnated with Islamic dogma, as interpreted by specially chosen NCP mullahs. That was the army of Sudan in which unity was to be made attractive to both Muslim and non-Muslim citizens. As for international observers, including U.N. military observers, they took cover behind the abstruse language of U.N. Security Council resolutions, which in one paragraph allowed UNMIS to take all actions to maintain peace in conflict zones but disallowed such actions in the next paragraph. That was perhaps why the U.N. Security Council's verbal admonishments to the Government of National Unity for breaches of the agreement remained only that.

7.4 National Census

The CPA and the INC stipulated that a nationwide census should be conducted by July 2007. Other than providing a statistical count of the country's population in preparation for national elections, the southern Sudan referendum, and popular consultation in the two areas, the census was also to furnish baseline information essential for the formulation of economic, social, and cultural policies as well as for determining public spending priorities.

Despite its direct relevance to those activities, the census was repeatedly delayed, allegedly for lack of funding. In 2006, the Multi-Donor Trust Fund (MDTF) approved funding for the census operation based on a proposal submitted by the National Bureau of Statistics (NBS) and the Southern Sudan Centre for Census, Statistics, and Evaluation (SSCCSE). A budget of $73 million was proposed, of which $44 million was earmarked for northern Sudan and $29 million for southern Sudan. The Government of National Unity and the Government of South Sudan were to provide 55 percent of the cost, and the MDTF would make the remainder available.[58] The Government of National Unity's tardiness in making its share of the cost available led to suspicions that it was not in a hurry to carry out the census. The census operation also received technical support from the U.S. Bureau of Labor and Statistics, France's Geographic Information Systems (GIS), the Danish International Development Agency (DANIDA), and the European Union. Eventually, the two parties scheduled the census for the end of 2008 instead of the period between April 15 and 30 of that year, as earlier agreed upon between them. The government of South Sudan's minister of information and broadcasting gave various reasons why his government decided to consent to that delay, among which were the need to repatriate southern Sudanese citizens who were still living in the North, lack of progress on border demarcation, regional insecurity, and, surprisingly, the ongoing conflict in Darfur. The latter reason was received with jubilation in Darfur.[59] The minister, however, was silent on an issue that had figured prominently in the face-off between the two parties in 2007: inclusion into the census questionnaires of information on ethnic origin and religion.

Evidently, there were legitimate causes for the delay in conducting the census, as agreed upon in the CPA, such as poor infrastructure, nonresolution of the knotty issue of border demarcation, and resettlement of returnees. Even with funding available, these causes should not be underestimated. The United Nations Population Fund (UNFPA), the United Nations agency responsible for providing technical support to census operations in Sudan, listed among the problems besetting the operation coordination, management, planning, resource mobilization, advocacy and publicity, cartography, enumeration and data processing, tabulation and analysis, publication and dissemination of results, procurement of equipment and logistics, and human resources development. UNFPA also observed that in 2005 few current maps existed for South Sudan; thus, the territorial units that constituted the states in that region and their respective counties, districts, and villages had to be mapped anew.

On the NCP side, there were also undeclared concerns such as fear that the census might reveal a population size in southern Sudan that might weaken the NCP's control of the national legislature, executive, or civil service. Recall, if you will, the protracted debate at Machakos in June 2002 between the two parties regarding equitable distribution of parliamentary seats, executive positions. and civil service posts based on demographic weights. The population results were announced in April 2009, one year after commencement of the census operation. According to these results the population of southern Sudan was counted at 3.8 million while that of the whole country added up to 39 million. According to past censuses, the population of southern Sudan was estimated to be one third of the country's population. The 1993 national census, for instance, put the figure at 4 million, based only on counting people living in areas under government of Sudan control. Little was known then about the population residing in areas controlled by the SPLM/A in southern Sudan. It would thus appear that the results of the 2008 census in South Sudan were simply guesstimates based on a scale-down of the 1993 figures. The results of voting at the referendum validated this assumption, as 3,770,600 citizens registered as voters. That figure was almost equivalent to the 3.8 million the census committee reported to be the total population of South Sudan. However, if we take into account hundreds of thousands who were ineligible to vote for reasons of age (below the minimum age for voting) or infirmity, then the discrepancy shall be obvious.

The census results, nonetheless, revealed disturbing anomalies. For example, the population of the Arabized tribes of Darfur increased by 90.22 percent, compared to 1992 census figures. This rate of population growth was double the average national growth. Also, the number of nomads in that area jumped from 695,000 to 2,950,000, a threefold increase at a time when nomadism was on the decline. As a result, the population of Dar Fur, counted to be 4,500,000, became higher than that of South Sudan, an enumeration that did not tally with previous census figures. Furthermore, the number of southern Sudanese in the national capital was counted to be no more than a quarter of a million persons, a figure that neither corresponded to those provided by repatriation agencies nor with the national elections register that was prepared later. Those anomalies raised doubts about the integrity of the census process and were subject to howls of protest by the SPLM.[60] Chairman of the SPLM, Salva Kiir conveyed to the presidency his party's rejection of the census results.[61] Rather than investigating the grave accusations raised by the SPLM about the census process and results, the NCP proposed a political solution to the problem, which entailed an amendment of the national electoral law to allow for additional appointed members from South Sudan, South Kordofan, Blue Nile, and Abyei in the National Assembly in order to safeguard against any tampering with the CPA quotas.

7.5 Voluntary Return, Reintegration, and Recovery

Related to the census was the issue of resettlement of returnees, refugees, and internally displaced persons (IDPs) in their traditional home areas. According to U.N. Security Council Resolution 1590, UNMIS was to "facilitate and coordinate, within its capabilities and in its areas of deployment, the voluntary return of refugees and internally displaced persons." Toward that goal, the UNMIS Return, Reintegration, and Recovery (RRR) operation was established to coordinate and plan return activities undertaken by U.N. agencies. Nongovernmental organizations and donors also played a supporting role to government return activities. The operations of UNMIS RRR, as defined in the U.N. 2005 Work Plan for Sudan, were to be rooted on three principles: the right to return in safety and dignity, free and informed choice, and the right to choose the destination of return. All programs of reintegration and recovery were to be community-based, benefiting equally those who left and those who stayed, according to their needs. These objectives, however, remained aspirational goals.

According to the United Nations High Commission for Refugees (UNHCR), 260,000 registered Sudanese refugees were in exile with the majority (216,000) living in refugee camps in Kenya, Uganda, and Ethiopia. This figure was much lower than the number of southern Sudanese known to have taken refuge in those countries. The discrepancy was probably due to the fact that UNHCR's statistics only accounted for refugees registered with the commission in the host countries. Since the launch of UNHCR's voluntary repatriation operation in December 2005, only 68,000 refugees had returned home with the help of the UNHCR from the Central African Republic, the Democratic Republic of the Congo, Uganda, Kenya, Ethiopia, and Egypt. An additional 92,000 had returned through their own means since 2005.[62] Thus, thousands of refugees still remained outside Sudan, the majority of whom was not counted in the April census.

In addition, untold numbers of southern Sudan IDPs living in northern Sudan were not included in the census count. Although the parties agreed that there was need to formulate a repatriation, resettlement, rehabilitation, reconstruction, and development plan to address the needs of those areas affected by the war, the resettlement of returnees, particularly IDPs, remained worrisome. Operational constraints, as well as political maneuvers, had impeded the movement and reintegration of those returnees in their home areas. According to figures provided by the national Ministry of Humanitarian Affairs, IDPs in northern Sudan were counted at 3,500,000 persons, of whom 2,300,000 were relocated in South Sudan, leaving behind 1,200,000. The discrepancy between those figures and the census figures, both coming from one and the same government, need not be emphasized. However, the same source reported that 500,000 of those repatriated to South Sudan became reverse returnees, giving either economic reasons (seeking employment) or family reunion as reasons for their trekking back.

Among the operational challenges that impeded repatriation, according to UNHCR, were weak infrastructure, incapacity of government institutions, limited or nonexistent services in areas of return, security reasons such as threats of attacks or prevalence of land mines and unexploded ordnances in areas of return, and limited funding and resources to support return and reintegration.[63] In September 2007, lack of funds forced UNHCR to stop buying and positioning basic assistance items such as plastic sheeting for shelter, blankets, sleeping mats, soap, jerry cans, hygienic clothes for women, mosquito nets, and cooking utensils. That was yet another example of the delinquency of the international community in providing support to a much-needed humanitarian operation that impinged directly on the peace-building process.

Pinning the blame only on the international community and humanitarian agencies would, unwarrantedly, absolve the Government of National Unity and the Government of South Sudan from responsibility. In order to achieve return in the manner agreed upon in the CPA, the two governments were required to provide basic services and livelihood schemes for the returning citizens. In effect, the Government of National Unity and the Government of South Sudan formed a High Committee for Resettlement chaired by Vice President Taha and co-chaired by Deng Alor Kuol, the then minister of cabinet affairs in the Government of National Unity. The committee included relevant ministers from both governments and did excellent work in drawing plans for repatriation. It also secured funding for the operation: $15 million from the Government of National Unity, $24 million from the Government of South Sudan, and $100 million from the United Nations. However, at the operational level, serious drawbacks existed, especially in preparing a hospitable environment for the returnees at their home base. There was also barefaced larceny by middlemen who were entrusted with transporting returnees to their home areas in South Sudan; none of those purloiners was made to account for his wrongdoing. Moreover, preparations at the receiving end were inadequate to the extent that some IDPs decided to return from where they had come from in northern Sudan, as alluded to earlier.

Nevertheless, the government of South Sudan recurrently blamed the NCP for actively discouraging, even preventing, IDPs from returning to the South, allegedly in order to influence the outcome of the 2011 referendum by having those southerners counted as residents of the North. On the other hand, some southern states were deeply concerned with the slow pace of return to the South to the extent that they decided to assume responsibility for the transportation of IDPs returning to areas within their states. Unity state officials, for example, claimed that up to February 2007, it had covered the transport costs of 50,000 people. With the approach of the referendum, the return of south Sudanese to their ancestral homes became an exodus, as shall be explained in Chapter Eight.

7.6 Elections and Democratic Transformation

National general elections, per the CPA, were to be completed by the end of the third year of the interim period (July 2008). During the negotiations, Garang, for expedient reasons, was not convinced of the wisdom of a midterm election, but he was prevailed upon by his colleagues who argued that elections were the only process through which the peaceful transfer of power could be achieved. Garang's fears emanated from two things. His first concern was the hegemony of the NCP over power and wealth for over a decade and a half, which he believed would neither give other parties the opportunity, nor the means, to compete with that party on level ground. With four aces in its hand, Garang thought the NCP was destined to be the winner. His second concern was apprehension that the elections might produce a government that would try to undermine the agreement. His first divination came true when national elections were held in April 2010. As to his apprehension that elections might produce northern parties who would try to undermine the CPA to which they were not signatories, the matter was agreeably addressed by the two parties before the signature of the CPA. To allay Garang's fears, the two parties, as observed earlier, incorporated in the CPA and the INC an article that obligated political parties who wished to contest elections to declare their commitment to faithfully abide by, and implement, the CPA. Any breach of that provision would have, therefore, become an unconstitutional act.

In reality, elections represent the *ne plus ultra* of democratic transformation. No matter how closely monitored and observed by international and local agents, elections would never be fair and free if the basic rights of citizens and groups were not respected. In a pluralist democracy, unlike a single-party system, free competition by enfranchised constituencies must be ensured without any hindrances. This right, as well as other political rights, was clearly defined in the CPA and entrenched in the INC's Bill of Rights. The SPLM had incessantly referred to the cardinality of the Bill of Rights to the sustenance of peace. But instead of faithfully addressing issues relating to democratic transformation, the NCP always skirted around the issue through unavailing tactics. One of those tactics was evasion of issues pertaining to democratic transformation in order to put them on hold until the end of the interim period and probably beyond. The other was taking cover behind the SPLM and government of South Sudan's alleged human rights violations in South Sudan. That evasion was counterproductive because it worked against the very thing the NCP, indeed all northern Sudanese, hoped to achieve: unity of the country. Despite the virtual independence southern Sudan enjoyed under the CPA during the interim period, a national system of governance in which the South was encouraged to partake would have added much political value to that independence. As for human rights breaches by the government of South Sudan—and they were not few—it was the responsibility of the people of the southern Sudan to make the government of South Sudan accountable for those breaches, not any other party. In addition, by insisting on the full implementation of the Bill of Rights, the SPLM was not acting as a human rights activist as much as it was acting as a contracting party demanding fulfillment of the terms of a contract. Ironically, the NCP seemed to have hoped that the SPLM would adopt in South Sudan the same style of totalitarian governance exercised in the North so that it would not set a role model for the North. That would have turned the one-country, two-systems into a two-countries, one-system rule. The NCP did no good to itself by exposing the party as insensitive to democratic rule. On the other hand, the chairman of the SPLM made it a ritual in all his speeches to remind his cabinet that respect for the rule of law was a red line. Even if he was only paying lip service to that ideal, he still showed sensitivity to values that should never be eroded by governors. As recent as May 2010, Salva Kiir had this to tell his government: "There is another aspect to peace. Peace, in the end, is a state of mind. Our constitution has embedded within it inalienable rights to citizens and other persons who live in our land. Those rights cannot—**and should not**—be infringed upon by any individual or government authority. They are part and parcel of the ideals for which we struggled. High up the ladder of those ideals is respect for the rights of all. Consequently, I want to say loud and clear that I shall not tolerate any infringement on the Bill of Rights. I shall also guarantee the independence of the Judiciary of Southern Sudan so that it jealously protects those rights. And I call upon Southern Sudan Human Rights Commission and all appropriate civil society organizations to be wide awake to such infringements, if they ever take place" (emphasis added).[64]

One may wonder then, why the NCP committed in the CPA to democratize the Sudanese state in the most profound manner since Sudan's independence, only to renege on that commitment when it came to implementation. We estimate that there were two reasons for that breach of promise: one political, the other attitudinal. Politically, the NCP seemed to be determined, come what may, to remain in power *ad infinitum*. That attachment to power is not only induced by lust for it, but more important, it is sustained by a growing phobia among powerful groups and individuals within the NCP known to have innumerable corpses in their cupboards. The NCP's longevity in power (16 years of uninterrupted absolute rule before the CPA) brought forth a peculiar frame of mind characterized by the arrogance of power and insensitivity towards others. It is within the context of this survivalist instinct that NCP's prevarication on consummating democratic transformation must be understood.

In the four years that preceded the elections, countless human rights violations occurred, including harassment of political activists, censorship of the press, unlawful confinement or molestation of political leaders, badgering of trade unionist, and shameful maltreatment of women. Those violations were further exacerbated by a serious justice gap at the level of the highest judicial body entrusted by the CPA and the INC with protecting and upholding human rights: the Constitutional Court. Not in one case had that court the courage to repeal any law, or question any administrative order, abusive to the Bill of Rights. Instead, the Constitutional Court invariably justified the legality of those breaches, including the most obnoxious of them.[65] Indeed, that court went into a trek of self-ridicule when one of its senior judges ruled that the Bill of Rights represented only guiding principles, not binding and enforceable constitutional edicts.[66] When judges descend from the sublime to the ridiculous with such a degree of cynicism, justice shall never be done, let alone be "manifestly and undoubtedly seen to be done."[67]

Of all the CPA's constituents, national elections—if fairly conducted—would have been the one to have the most transformative effect on Sudan. Elections, as intimated earlier, posed for the NCP the single greatest threat to its control over the military, intelligence, and the economic sectors—these three being the bedrock of its political power. Northern public opinion, which had pinned its hope on the transformation promised by the CPA, was disillusioned by the turn of events. The NCP never countenanced for a moment holding a free and fair election that would reduce its control of the executive and legislature or result in diluting its authority over institutions of official violence: army, law enforcement agencies, and security. As a keen observer of Sudan's political scene had argued: "losing power would potentially mean not just losing office but also being forced to abandon control of the security institutions, with potential consequences for individual accountability for past actions."[68]

The CPA was based on a degree of trust between Ali Osman Taha and John Garang, as well as on their understanding of how each side would gain from such a partnership. Taha hoped for a political partnership that would eventually culminate in an election that could bring the NCP a democratic victory. Yet after Garang's death, as we referred to earlier, some powerful elements within the NCP deluded themselves that Garang's vision was interred with his bones. Their attempt to recreate an SPLM in its image was based on this delusion, which to all intents and purposes meant the reincarnation of the pre-peace NIF as the dominant party in peacetime. Despite Salva Kiir's amenability to continuing a partnership with the NCP throughout the interim period, including going to elections on one ticket, the NCP's voracity for power seemed limitless; they wanted to take all. Thus by taking Salva Kiir for a malleable weak leader, they almost pushed him against the wall.

In all appearances, that clique's insensitivity to others had eventually become an occupational disease. Having excelled in fracturing or humbling political parties who made coalitions with them, the clique mistakenly speculated that the SPLM was one and the same. That was not the way to deal with a party and leader who had been fighting for two decades to achieve defined goals. The aim of that clique, in essence, was to keep the SPLM weak and focused solely on the South.[69] But, in reality, were the NCP to faithfully implement what it had agreed to do after the SPLM withdrawal from the Government of National Unity in 2007, an SPLM commitment to an electoral partnership would have been achieved. This would have enabled the NCP to gain popular legitimacy by emerging as the leading party in the North, if not absolutely dominating the northern political scene. The SPLM, after the crisis created by its withdrawal from national government, was ready to offer the NCP an electoral alliance and continue cooperation with it in order to make unity attractive. While there were signs that the NCP was receptive to an electoral partnership, it seemed to have wanted that partnership on its own terms: a partnership that relegated the SPLM to a junior southern partner, with its national role neutralized.[70] This was the same divide-and-rule, indeed divide-and-destroy, tactic that the NCP had mastered in dealing with all its partners from both the North and the South. This time the NCP did not realize the big gamble they were in for, as the stakes were very high: undermining the unity of Sudan.

Elections for the SPLM were also potentially divisive. The question of national identity had been at the root of the pseudoideological divisions within SPLM ranks since the movement's inception. For example, the desire to retain questions regarding ethnicity and religion in the census questionnaire was in part an electoral strategy by those in the movement who were betting on a united New Sudan. The exposure of a large percentage of citizens who were neither *ethnically* Arabs nor Muslims would have proven the multiple ethnic diversity of Sudan and also belied the claim that northern Sudan was a monoethnic region. Yet, for southern nationalists within the SPLM whose main concern was to deliver the referendum and ultimately protect South Sudan's independence, they did not mind letting that issue pass. The proponents of this idea never gave a second thought to winning elections or wresting power from the NCP in the center. Any strategy that involved a partnership with other marginalized regions or national parties opposing the NCP ran contrary to their main goal: southern Sudan independence. Indeed, some feared that an election victory would endanger the CPA by painting the NCP into a corner and forcing it to retreat from the agreement altogether.[71] Convinced that the NCP was more likely to safeguard the CPA than other northern parties such as the Umma or the Democratic Unionist Party (DUP), this SPLM faction seemed to have believed that any electoral partnership with opposition groups would not be a partnership against the NCP but against the

CPA.[72] This zany way of thinking reached such a level of absurdity that even the possible success of the SPLM in national elections (for example, electing Salva Kiir as president of Sudan) was considered by the separatists as a threat to self-determination. If this reading of events is correct, then it shall mean backsliding to Aggrey Jadden's vision of South Sudan, not that of Garang.

To the dismay of that group, the SPLM (Political Bureau) decided to field its own candidates in all national constituencies, including the presidency. Yassir Saeed Arman, the deputy secretary general of the SPLM,[73] was nominated by the SPLM for the presidency of the republic. That nomination came as a shock to the NCP for two reasons. First, it went beyond all their expectations; they thought that even if the SPLM decided to challenge NCP candidates in all parliamentary and gubernatorial elections, it would not dare challenge the president. The second was the presumption by the NCP that if the SPLM ever decided to field a candidate for the presidency, that candidate would never be a northerner, let alone a northerner whom the NCP would love most to hate. Arman later withdrew voluntarily owing to his own sensitivity toward southern nationalists whom he thought would not want him to upset the apple cart by becoming an encumbrance on the way to self-determination. The SPLM conceded to Arman's request, giving a flimsy explanation that the situation in Darfur would not make national elections comprehensive, free, and fair. To the chagrin of those who conceded to Arman's request to pull out of the race, as well as to those who claimed that his candidature would go against the wishes of the people of southern Sudan, the results of the elections were revealing. Arman, with 2,193,826, representing 21.69 percent of the total votes cast, came in second to Bashir who scored 6,901,694, or 68.24 percent of the votes. Surprisingly, votes in favor of Arman were cast both in the North and South, even though his name had already been struck off the list of candidates. The majority of Arman's support came from southern Sudan, which provided yet additional evidence that southern Sudanese were not innately averse to northerners. To the whole SPLM constituency in North and South Sudan, Arman's withdrawal from the race was not a faux pas, but a blunder.

The elections were unprecedented in their complexity. For example, the introduction of proportional representation and of special constituencies for women caught voters off balance who had no previous experience with such a system of voting. The confusion of voters was complicated because, for the first time, they had to vote in the same ballot for several candidates, including presidential, gubernatorial, and different categories of nominees for national and state legislatures. Parties other than the NCP and SPLM, therefore, found themselves in a disadvantageous position regarding resource mobilization, security of person, or ability to challenge irregular procedures.

In this confused atmosphere the national elections were held in April 2010. These were the first competitive elections to take place in 24 years since the last multiparty elections were held in Sudan (1986). It was also the fifth such elections since Sudan's independence 30 years earlier. A National Elections Commission (NEC) was formed and chaired by Abel Alier, the able Sudanese statesman and lawyer, with renowned academic Abdalla Ahmed Abdalla as his deputy. The formation of the commission was preceded by the promulgation of a new electoral law required by the CPA. Over 16 million (16,336,165) citizens were registered as eligible voters all over Sudan. Although the law satisfied all international requirements for free and fair elections, as international observers had maintained, the commission still came under heavy fire from different contenders, including the SPLM. Parties other than the NCP grumbled about the process of registration and the use by the NCP of government assets in election campaigns, which was contrary to the electoral law. However, complaints against the National Elections Commission did not receive the attention they deserved.

The electoral process was formally monitored by local and international observers, including the Carter Center from the United States and a high-powered team from the European Union that also included Canada, Norway, and Switzerland.[74]

In addition to logistical and operational inadequacies, serious infractions by the NCP of the electoral law and misuse of public resources and official media were reported by observers. If true, the misuse of public assets for electioneering purposes would have been an incriminating act under section 69 of the electoral law. That may have been the reason why the commission decided to let it pass. However, the most damning report came from the Carter Center team, based on its direct observation that the "vote tabulation was highly chaotic, nontransparent, and vulnerable to manipulation."[75] As a result, the observers expressed concern with "the accuracy of the preliminary results announced by NEC, as procedures and safeguards intended to ensure accuracy and transparency [had] been routinely bypassed."[76] The Carter Center observers also had "serious concern about election-related violence and intimidation in several states [in South Sudan], especially northern Bahr el Ghazal, Unity, and western Equatoria." Another damning comment came from European Union observers, not only about the election process itself, but also with regard to the clumsy manner in which both the NCP and SPLM agreed to resolve the problem created by the distortion of the balance of power between them in legislative and executive organs, as planned by the CPA. In this connection President Bashir and the NCP agreed to allow the SPLM to nominate parliamentarians from South Sudan, Blue Nile, and South Kordofan to restore the balance of NCP-SPLM membership in the national legislature to pre-election ratios. European Union observers remarked that this decision had "distorted the planned relationship between the equity of the ballot, equality between communities, and the competitive aspect of the elections."[77]

The elections also revealed the inconsequence of the majority of the opposition parties as well as their intellectual nudity. Elections are about competing agenda, not about persons, as they had often been considered by the majority of northern political parties. While the 72 registered opposition parties were legitimately striving to dislodge the NCP, hardly any of them came up with a competitive agendum that outrivaled that of the "discredited" NCP. This does not mean that the NCP had a superb agenda, but to many it represented "the devil they knew." Rather than being innovative, the 72 registered parties, as well as independent persons who were vying for high political positions in the legislature, executive, and the presidency, had nothing better to offer the public than rehashing old slogans or copying, without attribution, ideas and modes of action reflected in the CPA. The rest of what those parties offered to the electors was incessant lashing out at the NCP for misdeeds, and there surely was no scantiness of misdeeds for which that party deserved flaying.

Sudan is a country that has incrementally been afflicted by manifold hardships and miseries, which needed to be addressed by politicians vying for office. Electors were on the lookout for candidates with fresh ideas and plausible policies that would alleviate, if not erase, those hardships. Sudan's educational system continued to be in shambles and its health services in ruins, its judicial order had become a laughing stock of the legal fraternity, and its economy had been allowed to fall at the mercy of the presumed healing power of the free market. One would have expected, therefore, that candidates seeking power, especially political parties, would have engaged voters on the politics of these issues, rather than the politics of power and personalities. Woefully, the parties concentrated their efforts on yesterday's battles instead of addressing the problems of today and the challenges of tomorrow.

For two decades, those parties and politicians were engaged in attempts to restore the hold they had had on power but allowed to slip out of their grasp through a painless effort by the National Islamic Front. In their attempt to wrest power from the Islamist usurpers, these parties largely pinned their hopes on the sacrifices of the last SPLA warrior, despite persistent claims that millions of Sudanese were ready to launch a popular uprising inside Sudan to uproot the usurpers. Their claim to beat the NCP in popular contest proved to be as vacuous as their contention to forcibly wrest power from it. But, as proved by the national elections, the parties underachieved in voter registration; in mobilization of resources; in galvanizing popular support; and above all, in articulating convincing programs that would capture the imagination of voters. From July 1989, the success of the NIF/NCP in northern Sudan was a function of the inadequacy of its opponents, not the result of its matchless political ascendancy. Even following the conclusion of the CPA in 2005, the parties opposing the NIF/NCP failed to seize the opportunity to consummate the democratic transformation ushered in by that agreement, pretending that that was the prime duty of the two parties, especially the SPLM. For that reason, democratic transformation became an unimplementable charade.

There are, however, two factors that brought these parties to the nadir of their popularity. The first was the emergence of disenchanted regional movements, which traced their grievances back to policies that were initiated and perpetuated by those parties when they were in government. The second was intergenerational disparities and the inability of party leadership—on the left and right—to face up to those changes by reinventing themselves. But beyond everything, the parties almost lost their honor by succumbing to inducements offered by the NCP in the form of positions or material rewards. That was an art at which the NCP had become proficient. The readiness of the leaders of some political parties to be beguiled by those inducements caused them to lose respect in the eyes of many of their followers and the general public. Hence, despite all their rhetoric and grandstanding during the elections, people seldom listened. That left the honest citizens of the Sudan with only one alternative: resigning themselves to their fate, or to what the Italians call *la forza del destino*. Perhaps the *destino* shall come with the winds of change blowing on Sudan from the North and East. If it does, it shall not only carry in its wake political leaders who have been cleaved to power for over two decades and still seem to believe that people's acquiescence can be obtained through fraud, bribery, and terrorization, but shall also sweep away politically arthritic leaders who are given to believe that Sudan is destined to sustain them in perpetuity.

7.7 Border Demarcation

The north-south border extends for about 2,000 kilometers and cuts across nine states: South Dar Fur; South Kordofan; White Nile; Blue Nile and Sennar in northern Sudan; and Northern Bahr el Ghazal, Western Bahr el Ghazal, Unity, and Upper Nile in the south. Border demarcation was given prominence during the CPA negotiations, not only for administrative requirements, but also for its direct relevance to elections, particularly with regard to delimitation of territorial constituencies and referendum by the people of South Sudan. In this respect, the CPA matrix of implementation provided that the presidency shall establish a **Technical Ad Hoc Border Committee** to demarcate **precisely** the January 1, 1956 North/South borderline. This committee shall seek technical assistance and relevant expertise from both national and international sources in the pre-interim period after the adoption of the INC. What was envisaged, therefore, was a **precise technical exercise** that soon developed into a political problem and a bargaining chip in negotiating other issues. The Technical Border Committee (TBC) was formed in September 2005, but it actually commenced work in mid-2006 with a chair from the North and a deputy chair from the South. It comprised representatives of neighboring northern and southern states. Due to the overpoliticalization of its technical work, the TBC failed to complete it mission before the national elections, as envisioned by the agreement. Not even the commitment by the two parties in the trilateral talks held in Washington, D.C., in June 2009 was honored. In these talks, hosted by U.S. presidential envoy to Sudan Scott Gration, the parties agreed that "the border committee [shall] delimit undisputed areas not later than 1 September 2009." They also agreed "to request the United States and others to facilitate resolution of any disputed areas." As things stood in late 2010 (a few months before the southern Sudan referendum), the TBC declared that it had completed four-fifths of its work and was proceeding to the last leg of its mission.[78]

As Douglas Johnson observed: "The South's boundaries follow no natural geographical barrier. There [are] no clear dividing line…'The North' could no more be excluded, physically or economically, from 'the South' than 'the South' could be excluded from 'the North.'"[79] Conflict over land and resources, real or perceived, was patently behind the desire of both parties to put the issue of border demarcation at rest, but only after each party secured for itself the larger portion of the cake. The assumption that boundary conflicts, if they at all flare up, shall be over natural resources or mineral-rich areas is validated by the nature of the areas on whose demarcation the parties are presently at variance. Those areas include major sites of mechanized farming in Upper Nile, oil-rich areas in Unity state, and mineral-rich zones in western Bahr el Ghazal. The disputed areas, for example, include a 50-square-kilometer parcel of land that lies between Jabalain (White Nile state in the North) and Renk (Upper Nile state in the South). The area has been commonly used by southern pastoralists (Dinka Abialeng) and northern nomadic tribes (Seleim, Sabha, Ahamda, Rufa'a and Nezi). The populations in this area had lived in peace and shared equitably the benefits of the land until some northern nomads sought to acquire land and settle permanently in the area. That was why the area witnessed several tribal conflicts that brought the armies (SAF and SPLA) dangerously close to military intervention.[80]

In May 2010, the European Union stepped in with a view to ensuring a *modus vivendi* between northern and southern pastoralists in the region. It organized workshops in Kosti (northern Sudan) and Renk (South Sudan) in order to encourage these populations to live and let live as well as urge them to hand over small arms through joint border courts.[81] Another area of conflict was Kaka port on the White Nile, which was incorporated after January 1, 1956, in South Kordofan (Nuba Mountains), apparently to provide access to the Nile for Nuba and nomads from South Kordofan. A third flash point was the mineral-rich Kafia Kingi and Hufrat al-Nihas which were both subject to erratic changes of administration between April 22, 1924 and February 11, 1931. For example, Hufrat al-Nihas was part of the Raja district in Bahr el Ghazal during the colonial rule and remained so until 1960, when it was incorporated by General Abboud's government into Dar Fur. In the early 1990s it was officially included in Buram district (Dar Fur) by the NIF regional government minister, Ali El Haj. So, if the cutting date for border identification is January 1, 1956, as the CPA ruled, then there is no reason for disagreement on where the dividing line falls. But, evidently, the border problem had ceased to be an entirely technical question as it was originally conceived by the CPA, but one with political overtones and economic undercurrents. The September 2010 United States Institute of Peace report was really on the mark when it stated that the north-south border was more than a line.[82]

The non-demarcation of borders before elections was raised by the SPLM as one of the reasons that justified delaying those elections. That was a plausible cause since the delineation of borders was a prerequisite for drawing territorial constituencies. Nonetheless, the elections went ahead without border delineation. But as the referendum approached, the border issue became hot again, and this time it was the hawks of the NCP who maintained that the referendum would not be feasible without completing border delimitation. They sensibly argued that the north-south border, which was at that time only an internal administrative line of demarcation, would become an international border after secession. To that contention the SPLM answered that, with the exception of the western borders with Chad and Central African Republic, all international borders of Sudan to the north, east, and south were yet to be finally demarcated. To the north, conflict over Hala'ib Triangle had erupted only two years after Sudan's independence in February 1958, when the Egyptian government demanded return to Egypt of lands that lie north of the 22nd parallel. The problem persisted while both parties kept silent and let other people talk about it. Also, borders with Libya to the north were tentatively settled by an agreement signed in 1935 between the two colonial powers, England and Italy. That agreement assigned the Sara Triangle (formerly part of Sudan) to Libya, but the agreement had never been ratified by its signatories. Delimitation of the international border to the east is still subject of debate between Sudan and Ethiopia. The SPLM negotiators therefore argued that South Sudan, like other neighbors of Sudan, could still be independent without having definitive international borders with its neighbor to the north, especially if these borders were to remain on paper, as Salva Kiir had told the national cabinet on February 7, 2011. Coincidentally, the International Crisis Group observed that "if partition results in a 'hard' border, and access to the South [by pastoralists] is restricted, land and resource pressure [shall] intensify, as Northern governments and communities [will] depend even more on these areas. Too firm a barrier would create hardships for Southerners who rely on goods and services from the North and unnecessarily restrict communities which see the benefit of joint cross-border initiatives and interaction."[83]

7.8 Losing Momentum for Change

In Chapter Five we explained how the executive, legislative, and judicial institutions were radically reformed in Sudan in a manner never tried before independence, while in Chapter Eight we came across stiff resistance against that process of reform from elements within the NCP, who were never enthusiastic about change, as well as from bureaucrats, who were not beguiled by the virtues of decentralization. Be that as it may, one of the significant innovations of the CPA has been the creation of national commissions, independent of existing executive bodies, to carry out or superintend implementation of various aspects of the agreement.[84] Regardless of their shortcomings, the majority of these commissions were established in the first quarter of the interim period. In 2009, with less than one year left of the interim period, two cardinal national commissions were still to be formed: the National Land and the Human Rights Commissions. Both were crucial for two important aspects of the CPA: democratic transformation and land ownership. Nonetheless, performance of many of the commissions had been much below CPA expectations, especially with regard to public oversight on the government's performance in areas that fell within the purview of their responsibility or in making sure that targets established by the CPA were attained. Blame for that inadequacy has to be attributed to both partners. While the NCP was responsible for diluting the commissions' independence through interference in the way they carried out their mandates (for example, the relief of the chairperson of the Fiscal and Financial Allocations and Monitoring Commission referred to in Chapter Six above), the SPLM, wittingly or unwittingly, abdicated its responsibility in ensuring that members of the commissions were chosen from among independent-minded persons and that their secretariats were recruited from among nonpartisan professionals. In almost all cases, the SPLM limited its role in the formation of the commissions to selection of south Sudanese members, leaving the rest to the NCP, even though the CPA made the formation of these commissions in their entirety subject to the consent of the first vice president, the SPLM chairman. Glaring examples of such inattention were observed in the formation of institutions like the Constitutional Court, the secretariat of the National Constitutional Review Commission, and the Commission for the Protection of the Rights of Non-Muslims in the National Capital as well as in the secretariats and staff of the very crucial National Elections Commission. By way of illustration, the Constitutional Court appeared in several cases to be surprisingly meek toward the executive, and the Commission for the Protection of the Rights of Non-Muslims in the National Capital turned itself into a vehicle for maintaining coexistence between religious groups, rather than an ombudsman for ensuring that the rights of non-Muslims in Khartoum were protected and that the rules and regulations provided for in the CPA relating to rights of non-Muslims were enforced. Even the crucial CPA provision, which provided for the creation of special courts and public attorneys to handle cases in which non-Muslims were involved, never took place with the benign neglect of the commission and the SPLM. In addition to the unceremonious relief of the chair of the Fiscal and Financial Allocations and Monitoring Commission of his duties for no reason other than his insistence on carrying out his duties in the manner prescribed by the CPA, it was clear that the NCP treated all commissions as dispensable administrative adjuncts rather than supervisory bodies to ensure that government departments were acting within the bounds of the CPA.

The most glaring inadequacies, however, were in the constitution and performance of two principal commissions: the Assessment and Evaluation Commission (AEC) and the National Constitutional Review Commission (NCRC). The AEC was established, essentially, to alleviate misgivings by the SPLM that the exercise of the right to self-determination by the people of South Sudan might be frustrated. That was surely the reason why that commission figured in the Machakos Protocol under the chapter on self-determination. The commission was also meant to assure the NCP that unity had been given an adequate chance of success in the self-determination referendum. Consequently, the CPA empowered the commission to "conduct a mid-term evaluation of the unity arrangements established by the peace agreement." The CPA added that the commission, while composed of an equal number of members from the two parties, shall include "not more than two representatives from IGAD mediator countries [Kenya, Ethiopia, Eritrea, Uganda, and Djibouti] and two from the observer states [Italy, Norway, United Kingdom, and United States]." Thus, neither the international nor the independent nature of the commission should have been matters of dispute. This caveat appeared not to have been taken note of.

Furthermore, the preeminent role of the AEC in making judicious assessments and evaluations of the implementation of the CPA appeared to have been, purposely or inadvertently, disregarded by the parties. To cite an instance, the first chair of the commission, the Norwegian former foreign minister and diplomat Tom Vraalsen, was virtually driven to resign his position for no other reason than announcing his evaluation of the CPA implementation in a press conference in December 2007.[85] Vraalsen was reprimanded by the presidency for making his remarks openly, because it was alleged that the report should have been presented to the presidency privately. That interpretation of the agreement not only contravened the principle of independence of the commission, it also violated its transparency, a basic tenet of democracy recurrently referred to in the CPA. The CPA did not empower the presidency to oversee the work of the "independent commission" but only charged it with laying down the procedures and processes for its work.

Vraalsen's resignation came at a time when the relationship between the two parties was at its lowest following the suspension of the SPLM of its participation in the Government of National Unity. However, the SPLM was still not free from blame for attempts to frustrate the AEC's efforts to look critically on CPA implementation. One major shortcoming was the casual manner with which the SPLM treated the work of the very commission it sought to create at Machakos as the principal international mechanism for evaluating CPA implementation. Constant changes in SPLM membership in the commission was one factor that led to the commission's ineffectiveness, but the priority those members gave to their executive and political duties over those relating to the AEC was an unforgiveable mistake. Unlike the NCP, which continued to have permanent members at the AEC who were regularly briefed and debriefed by their principals, the SPLM members appeared to have been freelancers acting on their own. Small wonder many observers were perplexed about the equanimity with which the party that engineered the creation of the AEC as an international watchdog over the CPA implementation received the hounding of Vraalsen out of office. Those attitudes collectively not only defeated the purpose for which the AEC was formed, but it also reflected a shallow understanding of the politico-juridical underpinnings of the CPA.

The NCRC, on the other side, was formed to undertake two tasks. Initially, it was charged with drawing a constitution for Sudan based on the new political dispensation ushered in by the CPA. Its subsequent task was to organize "during the six-year interim period and without prejudice to the provisions of the Peace Agreement" an inclusive constitutional review process. That process was meant to provide political **inclusiveness** and **public participation** (2.12.10 Power Sharing Protocol). While one would not have expected the NCP to be much bothered with the operation of this provision, the SPLM had every reason to be concerned. First, the SPLM persisted on calling for inclusiveness in the institutions created by the CPA, and second, it was dissatisfied with the process of implementation, particularly insofar as the arrangements on national reconciliation and democratic transformation were concerned. As a result, that NCRC cardinal subsequent task was never exercised.

While the expectation was that the two parties would pull together in an uphill journey to reach a mutually agreed destination, one party was always busy identifying gaps in implementation resulting from recalcitrance by the other, and the other was exploiting frailties in its partner in order to frustrate CPA implementation on every step of the journey. In the process, the momentum for change created after the installation of Government of National Unity was irreversibly lost.

NOTES

1 Garang used the term in one of his speeches to caution the Khartoum political class not to take south Sudanese for granted or reduce them to a subhuman species.

2 Among the NCP negotiators who fell by the wayside when the Government of National Unity was formed were Yahya al-Hussein, Mutrif Siddiq, and Sayed El Khatib, who were crucial in bridging the gap between the two parties in the course of the negotiations.

3 The SPLM caucus in the National Assembly on numerous occasions aligned itself with opposition members of parliament to defeat laws that abridged press freedom, restricted operations of voluntary humanitarian organizations, or guaranteed unbridled powers to law-enforcement agencies.

4 The Protocol on Security arrangements established five steps for the deployment of SAF forces to the 11th parallel, which required that 74 percent of the forces were redeployed north by D-Day + 30 months. That target was not achieved in oil-producing areas in South Sudan.

5 Resolution 1590, Security Council Meeting, Nairobi, March 24, 2005 (See also Chapter Five).

6 Clause 1.5 of the Power Sharing Protocol calls on all levels of government to "perform their function and exercise their powers so as (i) Not to encroach on another level's powers and functions, (ii) Not to assume another level's powers or functions conferred upon it by the constitution."

7 The Power Sharing Protocol identifies "foreign affairs and international relations" at the top of national powers.

8 Douglas Johnson, *Gurtong,* February 14, 2007.

9 Roger Winter and John Prendergast, *Abyei: Sudan's 'Kashmir,'* Strategy Paper No. 11 (Washington, DC: ENOUGH, January 2008).

10 While the Ngok Dinka people were represented at the negotiations by highly placed politicians and officers in the SPLM/SPLA, the government's delegations included a Misseriya NCP-appointed local administrator and the lead lawyer in the government's delegation who hailed from Dar Misseriya.

11 *Sudan: Breaking the Abyei Deadlock,* Africa Briefing No. 47 (Nairobi/Brussels: International Crisis Group, October 12, 2007).

12 John Young, *Emerging North-South Tensions and Prospects for a Return to War,* (Geneva, Switzerland: Small Arms Survey, July 2007).

13 *Sudan's Comprehensive Peace Agreement: Beyond the Crisis,* Africa Briefing No. 50 (Nairobi/Brussels: International Crisis Group, March 13, 2008), 9.

14 See Bona Malwal, "The Future of the Comprehensive Peace Agreement" (paper presented at a symposium organized by the South Sudan Democratic Forum, Khartoum, December 12, 2007).

15 Douglas Johnson, "Why Abyei Matters: The Breaking Point of Sudan's Comprehensive Peace Agreement?" African Affairs 107/426 (Oxford University Press, 2008): 1–19.

16 Ibid.

17 ICG Supra note 11, 9.

18 The panel was presided over by Professor Pierre-Marie Dupuy (France) and comprised of Judge Awn Al-Khasawneh (Jordan), Professor Gerhard Hafner (Germany), Professor Michael Reisman (U.S.), and Judge Stephen Schwebel (U.S.).

19 In the Matter of an Arbitration before a Tribunal Constituted in Accordance with Article 5 of the Arbitration Agreement between the Government of Sudan and the Sudan People's Liberation Movement/Army on Delimiting Abyei Area...Final Award, The Hague, July 22, 2009.

20 The most important oil field in the Abyei area was Wafra, whose production dwindled from 16,000 to 6,000 barrels per day as a result of inefficient extraction technology. However, the rich Heglig oil field was deemed out of the Abyei area as demarcated by the International Court of Arbitration. Both Heglig and Bambo remained in the North (South Kordufan), while Wafra and Balome were in the South (Unity state).

21 Bronwen Manby, *International Law and the Right to a Nationality in Sudan* (New York: Open Society Foundations, 2011), 28.

22 Ms. Marie-Hélène Gillot v. France, Human Rights Committee, No. 932/2000, U.N. Doc. A/57/40 (2002).

23 The obscurantist Ugandan Lord's Resistance Army (LRA) used southern Sudan as a rear base for launching attacks on Uganda from southern Sudan (eastern and western Equatoria). The LRA staged attacks on villages in those regions mainly to loot food and medicine, abduct girls as concubines, and recruit young men as fighters. However, there were also unsubstantiated accusations that Ambararo/Fellata nomads from West Africa were being recruited by the NCP as a source of destabilization in South Sudan. In all probability the Ambararo/Fellata, who were known to have migrated from West Africa to Sudan during the dry seasons since the time of the colonial administration, were driven to move southward to Equatoria by desertification and loss of plant cover in the areas they used to migrate to during the dry seasons (Dar Fur and Kordofan).

24 These militias included the Equatorian Defense Force and the South Sudan Defense Force who participated, to varying degrees, in Khartoum's proxy war against the SPLA.

25 Mathew B. Arnold and Chris Alden, "'This Gun Is Our Food': Demilitarising the White Army Militias of South Sudan," *Conflict, Security and Development* 7:3 (2007): 316–385 and Young, *Emerging North-South Tensions and Prospects for Return to War.*

26 *Humanitarian Action in Southern Sudan Report*, prepared by the U.N. Office for the Coordination of Humanitarian Affairs, Issue No. 38 (Juba, South Sudan, November 6–20, 2009).

27 Richard Garfield, *Violence and Victimization after Civilian Disarmament: The Case of Jonglei* (Geneva, Switzerland: Small Arms Survey, December 2007).

28 *Jonglei's Tribal Conflicts: Countering Insecurity in South Sudan,* Africa Report No. 154 (Juba/Nairobi/Brussels: International Crisis Group, December 23, 2009).

29 Though originally organized for the purpose of protecting communities, the White Army was armed by Dr. Riek Machar after he parted ways with the SPLM/A in the early 1990s. The White Army was thus pulled into the broader civil war conflict. See Garfield, *Violence and Victimization after Civilian Disarmament.*

30 "The U.N. Strongly Condemns the Killing of an Indian Peacekeeper in South Sudan," United Nations Mission in Sudan Press Release, January 27, 2007.

31 Mareike Schomerus, *The Lord's Resistance Army in Sudan: A History and Overview* (Geneva, Switzerland: Small Arms Survey, September 2007).

32 "Ugandan Rebel Attack Shocks Sudan," *BBC News,* September 14, 2005; "LRA Attacks Threaten Sudan Talks," *BBC News,* June 2, 2006; Isaac Vuni, "30 Killed in Sudan's Eastern Equatoria After Ugandan LRA Attacks," *Sudan Tribune* (Kapoeta), January 16, 2007.

33 Arnold and Alden, "'This Gun Is Our Food.'"

34 "The Southern Front Reopens: Fighting between Khartoum's Soldiers and the Juba government Presages a New Crisis in the South," *Africa Confidential* 47/25 (December 15, 2006); "Militias in the South," *Africa Confidential* 47/25, December 15, 2006; "Khartoum's Proxies," *Africa Confidential* 47/25, December 15, 2006.

35 "Hundreds Killed, Wounded in Sudan Clashes," Reuters, December 1, 2006.

36 *The CPA Monitor: Monthly Report on the Implementation of the CPA*, (United Nations Mission in Sudan: December 2005), 20.

37 The Murle are a small Nilotic tribe whose traditional lands are located north of Juba (around the town of Terekeka), bordering to the north the Dinka Bor at Pariak. They are cattle-oriented, and that is the reason they engage in perennial cattle-raiding wars with the Dinka Bor during the dry season.

38 Young, *Emerging North-South Tensions*, 27.

39 Garfield, *Violence and Victimization after Civilian Disarmament*, 17.

40 Ibid.

41 Ibid.

42 Ibid.

43 "Southern Sudan Fails in Demobilizing 84,000 Soldiers," *Ajras Al hurriya,* September 2, 2010: James Gatdet Dak, "Since Peace Deal South Sudan Has Failed to Demobilize 84,000 Soldiers," *Sudan Tribune* (Juba), August 31, 2010. http://www.sudantribune.com/spip.php?article36137

44 Supra note 39

45 Robert Muggah, "Reflections on Disarmament, Demobilisation, and Reintegration in Sudan," *Humanitarian Exchange* 33 (March 2006), 33.

46 Ashraf Ghani, Clare Lockhart, and Blair Glencorse, "Assessing Linkages between Diplomatic Peacemaking and Developmental Peacebuilding Efforts," in *Ending Wars, Consolidating Peace: Economic Perspectives*, eds. Mats Berdal and Achim Wennmann (London: International Institute for Strategic Studies, Rutledge, 2010), 58

47 Muggah, "Reflections on Disarmament, Demobilisation, and Reintegration in Sudan," 38.

48 Ibid.

49 Ibid.

50 Ibid.

51 *CPA Monitor,* March 2006, 5.

52 Matthew Arnold and Matthew LeRiche "Neither 'Joint' nor 'Integrated': The Joint Integrated Units and the Future of the CPA," *Sudan Issue Brief* 10 (Geneva, Switzerland: Small Arms Survey, March 2008), 6.

53 Young, *Emerging North-South Tensions*, 39.

54 Twenty-four thousand were to be based in South Sudan, 600 in Abyei, 6,000 in the Nuba Mountains, 6,000 in Blue Nile, and 3,000 in Khartoum.

55 Arnold and LeRiche, "Neither 'Joint' nor 'Integrated,'" 6.

56 The term was first used in World War Two to signify the date for landing at Normandy. In the CPA it signifies the date agreed to by the parties for the commencement of operations provided for in the Security Arrangements Protocol such a cease fire, withdrawal of forces, demobilization, Disarmoment and reintegration.

57 Arnold and LeRiche, "Neither 'Joint' nor 'Integrated,'" 3.

58 *CPA Monitor*, March 2006, 11.

59 "Darfur Rebels Hail Decision by SPLM to Postpone Census," *Sudan Tribune* (London), April 12, 2008.

60 "The SPLM Calls Census Results Shameful," *Al Sharq Al Awsat*, May 9, 2009.

61 Ibid.

62 *Update on Southern Sudan and Blue Nile*, Geneva, Office of the U.N. High Commissioner for Refugees, March 2007

63 Ibid.

64 General Salva Kiir Myardit, inaugural address delivered after the southern Sudan elections on May 21, 2010, published as "Kiir's Inaugural Address Outlines Wideranging Priorities," *Gurtong* (Juba), May 22, 2010.

65 In 2009, Sudan's National Security Agency imposed censorship on the print media, which was challenged by some Khartoum publications before the Constitutional Court. To the dismay of all human rights supporters, that court, which had been charged by the constitution to uphold the Bill of Rights, rejected the plea because, in the eyes of the majority of its members, fundamental rights were not absolute.

66 El Haj Yousif El Haj Mekki v. Izeledin Ahmed Mohmed El Hassan, Constitutional Court (May 27, 2008).

67 Attributed to Gordon Hewart, lord chief justice of England (1922–1940).

68 Alex De Waal, "Prospects for Peace in Sudan," blog published on the Valentino Achek Deng Foundation website, posted December 16, 2008, http://www.valentinoachakdeng.org/blog/2007/12/16/prospects-for-peace-in-sudan/.

69 "Sudan's Comprehensive Peace Agreement Beyond the Crisis," Africa Briefing No. 50 (Nairobi/Brussels: International Crisis Group, March 13, 2008).

70 Ibid.

71 Ibid.

72 Ibid.

73 Arman, a northern Sudanese, joined the SPLM in the mid-1980s and stoutly fought in SPLA ranks throughout the war of liberation. He became a close confident of SPLM leaders Dr. John Garang and Salva Kiir and was admired by his SPLM/A comrades.

74 The European Union's mission was headed by Véronique De Keyser, a Belgian member of the European Parliament, and included 134 observers from 25 member states. *Sudan Final Report: Executive and Legislative Elections, 11–15 April 2010* (European Union Election Observation Mission, 2010)

75 Carter Center Reports Widespread Irregularities in Sudan's Vote Tabulation and Strongly Urges Steps to Increase Transparency (Atlanta, GA: The Carter Center, May 10, 2010).

76 Ibid.

77 Sudan Final Report: Executive and Legislative Elections, 11–15 April 2010 (European Union Election Observation Mission, 2010), 5.

78 "Sudan Resumes Demarcation of North-South Border," *Sudan Tribune,* September, 2010. Sudan Resume demarcation of north- South   border, *Sudan Tribune, Monday September 2010*

79 Johnson, *The Root Causes of Sudan's Civil Wars,* 62–63.

80 *More Than a Line: Sudan's North-South Border,* report prepared by a team of Sudanese and international consultants and Concordis International for the United States Institute of Peace (Washington, DC: United States Institute of Peace, September 2010).

81 Ibid., 94–95.

82 Ibid.

83 *Sudan: Defining the North-South Border,* Africa Briefing No. 75 (Juba/Khartoum/Nairobi/Brussels: International Crisis Group, September 2, 2010), 13.

84 The CPA provided for the creation of 14 independent commissions with clearly defined functions. The commissions were to come under the direct supervision of the presidency. They incorporated the National Constitutional Review Commission, Civil Service Commission, National Judicial Service Commission, Fiscal and Financial Allocation and Monitoring Commission, National Land Commission, National Election Commission, National Petroleum Commission, Abyei Boundary Commission, Assessment and Evaluation Commission, Ceasefire Political Commission, Commission for the Rights of Non-Muslims in the National Capital, Southern Sudan Referendum Commission, and Abyei Referendum Commission. Similar commissions, as appropriate, were created in South Sudan under the interim constitution of South Sudan.

85 "Sudanese Peace in Jeopardy as Former Norwegian Envoy Resigns," African Press International (Khartoum), December 4, 2007.

Chapter Nine
Southern Sudan's Multiple Transitions: Attainments and Foibles

■■■■■■■■■■■■❖■■■■■■■■■■■■■

> There is no failure except in no longer trying.
> —**Elbert Hubbard**,
> *The Note Book of Elbert Hubbard*

1. Introduction

This chapter deals with the crucial transitions southern Sudan and the Sudan People's Liberation Movement (SPLM) went through following the untimely departure of its founding leader. Before his death, Garang was set upon introducing unprecedented political, economic, and administrative reforms. These reforms included ethnic diversification of the administration, building a competent civil service as well as a professional army, and rehabilitating the rural economy. Since the effectuation of those plans was contingent on peace in southern Sudan and stability all over that country, Garang decided above everything else to give precedence to the neutralization of all other armed groups (OAGs) before he settled in his offices in Juba and Khartoum. To him, unless those groups were disarmed, there would be no stability in southern Sudan. Another problem that Garang wanted to put behind his back was the question of Darfur. Even during the Comprehensive Peace Agreement (CPA) negotiations when it appeared to him that peace was around the corner, Garang had premonitions that the Darfur conflict, if not resolved, could derail CPA implementation. Having failed to convince Vice President Taha to work with him toward reaching a pacific settlement with Darfurians, he drew his own plans to bring on board the two leaders of the Sudan Liberation

Movement (SLM), Mini Arco Menawi and Abdel Wahid Mohamed Nour, as well as Khalil Ibrahim, the leader of the then burgeoning new movement, Justice and Equality Movement (JAM). That meeting was to take place in New Site (Garang's home base in South Sudan) immediately after his return from his fateful trip to Uganda. In effect, Garang instructed one of his aides, Yassir S. Arman, to prepare that meeting in consultation with the Eritrean authorities who were by then hosting Darfurian rebels.

On the economic side, Garang was armed with the SPLM's own blueprints for the economic revival of Sudan and rehabilitation of southern Sudan, in addition to the Joint Assessment Mission (JAM) report (Chapter Six). Even before the conclusion of the CPA, he formed three committees to draw plans for South Sudan's economic development, building a competent civil administration, and professionalization of Sudan People's Liberation Army (SPLA). The first committee was headed by Wani Igga and the second by Riek Machar, while Salva Kiir was entrusted with the reform and restructuring of the SPLA. The economic plan was published under the title of "Peace Through Development: Perspectives and Prospects in the Sudan" and released in February 2000. Garang also supervised the production of another document, "SPLM Strategic Framework for War-to-Peace Transition," launched in August 2004. In these reports the SPLM leader framed an implementation matrix in which he identified targeted actions to be initiated during his first 180 days in office as first vice president of the republic and president of the government of South Sudan. In the meantime, Garang solicited advice from national[1] and international economists on the socioeconomic transformation of Sudan and reconstruction of the South. Of note was a layout of a South Sudan transformation agenda, which was presented by a senior World Bank advisor.

Garang's premature death caught both the North and the South by surprise. In Chapter Eight we elaborated on how the National Congress Party (NCP) made capital of the SPLM leader's death, including attempting to reinvent the SPLM to its image. This chapter shall analyze the situation in southern Sudan after Garang's eternal rest and how both the SPLM and the government of South Sudan had fared in the consummation of his agenda, especially in the areas of governance, security, economic development, and political organization.

2. Rising from the Ashes within Six Years

After the government of South Sudan was sworn in on October 24, 2005, and governors of the 10 southern states appointed, both the government of South Sudan and the SPLM were fully equipped with a road map for human and institutional capacity-building in southern Sudan, as well as with fairly detailed programs for reviving the economy. Evidently, the problems that South Sudan faced when the government of South Sudan took over the reins of power were colossal and beyond the capacity of a new and fairly inexperienced government. Though it occupied one-fourth of the surface area of Sudan (600,000 square kilometers), when the SPLM assumed power that territory lacked a single asphalted road, save for a few kilometers of derelict roads in Juba, the capital city of southern Sudan. As for education and health, those services were almost abandoned during the struggle to the Operation Lifeline Sudan (OLS) and foreign nongovernmental organizations. The SPLM's role at that time was limited to coordination of service delivery through its humanitarian arm, the Sudan Relief and Rehabilitation Association (SRRA). Evidently, the 21-year civil war was responsible for the ruination of the South, but war was a symptom of a larger problem that pervaded the whole country: marginalization of the peripheries. Only when the Machakos Protocol was signed in July 2002 did a national government recognize that problem and provide a window of opportunity for resolving it.

Garang's targeted actions addressed specific problems in both North and South Sudan, since he took his national role seriously. The 180-day plan, which is presented below, focused ahead to the consolidation of permanent peace and unity through coordinated and well-sequenced programs. To consolidate peace, for example, the program aspired to stabilize South Sudan, end the conflict in Darfur, and gear socioeconomic development toward the alleviation of poverty in order to put an end to economic want and marginalization. In this respect, the program gave priority to agriculture as the main engine of growth and proposed the creation of a national council of economic advisors under the first vice president to oversee the realization of the plan. The pride of place in the 180-day program was given to Garang's treasured project: **to take towns to rural areas**. Garang's idea was to provide work opportunities and social services in rural areas with a view to raising the living standard of rural population and inhibiting their gravitation into urban areas. That was to be initially achieved through the establishment of 1,000 community development centers in the 10 states of South Sudan (100 in each state) and 500 in the North to cover five states (eastern Sudan, Blue Nile, South Kordofan, Darfur, and Northern state). The centers were to be agents for the realization of Garang's strategy to take towns to the rural areas.

As recompense to SPLA warriors and veterans, the program included housing schemes for war veterans, widows, and orphans and a savings bank for these groups. In order to enhance the literacy and numeracy of SPLA men and women, Garang proposed the establishment of distance learning centers at the army's divisional headquarters. Garang also put at the top of his national priorities the issue of integration of the Joint Integrated Units (JIUs) and adoption of a common military doctrine for them other than those of the Sudan Armed Forces (SAF) and SPLA, which were deemed partisan. Garang was apparently looking forward to the creation of a national army in a united Sudan that would be imbued with the values, and constrained by the norms, established by the CPA. When these objectives were realized, he was also anticipating the cancelation of Sudan's debts, along with the normalization of relations with the United States and other Western donors. From the start, the late SPLM leader was determined to reform the Sudanese state as a whole without losing sight of the special needs of southern Sudan. That plan was entitled "Matrix of Targeted Actions to be Taken during the First 180 Days by John Garang in His Two Capacities as First Vice President of Sudan and President of the Government of Southern Sudan." The plan detailed the following actions:

As first vice president of Sudan	As president of government of South Sudan
1. Adoption of a common military doctrine for the JIUs with a view to making them a nucleus of the future Sudanese army. 2. Resolution of the Darfur conflict through a reconciliation effort between the government of Sudan and rebels, deployment of 5,000 SPLA forces together with an equal number from SAF to establish peace and security in Darfur, and return of internally displaced persons to their villages. 3. Approval of National Poverty Eradication Strategy (NPES) focusing on agriculture as the engine of growth of Sudan's economy, with oil as its legitimate fuel. 4. Formulation of an economic policy for the interim period with the triple objectives of sustained peace, economic growth, and poverty eradication	1. Establishment of 1,000 Community Resource Centers (CRCs), i.e., 100 for each of the South Sudan states. 2. Establishment of five distance learning centers at SPLA divisional headquarters to help raise literacy and numeracy levels of SPLA personnel. 3. Reorganization of the SPLA and its transformation into a modern army. 4. Construction of 60 kilometers of tarmac roads in Juba town and rehabilitation of 1,500 kilometers of priority roads in South Sudan. 5. Establishment of water and power stations in each of the 10 south Sudanese states. 6. Establishment of a lean and efficient civil service through the reorganization of the Civil Administration of New Sudan (CANS) and absorption of efficient / qualified personnel from the Coordination Council for southern Sudan. 7. Establishment of a savings scheme for the SPLA and war

5. Establishment of a Council of Economic Advisors under the direct supervision of the first vice president. 6. Establishment of 500 Community Resource Centers (CRCs) as key elements of the strategy to take towns to rural areas: 100 CRCs each for South Kordofan, Blue Nile, eastern Sudan, Northern state, and Darfur 7. Normalization of relations with the U.S administration and joint effort for addressing the issue of debts.	veterans, making use of the Rwandese model 8. Establishment of a pension scheme for former personnel of the civil service in areas in Southern Sudan liberated by the SPLM/A known as Civil Authority of New Sudan (CANS) in addition to a scheme for SPLA retired officers. The scheme was to be established according to plans prepared with the help of World Bank experts and approved by the SPLM Leadership Council in 2005.

In the process of drawing his economic map, Garang called on the World Bank, among others, for advice. The bank's advice came in the form of a very well-thought-out memorandum delivered to the SPLM leader in Cairo on June 19, 2005, by two high-ranking World Bank advisors: Ashraf Ghani and Clare Lockhart.[2] That memorandum cautiously began with an optimistic note, stating that "while an external reading of documents would make one quite sceptical of the success of the CPA in view of the enormity of the task, engagements on the ground left one with optimism." That sense of optimism was generated by what the authors of the report called "intelligent engagement on the ground" and the impression Garang left on the advisors. But with the disappearance of Garang from the scene, a discontinuation of "intelligent engagement on the ground" occurred, with SPLM leadership giving the impression that Garang's vision was increasingly being abdicated. That justified Ghani's scepticism. In his report, Ghani divined that despite all his optimism about the future of South Sudan, "a lot can still go wrong." Nonetheless, he was hopeful that "a coherent framework can result in the establishment of a stable polity in southern Sudan that shall be ready to embark on major economic development." For this to happen, Ghani averred, South Sudan leadership had to be fully aware of the assets in its hands. "If those assets were used within a strategy that combined short-, medium-, and long-term actions in a systematic way, this might result in a breakthrough on the path of state-building and institution creation that would have immense implications for Africa and **fragile states**" (emphasis added). The two advisors believed that if this were to happen, transformation would be achieved *within six years.* [3]

Southern Sudan assets recounted by the two advisors comprised political capital reflected in the support SPLM enjoyed as a result of its sacrifices in war and success in achieving an unprecedented deal for the South; institutional capital represented by pre-National Islamic Front (NIF) rules and regulations that governed Sudan and the many professionals within southern Sudan who were educated and/or trained in northern Sudan and neighboring countries; human capital manifested in former government of Sudan officials and southern Sudanese who received tertiary education in North Sudan and in the diaspora; natural capital characterized by oil, water, land, and timber; social capital evident in the complex coping strategies that enabled southern Sudanese to survive under stress, and financial capital in the assured financial resources made available to the government of South Sudan through oil revenues Those assets, according to the two advisors, were counterbalanced by the absence of physical capital in the form of roads, housing stock, schools, and clinics and information capital in the form of baseline data and security, which represented an overarching challenge. The two advisors predicted a "prosperous and stable southern Sudan," based not only on the above assessment, but also on what they called "Garang's compelling vision of the future." They told Garang, "If that vision were to be realized, the state of southern Sudan **in six years** would be characterized by a predictable system of decision making where issues that require political leadership would be separated from those that require management, and the two are linked through processes of monitoring and accountabilities" (emphasis added).[4]

In his first and only meeting with Ghani at Cairo, Garang expressed his appreciation of the extraordinary perspicacity with which the report was made and, concurring with the advisors' conclusions, promised to make their report an archetype for economic reform of southern Sudan. He was particularly enthused by Ghani's proposition to immediately dispatch, at World Bank's expense, hundreds of southern Sudan's young administrative cadres for short- and medium-term training courses in the Indian and South African civil services and other public administration institutions. Garang also seized the occasion to explain to Ghani that the heavy centralization and rigid command structures of the army (SPLA) and the party (SPLM) were dictated during the struggle by considerations of survival. Any laxity in command or allowance of disrespect to hierarchy and nonobservance of orders by superiors would not have only been breaches of law and order, but acts that might have put the whole movement and army in harm's way.

Ghani's penetrating and clear-sighted advice counted key decisions the SPLM could take to ensure that the six-year plan Garang dreamt of for developing South Sudan would come true. These comprised institutionalization of decision making, accountability, raising the capacity of the administration, improving service delivery, enhancing physical infrastructure, prioritization of programs, human resources development, judicial sector reform through upgrading the professional capacity of judges and guaranteeing independence of the judiciary, rationalization of economic policy, and engagement of citizens as legitimate stakeholders in the development process. On the latter issue, Ghani made a pertinent remark in which he said: "Many countries, especially in the post-conflict period, have made the wrong decision regarding the economy and the market, creating small elites with huge fortunes derived from natural resources or windfall profits from licencing [and] a major gap between the haves and have-nots developed through abuse or manipulation of public office." Ghani added: "If that was to happen, the public would quickly withdraw from being stakeholders in the peace process." Based on this assumption, Ghani asserted that the "realization of Dr. Garang's vision requires active participation of [all citizens] in the process of the creation of prosperity."[5]

The tragic death of Garang could not have come at a worse time for the SPLM/A. Even before Garang's death, Ghani and Lockhart identified multiple transitions that South Sudan would face. Those were "transition from an autocratic and security-dominated state into a pluralistic federal state; transition from violence to peace and political competition; transition from a single locus of decision making to pluralistic institutions of governance and the economy; transition from advocacy of social justice to delivery of services; and transition from the rule of the gun to the Rule of Law."[6] To those five transitions a sixth was added after the death of John Garang: leadership transition.

3. The Leader Is Dead: Long Live the Leader

With the death of the SPLM/A's founding father, not only did doom merchants predict that the glory of the two organizations would fade away, but even the rank and file of the movement and the army found themselves in an agony of doubt. Their fears and doubts were justified, since Garang was the only leader they had known for two decades, and responsibility for the realization of Garang's dream would lie on the shoulders of the new leader. These dreams were prodigious: uniting Sudan, rebuilding the South, and making Africa's largest country the driving force of African integration. However, the most immediate task facing Garang's successor was still full implementation of the CPA.

On the death of Garang on July 30, 2005, his widow, Rebecca Nyandeng, in a cool and collected manner, asked the SPLM/A leader who carried the tragic news to her, "Who is your Joshua?" Mrs. Garang, who endured all the sufferings and travails of war with her late husband, was clearly concerned about who would take the Sudanese to the New Sudan, the way Joshua took his people to Canaan after Moses' demise. Aside from the irony of such biblical parables and allegories issuing from the widow of a secular leader *par excellence*, the SPLM was a political party governed by established rules on assignment of roles and order of precedence. As early as the first SPLM convention (April 2, 1994, Chukudum), Salva Kiir Mayardit was elected by that convention as Garang's deputy (in the party) and second in command in the army (chief of general staff of the SPLA). As the only SPLM leader who was directly elected by the convention, alongside John Garang as chair of the party and Yousif Kuwa Mekki as chair of the convention, there should have been no doubt as to whom Garang's heir-apparent would be. More important, Salva Kiir was also one of the few SPLA top brass who firmly stood by the late leader during all the turmoil and uncertainties of the SPLM/A splits. He stood up for Garang in the aborted mutiny of Kerabino Kuanyin Bol, despite ties of kinship between him and Kerabino. Salva Kiir also remained loyal to the leader throughout the conflict between the leader and commander Arok Thon Arok[7] as well as in the Nasir split.[8] Even when a falling out occurred between the leader and his deputy in November 2004—mainly regarding Garang's style of management, not his political vision—the difference between the two was soon patched up in a historic meeting in Rumbek between November 29 and December 1, 2004.[9]

It is worth recalling that at the Rumbek meeting the preponderance of views expressed by the 240 attendees was overwhelmingly against Garang's style of managing the SPLA and SPLM, without challenging his vision or leadership. That encounter between the two leaders was followed by two other clashes between Garang and Salva Kiir, also in Rumbek, which were never made public. The first followed an intimidating decision taken by Garang as soon as he reached Khartoum. In that decision he unilaterally dissolved the SPLM high command, retired all SPLA commanders, including the chief of staff Salva Kiir, appointed Kiir as his deputy in the party and the government of South Sudan, and nominated three of the SPLM historical leaders as advisors: Daniel Awet, Samuel Abu John, and Lual Diing Wol. He also appointed Oyay Deng Ajak as SPLA chief of staff, the position that had been held by Salva Kiir. Salva Kiir was exasperated by Garang's decision, not because he was not consulted, but because his advice was sought and discarded by Garang without ascertaining from his deputy the rationale behind his observations. In effect, Salva Kiir raised both procedural and substantive concerns about Garang's decisions. At the procedural level, he thought that it would have been more tactful to call the then high command to a meeting, thank them for their services, and then disband them, even though that organ was not elected by the convention but handpicked by the chairman of the party. Of the three leaders elected by the convention to the party's highest leadership echelons, only Garang (the party chair) and Salva Kiir (the vice chair) were alive by 2005. The third, Yousif Kuwa, passed away on March 31, 2001. At the substantive level, Kiir questioned Garang's decision on the reorganization of the SPLA before discussing with Kiir the plan he, together with some of his subordinate officials, had drawn for the demobilization of SPLA commanders after giving them regular army ranks **and promoting them**. Kiir thought that dismissing commanders without disarming the forces under them might be a cause of unnecessary disorder, if not worse.

As a loyal and disciplined soldier, however, Kiir carried out the orders of the commander-in-chief, but was not happy. The occasion came for him to return like for like when Garang turned up in Rumbek to celebrate the SPLM anniversary in May 2005. Following the celebration, Garang called for a meeting of the high command, which he had already dissolved. Everybody either expressed their satisfaction with the leader's decision, or uttered meaningless words while Salva remained silent. Surprised by Kiir's muteness, Garang told his deputy that it would be unusual if the meeting ended without the deputy chair of the movement saying a word. It was at that point that Kiir exploded, calling the meeting unlawful and telling the late leader that he was acting in an authoritarian manner. He also reminded Garang that with the exception of himself (Salva), who was appointed deputy by Garang, and the three members who were made advisors to the SPLM leader, everyone else who was in attendance had no reason to be at the meeting by force of Garang's unilateral decree to dismiss the leadership council. At this point Garang made an ominous remark that soon proved prophetic: he assured Salva of his full trust in him, adding that "if anything happens to me you shall be the one to lead the movement."[10] Later on, Garang invited Salva to his residential quarters in Rumbek. In that meeting, the late leader not only repeated the statement he had earlier made publicly about his deputy, but he also made a revealing utterance. He told Kiir that despite the brief contrariety they had had at Rumbek, "he was still confident that his deputy would never abandon him *as some others might do."*[11]

Undeterred by all these factors that should have made his ascendancy to the leadership a matter of course, Salva Kiir, to the surprise of all his colleagues, resuscitated the defunct SPLM leadership council that had been dissolved by Garang a few months earlier. He told the revived council that regardless of his political and military seniority, he would leave it to the newly reinstated council to choose a successor to Garang and pledged full support to the person who would be chosen. That act alone revealed Salva Kiir's humility, as well as his awareness that Garang was a hard act to follow. Unanimously, the council endorsed Salva Kiir as successor. And sad as it had been, that occasion was also a moment of triumph for the SPLM/A, a party surrounded by many who were waiting to dance over its grave. Meanwhile, Salva Kiir did not wait long to show where he stood on the causes for which Garang had fought and eventually died. He chose the occasion of Garang's burial ceremony on August 8, 2005, to declare that he would stay the course charted by his predecessor and that the SPLM was "a vehicle with no reverse gear." As to his political priorities, he did not waiver in putting at the top of his agenda the unity of the people he was destined to directly govern: the people of South Sudan.

4. South-South Reconciliation

Salva Kiir is not Garang; he has his own style of leadership and modus operandi. So, rather than take on the OAGs the way Garang wanted to, he decided to engage them peacefully. The CPA, which focused attention exclusively on the North-South conflict, gave scant attention to the OAGs, save for provisions relating to their integration into Sudan's two standing armies. Certainly, Garang was never known to be always on the warpath, but he was renowned for being a leader who looked all ways and left nothing to chance. Equally, Garang was not averse to reconciliation between the SPLM and other groups as well as among opposing groups in southern Sudan; there were few attempts at South-South reconciliation under SPLA protection and the late leader's watch. The term South-south reconciliation was aptly described by two authors conversant with conflict in Southern Sudan as "Kiir's large tent strategy."[12] The meetings involved tribal chiefs, the New Sudan Council of Churches, and nongovernmental organizations.[13] However, in the case of the particular militia leaders who were bought over by the NCP, Garang believed that they were rebels without a cause; their only cause, as he saw it, was self-aggrandizement. Their greed, Garang estimated, was so rapacious that if the SPLM acceded to all their demands, a new set of demands would soon be raised. Future events had proven the validity of that judgment.

Salva Kiir, unlike Garang, decided to engage the OAGs, which led to his greatest post-CPA accomplishment: the Juba Declaration signed by the South Sudan Defense Force (SSDF)[14] and the SPLA on January 9, 2006. Unlike the CPA, which was in part a product of international pressure, the Juba Declaration[15] came about as a result of an internal process. It reflected good faith between Salva Kiir and Paulino Matip, the SSDF chief of staff, and responded to the two uppermost requirements of the people of southern Sudan: unity and security. The agreement officially disbanded the SSDF, integrated its command structures within those of the SPLA, and brought the bulk of the SSDF commanders to the SPLA. Most notably, it appointed the unlettered Paulino Matip deputy commander in chief of the SPLA, a position that made him senior to the SPLA war hero, Oyay Deng Ajak, the then chief of general staff of the SPLA.[16]

The diplomatic success of Salva Kiir's bringing Paulino Matip on board the SPLA was the finest achievement by Garang's successor; only remnants of the SSDF stayed behind and aligned with the SAF in a few remote areas of South Sudan. Having been taken off guard by the Juba Declaration, elements within the SAF sought retaliation by playing a spoiler's game. For example, they persuaded Brigadier General Gabriel Teng Ginye to remain with

Khartoum and dissuaded Commander Peter Lorot from joining those who flocked to Juba by transporting him to Khartoum from his base in Chukudum. Those efforts not only revealed a lack of good faith on the part of the SAF, but they also betrayed the very spirit of the CPA, since one of the main objectives of the Security Arrangements Protocol was the voluntary integration of OAGs into either the SAF or the SPLA. The determination by the SAF to control elements of southern Sudanese armed groups was perceived by the SPLM as a ploy that could serve one purpose: exploiting the OAG's in a proxy war against the government of South Sudan and as a source of destabilization of southern Sudan. Later experiences abundantly substantiated that fear.

Prior to the Juba Declaration, the SSDF represented the most serious threat to the implementation of the CPA, but a peace agreement was reached between the SPLM/A and the SDDF, not only was the SSDF's threat as a cohesive military force neutralized, it also became one of the tools for establishing security. For instance, 2,000 of Matip's former SSDF forces based near Juba airport, as well as some of his own bodyguards, were mobilized to contain a violent demonstration staged in Juba by SPLA (JIU) soldiers who were angry at delays in delivering their salaries, as referred to earlier. The Juba Declaration, therefore, demonstrated that the peace process required flexibility and attention to the immediate tasks at hand, rather than concentrating on the letter of the law. Nevertheless, the indiscriminate absorption of SSDF men into the SPLA came at a heavy cost to the professionalization of the SPLA and its downsizing, two prerequisites of the Protocol on Security Arrangements. The haphazard integration of nonmilitary elements into the SPLA complicated the transformation of a pyramidal military hierarchy, particularly when the integrated militias came with their own rank systems and command hierarchies. Nevertheless, the very guarded Salva Kiir chose to err on the side of caution. Making armed and unprofessional militias part of a regular army posed a threat to discipline and professionalism in that army, but excluding them from the peace deal would have been a threat to peace itself.

5. Security Strategy and Professionalization of the SPLA

The Interim Constitution of South Sudan (ICSS) called for the professionalization of the SPLA,[17] but that mission was fitfully undertaken. The major handicap to achieving it, as observed above, was the absorption into the SPLA of large numbers from OAGs, of whom some were only soldiers in name. Leaders of those groups inflated the numbers of their forces to cater to nonmilitary supporters and kinsmen. The penchant for inflating numbers of men under their command was not limited to commanders of former OAGs. Similar accusations were leveled against old-time SPLA commanders. To cite an example, Human Security Baseline Assessment (HSBA) reported in February 2011 that George Athor, the former deputy chief of staff for political and moral orientation who rebelled against the SPLA, was rumored to have been "accounting (and thus receiving salaries) for many more soldiers—in the thousands, according to some—than he had under his command in [Jonglie] state."[18]

This soaring inflation of the number of SPLA men, whether for reasons of political accommodation or nepotism, was not matched by an effort to raise the academic standard of the forces. The level of illiteracy within the ranks was almost as high as that of southern Sudan's overall average (85 percent). One of the reasons why Garang included the establishment of distant learning centers in his 180-day plan was precisely to enhance the alphabetical and functional literacy of the SPLA, a condition precedent to their professionalization. Even with all these shortcomings, the SPLA was firmly put under civil political control, represented by a minister for SPLA affairs and superintended by the president as commander-in-chief, per the CPA and the ICSS.

Garang, as president of the government of South Sudan, was also conscious of the need for an all-embracing security strategy to face the challenges emanating from the aftermath of war as well as carry out obligations imposed by the CPA on his government. But without a well-defined security strategy, the professionalization of the army would be purposeless. That strategy was announced by the end of 2008.[19] In his introduction to the strategy, President Salva Kiir wrote: "The signing of the CPA opened the door to new possibilities never before experienced by this generation of southern Sudanese. We look forward with high expectations as we embark on a new course. Yet, even in this environment of relative peace and progress we face many challenges and an uncertain future. If we fail to take full advantage of our current opportunities, we could fall back into the same struggle that has ravaged our people and our land for two decades."[20]

The objectives of the strategy were to:

- Provide physical protection of southern Sudan from external threats
- Strengthen alliances for peaceful subregional, regional, and global security
- Provide internal peace and stability in southern Sudan
- Strengthen capacity to provide public welfare through education, health, and food security
- Promote human rights, dignity, and harmony within southern Sudan cultural diversity
- Develop institutional frameworks to ensure good governance and rule of law through democratic processes
- Build an economic base that will alleviate poverty through employment and replace aid-dependency with self-reliance.

That strategy also included provisions and norms to govern behavior by SPLA forces and law enforcement agencies as well as operational goals to be achieved. The strategy, for example, reaffirmed commitment by the government of South Sudan to transform the SPLA into a force operating under civilian control and upholding human rights. On the other side, the operational goals focused on external threats, ethnic conflicts, and elite power struggles. As with all strategies, success hinged on two things: first, the priorities the government of South Sudan would give in funding to the strategy, and second, adherence by military and law enforcement agencies to the normative rules established by the CPA and ICSS. The former is yet to happen, as shall be explained later when addressing the government's budget priorities in general. As for adhesion to rules set in the CPA and the constitution, that objective is well-nigh impossible as long as the SPLA's political education is not geared toward instilling in the minds of men and women in uniform the culture of peace and the primacy of the rule of law, instead of boosterist propaganda of yesteryears that served its purpose during the struggle.

What the strategy omitted, however, was that the threat to security in southern Sudan might well come from the army-security complex itself. Presently, there are between 300,000 to 400,000 men and women in the SPLA, a figure well above its size during the struggle (100,000 to 130,000). There are also hundreds of generals, while the commander's corps in the SPLA during the struggle did not exceed 100, and the high command was made up of only 13 men. Any comparison between the size and hierarchical structures of the army of the newest state in the continent and those of fully established countries in sub-Saharan Africa such as Ethiopia, Nigeria, or Ghana is embarrassing. Over and above, each general in the SPLA was, at the time, allocated scores of men as protection forces, which almost turned the SPLA into a constabulary for the protection of senior officers. Those protection forces were often ostentatiously paraded wherever their commanding officers went—to offices, homes, or city restaurants. Apart from its unseemliness, this ostentation acted against the very idea of effective security protection; security is always more effectual when applied in an unobtrusive manner. Equally, nothing would make people shake in their shoes more than seeing their assumed protectors publicly appear to be in a state of fear or apprehensiveness. Moreover, in the absence of a well-run pay and records service and an audited payroll in the army, these protection forces became beholden to the generals who commanded them. The creation of military fiefdoms, owing allegiance to their direct commanders and not to a well-structured military command, would be the shortest route to indiscipline, if not disobedience, as was proved by the experience of some SPLA commanders who mutinied and carried with them the so-called "protection forces" under their command.

Above all, the heavy burden on the public purse caused by these deformities had, inexorably, undermined an important component of the security strategy: strengthening the state's capacity "to provide public welfare through education, health, and food security." The only way out of this predicament is for the SPLA to undergo serious and painful rationalization. Plans to achieve this rationalization had been envisaged but are continuously frustrated by interest groups. In contrast, the South African government had been involved after liberation in such an exercise in order to make the South African National Defense Force (SANDF) leaner, more effective, and efficient. A SANDF joint military coordinating committee found that the only rational and affordable army size for South Africa should not exceed 90,000 men, given the government's other obligations towards citizenry.[21] The Republic of South Sudan may have to draw a leaf from South Africa's book as well as from other African countries in this regard. For example, the army of Nigeria, a country with over 115 million inhabitants, comprises 162,000 men, and that of Ethiopia, with its population of over 90 million persons, does not exceed 138,000.[22] Indubitably, the size of the army in any country is determined, above all, by threat perceptions. But it is equally beyond doubt that the consolidation of peace demands the release of immense resources for the development of the country and the welfare of its citizens. The threats to security ensuing from neglect of these basic demands should never be underestimated by the military.

6. Democratization of the SPLM

One important decision of the Rumbek meeting (November-December 2004) was the call for the convocation, as soon as possible, of the second SPLM convention to address issues that had led to the standoff between Garang and his deputy. Throughout the struggle, Garang gave more attention to the SPLA than the SPLM, believing that both his adversaries at home and supporters throughout the world would only listen to his diplomatic pleas when his situation on the ground was credible. Evidently, Garang presumed true Mao Tse-Tung's dictum, "Power grows out of the barrel of the gun." More critically, the convention was also required to map out plans and programs for the post-CPA era. Garang did not survive to undertake that task, so it was left for his successor to do so. Another task awaiting the succession was the transformation of the party into an institution infused with participatory decision-making processes instead of one managed by command, as had been the case during the struggle. To that end, the new SPLM chairman created interim party organs to manage the SPLM, pending the holding of the second SPLM convention. On 2006, he declared the formation of an Interim Political Bureau (IBP), made up 47 members, and an SPLM Interim National Council

(SPLM, INC), comprising 119 members representing different shades of opinion within the party and balancing regional, ethnic, and gender representation. Thirty percent of the seats were allocated to SPLM members from the geographic North, a matter that was not observed in the first convention, probably because by then active enrollment in the SPLA was a prior condition to being part of the SPLM leadership. By assigning a percentage of seats to party members from northern Sudan, the new chairman clearly wished to affirm the national vocation of the SPLM. Those interim arrangements came to an end when the second SPLM convention met in Juba between May 10-16, 2008.

The convention was organized through a bottom-up elective process. It endorsed a new constitution for the party and revised the party's manifesto to address changes at local and global political arenas. The manifesto also took cognizance of obligations ensuing from the CPA. That revision was necessary since the original SPLM manifesto written in 1983 was interlarded with Marxist jargon by a minuscule group within the SPLM who distinguished themselves as Marxists. The label "communist" was also given to that document by dullards among the SPLM's opposition in both North and South Sudan to whom "communist" was a word of abuse, not a reflection of a political partiality. Whether the recital of Marxian shibboleths by SPLM self-styled Marxists was a result of genuine belief in that dogma or born out of a desire to pay court to the pseudo-Marxist regime of former Ethiopian leader Mengistu Haile Mariam who was by that time the main regional supporter of the SPLM. That jargon disappeared from the manifesto when it was reviewed by the first SPLM convention in 1994. Garang, who co-authored the 1983 manifesto,[23] had been inspired by Marx's interpretation of history, but he never lost sight of the inescapable local realities to which Marx was patently averse and, therefore, did not factor into his analysis. One such factor was ethnicity, which Marx dismissed outright as a bourgeois construct.[24] Furthermore, the 1994 convention came at a time when the political scene was dominated by three events. Locally, there was the split within the movement, which stirred up the issue of democracy and human rights abuses within the SPLM. At the international level, the collapse of the Soviet Union and its empire in Eastern Europe turned communism into a bugbear with which politicians, except for dyed-in-the-wool communists, would rather not be identified. In the meantime, the ascendancy of liberal democracy in the world made it hard for any politician not to be converted to it.

Aware of all those realities, Garang struggled hard not to be classified as an ideologue or identified with any ideology, including the "socialism" that the SPLM had openly espoused. On that he said: "The content of [the socialism we call for] cannot be determined mechanically and equated with Communism as Nimeiri would like the Western world to believe. The conceptualization and particularization of socialism in the Sudan shall unfold as the armed struggle

313

proceeds and as socio-economic development programmes are implemented during and after the war and according to Sudanese local and objective conditions."[25] Garang also used to good advantage the tradition of armed struggle in South Sudan, which enabled him find ready recruits for the cause he had sponsored. Nonetheless, party manifestos, for whatever they are worth, only become relevant when they address and resolve real problems in the real world, rather than satisfy the intellectual, or pseudointellectual, vainglory of their authors.

The new SPLM manifesto was authored, following wide consultations, by Dr. Wathig Kameir, a Sudanese academic who was close to Garang and edited a compendium of Garang's political dissertations.[26] The manifesto adopted in May 2008 was closer to the ground than the 1983 one. It defined the SPLM's concept of New Sudan (or the unity of Sudan on a new basis), analyzed the Sudanese crisis within an historical perspective, and diagnosed the ills of the old Sudan. It also highlighted political ideas and experiences that informed the SPLM's vision and had sharpened and enriched it through the struggle. Those included Marxian thought, African liberation philosophies, and experiences of nation building in North and South America. Nonetheless, the manifesto warned that the SPLM vision was not a dogma but a conceptual construct that shall evolve with unfolding new realities.

As for the new SPLM constitution, it established guiding principles for the work of the movement as a party competing with others in the political sphere and informed by a well-defined vision. The new SPLM constitution also entrusted the party with the safeguard and realization of values, norms, and institutions created by the CPA such as:

- Democracy, political pluralism, social harmony, and cohesion
- Decentralization of governance and devolution of power to states
- Voluntary unity of the people of Sudan based on historical and contemporary experiences, respect of diversity, and mutual economic interest
- Right to self-determination by the people of southern Sudan and popular consultation by the people of South Kordofan and Blue Nile.

In addition, the convention created governing institutions for the party. A 27-member Political Bureau (PB) was created, which included the chair, three deputy chairs, a secretary general, and two deputies to the secretary general (one for the North and the other for the South). A National Liberation Council (NLC) was also created, which encompassed 275 members of whom 80 percent were to be elected from states and 25 percent should be women. The convention was to meet every five years and the NLC once a year, while the PB would meet whenever the party chairman determined or as a result of a request to the chair by one-third of its members. Deplorably, while the PB chair called numerous meetings, the NLC did not hold a single meeting after May 2008 when it had its first and last meeting.

Despite numerous calls by NLC members to the SPLM secretariat general to convene a meeting for that body as per the party's constitution, those calls were disregarded. In effect, the NLC was expected to deliberate on the party's programs immediately after the conclusion of the meetings of the second convention, but that did not happen. Accordingly, the NLC decided to entrust that mission to the PB, with a view to presenting its recommendation for approval at the next meeting of the NLC. In what came across as a tennis game, the PB referred the matter to its specialized committees and the relevant secretariats of the party. However, neither were the PB's specialized committees established at the time, nor, when formed, did they hold a single meeting up to the end of the interim period, let alone carry out the missions entrusted to them by NLC.

As the referendum approached, murmurings within the NLC forced the PB to call for an NLC meeting to take place on September 15, 2010, more than two years after its establishment. Regardless of party rules on the regularity of meetings, the convocation of that meeting became imperative as the referendum was only four months away. If there was one event on which the NLC should have deliberated, that would have been the referendum that was to determine the future of the country and the party. In truth, that meeting did not take place because the party chairman sensed that the sudden urge to call an NLC meeting—already two years overdue—was impelled by the desire of some PB members to rally that body behind the cause of secession. Having been wary that SPLM NLC members from the geographic North, including those from South Kordofan and Blue Nile, might create complications, the chairman decided to put the whole issue on ice. By hindsight, that wise decision staved off an irascible breakup of the SPLM.

7. Shortfalls in Economic Policy Articulation and Implementation

The restructured SPLM did not live up to two basic expectations: translating the SPLM economic plans adopted in 2000 and 2004 into feasible programs of action and marshaling those programs through the Government of South Sudan, which it was leading, and the Government of National Unity, in which it was the major partner to the NCP. As explained earlier, the SPLM's economic agenda, though paying special attention to South Sudan, never lost sight of the party's national responsibility, especially toward economically marginalized groups in Sudan. All the same, slogans relating to SPLM's vision and mission continued to roar in public rallies, and the most garrulous SPLM leaders never ceased singing, with a delirium of desire, hymns to Garang's treasured ideas such as taking the towns to rural areas. Above all, the vision of the party and its leader was about delivering results in education, health services, and poverty eradication; ending economic marginalization; and setting the stage for the emergence of a robust self-reliant economy. As it were, that vision was virtually turned into a fetish rather than a feasible action plan that addressed real problems in a real world. Effectively, Garang wrote in his introductory remark to the "Strategic Framework for War-to-Peace Transition": "The aim is a community-driven development paradigm that promotes the concept of taking towns and services to the people in rural areas instead of the conventional development paradigm that results in attracting rural people to towns and trapping them in slums with a consequent reduced quality of life." This, he said "will be the SPLM's contribution to development economics." The fact that the rural populace continued to gravitate into urban centers in search of illusory green pastures proved beyond a doubt that the rural economy had come to grief, while the hymns of taking towns to rural areas became louder.

Being true to his cause, Garang came out with clear plan to achieve that economic goal as reflected in the matrix displayed above (see page 415) Underachievement by the SPLM in this regard might have been due to a lack of capacity to translate theoretical postulates to implementable plans of action. That, as Ashraf Ghani advised, could not be achieved without separation of the political from the managerial and uplifting the professional capacity of party managers. For two decades the SPLM leadership structures were permeated with a military culture. As a result, it was not easy to exclude from government and party managerial ranks SPLM cadres who gave the better part of their lives to the party in order to shift the balance of power toward those with experiences and skills that would match the new tasks at hand. Aware of this situation, the second SPLM convention resolved, under the title "Capacity Building and Cadre Development," to "develop a comprehensive strategy and programs of institution capacity building and human resources development in **order to transform the SPLM into an efficient political organ capable of realizing its objectives**" (emphasis added).[27] That resolution was almost forgotten. Sure enough, the party organized many external visits for top- and middle-level cadres to meet with their counterparts in like-minded parties or to be tutored on the art of party management and popular mobilization. But party management and popular mobilization, though important for party functions, should not have supplanted other cardinal party duties like translating social and economic strategies into programs. That was a job that could only be achieved when the party had been equipped with its own in-house planners and programmers supported by intellectual backstopping by party officers versed in economics, law, information technology, administration, and management. With the profusion of party cadres who were able, ready, and willing to serve their party in their respective fields of expertise, the problem was not paucity of competent party workers, but the immortalization of the culture of command that Ghani warned against. Hence, both the SPLM's economic blueprints and Ghani's report became of archival value at the party headquarters.

In the case of the government, it was unquestionably operating within a crippling environment, given the very low base from which it started. Yet, there were observable achievements by the government of South Sudan in building physical and social infrastructures and having functional governments at both regional and state levels. In a recent report on Sudan, the World Bank stated that in addition to the creation of functional governments at all administrative levels, "substantial rebuilding has taken place with rehabilitation and construction of key structures. A significant number of roads have been built and/or repaired and education and health facilities established across the region."[28] Admirable as those achievements had been, without clear prioritization of expenditure, neither would there be meaningful economic growth that delivers real peace dividends to the people, nor would the South Sudan government be practically able to realize the country's potentialities. As the World Bank observed, "Nowhere in the country is the gap between economic reality and unrealized potential greater than in South Sudan."[29]

The most serious economic challenge that faced the government of South Sudan was the gnawing gap in poverty levels between classes and within states. For that reason, both the national and southern Sudan constitutions described poverty eradication as the overarching goal of development.[30] Also, the constitution of the new republic established very clear and ambitious objectives for economic development. Article 37 (1) identified these objectives as eradication of poverty, attainment of the U.N. Millennium Development Goals in Sudan, guaranteeing equitable distribution of wealth, redressing income inequalities, and achieving a decent standard of living for the people of South Sudan. The same article in subparagraph (2) enjoined government, at all levels, to develop the economy in order to:

i.   Achieve prosperity through policies that increase production and assure an efficient and self-reliant economy.

ii. Ensure sustainable management and utilization of natural resources, including land, water, petroleum, minerals, fauna, and flora, for the benefit of the people.

iii. Facilitate development of the private sector, particularly indigenous entrepreneurs.

iv. Encourage and expedite rural development as a strategy for averting urban-biased development and policies that have been responsible for the neglect of rural communities.

The situation in South Sudan earnestly calls for such policies. According to a survey made in 2009 by the Southern Sudan Center for Census, Statistics, and Evaluation (SSCCSE), 50.4 percent of the people of southern Sudan were below the poverty line (poverty line calculated at 72.9 Sudanese pounds per person per month). The survey also reported that with an average monthly per capita consumption in southern Sudan calculated at 100 Sudanese pounds, significant variations were observed between the rural and urban poor (88 and 168 pounds, respectively). Among the poor, the average monthly consumption per person was only 39 Sudanese pounds. Those variations were also noticed between regions, with Greater Equatoria and Greater Upper Nile being the highest spenders (144 Sudanese pounds per person per month), while Greater Bahr el Ghazal remained with the lowest consumption level (60 Sudanese pounds per person per month) as well as the region with the highest level of poverty incidence—61.6 percent of its population were classified as poor.[31]

8. Delivering the Dividends of Peace

In its report referred to above, the World Bank reviewed Sudan's efforts to achieve growth and development and revealed some disturbing facts, especially regarding delivery of peace dividends.[32] The report maintained that "to deliver peace dividends and increase the likelihood of continued peace for the country, development of a medium-term growth strategy is a high priority for the South. Economic growth results in, and from, higher productivity and incomes, and a true peace dividend results in the transition from crisis and relief to sustained development." This, the report said "will contribute to all targets of [the government of South Sudan's] mandate: security and avoidance of conflict, higher employment, and the well-being of the population." This conclusion would take us back to advice Ghani had given to the SPLM before the government of South Sudan assumed power in Juba. In that advice he urged the SPLM to build on its physical, economic, and moral strength in order to succeed in the goals it had been struggling to reach for two decades. Achievement of these goals was entirely in the hands of the SPLM and the government it was leading, and both institutions were neither shorn of development strategies and economic transformation blueprints nor a guiding compass. What was lacking in the eyes of many political and economic analysts of the South Sudan dilemma was political will and perceptive understanding by its leaders of what the SPLM's greatest achievements—peace and liberation—meant. Peace is not solely manifested in the silencing of guns and cessation of hostilities, and liberation shall never be complete until swards are beaten into ploughshares and spears into pruning hooks so that implements of war become tools of development that liberate people from the servitude of poverty.

The Strategic Framework document, without equivocation, made poverty eradication the core of its economic philosophy. To that end, it affirmed that "agriculture is the engine of, and the key to, growth in South Sudan [where] more

318

than three quarters of the population live in rural or semi-rural areas and [their] labor force is engaged in agriculture." Heedful of the risk of dependency on oil at the expense of agriculture, the document went on to say: "Oil is a nonrenewable natural resource and we cannot anchor our development on it. Thus, our rationale for making agriculture the engine of economic growth to achieve effective poverty eradication is premised on the reality that 95 percent of our population [in South Sudan] live in rural and semirural areas." The document concluded: "In short, **the policy of the SPLM** will be based on using oil to literally **fuel agriculture** as the engine of growth" (emphasis added). Evidently, the document did not seek to underrate the contribution of the oil industry to Sudan's economy, since it was thanks to oil that Sudan became the fourth largest recipient of foreign direct investment in sub-Saharan Africa.

The booming oil sector left agriculture lagging behind in both North and South Sudan. According to International Monetary Fund figures (2007), Sudan's total export revenues reached $5.813 billion, of which $5.244 billion was derived from oil resources. Accordingly, non-oil revenues (mainly from agricultural products) were reduced to a skimpy $569 million, less than what Sudan's export earnings from agriculture used to be before the oil bliss. Those earnings were even less than earnings from agricultural exports in neighboring non-oil-producing countries Kenya and Uganda in that year. If that was the case at the national level, there was no reason why the South should have followed suit. One of the main reasons the Strategic Framework document gave agriculture the priority it had given was the alleviation of rural poverty. Both the national government and the government of South Sudan are constitutionally bound to reduce poverty by half by the year 2014. How on earth could that goal be achieved without reducing rural poverty. That was one reason John Garang made the concept "taking towns to rural areas" not only the pride and joy of his economic strategy, but also an exemplar of policy. Much as that policy can put a stop to the gravitation of rural populace to urban centers, its main objective is to rehabilitate the rural economy in order to release the immense potential of the rural work force, boost Southern Sudan's economy, and ameliorate the life quality of its people.

Beneficiaries of Garang's 180-day program were also to include citizens who, directly or indirectly, suffered from war: orphans, widows, incapacitated warriors, and herdsmen who lost their assets during the wars, including SPLM's own internal wars. Insensitivity to the woes of those hapless citizens is regrettable for two reasons. First, because it would reflect ingratitude to the thousands who gave their lives for the SPLM's struggle precisely against neglect and marginalization by former governments, and second, because it would constitute a threat to internal security. Nothing would be more threatening to public peace than a hungry and angry man or woman with a gun in their hands. Admittedly, commissions and ministries were formed to carry out those tasks, but without proper programming, allocation of resources, and follow-up, those institutions would only serve one purpose: providing jobs for the political elites who manage them. Fortunately, after five years in office, the government of South Sudan resolved to create a pension fund for veterans, which is a step in the right direction.

In all truth, had the SPLM succeeded in better articulating and operationalizing the party's policies proposed six years earlier, southern Sudan would have been relieved from the embarrassment of importing fruits, vegetables, bottled water, and even milk and eggs from neighboring countries. Incredibly, some senior SPLM and government of South Sudan officers never ceased to claim that southern Sudan was poised to be the "bread basket" of Africa and the Arab world. Evidently, southern, as well as northern, Sudan have the potential to be just that, but in the situation in which they are waddling, such a claim remains an illusion. Before making South Sudan the bread basket for anyone, it has to first and foremost ensure household food security within its own borders. Sadly, in 2009, the government of South Sudan Ministry of Agriculture and Forestry announced a grain shortage in southern Sudan rendering the states of Unity, North Bahr el Ghazal, Jonglei, East Equatoria, and Warrap food-insecure. One reason for that dire situation was the unpardonable failure to change the traditional mode of agricultural production in the region; nearly all the cereal production continued to be obtained through household gardening. The 1,000 rural animation centers proposed by Garang could have gone a long way toward enhancing food production methods and providing the basic infrastructure that would attract the private sector to invest in medium-, if not large-scale, farming. The SPLM could have also drawn upon India's experience under Indira Ghandi in the 1960s; Ghandi's greatest achievement during her rule was making India, with its one billion inhabitants, self-sufficient in food grains within one decade and after years of famine that was considered an inevitable phenomenon. Indeed India had been condemned to that fate by no less than the Nobel Prize Swedish economist, Gunnar Myrdal.[33]

Persistent grain deficit in southern Sudan, especially the coarse grains, resulted in a nontransparent purchase of grains in 2009 to meet the food deficit, purportedly for a cost of over 2.8 billion Sudanese pounds. In that year five states, including Warrap, the president's own state, were declared food-insecure by the Ministry of Agriculture. The purchase, however, turned into a fiasco as there was no dependable evidence that the grains were delivered to the people for whom they were bought; the only evidence of delivery was dubious certificates by some administrators acknowledging receipt of thousands of tons of cereals in areas where there wasn't a single grain silo. As some commentators observed, if grains worth that amount of money were actually delivered, stockpiles in southern Sudan would have been beholden from Kampala, if not Khartoum. That fiasco should have been turned into a *cause célèbre* and given officialdom sleepless nights, yet pressures to pay those behind the dubious deals came from the most improbable source: the Southern Sudan Legislative Assembly, the prime public oversight agency in the country. At long last a committee comprising the ministers for legal affairs, finance and economic planning, and commerce and industry was formed by the president to investigate that disastrous deal.[34] During his visit to the United Nations in October 2011, President Salva Kiir again highlighted the matter in briefings to the international media of South Sudan. Nonetheless, the fat cats who benefited from that deal are still at large in Juba, Khartoum, and Kampala.

9. International Do-Gooders: Much Ill and Little Good

Without absolving the government of South Sudan from responsibility for putting its house in order and properly identifying its priorities, southern Sudan development partners also failed to live up to the commitments they made in April 2005 at the Oslo conference. On that occasion, funders from Western countries committed themselves to make $4.5 billion available to help Sudan sustain peace, build administrative capacity and physical infrastructure, and deliver basic services. The funds, we recall, were to be managed by a Multi-Donor Trust Fund (MDTF) run by the World Bank. Nevertheless, by the end of 2009, of the $524 million dollars allocated to agreed-upon projects for the initial phase, only $181 million were dispersed. That was the situation at a time when the CPA was nearing its end (July 9, 2011). As a result, bilateral donors established their own independent recovery fund for southern Sudan: the Sudan Recovery Fund for South Sudan (SRF-SS). That fund was jointly managed by the government of South Sudan and other contributors, namely, the United Nations Development Program, Holland, and the United Kingdom.

Without underestimating the efforts made by the MDTF at the planning level such as aiding the government of South Sudan in ensuring effective prioritization of development plans, sequencing of projects, and improving (or struggling to improve) financial management, the MDTF's record in the rollout of committed funds was pitiful, as evidenced by the amounts disbursed up to the middle of the second half of the interim period. The culprit, as always, had been rigidities in, and bottlenecks caused by, the World Bank's procedures and its inability to remove these rigidities to meet a situation of emergency. Regrettably, that was one issue that the 2009 comprehensive report by the World Bank did not comprehend.[35]

Major donors also took shelter behind the Darfur conflict, claiming that resources were diverted to humanitarian relief in Darfur. That was a flimsy reason because Darfur is Darfur and southern Sudan is southern Sudan. Besides, Oslo funds were basically and voluntarily earmarked by donors to consolidate peace in southern Sudan after two decades of war wreckage and ruination. Apparently, with few exceptions, Oslo donors were under pressure in their own countries to give more attention to Darfur. The lesson that southern Sudan and others should draw from this episode is that external economic support is, in essence, a matter of power relationship in which pressures by domestic lobbies take precedence over the needs of recipients.

Lack of absorptive capacity had also been the recurrent justification for nondisbursement of pledged funds, even though human and institutional capacity building topped the priorities established by funding countries. Could the reason for not achieving that goal be that the government of South Sudan was averse to building its institutional and human capacity? The answer to this question came in a report commissioned by the U.S. Agency for International Development (USAID) in June 2010. That report concluded that "capacity building efforts in South Sudan are currently neither strategic nor focused." The report went on to say that "with few exceptions [the] objectives are sweeping, unspecific, detached from actual performance, impossible to measure, and thus unlikely to secure."[36] Hence, even the limited disbursed financial resources (compared to pledges) made available to southern Sudan were dissipated through lack of policy coherence. Ashraf Ghani *et al.* made a very pertinent remark on similar situations. They said: "The international community cannot operate through tools and   processes as currently conceived, with diplomatic and development personnel working in organizational silos and failing to fully understand, collectively, the nature of their environment, the objectives of their intervention, its time horizon, and the resources that need to be mobilized for its realization."[37]

Investors and academics reached another conclusion about external aid. A South African investor, Ian Alsworth-Elvey, who was reported to have spent $50 million in a Juba brewery, remarked that aid agencies were distorting the economy and the labor market. The investor, who had been employing 250 workers, said that no sooner had he trained locals in accounting skills than they were snapped up by aid agencies. Another distortion referred to by the investor was reflected in the exorbitant rents for hotel rooms and houses in Juba. He said, "I am staying at the Ritz in Chicago, and I am spending less than what I spend on some crappy hotel in Juba."[38] The most unsettling comment, however, came from William Easterly, a New York University economist and author of *White Man's Burden: Why the West's Efforts to Aid the Rest Have Done So Much Ill and So Little Good.* On aid to South Sudan, Easterly said: "You're flooding the place with aid and outside experts speaking in inconsistent voices and you have no body in the center."[39] Obviously, the key phrase in Easterly's comment is "the center," and who should have been at that center other than the ruling party and the government it led? That self-evident truth is also shared by observant aid advisors. Based on empirical evidence, Australia's principal advisor on aid wrote: "There is a longstanding and substantial body of evidence to show that real and sustained reform essentially comes from within the country itself." Reform, he said, "cannot be imposed through aid conditionality; nor can it be bought even by large promises of aid from bilateral and multilateral development."[40] Far from calling for the international community to disengage from the South Sudan development scene, or belittling that country's pressing need for external technical advice and assistance, it is maintained that without the government of South Sudan in the driving seat of development planning, South Sudan's plans shall end up being distorted and irrelevant. Socioeconomic development is about nation building, and no nation is known to have subcontracted nation building to others.

10. The Elite and the Fate of Their Government

For over two decades the SPLM regularly railed against GOS ruling elite for perpetuating a dysfunctional and self-serving economic development paradigm. If that paradigm was excoriated by the SPLM, it was only because it concentrated wealth in one area (North Sudan's riverain regions and urban centers), while abandoning the rest of the country. For two decades the late SPLM leader had been drawing attention to this phenomenon and warning that economic marginalization would lead the marginalized to rebel, since the cost of rebellion to them would be zero. That was a caveat that had been passed over by the ruling elite in Juba, where administrative expenditure on salaries, emoluments, perks, as well as a penchant for overseas travel and acquisition of expensive vehicles had never been measured in relation to funds required to meet the basic needs of the impoverished millions, the so-called marginalized people of southern Sudan. Even the South Sudan Legislative Assembly, the prime public overseer of government performance and the institution that brings together the representatives of the people lost no time in joining that gravy train by demanding salaries and perks for the heads of parliamentary committees commensurate to those offered to ministers, rather than calling for the scaling down of administrative expenditure. In the meantime, it was not difficult for the two institutions to realize the impact of this extravagance on activities that could have saved the rural populace from being entrapped in poverty. Inadvertence to such a serious matter not only reflected a glaring betrayal of SPLM's vision, but it also exhibited oblivion to basic human justice. Such an attitude would hardly befit a party whose declared mission had been putting an end to historical injustices.

To say that the people of southern Sudan were not fazed by the misdeeds of their political elite would be a grave underestimation of people's discernment. For example, in 2007 the National Democratic Institute (NDI) published a damning report based on a series of interviews with citizen focus groups in different locations throughout southern Sudan. Albeit a mere snapshot of public opinion, the report was revealing in that it indicated a plurality of attitudes toward CPA implementation. Even though the interviewed groups expressed pride in the SPLM for its role in bringing peace as well as respect for Salva Kiir as a leader, there was wide criticism of the government of South Sudan regarding corruption, tribalism, nondelivery of services, and slow infrastructure development. These critical remarks were also reiterated in the burgeoning news media in southern Sudan. Could it be that the Juba political elite did not realize that the fate of any government rested, to a large degree, on how ordinary citizens judged its performance in establishing peace in their community and uplifting their lives?

More disquieting was a recent study by a research team from the London School of Economics, with the help of Southern Sudan Peace Commission (SSPC) and the University of Juba's Center for Peace and Development Studies.[41] The study recognized academics in Juba and nongovernmental organizations in southern Sudan for their courage in raising alarms on matters that were apparently of little or no concern to official public overseers. The study team, which came out with harrowing observations on the misuse of resources, had undertaken 300 qualitative interviews with target groups, including government officials, ordinary citizens, nongovernmental organizations, and United Nations staff. On the misuse of funds, the report included the following implicating assessment: "The research team found numerous examples of situations where individuals appeared to act without reference to established conventional notions of social restraint, openly taking resources for their personal gain, acting in ways that violated ideas about moral probity, or in ways that were simply criminal or unconstitutional."[42] The most serious report, however, was presented by Stephen Wondu, auditor general of the South Sudan Legislative Assembly, which he submitted to the assembly in Juba in 2011. The report revealed the names of hundreds people who were receiving salaries without corroborating evidence of their even being employed; cash withdrawal from banks by the end of the fiscal year without supporting documents, which according to the auditor general, meant that the funds were "misplaced, misused, or misappropriated"; and acquisitions in Khartoum purportedly for use by the government of South Sudan, of property without following regular   government procedures. The auditor general also reported that a high percentage of contracts awarded in 2006 was not concluded on the basis of purchase procedures. More damning was the auditor general's conclusion: "Today this country stands at a crossroads; we either adjust our priorities in favor of human development and poverty alleviation, or we risk the loss of the peaceful and prosperous South Sudan we all sacrificed so much to earn."

Another worrisome aspect of the misuse of public resources is the extravagance that some senior government officials exhibit in the manner of the *nouveau riche*, not the modesty expected from "revolutionaries." Such extravagance is also not congruent with the conditions of a country that ranks among the world poorest. To illustrate, two-thirds of the population of southern Sudan are below the poverty level, child mortality is the highest in the world (135 out of 1,000 children do not reach their fifth birthday), maternal mortality is also the highest in the world (2,037 out of 100,000 women die from pregnancy or childbirth-related complications), and 60 percent of the rural populace lacks safe drinking water. These, and only these, figures should have determined priorities in public expenditure. For sure, neither the author nor any other southern Sudan observer would count on senior government officers to lead a spartan and straitlaced life. Nevertheless, all friends of South Sudan shall become very concerned when its senior government officials luxuriate at public expense with no pang of guilt. At no point did the majority of these wrongdoers realize that they were robbing from government coffers funds that were likely needed to save the lives of dying mothers or their offspring.

In tow with the mismanagement of public resources was the emergence of a dubious business class. Both phenomena had completely distorted national development priorities. The Interim Constitution of Southern Sudan urged the government to "facilitate the development of the private sector, particularly indigenous entrepreneurs and to establish and develop a viable private sector capable of participating effectively in reconstruction and development of South Sudan (Article 40 (c))." Based on these constitutional demands, the government of South Sudan was expected to encourage and nurture local entrepreneurship with a view to widening growth and employment opportunities for southern Sudanese citizens. Local entrepreneurship would have, in addition, put an end to the assumption prevalent among the elite of South Sudan that the only job an educated man or woman should ever yearn for is government employment. Aware of this phenomenon, the president of the government of South Sudan pointed out that in addition to able ministers South Sudan "is also in need of adept parliamentarians, competent department heads, bankers, and captains of industry." He also warned that the "prevailing culture that the only post worth aspiring for is a ministerial post shall, if it continues, devitalize Southern Sudan."[43] As it were, the continued scramble for ministerial posts confirmed that the devitalization of society was a matter of little concern to those who were jostling for such posts.

Tens of thousands of southern Sudanese, inside the country as well as throughout the diaspora, have gained experience or tutored themselves in business management. It is from this category of citizens, who wish to turn their expertise to advantage, that a class of indigenous entrepreneurs shall issue. Rather than encouraging and nurturing these upcoming businessmen or aspiring young men and women with a view to creating indigenous entrepreneurship, some murky decision makers in Juba opted for enabling fortune hunters from within and outside South Sudan to avail themselves to government contracts and government-mediated bank loans in lieu of illicit payoffs. In almost all these cases, wayward government officers acted illegally (outside government rules or structures) to grant favors to family and next of kin in addition to the perverse soldiers of fortune who had no time for clean and arduous business enterprise. Evidently, such government officers neither cared for the panorama of South Sudan economy, which was 98 percent dependent on oil revenues, nor for the challenges that this situation posed to the economic health of the country. For example, a recent International Monetary Fund report warned that the high oil prices that provided the basis for economic recovery in Sudan in the first decade of this century shall be cut by half in 2020.[44] Even so, reliable sources within the United Nations, World Bank, and the U.S. administration revealed to South Sudan's leadership that illicit payoffs to officials traced in foreign bank accounts added up to hundreds of millions of dollars. If this illicit money amassed by sticky fingers in the government were directed to revamping agriculture, it would have saved South Sudan the embarrassment of raising distress signals about famine only six months after the country's independence. In mid-December 2001, the United Nations World Food Program announced a plan to "provide emergency assistance to 2.7 million hungry and conflict-affected people in 2012," in addition to "providing highly nutritious supplementary foods to more than 500,000 children, pregnant women, and nursing mothers."[45]

This behavior cultivated a rent-seeking culture[46] that denied legitimate players equal opportunity in competitive business. Rent-seeking symptoms in South Sudan were generally a result of a manipulation of the economy instead of the encouragement of activities and transactions that would have produced added wealth. This aggravated distortions in the economy caused by ethnic polarization, which according to development experts, was less likely to provide higher levels of social capital.[47] According to research on the impact of secession on the country's economy, these distortions are an outgrowth of the "dysfunctional political economy of rent that infested the larger Sudanese state."[48] The researcher disputed a current impression among southern Sudanese that all their woes would be over with secession [without being aware] that splitting a fragile state could create more far-reaching political challenges, more so when the political economy of the state is rentier." The researcher went on to ask: "How can the state avoid the tripartite possibilities of unproductive autocracy, institutionalized rent-driven perpetual corruption and explosive communal violence?"[49] All those are indicators of state failure.

According to Seth Kaplan, an anatomist of failing states: "The businesspeople who flourish [in failing states] are not those with the best education or the best ideas but those connected by blood or marriage to the ruling clique, or those skilled at manipulating and bribing officials in charge of handing out licenses and contracts."[50] Stories abounded in South Sudan media about shady deals for the procurement of vehicles, foodstuff, construction, and telecommunication contracts, invariably with bogus contractors or redundant middlemen. This phenomenon, if allowed to continue, shall ultimately give rise to what the former Kenyan anticorruption tsar, John Githongo, has called "matatu capitalism,"[51] rather than to the emergence of a business class that shall make viable contributions to the economy of the country in the manner prescribed by article 37 of the Constitution of South Sudan. Matatu in Kenyan Swahili as refers to transport mini-vans which are privately owned and known for their disrespect for traffic rules. Instead of living up to the values they had been preaching for two decades, wayward elites chose with good grace to emulate Kenya's matatu capitalists. To add insult to injury, they flagrantly consorted with shady Khartoum businessmen who were known to have made their way to wealth in northern Sudan by a winding stair. Though sunk in iniquity, these businessmen were often tolerated on the northern side of the border for sharing part of their loot with the ruling party as a contribution to a common cause, whatever that cause was. On the southern side of the border, however, the loot was shared solely with few sticky-fingered kleptomaniacs.

But before seeking from outside Africa an *elixir vital* for curing South Sudan's ailment, it would be appropriate to draw comparison with the experiences of an African country that had succeeded in averting the disastrous path South Sudan might hurtle into. This country is Botswana, which like South Sudan, is landlocked, its size almost identical to that of southern Sudan (600,370 square kilometers), and its population about one-fourth of that of the new republic. But unlike Botswana, which had only 50 university graduates at independence, southern Sudan at present is endowed with tens of thousands of university graduates from Sudanese and foreign universities. Botswana was not racked with the problems from which southern Sudan had suffered such as wars, ethnic rivalries, and destabilization from its North. Nevertheless, Botswana is also a tribal society with an economy dominated by pastoralism and, like southern Sudan, it started from zero-level development. Also, with apartheid South Africa as its neighbor, Botswana was not in shortage of troublesome neighbors.

The success of Botswana, however, lay first in the ability of its elite to merge inherited decision-making practices with modern government applications bequeathed to them by the British. Traditionally, Botswana's tribal leaders were accountable to their people, and from the start, its elite (mainly cattle owners) focused on development plans that would enhance traditional wealth, values, and culture. To that end they concentrated efforts on rural development, including building rural roads, setting up modern ranching, and giving priority to education and human and animal health care. Even the discovery and exploitation of large reserves of mineral wealth, especially diamonds, did not detract the Botswana elite from that rural-centered path of development[52] the way southern and northern Sudan's political elites were led away from agriculture by oil. If Botswana succeeded in making a quantum leap in socioeconomic development, it was because it ensured stability within its borders and prudently managed its economy. Consequently, Botswana's gross domestic product per capita, which was US $283 (in constant US $2000) at the time of independence in 1966, rocketed in 2010 to $14,800, according to International Monetary Fund estimates. By 2006, Botswana became one of the upper-middle income countries, according to World Bank's world development index. Botswana's experience is one that rent seekers from oil wealth in both North and South Sudan would do well to take note of.

11. Integrity in Public Life

Lack of integrity in public life in any country is always a source of disquietude to citizens and governors. In Sudan, in general, and South Sudan, in particular, corruption in public office had become a cause of worry to citizens, civil society organizations, and the media for the last two decades. Transparency International the non-governmental organization that monitors corporate and political corruption in the world, classified Sudan, as it existed before the separation of the South, among the countries that ranked lowest in the scale of transparency in government, alongside Iraq, Myanmar, Afghanistan, and Somalia.[53] The report maintained that "corruption continues to lurk where opacity rules, where institutions still need strengthening, and where governments have failed to implement anticorruption legal frameworks."[54]

Aside from the overarching moral obligation to protect public assets, governments at national and subnational levels are constitutionally enjoined to fight corrupt practices, as explained earlier. Corruption, in short, is characterized by abuse of public office or position of trust so as to gain undue advantage. That is normally manifested in fraud, embezzlement, bribery, kickbacks, favoritism, or having direct or indirect (familial) interest in a decision. Many of those modes of corruption were reasonably established in the annual reports of the auditor general in Khartoum, and since 2011, in the reports of the auditor general in South Sudan. On the other hand, both the CPA and the constitutions (Interim National Constitution and Interim Constitution of Southern Sudan) emphasized the importance of accountability in the use of public funds and assets. The CPA, as an illustration, provided that "all levels of government shall hold all incomes and revenues in public accounts and subject to public scrutiny and accountability" (12.3 Wealth Sharing Protocol), while the Interim National Constitution provided, under the title "Morals and Public Integrity," that the state shall "enact laws and establish institutions to eliminate corruption, inhibit abuse of power, and ensure integrity in public life" (article 16 (12)). None of the institutions heralded by the constitution was created at the national level. It wasn't until January 2011, as the interim period was about to come to an end, that President Bashir announced his plan to create an anticorruption body. That declaration coincided with the shattering political earthquake that hit Tunisia and Egypt, leading to revelations of high-level corruption in the governments of those countries. Nonetheless, like in all totalitarian regimes, the merger of the state and the party made it possible for government and party officers to evade public oversight and encouraged creativity with accounting. Incontestably, when those who have fingers on the till and their public overseers are one and the same, constitutional edicts about accountability become meaningless.

In southern Sudan, the Interim Constitution of Southern Sudan catered in article 148 for the creation of an anticorruption commission charged with protection of public property and combating administrative malpractices in public institutions. Those practices comprised nepotism, favoritism, tribalism, sectionalism, gender discrimination, bribery, and embezzlement. The same provisions were maintained in the Transitional Constitution of the Republic of South Sudan, 2011. Nevertheless, southern Sudan has not been immune to the same ills from which North Sudan had suffered. Some of South Sudan's closest friends, as intimated earlier, drew the attention of its leaders to proven cases of misappropriation of funds and unlawful enrichment by certain government officers. The majority, if not all, of those accused were down-at-the-heels before assuming office. Those friends[55] were not only disturbed by that sudden wealth, but also by the apparent impunity with which corruption was treated by the government of South Sudan. This view was equally expressed by independent American analysts such as Thomas Talley, policy officer in the U.S. Africa Command. Talley wrote: "Even if we look past the fact that the SPLA has plenty of blood on their hands given the length and savagery of conflict, we still have to focus on the current reality. The current reality is that corruption in southern Sudan, particularly within the government, is stalling economic development."[56]

In addition to the creation of the Anti-Corruption-Commission ACC in southern Sudan, the president of the government of South Sudan in his first term of office unceremoniously ended the services of two ministers of finance and dismissed senior officials in that ministry for conduct unbefitting their duties. While these sanctions received applause, the question still remained as to why other government officers who were no less culpable of similar offences were allowed to get off scot-free with their illicit wealth. Cases relating to fiddling with government money for the purchase of vehicles, in addition to grains referred to earlier, were reported to the ACC, but for inexplicable reasons, no action was taken. That gave rise to one of two conjectures: either the corrupt officers were above culpability, or the SPLM appeared to be protecting its own. Apart from questions raised by South Sudan friends about this runway graft, similar questions were often asked by good and law-abiding citizens in South Sudan. When all is said and done, it is the sons and daughters of the land, and not foreign concerned observers, who need explanation regarding the continuance of corruption and why known abusers of public money are invulnerable to the law.

Despicable as it is, corruption cannot be analyzed solely on ethical and legal grounds; there are cultural, social, and institutional factors that allow that vice to persist and, in some instances, to be tolerated by society. This might be one explanation why the public remained passive about corrupt practices by co-ethnic colleagues in government. With such perception of public responsibility, those officers viewed government as a hazy institution and the people of South Sudan as an indistinguishable human quantum. Thus, despite all the populist brouhaha, the offending officers had never developed an emotional commitment to the "people" of the South, nor did they ever seem to realize that by injuring their government they were also injuring their communities and themselves.

Ethnic nepotism, all the same, is not a peculiarity of southern Sudanese. The term, according to sociobiologists, denotes the preference of people to those who belong to their own race or same ethnic group than to all other groups. However, in modern society, ethnic polarization hinders nation building and curtails the state's ability to deliver public goods in an equitable fashion. By its nature, ethnic nepotism also impedes the enlargement of social capital in society. American foreign affairs expert Robert Rotberg points out that "living standards deteriorate rapidly as elites deliver financial reward only to favored families, clans, or small groups [and] corruption flourishes as ruling cadres systematically skim the few resources available [or] stash their ill-begotten gains in hard-to-trace foreign bank accounts."[57] This phenomenon is becoming increasingly evident in South Sudan, including practices like the ones reported above by the Dustin research team,[58] which were too nefarious to contemplate in a young government with puritanical claims.

Leaving aside the academic research of sociobiologists on ethnic nepotism, there are also constitutional and legal rules that proscribe abuse of public funds and political alerts against corruption. The most significant political alert had been made by Salva Kiir at a time when the movement was in the thick of the struggle. In the confrontation at Rumbek (2004) between Garang and his deputy, corruption was one of the issues that figured high in the litany of complaints made by Salva Kiir against John Garang's management style. That statement came at a time when public assets were almost nonexistent within the SPLM realm, and the authority of the movement over the land it occupied was notional. Nevertheless, Salva Kiir's words still resonate today. Said he: "I would also like to say something about rampant corruption in the Movement. At the moment some members of the Movement have formed private companies, bought houses, and have huge bank accounts in foreign countries. I wonder what kind of system are we going to establish in South Sudan considering ourselves indulged in this practice."

By these words Salva Kiir established the standard by which people would measure his own performance.

On the other hand, southern communities are known to have had from time immemorial societal norms of behavior aimed at curtailing socially reproachable acts like thievery. These communities, especially Nilotics, were known to be loath to thieves, and the only punishment they normally reserved for them had been banishment from society. Nevertheless, in several cases when public officers were caught in the act of misappropriating public funds, they often rushed to claim that the whole community to which they belonged was being victimized. This sordid coercion has to be dismissed for what it is: a cover-up for criminal acts. The noble communities to which those miscreants belong shall never accommodate, let alone identify themselves with, thieves.

12. Leader with Two Hats

The dual role of the chairman of the SPLM as first vice president at the national level and president of the government of South Sudan at the regional level imposed an onerous task on Salva Kiir. That anomalous arrangement was designed with the unique person of John Garang in mind. After leading the movement for over two decades, Garang was perhaps capable of running the South from Khartoum through a web of trusted aides in vital positions in the army (SPLA) and government, while concurrently applying himself to CPA implementation and wining over northern allies to the cause of "New Sudan." Considering those attributes, the task would have been improbable for anyone else. By concentrating political power in his own hands and virtually holding all political ropes, in addition to the charisma with which he waded into politics, Garang turned into a leader with no coeval among his colleagues. Moreover, Salva Kiir's self-effacement and disinclination for political gamesmanship, as well as his total immersion in military affairs during the struggle, not only made him uninterested in politics, but also left no space for him to potter around it.

Even the simultaneous physical presence of the new leader in two places became problematic. Salva Kiir's absence from Khartoum would have created the impression that he was unconcerned about national politics and ambivalent to unity, while his absence from Juba would have made him appear uncommitted to the unity, stability, and reconstruction of southern Sudan. Salva Kiir's engagement in both causes at once could not have been taken without question in the same way Garang's would have been. Moreover, with Salva Kiir as his deputy in Juba, Garang was sure that he had a dependable second-in-command who, by his very nature, shrank from public gaze. Throughout the struggle Salva Kiir remained faithful to the SPLM cause and loyal to its leader despite the passing disagreements between them at Rumbek in 2004 and 2005. Moreover, the SPLM after Garang's demise did not unify in

331

such a way as to allow the new president to delegate responsibilities with the same degree of trust. Much as he had demonstrated an admirable altruism on his nomination as a successor to Garang, and despite his genuine desire to delegate authority, Salva Kiir appeared to have been frequently intimidated by some of the very aides he trusted with political positions.

Be that as it may, Salva Kiir emerged as a unifier and a team player who was always bent on accommodating all shades of opinion within the party as well as among all communities in southern Sudan. That attribute was sometimes taken for indecisiveness or procrastination. But without that deliberative—to some, ponderous—approach, Salva Kiir would not have been able to unite the often fractious southern Sudanese political forces. His patience with those forces was such that he was ready to accommodate infamous political opportunists whom Garang would not have tolerated for two seconds. Despite its oddity, that approach to leadership enabled Salva Kiir to keep his troops intact and lines of communication open with all southern political forces. In the meantime, he maintained cordial relations with Khartoum's political class in both government and opposition. Above all, Salva Kiir preserved respectful working relations with Bashir despite real and perceived efforts by Khartoum to destabilize his government and the unceasing calumniation showered upon him by the media in the national capital, including organs that were known to be sponsored or funded by the NCP.

Despite all its merits, Salva Kiir's approach to leadership had its downside: allowing the self-aggrandizers to take the president for granted, sometimes with utmost indiscretion. In Chapter Eight we touched upon maneuvers by a small group within the president's entourage who attempted to enfold the SPLM chairman while excluding other senior party members from communicating with him. That group, led by what was clandestinely called the Tuic mafia,[59] endeavored during his early years in office to isolate Salva Kiir from mainstream SPLM leadership as well as from famed warriors of the SPLA who were known to have been loyal to him for two decades. Rumors emanating from that group against these officers never ceased up to the end of the first half of the interim period; the rumors included accusations of attempted military coups against the leader. With the exception of a handful, that mafia was peripheral to the SPLA struggle. Not a few of them were lolling around in distant capitals throughout the struggle. Behind all these maneuvers was the desire by an ambitious group of politicians to create an undeserved space for themselves in the upper tiers of the party or government. Salva Kiir, however, proved that he knew better, while the rumormongers revealed their serious underestimation of the commander in chief's faculty to make sound judgment.

Alongside this handful of political mafiosi another group anointed itself as defender and protector of the president. These self-appointed presidential

332

"wardens" were even more harmful, because their only badge of identification had been their familial relations with the president. That relation became more unsettling when the "wardens" began burrowing into matters of politics of which most of them were not up to speed. Those included attempts to keep a tight rein on the leader's activities at the national level or with communities in southern Sudan other than those from which the presumptuous protectors hailed. For instance, attempts were made by that group to thwart the SPLM chairman's historic visits to South Kordofan and Blue Nile, the first by the leader to regions whose sons and daughters stood shoulder-to-shoulder with their comrades from South Sudan throughout the struggle. Much too often the president's movements were frustrated by this group because of alleged threats to his life. Apart from the fact that those threats were figments of the imagination of their authors, such claims were indeed very insulting to the president. First, what type of fool volunteers to become a private security advisor to the commander in chief of the army, the head of government, the comptroller of state finance, and the country's super ambassador at large? Giving his ear to such political trespassers, the president will effectively depreciate all the institutions that he heads. On the other hand, nothing could have been more fatuous than advising a leader who had been fighting in the bushes and marshlands of southern Sudan for over two decades to avoid public rallies held in his honor by his supporters in order to ensure his safety. Salva Kiir, to SPLM members, was known during Garang's life to be the officer who fearlessly commanded SPLA forces in battle. After the cataclysmic death of the late leader, he became the torchbearer of the party's vision and the shepherd who kept his flock united. Reducing a leader with such attributes to a notable of a section or a sultan of a tribe demeans the man and abases leadership. For that reason, Salva Kiir, the first president of the Republic of South Sudan, shall do his party and himself much good if he gives a wide berth to elements who only see in him a local celebrity or godfather of a community. Those closed-minded persons, however ethnically, regionally, or familially close they are to Salva Kiir, shall not add value to him as a political leader or ennoble him as a state president.

Salva Kiir's sedate style of leadership also proved to be counterproductive in another area that figured high in his political program: fighting corruption. That campaign assumed a farcical dimension when looters of public funds continued their larcenous activities despite the president's warning: "zero tolerance to corruption." One reason for the lack of progress in that campaign, it would seem, lay in the president's desire to fight corruption through public pronouncements and subtle warnings. He also seemed not to be ready to unnerve the "big boys" within the party or government, or irritate communities or sections within communities to which the offenders belonged. Corruption is as common a crime as street mugging or shoplifting. Consequently, wrongdoers among the big boys need to be named, shamed, and brought to justice like any other felon. Subtlety is invariably wasted on felons who are not ashamed of their misdeeds. As intimated earlier, there is every reason to believe that not a few of these wrongdoers had modeled themselves on Kenya's political class. According to John Githongo, "Kenyan history has always silently assumed that a minister was also a thief. Those who left office as paupers were laughed at." In order to win and retain public confidence in an "ethnically polarized and politically volatile environment," Githongo averred, "those presenting an anticorruption mandate must initially take on their own ethnicities and fellow party members. It is then when people begin to believe."[60]

If Salva Kiir, for whatever reason, opted in the past to accommodate the worthy and unworthy, after his resounding confirmation by the people of South Sudan across all ethnic divides and his victory in the South Sudan elections, his leadership should no longer be contested. The only way before him now is to cross the Rubicon and move forward. People shall judge him by his success in keeping South Sudan and the SPLM united, in keeping the SPLA under fairly tight control, and for daring to be the first person to raise the issue of corruption within the SPLM/A in the presence of Garang at the Rumbek meeting. But people shall also hold him responsible if, through inattention or lack of direction, he allowed those under him in the party or government to take South Sudan down the slope to state failure as a result of inefficiency in performance or impurity of motive. The territorial integrity of southern Sudan, the welfare of its people, and the reputability of the new republic are much more prized objectives to aim at than pandering to eminently forgettable cliques whose appetite for wealth is insatiable and greed for power unbridled.

At his inauguration as the first president of the Republic of South Sudan, the words Salva Kiir uttered were music to the ears of all those who wished the new state and its president well. Said he: "Our leaders, be they in politics, administration, churches, and the entire civil society are collectively responsible for serving the public interest first, and self last. Those who are unwilling or unable to make the sacrifices required in the public service will not be part of my government. They have options through which to satisfy personal aspirations and pursue other ambition outside government. Transparency and accountability are pivotal. Official corruption has been one of our major challenges during the Interim Period. In order to develop our country and deliver on the important goals of our national development plan, it is critical that we fight corruption with dedication, rigor, and commitment. As President, I pledge to you to do all I can to remove this cancer. We will work closely with our development partners as we move forward."[61] To such words, the good citizens of the new republic as well as well-wishers throughout the world cheered, "Hurrah." Probably, not a few among them, however, added, "We shall wait and see."

334

13. One Ideology: Conflicting Agenda

As the SPLM embarked on a process of change and assumed a new role and new responsibilities as the ruling party in southern Sudan, its internal contradictions became increasingly apparent. These contradictions became more egregious and unconcealed as the referendum approached. The SPLM, during the life of Garang, had maintained its official ideology of a democratic, secular, and united New Sudan. That position was richly elucidated by the late leader in his closing remarks to the Rumbek meeting in 2004. He said: "We must remain constant to our **objective of New Sudan and the right to self-determination**. After six years you will vote either for unity or separation. The allegation that there are separatists in the South led by a unionist, *me*, is a lie. The two scenarios go hand-in-hand. One scenario may fade away and the other survive. Which one survives will greatly depend on your decision to vote for separation or unity when the time comes. Sudan requires equality, and if that becomes accepted, **then there will be no need for a separate country**, and if not, then the northerners will be the ones who are separatists, and not the southerners. **If you achieve the objective of the New Sudan, then why not take the whole country**" (emphasis added).

Six months later, Garang addressed the public at a mass rally in the same town on the occasion of the 22nd anniversary of the SPLM, the first such meeting held after the signature of the CPA. In that address he appropriately focused on two issues: the right to self-determination and the national vocation of the SPLM. On the former he said: "At the end of six years, southerners will vote in a free and internationally monitored referendum on self-determination to choose whether to remain in a united Sudan under the [**one country two system**] arrangement, or opt for an independent southern Sudan. The challenge now for Sudan is to make unity attractive to southern Sudanese so that they vote for it during the referendum. If unity is not made attractive, why would any southerner vote himself or herself into second-class citizenship? If Sudan does not sufficiently and fundamentally change, why should anybody vote to become a servant instead of being a master in his/her own independent house? **Clearly the Sudanese must work hard during the Interim Period to make unity attractive if they want the Sudan to remain united as one country that accommodates all its citizens equally**" (emphasis added).

Those statements were preposterously vandalized in a manner that was slanderous to the late leader and disgraceful to the expurgators. In a memorandum issued by the SPLM Referendum Operations Room[62] dated November 30, 2010, the authors of that memorandum removed from the late leader's statement all references to unity of Sudan, the rationale for it, and the perils attending it. Certainly, southern Sudanese, including SPLM cadres, had umpteen reasons to turn their backs on unity. Nevertheless, the late leader was plenteously aware of the nuances in the unity/separation dialectic and had invariably reflected them in all his speeches. Thus, falsification of Garang's words by neoseparatists in order to legitimize their preferred option was below par. Unity, according to Mahmood Mamdani, is like the self, which "does not develop in linear fashion, in a straight line, from lower to higher levels, as if it were unfolding according to a formula." Mamdani adds that "political unity is the outcome of political struggle, not of utopian blueprints."[63] Such a struggle had been waged by the SPLM/A under Garang's leadership from 1983, in the course of which he made sure that it encompassed all Sudanese people with a view to reform the Sudanese state so that the country would accommodate "all its citizens equally." The story of that struggle, as Mamdani rightly opined, was not "a one-dimensioned story of northern oppression of the South, but there was a subsidiary story: the story of joint North-South struggle against that domination."[64] Armed and nonarmed warriors who joined that struggle from west, east, north, and central Sudan were not legionnaires of the SPLM/A but rebels who believed, like their southern combatants, in the cause of reform.

After Garang's demise pre-existing ideological fissures in the movement began to grow more apparent and were aggravated by the NCP's poor record in CPA implementation. In addition, the NCP's persistent efforts to split the SPLM and the continuing conflict in Darfur only made things worse. These factors combined made the idea of a united New Sudan increasingly untenable to a large number of the SPLM's cadres from South Sudan. In this connection, Jon Temin and Theodore Murphy were not off the mark when they pointed out that "the CPA in many ways was adapted into a regional agreement for governing the south and north-south relations during the interim period [and thus] the southern leadership viewed the CPA's provision for the southern referendum as by far its most crucial component, and made little effort at national reform."[65] And so was Temin and Murphy's remark that the vision of democratic transformation might have died with the death of Garang despite assertions that the CPA had been fully implemented with little grounding in reality, especially when it came to the agreement's democratic transformation agenda.[66] In effect, that issue was completely jettisoned by the NCP while it was made light of by not a few leading SPLM high rankers. The greatest letdown, however, came in April 2010, when the SPLM was on the verge of realizing its historic goal of seizing power in the entire Sudan but decided to give up that goal and opt for secession.[67] Mamdani made an interesting comparison between the failure of the Addis Ababa agreement and that of the CPA in keeping the country united. The failure of the Addis Ababa agreement, he said, was because it reformed the state in the South, but not in the North. In effect, the Addis Ababa constitutional arrangements (before they were abrogated by its two authors) granted the southern legislature powers to nominate or remove the government and president of South Sudan, while no such power was ever granted to the North. In the case of the CPA, the power-sharing arrangement boiled down to power sharing between two ruling parties to the exclusion of others. While there were justifications for such arrangement in the first half of the interim period in order to enable the two warring parties to consummate security arrangements, that situation continued even when the occasion for change came with the national election. That election, as demonstrated in Chapter Eight, was far from being free and fair; indeed, it unjustifiably appeared to third parties as if it was organized with a view to maintain the status quo, especially at the national level.

NOTES

1   In cooperation with Garang's in-house economic advisor, Lual Acuek Deng, Garang sought advice from two eminent northern Sudanese economists: Ali Abdel Gadir Ali and Ibrahim Elbadawi. That advice proved to be helpful to him in laying out his economic development plan and better articulating the SPLM's economic agenda.

2   Ashraf Ghani Ahmadzai is presently chairman of the Institute of State Effectiveness and before that was minister of finance in Afghanistan. Clare Lockhart is CEO of the same institute.

3   Personal recollection. The statement was made by the World Bank advisor to Garang during their June 2005 meeting in Cairo. The author, together with a few SPLM cadres, participated in the meeting.

4   Ibid.

5   Personal recollection

6   Ibid.

7   Kerabino Bol sought support from Ethiopian president Menistu Haili Mariam in 1987 to remove Garang from the SPLM/A leadership (see Douglas Johnson *Root Cause of the Sudan Civil Wars*, 92). Arok, a Dinka who hailed from Bor, Garang's home base, disagreed with the leader over his approach to negotiations with Khartoum and as a result was put in detention.

8   The split was engineered by Riek Machar and Lam Akol in 1991, denouncing Garang's pattern of leadership and what they described as lack of democracy in the party. However the SPLM's Political Military High Command met in Chukudum, Eastern Equatoria on September 12, 1991 and confirmed Garang's continued leadership.

9   The Rumbek meeting took place at a crucial moment when the CPA was virtually concluded. That meeting was attended by 240 of the SPLM/A cadres. It was triggered by rumors that Garang was about to remove Salva Kiir from his position as second in command in the SPLM/A and appoint Nhial Deng Nhial in his place. In his opening statement to. the meeting, Salva Kiir leveled accusations against Garang relating to his style in management in both the party and the army as well as his leniency toward corrupt elements in the system. Many officers, including those who were very close to Garang such as Oyay Deng Ajak and James Hoth Mai (both of whom later became chiefs of general staff of the SPLA) shared Salva

Kiir's criticism. Another allegation made against Garang related to his reluctance to organizing a South-South dialogue. The meeting ended with an agreement to reconstruct the party and army with a view to better organizing the SPLM and having a well-defined chain of command in the army.

10 Personal recollection; the full story was retold to the author by Salva Keir himself.

11 Ibid.

12 Matthew Le Riche and Matthew Arnold, *South Sudan from Revolution to Independence*, Hurst and Company, London, 2012, 145

13 The Wunlit conference, for example, brought together traditional leaders from western Nuer and Dinka from Tonj, Rumbek, andYirol who reached a peace settlement on grazing rights and protection from cross-border raids. Similar agreements were reached between the SPLA and SSDF in Jonglei. See Douglas Johnson, *The Root Causes of Sudan's Civil Wars*, 125.

14 The SSDF was a nonprofessional force that provided defense for oilfields and government garrison towns, and engaged the SPLA, alongside the SAF, in numerous battles. They controlled territory in central, eastern, and western Upper Nile, as well as parts of North and West Bahr El Ghazal. They also had a strong presence among the Murle of southeastern Upper Nile and East Equatoria. See Young, *Emerging North-South Tensions and Prospects for a Return to War*, 17.

15 Juba Declaration on Unity and Integration between the Sudan People's Liberation Army (SPLA) and the South Sudan Defence Forces (SSDF), January 8, 2006.

16 General Oyay Deng Ajak served as operations officer of the SPLA Bright Star campaign and director of military intelligence, and victoriously led famed SPLA operations such as the siege on Juba in 1991–1993, Jungle Storm in 1997, Thunderbolt in 1996, operation Deng Nhial in 1997, and operation Final Leap in 2001–2002.

17 Article 158 (1) provides: "The Sudan People's Liberation Army is a regular, professional, patriotic, productive, disciplined, nonpartisan military force subordinate to civilian authority as established under this Constitution."

18 *Sudan Update: Jongeli Fighting between George Athor and SPLA*, (Small Arms Survey, 2011).

19 Security Strategy of Southern Sudan (Government of South Sudan, Office for the President, Juba December 2008).

20 Ibid.

21 Colonel L. B. van Stade, "Rationalization in the South African National Defence Force: The Next Challenge,"*African Security Review* 6, No. 2 (1997).

22 List of countries by number of military and paramilitary personnel. http://en.wikipedia.org/wiki/List_of_countries_by_number_of_troops.

23 The 1983 manifesto was known to have been penned by John Garang, Martin Majiir Gai, Joseph Oduhu, and others at its initial stage. After the authors parted way, with some of them forced out of the leadership, the document was doctored in a way that portrayed the parting leaders as reactionaries and traitors.

24 Marx called ethnicity "a construct by the ruling bourgeoisie in capitalist states that was designed to divert the attention of the working class away from its economic grievances and focus attention on the identities and cultures that divided workers, rather than on the class interests that united them." Yivo Institute for Jewish

Research, "Communism," Yivo Encyclopedia of Jews in Eastern Europe, http://www.yivoencyclopedia.org/article.aspx/Communism.

25 Excerpt from a speech by John Garang delivered on March 3, 1984. See John Garang, *The Call for Democracy in Sudan*, ed. Mansour Khalid (London: Kegan Paul International, 1987), 24–25.

26 The compendium appeared in English. See John Garang de Mabior, *The Vision of New Sudan: Questions of Unity and Identity* (Cairo: Consortium for Policy Analysis and Development Strategies, 1998).

27 Capacity Building and Cadre Development, Second SPLM Second National Convention, Sudan People's Liberation Movement, Juba, May 2008, resolution 12.9.

28 *Sudan: Toward Sustainable and Broad-Based Growth* (World Bank: December 2009) 117.

29 Ibid.

30 Article 4 (1) of the Interim Constitution of Southern Sudan provides: "The overall goal of economic development strategy in Southern Sudan shall be the eradication of poverty, attainment the Millennium Development Goals, guaranteeing equitable distribution of wealth, redressing imbalances of income, and achieving a decent standard of life for the people of Southern Sudan." Article 10 (1) of the Interim National Constitution reflects the same provision.

31 Poverty in Southern Sudan, Isaiah Chol Aruai, *Poverty and Human Development in Southern Sudan* (Centre for Census, Statistics, and Evaluation: 2009).

32 Supra note 24 *Sudan: Toward Sustainable and Broad-Based* Growth, 117.

33 Gunnar Myrdal, *Asian Drama: An Inquiry into the Poverty of Nations* (London, Allen Lane, 1972).

34 "Government of South Sudan Investigates Waste of 2.8 billion Sudanese Pound Deal," *Al-Sahafa,* January 23, 2011.

35 Supra note 25 *Sudan: Toward Sustainable and Broad-Based* Growth, 117.

36 Kevin Peraino, "Sorry, Sudan," *Newsweek,* September 24, 2010.

37 Ghani, et al., "Assessing Linkages between Diplomatic Peacemaking and Developmental Peacebuilding Efforts," 54–55.

38 Supra note 36.

39 Ibid.

40 Ian Anderson, *Fragile States: What is International Experience Telling Us?* (AusAID, Australian Government, June 2005).

41 Mareike Schomerus and Tim Allen, *Southern Sudan at Odds With Itself: Dynamics of Conflict and Predicaments of Peace* (London: London School of Economics and Political Science Development Studies Institute, 2010).

42 Ibid.

43 Silva Kiir's inaugural speech after his election in 2010 as president of the government of South Sudan prior to the referendum.

44 Adolfo Barajas, *MENAP Oil Exporters: Benefiting from High Oil Prices Amid Growing Risks* (International Monetary Fund, 2011).

45 "South Sudan, World's Newest Country, Faces Hunger Crisis," World Food Programme, December 15, 2011, http//www.wfp.org/stories/south–Sudan–world's–newest–country–faces–hunger–crisis.

46 Rent in development economics, unlike rent of real estate, refers to spending resources without creating wealth. The term is derived from Adam Smith's

division of income into profits, wages and rent. In this particular case it refers to profits made by corrupt government decision makers by misapplying discretionary powers to ensure illegitimate gain to their clients.

47 Gustav Ranis, *Diversity of Communities and Economic Development: An Overview* (Tokyo: JICA Research Institute, March 2010).

48 Kenneth Omeja, *Dangers of Splitting a Fragile Rentier State: Getting It Right in Sudan* (Umhlanga Rocks, South Africa: African Centre for the Constructive Resolution of Disputes, 2010), 3.

49 Ibid., 5.

50 Seth Kaplan, *Fixing Fragile States* (Stanford, CA: Stanford University Hoover Institution, December 4, 2008).

51 Catherine Riungu, interview with John Githongo. *The East African, November 22-28, 2010.*

52 Philippe Martin, "A Closer Look at Botswana's Development: The Role of Institutions," *Paterson Review* 9 (2008).

53 *Transparency International Annual Report 2009* (Berlin: Transparency International, June 30, 2010).

54 Ibid.

55 Among those who drew the SPLM leader's attention to incipient corruption in southern Sudan were U.S. Vice President Joe Biden; Hilde Johnson, special representative of the UN secretary general to South Sudan; U.S. Congressman Donald Payne; and Susan Rice, U.S. ambassador to the United Nations.

56 Thomas Talley, "Southern Sudan—The Four Theses," Small Wars Journal (2010): 21.

57 Robert I. Rotberg, "Failed States in a World of Terror," (Council on Foreign Relations, July/August 2002).

58 Supra note 41.

59 The so-called Tuic mafia included the eminent SPLM politician, Justin Yac Arop, who served the movement on important diplomatic, political, and humanitarian missions, and Dominic Dim Deng, who fell out with Garang in the 1990s but was later reinstated in the SPLA and became minister of SPLA affairs. Both men sadly expired in a tragic air crash.

60 Supra note 51, Question and Answer with John Githongo, former Kenyan Anti-corruption Tsar, *The East African,* November 22 – 28, 2010.

61 President Salva Kiir's inaugural speech

62 In a military sense, the tern refers to the center that monitors, manages and controls operations in the battle field. The SPLM chose the term to describe the center that supervised and managed referendum operations.

63 Mahmood Mamdani, "South Sudan and the African Experience: The Quest for a New Political Order (talk delivered at Makerere University, Uganda, in March 2011), *The Indypendent* (May 20, 2011).

64 Ibid.

65 Jon Temin and Theodore Murphy, *Toward a New Republic of Sudan* (Washington, DC: United States Institute of Peace, June 2011) 6–7.

66 Ibid.

67 Supra note 57, Rotberg, "Failed States in a World of Terror."

Chapter Ten
Final Phase of the Interim Period: Referendum and Beyond

■■■■■■■■■■■■■❖■■■■■■■■■■■■■

> In the arts of peace Man is a bungler.
> —**George Bernard Shaw**,
> *Man and Superman*

1. Introduction

In earlier chapters, I emphasized how the Comprehensive Peace Agreement (CPA) had been structured with meticulous attention to detail. The agreement was also designed to include agreed upon principles and normative rules for governing the affairs of state in all of Sudan. Save for acts of God, the agreement was expected to be implemented with the highest degree of professional aplomb. That reasonable expectation was dampened by midterm of the interim period. In particular, Part A (entitled "Agreed Principles") in the Machakos Protocol provided for an unprecedented autonomy in southern Sudan as well as a groundbreaking devolution of power to other subnational levels. Those principles, which were further elaborated upon in the power and wealth sharing protocols, were ultimately encompassed in the Interim National Constitution (INC).

In enunciating these provisions, the two parties not only envisaged silencing guns in southern Sudan—vital as that was—but also contemplated restructuring national politics on a basis never tried before. The parties concluded that without erasing historical injustices and completely overhauling Sudan's dysfunctional politics at the center, voluntary unity between North and South Sudan, as well as stability all over the country, would not be feasible. Any attempt to disaggregate those elements would inescapably kill both dreams. Sadly, throughout the interim period the National Congress Party (NCP) seemed to have assumed that the CPA was an à la carte menu from which they only chose the dishes they savored most. As for the CPA guarantors who were expected to be guardians of the full implementation of the agreement, every so often they became absorbed in rewriting the CPA in order to accommodate flagrant breaches of its terms by the parties, mainly the NCP.

By the middle of 2010, a few months before commencement of the referendum process, disregard of multiple breaches of cardinal commitments in the CPA accentuated conflict between the two parties that cumulatively brought relations between them to an all-time low. At the heart of the conflict were needless squabbles over the conditions for referenda in southern Sudan and Abyei. The squabbles turned into a humorless farce when some NCP spokespersons, in intimidatory remarks, began to cast doubt about the feasibility of the referendum occurring in the time that was set for it. Those remarks became more pronounced as the referendum day drew closer and southern Sudanese appeared to be leaning toward secession. Indubitably, the people of southern Sudan were empowered by the CPA and INC to choose either unity by confirming "the system of government established under the CPA, or secession." The choice of either of the two options was entirely reserved for the people of South Sudan and was not to be made on their behalf by any political party or leader. Correspondingly, the SPLM's task became how to guide these people through the referendum process in order to enable them make an informed choice at the polls. Whatever choice the people would make had to be respected and upheld by the SPLM, NCP, as well as other national political forces and the international community.

Regardless of which way the vote went the referendum results were to create a totally new political situation and constitutional order in the country. In the case of unity—an eventuality that had become increasingly dim as the referendum drew near—a new permanent constitution would have to be agreed upon by the SPLM, the NCP, and other northern and southern Sudanese political forces. That was most likely to be achieved through amendments to the INC and the Interim Constitution of Southern Sudan (ICSS) through a revamped National Constitutional Review Commission (NCRC). Opposition parties who saw in the Power Sharing Protocol a raw deal would have appropriately seized the opportunity of the constitutional review to close lacunae in the INC and ICSS that had allowed breaches of the two constitutions. But as the people of southern Sudan had opted for secession, the national constitution review became a moot point for southern Sudanese. Consequently, it became incumbent upon the SPLM and other southern Sudanese parties to rewrite the ICSS into a constitution compatible with a sovereign state. That was what the SPLM-led government had done before the inauguration of the new state. As for the North, expectations of change became increasingly meager since the NCP appeared to cling to absolute power and made it obvious to all and sundry that if there were to be a role for other political forces, it would be no more than that of second fiddle. It must be added, however, that there was neither political discontinuity nor a constitutional hiatus at the national and South Sudan levels, as some opposition politicians in North and South Sudan seemed to think in their impetuous struggle for power.

Anticipating the two contingencies, Article 226 (10) of the INC provided that "if the outcome of the referendum on self-determination favors secession, the parts, chapters, articles, sub-articles, and schedules of this constitution that provide for southern Sudan institutions, representation, rights, and obligations shall be deemed to have been duly repealed." On the other hand, Article 208 (7) of the ICSS stated that "if the outcome of the referendum on self-determination favors secession, this constitution shall remain in force as the constitution of sovereign and independent southern Sudan and all the parts, chapters, articles, sub-articles, and schedules of the constitution that provide for national institutions, representation, rights, and obligations shall be deemed to have been duly replaced." Further, both constitutional clauses, which were to enact a political and constitutional separation between the two states, were not conceived to lead to administrative dislocation, economic destabilization, or social disharmony between the old and nascent states. Ironically, the "one country, two systems" model, which was devised in order to keep the country intact, had "inadvertently entrenched the very problem that it sought to address: the North-South division of Sudan."[1] Francis Deng, one of the authors of the model, wrote in retrospect: "The one country, multiple systems model would have facilitated crosscutting alliances that would provide a basis for democratic transformation and interaction among the people of the various regions [and] could incrementally generate a process of national unity toward a one country, one system model" that is ideal.[2] Sadly, the confederal system, the only framework within which that arrangement could have been possible, was rejected by the NCP at both the Abuja talks and CPA negotiations.

This chapter shall deal in two parts with these different but interrelated issues. Part I shall expose maneuvers by the NCP to derail the referendum process as well as reveal internal and external efforts to neutralize these maneuvers and how and why these efforts paid handsomely. Part II shall deal with, and display, the primacy of post-referendum challenges that have to be faced jointly by the two parties. The success or failure in finding a solution to these challenges shall determine the fate of the two states.

Part I. Referendum or Neverendum

1. Putting Spokes in the Referendum Wheel

The CPA stipulated that the self-determination referendum law should be enacted at the beginning of the third year of the interim period (July 2008) and a

343

referendum commission established soon after enactment of the law. Based on this time plan, registration of voters in the referendum was to start by the beginning of the sixth year of the interim period (July 2010) and voting held six months before the end of the interim period (January 9, 2011). None of the deadlines preceding the referendum on January 9 had been observed, much as other dates closely linked to the referendum were passed over. As broached earlier, the national census was only completed in 2008, three years after the date set by the CPA, and was, according to the SPLM, terribly botched. Also the demarcation of the North-South border, which was to be completed in the first two years of the interim period, was behind schedule up to November 2010. So were putting to rest the issue of Abyei and the formation of important national commissions such as the Human Rights and Lands Commission. Fears increased that the enactment of the referendum law would follow that pattern. NCP's dilatory tactics regarding such a crucial issue as the referendum gave rise to a not so far-fetched speculation that the NCP was maneuvering to turn the referendum into a "neverendum."[3] As a result, U.S. peace envoy Scott Gration took the initiative of calling the parties to talks in Washington, D.C., on June 21, 2009. The aim of the talks (dubbed the Washington Trilateral Talks) was to review outstanding issues on CPA implementation, with the promulgation of the referendum law at the top of these issues.

As if procrastination over the dates set for launching the referendum process was not enough, the NCP pulled out another trick from the bag. In what seemed to be an attempt to put off the referendum, it demanded a higher threshold of approval of the results of the ballot: two thirds turnout of registered voters and an affirmative vote of 70 percent of those voting. Speciously, the NCP was more concerned about a decision in favor of secession, not unity. As a result of U.S. persuasion, the SPLM gave in to a 60 percent turnout of registered voters but stood firm on a 50 + 1 percent of votes necessary to declare secession. The original proposition by the NCP was ill-advised on more than one count. First, the CPA, neither explicitly nor implicitly, had set any limitation on electors' turnout or a minimum vote requirement for validating the voters' choice. In all probability, the NCP at the eleventh hour realized that dismembering a country is too important a decision to be made by a skimpy vote. Nonetheless, in assuming that southern Sudanese people would opt for secession, the NCP could have looked deeper into the constituents of unity as defined by the CPA in order to make unity attractive, rather than play with the terms and conditions for the referendum enshrined in the CPA and INC.

Figure 3: Author with U.S. Presidential Envoy General Scott Gration in Washington, D.C. (June 2009)

There was nothing in modern state practice that supported the NCP's contention about requiring such a high approval rating for secession to be valid. According to Luis Aguiar-Conraria and Pedro Magalhães, "one particularly interesting aspect of referendum design concerns quorum rules. In many established democracies, the requirement of simple majority in order for a proposal to pass is coupled with a *participation quorum*, or, instead, an *approval quorum* requirement."[4] Aguiar-Conraria and Magalhães cite the Venice Commission's[5] guidelines for good practice regarding referendums, which "advised against the adoption of any sorts of quorums in referendums because of the temptation of 'falsification of turnout rates'...and the creation of awkward political situations where 'the majority will feel that they have been deprived of victory without an adequate reason.'"[6] While agreeing on setting a threshold for voter turnout as a reasonable demand in cases of popular consultation on consequential issues, the Venice Commission maintained that setting a quorum for the results might also enable a minority to frustrate the will of the majority. By way of illustration, if the affirmative vote is set at 70 or 60 percent, and the 51 percent vote in favor is rejected, then that shall mean putting a (51 percent) majority under the mercy of a minority of (9 or 10 percent). It was further observed that a quorum requirement may also give rise to political fraud through campaigns to dissuade potential voters from registering their names on voter lists and, thus, turn absentee votes into functional "No" votes. As for state practice, in the most recent experience of the separation of Montenegro from the Republic

345

of Yugoslavia, Serbia, and Montenegro (RYSM), the Montenegrin president announced before the referendum that he would declare independence if the vote passed by 50 percent. In that announcement he was supported by the constitutional charter which created RYSM and empowered any state member to demand, if it so wished, independence after three years of the ratification of the Charter in 2003. By the year 2006, Montenegro called for a referendum to separate from the union, and Serbia declared that it would abide by the results unconditionally, since its constitutional charter did not lay down any condition for the validation of results of separation referendum. Montenegrin separatists, however, had convincingly won with a high number of citizens participating in the poll.[7]

Having crossed the quorum hurdle, the parties were expected to immediately initiate the referendum process; with only one year left for that process, neither was the law promulgated nor the commission established. It was at this point that regional and international actors became anxious about the fate of the peace process. As the interim period began to wind up, the leadership of the United States and African Union lost no time in intervening in order to help Sudan make a smooth transition into the next phase. The trilateral meeting in Washington was the high point of those international pressures. However, three months after these talks in which the two parties reached understanding on all issues, the NCP appeared not to have been in a hurry to carry out the agreements reached in that meeting. In consequence, the SPLM called for an All Sudan Political Parties Conference to which the NCP was invited.

2. Internal Pressures on NCP

At its general secretariat level, the SPLM had been in constant contact with national opposition parties, especially those who were allied to it during the struggle. Salva Kiir also held regular meetings with leaders of major Sudanese political parties during his visits to Khartoum. However, coming at that particular moment, the All Sudan Political Parties Conference had put pressure on the NCP for three reasons: dragging its feet on holding national elections timely and properly, not making requisite arrangements for the referendum, and failing to repeal all laws repugnant to the CPA. All these issues were agreed upon by the NCP at the trilateral talks. Rather than exclude the NCP from the All Sudan Political Parties Conference in Juba, the SPLM extended an invitation to that party which it declined. The NCP would have preferred to have a closed, separate meeting with the SPLM, on the one hand, and major northern parties, on the other, rather than an open forum, especially if that forum was to be attended by local and international media. After four years of partnership with the SPLM, the NCP never brought itself around to recognize the SPLM as a party with a national role, even when it had been its major partner in a government called the **Government of National Unity**. The NCP was also circumspect that the Juba meeting might turn into a public scrutiny of its policies.

Even so, the Juba conference took place on September 26–29, 2009, and was attended by Sudanese political forces, except the NCP. It provided an occasion for the leaders of all participating parties to present their catalogue of grievances against the NCP, while enabling the SPLM chairman to underscore his party's determination to build national consensus on the implementation of the CPA as "a tool of transformation of the whole Sudan and national healing and reconciliation."[8] The SPLM chairman also argued that "without delivering peace to all of Sudan, implanting democracy in our soil, reaching consensus on major national issues, and finding an amicable solution to the conflict in Dar Fur, there shall be no comprehensive peace."[9] Salva Kiir also reminded the parties that by incorporating measures relating to democratic transformation into the agreement, the SPLM wanted to ensure Sudan's graduation from one-party rule to a multi-party democracy through negotiated settlement.

On issues relating to unity, Salva Kiir said that "unity is a noble cause" but adding that the unity the SPLM was calling for "is not any unity." That was why, he said, the SPLM coined the phrase "**unity on new basis**" (emphasis added). The SPLM chairman reminded the audience that irrespective of the SPLM's commitment to unity and determination to work with the NCP to make it attractive, there was still a lot to be desired before unity became an attractive option to the people of South Sudan. He also alluded to NCP's recalcitrance to implement overriding aspects of the agreement that were basic to achieving the unity goal. In addition, the SPLM chairman insinuated that separation, for all the above reasons, had become a probability. "The two probabilities of confirmation of unity or secession—without speculating on the results of the referendum— are real," he said.[10] He, thus, advised the congressists that the Sudanese should prepare themselves for both eventualities.[11]

3. The U.S. Gives a Kiss of Death to Democratic Transformation

As a result of all those internal maneuvers and external pressures, the two parties agreed that the long overdue referendum law should be passed by the sitting national legislature before its final recess. This was meant to avoid delaying the process until the election of a new legislature in April/May 2010. It was also agreed to disconnect the promulgation of the referendum law from ongoing negotiations by the partners on post-referendum arrangements, as some elements within the NCP called for. Moreover, the two parties committed themselves to organize a free, fair referendum and jointly seek technical assistance from the Assessment and Evaluation Commission, the United Nations, and the United States in order to ensure credible referendum results and mutually agreed upon post-referendum arrangements. The United States undertook in the Trilateral Talks of June 2009 referred to above this chapter to call on the international community to bring pressure to bear on Khartoum in order to respect and abide by the outcome of the referendum and to organize a donor's conference in 2011 to mobilize resources for post-conflict reconstruction.

On the related issue of making unity attractive, it is to be noted that during the trilateral talks the two parties agreed to begin a national reconciliation process as per the CPA and Presidential Decree 341/2007,[12] while committing themselves to work, with U.S. assistance, to solicit funding for development projects that would make unity attractive, including infrastructural development. They also agreed in Washington's Trilateral Talks to repeal "during the current national legislature all laws that are inconsistent with the CPA and INC **[especially] Popular Defence Act**" (emphasis added). That far-reaching concurrence of views in the trilateral talks, especially on unresolved CPA issues, confirmed awareness by the partners of the nexus between democratization, development, and making unity attractive. The failure of the NCP to carry through the commitments made in Washington in the presence of representatives of CPA observer states and organizations proved, one more time, the levity with which the NCP treated solemnly made agreements. That attitude haunted future negotiations between the partners on how to make unity attractive or translate the CPA into a tool of transformation. Given exclusive focus by the United State on referendum and elections, democratic transformation fell between two stools—indeed, it became a nonissue. That was regrettable coming from a mediator who never ceased repeating the sweet sounding refrains of full implementation of the CPA and democratic transformation. Less than one year after the trilateral meeting, the White House issued the U.S. National Security Strategy (May 2010), in which it highlighted the country's top national security concerns and priorities. In the preface to that strategy, President Obama wrote: "We [the United States] will strengthen international norms that protect these [human rights] and create space and support for those who resist repression. And we reject the notion that lasting security and prosperity can be found by turning away from universal rights. Our support for universal rights is both fundamental to American leadership and a source of our strength in the world." This universal support to democracy was not apparent in the U.S. mediators' dealings with the Sudanese government, despite Washington's endless singing about the virtues of democracy. By taking an extreme position on referendum, the NCP wanted to distract attention from all other issues, particularly democratic transformation. In that political poker game (one of its greatest survival skills since 1989), the NCP won by raising the stakes higher than anybody had expected.

4. The Referendum at Last

The referendum legislation was finally promulgated in the nick of time just before the dissolution of Sudan's National Legislature on December 31, 2010, but only when the SPLM was almost persuaded to overlook the issue of the repeal of laws that were repugnant to the constitution. Nevertheless, it took six more months for the Southern Sudan Referendum Commission (SSRC) to be established. The

SSRC was created by Presidential Decree 172 (2010) on June 29, 2010, under the chairmanship of Mohamed Ibrahim Khalil, a veteran Sudanese statesman and a practicing lawyer of renown,[13] with Chan Reec Madut, also a brilliant lawyer,[14] serving as deputy chair. Even though two senior lawyers were chosen as chair and vice chair of the SSRC, conversance with the law was not a condition for membership of the commission, as had been the case in some other international experiences.[15] The commission comprised seven other members of whom three were from the North and four from South Sudan. The SSRC had one woman member from the North and none from the South, despite all the political hue and cry about women empowerment.

Though it was formed two years after the date stipulated in the agreement for its creation, the commission hit the road running and conducted itself in a manner that eventually won it universal acclaim. Nonetheless, the SSRC faced a few hiccups as a result of conflicts that ensued between its chair and southern Sudanese members, between the chair and some SPLM leaders, and as a result of disagreement on the composition of the commission's secretariat.[16] In effect, before the SSRC resolutely began its work, Khalil was besieged with sideswipes and impingements by some leading SPLM politicians who were seemingly looking for a more malleable chair, without realizing that this would have obviated the idea of having a credible referendum. Equally regrettable was the campaign of denigration launched against Khalil by some senior SPLM politicians who, to all appearances, came to conclusions about him on anecdotal evidence. Attacks against Khalil also came from outside the SPLM and were probably engineered by the NCP with the hope of hounding him out of office. Were that to happen, agreement on a new chair would likely not have been possible in the foreseeable future. After a month of wrangling, the questions at issue—real or fabricated—were resolved in meetings Khalil held with the presidency and especially with the SPLM chairman. Not only did the chairman allay Khalil's fears, but he also promised him all the support he needed to carry out his mission. It was only then that SSRC began its work with undivided attention and redoubled efforts to make up for lost time. Registration of voters went on without a setback, except for few glitches caused by delays in the disbursement of funds, which caused logistical constraints. By the end of the year, the commission announced that 3,753,815 voters were registered, of whom 52 percent were women and 48 percent men.

Despite all the right vibes issuing from Khartoum, there were still fears that the NCP was not yet out of tricks. The most faithless attempt to thwart the operation of the SSRC seemed to have been instigated by high levels in the NCP. Soon after the formation of the commission following strong pressures from regional and international organizations, the chair of the commission received in his office an unexpected guest, Sudan's minister of electricity Usama Abdalla. Abdalla's message was to encourage the chair of the commission to resign, especially that rumours were circulating in Khartoum that the man was frustrated

349

by the attacks to which he was subjected from both sides. Khalil was so enraged by the minister's brazen advice that he told him off. Though he was brooding over resigning for his own reasons, Khalil told the minister that he changed his mind following the minister's intervention. In all likelihood Khalil thought that the NCP wanted to create a situation in which the referendum would be delayed further. Maneuvers by the NCP like this one, and unwarrantable attacks on the commission's chair from the SPLM, drove the U.N. Security Council to urge both parties on November 16, 2010, to make sure they held "peaceful, credible, and timely referenda both in southern Sudan and Abyei." In addition, U.N. Secretary General Ban Ki-moon cautioned the parties that "the commitment of the international community cannot supplant the willingness of the parties to meet their responsibilities."[17] During the Christmas holiday, both U.S. President Obama and Vice President Biden brought the full weight of their offices to bear on Sudan's president and first vice president so that they would live up to their promises to the Security Council to have a timely, free, and fair referendum. On December 26, 2010, Vice President Biden called Vice President Taha to underscore the U.S. government's concern over the referendum and post-referendum arrangements, while President Obama called Salva Kiir to appeal to him to work closely with Bashir toward resolving outstanding CPA issues.[18] Also on December 26, two unexpected guests landed in Khartoum: Hosni Mubarak of Egypt and Muammar Qaddafi of Libya. The two leaders held a closed meeting with Bashir that was attended by First Vice President Kiir and Vice President Taha. Qaddafi and Mubarak called for the timely conduct of the referendum and respect of the peoples' choice, whatever that choice would be. They also expressed hope for an amicable solution to post-referendum issues as well as consolidation of socioeconomic relations between the North and the South in the event southern Sudan chose secession.[19]

The referendum took place on time and with a high degree of professionalism. Despite the extreme tardiness in setting up the SSRC, preparing a voters' register, and carrying out enlightenment campaigns about the process, the commission did not need to exercise the power availed to it by the referendum act to postpone the process if need arose. The act empowered the commission, *inter alia*, to "postpone referendum procedures for any compelling circumstances in conformity with the provisions of the law and fix a new date after the approval of the national government and the government of southern Sudan."

After three days of voting, the SPLM announced that the 60 percent threshold was reached as 2.3 million voters had participated in the poll.[20] When the final count was made, 3,792,518 (98.83 percent) voted for secession while only 44,888 (1.17 percent) voted for unity. If the 14,588 (.38 percent) invalid or blank votes were added to this, the total number of voters would have added up to 3,851,994, which would have made voter turnout 97.58 percent. The referendum on the other side was heavily monitored by national and international observers. At the national level, domestic observation groups included the Sudanese Network for Democratic Election (SuNDE), the Sudan Domestic Election Monitoring and Observation Programme (SuDEMOP), and the Sudanese Group for Democracy and Elections (SuGDE). International observers were led by a team of prominent elders dispatched by the Carter Center, which comprised, among others, former President Jimmy Carter and former U.N. Secretary General Kofi Annan.[21] Other leading observers included Senator John Kerry, chairman of the U.S. Senate Committee on Foreign Relations, and the American actor George Clooney, who was supporting the Satellite Sentinel Project.[22] Other important observers included the African Union, the European Union, Intergovernmental Authority on Development (IGAD), and League of Arab States. On the other side, the United Nations, which did not deploy its own observer team, formed a special panel to follow up the referendum process through periodic visits to Sudan, with support on the ground by reporting officers. The panel was headed by Tanzanian former president Benjamin Mkapa and included former Portuguese foreign minister António Monteiro and former chair of the Election Commission of Nepal Bhojraj Pokharel.

On February 7, 2011, the SSRC chairman presented the final results of the referendum to President Bashir in an official ceremony attended by First Vice President Kiir and Vice President Taha. The presidency endorsed the results in a republican decree passed the same day. Later the same day, Bashir called a meeting of the cabinet to brief ministers of the results and secure their endorsement of them. In his address to the cabinet, Bashir said: "We promised to give the people of South Sudan the right to self-determination. Now that they have chosen independence we will keep our promise." Concerning post-referendum arrangements, Bashir said, "We are resolved to reach an agreement on [all outstanding issues] before the end of the interim period."[23] In turn, Salva Kiir lauded Bashir's action and added: "Secession is not the end of the road. We shall no longer become enemies of each other but will make sure that our relationship remains strong." He also declared that borders between North and South Sudan would only be on paper, as there would be no restrictions on movement of trade and citizens.

Part II. Post-Referendum Challenges

1. Sequels and Repercussions of Referendum

Article 67 of the Southern Sudan Referendum Act (SSRA) had provided for post-referendum measures in both eventualities—unity or separation. In the latter case, a score of crucial issues to be addressed by the two parties were enumerated, namely: citizenship, currency, public service, joint integrated units (JIUs), national security and intelligence, international agreements and conventions, debts, oil (field production, transport and export, contracts, and environmental impact), water, apportionment of assets, and debts, in addition to any other issue on which the parties agreed. This part of the chapter shall attend to the most salient of those issues as well as others that may have direct bearing on the viability of the two states such as economic integration and relations among pastoralist communities in North and South Sudan. Harmonious resolution to those issues would enable the two parties to turn liabilities into assets and make the two states a model of good neighborly relations.

Douglas Johnson recently wrote, "No geological fault line is going to open up separating the South from the North on July 9. North and South Sudan will remain physically, economically, and socially linked."[24] This truism was not that obvious to many within Sudan's political class in the North as well as to some political elites in the South who seemed to believe that they could wrap up southern Sudan and run away with it to wherever they wished to run southward. On the other hand, referendum and self-determination are two different things. The former is only a few months process that shall end with the tally of the polls; the latter encompasses lifelong processes in governance, economic management, internal and external security, and balanced and responsible external relations. Once the people of southern Sudan conclusively chose to have their own independent state, the new state would have to focus on the above issues, as they represented the kernel of self-determination. In preparing itself for the next stage, the new state had to gear itself up for addressing serious repercussions and important sequels that would ensue from secession. On the other hand, the two parties had to devise measures that would head off the repercussions, taking into consideration the interlocked economic, political, and social interests of the North and South. That was brilliantly set out in the SPLM chairman's speech to the All Sudan Political Parties Conference, referred to above. Careful political handling of those issues represented the greatest challenge to both states, particularly since neither the CPA nor the INC provided guidance in this respect. Article 223(10) of the INC, alluded to above, had only taken a formalistic approach to secession.

Notwithstanding, some of the rights, assignments, and liabilities mentioned in that article are governed by established principles of international law and practice within the context of the law of state succession. In simple terms, state succession occurs when one or more international persons succeed a preceding state in the responsibilities of that state for the international relations of the territory it has occupied or the liabilities it has incurred. Though there is a fairly established body of international law on state succession, that branch of the law of nations is one of the most inconsistent branches. Up to August 2008, the International Law Association was debating in Rio de Janeiro, Brazil, the principles governing the rights and obligations of preceding and succeeding states that were assumed to have been closed before the cataclysmic disintegration of Yugoslavia and dissolution of the former Soviet Union. According to Matthew Craven, senior lecturer in law at the London School of Oriental and African Studies, "there is one common theme running through all recent literature on the law of state succession; it is that the subject is largely confused and resistant to simple exposition."[25] However, diversities in legal research and doctrinal schisms on the issue of succession have often been generated by differing legal interpretations on the continuity and discontinuity of states, as the cases of the U.S.S.R. and Yugoslavia richly demonstrated. In the case of Sudan, however, there is no doubt about the disunion of the old state, both in law (CPA and INC) and in practice (recognition of the disunion by the mother country from which the new state had ensued and by the international community).

2. Challenges Facing the Two Parties

2.1 Petroleum Production, Processing and Apportionment of Revenues

During wealth sharing negotiations, the issue of oil production and revenue sharing was one of the most burdensome subjects under discussion. With a 98 percent dependency on oil revenues by the government of South Sudan, and a 65 to 40 percent dependency by the Government of National Unity,[26] one doesn't have to play up the importance of these revenues to the survival of the two states. Before oil development and exportation, Sudan's export earnings did not exceed half a billion U.S. dollars, compared to $9 billion after the oil boom. According to the 2009 International Monetary Fund Country Report, Sudan's exports in the period 2004–2008 were dominated by oil, which accounted for 80 percent of the country's exports.[27] The same report pointed out that non-oil revenues had dropped in 2004 from $677 million to $545 million. Consequently, if oil operations are to be abruptly shut down, Sudan shall lose $6.5 to $13 billion until oil production is resumed or an alternative source of revenue is found. Any drop in, let alone stoppage of, petroleum production shall wreak havoc on the economies of both countries. In reality, dependency by the two governments on oil revenues was such that even the Oil Revenue Stability Account (ORSA), which was created to specifically protect budget spending from volatilities in international oil prices, was raided by both governments at a time when oil prices were at their highest. This near-total dependency on oil in a country endowed with immense renewable resources made oil a curse rather than a blessing.

Map 3: Oil pipelines in Sudan

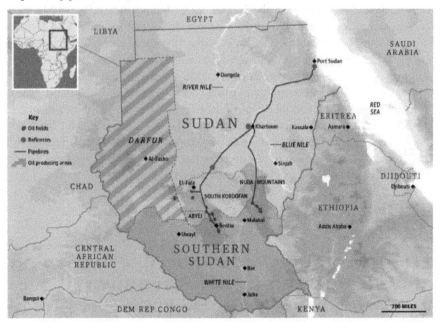

Sudan's petroleum reserves are the fifth largest in Africa following, respectively, Libya, Nigeria, Algeria, and Angola. By the end of 2009, approved oil production in Sudan amounted to 6.7 billion barrels, compared to 44.3 for Libya, 37.2 for Nigeria, 12.2 for Algeria, and 9 for Angola.[28] Recently, former Sudan minister of petroleum Lual Deng told the media that there might be more oil in North than South Sudan, citing preliminary studies in blocks AK and 12B (Southern Darfur), block 10 (Central Sudan between Gezira and Gadaref), and block 14 (northern borders with Egypt and Libya), block 6 (Halaieb area disputed by Egypt), and block 17 (Abyei). In addition, the minister announced that block 8 (Dinder) promised large commercial quantities of natural gas.[29] Of the presently 23 prospective plots, the only oil-producing ones are plots 1–7 in the Melut-Muglad rift basin. In total, the seven plots are reported to have 7 billion barrels of oil reserves. With few exceptions, all these plots lie in South Sudan, that is, south of latitude 12. On the other side, all the infrastructure of the petroleum industry is positioned in the north: pipelines, refineries, and loading points. Some of this infrastructure is being upgraded with oil produced in South Sudan such as block B, which is being exploited by the Total consortium.[30] Equally, 99 percent of the oil sector's national technical workforce is from northern Sudan. In view of this fact, and in order to avert collapse of the oil industry, both Sudan's Vice President Ali Osman Taha and the government of South Sudan's Vice President Riek Machar visited the oil production site at Melut on December 12, 2010, to reassure northern Sudanese working with Petrodar Operating Company that business would proceed as usual, even if southern Sudan seceded.[31] In April 2011, only four months after the comforting statements by the vice president of the government of South Sudan, the governor of Unity State ordered all northern personnel working in the petroleum sector to leave the state, claiming that southern Sudanese were competent enough to do the job. The decision caused commotion both in Khartoum and Juba, as it revealed discrepancies in decisions on issues that would have serious consequences. However, a few days later the governor's decision was quashed by the president of the government of South Sudan and the workers ordered back. Alarmingly, the minister of state in the Ministry of Petroleum in Khartoum predicted that if management of the petroleum sector were to be relocated to South Sudan, 90 percent of the workforce would resign.[32] Those contradictory statements did not augur well for future cooperation between the two states in the oil sector.

The CPA was clear about what needed be done during the interim period, that is, the period during which the country was one. First, it provided that the oil production agreements should remain intact through their lifetime. Second, it stipulated that management of the oil sector during the interim period would be a joint enterprise between the Government of National Unity and the government of South Sudan through a National Petroleum Commission (NPC). Third, the CPA established a detailed plan for the apportionment of oil revenues during the interim period, to which reference was made in Chapter Five. A completely new situation in the oil sector was expected to face North and South Sudan, were the latter to secede. In addressing this eventuality, two factors were to be kept in mind. First, petroleum produced in South Sudan would have no value without the existing oil industry infrastructure unless alternative facilities were found. Second, up until the time oil production in the North reached the levels announced by the minister of petroleum, that infrastructure would be rendered useless, if production from existing oil wells in the South were to be shut down. Some southern commentators argued that South Sudan could build its own infrastructure—a pipeline to Lamu in Kenya, refineries, storage facilities, etc. Though feasible, the building of such an infrastructure would take about three to five years to become operational. Were that to happen, another question would arise as to the ability of the new state to fund its administration and army, let alone carry out its own development programs.

Those speculations were authoritatively put to rest in a seminar organized by the Southern Sudan Referendum Commission on the future of oil after secession. John Luk, minister of legal and constitutional affairs and former minister of energy, who acted as the spokesperson for the government of South Sudan in that seminar, Luk said forthrightly: "The South does not plan to exclude the North [from the oil industry]; on the contrary it wishes to cooperate with it and seek its support in building the new state." He added that transporting southern Sudan's oil through Kenya is presently out of question. "Maybe the question shall arise if oil is discovered on Sudan's border with Kenya," said the minister.[33] As

355

noticed earlier, the shock caused by the drop in oil prices in 2007 had a marked effect on the operations of the government of South Sudan, so it would be madness to contemplate the termination of oil production even for one week.

Following a deadlock in the talks between the parties on Abyei and security arrangements, and the withdrawal of the SPLM delegation from the talks, the secretary general of the SPLM stated that southern Sudan "shall stop oil flowing to the North by shutting all oil wells operating in the South." He also added, needlessly, that he was under instructions from the chairman of the SPLM to commence negotiations for constructing a pipeline to the Indian Ocean.[34] The secretary general's flighty remark was taken by many to be grumpy brinkmanship. That brinkmanship was matched by the reckless attitude of the NCP in beating around the bush on issues like Abyei and border demarcation, as well as the NCP's whimsical decisions toward southern Sudanese living in the North. In response to the secretary general's saber-rattling, President Bashir irascibly reacted by threatening to deny oil produced in the South access to refineries and Red Sea outlets. Soon afterwards, the government of Sudan furnished the African Union mediators with a proposal to be presented to South Sudan negotiators, in which the government would charge $36 for each barrel, a figure much higher than the internationally applied rates. The SPLM secretary general described that as broad daylight robbery.[35] Embarrassed by the outrage caused by those unconscionable rates, the government explained the charges per barrel as covering transportation, sovereignty tax, handling at Red Sea export terminals, and $18 for treatment of crude at the Jablain terminal. Taking into consideration the volatility in world oil prices, the price of southern Sudan crude may drop, as it had done in 2007, to about the same amount charged by Khartoum for the use of oil facilities in northern Sudan. That alone revealed the level of absurdity of the government's proposition. Surprisingly, during the early negotiations with the government of Sudan, the government of South Sudan never made any claim to joint ownership of oil facilities in the North, since all these assets were built on Build, Operate and Transfer (BOT) terms and paid for *in toto* through oil produced in South Sudan. Thus, the agreement between the two parties on apportioning immoveable assets on the basis of territoriality never took into account the special nature of oil industry assets.

There is a wealth of world experience to draw on regarding the transboundary transportation of oil. For example, Algeria, presently the largest supplier of gas to Italy, transports gas to that country through the Mediterranean across Tunisia, while Russia, currently the largest gas supplier to western Europe, transports 80 percent of its gas to Europe across the Ukraine. In sub-Saharan Africa, Chad ferries oil to the Atlantic across Cameroon,[36] and in Asia a cross-border gas pipeline extending for 1,397 kilometers serves Myanmar and Thailand. Those experiences could have been taken as indicators, not necessarily examples, to emulate.

The oil transportation and treatment figures suggested by Khartoum were not based on a cost-benefit analysis but were concocted with a view to bridging the sharp drop in the government's finances as a result of losing 75 percent of its oil earnings. As a result, many southern Sudanese wondered why South Sudan should give preferential treatment to a government in the North whose intentions toward South Sudan were dubious. That was a far cry from the position Garang took during the negotiations at Naivasha. In one meeting, Garang was asked by some angry southern politicians why he had ceded 50 percent of South Sudan's oil to the North. To that question Garang tersely answered: "Before the CPA you had zero percent of the oil. None of the oil revenues except those used in the purchase of arms to kill southerners was used in the South. However, if anyone of you has the means—short of war—to recover the claimed 50 percent, I am all ears to listen to him." He then added: "At any rate, the decision I have taken reflects my way to **keep peace in the family**" (emphasis added). Garang, in place of a war in which the winner took all or both sides lost everything, was seeking another alternative: "keeping peace in the family" through equitable sharing. The situation after separation obviously became much different. Full ownership by the South of oil within its boundaries was no longer contested, and southern Sudanese were in full control of their region.

Nevertheless, South Sudan leaders lost no opportunity to say that they were concerned about the economic viability of the Republic of Sudan in view of the many interconnections between it and the new republic in South Sudan. They often added that they had no problem with the people of the North but only with their government. That position was underscored by President Salva Kiir at his address to the South Sudan National Legislative Assembly when he declared his government's intention to close oil wells.[37]

So, what are the sore points that made the South flush with such anger? Apart from the government's dragging its feet on important CPA issues, there were other things that had made a large number of southern Sudanese lose their cool with the NCP. In 2005, the NCP was acclaimed by the world for ending Sudan's civil war, a political masterstroke that no other party was able to achieve. Six years later, the NCP also achieved what no other northern party in government had tried, let alone achieved: conducting the self-determination referendum and abiding by its results. That achievement was lauded by the whole world. Rather than proceeding to cash in on these achievements by creating exemplary relations with the new state, the NCP turned sour against the very achievement it delivered. Its attitude after the emergence of the new state was marked, through and through, by anger, high dudgeon, and vindictiveness. This bizarre anger at all things southern following the southern Sudanese option for secession was reflected in a number of measures. Among those were the unpardonable wholesale expulsion of southern citizens from the North, dismissal of southern Sudanese officials from technical departments in Khartoum at a time when these departments were studded with expatriates, and incessant disinformation purveyed by government-controlled media in Khartoum against the South Sudan government and its leaders, with a view to presenting them as insufficient bunglers. Moreover, the NCP seemed not to have awakened to the fact that South Sudan became a sovereign state and, as such, it was not a ward to anyone. Nonetheless, President Kiir and many of his aides continued to underline the need for the viability of both states and the desire to continue with an oil-sharing formula that would ensure "peace in the family."[38] That might have been the reason that prompted SPLM secretary general Pagan Amum to tell Reuters, "The notion of sharing oil wealth will not be there. There is no continuation, whether 50 percent or anything."[39]

Prior to secession, several formulae for revenue sharing were floated, including a graduated ratio of 50/50, 60/40, and 70/30 within the first three years after independence. The highest ratio (50/50) would have ensured that earnings that had accrued to the North under the CPA were not tampered with in a manner that would destabilize its economy, while the (30/70) would have guaranteed the lion's share of oil revenues for the South, with 30 percent allocated to the North to cover fees for the use of oil facilities situated within it. Another formula that transpired in the course of SPLM musings was the extension of a medium-term, interest-free loan to the government of Sudan, equivalent to its present earnings under the Wealth Sharing Protocol, for an agreed upon number of years. The formula, if it had at all been accepted, would have achieved two purposes. First, it would have tranquilized those who were clamoring for their pound of flesh (100 percent of revenues of oil extracted in southern Sudan). Second, it would have forestalled any destablization of the economy of the North while giving its government breathing space to discover other sources of income. Even though there were indications attested by international financial organizations that the government of Sudan was moving in the direction of putting an end to its dependency on oil,[40] more recent reports revealed a gloomier picture. For example, Masood Ahmed, director of the Middle East and Central Asia Department in the International Monetary Fund (IMF) wrote that despite signs that "a marked increase in the country's oil production over the past decade has lifted growth rates, raised living standards, and brought in much-needed revenues, it has had only limited positive spillovers onto Sudan's non-oil sector, with the result that far too many Sudanese are still afflicted by wrenching poverty."[41] Following secession of South Sudan, the IMF reported that there would be a contraction in economic growth in Sudan as a result of losing 75 percent of oil revenues. The IMF's World Economic Outlook projected a negative real gross domestic product (GDP) growth of 0.2 percent in 2011 and 0.4 percent in 2012, down from the 6.5 percent achieved in 2010 and the 6.7 percent average registered growth in the years 2003–2009.[42] This situation worsened after the independence of the South, not only because of the dive in oil revenue, but also because of unrestrained military, security, and administrative expenditure. For example, despite its supposed farewell to arms on the signature of the CPA, the government of Sudan engaged in funding four wars in the country: Blue Nile, Darfur, Abyei, and South Kordofan. In addition, failure of the NCP to democratize governance and achieve national reconciliation resulted in more public disaffection and sometimes stout opposition. Rather than handling this situation politically, the government resorted to arm-twisting and, hence, enlarging expenditure on security agencies. Also, despite the country's loss of one-third of its territory, its leadership chose to increase its executive from 60 to almost 100 ministers, advisors, and assistants to the president. That was the price the NCP leadership decided to pay to politically accommodate job seekers. In a statement to Alex de Waal, executive director of the World Peace Foundation and a research professor at Tufts University, an SPLM leader observed: Why should we allow southern oil to go free to market, when the money from its sales is used to arm rebels who want to destroy us?" and "Why do we allow our oil to be stolen and the money used to kill our comrades in-arms?"[43]

Another problem in the oil sector that shall face South Sudan relates to existing contracts. In Chapter Five it was revealed how and why the CPA made these contracts immutable, save for "contracts deemed to have fundamental social or environmental problems." "Existing oil contracts" were defined as those signed before the conclusion of the CPA. Just as the government of Sudan hoped to see that all rights and obligations agreed upon under these contracts were assigned to the new state under the law of succession, the government of South Sudan believed that it had the right to challenge automatic succession to them for two reasons. First, "existing contracts" were virtually concluded under duress at a time when the government of Sudan was in dire need of resources to discharge its functions and carry out its programs (including the prosecution of war). In that period, the government of Sudan was shunned by the majority of Western donors as well as Sudan's traditional development partners, including Arab states, as a result of sanctions imposed by the U.N. Security Council in 1996, by the U.S. in 1997, and by the EU in 1994. The NIF's isolation in the Arab world was aggravated by its aborted attempt on the life of President Mubarak, supporting Saddam Hussein's occupation of Kuwait, denunciation of the Desert Storm War in Saudi Arabia, and harboring Osama bin Laden in Khartoum. Second, the government, in order to build its war arsenal, was ready to sign oil contracts at any cost with any operator who would promptly extract oil. For that reason new players from Asia moved with alacrity into oil fields in South Sudan, with China and Malaysia as leaders. The Asian players replaced the only three Western oil companies that were prospecting in Sudan: Canada's Talisman Energy, Austria's OMV Group, and Sweden's Lundin Petroleum. The three companies were hounded out of Sudan by the international community and civil society organizations in Canada and the United States for no reason other than their awareness of the role oil production played in intensifying war. Lundin, in actuality, is presently being sued by Swedish human rights groups for purported crimes against humanity as a result of its involvement in oil production in South Sudan during war.[44] To lure the new investors to risk producing oil in an inhospitable war environment, they were given lucrative conditions such as exemption from taxation and a 20 to 40 percent share in net profits at a time when the price of the barrel was computed at $20. When the oil price jumped to unrealistic levels, company net profits correspondingly shot up. This situation, irrespective of the reasons that had led to it, became untenable.

Other reasons that warrant a review of existing contacts include the damage wrought on the natural environment by the modus operandi of some companies in oil extraction as well as the total disregard by the companies concerned of human capacity building and preparation of southern Sudanese to eventually take over oil operations. Only in March 2011 did one of the major Asian players, Malaysia's Petronas, become cognizant of this fact. Though it was already training southern Sudanese students in Malaysia in different fields of expertise, Petronas did not have a well-structured plan for capacity building for southern Sudanese cadres in the oil sector. During the post-independence visits to Juba by Petronas chairman Nusral Danir, a memorandum of understanding was signed with the government of South Sudan's minister for energy and mining "for sharing experiences and expertise in the management of petroleum resources through capacity building and training programs."[45] Another important visitor to Juba after the declaration of independence was China's foreign minister Yang Jiechi. Yang promised a bright future for Chinese relations with Sudan and South Sudan and urged both of them to "have good neighborly relations based on mutual of benefits."[46] Manifestly, oil companies throughout the interim period shied away from any discussion with the government of South Sudan on matters relating to oil except through the National Petroleum Commission. After secession, however, all these oil companies burned up the miles to Juba in order to remain in the good books of its government. Conscious of the role of the two countries in the oil sector, the African Union High-Level Implementation Plan decided to engage oil companies from the two countries as legitimate stakeholders in its search for a final resolution of the conflict between the two states on oil. Thus, in January 2012, former Burundian president and AUHIP peace negotiator Pierre Buyoya held a briefing session with these companies to discuss how to guarantee continuation of the flow of oil.[47]

One other issue that had to be put to rest was the veracity of data on oil production and sales provided by the Government of National Unity and consistently doubted by the government of South Sudan. In September 2009, Global Witness came out with a report entitled "Fuelling Mistrust," which revealed discrepancies between oil revenue figures published by the Government of National Unity and those published by the China National Petroleum Corporation. The variations ranged between nine and 26 percent in the period 2005–2007.[48] Despite attempts by the Government of National Unity to rebut the accusations in a seminar organized in October 2010, Global Witness reported that it was standing by its findings.[49] For that reason President Bashir by the end of the 2010 announced the formation of an audit team comprising Dr. Lual Deng, minster of petroleum, as chair; Ali Mahmoud, minister of finance, as deputy chair; in addition to the auditors general in the Government of National Unity and the government of South Sudan, alongside a foreign audit firm. The audit team was to complete its report before the end of the interim period, but the presidential decision to form the audit group remained ink on paper. The lingering conflict on oil revenue figures prompted the AUHIP to propose the formation of a committee of the two parties, with two persons from each party to investigate arrears owed to the South. In case of disagreement, the matter would be referred to an audit firm, and if either of the parties was not satisfied with the conclusions of the audit firm, the matter would be referred to arbitration. That proposition, too, was held in abeyance until the parties accepted a framework agreement encompassing all issues pertaining to oil.

After a couple of years of bloody conflict between them over oil, the two states, at the behest of the AUHIP, reached an agreement on all contentious issues, including transportation and processing costs that came much closer to international rates. However, the Republic of South Sudan undertook to pay to Sudan agreed-upon amounts to alleviate the loss of its former share in southern Sudan oil. That agreement, denominated "Agreement between the Republic of South Sudan and the Republic of Sudan on Oil and Related Economic Matters," was signed in Addis Ababa on September 27, 2012, by the presidents of both countries.

2.2 Apportionment of Public Debt and Assets

As of December 31, 2010, Sudan's external debt was estimated at $36.27 billion, up from $33.72 billion on December 31, 2009, and it might jump to $38.8 billion by 2011. External debt refers to total public and private debts owed to nonresidents, repayable in foreign currency, goods, or services. This debt comprises monies owed to multilateral creditors such as the World Bank, the International Monetary Fund, and the African Development Bank, as well as bilateral creditors within, as well as outside, the Paris Club and debts to foreign commercial banks and suppliers. On the other hand, assets encompass all property, rights, and interests that belong to the predecessor state at the date of state succession such as real estate inside the country and premises outside it (e.g., diplomatic missions abroad), physical infrastructure (roads, bridges, and pipelines), foreign currency, and gold reserves, etc. Succession to property and debts is presently governed by the Vienna Convention on Succession of States in Respect of State Property, Archives, and Debts (1983). Even though the Vienna Convention is deemed by some states to be of dubious validity,[50] it still incorporates established principles of customary international law on the subject.

The convention, however, provides that: "where part of a state separates from another state, the debt of the predecessor state passes to the successor state in an equitable proportion taking into account, in particular, the property rights and interests which pass to the successor state in relation to that of the predecessor" (article 40). This apportionment, according to the convention, shall be made through agreement between the two states. The issue, therefore, shall be governed by two principles: agreement between the parties and equitable sharing of assets and liabilities.

Political convulsions that had racked Europe since the 1990s resulted in a rethinking of legal principles relating to state secession. For example, following the disintegration of the U.S.S.R., the Socialist Federal Republic of Yugoslavia, and the Czechoslovak Socialist Republic as well as the reunification of Germany, the International Law Institute resolved: "In the event of succession, the States concerned should, in good faith, settle by agreement amongst themselves the apportionment of State property and debts bearing in mind the criteria for apportionment enunciated in the Resolution."[51] These criteria included, *inter alia*, locality of assets avoiding unjust enrichment, apportionment of assets on the basis of territoriality, and equity in dividing assets to which the territoriality does not apply (article 11). The resolution also called for equity in the apportionment of debts, and if the apportionment did not produce equitable results and could not otherwise be corrected, the predecessor state and the successor state should settle the matter by equitable compensation (article 8).

Apportionment of assets, however, was not a cause of friction between the two Sudanese parties, as they both accepted territoriality as the governing principle for the division of assets. That principle implies that "immoveable property of the predecessor State situated on the territory to which the succession relates passes to the successor State on whose territory the property is located,"[52] while property situated outside its territory (e.g., premises of diplomatic missions) would be apportioned in equitable proportions.[53] This did not seem to be problematic, as the immoveable property abroad that was owned by the Sudan negligible. However, the two governments have yet to reach agreement on the apportionment of moveable property such as railway stocks, airlines assets, river barges, etc.

Unlike property, debts pose a special problem since they involve third parties. It is, thus, incumbent upon both predecessor and successor state to act in good faith with outside creditors. However, to ensure equitable apportionment, debts must be disaggregated so as to determine how, where, and for what purpose the borrowed funds were expended. For want of a better system, the easiest criteria for parceling out Sudan's foreign debts may also be on the basis of territoriality. Sudan's accumulated debts were mainly spent on development, budget support, or arms. Since independence, South Sudan hardly benefited from any major development project, although a small part of the external debts that accrued during the period between 1973 and 1983 was to meet the needs of the regional government in Juba established by the Addis Ababa agreement, or to launch a few development projects in southern Sudan. This included, among others, debts owed to Yugoslavia (succeeded by Croatia) for the construction of residences and offices for that government, and to Belgium for the Melut Sugar Project.[54] While the Yugoslav debts were actually expended on the purpose for which they were borrowed, debts for the Melut project did not benefit South Sudan, as that project never materialized, and the equipment bought for it remained in Khartoum and was partly cannibalized and used for similar projects in the North such as Assalaiya.[55] On the other side, the new state may be partly responsible for debts incurred by the national government for budget support, to be apportioned on a per capita basis. However, Sudan's largest portion of debts was accumulated through arms purchased from China, Bulgaria, Russia, and other countries that were part of the former U.S.S.R. That, for sure, is the type of debt that neither the NCP, nor any another government in Khartoum, would in good faith charge to the new state in southern Sudan.

To avoid the cumbersome process of disaggregating debts and identifying the purposes for which those debts were used and by whom, the two parties began to jointly explore ways and means of canceling Sudan's external debts. It would be worth recalling that a joint approach to extinguishing Sudan's external debts had been one of the issues highlighted by Garang in his 180-day plan. This process, however, was also encouraged by U.S. peace envoy Scott Gration and the United Kingdom. Realizing that Sudan's external debt caused greater distress to the North than it did to South Sudan, as the latter was neither encumbered by a heavy debt burden nor subjected to U.S. sanctions, the mediators surmised that debt forgiveness would be the most attractive inducement for the government of Sudan expedite efforts toward the resolution of outstanding conflictual CPA issues and putting an end to the Darfur conflict.[56] As a result of the above encumbrances, northern Sudan not only suffered from onerous debt burden, but also from a paucity of concessional financing from traditional funding agencies. At present only China, India, and Arab and Islamic funds continue to fund development projects in northern Sudan.[57] In April 2011, the government's anger turned to outrage when the Office of Foreign Assets Control in the U.S. Department of Treasury issued a statement excluding only the Republic of South Sudan from sanctions, adding "that sanctions imposed in 1997 on the government of Sudan shall continue."

Under normal circumstances Sudan's debts should have benefited from the debt cancelation initiative announced since 2005 by major lenders, including the Interntional Monetary Fund and the World Bank.[58] The two international financial institutions had established an approach to identifying countries eligible for debt cancelation known as the Heavily Indebted Poor Countries (HIPC) Initiative. Countries were expected to meet certain criteria to be considered for assistance ("decision point") and to receive assistance ("completion point). By 2009, thirty African countries benefited from that initiative by reaching the "completion point"; eight countries had reached the "decision point" and were being considered for assistance, while five, including Sudan, never reached the "decision point."[59] If Sudan had regularly been excluded from HIPC, it was not because it could not meet the technical criteria established, but for other reasons. These reasons were flagrantly political, as Lual Deng, Sudan's minister of state for finance, claimed during the France-Africa Summit in Nice, France, June 2010. Talking to the press, the minister said that "Sudan has met all the technical conditions for writing off its debts, but the super countries are linking this issue to political matters."[60]

Far from considering it a financial or political issue, international human rights groups and faith-based alliances treated poor countries' debts as a moral issue. These groups reckoned that reducing people to perpetual poverty under whatever political guise was not an issue of politics but one of justice and morality. In 1998, for instance, 750 bishops led by the archbishop of Canterbury gathered at Lambeth, England, in order "to make politicians see the evil of poor countries debts." The archbishop described the debts of poor countries as a "moral problem of enormous proportions."[61] This view was challenged by economists on two counts: legal and financial. Legally, says Sean Hagan,[62] general counsel of the International Monetary Fund (IMF), "states are generally bound by debt obligations contracted by previous governments and the concept of continuity is one of the most fundamental principles of international law." As a general matter, he said, "a state's rights and obligations under international law are not interrupted by a change in government."[63] From a policy perspective in economics and finance, Hagan maintained, "the introduction of an odious debt exception would most likely do considerable damage to the capacity of developing countries to borrow responsibly."[64] The IMF counsel was unerring in saying that developing countries should learn how to borrow responsibly, however, that argument ignored another consequential fact: over two-thirds of those debts related to interest and penalties, and that was from where the odium came. For that reason lenders, too, must learn how to lend to poor countries in a manner that is neither exorbitant nor unconscionable. It is interesting to note, however, that Sudan's debt to the IMF and the World Bank accounts for 75 percent of the global arrears owed to these organizations, according to an IMF report dated August 18, 2009.

Much as political pressure groups and activists have had serious grievances against the government of Sudan, especially in view of its policies towards Darfur and prevarication on implementation of the CPA, denying Sudan debt relief does not harm the callous politicians who were behind those policies but creates hardships to millions of ordinary citizens. According to the IMF, "Sudan will remain in debt distress in the foreseeable future even under a benign global environment and the implementation of appropriate policies."[65] The report also said that the government of Sudan "expressed concern that, despite [its] cooperation on policies and payments [to the IMF] for nearly a decade, no concrete progress has been made on alleviating Sudan's external debt burden, severely limiting the prospects for meeting the Millennium Development Goals (MDGs) and CPA commitments."[66] This is yet additional evidence of how measures taken by major powers and international organizations against targeted governments such as the government of Sudan do not only fail to hit their target, but also destabilize the economic strategic objectives of the world community such as achieving MDGs.

Leaving law and morality aside, the two parties eventually came to an agreement on September 27, 2012, at Addis Ababa regarding external and domestic assets and liabilities. The agreement was based on principles of international law, as expounded above, and the desire of both parties to ensure "mutual benefits derived from pursuing strategic cooperation on certain economic issues to maximize rather than prejudice the growth potential of each state."[67] Those sweet words were met with the indiscriminate actions of the U.S. Department of the Treasury, from which prominent apolitical Sudanese businessmen and professionals (not the government) suffered immensely for no other reason than their being domiciled in Sudan. Thus, Sudanese businessmen who kept bank accounts in, or transacted business through, banks in the United Kingdom and lived in Sudan suffered from the U.S. Treasury's random instructions. The banks were under threat to either suspend dealings with those bona fide clients, or be disallowed from doing business in the United States. Regardless of whether or not it related to debts or sanctions, laws promulgated by the U.S. administration were punishing the innocent rather their intended targets. This is the perfect example of what G.K. Chesterton has called good laws that turn, on application, into bad ones.[68]

2.3 Currency and Monetary Policy

In Chapters Five we explained how difficult the birth of Sudan's current asymmetric banking arrangement was. Also revealed in that chapter was the inclination of the SPLM to have a separate currency for South Sudan and how it eventually yielded to having one Sudanese currency based on the pound rather than the dinar. The emergence of both issues at the top of post-referendum measures under discussion by the parties was to be expected. Unquestionably, national currency is an important symbol of sovereignty, and for that reason the desire of southern Sudanese to have their own currency need not be misread. However, what caused misapprehensions about that desire was the tampering by some elements in the South with the wild idea of temporary dollarization of the southern economy before issuing a new currency instead of continuing, even for a short period, to use the Sudanese pound. That was an unnecessary and an ill-advised proposition as it did not take into consideration the historical, geographic, or economic factors that made countries like Liberia or certain central American republics adopt the U.S. dollar as a national currency.

Nevertheless, issuing a currency is not only about printing or minting money; it is a process that is closely tied to management of foreign currency reserves, macroeconomic stabilization measures, and confidence in the banking system itself. The contention by some SPLM negotiators that they would be ready with southern Sudan's new currency by the end of the interim period and before settling outstanding monetary issues nonplussed government negotiators and should have disconcerted southern Sudanese who had experience with the shambles of issuing, without due diligence or mandatory controls, a new pound in southern Sudan a few years before the conclusion of the CPA. That was an experience southern Sudan should never had thought of setting its heart on because of the troubles it had caused. Fortunately, this time, the government of South Sudan's Ministry of Finance established contacts with credible currency printers and the IMF to ensure that the operation was carried out properly. Those measures were necessary to avoid the sad experiences faced by other countries as a result of unstudied, or unprepared for, currency changes. In those cases the economy witnessed large deposit withdrawals, rapid exchanges of local currency into free currencies, hoarding of goods that led to severe commodity shortages, smuggling of money across borders, etc.

Realizing all those perils and the probability that the new currency might need a longer period to be printed, circulated, and recognized by the public beyond July 9, 2011, SPLM negotiators agreed that South Sudan would continue using the Sudanese pound for a period of up to six or nine months. To the surprise of everybody, the new South Sudan government declared that its new currency would be ready for circulation only one week after the declaration of independence (and not within six to nine months, as intimated to the NCP and conveyed to the IMF). This decision made the new republic seem to have acted in bad faith. In the meantime, Khartoum, which had never been known to be deficient in artifice, had already prepared itself for that eventuality. Once the new government of South Sudan announced the circulation of its currency, Khartoum immediately made public its decision to issue a new print of the Sudanese pound so that its old paper money would cease to be legal tender. That decision engendered a currency war between the two states, especially when the government in South Sudan called for redemption in foreign currency of the old Sudanese pounds accumulated in the South or, alternatively, permission to use that currency for trade with the North. The accumulated currency was calculated to be about two billion pounds. Not only did Khartoum reject the two requests, it also declared in a crude manner that that currency was only fit for burning.[69]

When the author inquired about what had prompted South Sudan to issue the new currency in defiance of its statements to the government of Sudan and the IMF that the process would take six to nine months, the governor of the Central Bank of South Sudan (BoSS) revealed a bizarre episode. He claimed that in May–June 2011, the government of South Sudan was in dire need of funds in local currency to meet its monthly operations expenses as well as the costs of preparations for independence day (July 9). The Bank of Sudan, according to the governor of the Central Bank of South Sudan, apologized claiming that there was shortage of notes and that the currency printing facilities were closed for maintenance. As a result, the government of South Sudan was forced to use foreign currency from its reserves to meet these pressing and vital obligations. The governor also presented to the author a five pound note of the new Sudanese pound, drawing attention to the date on which the banknote was printed: June 2011. That was the period when the printing facilities of the Central Bank of Sudan were alleged to have been closed for maintenance. It is, therefore, clear that there were reasons to make the government of South Sudan's Ministry of Finance and the BoSS expedite the issuance of its new currency, as well as fears that dependency on the Sudanese currency may, wittingly or unwittingly, jeopardize the functioning of the new state.

Apart from issuing its own currency, the new state was also faced with the arduous task of regulating its monetary policy. This task, which encompassed control of the money supply, management of foreign reserves, and regulation of the banking industry in the country was undertaken by the BoSS before independence of South Sudan. At that time, BoSS was not directly involved in any of those tasks, although it dealt indirectly with all these processes through its nominees on the Board of the Central Bank, (including the governor of BoSS). In that capacity, South Sudan nominees had an opportunity to contribute to the formulation of the bank's policies and the determination of policy instruments. However, by July 9, 2011, BoSS became solely responsible for managing the monetary policy of the new state. With limited experience in working out monetary policies, BoSS has to be professionally revamped if it is to efficiently and effectively carry out its main function: ensuring monetary and financial stability. As the Republic of South Sudan is soon to become an IMF member, the IMF has decided to provide technical assistance and training in areas of macroeconomics and fiscal, monetary, and financial policies. The IMF has also mobilized resources for a special IMF fund for macroeconomic capacity building in South Sudan.[70]

As important, if not more so, is BoSS's functional independence, which has not been firmly established in the last five years. During these years BoSS was constantly harassed by some of South Sudan's government officers who daftly maintained that BoSS was the government's bank and, accordingly, government ministers were entitled to meddle in the way it was run. True, BoSS during the interim period maintained the consolidated fund accounts of GOSS and also held, on behalf of Sudan's Central Bank, foreign exchange in South Sudan. It also acted as the country's bank of last resort for GOSS. Nevertheless, that did not give government officers in South Sudan, at any level and under whatever guise, the right to intervene in the operations of BoSS, let alone attempt to micromanage its operations. For example, in 2007 the minister of finance in the government of South Sudan accused the governor of expatriating the government of South Sudan's fund without the minster's authorization. Little did that minister know that BoSS was authorized by the CPA Matrix for Implementation to "open correspondent accounts in prime banks in favor of the government of South Sudan, deposit all of the government of South Sudan's foreign exchange resources in that bank, manage the account on the basis of the best banking practices in favor of the government of South Sudan, and disburse it in a way to ensure macroeconomic stability and national monetary policy objectives." Astoundingly, this meddling by the government in banking happened at a time when even the British government, which has been known for its possessiveness regarding monetary policy formulation, yielded operational independence over that policy to the Bank of England for the first time in history. These uncalled for interventions regrettably did not only reflect ignorance of how central banks function in the real world, but also of the banking regime established by the CPA.

To put order into the banking sector, the new state contemplated before secession the creation of a currency board instead of having a central bank and governor. Currency boards were common in former British colonies, especially in Asia and the Caribbean. Following decolonization, those countries opted for the creation of central banks, probably because they considered currency boards as vestiges of colonialism. Subsequently, there was an impressive return to currency boards as evidenced by the cases of Argentina, Ireland, Malaysia, Singapore, Hong Kong, and most recently—after the breaking up of Yugoslavia and the Soviet Union—in Estonia, Lithuania, Bosnia and Herzegovina, and Djibouti. Currency board regimes come with stringent conditions that may not be palatable to governments that recoil from tight monetary discipline. For instance, orthodox currency boards remove, or at least limit, the scope of discretionary credit policy, do not work as banks of last resort, and do not lend to governments or banks. In the latter case, they may only provide support to governments or failing banks either from their excess reserves, or through mediating borrowing from international capital markets. In addition, currency boards do not manipulate interest rates by setting discount rates. For it to function properly, a currency board must have at least 100 percent of its reserves in foreign currency to meet long-time commitments in local currency.[71] According to an IMF working paper, limiting the scope of discretionary funds results "in even greater discipline and confidence than simply pegging the exchange rate."[72] As to the effect of that system on growth, the paper stated that "countries with currency boards actually grow faster than the average of all countries with pegged exchange regimes," while inflation rates average 6 percent under currency boards, which is substantially lower than 15–20 percent under floating exchange rates. In light of all these considerations, the establishment of a currency board would have ensured better management of money and finance as well as control over public spending, which is now subject to little, if no, control. It shall also discipline the banking industry, enhance its ability to raise additional capital, and improve its governance through market discipline.

It might be interesting to recall that, if carried out, that would not have been the first time a currency board was created in Sudan. On January 1, 1956, and as a result of the fleetness with which independence was declared, the government decided to continue using the Egyptian pound for 16 months after independence, or up until August 4, 1957. Throughout this period, monetary policy and banking were administered by a currency board composed of three Sudanese economists[73] alongside three non-Sudanese bankers from Egypt, Sweden, and the United Kingdom. The three external bankers represented the National Bank of Egypt, the Central Bank of Sweden, and the Bank of England. One lesson to learn from that short-lived experience is the idea of seeking external help in the management of fledgling banking institutions. There is a wide range of reputable banking institutions from which the Bank of Southern Sudan may draw expertise such as the Bank of England, Bank for International Settlements, Bank of Sweden, etc.

Paradoxically, the splitting up of Sudan's monetary authority, which had been unified since independence, came at a time when African subregions were moving toward monetary unions and Africa was planning to have a common currency by 2028. Within subregions there is a progressive move towards intergovernmental monetary unions such as the East African Community (EAC). In a few years, the East African Monetary Union shall be the pinnacle of regional economic integration of the EAC. On the other hand, the West African Monetary Zone, spearheaded by Ghana and Nigeria at Accra in April 2002, was born to provide a stimulus to the integration of the Economic Community of West Africa.[74] The West African Monetary Zone, which comprises Gambia, Ghana, Guinea, Nigeria, and Sierra Leone, aims to create one currency; a governance council made up of ministers of finance, trade, and external affairs of the five countries; a technical supervising body made up of the governors of the central banks of the member countries; and a supreme body composed of heads of state. These options had, apparently, never been factored into discussions by the two parties, but they can serve as pointers to future developments in the continent that no country can evade.

After the secession of South Sudan, the government of Sudan announced its intention to join the EAC. When the North and South were united, the government had plenty of time to join that community the way Burundi and Rwanda had done because of its geographic contiguity to existing members, which has been a basic condition for membership of the EAC. Hence, making a hasty march into the EAC before the government of South Sudan had done, would have been counterproductive. Before the secession of the South, the Republic of Sudan could have been eligible for membership in the EAC by virtue of bordering two of its members, Kenya and Uganda. One wonders why Sudan sought economic integration in a common market where trade barriers would be removed; free movement of goods, labor, and services assured; and currency unified at the very time when it appeared determined to set barriers against all these activities within Sudan and South Sudan who were only one country six months earlier. This petulant act either reflected the inadequacy of Sudanese diplomacy or the fickleness with which its government treated the policy of regional economic integration.

Again, to the happy surprise of well-wishers for the two states, the twin issues of banking and trade were satisfactorily resolved in the Addis Ababa summit held September 27, 2012, between Bashir and Salva Kiir. On the issue of trade they agreed to establish a (JMCTR) within 30 days of ratification of the agreement. The JMCTR's primary responsibility is to enhance trade relations between the two states, including implementing a preferential trade regime. As for banking, an Agreement on a Framework for Cooperation on Central Banking Issues was also signed. As in the case of trade, a Joint Central Banks Committee (JCBC) was to be established within 30 days of ratification of the agreement. JCBC responsibilities include supporting "financial stability and sound banking policies in the two states" and developing "appropriate procedures and systems for enhancing cooperation in the areas of central banking, monetary policy, exchange rate policy, banking supervision, and the preservation of the value of the respective currencies of the two states." The committee shall also facilitate smooth payment system transfer operations between the two states, a matter which is cardinal for the enhancement of trade between them.

2.4 North/South Economic Cooperation/Integration

Closely related to the previous issue is that of economic cooperation and integration between the two states. Despite all political discords between North and South Sudan, people-to-people integration had been built through the years, especially in contiguous border zones. Those economic bonds need to be bolstered rather than weakened after secession. Above all, South Sudan shall be the only northern neighbor of the new state with the longest international borders. Despite incongruities in the economies of the two parts of the country, there are still convergences that are not to be overlooked. For example, the northern states, with a population of 30 million and a high population growth rate, shall be the main market for southern Sudan's tropical products, especially since all other countries neighboring the new state to the east, south, and west are either competitors in the production of those commodities or short of markets as elastic as that of Sudan. Also, East African markets, although close to Equatoria, are still geographically distant from the densely populated states of Bahr el Ghazal, Upper Nile, and Unity whose main supplies of basic food and other essential items such as cooking oil, soap, and sugar traditionally came from neighboring northern states. Thus, for secession to be smooth it had to be accommodative, rather than disruptive, of the interests of both states. A recent assessment published by Conflict Dynamics International warned that black-and-white choices, as some protagonists on both sides seemed inclined to, would harm both states.[75] Rather than a fragmented approach to post-conflict arrangements, Conflict Dynamics recommended a broad-based accommodative approach, since "structured reciprocity provides opportunity for more effective accommodation within northern Sudan, within southern Sudan, and between the two entities than issue-based reciprocity."[76]

In the contemporary world, integration of the economies of sovereign states has become the order of the day; economic unions have begun to bestride the world from the Pacific to the Atlantic and Indian oceans.[77] In Africa, eight regional economic blocks operate with different degrees of success.[78] The philosophy that inspired regional and subregional economic cooperation in Africa was, at the political level, pan-African solidarity and, at the economic level, collective self-reliance. In short, economic integration seeks to increase the GDP of the member countries, improve the welfare of their citizens, and widen opportunities for their economic growth. At the continental level, economic integration has been a target to which the fathers of the Organization of African Unity (OAU) have aspired to since the OAU's inception. In April 1980, that aspiration was translated into the Lagos Plan of Action for the Economic Development of Africa, 1980–2000. That plan was adopted by the African summit meeting in Lagos, Nigeria, in April 1980, although it was criticized as a reactive document to the World Bank's Berg report,[79] which blamed African leaders for the economic woes of the continent but lost sight of the economic shocks that had afflicted the continent as a result of inequitable terms of international trade, onerous debts, and the oil crisis in the 1970s. The Lagos Plan was also criticized by African economists for its lack of a critique of Africa's own role in messing up the continent's economies through economic mismanagement, corruption, maladministration, and inequities in wealth sharing. All the same, Africa's collective effort to integrate the economies of the continent culminated in the creation of the African Economic Community (AEC), signed by African heads of state and government in 1991,[80] in which shortcomings of the Lagos Plan were amply addressed. According to the AEC, full economic integration of Africa shall be achieved incrementally through a number of measures, including integration of subregional communities; creation of subregional blocks where these do not presently exist; and the establishment of free trade areas and customs unions in each regional block by 2017, a continent-wide African Common Market by 2019, and a continent-wide economic and monetary union and common currency by 2028.

Even though empirical research had proven beyond a reasonable doubt that unimpeded trade flows between states were beneficial to the economies of these states, some economic insularists within the continent persisted in believing in the erection of trade barriers and the maintenance of tax revenues as a bulwark

371

to the economy.[81] This short-sighted vision did not take into account that the benefits accruing from unimpeded trade within economic communities would outweigh those realized through trade controls and regulations and other insularist measures. Such insularist measures in Sudan were hardly informed by the vital interests of the two states, as they were meant to be punitive acts by one state against the other. For example, closure by the government of Sudan of trade routes between North and South Sudan was a retaliatory act against the Republic of South Sudan for what Khartoum thought to be procrastination on the resolution of a raft of CPA outstanding issues. On the other hand, more than a few closed-minded southern Sudanese nationalists, who despite their professed commitment to African economic integration, were outspoken about their desire to build a Berlin wall between North and South Sudan and turn their faces totally toward East Africa. That temerarious idea had neither taken note of the facts of geography nor of the dynamics of continental politics. The assumption by southern or northern Sudanese that North Sudan is not part of Africa is hollow to the core. On the eve of the referendum, Thabo Mbeki appurtenantly advised this group that "should the referendum vote be in favor of secession, Africa will welcome South Sudan as its 54th state. Rather than dividing Sudan into an 'African' south and an 'Arab' north, Sudan will become two equally African states, both marked by ethnic, cultural, and religious diversity, both facing the challenges of democratization, development, and unity in diversity."[82] Indeed, regional geopolitics and the dynamics of subregional economic integration shall impose on the new state participation in other subregional blocks such as the IGAD and the Common Market for Eastern and Southern Africa (COMESA),[83] in both of which the Republic of Sudan is a founding member and, as such, is there to stay. Insularists on both sides of the borders may have to wake up to new African realities: panAfricanism is no longer an ethnically based postulation but a grand design informed by geography, common economic interests, mutually enriching cultures, self-reliance, and communal security.

There is, however, a small group of insularists in southern Sudan who are not driven by ultra-Africanism, as they pretend to be, but by an unfounded belief that Western countries, especially the United States, wish to see South Sudan disconnected from its North. This belief obviously stems from a naive reading of international politics, which may have been encouraged by some U.S. advocacy groups who have an axe to grind with Khartoum for reasons that neither serve the interests of southern Sudan, nor of Africa. U.S. policy is often influenced by pressures from lobby groups, but it is never determined by them. Thomas Talley, a strategic plans and policy officer in the U.S. Africa Command, remarked that such ideas were "driven by an advocacy community with different or, probably, conflicting agenda."[84] The bottom line of U.S. policy in Sudan, as well as in other countries, is protection and enhancement of national interests. The United States also has national interest concerns in northern Sudan, not least of which is shielding that country from "international terrorism" and ensuring that it does not evolve into a center of destabilization in the region. It is very doubtful whether those who take pride (sometimes loudly) in being Washington's men in Juba have ever perused the history of U.S. politics toward southern Sudan, beginning with Senator Danforth's position on secession (Chapter Three) and Colin Powell's objection to having two standing armies in Sudan during the interim period (Chapter Five). Those who gladly wish to turn the 54th African Union into the 51st U.S. state shall neither give credence to the commitment of their leaders to panAfricanism, nor give pleasure to America, which is already saddled by more problems than it can cope with.

Another analyst, Wolfram Lacher, pertinently remarked that "the two sides should be encouraged to resist their likely reflex of erecting barriers and curbing ties between themselves." Lacher added that this reflex "is particularly relevant with regard to the southern government, which seeks the backing of Western donors as a counterweight to Khartoum's influence."[85] The analyst went further to say that the expansion (by the new state) of ties with its southern and eastern neighborhood and [neglecting the North] would deepen polarization between the two states. Lacher's remark was triggered by what appeared to be the southern government's search for economic development support from Western donors, as it had indeed been seeking (and receiving) political and moral support during the struggle. But surely those in the West who furnished support to the SPLM were not doing so became of a grudge toward the North, particularly since the North comprised large groups, which straddled the country from Darfur to Beja land and challenged, alongside the SPLM, the excesses of Khartoum. Besides, insinuating that southern Sudan's neighbors to the east and south wish to see it disconnected from the North is fulsome, as these neighbors have never hidden their wish to have Sudan united. When secession became imminent, they never spared an effort to ensure that would happen, if relations between the two states remained amicable and mutually rewarding. In general, the analyst was on the mark when he advised that, "Instead of hastening the south's uncoupling from the north and [raising] the risk of conflict between the two sides, external actors should seek to promote their integration, and prevent imbalances in north-south relations."[86]

2.5 Security

2.5.1 Border Conflicts

In Chapter Eight we had delineated security threats that faced southern Sudan and how its government grappled with these threats. After independence, southern Sudan security may still be at risk from three sources: border conflicts, external destabilization, and internal feuds. This part of Chapter Ten shall address the first two threats, while the third shall be discussed in the next chapter dedicated to challenges whose resolution shall essentially fall within the purview of the new state's responsibilities.

Concerning border security threats, those would naturally ease up, or be aggravated, as a result of the nature of relations the two states wish to have after secession; the more relations between the two states are informed by a concurrence of interests and mutual cooperation, the more peaceful southern Sudan will be. In the few months that preceded the referendum, the atmosphere on both sides was bristling with fear of return to war. These fears were generated by the unending conflict over Abyei, intimidating statements by NCP leaders and security operatives toward southerners living in northern Sudan, as well as the alleged increase of Sudan Armed Forces (SAF) and militias on the North-South border. More serious were accusations by the SPLM against the SAF of providing material support to SPLA renegades. If those claims were true, one would assume that there was an NCP endgame for these maneuvers, and if there was, it would be nothing other than return to war. Being alert to the repercussions of a reversion to war in southern Sudan, especially with the war in Darfur still going on and the revulsion by the international community of any new conflagration in Sudan, right-thinking elements within the NCP would not, in all likeliness, support such a gamble. Even when the two parties came close to full scale war after the occupation of Heglig by the SPLA on April 4, 2012, there were still inklings that all NCP moves (political, military, or diplomatic) were only impulsive tactical moves with neither a strategic frame of reference nor a calculation of risks. That would not come as a surprise to those who had been following the NCP's behavior in the last two decades. However, the NCP's rashness after the conclusion of the CPA had been encouraged by the slipshod manner with which observers treated many serious infractions of the agreement by that party. Whether through genuine belief or sheer make-believe, the NCP interpreted the silence of observers toward those infractions as a green light. When it had gotten away with all these breaches of solemnly made obligations without even a slap on the wrist, the NCP decided to raise the stakes, beginning with acting as if the referendum would not take place. The International Crisis Group rightly observed that "the NCP never expected the referendum would materialize and they would be faced with the stark reality of impending partition."[87] That view was even shared by NCP cadres who were deeply involved in the negotiations and should have been appreciative of the depth of SPLM's mistrust of northern politics and the intricacies of the peace agreement. Amin Hassan Omer, one of the active NCP negotiators at Machakos, told a Khartoum daily that repeated talk about impending secession of the South reflected a phobophobia not supported by real and objective indicators. He added: "I don't believe that any person who bases judgment on objective facts shall come to the conclusion that southerners shall vote for secession."[88] Indubitably, without the combined efforts of the United Nations, United States, African Union, the IGAD, and very close Arab neighbors to Sudan, the NCP's playacting regarding the referendum would have continued. However, once the referendum appeared to be inevitable and secession increasingly probable, the hawks within the NCP became more impetuous in their remarks and actions.

To head off any post-referendum risks to the new state's security, the president of the government of South Sudan called for cross-border international monitoring, including a role for the United Nations, in order to ensure the protection of civilians on both sides of the border. The request was made to a high-level delegation from the U.N. Security Council, which visited Juba in 2010 and was reaffirmed by the government of South Sudan's president during his visit to the U.N. Headquarters in September of the same year. Even though fears lessened as a result of a concerted effort by neighboring countries, regional organizations, and the international community, it did not entirely dissipate, as can be gathered from a statement by Deng Alor Kuol, the government of South Sudan's minister of regional cooperation. The minister told a Khartoum daily correspondent in Washington that plans were under way to extend the mandate of the United Nations Mission in Sudan (UNMIS) in southern Sudan for peacekeeping during a reasonably short period.[89] Those fears were shared by the IGAD countries during the IGAD Assembly of Heads of State and Government meeting in Addis Ababa in July 2010. On that occasion, Ethiopian Prime Minister Meles Zenawi told the media that a new war in Sudan was possible but not inevitable. He added that if such a war broke out it would be more dangerous than the Ethiopian-Eritrean war, since it would engulf the whole of Africa. Zenawi, who probably had a hunch that war might escalate as a result of reprisals for small incidents, said: "If an eye for an eye vengeance is to happen, there shall be many eyeless people in Sudan.[90] The IGAD summit urged the two parties to avoid any tension that might turn into violence and disrupt the referendum. In effect, the surprise visit by President Bashir to Juba on April 1, 2011, five days before the referendum, seemed to have dampened fears, particularly when he declared the commitment of his party to abide by whatever decision the people of southern Sudan settled for.

Eventually, on July 8, 2011, the U.N. Security Council adopted Resolution 1996, authorizing the creation of a 7,000 man United Nations Mission in the Republic of South Sudan (UNMISS) as a successor to UNMIS. The mandate of the new force was to support peace consolidation, economic development, and state building in South Sudan. In addition, the U.N. force was to provide civilian protection under article VI of the charter and advise the government on policies relating to governance such as constitutional development, elections, human rights protection, and promotion of media independence. Hilde Johnson (Norway), one of the peace architects, was nominated by the U.N. secretary general as his special representative to the new republic on June 13, 2011. A breakthrough, it may be recalled, was also made by the two parties through the intermediation of the African Union High-Level Implementation Plan (AUHIP) on September 18, 2011, when the two parties—led by the ministers of defense of the two governments, Abdel Rahim Mohamed Hussein on the part of the

Republic of Sudan, and John Kong Nyuon on the part of South Sudan Republic—agreed on the establishment of a 300-man protection force to be provided by the United Nations.[91] The area on both sides of the border was to be demilitarized, and 10 entry points in the 2,000-kilometer border were identified by the two parties to ensure free flow of persons, goods, and services. But as the ICG had rightly observed, this process would be incomplete without "a complement of civilian monitors…to support cross-border initiatives, dispute resolution, local border management, and effective and transparent information gathering and reporting."[92]

The ICG observation was more than an intuitive remark, as future developments proved. The escalation of activities in South Sudan, especially in Unity State, by southern insurgents supported by Khartoum, coupled with the intensification of war in Nuba Mountains involving SAF and contingents of the SPLA and the Heglig conflict involving SAF and SPLA, were all cases in point. Sadly, all those accidents were a direct result of failure to address in a conclusive manner clauses in the CPA relating to outstanding border security issues. Acknowledgement of the necessity to reach "final agreements on all key border issues in an integrated manner and to provide appropriate mechanism for their implementation"[93] was only reached by the end of September 2012. That agreement provided that borders between the two states would be soft in order "to maintain a peaceful, safe, and secure border along which people can move and goods and services can flow easily." In addition, it stated that, "Given the special character of the border and the need to regulate, protect, and promote the various interests of public and community nature along the border," an integrated border management approach should be adopted in order to put the above objectives into effect. That approach, according to the agreement, would encompass bilateral cooperation, inter-agency and intra-agency cooperation, and stakeholders' participation. Regarding border demarcation, the agreement decided that, within two weeks of its ratifications, a Joint Demarcation Committee (JDC) should be established, supported by joint technical teams (JTT). This agreement had surely closed any loopholes in the previous arrangements on borders.

2.5.2 Proxy Wars

In previous chapters, reference was made to numerous attempts to destabilize the government of South Sudan by other armed groups (OAGs) aligned to the SAF. Those proxy wars were waged against the government of South Sudan by forces commanded by Gordon Kong, Simon Gatwich, and Gabriel Tanginya, as well as by southern Sudanese elements serving within joint integrated units (JIUs). While accusations against the three were amply proved, there were also spurious accusations by the government of South Sudan against other groups. One such example is the insinuations that the Ambororo roaming tribesmen were armed militias of Khartoum.[94] Nevertheless, attacks by OAGs continued even after

Salva Kiir's successful reconciliation with all armed and nonarmed southern opposition groups. That reconciliation included the OAG rebel Tanginya, who was received by the first vice president at his official residence in Khartoum two weeks before the referendum, as well as with George Athor, who broke rank with the SPLA after his defeat by the SPLM candidate in the gubernatorial elections in Jonglei.[95] A cease-fire agreement between Athor's forces and the SPLA was signed on January 5, 2011.[96] Both agreements should have meant that south Sudan had, to all intents and purposes, bid farewell to arms. However, the conflagration of war in Jonglei and Upper Nile states at the bidding of the two rebel soldiers raised doubts as to their real motives as well as the source of their heavy armament. No sooner had the referendum ended than Athor waged a full-scale war against SPLA garrisons in Jonglei and extended his attacks to Fangak, a center of Lou Nuer. That attack resulted in the death of scores of Nuers in addition to plundering the town. That was hardly the way to even up the score for his defeat in the elections. Tanginya, who reached agreement with the government of South Sudan president, went back to southern Sudan to wreak havoc and declare, likely with encouragement from certain political aspirants, a war against the government of South Sudan and the SPLA. After skirmishes in which hundreds of people perished, he was arrested and brought to justice. It is to be recalled that the government of South Sudan president had requested, to no avail, the extradition of this officer from Khartoum to Malakal to answer for the massacres he caused in that town. With this history of double dealing, and the blood bath caused by the two renegade officers, suspicions increased as to the support they were receiving from Khartoum in order to destabilize the government of South Sudan and humiliate the SPLA. Hence, the SPLA came to a not far-fetched conclusion that its former officers were masterminded and supported by the SAF, particularly in view of the heavy weaponry they were able to amass in a very short time. SAF, as usual, hastened to deny the accusation.[97]

2.5.3 War of Documents

In mid-March 2011, the SPLM secretary general accused President Bashir of personal involvement in the attempts to overthrow Salva Kiir before independence day. In support to the allegation, he produced documents purportedly emanating from SAF and NCP. Both SAF and NCP speedily denied the accusation and claimed that the documents were fraudulent.[98] Two days after the secretary general's press conference, South African President Thabo Mbeki held a meeting with the presidency in Khartoum to jump-start the talks, but before that, to get to the bottom of the SPLM's serious accusation. The presidency, after deliberation on the matter, decided to form a technical committee to investigate that matter and verify the authenticity of the documents. The investigation was immediately started by Thabo Mbeki, with technical help from UNMIS. What was startling in this episode was the secretary general's choice of the venue at which he revealed accusations of such magnitude.

According to a senior security source in the government of South Sudan, those documents, if proved authentic, would have been tantamount to a declaration of war. In that case the documents should have been subjected to serious analysis by the government of South Sudan, the U.N. Security Council, and intelligence experts, otherwise both the credibility and professionalism of the government of South Sudan would suffer if the documents were proved to be inauthentic. But while no decision was yet reached investigation of the documents was still out, the secretary general decided to up the ante once more, this time by taking the matter to a consultative private meeting held by the U.N. Security Council on March 21, 2011. That meeting was called to review the situation in Sudan, especially regarding the Abyei conflict. Nevertheless, the secretary general chose to raise the issue of the "incriminating" documents with Security Council members. That in itself was an impolitic act since the matter had already been referred to the African Union-United Nations chief mediator to investigate with the help of UNMIS. As if all these gaffes were not embarrassing enough, the secretary general went a step further and announced that the Security Council had decided to take up the matter.[99] Understandably, politicians often go hyperbolic in their statements even if it does them no favor, but twisting facts in a situation of crisis is indefensible. In effect, the council's report on the meeting said: "The Council held a private meeting on 21 March, in which [Atul Khare, assistant secretary general for peacekeeping] again briefed the Council on the situation of Abyei and representatives of the Government of Sudan and the Government of Southern Sudan each put forward their perspective on the accusations leveled by the SPLM against NCP regarding support to armed militia. Sudanese representatives said the southern government needed to stop blaming others for its internal problems. There was no specific outcome from the meeting, but it is understood that Council members were pleased to note that the parties had agreed to resume talks and that UNMIS was chairing a joint investigation into the violence."[100]

Whether southern Sudan's small wars were proxy wars orchestrated by Khartoum or local wars initiated by greedy soldiers aspiring for political positions, initiators of these wars seemed to have cared less for the appalling cost of war to northern and southern Sudan, as well as to the region. According to a recent study, rekindling war in South Sudan would entail loss of over $100 billion over 10 years.[101] That amount, according to the study, comprised a $50 billion loss in GDP to the whole of Sudan, a $25 billion loss of GDP to neighboring countries relative to a more stable situation, and $30 billion in peacekeeping and humanitarian costs to the international community. These figures alone should have been enough to persuade both parties to avert war. Nonetheless, endless rebellions against the government of South Sudan continued to raise their ugly heads, making Salva Kiir's calls for peace futile cries in the wilderness. These rebellions signified one of two things: either the rebels had genuine public (not personal) grievances that had to be addressed forthwith in order to consolidate

378

peace or, as appeared to be the case, their motives were essentially personal, aimed at either political aggrandizement or material gain. The latter motives were repeatedly made obvious, particularly in the case of rebellions by SPLM/SPLA cadres who had challenged official party candidates in elections and, failing to win popular support, resorted to arms. Little did those political aspirants know that no democracy would ever survive with election losers who never lose. Consequently, the new state has to put an end to this travesty and exposed this group of rebels for what they are: selfish enemies of the people. The policy of accommodating political coercionists would only encourage more blackmail and, if succumbed to, end up in creating a top-heavy government that would eventually collapse under the weight of its own unwieldiness.

Concerning the viability of the two states, it became clear that the exchange of accusations and counter-accusations should cease and the two states move forward to develop a formula for peaceful coexistence, beginning with the removal of any lingering mistrust between their two armies and scepticism by one state of the final intentions of the other. The partition of the old Sudan into two states had been a voluntary political partition unlike liberation from a colonial power. Ultra-separatists should have remembered that Salva Kiir, up to July 9, 2011, was the first vice president of Sudan and that the Republic of Sudan remained, after secession of its southern part, the only neighbor of the new state to the north with the longest international border. Also, unlike a colonial occupying power that left its former colony lock, stock, and barrel, North Sudan remained an important neighbor of the new state. As Mamdani observed, the two states "have a history and history overlaps geographical boundaries."[102] Happily, the majority of southern Sudanese as well as the SPLM leadership did not share the ultra-separatist's obtuse vision. In truth, President Salva Kiir, on the occasion of lowering the old Sudanese flag and raising the flag of the new state, kept President Bashir guessing until the last minute about what he wanted to do with the old flag. Bashir was expecting that flag to be handed over to him on Sudan's independence day the way the Union Jack and Egyptian flags were handed to the representatives of the two colonial powers. When the time came, Salva Kiir declared that the Sudanese flag would be kept by the new republic because it was part of its history. This spirit should have guided the dealings between the two states manifested by mutual cooperation in all walks of life: unimpeded movement of capital, goods, labor and services, cultural and familial interaction, and eventually, for purposes of mutual security, a nonaggression treaty guaranteed by third parties and deposited with the appropriate regional and international organizations. That was not to happen for the first two years that succeeded South Sudan's independence. However, to the utter satisfaction of the people of the two states and the region, the two states again reached an agreement on September 27, 2012, at Addis Ababa, with a view to putting into effect a series of compacts that had remained inoperative since their adoption. Those included:

- Joint Position Paper on Security Arrangements, signed on December 7, 2011
- Joint Position Paper on Border Security, signed on May 30, 2011
- Agreement on Border Security and Joint Political Security Mechanism, signed July 29, 2011
- Agreement on the Border Monitoring Support Mission, signed July 30, 2011
- Memorandum of Understanding on Nonaggression and Cooperation, signed on February 10, 2012.

The prompt implementation of those agreements in their totality would have saved the country the agony it had gone through for almost two years.

2.5.4 Threats by an Elusive Enemy

Threat to security from outside South Sudan intermittently issued from operations by the Lord's Resistance Army (LRA) led by the illusive Joseph Kony. The LRA remained a threatening, transboundary, destabilizing force, not because of its size, but in view of the barbaric methods with which it had been carrying out its predatory attacks as well as the cryptic nature of its ultimate objective. The government of South Sudan had, to no avail, bent over backwards to engage the LRA in negotiations to bring about peace to the region. Nonetheless, LRA marauders continued their forays into southern Sudan, particularly Western Equatoria and Western Bahr El Gazal in Sudan as well as in the Central African Republic and the Democratic Republic of Congo. This ubiquitousness of its operations belied the LRA's claim to be a Ugandan liberation movement. Accordingly, the government of South Sudan, in cooperation with concerned neighboring countries and support from the international community, engaged in a joint effort to rid the region from that primitive force. In December 2009, armies from Uganda, Democratic Republic of Congo, and South Sudan launched "Operation Lightening Thunder," backed by U.S. intelligence and logistical support to track Kony and his armed followers. In November 2010, President Obama presented a plan to the U.S. Congress to disarm that bloodthirsty army in pursuance to a law passed by Congress six months earlier requesting the administration to defuse the spiraling bloodshed in Central Africa, protect the civilian population, and bring the LRA to justice.[103] However, that was not the first time the United States had called for the apprehension of Joseph Kony and his senior commanders as the world's most elusive war criminals.[104] According to Colonel Stefano Mugerwa, an Ugandan army officer in the field, "the LRA had developed a range of effective evasion tactics, including changing clothes to blend in with the local population."[105] On October 14, 2011, President Obama announced that he had authorized "a small number of combat-equipped U.S. forces to deploy to Central Africa to provide assistance to regional forces that are working toward the removal of Joseph Kony from the battlefield."[106] It is hoped that with the added intelligence and logistical support provided by the United States, the dwindling predatory army (now reported to have shrunk to 300 fighters) would be eliminated so that peace returns to the region. By September 2012, it was not only the US and South Sudan who were tracking Kony, also the African Union launched an initiative in South Sudan to take control of the fight against the LRA in Western Equatoria.[107]

2.6 The Nile Waters

Political historians throughout the last century treated the Nile waters question as a matter of primary concern only to Egypt and Sudan. Since the 1990s, the Nile assumed a basin wide bearing. In that decade, 10 Nile riparian countries agreed on a cooperative framework under the name of the Nile Basin Initiative (NBI).[108] The NBI is led at the top by a council of ministers known as the Council of Ministers (Nile-COM), which brings together ministers in charge of water affairs in member states. The Nile-COM supported by a Technical Advisory Committee (Nile-TAC) and a secretariat (Nile-Sec). The NBI is charged with handling all aspects relating to the development and utilization of Nile water resources, including review of contested claims over those waters. In addition, the NBI is entrusted with the basin's environmental and biodiversity conservation as well as the identification of agricultural needs of different riparian and lacustrine states. Nevertheless, differences over relative shares of water continued to exasperate relations among member countries. Those differences are mainly between downstream riparians, especially Egypt and Sudan on the one side, and upstream countries, particularly Ethiopia and the lacustrine countries of East and Central Africa: Kenya, Uganda, Tanzania, Democratic Republic of the Congo, Rwanda, and Burundi.

Since the last century, the Nile has been haunted by two agreements: the 1929 Nile Waters Agreement signed with Egypt by Great Britain on behalf of the Nile basin countries that were then under British tutelage: Sudan, Kenya, Uganda, and Tanganyika. The second was the Nile Waters Agreement signed between Egypt and Sudan in 1959. The 1929 agreement was embodied in an exchange of notes in May 1929 between Lord Lloyd, the British high commissioner in Cairo, and Mohamed Mahmoud Pasha, the then Egyptian prime minister. In that exchange of notes the British guaranteed "Egypt's natural and historical water rights," a clause that was framed in a manner that defied principles of customary law and had all the marks of political mollification. Britain then wanted to mend fences with Egypt after the disharmony between the two countries that followed the assassination of Sir Lee Stack.[109] In an attempt to appease Egypt and quell its fears, Britain never gave a thought to the future interests of the countries she claimed to represent. For example, without any corresponding obligation to Egypt, the British agreed that "save with the previous agreement of the Egyptian Government, no irrigation or power works or measures are to be constructed or taken on the River Nile or its branches or on the lakes from which it flows so far as these are in Sudan or in countries under British administration, in such a manner [that entails] prejudice to the interests of Egypt, by either reducing the

381

quantities of water arriving in Egypt or modifying the date of its arrival or lowering its level."[110] In spite of protests from Ethiopia and from the colonial office on behalf of Uganda, the British government refused to budge from its position. In reality, Lord Allenby, the British high commissioner in Egypt, argued that "the principle of safeguarding the **natural and historic right of Egypt would be observed at all times and under whatever conditions that may arise**" (emphasis added).[111] By creating a historical vested interest for Egypt in the Nile waters, that commitment, according to a Kenyan jurist-turned-statesman, "totally dispossessed for good other riparians of their rights in these waters."[112] No matter how valid those rights were in actuality and at the time they were made, they could not extend beyond the limits of the actual usage at that time.[113] Probably for that reason, the new Sudanese government, upon independence, spurned succession to the 1929 agreement, a decision which triggered the first water conflict between Sudan and Egypt in July 1959.

At that year the government of Sudan decided to withdraw additional waters from the Nile for the irrigation of the Gezira-Managil extension, the first extension to the Gezira scheme since its establishment.[114] The extension increased the acreage of the scheme by 807,139 feddans (acres). Egypt then argued that withdrawal of additional waters from the Nile would endanger her own agricultural plans, an unfortunate remark suggesting that Sudan was expected to forestall its own development for the sake of Egypt's. In reality the clamors against the restrictive and pre-emptive nature of the 1929 agreement went back to 1945 when Mekki Abbas, the renowned Sudanese educator, later the first Sudanese managing director of the Gezira Board, raised the issue at the first session of the governor's Central Advisory Council.[115] In effect, the 1929 agreement was never recognized by the Nile countries in East Africa; in particular, Tanganyika declared, upon independence in 1962, that it would not automatically succeed to agreements signed on its behalf by the colonial power before weighing their costs and benefits. That selective succession to treaties came to be known as the Nyerere doctrine, after Julius Nyerere, who was serving as the first president of Tanganyika at the time. Nyerere's main reason for refusing automatic succession to the 1929 Nile Waters agreement was that it obligated his country, among others, to seek Egypt's consent for any works they intended to undertake on the Nile at its source.

In November 1958, the Sudanese military, under General Ibrahim Abboud, took over the reins of power in Sudan. One of the first foreign policy decisions taken by that government was to negotiate, and conclude, a Nile waters agreement on terms shunned by Sudan's civilian government. That agreement continued to plague relations between Egypt and Sudan, on the one side, and upper riparians, on the other. The latter states, understandably, could not resign themselves to abiding by the terms of an agreement that totally disregarded their interests. However, the apportionment agreed upon between Egypt and Sudan was based on an average annual discharge of the Nile at Aswan calculated as 84 billion cubic meters (bcm) as follows: Egypt at 55.5 bcm (i.e., 4–5 bcm more than its share under the 1929 agreement); Sudan at 18.5 bcm(14.5 bcm more than its share in the 1929 agreement). As it had been assumed at the time, Sudan would not be able to exploit the amount of water allocated to it by the agreement; consequently, it yielded to Egypt 1.5 bcm of its share as a water loan up to the end of 1977. In addition, 10 bcm were written off to evaporation and seepage.[116] Not only were the two parties remiss about the interests of other riparians when they apportioned the Nile waters, they also agreed that in the eventuality that the issue of water sharing arose with other riparians, the two parties would take a joint position on the subject. That clause was not only unnecessarily exemptive, it was also presumptuous as it meant in effect that lower riparians had arrogated to themselves the prerogative to determine the rights of upper riparians.

The 1959 agreement also provided that the two governments would work jointly to salvage water losses from evapo-respiration and seepage estimated at 42 bcm. A permanent joint technical committee was created to oversee, among other things, the implementation of such Nile development projects. The first of those projects was the Jonglei Canal, which was originally conceived to provide an additional 4 bcm of water to be captured through the diversion of waters from Bahr el Jebel at Bor into a 340-kilometer canal directly into the junction of the Nile and Sobat rivers. Those waters were to be equally shared between Egypt and Sudan. So, even when the two lower riparians envisaged harvesting additional waters, they utterly overlooked the interests of other countries. Work on that canal, however, started in the mid-1970s after the break of peace following the Addis Ababa agreement, but its history went back to 1904, when Sir William Garstin, the British undersecretary of public works in Egypt, came out with that recommendation.

The Jonglei project promised great benefits to the region in socioeconomic development, employment opportunities, and improvement of pastoralist livelihood; nonetheless, it caused consternation among the people of the affected areas.[117] Work on that huge project was undertaken by the French company Compagnie de Constructions Internationales, whose experience in the construction of the Jhelum-Indus canal in Pakistan made it preeminently qualified for the job. The project was eventually stopped upon the outbreak of war in 1983. Notwithstanding, the SPLM late leader, who was aware of the benefits of the project, wrote commendably about it in his doctoral thesis at Iowa state University[118] while castigating the manner in which the project was presented to the public. That was the reason why Garang made it a point in his various contacts with those concerned to indicate his concern for the destiny of the project.[119] The second phase of Jonglei was to drain a large part of the swampy areas of Bahr el Ghazal and Bahr el Zaraf. Though this project is expected to save a volume of water similar to that of Jonglei, no final determination can be made on that phase of the project before assessing the White Nile's capacity to carry additional waters.

The need for the waters to be harvested through these projects is still real and may increase in importance if North and South Sudan are to become among the countries that shall help reduce the deficit in world food supply. The proposed allocation of the original two bcm to Sudan was meant to satisfy agricultural development needs in the whole country, including areas in the South where rainfall was scarce or unreliable. Also, despite having the largest irrigated area in sub-Saharan Africa (4.4 million feddans), North and South Sudan shall still require more water to meet the needs of their expanding populations. As things stand today in Sudan, only the North benefits from the 18.5 bcm allocated to it by the 1959 agreement. Of this volume, 8 bcm (40 percent of Sudan's share) goes to the Gezira scheme and about 8 bcm to other agricultural schemes such as New Halfa, Suki, Kenana Sugar Company, and White and Blue Nile pump schemes. That still leaves 2.5 bcm of Sudan's share unutilized. Those waters, without additional waters from Jonglei, could have been enough for irrigating the agricultural development projects that were envisaged for southern Sudan in the 1970s such as sugar plantations in Melut and Mangala, and the Tonj Kenaf fiber factory. Nevertheless, looking into Sudan's future needs based on population growth, the country may require 23.83 bcm for agriculture and .55 bcm for nonagricultural uses (domestic and industrial).[120]

Undoubtedly, the new state in South Sudan shall be part of the NBI, not only by virtue of being a Nile riparian but also a source country. In this regard, it is interesting to note that northern Sudan, after separation of the South, had ceased to be a source country since all the Nile tributary feeders in Sudan such as Lake No, Bahr el Ghazal, and Bahr el Zaraf were all situated in southern Sudan.[121] Notwithstanding, important issues relative to the Nile waters shall await the new state in Juba. These include recommencement of work on the Jonglei Canal and decision on the share that shall be allocated to other riparians in the Nile Waters, which is greatly circumscribed by the 1959 agreement. Ironically, that agreement was called "Agreement for the **Full** Utilization of the Nile Waters" (emphasis added). As things stand today, there shall be no way to satisfy the legitimate needs of theses riparians unless the volume of the Nile waters is increased, or riparians (especially lower riparians) review their water usage practices in order to reduce leakages and water misuse. This is even more critical in view of the limited volume of the Nile water. According to a renowned water expert on the Nile, the volume of the Nile waters, which is the longest river in the world (6,650 kilometers), is minimal compared to other rivers, including those in Africa. For example, the volume of Nile waters represents two percent of that of the Amazon, six percent of that of the Congo, 17 percent of the Niger, and 26 percent of the Zambezi.[122]

Currently, there is no alternative within the realms of possibility to increase the volume of the Nile waters other than water harvesting. For that to happen, the states concerned must be conscious of the social dislocation and environmental damage that may be caused by such operations. That much was learned from the experience of Jonglei in the 1980s. Consequently, for such projects to be realized, the stakeholders have to be assured about the utility of the projects and its direct benefits to them. Doubts about Jonglei in the early 1980s were played up by politicians as part of their senseless opposition to Abel Alier's government; nonetheless, there were genuine popular concerns. The new state in South Sudan may, therefore, need to investigate the matter objectively with only public interest in mind. In that investigation, it may also have to look into the manner in which the project was presented to the public, since there was a lot to be desired in the way it was publicized in the decade of the 1970s and 1980s. For instance, issues like compensation to pastoralists for land expropriated and direct and immediate benefits that would accrue to them were not sufficiently explained to the communities. The issue of environmental impairments may also be a cause of concern to local and foreign environmentalist. Those claims persisted in the 1970s and 1980s in spite of the many environmental impact assessments carried out by the National Council for the Development of the Jonglei. In fact, environmental concerns may increase, not subside, as a result of the identification in 2006 of the Sudd area as a wetland of international importance under the Ramsar Convention.[123]

The apportionment of Nile waters shall, without doubt, remain the most hotly contested issue. At present it represents the hardest bone of contention between Egypt and Sudan, on the one side, and Ethiopia and East and Central African riparians, on the other. In this regard, five upstream riparians (Kenya, Uganda, Tanzania, Ethiopia, and Rwanda) signed a cooperative framework agreement to allocate more water for themselves, irrespective of the limitations imposed on them by the 1929 and 1959 agreements. The situation was further aggravated when Burundi joined the five countries on February 28, 2011, which brought the signatories to the agreement to a number that would make the agreement operative once it was endorsed by their parliaments. Both Egypt and Sudan took exception to that agreement and refused to join in, even though Egypt recognized the need for such agreement. However, Egypt maintained that it would not partake in a treaty that would affect its present share of the water. As an alternative, both Egypt and Sudan proposed that the parties work together for drawing a new arrangement for water sharing, provided that such an agreement "would not adversely affect the water security and current uses and rights of any Nile basin state; obviously, they were referring to Egypt. Egypt also required prior informed consent by concerned riparians before the building of any dam on the Nile. That proposal, which was tantamount to a reiteration of the 1929 pre-emptive clause, was rejected by the signatories of the May 2010 agreement, particularly Ethiopia, which had already started constructing dams on the Blue Nile.

The Ethiopian case, in particular, deserves attention in order to dispel misconceptions by some riparian states and unwarranted fears by others. As likely as not, Ethiopia is the richest country in water resources within the Nile complex; it has abundant rainfall and numerous water sources such as lakes and internal rivers and rivulets. It also provides over 80 percent of the Nile waters. Still, it is the riparian country that benefits least from those waters. Every so often, in order to justify depriving it of a fair share in the Nile water, lower riparian countries argue that Ethiopia does not depend entirely on Nile waters as other countries do. However, this argument never took into consideration climatological changes and extreme temporal and spatial variations in rainfall that make Ethiopia subject to successive droughts and famines. The population explosion in that country (presently 88 million, which makes its population second to Nigeria and above Egypt's) only adds to the country's crises.[124] Besides, in its attempts to diversify its economy, Ethiopia is apparently endeavoring to become a major producer and exporter of hydroelectric power in order to benefit from its abundant waterfalls. Incredulously, even Ethiopia's desire to establish dams to produce much-needed power for local consumption became a matter of concern to lower riparians.[125] Small wonder, when Ethiopia commenced work on dams on rivers Tikzi (Atbara), Tana, and Benishangoul (40 miles from Sudan borders), the furor became a frenzy. Ethiopian Prime Minister Meles Zenawi called on both Egypt and Sudan not to worry as those dams, according to Zenawi, would not curtail the flow of the Nile downstream.[126] If anything, they shall regulate that flow.

For them to live in peace and ensure equitable sharing of water, both upper and lower riparians have to move away from hard positions and seek to understand each other's legitimate concerns. For example, waters that were already appropriated to, and utilized by, Egypt should never be tampered with, as denying them would make people perish. That could not be justified morally or legally. On the other hand, recognizing to Egypt an *apriori* vested right in unappropriated waters would amount to granting Egypt a pre-emptive right in these waters, irrespective of the interests of other riparians. Instead of playing the zero-sum game of political alignment with either of the two groups, the new state shall be well placed to play the role of a go-between in order to bring all parties together. For example, rather than taking a negative position toward Ethiopia's, and for that matter Uganda's,[127] intention to construct dams on the Nile for hydropower generation, the NBI should envisage a basin-wide scheme for that purpose, bringing together Ethiopia (the proposed dams), Egypt (Aswan dam), Sudan (Merowtre and Rosseiris dams), Democratic Republic of the Congo (Inga), and South Sudan (Biden). Such an ambitious, though feasible, scheme shall create a continent-wide market for electricity and, probably, a world market by linking together African and European grids. There are comforting signals that the new state shall be disposed to doing that. By way of example, the government of South Sudan's minister of water resources has already reached agreement with the Government of National Unity's minister of irrigation and water resources that water sharing between North and South Sudan would be governed by the agreed quotas established by the NBI.[128] On the other hand, Egypt should continue giving support to the Republic of South Sudan in water management projects in Bahr el Ghazal; establishing stations for gauging water levels in Juba,

Malakal, and Wau; and building capacity of local personnel in water management and environmental control. Cooperation between Egypt and the new state was highlighted in the meeting between President Salva Kiir and Egyptian Prime Minister Issam Sharaf during the visit in March 2011 by the latter to Juba.[129] The Ministry of Irrigation and Water Resources in Juba had also remained in contact with ministries of water in Ethiopia, Uganda, and Kenya to iron out differences and identify additional water resources. By playing a positive role in the promotion and development of water harvest in projects in Jonglei and Bahr el Ghazal, the new state may turn out to be the holder of the key to unlocking the Nile waters gridlock.

2.7 Pastoralists and Grazing Rights

Pastoralists—itinerant people who move with their herds after pastures—are to be found throughout Africa. They include the Tuareg and Ambararo in North and West Africa; the Borana in East Africa (Kenya, Ethiopia); the Afar between Ethiopia and Somalia, and the Masai between Kenya and Tanzania. Within South Sudan, nilotic pastoralists span the whole region from Eastern Equatoria to Upper Nile and Bahr el Ghazal and encompass herdsmen from Didinga, Toposa, Murle, Dinka, and Nuer ethnic communities. Across Sudan's north-south border, pastoralists continue to live together and seasonally move without impediments across that border. Whenever clashes erupted between them, those clashes were promptly resolved through traditional reconciliation mechanisms. Concern about these time-honored practices was, to be sure, what prompted the parties at the CPA negotiations to provide in the Abyei Protocol that "the Misseriya and other peoples retain their traditional rights to graze cattle and move peoples across the territory of Abyei." If that process was frustrated during the war, as indeed it had been, it was only because of the entanglement of northern nomadic tribes in a war that they had neither started nor benefited from.

The border grazing areas shared by northern and southern pastoralists fall between latitudes 7–13 degrees north of the equator and longitudes 14–34 degrees east of Greenwich. This area is occupied by 14 percent of Sudanese tribes. That was the reason why President Salva Kiir pertinently observed that borders between these tribes shall only be on paper. On several occasions, John Garang called for turning areas where the two states come into contact (described by geographers and sociologists as areas of *tamass*, or contact) into an area of *tamazuj* (fusion). In that area, freedom of movement is to be assured, resources equitably shared, and mutual interests preserved. In December 2010, the Austrian government intervened to play a role in the consolidation of existing interdependences between North and South Sudan, including maximizing interdependences in the *tamazuj* zone.[130] The process involved research on the phenomenon of pastoralism and designing programs that would enhance cooperation among pastoralists, visiting Sudanese pastoralists to expose them to cooperative arrangements within pastoral communities, mapping out an economic development plan for the area, as well as ensuring funding for the realization of that plan. Regrettably, for whatever reasons, Austria withheld its labor on this project. Austrian engagement in pastoralism in Sudan was preceded by similar efforts by two Western countries: Holland and Canada (Canadian International Development Agency). The two countries funded a United Nations Development Programme (UNDP) project for reduction of resource-based conflicts. The UNDP report, which was produced before the signature of the CPA, could have been instructive to policy makers, especially those concerned with natural resources use and management.[131]

Pastoralism, like transboundary waters, is now more than a bilateral or monolithic issue; it is a multifaceted phenomenon that requires a multidisciplinary approach. It has also developed into a matter of regional consequence and concern and, therefore, calls for international cooperation and assistance. Conscious of the interstate problems issuing from pastoral practices, the African Union has been working on the formulating an Africa-wide pastoral policy framework with a view to safeguarding traditional rights and addressing the underlying dynamics of conflict among pastoralists, on the one hand, and between them and states on the other. Five years ago (July 2007) 15 African countries met at Isiolo, Kenya, to formulate a continental pastoral policy framework based on awareness of the interconnectedness of issues relating to land, governance, education, finance, marketing, conflict, and poverty risks. Furthermore, both the African Union and the United Nations have agreed on programs for reducing, within the above mentioned framework, pastoral poverty as an important element in national programs to achieve Millennium Development Goals.[132] Equally, the IGAD has established a Conflict Early Warning and Response Mechanism to address cross-border pastoral conflicts. All those are mechanisms from which both North and South Sudan may benefit if and when they decide to approach pastoralism as a multifaceted phenomenon.

Recently, the future of pastoralism, with accent on East Africa, was subject of a multidisciplinary discussion at an international conference held in Addis Ababa to examine the gamut of issues pertaining to pastoralism, including land, climate variabilities, transborder infrastructure, human and animal health, education, and better resource management techniques.[133] Also, given its awareness that pastoralism is increasingly threatened by urbanization and the demands that urbanization shall create for livestock products, the United Nations is adumbrating policies to prepare for the eventuality of the demise of pastoralism in some African countries with a view to creating alternative modes of livelihood for pastoralists and measures to preserve and enhance their animal wealth. Since the largest portion of Sudan's animal wealth is found in pastoralist regions, the two states may have to begin identifying ways and means to modernize that sector, especially through creating large-scale ranching projects, modern animal husbandry techniques, and up-to-date practices in meat production and marketing. Regrettably, the two states persist in treating pastoralism as only a

388

security issue, probably because of its impingement on border issues and that of Abyei. Since 2010, this approach to the issue has neither resolved pastoralist problems nor ensured security. In effect, this non-integrated approach to pastoralism did not even provide a palliative to the problem.

It was observed earlier that President Salva Kiir, in the last meeting of the national cabinet (February 7, 2011) he attended, declared that the borders between the two states shall be soft. However, in the two years succeeding the referendum, the borders between North and South Sudan, if anything, became harder and fraught with danger. That was due to two factors: lack of common understanding as to what soft borders meant and perpetual mistrust between the two states, which unfortunately percolated to communities across the borders. Even so, in the tide flow of agreements reached on September 27, 2012, the two states had put the question at rest. The agreement on border issues established that "the parties shall regulate, protect, and promote the livelihoods of border communities without prejudice to the rights of the host communities and, in particular, those of the nomadic and pastoral communities, especially their seasonal customary right to cross with their livestock the international boundary between the parties for access to pasture and water." In the meantime, the agreement established a Joint Border Commission (JBC) and a Joint Political and Security Mechanism to coordinate activities, especially with regard to management of movement routes and corridors for the use of transboundary communities. Those bodies are to become operative two weeks after the ratification of the agreement.

2.8 Citizenship

Citizenship is a status that entitles a "natural person" i.e. (human beings as opposed to a corporate body) to an assortment of political, economic, social, and security rights such as the right to vote, the right to work, and right to receive protection. It also subjects that person to correlative duties and obligations. In customary law this status is acquired either through the right of blood (*jus sanguinis*), i.e., descending from parents who are citizens by birth, or through being born in the land (*jus solis*). Some states accord citizenship on the basis of nativity of at least one of the parents or through marriage to a person holding citizenship (*jure matrimonii*). The issue of citizenship ranked high in the discussions of post-referendum measures when it became clear that the people of southern Sudan were more inclined to have their own state.

Before addressing the issue of citizenship, parties to the CPA had to grabble with two immediate relative questions: conditions for eligibility to vote in the referendum and eventually become citizens of the new state, and the destiny of citizens of the new state who wished to remain in the North or South. Regarding the first question, the act established clear conditions for eligibility to participate in the referendum. Article 25 of the referendum law provided:

The voters shall be:

(1) Born to both parents or one of them who belong to an original ethnic group dwelling in southern Sudan before January 1956, or before that date his or her origins are traceable to one of the ethnic groups in southern Sudan, or

(2) Permanently or uninterruptedly resident, or whose parents or grandfathers have been permanently or uninterruptedly resident, in southern Sudan on the first of January 1956.

For the purposes of verification of voter's identity, the presumptive voter was required to present written or oral testimony from the sultan of the community to which he or she belonged.

The presence in northern Sudan of hundreds of thousands of citizens whose ancestors originated in the South should not have constituted any problem, since all of them were settled in the North and none of them expressed a desire to return to the land of their ancestors. Woefully, even some of those citizens who were born and habitually lived in the North were harassed and effectively reminded of a past they had forgotten or wished to forget: the transport of their ancestors to the North from South Sudan in bondage. Within South Sudan itself there had been hundreds of thousands of Sudanese citizens who did not belong to any indigenous group in that region but had become southern Sudanese either through marriage or permanent residence.

Having settled the issue of eligibility for voting in the referendum, the two parties turned to the question concerning the fate of southern Sudanese domiciled in the North in the post-independence era. As it transpired, there were large numbers within this group who had no intention to abandon their domicile in the North and, therefore, wished to acquire citizenship in both states. Those comprised professionals such as doctors, teachers, and engineers who lived, worked, and raised families in northern Sudan. It also transpired that among northern Sudanese living in South Sudan and entitled to the nationality of the new state, there were some who wished to retain their original nationality. The desire to acquire dual nationality by either of the two groups neither contradicted the Interim National Constitution (INC) provisions on nationality [article 7 (4)], nor was it incompatible with the Sudanese Nationality Act of 1994. That law stipulated in section 1 (4) that "any person born before the coming into force of the law shall be Sudanese by birth if he satisfies the following conditions:

i. (a) has acquired the nationality on birth
   (b) he or his father were born in Sudan
ii. had been living in Sudan on the coming into force of the law and he, or his forbearers from the father's side, had been living in Sudan since January 1, 1956

Sections 2–4 of the law dealt with persons born after the coming into force of that law as follows: a person born in Sudan shall become Sudanese by birth on the time of their birth; a person born of a Sudanese mother by birth is entitled to Sudanese nationality on request; and a person born to Sudanese nationals by adoption shall be deemed Sudanese if his parents obtained the Sudanese nationality before his birth

The term "national (citizen) by adoption referred to an adult alien who had lived in the country for five years or more and satisfied the conditions for naturalization specified in the law. All southern Sudanese, whether they had lived in the North or South, would satisfy the conditions stipulated in the law. Besides, a nationality so acquired, according to the law, could only be withdrawn by an express request by the holder of such nationality presented to the president. The president might accept or reject the request under specific conditions, for example, if the request was made by the citizen in the course of a war to which Sudan was party. That citizen might also lose his or her nationality through presidential order if it was proved that he had joined the service of a foreign country in contradiction to an existing law that criminalized that act. On the other hand, the INC stipulated, as referred to above, that "a Sudanese national may acquire the nationality of another country as shall be regulated by law" [article 7 (4)].

On the basis of the above constitutional and legal provisions, it was stunning to note that the government of Sudan, which afforded generous nationality rights to residents of the country of non-Sudanese origin irrespective of culture, religion, or race, had decided to begrudge southern Sudanese such rights for no reason other than a decision taken by the people to whom they ethnically belonged to secede from the mother country. The irrationality of the decision reached its apogee when the government decided to apply it even to southern Sudanese who voted for unity, or those who did not participate in the referendum. Such a decision was not only irrational, it also smacked of racism, especially when a large number of the affected citizens either continued to be tied to the mother country in more than one respect or had substantial connections or interests in it. One really wonders whether those who took or justified this decision were aware of the African Charter of Human and Peoples' Rights, which prohibited the mass expulsion of non-nationals based on national, racial, or religious reasons.[134] That irrationality became compounded when it was discovered that innumerable high-level NCP politicians were enjoying the privilege of dual nationality, including citizenship of countries like Britain, Canada, and the United States.

The extreme position taken by the NCP toward southern Sudanese living in the North was patently inspired by resentment of the gathering momentum in favor of separation. Those who wished to save the NCP the embarrassment of being depicted as racists saw in its decision a ploy to discourage southern Sudanese living in the North from voting for secession. But if that was the case, then the proponents of this ploy had preposterously gone to extremes, as evidenced by the declaration by Sudan's minister of information on Sudan

391

television on September 25, 2010. In that declaration the minister said that all southern Sudanese living in the North would be denied all the rights they had been enjoying as citizens, if South Sudan opted for secession. "They shall not enjoy citizenship rights, jobs, or benefits. They shall not be allowed to buy or sell land in the Khartoum market. And they shall not be treated in hospitals; even an injection shall not be administered to them," said the minister, in his statement telecast through Sudan Television on September 25, 2010. Little did the ill-informed minister of information know that some of those rights could not be denied even to a transient visitor by any law-abiding government in today's world. Besides, the minister did not reflect for a second that the measures he called for would put him in league with Nazi Germany, the only country in modern times that denied similar rights to Jews and Romas (gypsies).

Some NCP politician said, *sotto voce*, that their abrasive reaction toward southern Sudanese living in the North was in response to irritating remarks made during the referendum campaign. One of these remarks was an announcement attributed to the SPLM asking southern voters to choose between "being free in the South or remaining as slaves and second-class citizens in the North." Rather than argue that the presence of a large community of southern Sudanese workers, traders, and professionals living in the North and socially moving upward within its society belied the claim that they were living as slaves or second-class citizens, the NCP militants made a peaceful community incur the wrath. Telling that community to go to where they would live as "first-class citizens" was an apathetic response from Khartoum to a daft announcement emanating from Juba. The frictional remarks by the minister caused angst within the southern Sudanese community in the North as well as disquietude within the international community. As a result, thousands of southern Sudanese hurriedly began to pack up and dispose of their belongings at any price before they hit the road to South Sudan. Those included families that were born and raised in northern Sudan: professionals, traders, artisans, and laborers, some of whom were the mainstay of occupations such as the construction industry. Fears of wholesale expulsion of southern Sudanese from the North also threatened 20,000 students and 1,384 teachers in northern or northern-based southern universities at a time when any right-thinking person should have known that teaching institutions provide the perfect melting pot for people of different cultures. The NCP's excessive reaction, whatever its motives were, had backfired and made secession, not unity, attractive even to avowed southern unionists.

To ward off any forcible expulsion of southern Sudanese from Khartoum, the government of South Sudan, with the help of international organizations, established an emergency returns program (ERP) to ensure the peaceful and organized return of southern citizens to their homes.[135] The international community also called for protection of the rights of minorities in both North and South Sudan, especially in view of expected reprisals against the 1.5 million southern Sudanese living in the North, if and when south Sudan voted for secession;[136] the memory of the carnage that took place in Khartoum in 2005 after the death of Garang, in which hundreds of innocent southern and northern Sudanese citizens perished, was still fresh in people's minds. Human Rights Watch appealed to the NCP and SPLM, as they negotiated post-referendum measures, to adopt a progressive and inclusive framework for addressing citizenship in the event of secession. It proposed that since dual nationality was rejected by the NCP, the two parties were to find "an arrangement whereby minority nationals living in both northern or southern jurisdictions may choose to continue to live there with basic civil, political, economic, social, and cultural rights on equal footing as citizens."[137] Without question, international law prohibits mass expulsion, forced eviction, and discriminatory rules of citizenship.

The mass exodus of southern Sudanese from the North evoked memories of the mutual expulsion of citizens in Eritrea and Ethiopia after the war between the two countries, or of Ugandan Asians by General Amin. Whoever was directly or indirectly behind those calls for the repatriation of citizens neither did justice to the tolerance of ordinary northern Sudanese citizens toward their southern brethren who lived with them in the North under one flag, government, and constitution, nor to that constitution. If at all, mutual repatriation or expatriation in both directions should have been voluntary and handled in a manner that did not cause disruption to the livelihoods of individuals and communities.

During all those bizarre happenings, the government of South Sudan kept its cool before coming up with a well-reasoned proposition to diffuse the tension. It maintained that the citizenship of all Sudanese during the interim period up to July 9, 2011, should not change, regardless of the result of the referendum, and their rights should remain intact wherever they chose to stay. After July 9, 2011, citizens would be allowed to choose the nationality of either state compatible with international law and practice. It also added that any person deemed eligible to vote in the referendum would be entitled to southern citizenship and lose citizenship rights in the North unless if he or she opted to remain with that citizenship. However well-reasoned that proposition was, the NCP dwelt on saying "No" to dual nationality, even though Sudan's constitution warranted that. But to the surprise of the persons concerned, the expulsion of southern Sudanese from the North to southern Sudanese living in the North reached farcical proportions when the government decided to dismiss *en masse* southern government officials, including second-generation citizens among whom were doctors, nurses, teachers, and university professors. Choosing citizenship of any country is a matter of voluntary choice, but none of these citizens was asked whether he or she wanted to remain domiciled in the North or intended to relocate to the south.

The position taken by Khartoum on the issue of citizenship was stupefying as it also went against international law and practice. As it stands today, international law enjoins states, in the case of secession, dissolution, or disintegration of existing states, to ensure that no person is rendered stateless.

393

The Convention on the Reduction of Statelessness (1961) has precisely been enacted to guarantee that no person is denied civil rights or the ability to endow his children with a nationality or a home to which he shall be ensured automatic return. In particular, the convention calls on countries involved in secession of territory to ensure that no person becomes stateless as a result of change of sovereignty.[138] In this regard, no southern Sudanese living in the North before secession, nor any northern Sudanese living in the south, shall be stateless. However, problems still remained for southern Sudanese citizens who habitually lived in the North and wished to retain their northern Sudanese nationality. In this respect, the International Law Commission's report entitled "Nationality of Natural Persons in Relation to the Succession of States (1999)" provides some guidelines. Article 1 of the report states that "every individual who, on the date of the succession of States, had the nationality of the predecessor State, irrespective of the mode of acquisition of that nationality, has the right to the nationality of at least one of the predecessor States concerned, in *accordance with the present articles.*" Although the article states the obvious, the caveat at the end was important, as it provides safeguards to citizens, especially concerning the voluntary nature of acquiring nationality. In this connection Article 11(2) provides that "each State concerned shall grant a right to opt for its nationality to persons concerned who have appropriate connection with that State." The right of option was described by the International Law Commission as an attribute of the right to self-determination. Granting the right of option to southern citizens could not be rebutted by the assertion that the citizens in question would not become stateless because of their entitlement, as of right, to become southern citizens. In the case of habitual residents in a territory, Article 14 provided that the states concerned shall not, because of events connected with the succession of states, force residents to leave their habitual residence on its territory or deny them the right to return thereto. In its commentary on this Article, the commission ruled that the succession of states, as such, should not entail negative consequences for the status of persons considered habitual residents. Article 12 also ruled that "where the acquisition or loss of nationality in relation to the succession of States would impair the unity of a family, States concerned shall take all appropriate measures to allow that family to remain together or to be reunited."[139] This view was expressed earlier by the Harvard Law School in a comment to article 19 of the Draft Convention on Nationality. In that draft it was stated that "it is desirable in some measures that members of a family should have the same nationality [since] the principle of family unity is regarded in many countries as a sufficient basis for the application of this simple solution."[140] Article 15 of the commission's document stipulates that "states concerned shall not deny persons concerned the right to retain or acquire a nationality or the right of option upon the succession of States by discriminating on any ground."[141] The irrational decisions taken by Khartoum to deny southern Sudanese born and raised in North Sudan when they and their families had been habitual residents in that territory were, by all standards, discriminatory and neither congruent with domestic law nor international practice.

In addition, there was a wealth of state experience the two parties could draw from in the matter of citizenship in countries that had seceded from an existing state or in new states originating from the dissolution or disintegration of a federal state. The most recent experiences of the disintegration of the Socialist Federal Republic of Yugoslavia (SFRY), the dissolution of the Union of the Soviet Socialist Republics (U.S.S.R.), and the dissolution of the Czechoslovak union may offer some guidance. For instance, Yugoslavia (Serbia) did not require citizens of states that seceded from it to relinquish the nationality of the mother country. Also countries that seceded from the SFRY, though they differed in their policies regarding dual nationality, had all showed sensitivity toward the wish of their citizens to optionally retain the citizenship they had held before secession or dissolution of the union. In this respect, the Slovenian nationality law, which based citizenship primarily on *jus sanguinis* (descent from a parent), had nonetheless recognized Serbians who were resident in Slovenia on December 23, 1990 (the date of declaration of independence) as citizens of the new state by operation of the law. Also, article 29 of the citizen law of the Republic of Bosnia and Herzegovina (RBH) granted citizenship to Yugoslav citizens who were domiciled in RBH, even though article 2 of that law would not recognize dual citizenship. In the most recent case of the secession of Montenegro from Serbia, the government of the Republic of Montenegro bestowed on citizens of Serbia living in its territory all rights enjoyed by its citizens except the right to vote. That unilateral declaration, however, was to be formalized through a treaty between the two states.

In the case of the Russian Federation, article 18 of the Russian citizenship law provides that "citizens of the former U.S.S.R. residing in the territories of states which were part of the U.S.S.R. can acquire Russian citizenship through registration as long as they have not acquired another citizenship." And even though the Russia Federation did not recognize dual nationality, President Vladimir Putin proposed to the Duma (Russia's chief legislative body) in April 2001 that exceptions should be made for citizens of the former union. The Russian Federation bestowed certain rights on citizens of the erstwhile union that were only enjoyed by citizens of the federation. As an example, citizens of the Ukraine and Belarus, though they retained national passports, were granted by the two countries the right to settle permanently or work in either country without formal immigration procedures that are mandatory for other foreign nationals.

Despite the above hindrances to southern Sudan citizen's desire to remain domiciled in the North, President Bashir told Salva Kiir during the former's visit to Juba on the eve of the referendum, that in case of secession, he looked forward to having a union between the two states comparable to that of the states of the European Union. If that was what the president wanted, then he and his party should have desisted from the tendency to create unnecessary rigidities into the citizenship law that would work against the aim Bashir desired to achieve: creation of a Sudanic Union. In this connection, it is to be observed that the European Union has two levels of citizenship: union and national. According to the Maastricht Treaty, the instituting document of the European Union: "Every person holding the nationality of a member state shall be a citizen of the union" [article 17 (1)]. That citizenship complements, and does not replace, national citizenship." In addition, the European Convention on Nationality signed in Strasbourg, France, on November 6, 1997, contains relative provisions such as article 16, which states: "A State Party shall not make the renunciation of another nationality a condition for the acquisition or retention of its nationality where such renunciation or loss is not possible or cannot reasonably be acquired." But before going the European way in the matter of citizenship, the two states had to create their own all-embracing Maastricht Treaty. The ingredients of such a treaty could have been found in the September 2012 Cooperation Agreement, which was presented to the two parties by the African Union mediation panel headed by Thabo Mbeki.

Those erratic decisions by the NCP, which would not have led to a panSudanic union, cannot simply be explained away as a petulant reaction to secession; it was calculated. Up to that point in time, the NCP could not forget that the SPLM had emerged at the April 2010 national elections as its prime challenger in the North. Having assumed that the bulk of support to this political "parvenu" had come from southern Sudanese living in the North, it decided to dispossess the SPLM northern sector of that support base.

All the same, after two years of mutually self-inflicted harm, the two parties came to realize that there was no alternative for them other than to perpetually live together in peace and amity. In the preamble to the March 2012 Framework Agreement on the Status of Nationals of the Other State and Related Matters, the two parties stated what had been obvious to all: "Concerned that for the social and economic viability of the two states it is necessary that Sudanese and southern Sudanese people continue to interact with each other and enjoy the freedom to reside, move, acquire, and dispose of property and undertake economic activities within the territories of the two States." Those rights were dubbed in the agreement "The Four Freedoms." A Joint High-Level Committee was to be established two weeks after the ratification of the agreement, with a view to oversee the implementation of joint measures relating to the status and treatment of nationals of each state in the territory of the other. The first meeting of the Committee was to be conveyed by the African Union High-Level Implementation Panel.

Notes

1   *Stabilising Sudan: Domestic, Sub-Regional and Extra-Regional Challenges* (Cape Town: University of Cape Town Centre for Conflict Resolution, August 2010), 7.

2   Francis M. Deng, *Sudan at the Brink: Self-Determination and National Unity* (New York: Fordham University Press and the Institute for International Humanitarian Affairs, 2010), 41.

3   Mansour Khalid, "Toward the Self-Determination Referendum and Beyond," in *New Sudan in the Making? Essays on a Nation in Painful Search of Itself*," ed. Francis M. Deng (Trenton, NJ: Red Sea Press, 2010), 340.

4   Luís Aguiar-Conraria and Pedro Magalhães, "Referendum Design, Quorum Rules and Turnout" (working paper, Departmento de Ciencia Política y Relaciones Internacionales, Universidad Autónoma de Madrid, 95/2008), 3.

5   The Venice Commission is an advisory body of the Council of Europe created in 1990 to give advice in drafting constitutional amendments and para-constitutional law matters such as minority legislation and electoral laws. The commission started with a membership of 18 states, but by 2010 the number had increased to 57 states, the majority of whom were nonEuropeans, including Algeria, Argentina, Brazil, Belarus, and South Africa.

6   Aguiar-Conraria and Magalhães, "Referendum Design, Quorum Rules and Turnout," 4.

7   Eighty-eight percent of voters participated in the referendum, with 55 percent voting for independence and 44.5 percent against.

8   Salva Kiir (opening keynote remarks delivered by chairman of SPLM to All Political Parties' Conference, Sudan: Towards Full Implementation of Peace Agreements and Democratic Transformation, Juba, September 26–29, 2009.

9   Ibid.

10   Ibid.

11   Ibid.

12   Presidential Decree 341/2007 was issued by president Bashir in response to the withdrawal of SPLM advisors and ministers from the Government of NationalUnity in protest against non-complementation of certain CPA clauses including the initiation of a process of national reconciliation.

13   Mohamed Ibrahim Khalil (SSRC chair) is a longtime lawyer who served as dean of law at the University of Khartoum and minister of justice in the government of South Sudan in 1960. He also served as foreign minister in the decade of the 1960s and was a resident fellow in United States Institute of Peace in Washington, DC.

14   Chan Reec Madut (SSRC deputy chair) was former judge of the National High Court, legal advisor to the first vice president in Khartoum, and deputy chief justice of South Sudan. In August 2011, Madut was appointed chief justice of the new republic.

15   Members of the Referendum Commission in Ireland were required to be members of the High Court.

16   Khalil's nominee for secretary general was ambassador Omer Elsheikh, a refined diplomat who served with the United Nation's mission in Western Sahara and, thereafter, with the Joint Assessment Mission following the conclusion of the CPA. He was, therefore, an eminently qualified candidate for the job.

17   UN News Services 15/11/2010: http://www.un.org/news/printnews.asp

18   "Obama Urges Sudan's Kiir to Reach Agreement with NCP," *Sudan Tribune* (Washington, DC), December 22, 2010.

19 "Mubarak, Qaddafi to Discuss Referendum Development with Sudanese President," Agence France-Presse on *Almasry Alyoum,* January 26, 2011.

20 "South Sudan Voter Turnout to Reach 60 Percent Threshold," *Voice of America,* January 12, 2011.

21 "Jimmy Carter, Kofi Annan, Joseph Warioba, and John Haardman to Lead Carter Center Delegation to Observe Referendum on Self-Determination of Southern Sudan," The Carter Center, http://www.cartercenter.org/news/pr/sudan-010311.html

22 The project, sponsored by the United Nations and Google, was established to use satellites to track any suspicious movements that might appear to be intended to frustrate the referendum process.

23 "Jubilation as Final Referendum Results Favour Secession, Bashir Accepts Results—Mbeki AUHIP Congratulates Sudanese Leaders," *Sudan Watch* (South Sudan), February 8, 2011.

24 Douglas H. Johnson, "Fifty Five Years of Bananas?" *The Pioneer, Juba,* March 1, 2011.

25 Matthew C.R. Craven, "The Problem of State Succession and the Identity of States under International Law," *European Journal of International Law* 9 (1998), 142–162.

26 The 65 percent represents expenditure by the Government of National Unity on national government, states, and southern Sudan. However, when expenditure from oil revenues on the latter two beneficiaries is deducted, the ratio comes down to 40 percent. In addition, dependency of the national budget on oil revenues is contingent on the Government of National Unity's performance in raising non-oil revenues, a source that is not effectively tapped by the government of South Sudan.

27 *Sudan: Midyear Review of the 2005 Staff-Monitored Program,* International Monetary Fund Country Report 05/430 (Washington, DC: December 2005).

28 Christof Rühl, "BP Statistical Review of World Energy 2010," (speech delivered June 9, 2010), www.bp.com.

29 Lual Deng, "Petrol Reserves in Northern Sudan Are Larger Than That of South, *Alsharq Al-Awsat* (London) November 14, 2010.

30 The consortium brings together Total (France), Kupek (Kuwait), and Marathon (USA). The latter had withdrawn as a result of American sanctions against U.S. companies operating in Sudan. Talks are currently under way with Qatar Petroleum to acquire these shares.

31 "'Don't Panic' Machar Tells Oil Workers from North Sudan, *Sudan Tribune* (Juba), December 12, 2010.

32 "Minister Estimates That Workforce in Oil Companies Shall Resign If Petroleum Management Is Relocated to South Sudan", *Al-Ahdath* (Khartoum), April 9, 2011.

33 Alawya Mukhtar, "Juba Discusses Petroleum and Security Arrangements," *Al-Sahafa* (Khartoum), January 8, 2011.

34 Maram Mazen, "South Sudan Studies Routes Other Than North for Oil Exports," Bloomberg, March 12, 2011, http://www.bloomberg.com/news/2011-03-12/south-sudan-studies-routes-other-than-north-for-oil-exports-1-.html.

35 "South Sudan Accuses Khartoum of 'Currency War,'" *BBC News Africa,* July 25, 2011.

36 The whole of Chad's oil is transported to the Atlantic through Cameroon via the Chad-Cameroon pipeline.

37 See "Statement by H.E. Salva Kiir Mayardit, President of the Republic of South Sudan, to the National Legislature on the Current Oil Crisis," *Sudan Tribune,* January 23, 2012.

38 Luka Biong Deng, former minister of presidential affairs, government of South Sudan, told the *Financial Times:* "The economic viability and unity of the North will make us even see whether we can continue with the same oil arrangement that we have," *Sudan Tribune* (Juba), February 15, 2011.

39 "South Sudan Rules Out Sharing Oil Revenue with North," *Sudan Tribune* (Juba), February 15, 2011.

40 A report by Peter Ngumbullu, IMF executive director for Sudan, and John Mafararikwa, senior advisor to the IMF executive director, stated that the government of Sudan, with strong performance of agricultural manufacturing, construction, power, and services sectors, had appropriately managed to avoid a Dutch Disease following oil discovery. See "Statement by Peter Ngumbullu, Executive Director for Sudan and John Mafararikwa Senior Advisor to Executive Director, April 29, 2005," in *Staff Report for the 2005 Article IV Consultation, Final Review of the 2004 Staff-Monitored Program, and the 2005 Staff-Monitored Program* (Sudan: International Monetary Fund, April 15, 2005), 2.

41 Masood Ahmed, "Sudan and South Sudan: New Era, New Opportunities," *Asharq Al-Awsat,* July 23, 2011.

42 "Sudan: Economy Seen Shrinking in 2011–2012: IMF," *Sudan Tribune* (Washington, DC), September 21, 2011.

43 Alex de Waal, "South Sudan's Doomsday Machine," *New York Times,* January 24, 2012, Op-Ed.

44 Ritt Goldstein, "Swedish NGOs sue Lundin for Crimes against Humanity in Sudan," *Christian Science Monitor,* June 22, 2010.

45 "PETRONAS Signs MoU with Ministry of Energy and Mining," *The Pioneer* (Juba), March 2011.

46 "China's Foreign Minister in First Visit to South Sudan," *BBC News Africa,* August 9, 2011.

47 "Eight Oil Firms Facilitate Talks to Resolve Oil Logjam," *Africa News,* January 30, 2012. The companies included China National Petroleum Corporation, Greater Nile Petroleum Operating Company, India Oil and Gas Company India Oil and Gas Company, Petrodar Operating Company, Petronas (Malaysia), Tri-Ocean Company (consortium of Arab investors), Sudapet, and White Nile Petroleum Operating Company.

48 *Fuelling Mistrust: The Need for Transparency in Sudan's Oil Industry* (London: Global Witness, September 2009).

49 "Global Witness Stands by Finding on Sudan Oil Data," *The Citizens* 5:272 (October 5, 2010).

50 The Convention was completed on April 8, 1983, but did not come into force as it had not yet been ratified by the requisite number of states. The Convention

shall only come into force on the thirtieth day following the date of deposit of the fifteenth instrument of ratification or accession.

51 State Succession in Matters of Property and Debts, Institut de Droit International, August 26, 2001, article 6.

52 Ibid., article 19 (1).

53 Ibid., article 19 (3).

54 The Melut sugar scheme was one of a number of major industrial projects, launched by Nimeiri's government following the conclusion of the Addis Ababa agreement (1972).

55 Assalaiya is one of a series of government-owned sugar production plants established during Nimeiri's era. The scheme lies two hundred and eighty miles south of Khartoum and had become operational in January 1980.

56 The Darfur Peace and Accountability Act of 2006, January 3, 2006, (H.R.3127/S.1462) provides, among other things, for countrywide blocking of government of Sudan property and prohibits transactions relating to petroleum and petroleumical industries in Sudan.

57 Presently, Sudan is indebted to these countries as follows: China $377.7 million, India $316.18 million, Saudi Fund $190.2 million, Kuwaiti Fund $184.4 million, Arab Fund for Social and Economic Development $532 million, Islamic Development Bank $176.7 million, Arab Monetary Fund $15.7 million, and OPEC Fund $14.3 million.

58 The G8 Summit, held in Gleneagles, Scotland, July 6–8, 2005, pledged to cancel the debts of the world's most indebted poor countries. In September 2005, the Board of Governors of the International Monetary Fund and World Bank endorsed the principle of a 100 percent debt cancellation under what they called the Multilateral Debt Relief Initiative.

59 By the end of 2009, 40 countries were identified as potentially eligible to receive debt relief, of which 30 received full or partial relief. See "Factsheet: Debt Relief under the Heavily Indebted Poor Countries (HIPC) Initiative," International Monetary Fund, April 2, 2013, http://www.imf.org/external/np/exr/facts/hipc.htm.

60 "Sudan Seeks French Support for Debt Cancellation, ICC," *Panapress*, June 2, 2010.

61 "Poorest Countries are Enslaved by Debt, Says Bishop," *Daily Telegraph*, July 25, 1998.

62 Hagan is general counsel and director of the Legal Department at the International Monetary Fund. His views were presented at a symposium on nation building in 2005. See Sean Hagan, "Donor Interventions" (comments made during a panel discussion at "Rebuilding Nation Building," symposium held at Case Western Reserve University School of Law, April 8, 2005), webcast at http://www.law.case.edu/centers/cox/content.asp?content_id=67

63 Ibid.

64 Ibid.

65 *Sudan: Article IV Consultation—Staff Report; Debt Sustainability Analysis; Staff Statement; Public Information Notice on the Executive Board Discussion; Statement by the Executive Director*, IMF Country Report 10/256 (Washington, DC: International Monetary Fund, June 2010), 41.

66 Ibid., 16.

67 Agreement between Republic of southern Sudan and the Republic of Sudan on Certain Economic Matters signed at Addis Ababa on 27th September 2012 by President Bashir and Salva Kiir. http://sites.tufts.edu/reinventingpeace/files/2012/09/The-Cooperation-Agreement-Between-Sudan-and-South-Sudan0001.pdf

68 G.K Chesterton, *All Things Considered* (New York, J. Lane, 1913). To paraphrase Chesterton: good laws that are meant to restrain bad people sometimes turn out to be bad laws that would restrain good people.

69 "North Asks South Sudan to Burn Two Billion Pounds," *Al-Ahdath*, July 24, 2011.

70 See International Monetary Fund Country Report 05/430, December 2005 and "IMF Statement on South Sudan," press release 11/292, July 25, 2011.

71 Niina Pautola and Peter Backé, "Currency Boards in Central and Eastern Europe: Past Experience and Future Perspectives," *Focus on Transition* 1/1998 (Austria: Oesterreichische Nationalbank, 1998), 72–113.

72 Atish R. Ghosh, Anne-Marie Gulde, and Holger C. Wolf, *Currency Boards: The Ultimate Fix?* (working paper, International Monetary Fund 98/8, Washington, DC, 1998), 5–10.

73 The three were Mamoun Beheiry, undersecretary of finance (who later became the first governor of the Bank of Sudan); Ibrahim Osman Ishaq, director for trade and Professor Saad el Din Fawzi, professor of economics at Khartoum University.

74 The integration of this economic block is severely hampered by the attachment of francophone Africa to the franc zone. The CFA franc is used in fourteen countries, twelve of which were former French colonies and two former Portuguese colonies, Guinea **Bissau** and Equatorial Guinea.

75 Conflict Dynamics International, Governance and Peacebuilding Series, *Briefing Paper No 3*, Envisioning the Future, Options for Political Accomodation Between North and South Sudan Following the Referendum. Cambridge Mass, September 2010.

76 Ibid., (iii).

77 Economic integration associations bestride all continents: the European Union (EU), Association of South East Asian Nations (ASEAN), the Asia-Pacific Economic Cooperation (APEC), the North American Free Trade Agreement (NAFTA), and the Gulf Cooperation Council (GCC).

78 Community of Sahel-Saharan States (CEN-SAD), Common Market for Eastern and Southern Africa (COMESA), East African Community (EAC), Economic Community of Central African States (ECCAS/CEEAC), Economic Community of West African States (ECWAS), Intergovernmental Authority for Development (IGAD), Southern African Development Community (SADC), and Arab Maghreb Union (AMU/UMA).

79 Elliot Berg, *Accelerated Development in Sub-Saharan Africa: An Agenda for Action* (Washington, DC, World Bank, 1981).

80 Commitments in the Lagos Plan of Action were ultimately translated in the treaty establishing the African Economic Community (AEC) during the 27th session of the African Union Assembly of Heads of State and Government. From then on, the Organization of African Unity (OAU) was officially called the OAU/AEC.

The African Economic Community (AEC) was sometimes referred to as the Abuja Treaty.

81 Jacob Viner, *The Customs Union Issue* (New York: Carnegie Endowment for International Peace, 1950), Also Richard G. Lipesy, *The Theory of Customs Unions: A General Equilibrium Analysis* (London: Weidenfeld & Nicolson, 1970).

82 *The Observer*, London, Sunday 9 January 2011.

83 The COMESA serves a population of 290 million in twenty countries: Angola, Burundi, Comoros, Democratic Republic of the Congo, Djibouti, Egypt, Eritrea, Ethiopia, Kenya, Libya, Madagascar, Malawi, Mauritius, Rwanda, Seychelles, Sudan, Swaziland, Uganda, Zambia, and Zimbabwe. With its 29-member states, COMESA's main objective is to conjoin the states of the association into a large economic and trading unit with a view to overcoming barriers faced by individual states.

84 Talley Thomas, "Southern Sudan—The Four Theses," Small Wars Journal, October 22, 2010.

85 Wolfram Lacher, *Sudan: Negotiating Southern Independence. High Stakes on the Talks in Post-Referendum Arrangements* (Berlin: German Institute for International and Security Affairs, 2010), 7.

86 Ibid.

87 *Negotiating Sudan's North-South Future*, Africa Briefing 76 (Juba, Khartoum, Nairobi, Brussels: International Crisis Group, November 23, 2010), 2.

88 Amin Hassan Omer, "Talk about secession reflects phobophobia," *Al Sahafa* (Khartoum), January 8, 2009.

89 Abdel Fatah Arman, "Interview with Minister Deng Alor," *Ajras Al-Hurriya*, February 20, 2011.

90 *Al Sudani* (Khartoum), July 24, 2010 and *Al Ahdath* (Khartoum), July 24, 2010.

91 "Sudan: North and South Sign Border Pact," *Spero News*, September 20, 2011.

92 *Sudan After the South's Independence* (International Crisis Group, July 9, 2011).

93 "Preamble" to Agreement between the Republic of Sudan and the Republic of Southern Sudan on Border Issues, Addis Ababa, September 27, 2012.

94 Schomerus and Allen, *Southern Sudan at Odds with Itself*, 66–67.

95 George Athor signs ceasefire agreement with SPLA: *Al Jazeera English 6 January 2011* http://English.aljazerra.net Also, "South Sudan and Athor Sign Ceasefire Agreement Days Before Referendum, *Sudan Tribune* (Juba), January 5, 2011.

96 The cease-fire agreement was signed by Abraham Thon Chol on behalf of Athor's forces and by General Michael Majur Akeer on behalf of the SPLA. The agreement was mediated by Revered Daniel Deng Bul.

97 SAF Reject SPLM Accusations; Colonel Saad Al Swarmi, SAF Spokesman, *Sudan Vision*, February 17, 2011.

98 Khalid Ahmed, "Khartoum and Juba, War of Documents," *Al Sudani*, March 16, 2011.

99 "Security Council Investigates Complaint Against Government of Sudan for Aggression on the South Through Arming Militias," *Ajras Al-Hurriya* (Khartoum), March 21, 2011.

100 *April 2011 Monthly Forecast: Africa, South Sudan* (U.N. Security Council, March 31, 2011) 9.

101 *The Cost of Future Conflict in Sudan* (Nairobi: Frontier Economics, Institute for Security Studies, Society for International Development, and Aegis Trust, 2010).

102 Mahmood Mamdani, "South Sudan and the African Experience: The Quest for a New Political Order (lecture delivered at Makerere University, Uganda, May 20, 2011). http://www.indypendent.org/2011/05/20/south-sudan-and-african-experience-quest-new-political-order

103 Agence France Presse (Washington, DC), November 25, 2010.

104 Ibid.

105 "Uganda: On the Trail of the LRA," Integrated Regional Information Networks (Kampala), January 12, 2011.

106 "Obama Sends US Military Advisers to Uganda," Reuters (Washington, DC), October 14, 2011.

107 Lord's Resistance Army, http://en.wikipedia.org/wiki/Lord's_Resistance_Army

108 The NBI encompasses Burundi, Democratic Republic of the Congo, Egypt, Ethiopia, Kenya, Rwanda, Sudan, Uganda, and Tanzania. Eritrea participates as an observer.

109 Sir Lee Stack (Sirdar), commander of the Anglo-Egyptian Army, was assassinated in Cairo on November 19, 1924. The British accused Egyptian Prime Minister Saad Zaghloul and his Wafd Party of the attack. One of the penalties imposed on Egypt was a notification that "the Sudan government will increase the area to be irrigated in Gezira [Sudan] from 30,000 feddans to an unlimited figure as need may arise."

110 Bonaya Adhi Godana, Africa's Shared Water Resource: Legal and Institutional Aspects of the Nile, Niger and Senegal River Systems, London: Frances Pinter 1985, 70-71.

111 Ibid., 171.

112 Ibid.

113 Ibid. Also see Terje Tvedt, *The River Nile in the Age of the British: Political Ecology and the Quest for Economic Power* (London, New York: I.B. Tauris, 2004), 143–48. *American University in Cairo Press, 2004 PP 143 – 148.*

114 The Gezira scheme was established in the 1930s in the area lying between the White and Blue Niles, although its establishment was the subject of debate in the British Parliament since 1913 at the behest of the British Cotton Growing Association. The project—originally funded by the Sudan Plantations Syndicate—turned out to be the main source of raw material for the cotton industry in Yorkshire.

115 The Advisory Council for Northern Sudan, *Proceeding of the First Session, Governor General's Palace, Khartoum 15 – 18 May 1944*, Mc Corquodale Company, 29.

116 John Waterbury, *Hydropolitics of the Nile Valley* (Syracuse, NY: Syracuse University Press, 1979), 72–73.

117 Salman M.A. Salman, "Water Resources in the Sudan North-South Peace Process: Past Experiences and Future Trends," *African Yearbook of International Law* 16 (2010): 317.

118 John Garang, "Thesis on the Agricultural Development in Southern Sudan" (master's thesis, Iowa State University, in agricultural economics in 1979 and Ph.D in economics from the same university in 1981.

http://www.lectures.iastate.edu/lecture/397. Garang's doctoral thesis related to political, economic and social aspects of the Jonglei scheme.

119 In his first meeting with former Egyptian President Hosni Mubarak, John Garang requested Mubarak to send Egyptian engineers to examine and maintain the bucket-wheel (the mammoth excavator brought by Compagnie de Constructions Internationales from Pakistan for the project). Garang also repeated the same request to the Sudanese engineers whom he met in Koka Dam, Ethiopia, in 1986.

120 Cesar A. Guvele, *The Nile Basin Initiative and its Implications in Post-Conflict South Sudan* (prepared for a workshop supported by United States Agency for International Development, June 2003).

121 While 59 percent of the Nile waters flow from the Blue Nile and 13 percent from the Atbara River (both originating in Ethiopia), the White Nile, with its tributaries in South Sudan, contributes only 28 percent.

122 Salman M.A. Salman, "Fallout of the Signature of Burundi on the Nile Framework Treaty," *Al-Sudani*, March 7, 2011.

123 The Ramsar Convention on Wetlands of International Importance, especially as waterfowl habitat was concluded at Ramsar, Iran, on February 1972. The number of signatories of the convention jumped from 18 in 1971 to 119 in 2000. Sudan became a contracting party in 2005.

124 Salman M.A. Salman, "Ethiopian Dams and the Nile Water Dossiers," *Al-Sahafa* (Khartoum) April 7, 2011.

125 In 1973, Ethiopia established a dam on the Fincha River to produce 100 megawatts of electricity. A lot of furor was caused in Egypt, despite the fact that construction of that dam would have neither affected the flow, nor quantity of, waters passing to Sudan and Egypt.

126 Statement to the media by Ethiopian Prime Minister,, "Dams Shall Not Affect Nile Flow," *Al-Sahafa* (Khartoum) March 20, 2011.

127 Egypt had consistently objected to Uganda's plan to build a dam on the Nile for generating hydropower based on the 1929 treaty prohibitive clause.

128 "North, South Sudan Reach 'Preliminary' Deal to Share Nile Water after Referendum," *Sudan Tribune* (Khartoum), November 28, 2010.

129 "Signature of MoU on Development of Energy, Gas, Agriculture, Animal Resources and Fisheries between Egypt and Southern Sudan," *Al-Sahafa* (Khartoum), March 29, 2011.

130 The Vienna process was initiated in November 2010 by the foreign ministers of Austria and Sudan and held two meetings in Khartoum in December 2010 and in Addis Ababa, also in December 2010. A third meeting was envisaged to take place in Juba but that did not happen. Though sponsored by the two governments, work on the Vienna process is undertaken by the Austrian Study Center for Peace and Conflict Resolution.

131 UNDP Sudan, http://www.sud.undporg/projection/cp3.hta

132 "Can Pastoralism Survive in the 21st Century?" Integrated Regional Information Networks (Isiolo), July 13, 2007.

133 The Future of Pastoralism in Africa, conference organized by the Future Agricultures Consortium, Institute of Development Studies, University of Sussex; and the Feinstein International Center, Tufts University, Addis Ababa, March 21–23, 2011.

134 African Charter on Human and Peoples' Rights, adopted June 27, 1981, entered into force October 21, 1986, Part I (Chapter I, Article 12-5).

135 The program was undertaken by the government of South Sudan in cooperation with Office of the U.N. High Commissioner for Refugees and the International Organization for Migration, with state-level structures created for the reception of returnees. OCHA Humanitarian Bulletin, Issue 5 (September–October).

136 "Sudan: Guarantee Post-Referendum Citizenship Rights," *Human Rights Watch* (New York), December 16, 2011.

137 Ibid.

138 Malcolm N. Shaw, *International Law* (Cambridge: Cambridge University Press, 2010), 1005.

139 Nationality of Natural Persons in Relation to the Succession of States, text adopted by the International Law Commission and submitted to the U.N. General Assembly, 1999.

140 "Draft Conventions on Nationality, Responsibility of States for Injuries to Aliens, and Territorial Waters," *Supplement to the American Journal of International Law* 23 (Cambridge, MA: Harvard Law School, 1929): 13, quoted in Draft Articles on Nationality of Natural Persons in Relation to the Succession of States with Commentaries, text adopted by the International Law Commission and submitted to the U.N. General Assembly, 1999: 35.

141 Ibid.

Chapter Eleven
Challenges Facing the New State

■■■■■■■■■■■■■■❖■■■■■■■■■■■■■■

Liberty means responsibility. That is why most men dread it.
—**George Bernard Shaw**,
Man and Superman

1. Introduction

On January 9, 2011, the people of southern Sudan swarmed around polling stations in South and North Sudan, as well as in the diaspora, to exercise their right to self-determination promised by the CPA. Four weeks later the chairman of Southern Sudan Referendum Commission (SSRC) announced the results of the poll, which were massively in favor of secession: 97.58 percent of the voters who turned out chose to secede. But the referendum, as observed earlier, is a limited procedure to ascertain the people's will to opt for unity or secession. Veritable self-determination would only come when the political dust bestirred by polling had settled, the flag of the new state was raised aloft, and the fiesta was over. This chapter deals with a myriad of problems that the new state has to face and brood about after the fiesta.

Among these problems, three deserve utmost attention: internal security, ensuring dividends of peace to the people, and good governance. To begin with, before independence, instability in southern Sudan was customarily attributed to the Sudan Armed Forces (SAF) or the National Congress Party (NCP). Some of those accusations were corroborated by demonstrable evidence, while others were only based on anecdotal reports. But after independence of South Sudan, Khartoum would no longer be available as a scapegoat for internal conflicts in South Sudan. Second, it would be fair to say that the people of South Sudan had not shed blood and suffered the torment of war for two decades only to see a new flag raised or their political leaders ensconced in power. Before anything else, they had gone through all those sufferings in order to live in peace, dignity, and freedom from want. Third, as demonstrated in previous chapters, maladministration and a deficit of probity in public life led to anxieties within South Sudan, as well as among some of the government of South Sudan's eminent external supporters.

While Chapter Ten was dedicated to the consequences of separation both parties were expected to jointly address, this chapter will deal with problems that the new state, and the party leading it, should solely address. These problems cover factors that may either put at risk the territorial integrity of, and public tranquillity in, the new state or presage a worse fate: state failure. In this respect, the chapter shall lay stress on the ethnicization of politics, i.e., the exploitation of ethnic cleavages for political ends, in addition to profligacy in public spending and infidelity in public life. Furthermore, it shall address the future of the Sudan People's Liberation Movement (SPLM) as a national party, which as a result of secession, has been constrained to retrench its national role. Betwixt these subjects the chapter shall also deal with two other issues that have in the past been made light of, even though they have deserved the utmost attention by the state: protection of southern Sudan's threatened natural environment and problems pertaining to the international boundaries that the new state has inherited from the predecessor state. Two other important issues to be brought to light are myths about secession that were trumped up by the Khartoum media in the build-up to the referendum, and the evolution of the SPLM from a party that has been for two decades the standard bearer of Sudan's unity into a propagandist for secession.

Evidently, the result of the referendum came as a shock to all northern Sudanese. That shock was incomprehensible in a country where the issue of self-rule for southern Sudan was on the table since December 15, 1955, and where the right of the people of South Sudan to secede, if unity appeared to be unattainable, became cast in stone in Sudan's 2005 Interim National Constitution (INC). Nevertheless, the shock in all probability was sparked by the size of the majority that had voted for separation. And though one may sympathize with the lamentations of ordinary northern citizens over the mutilation of a country they have known to be united throughout their lives, it shall be very difficult to comprehend shocks over secession evinced by Khartoum's political class and part of the northern media. Hundreds and hundreds of those had for half a century conjured up a vision that peace agreements with the South could be treated lightly, indeed trivialized. In case of the CPA, trivialization was not only limited to the blatant breaches of the agreement by one of its signatories, but also reflected in the nonchalance with which the government's media accessories relapsed into silence when those breaches took place. This was what made of their lamentations only crocodile tears. Secession of the South was, in effect, the most glaring proof of the failure of the NCP to do what it was supposed to do in order to maintain the unity of Sudan as defined in the CPA. It was also evidence of the complicity of the obliging media and political commentators who never raised the alarm when the NCP failed to implement not only cardinal clauses in the agreement relating to democratic transformation, but also the road map agreed to by the parties in December 2007 and reflected in Presidential Decree 341/2007. That decree was meant to conclusively remove all impediments that hampered the democratic transformation process (Chapter Eight). In reality, the NCP deluded itself that it could be in two places at once: paying lip service to all aspects of the CPA, while maintaining business as usual in Khartoum. Still, the NCP had political precursors in this infamy: past Sudanese regimes that had become adept in dishonoring solemnly made agreements on South Sudan. Northern parties, especially the NCP, appeared as if they had never heard Garang's warning that the CPA represented the last chance for unity. Thus, while it was five years late in creating a political environment hospitable to Sudan's unity-in-diversity, the NCP, together with other national parties, were effectively 50 years behind time.

Nonetheless, the shift toward secession by the SPLM did not come without wrangles between SPLM senior cadres in South Sudan and their unionist comrades in the North. Until the declaration of the results of the referendum, SPLM adherents from northern Sudan continued to believe that ruling out unity of Sudan on a new basis was almost an argument against the sun. But at no point in time did they begrudge the right of southern Sudanese to independence, if unity on a new basis proved to be unlikely. The wrangle, as will be elaborated upon in the chapter, had been over what appeared to SPLM unionists to be an underhanded approach to secession by neo-secessionists in Juba.

2. Jitters in the North, Jubilation in the South

The gathering momentum for secession began to cause jitters in Khartoum, leading eventually to a deepening gloom. That was reflected in media commentaries and in articles by scribes who were assumed to have been versed in the history of Sudan's conflict. For all that one knew, the self-determination provision signed in the Machakos Protocol on July 20, 2002, was also affirmed in article 222 of the INC, which stipulated that the referendum would lead to one of two options: unity or secession. That article came in a chapter entitled "Affirmation of the Right to Self-Determination." So, given political commitment to it in the CPA and its confirmation by Sudan's Constitution, the right to self-determination became unassailable both politically and legally. In the case of the secession of Quebec, for instance, the Canadian Supreme Court put the issue as follows: "[for secession to be legal]" it must be carried within the constitutional framework of the parent state."[1] Also, five years before the conclusion of the CPA all Sudanese political parties committed themselves in the

409

1995 Asmara Resolutions to granting that right to all people of Sudan who demanded it.[2] Consequently, commitment to the right to self-determination to the people of southern Sudan, even if it was to lead to secession, had been idiot-proof. The results (whatever they might have been) were, therefore, not to be cause for grouses by anybody. But to conceal its failure in doing what it was obligated by the CPA to do in order to keep the country intact, the NCP began to moan and groan and eventually acted as though its recognition of the results of the referendum was a goodwill gesture toward South Sudan, not a performance of a duty to which they were beholden.

On the other side, grief by ordinary citizens in northern Sudan was not surprising, as it was driven by shock at seeing Sudan disintegrating as well as disbelief that their rulers could have ever pursued policies that made secession inevitable. Genuine as these sentiments were, and real as the psychic trauma caused by separation had been, it would still be foolhardy to assume that politics is akin to an *affaire de coeur*. History is replete with stories of countries and peoples who lived for centuries together but ultimately had been made to withdraw from each other. The term secession itself is etymologically derived from the Latin word *secedere* (withdraw) or the Latin term *secessio plebis* (separation by *plebis*, i.e., people). Such withdrawal indicates either uncongeniality between one group and another or rejection **by** an underprivileged group of domination, real or perceived, **by** a privileged group. Since the emergence of nation states, there have been plenty of cases of peoples who seceded from mother counties as a result of political, cultural, or religious incompatibilities. For example, in 1930 Belgium declared its independence from Holland, of which it had been part since the Congress of Vienna (1815). Luxembourg, which remained under the Dutch crown, seceded from Holland to later become the independent Grand Dutchy of Luxembourg. Norway seceded in 1905 from the Kingdom of Sweden, even though it had enjoyed a large measure of autonomy under that kingdom. On the other hand, present day South American states issued from continuous processes of secession and separation. For instance, Venezuela and Quito (today's Ecuador) were born as a result of separation from Gran Colombia, which comprised Colombia, Venezuela, and Panama. Panama, with U.S. support,[3] became the Republic of Panama in 1930. Equally, Uruguay sprang from the Empire of Brazil and the United Provinces of the Río de la Plata (today's Argentina) following the 1828 Treaty of Montevideo.

More recently, the world witnessed in 1947 the partition of the Indian subcontinent into India and Pakistan and later the separation of Bengal from Pakistan (Sindh), leading to the creation of Bangladesh. The decade of the 1960s marked the dissolution of the Federation of Malaysia after the expulsion of Singapore from that federation by Prime Minister Tunku Abdul Rahman.[4] Very recently the world also viewed the secession of the Baltic States from the Soviet Union and the disintegration of the Soviet Union itself into a so-called Commonwealth of Independent States (CIS).[5] Indeed, when the CIS emerged initially to comprise Belarus, Ukraine, and Russia as independent sovereign states with defined borders, the eye of heaven did not cease to rise in the east and set in the west, much as Lenin predicted when he said, "Ukraine is the head of Russia, and if Russia lost the Ukraine it shall be headless." Around the same time the Socialist Federal Republic of Yugoslavia (SFRY) was divided in the beginning into four independent republics[6] and later into six as a result of the withdrawal of Macedonia and Montenegro from the federation. That was followed by the dissolution of Czechoslovakia in 1992 into the Czech and Slovak Republics, probably to satisfy an historical yearning by the Slavs to have their own land.

In the face of all the above history, moaners and groaners in Khartoum never seemed to have cast their minds back to that history, much the same way their predecessors in mid 1950s failed to realize that federalism, which kept countries like Brazil, Canada, Germany, India, and the United States united, was not a colonialist ploy (Chapter One). Nonetheless, it might be argued that secession of states had never been favorably looked at in Africa, especially since the Organization of African Unity (OAU) summit resolution in Cairo (1964) about the sanctity of borders of existing states. Save for the case of the separation of Eritrea from Ethiopia and the much-forgotten dissolution of the union of Rwanda-Urundi,[7] Africa had never given the glad eye to claims for secession. That had been the case despite murmurings by people in a number of African countries calling for separation for ethnic or economic reasons: the Casamance in Senegal, Katangans in the Congo, Biafrans in Nigeria, or Sahrawis in Western Sahara. African leadership at independence had decisively given precedence to the unity of the new states as building blocks for continental unity. That view was firmly held by the likes of Kwame Nkrumah, Ahmadou Sekou Toure, and Julius Nyerere. However, as two African researchers on the subject had recently observed, concentration by African leaders on "developing a sense of collective belonging among the divided populations" made them overlook other challenges like liberty, democracy, and universal human rights.[8]

The lofty aims of the fathers of African Unity were, however, undermined by two events. The first was competition between the two superpowers during the Cold War to have foothold in the continent. The second was the willingness of a large number of African leaders, to the right and left, to be used as pawns in that war by either of the superpowers. These leaders were sustained in office by their superpower mentors, often to support policies that were not necessarily in congruence with the ideals that had informed the continental strategy of the founding fathers. In effect, during the first two decades of independence, many independent African countries were turned into fiefdoms monopolized by oligarchs under quasi-tutelage by the superpowers. It was only in the decade of 1980s, when the Cold War was in its final death throes, that the grand design of the founding fathers to inculcate in nation states a sense of collective African belonging was revived in the form of the Lagos Plan of Action. Ironically, even at the regional level, the unity that had been forcibly achieved by colonialists was shattered after independence. The common platitude that colonialism had dismembered Africa was exploded by Ugandan political commentator, Mahood Mamdani, when he observed that "France created two political units in Africa: French Equatorial Africa and French West Africa. Britain created two great federations: the Central African and the East African Federations." Those federations, Mamdani said, "were split up, not at the moment of colonialism but after it."[9]

Many northern Sudanese were also secure in their belief that secession was a result of an American plot to dismember Sudan. This view was held by not a small number of northern politicians, political commentators, and newsmen, as if the long history of betrayal of promises made to southern Sudanese by those very leaders were not cause enough for alienating them. Even if all that history was deemed insufficient to justify secession, the measures agreed upon by the Sudanese themselves to resolve the North-South conflict, including granting the people of that region the right to secede, should have been enough explication as to why secession took place. Notwithstanding the foregoing, the United States, as was made abundantly clear in Chapter Five, was ambivalent about the limits and purport of self-rule in southern Sudan. Examples of attempts by the United States to keep its distance from calls of secession came galore. That was obvious in Senator Danforth's trials to dissuade the SPLM leadership from contemplating a self-determination process that would lead to secession and in assistant secretary of state for African affairs Walter Kansteiner's observation after the conclusion of the Machakos Protocol that autonomy, not secession, was what the United States would expect from the Machakos talks. This position was maintained by the U.S. administration at the highest level; for example, in a meeting between President Bush and Salva Kiir at the White House on November 15, 2007, to which the author was privy, the SPLM leader briefed President Bush about preparations for the referendum, among other things. Bush remarked: **"I hope you are going to keep Sudan united"** (emphasis added). Salva Kiir, in response, said: "President Bashir is not helping us make unity attractive." To that response Bush said, "Why don't you kick his ..." Bush, noticing the presence of a lady in the meeting (Anne Ito, SPLM deputy secretary general) added in an embarrassed tone: "Sorry, madam, but I was talking like a Texan." Texan or no Texan, the speaker was the president of the United States addressing a foreign head of government at the Oval Office. If all those incidents were not enough to convince Khartoum's doubting Thomases, who were often on the lookout for a red herring to mask their own inadequacy, nothing else would. In effect, these speculations are but symptoms of the irrationality of conspiracy theories. And though conspiracy theories are often the last refuge of simpletons, they still have a compelling power to convince the unaware public, on the one hand, and satisfy, on the other hand, self-congratulatory elites who hardly have any time for introversion. That said, and getting away from the official position taken by the United States administration on Sudan's unity, there

412

had been an underground movement by political activities in Washington who were hell-bent on promoting the separation of South Sudan for no reason other than their intense hate of Khartoum. During Garang's lifetime, this group of activists was not only subdued, but also persuaded to promote Garang's policy of cooperation between like-minded political forces in North and southern Sudan.

3. Jumping on the Separation Bandwagon

While jitters were palpable in Khartoum, a rash of politically incorrect games were being played in Juba, causing distress within the SPLM ranks. Those games were reflected in statements issuing from some senior officers of the party in favor of secession, even before their party had taken a position on the question. Given the vestiges of southern nationalism in the inner minds of southern elites, including some SPLM cadres, that turn of events did not surprise those who knew the movement deep down. Added to that was the growing confidence among this elite in the ability of southern Sudanese to govern themselves after five years of self-rule. Among those who were most categorical about separation were firebrand rabble-rousers who had been close disciples of the SPLM founding father and regularly recited, chapter and verse, the New Sudan Gospel according to St. John. To the credulous, that retraction was a betrayal of a cause for which John's disciples appeared to have been fighting for decades. Skeptics, however, were more damning in their censure: to "betray", they said, "you first have to believe." In reality, if the statements in favor of secession were pronounced as personal views, unionists would have swallowed them, though with bad grace. On a number of occasions, Salva Kiir and his two deputies, Riek Machar and James Wani Igga, made statements about the growing secessionist wave in South Sudan and revealed that their personal inclination was toward that choice. But, invariably, they hastened to add that the SPLM, as a party, was yet to take a decision on the matter. Other senior SPLM leaders may have held the same view about the inevitability of secession, but they kept their tongues tied until the jury was out.

There were several reasons for the anxiety felt among SPLM membership in northern, as well as southern, constituencies such as Blue Nile and Nuba Mountains. First, regardless of the commitment by all party members to respect the will of the people of southern Sudan if they chose separation, the party was nevertheless obliged to work for unity. That much was affirmed by the party chairman, Salva Kiir, in his first appearance before a public rally in South Kordofan only six months before the referendum.[10] Any deviation from that course would have required preparing the ground for it, since it would be clumsy for any political party to make a volte-face before undertaking thorough consultations within its ranks. Second, highjacking the party by any of its senior

413

officers would be a seriously presumptuous act in the eyes of members who did not share the views of the hijackers. The SPLM as a structured institution with well-defined decision-making processes and channels of communication was not expected to tolerate freelancing in policy decisions on vital issues. Third, claims by neoseparatists that secession represented an exit strategy for the SPLM were only half-truths. Southern Sudanese represented the mainstay of the SPLM, and any leader who ignored that reality would do this at his own peril. However, while secession would obviously be the appropriate exit option for the people of southern Sudan (including SPLM members, if they were not sufficiently persuaded of the attractiveness of unity), it would never be an exit strategy for SPLM non-Southern constituencies. To those, the only egression would be to a New Sudan. Fourth, the issue had never been about the right of the people of southern Sudan to secede, as remarked earlier, but about party discipline and faithfulness to principles.

The existence of separatists within the ranks of the SPLM was not a secret, even to the party's leader. John Garang was well aware of the existence of hibernating southern nationalists, some of whom were threateningly close to him. In one of his statements, Garang said: "I have separatists around me, even in my own bedroom." In a 2011 statement to the media, Mrs. Garang had the courage to admit this.[11] Garang obviously had counted on persuading unbelievers in the merits and feasibility of unity through demonstration. In the meantime, the SPLM had consistently described itself as a vanguard party, and vanguards are trendsetters and trailblazers, not rear guards of a procession. To cite an instance, during the first SPLM convention at Chukudum there was a perceptible support by convention delegates to the right to self-determination leading to secession. Those who maintained that position within the convention obviously wanted to cut the wind off the sails of the SPLA-Nasir faction who championed the cause of secession through the process of self-determination. When Garang stood his ground, Atem Yaak Atem, an inquisitive SPLM journalist, asked him, "Why are you so insensitive to the floor?" To that question Garang answered: "I am the leader, and leaders command from the front, not trail behind."

Garang never wavered in his political pronouncements on the issue of unity, especially after the CPA signature. On his inauguration as first vice president on July 9, 2005, he said: "I want to assure you that the SPLM is a national Movement for all of Sudan, a movement for the New Sudan that will work with all political forces in the country for national consensus and a new beginning for the Sudan. In this regard the SPLM will set up offices everywhere in the Sudan, in the South, in the North, in the Center, in the West, and in the East, and I appeal to all Sudanese to join the SPLM and safeguard the unity of our country by making unity attractive."[12] In Chapter Nine we made reference to Garang's statements at Rumbek on the occasion of the 22nd anniversary of the SPLM/A, as well as attempts by the SPLM's referendum operating rooms to truncate that speech in order to put Garang's imprimatur on a U-turn.

414

This distortion of the late chairman's words did not behoove a party that prided itself in giving a straight answer to a straight question. More important, Garang's fine balancing between his commitment to unity on a new basis and his awareness of the aspirations of southern Sudanese for secession was always accompanied by the fine calibration of those aspirations with the cravings for unity on new basis by likeminded political forces in all parts of the country. Neo-secessionists within the leadership of the SPLM would have done themselves a lot of good if they had claimed that they had tried hard to build a new Sudan, but their efforts were consistently frustrated by their partner, rather than seek to persuade the world that secession was the objective they had been struggling for from the beginning. These SPLM neo-secessionists had been bred on the SPLM manifesto, which clearly established the objectives of the movement. Chapter VII, paragraph 21 of the manifesto stated: "It must be reiterated that the **principal objective of the SPLA/SPLM is not separation for the South.** The South is an integral and inseparable part of the Sudan. Africa has been fragmented enough by colonialists and neo-colonialism, and its further fragmentation can only be in the interest of her enemies" (emphasis added). Garang, with deep percipience, had conceptualized and trained his sight on creating a new Sudan that was to be a building block of continental unity. The author had been close enough to Garang to say that it was neither because of his attachment to South Sudan that he yearned for the separation of the South, nor for extreme national fervor that he strove to ensure unity between North and South; his master plan was to keep the largest country in Africa united as a solid building block for African unity. Garang's innermost thought ceased to be uppermost in the minds of latter-day separatists, who for two decades had considered him a role model. Therefore, those "comrades" who wished to reinvent the SPLM or rewrite the words of its leader should be reminded of the leader's words in May 1985 speech he made on the anniversary of the Bor, Pibor, and Pochalla resistance and Ayod revolution. In that speech Garang described the forces of separation as "defeatist reactionaries and opportunists" (Chapter One of this book). Far from wishing to assign such epithets to SPLM combatants who sacrificed everything for the struggle, one can still not escape recalling that statement when these combatants expediently attempt to rewrite the history of their own party's struggle.

A sense of alarm was also sparked off by utterances of some neo-separatists who portrayed secession as a total divorce between North and South Sudan rather than a political option of last resort forced by political circumstances. Neither the people of the North nor those of the South had any hand in the creation of these circumstances. On the contrary, there was abundant evidence to confirm that the New Sudan project, as well as the objectives the SPLM had been struggling to achieve, enjoyed preponderant support among the rising generations in northern Sudan. There was no more telling proof of this contention than the espousal by almost all political factions in the country, with or without attribution, of the main tenets of that project: recognition of Sudan's multiple diversities, ending all manner of marginalization, acknowledging citizenship as the only attribute for determining the civil and political rights of citizens, elevating women rights in the scale of national concerns, radical decentralization of the system of rule, and honoring all universal human rights covenants. In reality, punishing the whole of northern Sudan for malevolent acts by the NCP is like cutting one's nose to begrudge one's face. Ergo, some of the SPLM's "neo-separatists" were even embarrassed to call the new state "New Sudan," the name that was habitually given to areas under the SPLM control in southern Sudan. Fortunately, Salva Kiir and those who supported him settled on calling the new state the Republic of South Sudan, perhaps as a pointer toward a possible reunion of the two republics in the future, the way the two Germanys were reunited.

Those ill-advised actions and utterances by SPLM neo separatists had come in the face of two important SPLM Political Bureau meetings: the extraordinary session held between April 15–17, 2010, and the eighth regular meeting held between August 13–16, 2010. Though the neo-separatists expected the two meetings to mark the tipping point in favor of secession, the conclusions reached at both meetings were not to their liking. The first meeting clarified the party's position on the referendum and its possible outcomes, with a view to putting an end to an already growing confusion within the party as to where it stood on the issue of secession, as well as guarding against uncalculated risks inherent in instinctive decisions. The meeting, it might be added, was prompted by the groundswell of support for separation, which induced some Political Bureau members to suggest that the party should espouse a position that favors secession, even if that position went against SPLM imperatives such as:

i) The historical position of the movement on unity, which was reaffirmed by the Second Convention in 2005,
ii) SPLM commitment in the CPA to work with its partner during the interim period to make unity attractive, and
iii) The implication of such a decision on SPLM structures outside southern Sudan.

Members of the Political Bureau who argued against the change of course maintained that the SPLM should not make a volte-face without adequate reasoning to its grassroots members; otherwise it would emerge as an undependable organization. In fairness to those who advocated a change of course it must be added that they were under pressures from three quarters: political opponents from southern Sudan such as the Kenana Group,[13] traditional southern Sudan nationalists, and some SPLM grassroots organizations. The first group only wanted to conjure up a vision of the SPLM as the party that was betraying the South by not taking a clear stand on the issue of secession, even though none of the Kenana participants had by then the courage to utter the "S" word in Khartoum, which was harboring and maintaining them. On the contrary, some of them became unity standard-bearers in the NCP's national campaign during the referendum. As for Southern nationalists who had historically favored separation, none of their leading lights was known to have contributed to the SPLM struggle to realize their cherished objective (if separation was the objective to live and die for). Instead, they left the struggle to the SPLM/A while they sought protection in distant capitals of the world or laid in waiting in bolt-holes in Khartoum. The pressure from grassroots factions in South Sudan was more decisive, particularly when they appeared to have been looking for guidance from the top. That pressure would have been a more convincing cause for explaining the change of direction by the new separatists than claiming that secessions had always been an SPLM option or that they were constrained to sheepishly "follow the surge towards secession, otherwise it would lose popular support." Expediency is a function of realpolitik, but not so attempts to deliberately misconstrue Garang's words, as referred to earlier, in order to justify a political tergiversation. It was indeed that unscrupulousness that inconvenienced unionists most, especially when it came from leaders who presented themselves for over two decades as paragons of dedication to the cause for which the late leader lived and died.

The Political Bureau, as mentioned earlier, revisited the issue in its regular eighth meeting in August 2010. Wisely, it came out with a measured political statement in which it reiterated that "**the preferred option** for the SPLM, for which it has been struggling for a quarter of a century and recently repeated in its 2008 Manifesto, is the creation of a democratic and secular Sudan united in diversity" (emphasis added). This resolution was adopted by the SPLM leadership assembled in Juba five years after the late leader's demise. The Political Bureau's resolution, however, went on to say that "requirements for unity are faced by the desire of [the SPLM's] partner—the NCP—to consolidate a nondemocratic and religion-based state that does not, by its very nature, recognize even the minimum rights guaranteed by the CPA and INC to nonMuslims, indeed, even to Muslims who do not share its political inclination."[14] In this respect, the Political Bureau recalled that on several occasions it was constrained to distance itself from "unconstitutional measures that were taken by a government, of which it was assumedly part, against journalists, doctors, political leaders, women, and entire ethnic groups as characterized by what continued to take place in Darfur."[15] This environment, the statement added, "shall inevitably discourage southern Sudanese from being part of a state that neither respects its own constitution, nor cares for reducing some of its co-citizens to a second-class status." That was indeed a fair depiction of the NCP government, which turned out to be comprehensively a government of the NCP, by the NCP, and for NCP. That statement alone provided enough grounds for the SPLM secessionists to rest their case without having to falsify Garang's words or strain their meaning.

The Political Bureau also made an historic declaration that should have put to rest misapprehensions about alarming statements originating from some the

417

SPLM leaders. That statement seemed to present secession as a total divorce between the North and South, not only a political separation. In its resolution the Political Bureau maintained that if secession was to be the option of the people of southern Sudan, then it would leave no stone unturned to guarantee that **"there shall be two viable sisterly states bound together by historical, economic, cultural, and social bonds, co-existing in peace, sharing common resources for the mutual benefit of both of them, and ensuring for their citizens mutually beneficial rights guaranteed by natural law and international practice"**[16] (emphasis added).

4. Southern Sudan: A Complex Web of Antipathies

Internal conflicts in southern Sudan are neither entirely due to external factors nor to congenital ethnic animosities; they are symptoms of underlying political, managerial, and economic causes. Although the government of South Sudan had been doing its level best to resolve those conflicts, low-intensity violence and lawlessness abided in areas such as Jonglei, Unity, and Upper Nile states. Southern Sudan thus remained a house divided, and "if a house be divided against itself, that house cannot stand." In its excellent research on the underlying causes of conflict in southern Sudan, the Development Studies Institute (DESTIN) research team at the London School of Economics and Political Science observed that conflicts, be they intertribal (Dinka against Nuer) or intratribal (Dinka Gok and Dinka Rek in Warrap and Lakes States), were rampant and were components of "a complex web of political power, marginalization, competition over resources, and unaccountable government structures."[17] To properly analyze this complex web of problems, we may have to address the dynamics of conflict at three levels:

(i) Political manipulation of ethnic cleavages by political elites for self-serving purposes;

(ii) SPLM's role in curbing tribal proclivities and its success or failure in unifying southern Sudanese across tribal fault lines; and

(iii) Guaranteeing for the people dividends of peace that are fundamental to the consolidation of peace and stability in South Sudan.

Thinking too little of those interlinked factors and attributing conflict solely to tribalism would not lead to a proper understanding of the problem, let alone a solution.

Ethnic, religious, or sectarian-based conflicts are profuse in many parts of the world, from Kosovo to Kenya. In those innumerable conflicts, one sectarian group is inevitably set against the other (Lebanon), one religious denomination of the same religion is set against another (Protestants and Catholics in Northern Ireland and Shiá and Sunnah in Iraq), and one ethnic entity is set against another even when both adhere to the same religion (Turks and Kurds in Turkey). The ubiquitousness of this phenomenon confutes claims by some foreign and northern Sudanese political commentators that the South is destined to fail in running its internal affairs as a result of the heterogeneous nature of its tribal composition or antagonisms among its diverse ethnic groups.

Unlike the above cases, the situation in southern Sudan has been aggravated by primal factors often highlighted by southern Sudan observers such as competition over natural resources or primordial claims of ethnic superiority. While there is some truth here, this indictment needs to be closely scrutinized since it sounds both peremptory and arrogant. To begin with, a long history of antipathy between tribes exists, especially between the two major ones, Dinka and Nuer. Aside from competition over resources and lusting after each other's assets, mythical folk tales among Nuers have shaped their thinking about Nuer superiority to others. Also, elites of the Dinka assume that they have a prerogative to lead the South, given the cardinal role their community claims to have played in the second civil war. The simulated superiority nurtured by the elites of one group (Nuer) and the presumed justification for ascendancy over others claimed by the other (Dinka) contributed immensely to disunion among communities and heightened animus between them. According to the DESTIN research team, the so-called tribal conflicts, while "demarcated along tribal lines," represent "the best example of such politicalisation of identities in which tribal belonging is emphasised whenever politically useful."[18] Barring elite manipulation of the fears and myths of the two communities, there is no evidence to prove that Nuer and Dinka are inveterately cantankerous or innately prone to violence. This contradicts default explanations that conflicts are attributable to a tribal propensity for violence rather than to political manipulation by elites who inflamed the conflict, or *agents provocateurs* who actually set the fire.

One of the most pernicious sources of conflicts is that which is often related to so-called Dinka domination. That accusation has been recurrent since the 1970s and led to the disintegration of the southern Sudan region. The agitation about Dinka domination, despite perceived fears from the Dinka numerical weight, did not come from ordinary citizens; it was always initiated by educated leaders. The elites who purveyed that claim were only concerned with their immediate political gain through the conflict and cared less for the harmony and unity of the South or for the damage wrought on southern communities by such conflict. This almost pathological revulsion of the Dinka was expressed in 1994 by Angelo Beida, an Equatorian who was then deputy speaker of the National Assembly in Khartoum. In a visit to Copenhagen on December 12 of that year in company of Sudan's foreign minister, Mustafa Osman Ismail, Beida said, in answer to a question on self-determination, "I don't support self-determination for the South because I prefer to be ruled by the Jellaba and National Islamic Front (NIF) than the Dinka." Such inveterate fear only reflects a pathological hatred. In his well-researched work on the causes of conflict in Sudan, Douglas

Johnson pertinently observed that the Dinka, who represented at least one-third of the southern Sudan population (according to the 1983 population census) and are the second largest linguistic group in Sudan (after Arabic speaking groups), included sections and subsections spread over a number of states (Bahr el Ghazal, South Kordofan, Lakes, Jonglie, and Upper Nile). Nevertheless, the Dinka, according to Johnson, never developed a tendency to unite within one party.[19] As a result, Dinka politicians were spread across an array of political parties during multiparty democracy as well as in periods of armed struggle when an illustrious Dinka warrior did not shy away from being led by non-Dinkas.[20] Also, purveyors of claims about Dinka domination seemed not to have ever mulled over the fact that only one (Abel Alier) of the four elected presidents of the South Sudan Executive Council throughout its lifetime (1972–1983) was a Dinka, despite the Dinka preponderance in the legislature, which constitutionally nominated the president.[21] Nonetheless, the swaggering by some Dinka elites about their unparalleled contribution to the struggle and claims that the prominent positions they occupied in government, politics, and business were a reward to that contribution, had brought unwarranted tongue-lashing to their community by other ethnic groups. The SPLM struggle had many unsung heroes from communities other than Dinka. Thus, for the sake of peace in the South, the swaggering and the tongue-lashing have to cease. In his inaugural speech on May 21, 2010, President Salva Kiir made an appurtenant remark in which he said: "With the elections over, let us not be dominated by the elation of victory. Wisdom and charity of spirit counsel us that a minority, however small, should not be banished or taken for granted." By that statement Salva Kiir delineated common goals that transcend ethnic identities. If South Sudan is to remain united within the framework of democratic pluralism, its elite shall have to accept that electoral democracy is a game of numbers. Nevertheless, political wisdom, if not charity of spirit, dictates that political space must be yielded to minorities within the bounds of the constitution and the law in order to enable them develop into a majority in the fullness of time.

Even fighting over land and natural resources such as pastures, which were dwindling as a result of environmental causes, did not escape politicization. These conflicts were not limited to Dinka and Nuer; they extended to other communities and were unnecessarily politicized. One such case is the growing conflict between Dinka and Shilluk in Upper Nile. The Shilluk within South Sudan's social fabric are distinguished by clear hierarchical social structures and occupy, unlike the Dinka and Nuer, a physical landscape that is conducive to centralized political organization.[22] However, the social disruption of communities as a result of the war had engendered movements by Dinka to Shilluk land east of the Nile and generated conflicts between the two communities relating to land, grazing, and fisheries.[23] These conflicts reached their zenith when Padang Dinka in Jonglei locked horns with the Shilluk to the surprise of the authorities, as there had never been any conflict between the two communities in the past. Instead of limiting conflict to competition over dwindling resources, it extended to the location of villages such as Pigi as well as to where the county headquarters should be situated.[24] That conflict, which was reportedly whipped up by Dinka elites, culminated in clashes on who owns Malakal, the state's capital, even though its own name is derived from the Shilluk word *makal*. As a result, Shilluk spokesmen reacted violently, claiming that "Dinka are using their dominant position in the government and the military to consolidate territorial expansion made during the war."[25] This accusation should not be dismissed as wildly speculative, since meetings to reconcile Dinka subclans in the area did not include a Shilluk representative, even though the conflict was on Shilluk land.[26] Consequently, in September 2009 the Dinka-Shilluk conflict in Upper Nile led to serious clashes between the two communities and resulted in horrendous losses, including the assassination of leaders, torching of villages, and destruction of property. In additions to the Dinka-Shilluk dispute in Upper Nile, a group of Ndogo elders in Western Bahr el Ghazal complained to the DESTIN team about incursions by Dinka on fishing sites they habitually used. The Ndogo spokesperson hastened to add that "[t]he Dinka did not come here before the war. They have their own river, fish, and cattle. There is no reason why they should come here, other than a pretext to cause ethnic tensions."[27] The same source reported a conversation with Ndogo elders in Bisselia in Western Bahr el Ghazal in which they claimed that before the war Dinka used to ask permission to graze their cattle on their land, but that had stopped after the war.[28] That remark was only meant to persuade the listener that the "victorious" Dinka began to take others for granted.

Recently, Equatorians who kept their cool throughout the Interim Period decided to stand up and be counted. In April 2011 a conference comprising 600 political, civil society, and traditional leaders from Greater Equatoria met to voice their litany of concerns. Those concerns included the alleged predominance of three communities—Dinka, Nuer, and Shilluk—in the government and administration, and inadequate representation of Equaorians in the upper tiers of government and army. They also rightly drew attention to their role in curbing internal conflict; Greater Equatoria during the war became almost the only oasis of peace in South Sudan and a bastion of support to the SPLM/A. Much as all these claims were true, they were founded on a wrong premise: pluralistic democracy is based on counting numbers of voters, not weighing votes. Accordingly, numerical weights shall always be a determinant factor in the allocation of jobs and positions. Nonetheless, there shall be no peace in South Sudan unless a formula is devised to ensure equitable representation of all communities at all levels of the government and administration. This formula must not be allowed to degenerate into the hilarious situation prevailing in Belgium where even posts in the Brusseles fire brigade are apportioned according to population ratios of ethnolinguistic groups. Undoubtedly, some of the Equatorian grouses were justified, but what caused alarm was the predominance of elitist demands in the Equatorian conference. Among those demands was a call for the creation of a post of second vice president to be occupied by an Equatorian and the allocation of 30 ambassadorial posts for Equatorians. If that is to be the case, then the new state may have to brace itself for creating a global diplomatic service that incorporates missions to Fiji, Solomon Islands, and Liechtenstein. Obviously, these claims never paid any consideration to costs, let alone comparing costs to the overall finance of the new state. Equatoria had a head start in education, which enabled it to provide South Sudan with top-quality civil servants and academics in addition to contributing some of its better managers and spokespersons to the SPLM. But as it were, those who congregated in Juba failed to see the wider picture, as they had only one objective in mind: to catch up with the Joneses.

Throughout his political life, the late SPLM chairman described ethnic groups in North and South Sudan as nationalities. Apart of his abhorrence of the derogatory term "tribe" ascribed by European anthropologists and ethnohistorians to African ethnic groups, Garang wanted these groups to be identified as collectivities of people sharing an identity based on ethnocultural roots but still have a common destiny and mutual economic interests. To colonialists, tribalism typified groups whose primordial social ties were parochial and whose livelihood systems were thought to be unbefitting, and inadaptable to, the requirements of modern states. That demeaning typification is belied by the fact that in today's world, many ethnic groups call themselves nations even though they have no defined land such as the Kurds. Others identify themselves as nations despite their being part of a nation-state: for example, the Basques and Catalan in Spain. Some ethnic communities, such as the Chechens in the Russian Federation, take pride in their ethnocultural roots even though they are incorporated in a political union. And despite his recognition of the ethnic identities of such as "nationalities," Garang also had a grand design to merge them into one nation, which would, in turn, be a building block for African union. By seeking to create a superior national identity, Garang thought that parochial identities had to be moderated and toned down. That, to Garang, was only doable if ethnic chauvinism displayed by power-hungry elites was curtailed. Ethnic chauvinism, he believed, was not an idiosyncratic trait of character of southern Sudanese but a phenomenon born out of cultural factors that would only wane through modernization and good management of diversity. His ability during the struggle to merge and blend men and women of different ethnic origins into an effective unified army was proof enough that transcending ethnic cleavages was possible. As experience during the struggle testified, every time so-called ethnic conflicts surfaced, power-hungry politicians were always behind them, exploiting ethnic cleavages and fanning the fires of conflict into a blaze.

5. Governance and De-Ethnicization of the Administration

On assumption of power in July 2005, Garang decided to put an end to ethnic-based governance by appointing state governors/political overseers in southern Sudan states from ethnic groups other than the one dominant in the state. Not only was this system abandoned after Garang's demise, even county commissioners—the level of administration closest to the grassroots—were often chosen on the basis of tribal emanation. Interestingly, a youth focus group in Shilluk land told the DeSTIN team that "Dr. Garang has set up an initial system of caretakers. He made that arrangement to diffuse tribalism. When he died, the leadership broke Garang's arrangement...They came with an ideology that counties should be based on tribes. That has led to tribalism and nepotism...We need to return to Garang's ideology of caretaking."[29] Those were the words of a young Shilluk, probably an SPLA young warrior with fire still in his belly. Some may unjustifiably dismiss this statement as a juvenile remark, but sometimes grownups have something to learn from adolescents. In reality, the partisan manner in which administrators belonging to one ethnic group or the other dealt with official matters in the state they superintended made the ethnicization of the administration a stimulant, rather than a depressant, of conflict. Ethnicization was not limited to state levels but also pervaded at all levels of the central administration, with some senior civil servants assuming that government departments under their watch were bureaucratic fiefdoms to which they were granted a *carte blanche* to fill mainly with employees who belonged to their ethnic group. The prevalence of this culture, especially within the central administration, and the apparent impunity it enjoyed dealt a heavy blow to Garang's policy to de-ethnicize government and also impaired work ethics. Such a mode of governance, more than anything else, would inexorably lead to state failure and, according to foreign policy analyst Seth Kaplan, might engulf already weak governing bodies. That process of tribalization, says Kaplan, would prevent the emergence of any political/bureaucratic structures that could gain some allegiance from the [whole] population.[30] That, in turn, would make "each identity group fall back upon its traditional loyalties because such loyalties are the only form of protection and support available."[31]

In effect, tribalization of government departments, even if limited, undermined southern Sudan's own constitution. Articles 112 and 141 of the Interim Constitution of South Sudan (ICSS), for example, set golden rules for appointments to the cabinet and civil service. In the case of cabinet appointments, the ICSS identified "competence, integrity, gender, ethnic, and regional diversity" as attributes for officeholders; in the case of the civil service, it provided that it should be "broadly representative of the people of southern Sudan with employment and personnel management practices based on ability, objectivity, fair competition for jobs, and the need to redress any imbalances of the past to achieve broad representation through affirmative action." While no wise politician would ignore the imperative of regional, ethnic, or gender diversity in appointments to cabinet and recruitment in the civil service, obliviousness to other requirements such as competence, integrity, ability, and objectivity shall eventually bring any government to its knees. That need not happen in a region that has hundreds of academics, professionals, and trained civil servants who have served in national governments and in the diaspora and who are all available for recruitment. Inattention to these requirements that are clearly stipulated in the ICSS shall inevitably lead to the creation of an ineffective governments and an inept public service. Garang did not live to carry out his policy for de-ethnicizing governance, but the SPLM's vision remained centered on weaning people from ethnic proclivities. This imposes on SPLM leaders the arduous task of restraining ethnically programmed reflexes in politics and the administration, as those visceral reflexes, as experiences of the decade of the 1980s has taught us, would inevitably lead to the dismemberment of South Sudan itself.

6. Traditional Leadership in a New Era

After the death of Garang, President Salva Kiir made praiseworthy efforts to ensure intercommunal peace, mitigate intertribal tensions, and empower traditional leadership to play a more effective role in the country's administration. The importance of this level of administration is recognized by the ICSS in article 174, which provided for:

1) The institution, status, and role of traditional authority, according to customary law, are recognized under this constitution.
2) Traditional authority shall function in accordance with this constitution and the law.
3) Courts shall apply customary law subject to this constitution and the law.

Open-ended and vague as it had been, these provisions were reproduced in the interim constitution of the new republic under the article 167. There is, therefore, something to be desired with regard to the role of traditional leadership, particularly concerning the administrative, social, and developmental responsibilities of those leaders. During the colonial period, traditional leaders were reduced to a tool of domination and a medium for indirect rule. Even though southern Sudan had witnessed in precolonial times highly structured governments such as those of the chollo (Shilluk) and the Azande kingdoms, those kingdoms were emaciated by the colonial administration and turned into structures that only served colonialist political ends (maintenance of peace and security) or economic requirements (tax collection). The traditional system did not remain frozen in time but moved on through the education and social upward mobility of the leader's sons and heirs.

During the struggle, traditional leaders gave much-needed support to the SPLM in direct and indirect ways, including encouragement of their sons and daughters to join the struggle. They also provided, within their limited means, material support to warriors, mainly in the form of food. Nevertheless, this generosity did not stop SPLA fighters in a state of dire need from swooping down on communities looking for food. That was a sad chapter in the history of the struggle for which Garang profusely apologized in his meeting with southern Sudan elders at New Site after the conclusion of the peace agreement. Amazingly, some of the same citizens who considerably suffered from the behavior of unruly SPLA soldiers during the war told the DESTIN team: "During the war, we had a very strong law [because of the relatively tight control exerted by the army and CANS].[32] You do [something bad] and you will be penalized. But now after the peace, the army is not in one place and everybody has a gun and nobody respects anybody."[33]

Despite this seeming ambivalence towards the SPLM, traditional leaders had come in droves to support the movement and its army, save for a few who believed that their bread was better buttered by the NCP. Regardless of the above and the proliferation of chiefs and sultans in the North within communities of internally displaced people (IDP), traditional leaders remained a bulwark of administration in south Sudan. Their recognition and support by the SPLM government was not in doubt. For instance, in 2009, the government of South Sudan organized in a conference that brought together 1,000 traditional leaders in order to acquaint them with the CPA and mobilize their support to the government in facing the challenges ahead.[34] That conference came out with sober decisions that were not only limited to the SPLM's immediate demands, but also touched on issues of local government, development, and corruption. The problem that awaits the new state is how to bring that level of administration, without belittling its many redeemable virtues, in line with the values and norms established by the ICSS or embodied in the SPLM political culture. One example is upholding the Bill of Rights and ensuring women's rights within a male-centered patriarchal system. A day shall soon come when women demand the 25 percent minimum share allocated for them in the SPLM Manifesto in the structures of traditional administration. Another problem that needs to be addressed relates to the administration of justice, especially concerning relations between the judiciary and the traditional justice system. Even though local people prefer restorative justice and consensual dispute resolution,[35] the two systems overlap in some areas. According to a study by the United States Institute of Peace and the Rift Valley Institute, there had been heavy criticism of the "courts at all levels for perceived increasing prevalence of bribery, favoritism, and excessive delays which significantly disadvantaged the poor."[36]

There are, however, apposite experiences in Africa from which the new state can pick regarding organization, powers, and remuneration of traditional leaders. For instance, the 1992 Ghanaian constitution of the Fourth Republic assigns both statutory and nonstatutory functions to traditional leaders. Statutory functions include collection, refinement, and unification of customary law, adjudication in chieftaincy disputes, determination on issues of succession to traditional offices, mobilization of people in development efforts, etc. A National House of Chiefs was also created to regularly deliberate on matters of concern to chiefs. Under the South African constitution, on the other hand, a Traditional Leadership and Governance Framework Act was promulgated in 2003, which established hierarchies, appointment and removal procedures, and functions of traditional leadership. Like Ghana, the act required that a National House of Traditional Leaders be established in accordance with article 212 of the South African constitution. In addition, a Commission on Traditional Leadership Disputes and Claims was created to deal with leaders' claims and disputes, health, administration of justice, security, management of environment and natural resources, and registration of births and deaths. Uganda's experience, though different, also offers something to learn from. The Ugandan constitution, which does not recognize a role for traditional leaders in the public domain, provides in article 246 that the government regulates activities of traditional and cultural leaders—activities that are, to a large extent, ceremonial. However, the recently passed act regarding functions, rights, and privileges of traditional/cultural leaders ensures ample financial support to this group, including free education to two of the leaders' biological children up to university level. In its effort to reorganize that level of administration, the new state does not need to look far for appropriate examples to emulate or help refine its attempts to develop the present constitutional and legal framework for traditional leadership. But closer to home, it has to give effect to the very laws it enacted (for example, the Local Government Act) to ensure devolution of power to subsidiary levels of government. Calls for the effectuation of that law made by traditional leaders in their conference, referred to above, had also become a matter of concern to civil society organizations.[37]

7. State Failure and How to Fend it Off

Attention was drawn in Chapter Nine to eminent dangers besetting southern Sudan which, if not curbed, might lead the new state to join a league of failed states. That danger is reflected in a triumvirate of debilitating factors: maladministration, mismanagement of the economy, and venality in public life. The three factors are all the more alarming since they persisted despite a battery of laws, including constitutional edicts, regulations, and presidential cautionary notes. So, if there is one area that requires weighty intervention from the leadership of the new state, it is this one. With no "northern" peg to hang responsibility on for the woes its people shall face after secession, the new state has four paramount priorities to earnestly get on with: state building, economic rehabilitation, ending venality in government, and ensuring social justice for the people. Failure of states and erosion of confidence in them are never caused by natural disasters; they almost always issue from leaders' inadequacy or improbity.

A recent working paper issued by the United Kingdom Department for International Development identified three areas upon which state building hinges: political settlement, survival functions, and expectational functions.[38] Political settlement, unlike peace settlement, refers to inclusivity in the state structures of persons or groups who either forgo being part of those structures for reasons of personal insecurity or because they are waiting for an opportunity to become the government. Survival functions signify competence and ability of the state to strengthen its institutions in order to enable them fulfill their core functions: security, rule of law, and revenue collection. Failure to undertake those functions, according to the working paper, shall inevitably lead to the demise of the state. As for expectational functions, the paper enumerated the ability of the state to satisfy citizens' basic demands such as health and education services, efficient policing, better roads, etc. Attention to these three requirements represents a survival kit for any regime.

Governments are humanly devised institutions governed by equally humanly conceived values and normative rules. Hence, success or failure of any government is measured by its ability to achieve the ends, and abide by the rules, it has set for itself. No government would be taken seriously by its citizens, or by anybody else for that matter, if it did not take seriously its own laws and the value systems it had established. Under the leadership of Salva Kiir, the government of South Sudan had scored a large measure of success in realizing political settlement, as detailed in previous chapters. Nonetheless, the president's efforts to achieve survival functions often fell short as a result of disunion caused by a conflicting private agenda. For example, the irresoluteness shown by some members of government in facing its most serious challenge—mutinies in Jonglei and Unity states—led to unnecessary losses of assets and lives of military and civilian persons. That irresoluteness was attributable less to faint-heartedness as it was to political calculation. On the other hand, the perseverance of elements within the SPLA leadership, as well as within the president's own entourage, in fighting factional wars of yesterday at a time when their government was facing new and immeasurable challenges, spoke volumes about the lack of awareness of those leaders of south Sudan's real problems. In Chapter Eight, reference was made to SPLM cadres, some close to the president, who spared no pains in picking a quarrel with the so-called "Awlad Garang." For such fights to continue six years after the death of the late leader revealed not only how behind the times those leaders were, but also their inability to measure up to the daunting tasks presently facing South Sudan. The president, with the overwhelming problems he is facing, neither has time for such antics nor for sycophants who want to creep into his good graces. These sycophants, if anything, are the enemies within the gates. What the president needs and cannot do without if he wishes to succeed in his mission are competent, efficient, and selfless ministers and aides who shall help him take South Sudan to new horizons rather than keep him a hostage of the past or a prisoner in a political luak.[39]

That said, the government of South Sudan's underachievement in the expectational function lay squarely on the shoulders of its political elite. On more than one occasion, failure could be attributed to inattention to problems such as rural poverty, unwieldy administrative expenditure that only satisfied the elites' caprice, and the equanimity with which corruption was treated. Inattention to these shortcomings is not only due to the contradiction with the principles on which this elite was raised, but also to lack of remorse by a large number of them for these venal acts. Disloyalty to time-honored principles and codes of ethics declared by the SPLM, as well as to constitutional injunctions designed by the elite itself, were the main reasons why southern Sudan was perceived as a fragile, if not failed, state in the making.

According to Robert Muggah, the fragility of states is easier to describe than define. Nevertheless, Muggah still assigns the term to states "that are incapable or unwilling to deliver core services to their people." Ashraf Ghani whose views on the future of southern Sudan were reflected earlier in Chapter Seven, described the fragility of states as a sovereignty gap reflected in the "social distance between elite decision making and those on the receiving end of these decisions."[40] State fragility, therefore, is not defined by the government's incapacity to project power and assert authority within the borders of the territory it controls, but, more important, it is characterized by its inability to provide public goods to citizens. Nonetheless, many sovereign countries in the developing world, especially those endowed with vast natural resources, are ever obsessive about enjoying, inside and outside of their countries, the trappings of power, which they seem to believe are the only attributes of sovereignty. Those include sumptuous residences, unnecessarily large presidential motorcades, oversized delegations to foreign countries, etc. What this elite seems not to be aware of is that delivering basic services to their people, before everything else, is the principal attribute of sovereignty.[41]

Attention to failed/fragile/failing states gained prominence in Western political and academic circles, especially in the United States, after the war against international terrorism was initiated. According to Seth Kaplan, political analysts who only worried during the Cold War about competing powers such as the Soviet Union and China began to consider even the weakest of countries in the world as potential threats to international peace.[42] More pertinent to South Sudan was Kaplan's remark, in which he quoted a U.S. national security source who said: "Poverty may not turn people into terrorists, but poverty, weak institutions, and corruption can make weak states vulnerable to terrorist networks and drug cartels."[43] Incidentally, in the same month the CPA was signed (January 2005), the United States Agency for International Development (USAID) issued its first report on the subject under the title *Fragile States Strategy*. In several instances

428

Sudan (the Republic of Sudan) was lumped together with failed states, mainly conflict-ridden states such as the Democratic Republic of Congo, Liberia, Sierra Leone, and Somalia. The indictment of these countries was based on criteria set by Kaplan, and in particular, Gerald Helman and Steven Ratner in their article on failed states.[44] The two writers identified the decade's failed states as Afghanistan, Angola, Burundi, the Congo, Sierra Leone, and the Sudan, while Somalia was described as a collapsed state. What these countries had in common was their inability to put an end to civil strife within their borders, divert assets wasted in war to development, and set right their priorities in governance and development. States who do not adhere to this prescription shall irretrievably be doomed to failure, according to the two authors. Paradoxically, the SPLM secretary general never wasted an opportunity to describe the Republic of Sudan as a failed state,[45] based on Helman and Ratner's report. Spokespersons of both North and South governments much too often took pleasure in pointing out each other's failures, and there was sufficient evidence to validate these accusations and counteraccusations. But, assuming a holier-than-thou attitude by either state betrays a misreading of the meaning of the term "failure" in the literature. It behoves both sides to be more inward looking in order to identify potential causes of failure so that they can take appropriate measures to forestall failure.

Be that as it may, many friends of Sudan held high hopes after an agreement had been reached that put an end to the longest civil war in Africa. Those friends were, for good reasons, under the impression that Sudan would set an example to Africa of good governance. Those friends viewed the agreement as a fresh breath of sanity. In the case of southern Sudan, the high expectations were based on the way the SPLM leadership had projected itself during the struggle as a principled and high-minded movement that was not only fighting for a noble cause, but also capable of living up to the ideals it was fighting for. That cause was not only lauded by outsiders, it also received popular legitimization inside the country, as attested by the millions who met the SPLM leader upon his arrival in Khartoum and the sustained support his successor continued to receive in southern Sudan. That alone proved that the SPLM, with the CPA as a tool of change, had cultivated a sense of hope in the hearts of average Sudanese when hope in national politics was about to be completely lost. To all those well-wishers and supporters, the CPA and SPLM vision had become more than a legal and constitutional document; it developed into a citizen's manifesto.

Those hopes began to wither as a result of the slovenly practices referred to above. But despite these practices, northern Sudan shall not evolve into a Taliban state, as some commentators predict, or southern Sudan degenerate into a Somalia, as some Cassandras divine. Even so, that is no reason for jubilation by either country. That cautionary is important so long as state failure is defined by the inability of the state to deliver public goods to its citizens, not by failing to use the physical power available to it in order to control the territory it rules. Excluding the possibility of the "somalization" of Sudan, the eventuality of both

North and South going the way of Yugoslavia, however, is not remote so long as those on the helm in both states believe that the situations in their countries is roses all the way. With conflict in Darfur, South Kordofan, and Blue Nile in northern Sudan and the continuing carnage in Jonglei and Unity states in southern Sudan, that is not a far-fetched surmise. Equally, international media is now drowned with news of what may happen to rulers who take their people for granted. The assertion, frequently expressed by Sudanese rulers in the North and South, that "this will not happen to us" is an assertion of the unthinking, if those rulers believe in it, and a futile consolatory statement if it is only meant to gladden the soul.

Rather than grumbling about the description by some foreign commentators of southern Sudan as a fragile regime, its leaders would do themselves and their people plenty of good if they engaged in a process of self-examination. Experience has taught us that blaming the outside world for Sudan's self-inflicted woes has never done the Khartoum government any good; likewise, Juba's frowning on condemnations by international observers of the new republic's poor prioritization of needs and tolerance of corruption would not do South Sudan any service. Theses friends are only being cruel to be kind. President Salva Kiir seized the opportunity in his first visit to the United Nations in New York as president of the new republic capacity to announce five critical steps to ensure probity in governance: "Land sales shall be reviewed, public contracts shall be subject to new laws, and officials will be expected to publish their assets and earnings" said the president.[46] The president also admitted that public money had apparently been stolen and would be investigated and the results made public. The president, who later met U.S. President Obama in New York, reiterated his pledge to fight corruption and investigate diverted funds.[47]

A few months later, President Kiir attended a U.S.-sponsored conference on the economic rehabilitation of South Sudan, in which a number of governments and international and regional organizations participated. In opening the conference, USAID administrator, Rajiv Shah, expressed "hope that there will be a major theme of mutual accountability as part of this conference." Shah added that "the southern Sudanese government and President Kiir have made commitments to implement a public financial management law to bring transparency to the private investment sector" and "to take critical decisions to ensure that oil revenue and revenue that's generated from the oil sector is transparent and is reinvested against the core human needs."[48] In that conference Secretary of State Hillary Clinton described South Sudan as a country that "survived by being born" but needs "intensive care from all of us."[49] She also reflected on the management of oil wealth with transparency and accountability and went on to say: "We know that it will either help your country finance its own path out of poverty, or you will fall prey to the natural resource curse, which will enrich a small elite, outside interests, corporations, and countries, and leave

430

your people hardly better off than when you started."[50] In response President Kiir said: "We can have well-written and thought-out dreams, but if we do not practically improve our governance system, this dream is as good as not being there."[51] Well said, but at the end of the day what matters is not what President Kiir has said in New York and Washington, but what he will do in Juba. Before his trip to Washington, President Kiir ordered all political officers and senior bureaucrats in his government to declare their assets and those of their spouses and offspring. A date was fixed for the submission of these declarations, after which those who failed to do so were required to vacate their offices. Another decision by the president was calling upon the former Kenyan anticorruption expert, John Githongo, to advise the government on anticorruption strategies and measures. While the words of Hillary Clinton represented a fair warning, those of Salva Kiir were music to the ears of those who heard them. Deplorably, at the very time when the warning was solemnly made and the music dextrously played, happenings in Juba told another story. The government signed a contract with a northern Sudanese business man for the establishment of a telecommunications outfit, dubbed South Gate. The idea itself was bad enough, since governments throughout the world were divesting in an industry that had been increasingly taken over by the private sector. To add insult to injury, all major assets for the joint venture were to be paid to a Chinese supplier by the government through guarantee from the Central Bank of Southern Sudan. In the meantime, the government's share in a project that it would almost totally fund would be 30 percent, while the 70 percent would go to the private investor who neither had a penny to invest nor was known to have skill and proficiency in the industry. While the story was circulating in Juba about the man who had found his El Dorado in south Sudan, even those who enjoyed being called "Mr. Clean" in the government of South Sudan treated the matter as a non-event. If anything, Hillary Clinton's words were proved right: that the choice available to South Sudan is either to expend its new riches in a manner that would finance its own path out of poverty," or "fall prey to the natural resource curse, which will enrich a small elite, outside interests, corporations, and countries." These words came from a person who had been considered by those elite as a caring friend. But if those elite thought that the Clintons of this world could be mollified by words while business went on as usual in Juba, then they would have to be reminded of what they seem to forget; what should always matter to governments is not advices from friends but judgments of its people. There is sufficient evidence to prove that the people of southern Sudan are not amused by kidology from men of straw.

The new state may also have to call the bluff of elites who seek to justify purloining public funds by claiming that they were engaged in that heinous act for the benefit of their communities. In Chapter Eight we alluded to how ethnic communities kept their distance from thievery and banished thieves from their communities. In their meeting between May 18–24, 2009, referred to earlier in the chapter, southern Sudan traditional leaders applauded Salva Kiir's declared position on zero tolerance to corruption and called on him to "effectively address the issue of corruption using all available institutions, including the investigative and prosecutorial powers of the Ministry of Legal Affairs."[52] However, that corruption continued, neither because the laws were unclear nor because leaders were ignorant of the pernicious nature of the offence. What is lacking is the political will to fight it. Indeed, if there is a chink in the SPLM's armor and that of the government it leads it is the existence in their midst of few acquisitive fortune hunters who neither mind ripping off the government nor give a second thought to the impact of their ill deeds on millions of citizens who are mired in destitution. People who wish to govern others must first learn how to govern themselves.

Without underestimating efforts by South Sudan Anti-Corruption Commission, that institution still needs to rally public support through systematic engagement of civil society organizations and sensitization of citizens to the deleterious effects of corruption. In addition, the commission may have to continually carry out empirical investigations on corruption, especially in cases where the corrupt and corruptors are allowed to get away with unlawfully acquired gains. Those observations shall help uncover gaps in the administration of justice that allow looters of public funds to be immune to justice. The commission may also have to highlight the successes and failures of law enforcement agencies such as the police and public oversight organs such as the legislature in exposing corruption. War against corruption cannot be fought single-handedly by the commission, for as long as there are loopholes in the laws, offenders and sacred cows shall always find exit routes that enable them escape blame or circumvent justice. The commission may also envisage making an annual integrity survey similar to the one introduced by Uganda, which includes receiving information from the public on perceptions of corruption by ordinary citizens. Without prejudice to due process of the law, the commission should also be empowered to name and shame wrongdoers whenever there is irrefutable evidence to support charges against them. The Ministry of Justice, on the other hand, may consider promulgating a Freedom of Information Act that enables the public and the media to access all information relating to corrupt practices as long as that evidence is not subjudice, or its revelation shall prejudice ongoing investigation.

At the international level, the commission has to enhance its cooperation with Transparency International in all fields, including capacity building, data gathering, and human resources development, since failure to combat corruption is, in part, attributable to human asset weaknesses. Two other international institutions the commission may tap for support are (i) Stolen Asset Recovery (STAR) program, initiated by the U.N. Office on Drugs and Crime and World Bank Group, and (ii) the Extractive Industries Transparency Initiative [EITI]. STAR was established in order to help countries recover stolen assets. The process of recovering stolen assets, though time-consuming, has had remarkable success in the Philippines, Nigeria, and Peru. More important, it represents a deterrent to offenders when they know that there is no longer a place for them to hide. The EITI, on the other hand, was born in Johannesburg in September 2002, following the U.N. World Summit on Sustainable Development and was joined at its inception by Ghana and Nigeria. By January 2001, 33 resource-rich countries joined the process.[53] The philosophy behind the EITI is to ensure transparency in operations of, and payments by, companies engaged in extractive industries (oil and minerals) to governments and public corporations. In fact, if there is any fear of mega-corruption in the Republic of South Sudan, it shall be in this sector, particularly in the areas of exploration licences and marketing. Past experiences attest to contracts on oil exploration signed with dubious middle men without proven expertise in the industry or financial capacity.

8. Environmental Protection and Management of National Resources

In Chapter Nine a cursory remark was made on the social and environmental impact on humans, animals, and plants caused by hasty and intensive oil drilling. The most egregious environmental damage was generated by failure to isolate water from oil and the casual manner in which toxic waters were disposed. Whether that failure had been due to deficiency in production technology or to lack of environmental concern by the operating companies or by those who concluded such deficient agreements with them is of little account; the point of concern is how to stop the damage caused to the natural environment as a result of discharge of untreated water into surface areas and of noxious effluents into water courses. This situation necessitates immediate renegotiation of contracts with the concerned oil companies that had allowed this environmental hooliganism. Hopefully, as stated by the state minister for the environment in South Sudan, "independence would give [the new state] great leverage over the [oil] industry."[54]

War also wrought incalculable damage on the environment characterized by deforestation, game poaching in national parks, dumping of solid waste on land and into waterways, illegal trade in ivory and skins, and heavy pressures on land as a result of growth in human and animal population. In the case of the latter, the United Nations Environmental Programme reported that Sudan witnessed a 400 percent increase in livestock in the period 1961–2004.[55] That explosive increase in both human and animal population resulted in an extensive loss of plant cover. According to one source, five to six million acacia trees disappeared in South Sudan as a result of logging wood for charcoal.[56] In addition, lack of safekeeping of protected areas during the war seriously impaired those areas.[57] The responsibility of the government in regulating and protecting such areas needs no emphasis. Moreover, the accumulation of municipal waste (including hazardous waste) in South Sudan's capital city is not only unsightly, it also has an odious effect on the natural environment and the well-being of humans. Local administrations have utterly failed in undertaking this mundane function, and if a local administration is not able to properly dispose of municipal waste, then it may fairly be assumed that it is not capable of doing anything else.

Nonetheless, there is also good news in the area of environmental protection and safeguard of biodiversity. For instance, the joint work undertaken by South Sudan's former Ministry of Wildlife Conservation and Tourism, in cooperation with USAID and American environmentalists, revealed that conflict in Sudan, unlike that in Angola and Mozambique, had not seriously affected wildlife east of the Nile. Not only did wildlife survive the conflict, it also thrived. The return to southern Sudan after the war of hundreds of thousands of wildlife, including rare species, especially in the Boma plateau, shall be a boon to the economy and has been called by some observers an animal El Dorado.[58] The discovery was made by the New York-based Wildlife Conservation Society (WCS) in cooperation with the government of South Sudan's Ministry of Environment and Ministry of Wildlife Conservation and Tourism.[59] The aerial survey conducted by WCS revealed the existence of 800,000 white-eared kob in addition to tens of thousands of species such as topi and Mongalla gazelle. The total number of migratory animals was determined to be 1.3 million, approaching the Serengeti migration of wildebeest and zebra across East Africa.[60] On that account, environmental conservation and economic growth should be treated as interlinked issues. For example, the government cannot put an end to disorderly woodcutting without providing alternative sources of energy to people, especially in rural areas. People rationally cut trees in order to satisfy domestic energy needs such as cooking and heating. Also, nature-based tourism cannot survive if the natural landscape on which that tourism depends is not properly managed. The question raised by *Environment News* is to the point: "Wildlife survived Sudan's civil war: can it survive the peace?"

All this adds a burden to the ministry that requires commensurate support from the government. Environmental protection which had always been treated as an add-on or adjunct to activities of another ministry should now be provided with the necessary resources to enable it carry out its functions, both as a service and an income-generating department. In addition, the new state may consider creating a South Sudan Environmental Council/Commission comprising all relevant ministries in addition to academics and pertinent civil society organizations. That council/commission need not be an executive agency or a replacement to an existing ministry but rather a regulatory body that provides guidelines to the government on environmental policy and oversees the implementation of that policy. The Republic of Southern Sudan also has in hand two road maps for conserving the natural environment, presented in 2007 by the United Nations Environmental Programme[61] and USAID.[62] To sustain environmental protection plans, the new republic also needs to ensure that an environmental dimension is incorporated in the design of all economic development projects. Lack of proper environmental impact assessments in the oil industry was proof of the damage that might ensue from lack of prior assessment of potential damage. As long as protection of the environment and development are closely interrelated functions, it is imperative to create a high-level coordinating mechanism for all activities that impact the environment such as agriculture, forestry, management of water resources, industry, road construction and transport, etc.

9. International Borders

Among the post-referendum issues in which the parties were deeply engrossed was the North-South border delineation. After secession, the new state in southern Sudan shall also be saddled by problems relating to borders to the south, east, and west. Those include part of present Sudan's borders with the Central African Republic (CAR) and Ethiopia, and all borders with the Democratic Republic of the Congo (DRC), Kenya, and Uganda. The least nettlesome of the five borders shall be those with CAR and DRC. In the case of the former, which was known as Ubangi-Shari in the colonial era, borders with Sudan were identified by a series of treaties concluded by France on behalf French Central Africa, and by the United Kingdom on behalf of Anglo-Egyptian Sudan, in 1898, 1899, and 1919. However, after decolonization, the borders were not completely demarcated on the ground. This did not seem to cause problems between the Sudanese Azande on the eastern border with their coethnics to the west. As for the border with the DRC, which was also delineated by the colonial administrations in the two countries, the only technical point remaining is to define the borders on the ground. The contours of the 660 kilometers that separate DRC from Sudan were established in a May 9, 1906, agreement with the Congo Free State (CFS) signed by Great Britain on behalf of Sudan. That agreement also allocated the Lado Enclave to King Leopold of Belgium, the presumptive proprietor of the Congo. The enclave was returned to Sudan on June 16, 1910, after Leopold's death. What remains to be settled between the two countries is actual border demarcation.

Sudan's border with Ethiopia was subject to dialogue between the two countries since Sudan's independence, covering borders in both the north and south rims. The most vital issue relating to the southern rim was the Gwynn border line (1903–1909),[63] which Ethiopia refused to recognize. That matter shall be of direct concern to the new state because it relates to Ethiopia's borders with South Sudan as well as borders contested by the two countries and Kenya. On July 18, 1972, the author, in his capacity as Sudan's foreign minister, exchanged notes with Ethiopian foreign minister Minasse Haile that reflected, for the first time, recognition by Ethiopia of Major Gwynn's line as a line of border demarcation between the two countries. To avoid any embarrassment as a result of its nonacceptance of the validity of that line by successive Ethiopian regimes since the time of Emperor Menelik, Ethiopia formulated its acceptance as follows: "Basic acceptance of Major Gwynn's demarcations on the basis of the 1902 and 1907 treaties as the boundary line between Ethiopia and the Sudan, regardless of the issue concerning the validity of Gwynn's demarcations."[64]

Problems, however, obtained regarding Elemi Triangle and the trilateral junction of Ethiopia, Kenya, and Sudan borders. The triangle covers an area of 8743 square miles, of which the western Elemi bordering Sudan covers 5,013 square miles. Since that area was inaccessible from Sudan, the colonial administration in Sudan entrusted its administration to Kenya in 1931 for a onetime fee of £20,000, in addition to £5,500 for road clearance. Though the main beneficiaries of this land were Turkana pastoralists from Kenya, the Toposa and Dedinga tribesmen from Sudan and the semi-nomadic Dassanech and Mursi tribes from Ethiopia also used the area for cattle grazing. The Sudan government, through the governor of Equatoria up to the end of General Abboud's rule, annually wrote to the Kenyan government reminding it of this agreement. In 1938, a joint Kenyan-Sudanese committee was formed to draw an international line between the two countries; the colonial power then wanted to identify definitive lands for Turkana grazing. But fear of enraging Egypt caused the other colonial partner to hesitate to do the same. Egypt, which was then claiming sovereignty over Sudan, would not have accepted attaching part of Sudan to another country. Accordingly, the British ambassador conveyed to the Egyptian government a memorandum of understanding (183) dated March 6, 1940, describing the line of demarcation established by the Sudan government and the British authority in East Africa as a temporary administrative line. The situation was further complicated by order (214) of the Colonial Office, dated April 21, 1914, which identified the border between Sudan and "Crown Properties" in East Africa by the dividing line from Lake Rudolf (Turkana) and the line between the Nile and Congo river basins referred to as the Uganda line. However, in February 1926, when Rudolf Province was separated from Uganda and annexed to Kenya, the Uganda line became the dividing line between Sudan and Kenya.

The reason the borders between Kenya, Sudan, and Uganda did not cause any conflict for the local administration was because the three were either *de jure* (in the case of Kenya and Uganda) or *de facto* (in the case of Sudan) under the same sovereign (Britain). After independence, problems began to emerge. Those problems were aggravated (as was the case with the Hala'ib Triangle in the north) by reports that the Elemi Triangle was rich in mineral wealth. Nevertheless, in view of the close relations at the time between President Nimeiri and Emperor Haile Selassie, on the one side, and the Emperor and President Kenyatta of Kenya, on the other, the Sudanese president decided, in agreement with the Ethiopians, that Sudan should probe with Kenya the possibility of reaching a tripartite agreement on borders. Consequently, the author wrote on June 21, 1973, to Kenya's Vice President Daniel Arab Moi, who was then holding the docket of home affairs, requesting a meeting to discuss border issues with a view to amicably reaching an agreement among Ethiopia, Kenya, and Sudan. It appeared then that the Kenyans were not ready to open a tin of worms. One meeting was held in Nairobi in 1974, after which Kenya consistently evaded further meetings. With the onset of Sudan's second civil war, the matter was left in abeyance. Neither was the government of Sudan in control of that part of southern Sudan, nor was the SPLM, which was in virtual control of southeastern Sudan, bothered with borders.

Sooner or later this situation may have to be revisited in peacetime. Even an accident may force the issue on the two neighbors. For example, border skirmishes took place between Toposa tribesmen and Kenyan police during the interim period when the police demanded the tribesmen present passports and other national identity documents in order to enter Kenya.[65] During the same period a Kenyan minister who was denied entry into Sudan came back with a military force to gain entrance to what he considered to be part of Kenya and to arrest and beat up Sudanese in the marketplace.[66] That unhappy incident was explained by the failure of the Sudanese border guards to identify the minister, as there was no high-level official to meet him at the border. However, as Kenyan President Moi did not want to open that tin of worms in 1973, so would probably be the new South Sudan government. However, it shall do peace in the region a lot of good if the new state, in cooperation with Ethiopia, initiated negotiations at the appropriate time in order to jointly develop the area for the common benefit of all parties concerned.

On the Ugandan side, even though the Uganda Line was assumed to have permanently settled the border issue between that country and Sudan, there still remained conflictual issues relating to tribal lands. Those conflicts kept cropping up, even though the international borders between Sudan and Uganda had been officially confirmed in a Colonial Office declaration dated September 17, 1926, and published by the governor general of Sudan in Sudan's official gazette on December 26, 1926, under order (484). Examples of such conflicts were reflected in disputes over tribal lands between the Dedinga of Sudan and Ugandan authorities as a result of encroachments by the former into Kidepo Valley National Park, or between the Kuku relating to the limits of the southern borders of that tribe. Recently the Madi of Moyo and Yembe claimed that their coethnics on the Ugandan side of the border were extending their administrative structures into Sudan.[67] However, unlike differences over international borders, local community problems can be addressed through mediation by elders and resolved by administrative measures. Even so, they should never be allowed to putrefy.

10. SPLM Vision: Forward or Backward March

10.1 CPA: Achievements and Infirmities

(i) The SPLM was born in southern Sudan, shored up by southern Sudanese warriors, and led by officers who, without exception, hailed from the South. But, as I have tried to demonstrate, the SPLM soon developed into a national political party whose prime cause was to restructure the center in order to reshape Sudan into a country where historical injustices were erased and universal human rights upheld. That was the first time in Sudan's political history that a political party of southern Sudan origin assumed such a visible national profile. Numerous reasons had driven large groups from northern Sudan to the SPLM and, particularly, to its founding leader, John Garang. Chief among those reasons were Garang's vision and foresight in addressing Sudan's multiple crises, including the problem of the South as a subset of a national problem,

(ii) skillfulness in conducting sustained political and intellectual intercourses with all social groups within Sudan across ethnic, cultural, and political divides, either to win them over to his side or to agree with them on a minimum political agenda for cooperation, and

(iii) talent in differentiating between what is possible and what is impossible in politics, a talent that enabled him to reach out to, and conclude agreements with, all political forces, including the NIF/NCP, with whom he was at war for nearly two decades.

With those traits of character and intellectual acumen, the SPLM leader was able to capture the imagination of countless educated northern Sudanese, while his new-look political program resonated with many ordinary northern citizens who were craving for change. Their empathy toward the SPLM leader, as remarked earlier, was reflected in the millions of northern Sudanese who thronged around him when he made his first appearance in Khartoum after the signing of the CPA. Without his discerning understanding of Sudanese political realities and his adroitness in relating to the common man, John Garang would not have been able to successfully negotiate his way through the muddy and turbulent waters of Sudanese politics and eventually conclude an unparalleled peace agreement. Even though it had brought immense benefits to southern Sudan, as well as to the whole country, that agreement, even in its totality, did not represent Garang's complete vision. The sum total of Garang's vision, which he continued to uphold until his demise, was the creation of a New Sudan united on a new basis. Nevertheless, the CPA laid strong foundations on which the SPLM and other political forces were to continue building. To be sure, the idea of a New Sudan is neither an abstraction nor a metaphysical concept. As the late leader used to say, "creation of the new Sudan is a process, not an event."

438

What did the CPA achieve for the SPLM and other Sudanese political forces to build upon? Though the author may be repeating himself, he would still do so in order to properly contextualize his above thesis. The CPA, first, achieved peace for a country that was at war with itself since independence, save for a 10-year respite between 1972–1982. Without peace, there would have neither been stable governance, good or bad, nor development. In addition, the CPA initiated a fundamental change in the system of rule through radical decentralization of power centers. That was a feat, for despite all the lip service paid in the past to decentralization by national Sudanese governments since the mid-1960s, none of those governments was ready to concede the hold of Khartoum on the peripheries. Moreover, the agreement laid the ground for a paradigmatic shift in the economy by enshrining in the constitution ground rules for equitable apportionment of national wealth and equalization of revenues. It also gave worth to ignored—sometimes disdained—Sudanese cultures and languages and elevated them to the status of national languages and cultures. Over and above, the agreement established that citizenship, and not ethnic, gender, or religious affiliation, would be the basic determinant for occupying national offices, including the presidency. Up to the close of the 1960s, Sudanese politicians were debating whether Christian citizens had the right to aspire to that office. The CPA gave the pride of place in Sudan's Constitution to human rights and promulgated, for the first time in Sudan's constitutional history a Bill of Rights. It also set in motion a democratization process that was meant to create a level ground for political competition. Admittedly, that transformation, despite the entrenchment of its requisites in the constitution, is far from being realized. Rather than dismissing democratic transformation as an impenetrable charade, all Sudanese political forces who were to benefit from it were under obligation to struggle for its realization. Finally, the agreement gave meaning to what the SPLM used to describe as "unity on new basis" and expounded the manner in which that unity would be voluntarily realized. In reality, those accomplishments might have been the reason why self-admiring northern leaders, who had foundered through nearly half a century in their attempts to resolve Sudan's conflict, became green with envy and, therefore, continued to be resentful of the CPA and its authors.

One would assume that SPLM was bound to struggle to make unity attractive, not only because that was one of its credos, but also because it was constrained to do so by the CPA. In reality, being the party that first championed the call for New Sudan as well as the one endowed with the political wherewithal to make it happen, the SPLM was the only political force that could have made unity a reality. That had been a responsibility the SPLM never shook off in principle, as attested by resolutions passed by its second convention and confirmed in subsequent sessions of its Political Bureau. In practice, however, the matter was different. The attractiveness of unity hinged on faithful implementation of the agreement by the two parties, especially insofar as governance and development are concerned. On the issue of governance, the

NCP/Government of National Unity had religiously adhered to the CPA where the autonomy of South Sudan was concerned. From July 9, 2005, and regardless of attempts by Khartoum to destabilize its government, southern Sudan became a semi-independent country with its own legislative, executive, and judicial organs. It was also guaranteed an army independent of the national army, in the teeth of rejection by Khartoum and international observers, with the United States at the head of those opposing the creation of an independent army in Southern Sudan in the interim period (2004-2010). Even at the level of foreign relations, South Sudan had developed its own diplomatic channels with foreign countries with the benign silence of Khartoum.

At the national sphere, the case was different at the political, economic, and institutional levels. In the appropriate chapters of the book we elaborated on the failure of the NCP to deliver its part of the deal in areas of democratic transformation, establishment of national commissions, fiscal decentralization, etc. As for institutions, the NCP made a mockery of the power sharing agreement: the majority, if not all, SPLM ministers in the Government of National Unity were ministers in name. All government departments assigned to them were occupied at their higher and middle civil service levels by NCP partisans who owed allegiance to their party, not to their ministers. In fact, some of them never minded making this known. The ratios established by the CPA and the Interim National Constitution for southern Sudanese in the civil service were far from being attained. Without a shadow of doubt, Sudan's public service had been comprehensively privatized by the NCP.

With regard to the economy, we recall that the leaders of that two negotiating teams described the Joint Assessment Mission (JAM) report as "a strategy and a vision that will give the unity of Sudan a chance during the interim period by making it attractive through a reformed and fully developed system of governance on which all Sudanese are equal stakeholders." That too was not realized. It became apparent that the minds of the two parties were not at one on the meaning of attractive unity. The unity promoted by the CPA was a unity in which all Sudanese were equal stakeholders. That unity is neither in character with what northern politicians assumed, or were given to believe, unity meant since Sudan's independence, nor was it equivalent to the one mutilated by the NCP, with the benign neglect, indeed ineffectiveness, of the SPLM in the Government of National Unity.

In these circumstances, the SPLM found itself on the advent of referendum in a delicate situation: either to educate voters in southern Sudan about what unity meant (i.e., a united Sudan) while leaving them to voluntarily make their choice, or stay the course of unity up to the referendum day, even when it had become clear to its leaders where the wind was blowing. At a certain point in time it dawned on this author that abnegation by the SPLM of the vision of a united Sudan, for which it had struggled to achieve for two decades, was no less erroneous than the NCP's delinquency in observing the terms of the agreement

440

in a manner that would have made unity winsome to southern Sudanese. The results of the referendum, with 98.83 percent of voters (3,792,518) opting for secession, revealed that what was thought to be a blowing wind in favor of secession was truly an outburst of a hurricane. It also proved beyond a doubt that the people of southern Sudan were not only dissatisfied with the way the CPA was implemented by the NCP, but were also riled by its meddling in SPLM politics, reflected in its support to SPLM renegades and attempts to frustrate the referendum process. That was the sad end to which peacemaker Bashir had led southern Sudanese, much as peacemaker Nimeiri before him had done. What the NCP failed to take into account was the refrain in Garang's speeches that the CPA represented the last chance for unity. Even with all these reservations, the author for two reasons still stands by his earlier statement on the defeatist attitude of SPLM leaders who, with great haste, jumped into the separation bandwagon. The first reason was their throwing in the towel at the national elections (April 2011) without sufficient explanation to the party grassroots and the Sudanese public at large of the reason for shifting ground. The second was evasion of an open debate within the party on the issue of unity and secession. By acting clumsily on vital political questions in the first case, and evasively in the second, their action became a matter of concern both politically and ethically.

10.2 New Sudan Writ Small

As mentioned earlier in this chapter, the referendum is not the end and, in conformity with Winston Churchill, "It is not even the beginning of the end. But it is, perhaps, the end of the beginning."[68] The beginning was the interim period, during which a serious effort was made to restructure the Sudanese state, for the first time in Sudan's modern history, in order to make the country home for all Sudanese in their multiple diversities. If that has regrettably not been achieved at the national level, a similar task awaits the new state, namely to homogenize all southern Sudanese diversities. In one of his many lucid messages to the Sudanese people, President Thabo Mbeki wrote on the eve of the referendum: "Virtually all civil wars and other violent conflicts in post-colonial Africa have occurred because of the failure to manage properly the diversity that characterizes these countries....it is only by respecting our diversity—ensuring that each social group enjoys a shared sense of belonging, rather than feeling marginalized and excluded—that the state's unity and peace can be guaranteed."[69] Fortunately, this matter was not out of President Salva Kiir's mind following his assumption of power as president of the Republic of South Sudan. In a public speech on Martyrs' Day, July 30, 2011 he told the nation that "unless we cultivate the spirit of nationalism cemented by the blood of our martyrs, we cannot prosper. Therefore, I appeal to all, especially the young generation, to cease tribal tendencies and remember always that we will not be the only people to live in a diverse society."[70]

If a profusion of challenges are in store for the government of the new state, as noted above, challenges aplenty await the SPLM as the party that promised the people of New Sudan to be a lodestar and a beacon that would shine on the country's horizon and beyond. The SPLM leadership had envisioned the New Sudan "writ large," and there had been adequate reasons for that. The country that the SPLM had hoped to redesign was the largest country in Africa, endowed with an illustrious history, mutually enriching cultural and human diversity, bountiful resources, and immense social capital. Nevertheless, there is no reason why that dream cannot be achieved in a New Sudan "writ small." This, however shall only be feasible if the SPLM lives up to the values, and continues to be guided by the vision, that was bestowed upon it by the founding father. Much as the Sudan writ large needed Garang's vision to unify the country on a new basis across multitudinous divides, so would South Sudan need that vision to transcend ethnic, linguistic, religious, and cultural cleavages. That vision, it was repeatedly observed, was designed to create a badge of identification for Sudanese "nationalities," superior to parochial attachments, ethnic chauvinism, cultural particularities, and primal loyalties. Kenneth Omeje, a Nigerian academic who has written extensively on conflicts in the global South, observes that South Sudan is "an agglomeration of polarized ethnic communities. What has united them over the years is the war against the north....their differences will show more because north Sudan is not likely to remain a formidable enemy in the years to come."[71] To prove such academic prognostications wrong, the SPLM has only to stay the course charted by the SPLM late leader.

Between October 13–17, 2010, Salva Kiir assembled in Juba leaders of all southern political parties, nonpartisan southern Sudanese politicians, and civil society leaders. That congregation met in Juba to discuss preparations for the then imminent referendum. The conference agreed on "a timely and unhindered conduct of the referenda (South Sudan and Abyei). It also dealt with reconciliation among, and the preparation of, southern Sudanese for that period. On reconciliation, the conference recommended the formation of reconciliation committees at different levels to consolidate peace in the whole South. As for preparing south Sudan for the post-referendum period, the conference agreed that, in case of secession, a constitutional review process would be initiated by the president. However, the clause in the final communiqué of the conference on the constitutional review was extremely confused and confusing. For instance it provided:

(i) The government of Southern Sudan shall establish a National Constitutional Review Commission to review the Interim Constitution for South Sudan (ICSS) for adoption by the South Sudan Liberation Army (SSLA) as a transitional constitution.

(ii) The government of South Sudan shall convene an all-party constitutional conference to deliberate [on] and adopt a constitutional system for the new independent and sovereign state in southern Sudan.

(iii) The constitutional conference shall discuss and agree on the formation of an interim, broad-based government under the current president of government of South Sudan, Salva Kiir.

(iv) The draft constitution shall be presented to the SSLA for promulgation before the end of the interim period.

(v) A constituent assembly shall be formed after the interim period in accordance with the provisions of the transitional constitution.

(vi) The permanent constitution shall be passed by the constituent assembly, after which the transitional government shall organize and conduct general elections.[72]

That jumbled resolution was signed by the SPLM secretary general on behalf of the SPLM. For that reason the SPLM Political Bureau was about to distance itself from the obligations inherent in the resolution because they ran against the ICSS and appeared to have been intended to rob the SPLM not only from its peace laurels, but also of its elections victory in 2010. Finally, the Political Bureau yielded to its chairman's proposal that a better path would be to explain to the signatories of the communiqué the serious contradictions in that document with the ICSS. It may be recalled in this respect that article 208 (7) of the ICSS provided that that constitution, after amendments referred to in the article, "shall remain in force as the constitution of a sovereign and independent Southern Sudan." The amendments referred to only related to powers conferred by the constitution on the national government in southern Sudan. Consequently, the legitimacy of the president and legislature of southern Sudan would continue to be derived from their popular elections under ICSS and not through approbation by an ultra-constitutional authority such as the October 2010 Juba conference, as members of that conference seemed to suggest or hope for. There was a high probability, almost certainty, that not a few participants in that conference had their minds simplistically set on dispossessing the SPLM of all its gains and inheriting the earth thereafter. That was not surprising, since the conference brought together a medley of parties and individuals who included political axe grinders, veteran politicians, whose wisdom and experience were thought to add insights to the debate, and leaders of historical parties, who though out of operation for decades, were still able to contribute to the conference lessons they learned in the past. Over and above, there were loud-mouthed, briefcase politicians with no faculty to illuminate the debate, or a social base of support to woo or contend with. It was the last group that caused too much noise and almost turned the conference into a jamboree. What struck a jarring note in all these maneuvers was the expectation by the briefcase politicians not only to share governance with the SPLM, but also to share it on the basis of parity. At no point in time did the SPLM's leader, Salva Kiir, shirk the idea of accommodating others in his government, but abdication by his party of all political entitlements it earned through two decades of struggle was the last thing he could have bargained for. At no point in time did the SPLM claim that it would draw up a permanent constitution for southern Sudan by itself. The constitution under review was, by its very nature, an interim constitution that would govern the new state up to 2015, the time when the present government's mandate would come to an end. In the meantime, a permanent constitution for the Republic of South Sudan is now being drafted by a constitutional review commission chaired by one of South Sudan's most able lawyers: Professor Akolda Man Tier. Under the steady hands of its chair, the commission shall prepare a draft constitution for the new republic that will be presented for pubic confirmation through plebiscite. In light of the foregoing, the Republic of South Sudan is duty-bound to open the political space to all competitors and guarantee for them all rights incorporated in the Bill of Rights so that they can legitimately partake in national politics. However, political accommodation is often called for by shady southern politicians as a gateway to power by counterfeit politicians. Given the number of political parties in South Sudan, of whom the vast majority lacks substantial following, political accommodation has increasingly become a euphemism for satisfying the voracity for power of self-acclaimed politicians.

If only for this reason, the Republic of South Sudan may have to consider as an urgent priority the promulgation of a new code for political parties, not only to humble grasping politicians, but above all, to put order into political life. Neither Sudan nor South Sudan is England, where laws on party registration such as the Registration of Political Parties Act (1998) or the Electoral Commission for the registration of political parties are only meant to list parties qualified for elections. The acts were promulgated with parliamentary elections in mind, and the political parties knew their place very well. For example, community-based parties in the United Kingdom who under the law are only allowed to contest community elections; they neither make a bid in national elections nor seek a place in national government. Also, single issues or special interest parties such as animal rights or environmental protection groups invariably limit themselves to the specific causes to which they have dedicated themselves. In the United States there are 33 minor political parties with no federal representation or claim to have an institutional federal role. Nevertheless, whenever support for the cause espoused by these groups swells, and the cause they are fighting for becomes a matter of national interest, the groups concerned may well decide to veer into national politics and engage in national elections, as has been the case with the so-called green parties in Europe. The proposed party law for South Sudan may have to require a minimum number of party adherents across different states before it is registered. In a country fragmented by ethnic and cultural divides, this requirement may help create fairly inclusive political organizations rather than ethnic-based ones. The Nigerian party law provides a good model to follow. It stipulates that a party shall have a registered national office and national officers who must have a Nigerian federal character (i.e., not drawn from one region or ethnic group). It also provides that each political party shall have a constitution and rules and also organize periodical elections on a democratic basis. The party, in addition, shall have aims, objectives, and programs that must conform with the national constitution. Over and above, every political party is required to submit to the Independent National Electoral Commission a detailed annual budget analysis of its expenditure and sources of funding. No political party is allowed to hold or possess any funds or other assets outside Nigeria, or be entitled to retrain any funds or assets remitted or sent to it from outside Nigeria. The latter case is very important in the case of Sudan, since there is abundant evidence to prove that the life-support machine of the noisiest southern parties challenging the SPLM is in Khartoum.

Nonetheless, the political ascendancy of the SPLM in southern Sudan, for historical or contemporary reasons, should never be a reason for inculcating into the country a culture of political totalitarianism. The SPLM has to be sensitive to genuine demands of opposition groups, no matter how small these groups are. That will be the only way to ensure building a vibrant, multi-party democratic state. In a recent statement to the United States Congress during a congressional hearing, the U.S. special envoy to Sudan stated that "the United States is especially concerned about allegations of human rights abuses perpetuated by the security services of South Sudan and the increasing reports of transgressions by the police." The envoy added: "The police are a critical institution for establishing public trust in the government and must be seen not only as respecting human rights and fundamental freedoms, but as promoting them as well."[73] Such allegations must be thoroughly investigated rather than treated lightly.

10.3 Delinking SPLM Regional Sectors

As political separation between North and South Sudan materialized through a process of soft landing, so should the eventual delinking of the SPLM northern from the southern sector proceed. That delinkage would bring an end to the fictitious incorporation of the Nuba Mountains/South Kordofan and Blue Nile in the SPLM southern sector. The incorporation of the two areas in that sector, far from being induced by ethnic empathy as some had assumed, was dictated by compelling strategic considerations. For example, the SPLA forces in Guffa are predominated by men drawn from Southern Blue Nile, while the Nuba count thousands of men in Division Four of the SPLA based in Bentiu as well as in Equatoria. The delinkage would not have had to take place were it not for the prevailing mistrust between the SPLM and NCP. As a result of that mistrust, not only did the NCP leaders look forward to delinkage of the two sectors, some of them seemed to hope that the SPLM in the North would be crushed to smithereens. That position was surprising since throughout the interim period the NCP had been cohabiting with several political parties that had been closely (sometimes organically) linked to parent parties outside Sudan. But, the NCP has never been threatened by the presence of parties allied with, or organically attached to, foreign parties like the radical Islamic Hizb Al-Tahrir, the Syrian-based Ba'ath Party, or Gaddafi's congresses. Were it not for these forebodings, the NCP could have seen the SPLM northern sector as an asset, since it might have provided a political bridge between North and South Sudan and a conduit for communication between it and the SPLM.

The NCP never hid its revulsion of the SPLM's call for secularism. Two weeks before the commencement of the referendum, President Bashir made two important declarations: one in Gedaref, Eastern Sudan, on December 19, 2010, and the other and in Gezeira on January 8, 2011. In the two declarations Bashir promised that after independence of southern Sudan, Sudan's constitution would be transformed into an Islamic constitution and all the *"nonsense"* talk about multidiversity would cease.[74] Having tolerated, indeed cooperated with, the Sudan Communist Party throughout the interim period, the president's grumble about SPLM's secularism was but a fragile argument that confirmed the inconsistencies and contradictions that had blighted NCP politics in recent times. As for Bashir's denunciation of cultural diversity as "nonsense," that statement might have shocked the president's emissaries to the Doha talks on Darfur, as they were at that very time refining a document that incorporated provisions on respecting cultural diversity. By making such corrosive statements, President Bashi might first have wished to cover the radical flank in his party, a growing constituency of Islamic fundamentalists. These groups had always seen the CPA as a sell-out document. Second, he might have wished to cut the ground from under the feet of the SPLM which, after the separation of the South, increasingly became a pole of attraction of large groups of Sudanese, especially among the young, women, and other social groups disenchanted with traditional politics in North Sudan. The SPLM appeared to be the only national party with the power to attract regionally based parties. That fear on the part of the NCP, we might recall, has been the reason for denying citizenship to hundreds of thousands of southern Sudanese living in the North and whose political home, if they ever wanted to engage in politics, was assumed to be the SPLM.

The president's statement, however, caused consternations within and outside Sudan. A Khartoum daily dismissed it as a political ploy to appease NCP radicals, particularly since it contradicted Sudan's constitution.[75] The first article of that constitution describes Sudan as "multicultural, multilingual, multiracial, multiethnic, and multireligious." The president also never took stock of the cultural underpinnings of the conflict in Darfur, the murmurings in the Nuba Mountains and Blue Nile, and the revivalist movements among Nubians of the North. All of those groups are part of the mosaic that makes up northern Sudan. In addition, article 8 of the INC provided that "all indigenous languages of Sudan are national languages and shall be respected, developed, and promoted." The last annual report published by the Council for Promotion and Development of National Languages (created according to CPA requirement) counted 60 non-Arabic spoken languages in northern Sudan, found in Nuba Mountains, Darfur, Blue Nile, and Eastern and Northern Sudan. A *Guardian* correspondent was, for this reason, was on target when he maintained that Bashir's statement reflected his regime's dilemma. Going back to the pre-CPA era, said the correspondent, "should be a no-brainer" as it would "condemn Khartoum to a situation of constant confrontation with the outside world and with its own population...[who had] rejected hardline Islamism." The correspondent divined that "returning to centralization and shari'a is likely to hasten the demise of al-Ingaz through a violent disintegration of northern Sudan, as neither the people in the peripheries (Darfur, South Kordofan, Blue Nile) nor those in Khartoum [secular or Christian groups] would accept a monocultural, mononreligious "Arab" state."[76] Before that disintegration happens, one of Bashir's senior advisors has had the courage to take exception to President Bashir's statement made in Gedarif. Presidential advisor Ghazi Salahuddin told a Khartoum daily that the "Islamic movement needs redefinition. Now I feel that some of those whom I used to classify as foes are closer to me than some Islamists. The Islamic project, after separation of the South, has to still be nationalistic and encompassing all shades of the rainbow, including the left."[77]

The SPLM-northern sector (SPLM/N), or whatever new appellation it shall give to itself, is constrained to reinvent itself into an all-embracing national party functioning within the bounds of the country's constitution and laws while dedicating itself to the national ideals of, and guided by the vision articulated by, the founding father. To that end, an interim leadership was formed to prepare for the transition. That leadership comprised members of the SPLM Political Bureau from the North, in addition to party secretaries in all northern states. A team chaired by Wathig Kameir was entrusted with drawing up a manifesto, work plan, and other statutory documents for the party. That process was almost discarded. Earlier, in a meeting February 12–15, 2011, the SPLM/N presented to the SPLM Political Bureau recommendations for the delinkage of the two sectors. The Political Bureau endorsed the recommendations but also added: "The Political Bureau:

i. Underscores the importance of maintaining viable and functional SPLM in the two states guided by the vision of New Sudan in the interest of peace, stability, good neighbourliness, and prosperity for the Sudanese people;

ii. While endorsing the leadership structures proposed for SPLM/N, calls for the inclusion of women at all levels of decision making in line with the SPLM policy of empowering women and enhancing their participation in public life."

These hopes were dashed after the conflagration in Blue Nile and South Kordofan.

NOTES

1   Re Secession of Quebec, Supreme Court of Canada (1998) 84 SCR 15.

2 All opposition parties in North and South Sudan, including the SPLM, solemnly acknowledged during a meeting in Asmara, Eritrea in June 1995 the right to self-determination for all Sudanese nationalities who demand it.

3 The United States was then on the lookout for an impressible Colombian government that would agree to the construction of the Panama Canal.

4 In September 1963, Singapore merged with Malaysia alongside Sabah and Sarawak to form the Federation of Malaysia. Due to ideological differences, especially on economic policy, the prime minister expelled Singapore from the federation, and the federation was formally dissolved in August 1965.

5 Following the Minsk Agreement, which created the Commonwealth of Independent States in 1991, another treaty, the Alma Ata Declaration, brought into the commonwealth nine countries: Armenia, Azerbaijan, Kazakhstan, Kyrgyzstan, Moldova, Tajikistan, Turkmenistan, Uzbekistan, and Georgia.

6 Croatia, Slovenia, Bosnia, Herzigovina, and Serbia-Montenegro

7 Rwanda-Urundi country, which was under German colonization prior to World War I but after that war became a trust territory under Belgian administration. In 1959, Burundi's King Mwambutsta IV requested the separation of the country into Burundi and Rwanda. In 1962, the union was dissolved, and both Burundi and Rwanda joined the United Nations on September 18, 1962.

8 Mupenda Wakengela and Sadiki Koko, "The Referendum for Self-Determination in South Sudan and its Implication for the Post-Colonial State in Africa," in *Peace and Security in Africa*, Conflict Trends, issue 3 (Umhlanga Rocks, South Africa: African Centre for the Constructive Resolution of Disputes [ACCORD], 2010), 22.

9 Mamdani, "South Sudan and the African Experience."

10 President Kiir told a public rally in Kadogli that he was committed to unity as the first option for the SPLM in the referendum. *Al-Ahdath*, July 8, 2009.

11 In an interview with *All Africa*, Rebecca Garang reported that she "was a real southern separatist." But, she added, her husband convinced her otherwise. Tami Hultman, "Rebecca Garang Promotes Accountability for New State," *All Africa* (Juba), February 14, 2011.

12 First Vice President John Garang de Mabior, "Address on Inauguration of the Sudan Collegiate Presidency," (Khartoum, July 9, 2005).

13 A group of 64 southern Sudanese politicians and public figures met from April 1–3, 2009, at the complex of Kenana Sugar Company in Kosti, northern Sudan. The meeting basically concentrated on the performance of the government of South Sudan in government and the alleged prevarications by the SPLM on CPA implementation.

14 SPLM Political Bureau Resolution 5 (ii) Post – referendum Arrangements, Regular Eighteenth Meeting, Juba, 13th – 16th August 13–16, 2010.

15 Ibid.

16 Ibid.

17 Schomerus and Allen, *Southern Sudan At Odds with Itself*, 20.

18 Ibid., 21.

19 Johnson, *The Root Causes of Sudan's Civil Wars*, 51–52. The Dinka comprises a score of subdivisions: Atout, Aliab, Bor, Chij, Agar, Gok, Rek, Wij, Malual, and Ngok. The

Malual, whose members are estimated to be one million persons, is the largest Dinka subdivision.

20 The SSLM was led by Joseph Lagu from a minor Equatorian tribe (Madi). His second-in-command was an Anuak, Joseph Akwon. Only Lagu's third-in-command, Emannuel Abur, came from the "dominant" Dinka. Abur was an eminent and courageous Dinka warrior who gave his life in order to discipline a mountainous group of soldiers.

21 The other three elected presidents came from different ethnic groups: Joseph Lagu (Madi), Joseph Tumbura (Zande), and Peter Gatkuoth (Lou Nuer).

22 Schomerus and Allen, *Southern Sudan At Odds with Itself*, 52.

23 Ibid., 49.

24 Ibid., 48-49

25 Ibid., 21

26 Ibid., 52

27 Ibid., 21.

28 Ibid., 21

29 Ibid., 41.

30 Seth Kaplan, *Fixing Fragile States* (Stanford: Stanford University Hoover Institution Policy Review 152, December 4, 2008).

31 Ibid.

32 The Civil Authority of New Sudan (CANS) was the SPLM administrative arm in southern Sudan during the struggle.

33 Interview with a local nongovernmental organization coordinator in Wau, Bahr el Ghazal, on October 17, 2009, in Schomerus and Allen, *Southern Sudan At Odds with Itself*, 58.

34 Kings, Chiefs, and Traditional Leaders Conference, Bantiu, May 18–24, 2009.

35 Cherry Leonardi, Leben Nelson Moro, Martina Santschi, and Deborah H. Isser, *Local Justice in Southern Sudan* (Washington, DC: United States Institute of Peace and Rift Valley Institute, 2010).

36 Ibid., 5.

37 Southern Sudan Civil Society Organization, Consultative Meeting, World Bank Headquarters, Juba.

38 Alan Whaites, "States in Development: Understanding State-Building" (London: Department for International Development, 2008).

39 Dinka settlements in the rainy season comprise two main strucures, luaks as cattle byres and jongs as granaries.

40 Robert Muggah, "Stablilising Fragile States and the Humanitarian Space," in *Ending Wars, Consolidating Peace: Economic Perspectives*, eds. Mats Berdal and Achim Wennmann (London: International Institute for Strategic Studies, 2010), 33–52.

41 Ghani and Lockhart, *Fixing Failed States: A Framework For Rebuilding A Fractrued World*, Oxford University Press, 2008, 17-19.

42 Seth Kaplan, *Fixing Fragile States*, Supra note 30

43 Ibid.

44 Gerald B. Helman and Steven R. Ratner, "Saving Failed States," *Foreign Policy* (originally published in Winter 1992–1993. Republished June 21, 2010).

45 Pagan described the government of National Unity as a failed state. Press symposium, *Ajras Al-Hurriya,* July 24, 2008.

46 "South Sudan's President Salva Kiir to Fight Corruption", BBC, *News Africa*, September 21, 2011.

47 "South Sudan President to Meet Obama," Voice of America, September 20, 2011.

48 International Engagement Conference on South Sudan, Washington, DC, December 13, 2011.

49 David Lerman, "Clinton Urges 'Intensive Care' for Independent South Sudan," Bloomberg Businessweek, December 15, 2011.

50 Ibid.

51 From statement by Salva Kiir at the International Engagement Conference on South Sudan organized by US government and business and held in Washington DC on December 14, 2011. The conference was opened by US Secretary of State Hilary Clinton.

52 Kings, Chiefs, and Traditional Leaders Conference, Bantiu, May 18–24, 2009.

53 The African countries included Burkina Faso, Cameroon, Central African Republic, Chad, Congo, Côte d'Ivoire, Democratic Republic of the Congo, Ethiopia, Gabon, Mali, Madagascar, Mauritania, Mozambique, Niger, Tanzania, and Zambia.

54 Rebecca Hamilton, "Looming Challenge for Southern Sudan: Regulating Oil Companies," *The Washington Post* (In Bentiu, Sudan), February 12, 2011.

55 Sudan Post-Conflict Environmental Assessment (United Nations Environment Programme, 2007).

56 "Unpaid Debt: The Legacy of Lundin, Petronas, and OMV in Block 5A, Sudan 1997–2003" (Utrecht, Netherlands: European Coalition on Oil in Sudan, June 2010).

57 Protected areas are defined by the International Union for Conservation of Nature as "areas of land especially dedicated to the protection and maintenance of biological diversity managed through legal or other effective means."

58 Stephanie McCrummen, "After War, Wildlife Return to Sudan," *Washington Post* (Boma, Sudan), October 11, 2009.

59 "Wildlife Survived Sudan's Civil War, Can It Survive the Peace?" *Environment News Service* (New York) June 18, 2007.

60 Ed Pilkington, "Sudan's Breathtaking Migration," *The Guardian* (New York) June 13, 2007.

61 Sudan Post-Conflict Environmental Assessment (United Nations Environment Programme, 2007).

62 *Southern Sudan Environmental Threats and Opportunities Assessment: Biodiversity and Tropical Forest Assessment*, prepared by the International Resources Group for United States Agency for International Development (Washington, DC: September 2007).

63 Major Gwynn was appointed by the British government, with the consent of Emperor Menelik, to demarcate the borders between Ethiopia and British East Africa based on the December 6, 1907, agreement between the two countries. Sudan did not figure in that agreement except when the territory between Mount Birino and Lake Rudolf (presently Lake Turkana) was transferred to Sudan by the Uganda Order in Council on April 21, 1914.

64 See Faisal Abdel Rahman Ali Taha, *The Sudan-Ethiopia Boundary Dispute* (Abu Dhabi, United Arab Emirates: Abu Dhabi Printing and Publishing, 1983).

65 Schomerus and Allen, *Southern Sudan At Odds with Itself*, 44.

66 Ibid.
67 Dradenya Amazia, "Uganda-Sudan Border Dispute: Is There Still Room for Customary Boundaries?" *New Vision* (Kampala, Uganda), January 4, 2010.
68 Winston Churchill, Lord Mayor's Luncheon, Mansion House, London, November 10 1942.
69 Thabo Mbeki, "Sudan and Africa's Future," *Project Syndicate*, December 16, 2010, http://www.project-syndicate.org/commentary/sudan-and-africa-s-future.
70 Kiir's speech on Martyrs Day, Gurtong. http://www.gurtong.net/ECM/ Editorial/tabid/124/ctl/ArticleView/mid519/articleId/5519/Kiir's-speech-on-Martyrs-Day.aspx
71 Kenneth Omeje, "Q+A: South Sudan May Be More Conflict-Ridden after Independence Than Before," interview by Katy Migiro, Thomson Reuters Foundation (Nairobi), April 8, 2011, http://www.trust.org/item/?map=qa-ssudan-may-be-more-conflict-ridden-after-independence-than-before-academic/. Kenneth Omeje, presently teaching at the United States International University in Nairobi, has written *Dangers of Splitting a Fragile Rentier State: Getting it Right in Southern Sudan* (Durban: ACCORD, 2010) and *Conflict and peacekeeping in Liberia and* edited *Extractive Economies and Conflicts in the Global South: Multi-Regional Perspectives on Rentier Politics* (Burlington, VT: Ashgate, 2008), among others.
72 All Southern Sudanese Political Parties' Conference, Juba, Southern Sudan, October 13–17, 2010.
73 Princeton Lyman, "A Comprehensive Assessment Toward U.S. Policy in Sudan," testimony before the U.S. House of Representatives Subcommittee on Africa, Global Health, and Human Rights, Washington, DC, October 4, 2011.
74 Gamal Abdel-Gawad, "Will North Sudan Become a State Ruled by Shari'a Law? Bashir says yes," *Ahramonline,* December 22, 2010.
75 "Application of Shari'a Is Political Not Religious Debate," *Al-Sahafa* (Khartoum), February 19, 2011.
76 Harry Verhoeven, "Northern Sudan at a Deadly Crossroads," *The Guardian*, January 18, 2011.
77 *Al-Sudani*, December 21, 2010.

Chapter Twelve
Darfur and the CPA: Shady Foreign Interventions and Unpardonable Local Concealments

■■■■■■■■■■■■■❖■■■■■■■■■■■■

> If you want peace, work for justice.
> —**Pope Paul VI**
> World Peace Day, 1972

1. Introduction

Armed conflict in Darfur broke out when the Comprehensive Peace Agreement (CPA) negotiations were ongoing, yet it received much more attention in academic literature and international media reports than the twenty-one year war in southern Sudan ever received. With few exceptions,[1] the literature and reports on Darfur rarely contextualized that conflict within the broader politics of Sudan. Even if its roots were no different than those from which conflict in southern Sudan sprouted, the Darfur conflict was not directly addressed by the CPA; only a general clause in that agreement called for the emulation of the CPA in the resolution of conflicts in Sudan akin to the North-South conflict.[2] The Darfur Peace Agreement (DPA) signed in Abuja in May 2006 and the Eastern Sudan Peace Agreement (ESPA) signed in Asmara in October of the same year were both structured on, and drew extensively from, the CPA. The lack of full implementation of these agreements, especially the DPA, led to the disaffection of Darfuris, including the leader who had affixed his signatures to the DPA. The horrific dimensions reached by the Darfur conflict could not have passed unnoticed by the international community, but the measures taken were hardly coordinated, or sometimes even related, to cardinal objectives like ensuring peace and restoring community harmony.

This chapter shall first touch on the genesis of the Darfur crisis, origins of the relationship between the Sudan People's Liberation Movement/Army (SPLM/A) and Darfurian rebels, and the deliberate ethnicization of that conflict by external players and, wantonly, by local actors. To all ends and purposes, the Darfur conflict had been a political strife with economic, social, and cultural dimensions. Thereafter, the chapter shall attend to the cruel manner with which the National Congress Party (NCP) had initially handled that problem, as if it had learned nothing and forgotten everything from the experiences of two civil wars in Sudan. The government's brutal handling of the rebellion and the dislocation of Darfurian communities as a result of that brutality generated a critical humanitarian crisis, causing hue and cry across the world. Unfailingly, the NCP's response to the international outcry was denials, concealments, and spurnings. In view of these unconvincing denials and the continuation of brutality and what seemed to be utter lack of concern by the NCP for the unfolding humanitarian crisis, international pressures culminated in accusing the government of genocide, with accusatory fingers pointed at no less than the president of the republic. Much as international concern with Darfur conflict was abundantly justified, it still lacked focus on the main objectives of the intervention: bringing peace to Darfur and alleviating humanitarian crisis. In addition, some interventions were driven by motives impertinent to the crisis. In particular, a concentration of efforts by special interest groups, mainly in the United States, on hauling President Bashir to the International Criminal Court (ICC) signified a complete lack of prioritization of issues and revealed an agendum likely to be hurtful to the cause of Darfurians.

The last part of the chapter shall deal with how all these factors aggravated, rather than relieved, the suffering of Darfurians. The perpetuation of the conflict led to almost a complete shift of international attention from the CPA to the DPA and its sequels. That shift was a result of the disproportionate intentness that the outside world, led by the United States, began to give to Darfur to the exclusion of other crises in Sudan, including the tentative peace in southern Sudan, on whose achievement the United States and its partners invested considerable energy and resources. As a result, concentration on the CPA implementation in all its elements became less intense internally and externally. Internally, the preoccupation of the Government of National Unity with Darfur distracted it from its prime duty during the interim period.[3] Externally, relations between Sudan and the outside world, including the United Nations, became poisoned by Khartoum's compulsive reactions to outside interventions in Darfur and, thus, negatively affected the contribution of international players to the resolution of other Sudanese problems. Those included much-needed funding for CPA implementation and post-conflict reconstruction in southern Sudan and other war-ravished areas. This lack of focus almost destabilized the CPA peace process and never came close to resolving the Darfur crisis. For this reason, the last part of the chapter shall examine the dynamics of external interventions, especially by the United States, in the post-CPA era to ensure the peace building ushered by the CPA, on the one hand, and to realize peace in Darfur, on the other hand.

2. SPLM and Darfur Conflict

In Chapter Five we hinted at the offer made by John Garang to Vice President Taha for a joint SPLM/NCP effort to stave off the deterioration in the Darfur conflict, while in Chapter Six we made reference to plans by the SPLM to engage Darfurian leaders in order to reach comprehensive peace with the government. Much as Garang's offer was summarily dismissed and his plan for Darfur lapsed after his death, Garang's successor became engrossed in bringing peace to South Sudan. Subsequent to the formation of the Government of National Unity, the new SPLM leader proceeded to make capital of both his participation in the Government of National Unity as well as his relations with the Sudan Liberation Movement (SLM) [4] in order to narrow the gap between the two conflicting parties. To that end, he dispatched an SPLM delegation to Abuja as part of the government's delegation. Different factors contributed to the failure of the Abuja negotiations, including lack of clarity of vision among Darfurian leadership about the endgame to the process and the highhandedness of the mediators in rushing rebel leaders to a half-baked agreement, according to an observer of those mediators who ran the negotiations through "deadline diplomacy."[5] Having failed to turn things to its liking, the government delegation (which was essentially an NCP delegation) resorted to what that party knew best: splintering and weakening rebel groups, and dividing communities in Darfur such as Fur, Masalit, and Zaghawa in order to keep Darfur unstable and prevent the emergence of a unified opposition. Hence, the door for a just and final settlement of the conflict appeared almost to have closed, especially when the government began to brazenly favor so-called Darfurian "Arabs" against "non-Arabs," labeled *Zurga* (black).[6] That dubious distinction between two African peoples provided ammunition for Western commentators who delighted in describing the conflict in Darfur as one between armed "Arab" militias and innocent "African" victims.

The SPLM's involvement in the Darfur conflict was essentially driven by its commitment to a cause for which it had struggled shoulder-to shoulder-with other marginalized groups in order to establish justice for all. The first contact between Darfurian rebels and the SPLM was in the early 1990s when the former Islamist activist, Daoud Yahya Bolad, sought help from Garang, which was readily given. The fallback by an Islamist cadre, who was highly regarded by his brethren, on the man who was depicted by the National

Islamic Front (NIF) as the devil incarnate revealed Bolad's disenchantment with the NIF. That disenchantment assumed what appeared to be a racist dimension when Darfurians issued their Black Book, to which reference was made in Chapter Two. In that book Darfurians claimed that they were pejoratively identified by "northerners" as *awlad al-gharib* (sons of the west) as opposed to *awlad al-Bahr* (children of the Nile). Bolad's incursion into Darfur was ruthlessly crushed by the NIF, with him summarily executed.

Distracted by the split within its ranks in the mid-1990s, the SPLM was not able to give undivided attention to Darfur. However, one lesson to be learned from that episode was that social, economic, and ethnic factors could not be concealed under the cloak of brotherhood in Islam. If Bolad's rebellion was not enough to reopen the eyes of the NCP to that fact, then that of Dr. Khalil Ibrahim, dubbed "*Amir al-Dababeen*,"[7] should have. The neglect Darfur suffered from the central authority was not a phenomenon that had surfaced after the NIF's assumption of power; it was symptom of the center-periphery dialectic since colonial times. It also reflected the condescendence with which the political elite at the center treated communities in the peripheries. Rather than addressing the root causes of impoverishment and disenfranchisement that these communities suffered, the central authority chose to subdue their anger by enlisting from within their ranks retinues who were willing to tag along with Khartoum and ensure that a patron-client relationship was established with it. Ultimately, that approach neither succeeded in quelling rebellion nor in maintaining the status quo.

After the virtual collapse of the DPA and the impatience expressed by Minni Arkuwa Minnawi over unwarranted delays in its implementation,[8] the SPLM chairman established a Darfur Task Force (DTF) to engage Darfurian rebel groups in consolidating their ranks and better articulating their demands. The rebel groups had by then multiplied from two to nearly twenty groups. The DTF made several trips to neighboring countries to meet leaders of these groups in order to reconcile their views on peace at the ongoing negotiations. The SPLM chairman also visited Ndjamena on March 19, 2007, to meet with Chad's President, Idriss Déby of Chad in order to exchange views on how to end the Darfur Conflict, while the government of South Sudan vice president, Riek Machar, made use of a visit to Paris in the same year to establish contacts with Abdel Wahid Mohamed Nour, who was known to have been playing the role of "hard to get." In the meantime, the SPLM maintained contacts with Eritrea, which had by then open lines of communication with all Darfur rebels. These contacts climaxed in the first official visit to Eritrea by then First Vice President Salva Kiir in 2007. In that visit, Eritrean President Isaias Afewerki, who by then was not on friendly terms with Khartoum, proposed that the Darfur file be handed to the first vice president with whom, he said, Eritrea would cooperate. Afewerki made that offer in the presence of a Sudan government delegation, which Salva Kiir headed and which included the government of Sudan's chief negotiator in Darfur, the late Dr. Magzoub El Khalifa. Khartoum flew into a temper, and President Bashir, on receiving the news, exploded with rage. Bashir thought the proposition made by Afewerki was an intervention by Eritrea into Sudan's internal affairs. It didn't seem to matter to him that entrusting the matter to the first vice president of the republic would elevate the Darfur dossier to a higher level in his own government, or that Eritrea had been ever present in the Abuja negotiations as an observer trusted by the Darfurians and the SPLM. It seemed that the NCP was mistrustful of any breakthrough in the Darfur conflict that might be achieved by the SPLM. That was probably the same reason why Taha rejected John Garang's offer at Naivasha. The NCP was equally wary that any success scored by the SPLM in Darfur might raise the status of the movement at both the national level and among Darfurians. With that level of pettiness, the SPLM settled for moving ahead alone with its efforts to help resolve the Darfur crisis, especially by concentrating on making Darfurians speak with one tongue.

3. Who Are the Darfurians?

Alex de Waal, a British scholar on African issues, appropriately asked that question in a February 2008 symposium organized in Addis Ababa by Cornell University and the Prince Claus Fund-Library.[9] The term "Darfur" literally means "home of the Fur," who are one of more than 20 ethnic communities who occupy the land in western Sudan.[10] The term, therefore, denotes a geographic space inhabited by a multitude of tribes, including the Fur. Those ethnic groups lived in peace for hundreds of years, and though sharing the same religion (Islam) and using Arabic as a *lingua franca*, the majority of them persisted in using their local languages and drawing on their local cultures. In view of those shared cultural characteristics, animosities based on ethnic origin or color were alien to the people of Darfur. In effect, intertribal feuds over resources were more common among tribes of the same lineage such as the "Arab" Maalia and Rezeigat or Beni Halba and Habaniya than across racial divides. Even the supposed divides among groups based on color of skin were attenuated by intermarriages among both groups. However, a sense of jealousy and possessiveness came to light during the Nimeiri regionalization policy, when the first governor of the region appointed by Nimeiri, Ahmed Ibrahim Direig, happened to be a Fur. Historically, governors were recruited from outside the region, as was the case in other so-called less-developed regions like South Sudan and Kassala. The appointment of Direig as the first governor of Darfur under the new regionalization policy caused resentment among major tribes, particularly Darfurians who marked themselves as Arabs, even though the majority of Direig's government came from these tribes. Those who resented Direig's ascendency to a position to which he was qualified by his education and experience appeared not to have looked at the man as a

457

regional compatriot qualified for the job, but simply as a Fur.[11] One may dismiss the insinuation that resentment toward Direig was a group position much as it had been a reflection of jealousy by elites from other communities who were coveting the position.

In the mid-1980s, West and East Africa were hit by the severest drought in a century, from which Darfur and Kordofan suffered most. Consequently, Arab nomads made a swoop into the verdant lands of the sedentary Fur in search of water and pasture. Trespass on Fur land, unlawful as it had been, was actually triggered by drought and struggle for survival. Nevertheless, the government of the day (headed by Prime Minister Sadiq al Mahdi) closed its eyes on incursions by "Arab" nomads into Fur land in deference to "Arab" tribes who represented at the time the Umma Party's bastion of support in Dafur. In addition, Al Mahdi's government might have been paying Qaddafi back for the military support he had given him in the mid-1970s in a failed attempt to topple Nimeiri's government, as well as the economic support he promised to Al Mahdi's post-Nimeiri government. In addition to this *quid pro quo*, Qaddafi also succeeded in winning over Al Mahdi's support to his fanciful idea of establishing an Arab empire across the Sahara. Qaddafi established a so-called Islamic Legion composed of recruits from "Arab" tribes and coordinated by a front man and protégé called Sheikh Ibn Omar Saeed, who replaced another protégé, Balani Aseel Aghbash, who was killed in Chad in July 1982. When Qaddafi's bid to overthrow the Chadian government failed, Ibn Omar retreated from Chad into Sudan and was hosted by Musa Hilal, the sheikh of the Mahameed "Arab" tribe. The Mahameed became armed to the teeth through weapons obtained from Libya in the course of the Chadian-Libyan war as well as from those left over by Ibn Omar. From this nomadic community emerged the Janjaweed, a blanket name for heavily armed nomadic camel herders attacking Fur farmlands. According to Mamdani the Janjaweed phenomenon had a social side to it, all Janjaweed recruits were mainly in their teen or preteen years and was reflective of an "economic, social and generational crisis." The Janjaweed, according to Mamdani, were an "antisocial outlaw phenomenon."[12] Only with the intensification of conflict was Janjaweed material incorporated in the government's counter-insurgency structures.[13]

Two more serious developments occurred and inordinately changed the balance of power. The first was the decision by the NIF government to engage the Janjaweed on its side in the incipient rebellion in Darfur. As in the case of the *murahaleen*[14] in South Kordofan, such undisciplined armed hordes would not hesitate to exploit the opportunity to maximize their gains, particularly when they were not receiving any remuneration for their military services. This freelancing in war, armed by additional weapons from Khartoum governments as early as that of Sadig al Mahadi, enabled the Janjaweed to qualitatively escalate the Darfurian conflict into an ugly racial divide.[15]The monstrosity of the Janjaweed exploits reached such a height when their battle cry became "*almat mat shaheed wal hiya lehu mal al abeed*" (he who dies shall die a martyr and he who lives shall acquire a wealth of slaves). Hence, the cleavage between the nomad populations and the sedentary Fur (the former depicted as Arabs, the latter as Africans) became established, with a disastrous effect on communal peace in the face of a long history of peaceful coexistence between the two communities. That ethnicization of conflict led representatives of 21 non-Arab Darfurian communities to meet in Nyala, the capital of South Darfur, to document that "they felt great pain witnessing the destruction of homes by a racial sedition and ignorant rooted call" against their ethnic groups.[16]

The second development was the government's implantation of trusted non-Darfuri NCP cadres in the higher echelons of government in the state in view of its wariness of Fur loyalty to the regime, especially after the aborted insurrection led by one of their own (Bolad) and the split within the NCP led by Dr. Hassan al-Turabi. That spilt was reported to have driven in its wake large numbers of Darfuris to Turabi's camp. The NCP-appointed administrators wittingly became part of interethnic disputes that appeared to be pitting "Arabs" against "non-Arabs." That development was soon exploited by lobby groups in the United States to play up the conflict and present it as an onslaught by "Arabs" against "Africans." Apart from this willful distortion of identities, indiscriminate killings by the army in Darfur provided international nongovernmental agencies (NGOs), especially in the United States, with the evidence they needed to corroborate their claims on mass killing. In addition, there could have been no more invaluable present the Sudan government could have given to international NGOs than a decision it had taken on October 22, 2006. On that date, the top U.N. representative, John Pronk, was asked to leave the country within three days. The Sudan Armed Forces (SAF) was raging mad at an assessment Pronk made on his personal blog in which he claimed that the morale of the army in North Darfur was low, and some generals were sacked.[17] Pronk's expulsion was condemned by the NGO community and mildly described in the United Kingdom by foreign office minister, Lord Triesman, as "counter-productive and will contribute nothing to solving the problems of Sudan."[18]

Coincidentally, just over a week before Pronk's expulsion (October 13, 2006), the U.S. Congress enacted Public Law 109/344, entitled the "Darfur Peace and Accountability Act." Section 4 of the act stated that "the genocide unfolding in the Darfur region of Sudan is characterized by acts of terrorism and atrocities directed against civilians, including mass murder, rape, and sexual violence committed by the complicity and support of the National Congress." The act imposed sanctions on the government of Sudan "in support of peace in Darfur" comprising the blocking of assets of appropriate senior officials of the government and restrictions of visas to individuals identified by the United States president. It also called for denial of access by

459

the government of Sudan to oil revenues. With China, India, and Malaysia as the main beneficiaries of Sudan's oil, that denial was easier said than done. Nevertheless, the Darfur Peace and Accountability Act also called for the prohibition of entry to U.S. ports by cargo ships or oil tankers engaged in business or trade activities in the oil sector of Sudan or involved in the shipment of goods for use by the armed forces of Sudan until such time as the government of Sudan had honored its commitments to cease attacks on civilians and demobilize and demilitarize the Janjaweed and associated militias, etc.

4. Early Attempts to End Conflict

In 2006, hopes of imminent peace were raised after the conclusion of the DPA as a result of considerable cajolement by President Obasanjo of Nigeria, U.S. Deputy Secretary of State Robert Zoellick, the African Union, and a host of observers from the United Kingdom, Norway, and Eritrea. These hopes were soon dashed when the then leading Darfurian rebel group leader Minni Minnawi signed the agreement, but Abdel Wahid Mohamed Nour[19] and Justice and Equality Movement (JEM) leader Khalil Ibrahim refused to sign it. The haste with which mediators and observers wanted to conclude an agreement between the parties was reminiscent of attempts to resolve the North-South conflict through quick fixes. It may be recalled that the conclusion of the CPA took about 10 years (from the beginning of the Intergovernmental Authority on Development (IGAD) initiative in 1994 to the initialing of the CPA in December 2004), while the Abuja process took a few months to conclude. The apparent penchant for power among the two SLM leaders, especially as to who should come at the top in any future arrangement, caused disarray in their ranks, or as political analyst Julie Flint aptly described the Movement's disorganization and erratic isolated approaches to decision making.[20] If the external factor, which was ever present in the Darfur conflict long before the rebellion, is added into the mix, then the unmaking of the Abuja agreement would not come as a surprise to any person conversant with Darfurian politics. Rather than extinguishing the flames of war, the DPA actually deepened fragmentation in Darfur and, consequently, heightened international pressures. With African countries such as Chad, Eritrea, and Libya deeply embroiled in the conflict; France and the European Union standing behind the enfeebled Chadian government; and the United States driven by worthy and unworthy causes to be directly enmeshed in the conflict, Darfur became a free-for-all. Eventually, Minnawi settled in his new position as senior assistant to President Bashir. That position, for those who knew, was little of littleness. Minnawi was hoping against hope to ensure implementation of the agreement he had signed with Khartoum. As for Abdel Wahid Mohamed Nour, he made Europe, especially France, a firm base for launching propaganda campaigns against the government of Sudan. In the meantime, he did not relent in seeking military support from Europe and Israel for his forces on the ground, which kept breaking into fragments with the help of Sudan's security. Khalil, on the other side, pursued building up his war arsenal and ultimately staged a daredevil attack on Omdurman in May 2008 with the compliant support of Chad and funding by "peacemaker" Qaddafi.

Two years before the Abuja talks the African Union brokered a cease-fire agreement between the government of Sudan and rebel movements in Darfur in order to facilitate delivery of humanitarian assistance to innocent citizens who were entrapped in the war zone. The African Union Mission in Sudan (AMIS) was formed and promised to stabilize the situation in Darfur, based on the cease-fire brokered on behalf of the government of Sudan by President Déby with Darfurian rebels.[21] The agreement was signed on September 3, 2003, and extended further in November 2003. The first peacekeeping observers were deployed in July 2004, but rather than concentrating on cease-fire maintenance, they were soon engulfed in the protection of civilians. Despite commitments by several Western countries to support AMIS financially and materially, it appeared that "their preference was to run down the capacity of the AU force in favor of strengthening the case for a UN force."[22] Nevertheless, Western activists, who were unmindful of their own governments' failures to provide that force with the tools it needed to carry out its mission, condemned AMIS for ineptness. Darfurian rebels, especially from JEM and Nour's SLM faction, joined the campaign against AMIS, probably in an attempt to make it a scapegoat for the failure of Western countries who had by that time become the main benefactors to at least one of the two rebel movements.

Pressures continued to mount against the "ineffective" African Union force, calling for its replacement it with the United Nations Mission in Sudan (UNMIS), which was operating in Sudan as part of the security arrangements stipulated in the CPA. UNMIS was already spread thin on the ground with its mandate covering southern Sudan, South Kordofan, and the Blue Nile. The NCP was reluctant to see the UNMIS mandate extended to Darfur and insisted on maintaining the African nature of the peacekeeping force in that region. However, as a result of pressures on it, mainly by African countries, the NCP consented to the creation of a hybrid force under the command and control of the United Nations. On July 31, 2007, the UN Security Council passed Resolution 1769, ordering the deployment of a 27,000 strong military force to join the miniscule AMIS force and be called the United Nations-African Union Mission in Darfur (UNAMID). The new force was mandated to maintain peace, protect its personnel, guarantee the safety of civilians, and support the implementation of the DPA "without prejudice to the responsibility of the government of Sudan." The DPA, which UNAMID had been called upon to implement, was the very agreement that was rejected by JEM and Abdel Wahid Nour's faction of SLM. Minni Minnawi, the very man

461

who had signed the DPA, criticized its lack of implementation. The clause about the government of Sudan, which might have pleased the government immensely, could not have been inserted in the U.N. Security Council resolution by anybody who was *au courant* with the realities on the ground.

Meanwhile, international campaigns against the government intensified and were egged on by that government's ruthless prosecution of the war with complete indifference to serious human rights abuses. The indifference was such that even reports of human rights abuses compiled by a group of distinguished Sudanese lawyers whom the government had handpicked, mattered less to the government.[23] As a result, the United Nations, upon prompting by the U.S. administration, established in October 2009 a five-member International Commission of Inquiry on Darfur.[24] Though it did not validate claims of genocide proffered by the United States and American human rights activists, the commission reported that there was a pattern of indiscriminate governmental violence that was "manifestly disproportionate to any threat posed by the rebels" [and was] "conducted on a systematic as well as widespread basis...and **may constitute persecution as a crime against humanity**" (emphasis added).[25] The Commission also held rebel leaders (especially of SLA and JEM) responsible for serious violations of international human rights and humanitarian law that may amount to war crimes.

5. Defining a Framework for Negotiations

No serious progress was registered in efforts to find a political solution to the Darfur crisis after the signature of the DPA. Absence of a defined framework for talks and disunity among Darfurian political groups as to the endgame of the peace talks hampered any progress or even meaningful dialogue. Conflicting agenda of outside powers, proxy wars between Sudan and some neighboring countries, and non-inclusion of nonarmed Darfurian groups in the peace talks conspired to make negotiations purposeless. As a result, U.N. Secretary General Ban Ki-moon and the African Union chairperson, Alpha Oumer Konaré, appointed Djibril Yipènè Bassolé, former foreign minister of Burkina Faso, as a full-time mediator for the Darfur peace process. Bassolé, who had been coordinating the peace process from his base in El Fasher in North Darfur, was criticized from the outset for being too inexperienced, noncollaborative, and lacking a peacemaking strategy beyond cease-fire maintenance. "His disinclination to give a public narrative of his strategy further alienated Darfurians...[while] U.S. officials in Khartoum complained that the mediator was not using international leverage and was insisting on 'charting his own way.'"[26] Before the appointment of a full-time diplomat, the mission had been entrusted since February 2007 to two eminent diplomats working part time: Salim Ahmed Salim, on behalf of the African Union, and

Jan Eliasson, representing the United Nations. The appointment in June 2008 of Bassolé as Joint African Union-United Nations chief mediator for Darfur at least had the saving grace of ending the two-headed mediation effort. But given Bassolé's proven inexperience and peremptory style, there was fear that he would resort to a quick fix akin to the "stillborn" agreement signed in Abuja in 2006, without the international cover that that agreement had enjoyed.

The major shortcoming that the Abuja agreement suffered from was its exclusivity and the constitutional limitations ensuing from that exclusivity, including the rigid CPA framework which apportioned power between the two major ruling parties, the NCP and the SPLM. Even though, the CPA created some limited space for other political forces during the interim period, it did not allow for tampering with the institution of the presidency or powers allocated to South Sudan. For example, the propositions made by some constitutional experts for the creation of a council at the top of the pyramid (presidency) composed of governors from all Sudanese states with a rotating chairmanship, similar to the Swiss arrangement, had simply no chance to fly within that rigid constitutional system created by the CPA. This idea might have been inspired by Sudan's former experience at independence, when the presidency was entrusted to a Supreme Council made up of five members chosen by the Parliament from within the dominant parties. But in a system of rule encompassing 15 states (and rising), that system would have turned into a mimicry of the Supreme Council model, not a replication of it.

Another proposition advanced by Darfuris during the early negotiations called for granting Darfur a vice presidential slot in the institution of the presidency. Though the SPLM was not against the proposition, it was wary that any radical revision of the CPA, or modification of the Interim National Constitution (INC), might make the CPA unravel. Both the NCP and the SPLM had also maintained that the peace agreement provided the framework for solving the Darfur problem as well as problems relating to power and wealth sharing in other regions. It is to be observed that the INC, by its very nature, had been an interim constitution. Thus, genuine concerns of all regions, including Darfur, could only be considered when a permanent constitution for Sudan would be drafted. All the proposed constitutional tinkering never addressed the problems of the people of Darfur, but rather was done in response to the avidity of some of their elites for power. In consequence, the debate on power sharing arrangements appeared to be mainly about who would get what, how, and when peace was achieved.

Come January 2009, a new round of peace talks between the Sudan government and rebel movements kicked off in Doha, Qatar, and reflected an attempt by that Gulf state to assume a role in international diplomacy similar to its role in bringing peace between Lebanese sects in May 2008 after a vicious sectarian war that threatened Lebanon with disintegration. There were, however, wild surmises that the Qatari initiative was "a pure Islamic fundamentalist initiative" to reunite Sudan's Islamists. While it was true that Qatar wanted to carve a niche for itself in international mediation as it had done in Lebanon, seeing that intervention as an Islamic fundamentalist ploy was wide off the mark. The initiative, however, suffered from the same mediation shortcomings as Abuja. Qatar had the capacity to provide logistical support to that mediation without being restricted by bureaucratic limitations, as was the case with Abuja, but that had a downside. Julie Flint, for example, questioned the logic of giving rebels "material benefits" such as "flights all over the world, accommodation in luxury hotels, generous per diems." To Flint that largesse resulted in "'leaders'…who were driven by economic, not political, motives."[27]

In 2010 glacial relations between Sudan and Chad began to thaw. One important development that came out of the improvement of relations between the two countries was President Idriss Déby's success in persuading JEM's leader, Khalil Ibrahim, to join the Doha talks. On February 20, 2010, after many months of stalled negotiations, JEM signed a framework agreement with the Sudan government that would be the basis for further negotiations. The framework agreement included a two-month cease-fire, release of JEM prisoners in Khartoum who were detained after JEM's attack on Omdurman, and recognition of JEM as a political party. Soon afterwards, President Omar al-Bashir announced that he was quashing death sentences handed down by Sudanese courts against hundreds of JEM fighters for their part in the assault on Omdurman in May 2008.[28] Albeit, the framework agreement between Khartoum and JEM was essentially a bilateral agreement as it left out many other Darfurian groups, including some who were present in Doha—a shortcoming that made the deal inauspicious.[29] As there was no palpable incentive for other rebel groups to negotiate since they were a priori excluded from the negotiations, the government of Sudan-JEM agreement created more disaffection among Darfurian groups and failed to achieve the goal it was ostensibly meant to achieve: signing a final agreement before March 15, 2010, in time for legislative elections due in April. That date came and passed and the peace agreement was still far from sight. Nonetheless, the framework agreement caught the mediators by surprise, including Bassolé. Julie Flint noted that "Bassolé was surely ambushed by this latest NCP-JEM agreement" which "had been done behind his back."[30]

Though happy with the thaw in relations with Chad and the success of the latter to bring JEM to the negotiation table, the NCP became increasingly aware that divisions between the various rebel groups were impeding efforts to reach a comprehensive peace in the region.[31] Ironically, many of these groups were virtually created by the NCP as part of its policy to "divide and destroy." Having failed to learn anything from the folly of this policy during its war with the SPLM, the NCP reverted to the same path when it encouraged on February 23, 2010, the merger of SLM splinter groups into another

Darfurian group, the Liberation and Justice Movement (LJM), led by Tigani el-Sissi, a former governor of Darfur. It was however, rumored that the creation of the new movement was blessed by U.S. envoy Scott Gration, who tried and failed to unify those splinter groups. The LJM announced its readiness to engage in separate talks with the government; however, it refused to merge with JEM, saying that they would only accept coordination. JEM, on its part, refused LJM's participation in the negotiations unless they became part of its negotiating team. JEM, in all probability, was suspicious of the legitimacy of the new organization and thus treated it as a fictitious government creature. To assert his independence from the government, el-Sissi told a Qatari daily that the DPA created more problems than it had solved and expressed skepticism about the seriousness of the government in reaching a comprehensive solution. He added that given the support the DPA was receiving regionally and internationally, Doha represented the best venue for talks.[32]

With Darfurian groups multiplying, the SLM (Abdel Wahid's faction), ever shunning peace talks, and Minni Minnawi's faction becoming increasingly soured by the nonimplementation of the DPA to the point of resigning his position in the government, the Doha talks appeared to have turned into an exercise in futility; only the Qatari government took the matter seriously. In the meantime, emboldened by the clandestine support it was receiving from Cairo and Tripoli, JEM progressively raised the stakes. Both capitals, each for its own reasons, did not want the Doha talks to progress. The government, on the other hand, seemed to have learned, parrot-fashion, Nimeiri's tactics towards South Sudan, so it also decided to up the ante. As alluded to earlier, Nimeiri after the 10 years of peace brought to Sudan by the Addis Ababa agreement, decided to repudiate that agreement. Bashir, on his side, had no patience to wait 10 years as Nimeiri did with the Addis Ababa agreement. In only a few years he decided to practically go back on the DPA and, in so doing, drove the only Darfurian signatory of that agreement to go back to arms. By being unfaithful to implementing the DPA, it was the government, not the rebels, who became responsible for undermining peace. With the Doha talks progressing very slowly, President Bashir, on the eve of Sudan's independence anniversary, declared that December 31, 2010, would be the final date for negotiations, after which there would be no more talks with armed groups. In a public rally at Nyala, the capital of South Darfur State, the president announced on December 29, 2010: "I've told the government negotiation team to quit the talks tomorrow whatever the outcome might be."[33] Bashir also said that "the armed groups have an ultimatum until tomorrow...to either sign the draft peace deal or wait for a new round of talks, which will take place inside Sudan."[34] Meanwhile the NCP heaped abuse on the SPLM and neighboring countries for meddling in Darfur[35] but at no time exercised any self-analysis of the government's own performance in peacemaking. Coming from the highest level in the government and party, that announcement should have meant bringing the Doha process to a close by January 1, 2011. As a matter of fact, talks continued without an explanation to Darfurians, mediators, or the world at large. If anything, that episode reflected the haphazard and casual manner in which the government treated the most serious problem it had been facing.

The Doha talks continued unabated despite the president's ultimatum, while JEM refused to yield to local and regional pressures, Abdel Wahid played hide-and-seek, and Minnawi almost sought refuge in Juba. As if all those self-inflicted agonies were not enough, the government made another *faux pas* by deciding to conduct a plebiscite on the administrative division of Darfur, likely with a view to creating more states in the region. The decision was officially announced in Presidential Decree (4) in the beginning of April 2011, when the government was struggling to come to a halfway house with Darfurian armed groups on a range of issues, including the administration of the state. As to be expected, the government's decision came as a surprise to rebel groups leading three of those armed forces—JEM, SLM (Minnawi faction), and SLM (Abul Gasim Salih faction)—who denounced it.[36] A statement issued by the three groups and circulated through the media stated that:

i.   Darfur had been one state up to 1994, when it was divided by the Ingaz into three states.
ii.   Throughout negotiations with the government, Darfurian negotiators consistently called for the reunification of the three states.
iii. The Presidential decree on the Darfur plebiscite was a unilateral act, in addition to the fact that it related to a subject under negotiation.

The statement also called on Darfurians to boycott the plebiscite and urged the international community to stop implementation of the decree, without saying how that could be done.

In response to that statement, Dr. Ghazi Salahuddin in a lecture he delivered in London, announced that the government was acting within its constitutional powers and according to the Abuja agreement.[37] Emanating from a man who pondered seriously before he talked, that statement was fortuitous; 24 hours later, JEM announced its withdrawal from the talks until they received clarification from the presidency.[38] The government's action was yet another example of the NCP's talent for shooting itself in the foot or engaging in irrelevancies that would distract it from functions that require total concentration. Would it not have been more appropriate to concentrate on answering questions raised by Minnawi, the only Darfurian leader who signed with the government the regionally and internationally recognized Abuja agreement? Minnawi's concerns were unambiguously about nonimplementation of that agreement. Hence, making a contentious decision under the guise of implementing an agreement whose authority was already challenged by its sole Darfurian signatory bordered on a travesty.

Having given up on bringing around fractious rebel groups, the government decided to work toward "peace from within" in a manner different than that tried with Riek Machar. An All Darfur Stakeholder Conference (ADSC) comprising nearly 500 delegates was held in Doha in an attempt to reach a permanent cease-fire and a comprehensive and inclusive peace settlement for the Darfur conflict. The ADSC brought together political activists, retired civil servants and army officers, traditional chiefs, etc. Rebel groups took either a standoffish position toward the stakeholder conference or denounced it totally (JEM and SLM). All the same, after 30 months of marathon talks, the Doha conference produced a document purported to be the final peace document. It was signed at Doha on July 14, 2011, by government of Sudan representative, Amin Hassan Omer, and LJM chair, Tigani Sissi.[39] The JEM, which triggered the Doha talks with the government in February 2010 and remained a player in those talks, distanced itself from the final peace document. Unfortunately for JEM's leader, Khalil Ibrahim, he was stranded in Libya during the Libyan revolution when the last phase of the Doha talks took place. Rather than giving attention to the unfolding events in Doha, he was busy shielding himself against alleged attempts by Khartoum to capture and whisk him out of Libya. That was not to happen, as Khalil, after the fall of Tripoli, managed to make his way to Darfur with heavy arms.[40] Commenting on attempts by Khartoum to exploit the uncertain situation in Libya in order to put paid to JEM, the external relations spokesman of the movement told the media that betting on an external factor to enfeeble JEM would be a losing bet. A few months later (December 26, 2011) JEM's leader, Khalil Ibrahim, was slayed by the SAF in a rocket attack while he was leading a convoy in West Kordofan, probably on his way to South Kordofan to join rebels in that area.

The Doha document came in seven chapters covering human rights and fundamental freedoms, power sharing, administrative status of Darfur, wealth sharing, compensation, return of internally displaced persons and refugees, and justice and reconciliation. The document also comprised four other parts dealing with cease-fire, final security arrangements, internal dialogue and consultation, and implementation. On the latter issue an Implementation Follow-up Committee (IFC) was formed, to be chaired by Qatar. The weakness of the Doha document lay in lack of support from some internal players, especially armed groups, even though it received considerable support from outside actors. Without bringing these groups on board, the provisions in the agreement relating to cease-fire, consolidation of peace, and security arrangements shall be inconsequential. No matter how devitalized the armed groups are, they still remain a source of destabilization of Darfur, making the territory, or parts of it, ungovernable, and this is what guerrilla warfare is about.

Consequently, much as the engagement of all legitimate stakeholders is cardinal for making peace comprehensive, trivialization of armed groups may still undermine all peace efforts and negate other gains made in the negotiations.

At the external front, however, the United States, in particular, declared its support to the Doha peace accord. President Obama was reported to have called the emir of Qatar, thanking him for the role he had played and presidential envoy to Sudan, Princeton Lyman, told the media that the Doha document was a well-studied document. He added that "what we want now is a cease-fire and an appropriate environment for the political process to begin."[41] On the other hand, U.S. envoy to Darfur, Dennis Smith, announced the desire of his government to hold a Darfur forum in Washington in September in order to bring Darfur rebel groups in line with Doha.[42] While LJM leader Tigani Sissi and Sudan's foreign ministry spokesperson welcomed the initiative, the government's chief negotiator at Doha expressed reservations about it.[43] Nonetheless, Dennis Smith, according to a Khartoum daily Al Tayar, met with representatives of JEM and SLM in London to persuade them to join the Washington forum.[44] As a result of hesitations on the part of the rebel movements and doubts about the intentions of the U.S. administration by the authors of the Doha document, September came and passed without the forum being held. Doubts harbored by the government about the intentions of the United States were not alleviated by Dennis Smith's statements to the press. In one statement, Smith said the United States was concerned that the war in Darfur might engulf South Kordofan in the conflict.[45] Eventually, the Washington meeting took place in November 2011, with the Sudan government conspicuous by its absence. However, the government was evidently pleased when the two U.S. emissaries to Sudan, Scott Gration and Princeton Lyman, asserted that their government was urging Darfurian armed groups to seek peace through negotiations, not war. With endorsement from the U.N. Security Council and acquiescence to it by the United States and other European powers attending the Washington meeting, the Doha process became the only game in town.

6. Sudan Government and Genocide

6.1 Confusing Law with Politics

A chorus of campaigns were launched against the Sudan government and the NCP for alleged war crimes (which were confirmed by the U.N. commission) and genocide (which the commission found no evidence to substantiate). That campaign reached its high noon when the International Criminal Court leveled accusations against some leaders of the two institutions for war crimes and called for bringing them to international justice. That chorus was led by the United States at the highest level. President G.W. Bush, in an address to the

U.N. General Assembly on September 21, 2004, told the assembly: "This hour, the world is witnessing terrible suffering and horrible crimes in the Darfur region of Sudan, crimes my government has concluded are genocide."[46] A few weeks before the president's declaration, Secretary of State Colin Powell told the U.S. Senate Committee on Foreign Relations on September 9 that "genocide has occurred and may still be occurring in Darfur" and "the government of Sudan and the Janjaweed bear responsibility."[47]

Although neither the purpose nor purport of this book allows for a legal analysis of the crime of genocide, the convoluted way in which the Sudan government became the first government to be charged under the United Nations' Convention on the Prevention and Punishment of the Crime of Genocide (CPPCG) since its adoption in 1948 raises serious questions that need to be addressed. At the outset, what was astounding about the U.S. administration's position on genocide in Darfur was its contradiction with both the law and practice in the United States regarding genocide. From 1948, when the CPPCG was adopted, up to January 1951, when it came into effect, the U.S. administration (which became the leading light of the Darfur campaign) had been very staunch in its refusal of the principle of universal jurisdiction relating to genocide crimes. Indeed, the United States maintained that position up to 2007, when the Genocide Accountability Act was signed by President Bush. When President Bush accused the government of Sudan of genocide before the U.N. General Assembly, and when his secretary of state leveled the same accusation against that government before the Senate, the act had not yet been signed by the president. The United States was not alone in lingering with regard to the domestic application of the CPPCG. The five permanent members of the Security Council, apart from France, took time in bringing the convention into effect: the Soviet Union in 1954, United Kingdom in 1970, and the Republic of China in 1983. Despite this dubious distinction of shielding its own citizens against universal jurisdiction over crimes against humanity, the United States did not balk at joining other council members in entrusting to the Security Council the implementation of the U.N. Summit's resolution on April 28, 2006, regarding the responsibility of states to protect populations from genocide, war crimes, and crimes against humanity.

Genocide is a heinous crime entailing the destruction of an ethnic group physically or biologically, in whole or in part. For that reason, such crimes should never be allowed to be open to wide, let alone open-ended, interpretations. Any such interpretation of the law or definition of the crime shall never allow justice to be done. Kurt Jonassohn and Karin Solveig Björnson, two legal scholars who made an historical study of genocide and did not limit themselves to the twentieth-century experience dominated by the Holocaust, argued that current definitions of genocide are expansive and that academic studies of the crime are too young to have a canon of work on which to build an academic paradigm.[48] The debate in the United States over universal jurisdiction and its implications on national sovereignty and U.S. internal peculiarities confirmed the thesis of the two scholars. There were strong reasons for American jurists and legislators to worry. Given the extraterritorial nature of genocide, universal jurisdiction might extend to offences "generally recognized as being of international concern, regardless of the *situs* of the crime and the nationalities of the offender and the offended."[49] The most obvious fear in the United States was giving license to other countries to implicate American service men in such crimes. That was precisely the reason why the United States refused to endorse the Rome Statute that gave birth to the International Criminal Court (ICC). The prevailing view in US legal circles had been put forward by John Bolton a former Assistant Secretary of State for International Organizations in the Bush Administration. Bolton's view is that the ICC's failing "stems from its purported authority to operate outside (and on a plane superior to) the US Constitution and thereby to inhibit the full constitutional autonomy of the three branches of the US government."[50] Long before the creation of the ICC, concern was also expressed during U.S. Congressional hearings in the 1950s on article VI of the CCPCG (creation of an international criminal court). No less than the representative of the American Bar Association stated in these hearings that intent to destroy a group in whole or in part could mean an individual. This, it was claimed, might open the door for African Americans, during a period of high racial tension in the States, to sue American citizens or institutions for lynching, a practice that was common at the time. Debate on this issue was raging since mid-1940s when US representative Emmanuel Cellar asked "whether a change of genocide could be brought against a signatory country in the case of a mob lynching in Mississippi?" Cellar added "and if so would the US agree to extradite the citizens involved for trial in another country?"[51] It was, therefore, not surprising that the 1987 Proxmire Act,[52] which implemented the International Convention on the Prevention and Punishment of Genocide, included a sovereignty package proposed by Senators Richard Lugar, Jesse Helms, and Orrin Hatch, which considerably watered down the purport of the convention. As a result, U.S. jurisdiction in the case of genocide was only limited to offences committed within the U.S. or if the alleged offender was a citizen thereof. That remained the situation until the enactment of the Genocide Accountability Act (2007), which added the following categories:

- Alien alleged offenders who are admitted for permanent residence in the United States,
- Stateless persons whose habitual residence is the United States,
- Alleged offenders who were brought into, or found in, the United States even if the genocide was committed outside.[53]

Despite the legal rhetoric about genocide in the Nuremberg trials, both the United States and U.S.S.R. argued during the drafting of the CPPCG (1948) against punishment of genocide offences alleged to have been committed in territories outside the United States and U.S.S.R. Robert Jackson, the U.S. prosecutor at the International Military Tribunal at Nuremburg, famously said that the real complainant in genocide cases is humanity. That was tantamount to considering such crimes *erga omnes* (owed to the entire world community) as well as *jus cogens* (a law obligating all states that could neither be circumvented by national law nor by treaty obligations). That interpretation of the law was evidently inspired by principles of international law relating to piracy in which extraterritoriality was rooted in the belief that pirates were *hostis humanis* (enemies of humanity). While this was the situation as far as legal theory and rhetoric were concerned, reality and practice have diverged in the United States since 1948, indeed up to 1987, when a watered-down version of the convention was signed by President Reagan, and in 2007, when President Bush signed a Genocide Accountability Act honeycombed with protective exemption for U.S. citizens under a professed sovereignty package.

Those in the United States who were in a hurry to equate war crimes committed by the government of Sudan against Darfurians with genocide were neither known to be strict constructionists of the CPPCG since its adoption in 1948 by the United States, nor troubled by the U.S. administration's rejection of the Rome Statute because of their alleged infringement on national sovereignty. Instead, there had always been a burning desire by some U.S. politicians to see the NCP consigned to oblivion as long as it refused to behave itself the way it should as a peace-loving and law-abiding government. That desire had been shared by Sudanese political forces that were increasingly turned into aliens in their own country by the NCP's intemperate totalitarianism. There was also deep concern among a vast number of human rights activists who were genuinely distressed by the opprobrious acts of the NCP in Darfur and, therefore, wanted to see the perpetrators of these acts booked for their offences. But, there were also pro-Israeli lobbies whose concern with Darfur, indeed with the Sudan as a whole, was a function of the government of Sudan's (read NCP's) attitude towards the Arab-Israeli conflict, especially its relationship with Hamas, which the NCP openly flaunted. Aware of all those legal intricacies and political subterfuges, the U.S. administration saw to it that the genocide dossier was pushed to the U.N. Security Council. By throwing the Sudan government and its leader, President Bashir, to the ICC prosecutor, the U.S. administration was mostly aiming at keeping its howling wolves at bay. That decision marred the United States' ability to be an honest broker or a trusted mediator, as it had been during the CPA negotiations, and made the NCP more abrasive and nasty, like any threatened, cornered cat. Had those who sponsored this policy taken a leaf from Henry

471

Kissinger's book, they would likely have had second thoughts. Kissinger maintains that universal jurisdiction risks creating universal tyranny by judges and could degenerate into politically driven show trials to place a quasi-judicial stamp on state enemies or opponents. He also advised that applying universal jurisdiction to cases of international crimes might make it difficult to reach political agreements that would encourage those who committed such crimes to step down.[54]

In practice, however, with the exception of the trial of Slobodan Milosevic, former president of Yugoslavia, before the International Criminal Tribunal for Yugoslavia (ICTY) in 2000, no head of government or state was brought to justice for such crimes. This is not to exclude cases against Rwandese politicians for massacres in that country amounting to ethnic cleansing by one ethnic group (Hutu) of the other (Tutsi).[55] In this case it was proved beyond reasonable doubt that all the accused were Hutus and the totality of their victims were Tutsis, irrespective of their religion or political leanings. It may be noted, however, that Bosnia accused the Serbs of genocide in the 1995 Srebinica massacre, but the ICTY ruled that while that massacre constituted genocide, the Serbian government could not be deemed to have participated in the genocide as Bosnia claimed. That ruling was upheld by the U.N. International Court of Justice.[56] Crimes against humanity, including genocide, are not limited to the above cases; such crimes were perpetrated in Iraq at the very time that country was under U.S. occupation, especially with regard to religious and ethnic conflicts between Shia and Sunni Muslims. Though the U.S. media never hesitated to highlight such crimes against humanity, including religious and ethnic cleansing, the U.S. administration was too reticent to talk about those heinous crimes, let alone pursue perpetrators the way Saddam Hussein was for his unspeakable atrocities against the Kurds.

In the case of Sudan, the Security Council, under Chapter VII of the U.N. Charter, adopted Resolution 1593 (2005) to refer the matter to the International Criminal Court (ICC) based on the report of the International Commission of Inquiry on Darfur, without mentioning specific crimes. There were eleven votes in favor, one against, and four abstentions, including the United States and China. Of the five permanent members of the council, not only China, but also the United States abstained. The ICC prosecutor informed the council that he had found crimes committed against humanity and war crimes,[57] without mentioning genocide. Those charged with committing the crimes were described as "the identified persons." About 50 names were sealed in a document that the Security Council presented to the prosecutor. The list comprised names of government officers, rebel leaders, and Janjaweeds.

Based on further investigations by the ICC prosecutor, judges of the Pre-trial Chamber issued warrants of arrest against a Sudanese minister, Ahmed Haroun, for crimes he had allegedly committed when he was minister of state for the interior, and a Janjaweed leader, Ali Kushayb, for crimes against humanity and war crimes. Incommoded by the violent reception of his indictment of the two Sudanese and the insults directed against him by the president himself, the prosecutor decided to up the ante. On March 4, 2009, the ICC issued a warrant of arrest against President Bashir for war crimes and crimes against humanity; the Pre-trial Chamber, however, did not include genocide in the charge sheet because of insufficient evidence. Targeting Bashir, the first serving president to be brought to trial before the ICC for serious human rights crimes including mass murder, generated a wave of negative reactions in Arab and African states, including countries that were parties to the Rome Statute. In consequence, the African Union Summit meeting in Sirte, Libya, on June 28–July 2, 2005, denounced the indictment of President Bashir, except for Botswana and South Africa. The two dissenting countries (both signatories of the Rome Statute) argued that since the statute had become part of the law of the land, its provisions relating to international cooperation with the court or seeking judicial assistance from it had the force of law in their countries. That was why Bashir's visit to Kenya to attend the launching of the new Kenya constitution in September 2010 created serious tension between the Kenyan government and some Kenyan parliamentarians, media, and nongovernmental organizations who demanded their government to apply the law to Bashir. Kenya, who had been a key player in the CPA implementation, opted not to do so, arguing that its primary attention should be given to CPA implementation in which Bashir was playing a key role. A year later France requested Malawi, a signatory of the Rome Statute, to apprehend the Sudanese president who was attending a Common Market for Eastern and Southern Africa (COMESA) Summit in Lilongwe, Malawi's capital, on October 14, 2011. The same request was made by Catherine Ashton, high representative of the Union for Foreign Affairs and Security Policy for the European Union. Both requests were spurned by the president of Malawi.[58] It is interesting to note that none of the "Permanent Five"[59] members in the Security Council, who continued to exhort African member states to live up to their obligations under the Rome Statute and the U.N. Charter and apprehend the Sudanese president, ever tried to invoke Article 103 of the U.N. Charter. In effect, while African countries maintain that they are obligated by African Union resolutions not to apprehend sitting African heads of state, Article 103 provides that the obligations of member states under the U.N. Charter override commitments under other international agreements. To all appearances, therefore, the hubbub from Western capitals calling for the apprehension of the Sudanese president in the territories of African countries he visited was not impelled by a desire to ensure due process or uphold U.N. Charter provisions as it was to appease lobby groups in the various countries.

473

The issue of apprehending the Sudanese president took a turn to the worse when the Kenyan section of the International Commission of Jurists (ICJ Kenya) made an application to the Kenyan High Court to issue an order to Kenya's attorney general and minister for internal security (as respondents) to apprehend the Sudanese president under Article 12 (1) of the Rome Statute, which obligated countries who adhered to it to recognize the ICC jurisdiction. On November 28, 2011, Judge N.R.O Ombija upheld the application. That decision caused a furor in Sudan. The Sudan government declared the Kenyan ambassador in Khartoum *persona non grata* and gave the Kenyan government two weeks to reverse the decision, threatening, if it did not, to stop all trade relations with Kenya, expel Kenyans who live or work in Sudan, and put an embargo on all flights over the Sudan emanating from, or traveling to, Kenya. The Kenyan government, which was taken off guard by the court decision, appealed to the Court of Appeal of Kenya to temporarily set aside Judge Ombija's ruling pending its review on the basis of an appeal made by Kenya's attorney general. To the chagrin of the two governments, the Court of Appeal refused to set aside the High Court's decision.

Though the concern by the two governments of the fallout of the High Court's decision was predictable, it was also embarrassing to both. In the case of Kenya, which had recognized the ICC's jurisdiction in the case of six high-profile Kenyan politicians accused of masterminding violence after the 2007 elections, hesitating to take the same action in the case of a foreign head of state was, to say the least, galling. As for Sudan, the assumption by its government that court decisions in Kenya rendered at the highest level of the judicature could be easily reversed by the executive reflected utter disregard for the independence of the judiciary. If that was the way the Sudan government envisaged the relation between the two arms of the state, then the international community, including the African Union, would need no further evidence of the inveracity of that government's claim that justice in Sudan is above suspicion.

6.2 The African Union's Rescue Mission

The African Union became involved in the Darfur conflict in 2004, even though its performance was racked by incompetence as a result of slenderness of resources. The Darfur crisis was thrust upon the African Union when it was at its infancy,[60] with little preparation to handle a complex problem like that of Sudan. The African Union inherited the Organization of African Unity (OAU), which was known for structural weakness and dearth of accumulated experience in peacemaking. Nevertheless, on its creation, the African Union established a five-year African peacekeeping program supported by readily available peacekeeping brigades to move into any African crisis in the different African subregions. The Darfur crisis occurred twelve months into the five-year program.[61] With such limited preparedness, the African Union was not fully equipped to face Darfur's arduous mission. It was, thus, constrained to seek help from the United Nations in order to properly carry out the mission with which it had been shouldered. As a result, in 2006 the U.N. Department of Peacekeeping Operations (DPKO) developed a plan to augment the African Mission in Sudan (AMIS). Following intensive private and public contacts by U.N. Secretary-General Ban Ki-moon and other senior U.N. officers, an unprecedented joint African Union and United Nations peacekeeping operation was established to replace AMIS in 2007. U.N. Resolution 1769 authorized the establishment of the United Nations African Mission in Darfur (UNAMID) for an initial period of 12 months. Its 26,000 force was deployed to the region in October 2007, and it formally took over from AMIS on December 31, 2007. UNAMID's mandate was extended twice. On July 29, 2011, following the separation of South Sudan, the U.N. Security Council extended the mission for another year, to July 31, 2012.[62]

The most crucial intervention of the African Union in the Darfur conflict came after the indictment of President Bashir by the ICC. Despite the prevarication of a number of African states, the majority of the African Union members were detectably displeased with the U.N. Security Council's decision to refer a matter concerning a serving African head of state to the ICC. That displeasure was augmented with the council's reluctance to favorably respond to Africa's request for the deferral of the proceeding against the Sudanese president, a prerogative given to the council under Article 16 of the Rome Statute. Nevertheless, the African Union acknowledged the ICC's role as a court of last resort but expressed keenness to find an "African" solution for transitional justice in Darfur, thereby setting a precedent for conflict resolution in the continent. It also pointed out that the ICC process did not preclude local and national justice processes. In July 2008, the African Union Peace and Security Council (AUPSC) called for the formation of an African Union High-Level Implementation Panel on Darfur (AUHIPD), and the decision was endorsed by the African Union Summit in February 2009. The AUHIPD held its first meeting the following month. The panel was to be chaired by former president Thabo Mbeki of South Africa and comprised two former heads of state in addition to a group of distinguished African statesmen and human rights activists.[63] Mbeki, an African freedom fighter, dexterous diplomat, and a statesman with extraordinary depth and breadth of knowledge, had the job cut for him. With those attributes, in addition to support by the whole of Africa, Mbeki belonged to a class of mediators who should neither be taken lightly by protagonists nor sidestepped by foreign observers. The mandate of the panel was to examine the situation in Darfur in-depth and submit recommendations on how best to address the issues of accountability, peace, justice, and reconciliation.

Regarding the indictment of the president, the panel's report stated, "The ICC is a court of last resort as well as of limited practical capacity: it can only target a few people for prosecution." It added that in view of the limited resources available to the ICC, the prosecutor "has adopted a policy of focusing only on those few whom he believes bear the greatest responsibility for the most serious crimes that have been committed in each situation. This prosecutorial policy, inevitably, leaves the overwhelming majority of individuals outside of the ICC system and still needing to answer for crimes they might have committed." Furthermore, the AUHIPD maintained that "justice from the ICC, exclusively, would give impunity for the vast majority of offenders in Darfur, including virtually all direct perpetrators of the offences."[64] To give effect to its proposition, the panel called for the establishment of a hybrid court for Darfur, which would combine national and international staff, as well as domestic and internationally recognized criminal justice procedures. This, according to the AUHIPD, would be more cost-effective, efficient, and perhaps also more acceptable in the domestic or regional context.

That coherent and well thought out report represented the first attempt to address the Darfur crisis in all its manifestations and contextualize it within a broader background. Alex de Waal rightly assessed that the report represented a "substantive and principled" analysis of the situation and delivered the central message that "Sudan is ruled by a minority elite, which must share power or face the demise of the country."[65] Julie Flint agreed: "The AUPD's recommendations were superb on what the Sudanese government needs to do to start re-legitimizing the state."[66] Hybrid courts, she went on to say, were "the least bad option."[67] Such courts are a new phenomenon in the international legal system and gained prominence in the 1990s following conflicts in Cambodia, Sierra Leone, and Timor-Leste.[68] The birth of these courts was far from easy. For example, the hybrid court that dealt with the Khmer Rouge genocide killings between 1975–1979 in Cambodia only became operative in 2005, despite the heavy involvement of the United Nations in the process of establishing that court. Throughout these years the government of Kampuchea (Cambodia) expressed worry and concern that a strict legalistic approach to the cases under consideration might jeopardize the reconciliation process.

In its report, the African Union panel had reflected an insightful analysis of the Darfur situation as well as of the challenges facing Sudan as it was entering the last and most decisive phase of its transition. Unlike the mechanical approach by other mediators, including U.S. and U.N. mediators, pragmatic as their approach might have been, the panel appeared to have been inclined to find a resolution for the Darfur conflict, not within a provincial or a national context, but within a regional one. The African Union initiative was also not detracted by pressures from groups with an agenda that was palpably extraneous to that of the people of Darfur. If the African Union initiative was at all to be disregarded or frustrated by the parties, that would only have been as a result of a lack of political will on one side, or the absence of a genuine desire for comprehensive peace, on the other. The lack of political will was perceived in the dubious silence with which the government received the panel's suggestion on the creation of hybrid courts, arguing that the Sudanese judicial system was sufficiently competent to undertake that task. That judgment was not shared by the majority of Sudanese lawyers. It was also corroborated by the fact that domestic legal institutions had, up to the point in time in which the panel presented its report, failed to take credible measures against crimes unearthed by the former government of Sudan chief justice and his panel. As recent as December 2010, the government's own general prosecutor for war crimes in Darfur boasted before a press conference in Khartoum that "no one would escape justice for war crimes."[69] His definition of war crimes, however, was restricted to alleged offenders from rebel groups accused of attacks on UNAMID, or so-called armed robbers. Offenders such as the Janjaweed militias or government officials who stood accused by the Security Council of crimes against humanity had conveniently fallen off the screen of the national prosecutor. This bare-faced trivialization of serious offences that distressed the world caused distrust in Sudan's legal system and also confirmed the suicidal disposition of the government: every time the world volunteered to unhook it from a self-inflicted predicament, it cleverly sought to take the world for a ride.

The report of the African Union Panel on Darfur was submitted in October 2008, emphasizing existing agreements and taking the position that the disintegration of Sudan would have an adverse impact on the country as well as on the continent. It also emphasized the imperative of a fundamental renewal of Sudan as a whole. In this regard, the report asserted that what is best for Darfur is to remain incorporated in a united, democratic Sudan. One part of the tragedy of Darfur, it stated, was that "ordinary Darfurians stand more to gain from the CPA's stated primary goal of national unity on the basis of democratic equality than any other group in north Sudan, and conversely, they have more to lose should the CPA fail in this aim and the southerners opt for secession." The panel, taking a holistic approach, concluded that the Darfur crisis was part and parcel of a national predicament. In consequence, it maintained that a composite of initiatives was needed in order to achieve peace in Darfur, namely:

- Ending conflict through negotiated settlement,
- Allowing Darfur equitable access to power and wealth,
- Accelerating economic development in Darfur,
- Promoting reconciliation and building mutual trust,
- Making the continued existence of Darfur within a united Sudan attractive,
- Encouraging political forces in Sudan to commit themselves to the fundamental reconstruction and development of Sudan, and

477

- Normalizing relations between Sudan and its neighbors and between Sudan and the wider international community.

Furthermore, the panel drew attention to the lack of "political will and practical support" to the various peace agreements that were thought to have put an end to previous rebellions in Sudan, notably in the East, South, and Darfur itself. Finally, the report was on target when it stated: "To the extent that the Agreements acknowledge the need to attend to the issues of democratization, power sharing, and wealth sharing in order to address the root causes of the conflicts in Sudan, they constitute the basis upon which Sudan can, and should, reconstruct its system of governance." It went on to add that, "The Agreements make it possible to institute programmes to manage the diversity of Sudan in such a way that reinforces national cohesion and serves as a source of strength, harmony, and inspiration."[70]

If that advice was heeded by all concerned, Sudan would have still been united and war in Darfur happily ended. The panel's approach to peace-building in Sudan reflected the vision of the African Union as a regional organization inspired by, and devoted to, Africa's unity and territorial integrity. But despite all the political breakthroughs the African Union made in Sudan's multiple crises, its efforts were often frustrated by the small-mindedness of the protagonists. Earlier, we had occasion to expose the political shenanigans to which some elements within both parties to the CPA often resorted, even at times when the whole country was on the brink of disaster. As for some Darfurian leaders, they seemed to believe that there would be no peace until the NCP was removed root and branch and Bashir delivered to the Hague. That perhaps was the reason why the proponents of this idea spread disparaging rumors against the African Union mission to the effect that it was only made of Khartoum's hangers-on. Those who plodded such views had neither veneration for the African Union nor deference to Africa's senior statesmen. A smaller annoyance to the AUHIPD was caused by an incident from inside the African Union's own house. African Union-United Nations joint mediator Bassolé created unnecessary confusion in the minds of the parties, given his disjointed and out-of-focus approach to mediation in addition to his desire to become the *prima donna* of peacemaking. Bassolé did not help a process that required utmost discretion and quiet diplomacy. His disrespect to others, including the African Union's High-Level Panel added to the problems he had created. That nuisance, however, led the AUPSC to call the mediator to attention in its April 2011 meeting. Bassolé was advised by the AUPSC not to deviate from its policy directives and to coordinate his activities with those of the AUHIP.[71] Bassolé resigned his mediation job soon afterwards and returned to his former post as foreign minister in his country.

6.3 Doha Revisited

Coming back to the Doha document, especially insofar as transitional justice is concerned, two important paragraphs of that document need to be highlighted: paragraphs 49 and 50, which deal with justice and reconciliation. Rather than being guided by the well-thought-out propositions made in the AUHIP report, the Doha articles prescribed the creation of a special court to prosecute cases of grave human rights abuses. The court was to be empowered to apply, alongside Sudan's penal laws, "international criminal and humanitarian law" as well as universal human rights codes. Paragraph 49 of Chapter Five stipulated that a special team of experts associated with UNAMID would oversee the conduct of trials held by the special court with a view to ensuring their compliance with "principles of justice and equity provided for in international laws." Behind this diffuse wording was obviously a desire by the authors of the document to stick to the government's position that Sudan laws and justice system were unblemished and could, therefore, be counted on to duly administer justice to those accused of serious human rights crimes. Reference to international laws that would guide the special courts processes, without identifying these laws, amounted to sweet nothing. In addition, empowering UNAMID with power to oversee the court's procedures was a ridiculous proposition; neither UNAMID's mandate, nor its composition, would allow it to undertake such a task. Special courts could only function within an international or regional legal framework if their constituent instrument allowed a right to appeal their decisions to a higher regional or international legal authority. It is, thus, surprising that the authors of the Doha document, especially on the issue of justice and reconciliation, did not find it fit to make use of the AUHIP report in this regard. Nevertheless, in January 2012, the chief justice of Sudan issued a circular creating a special court headed by a justice of Sudan's Supreme Court and comprising two judges.[72] According to the circular, the special court would deal with "serious crimes" committed since February 2003. The special court, as per the circular, shall follow procedures set by the chief justice. The circular further provided that the African Union and the United Nations may send observers to follow the court's proceedings, provided they are chosen by their principals in consultation with the government of Sudan. Appeals of the special court's decisions shall be made to a special appeals court also to be established by the chief justice.

One would have thought that with the clamors of Darfurians for justice, the ICC's Damoclean sword over its head, the Security Council resolution on that matter ever present, and the African Union as the only organization that had offered to bail it out from both eventualities, the government would cling to the AUHIPD. Trying to be clever in such a situation is simply being clever by half. What the AUHIPD had offered was accountability that takes into account truth, justice, and redress. Truth and reconciliation, in the literature, represents a transition from past conflicts to future reconciliation.[73] According to an eminent human rights jurist, the fundamental principles of such accountability shifted to cessation of conflict, prevention of further conflict, deterrence of future conflicts, rehabilitation of society, and reconciliation between peoples in that society rather than penalizing offenders for past deeds.[74] Viewed in this light, justice shall never be done within an arrangement that is designed to grant impunity to alleged wrongdoers. Such impunity shall not only be the antithesis of accountability and justice, but also of sustained peace. Thus, by endorsing the Doha document without expressing any reservation about the clauses on justice and reconciliation, both the U.N. Security Council and the United States had not only compromised the role of the African Union panel, they also undermined the very processes they had initiated to achieve peace, justice, and reconciliation.

6.4 Genocide in Darfur: Myth or Reality

Clearly, there had been an odd fixation among the Darfur lobbies on two phenomena: conflict between Arabs and Africans and the perpetuation of genocidal policies by the government of Sudan. That fixation side-tracked efforts from peacemaking to identifying and punishing alleged wrongdoers. Several reasons were behind this fixation. To begin with the government's wholesale and indiscriminate violence against Darfurians, particularly after the humiliating attack on Fashir airport in April 2003, provided anti-Khartoum activists with the evidence they needed to substantiate their accusation. Punitive, indiscriminate attacks neither destroy enemies nor win friends; they only kill innocent people through "friendly" or unfriendly fire. The major part of the evidence gathered by the ICC was from events that occurred during that period. Second, the government's sponsorship of Janjaweed and exploitation of them as a destabilizing force against so-called non-Arab Darfurian rebels made that government appear to be ethnocentric, if not engaged in ethnic cleansing. The government's lack of sensitivity toward grudges expressed by the Fur and palpable concern by the international community, especially the U.N. Security Council with the issue of the Janjaweed confirmed suspicions that the government had something to hide. That insensitivity was such that one of the Janjaweed leaders (Musa Hilal) was appointed senior advisor to the minister of regional government, as if there was no other person in his tribe who was qualified for the job. Whoever was behind the policy of "we see nothing, hear nothing, and say nothing" failed to distinguish between defiance and provocation. Third, the almost paranoid attitude of Sudanese security agencies and operatives, as well as insular northern Sudanese journalists towards foreign humanitarian agencies, complicated things immensely. By invariably treating them as foreign spies, these agencies were turned into foes rather than development partners. Actions taken against those agencies were often vindictive or punitive. For example, following the indictment of President Bashir by the

ICC prosecutor, a number of organizations were expelled, including Oxfam and Mercy Corps, on the allegation that they were spies in the service of foreign regimes.[75]

Even though those factors combined were enough to attract the interest of the international community in what was happening in Darfur, there was still another factor that led to the emergence of activist individuals and groups who made of Darfur a blockbuster with predetermined villains and heroes. While support to southern Sudan in the decades of the 1980s and 1990s was galvanized by a coalition of academics, legislators, human rights activists, and congressional aides conversant with the issues who were in a position to shape foreign policy and raise public awareness about Sudan, support for the Darfur cause originated within an *omnium gatherum* of concerned human rights and relief organizations led by special interest groups such as the Save Darfur Coalition, whose motives appeared not to be above suspicion. In view of the dubiety of the motives of those groups, Mahmood Mamdani expressed concern about their being creative with facts and engaging in inflammatory rhetoric, which ultimately became an impediment to the long-term goal of peace building in the region.[76] Mamdani methodically analyzed operations by the Save Darfur Coalition, challenging the popular assumption (which is shared by some scholars) that the primary cause of the war in Darfur was ethnic or racial hatred. He also argued that casualty rates had been severely inflated and that activists had been selective with the information they distributed through their awareness campaigns. Over and above, Mamdani maintained that in the political context of the war on terror, groups like the Save Darfur Coalition had been able to use the language of race and genocide to mischaracterize the Darfur conflict, pitting Arab "villains" against black African "victims."

Genocide is not defined by mortality rates; it is a matter of mind-set, perspective, and intent. Even an hundred people killed on the basis of their race or culture with intent to destroy that race or culture is enough evidence of genocide and an act so grisly it makes one's blood run cold. Nevertheless, when those groups lump together horrific mortality figures resulting from war violence, disease, and malnutrition as genocidal deaths, their credibility becomes doubtful. In 2009, for instance, the *Lancet* published a survey of Darfur mortality undertaken by analysts Olivier Degomme and Debarati Guha-Sapir. The survey, unlike earlier studies, included data up to the end of 2008.[77] The analysis concluded that in the initial period, the majority of war-related deaths had increasingly subsided, while deaths attributable to disease accounted for about 80 percent of the overall death toll. This, however, should give no comfort to the government because whatever the causes of death had been, they were still a function of a war that the government had started and had yet to resolve. It should also not absolve the government from the responsibility for bringing to justice all persons, whatever positions they occupied, for crimes committed against innocent citizens in the manner prescribed by Mbeki.

There are two reasons to question the authenticity and legitimacy of the fixation of the U.S. administration and Congress on genocide in Darfur. On the one hand, the constituency that cajoled both the administration and Congress to take an extreme position against Khartoum appeared neither to have been concerned with peace in the region, nor the well-being of the Darfuris. Neither did that constituency's plan for Darfur allow a path for political settlement, nor was a single cent of the millions of dollars it had collected in the Save Darfur campaign spent on needy Darfurians directly or through relief organizations. The Save Darfur hidden agenda was, in fact, far from hidden; it was not so much concerned with the plight of Darfur as it was loath to the close relations between the NCP and Hamas an organization with which Bashir maintained close relations.

7. Evolving U.S. Policy on Darfur

7.1 Obama Administration and the Policy of "Engagement"

In previous chapters we dwelled considerably on the reasons behind the involvement of the United States in Sudan's conflict during the administrations of Presidents Clinton and George W. Bush. Following the ascension of Barak Obama to power, that interest did not subside, though the policy became more nuanced despite his strident remarks on Sudan's regime during the elections. For example, during the presidential campaign, Barack Obama and some of his foreign policy advisors went public about a humanitarian crisis and human rights abuses carried out by the NCP in Sudan, to say nothing of crimes against humanity in Darfur. No sooner had Obama took office, however, than the Sudan conflict became subsumed within a broader policy shift in U.S. foreign policy. Obama's shift, referred to as the policy of "engagement," was predicated on reaching out to the Arab and Islamic worlds who had both become alienated during the Bush administration's War on Terror. The worsening situations in Afghanistan, Iraq, and Pakistan demonstrated that the post-9/11 global security strategy was not only ineffective, but it was also a contributing factor to insecurity. The "engagement" policy was premised on the assumption that neither building peace nor achieving American security interests in that part of the world could be achieved through "us and them" dichotomies. According to the authors of the new policy, preserving those interests required a culturally sensitive and politically constructive approach in which diplomacy played a central role.

Hence, the Obama administration had to shift its policy toward engagement and away from earlier policy statements that condemned the government of Sudan for alleged crimes against humanity, including genocide in Darfur. Some of those condemnations, surprisingly, were made before and during Obama's election campaign by the some of his closest advisors. For example, in October 2006 Susan Rice co-authored an article that stated, "History demonstrates that there is one language Khartoum understands: the credible threat or use of force."[78] The authors of that appeal called for a no-fly zone in Darfur and, if need arose, U.S. boots on the ground. Thus, the idea of "engagement" with a regime presided over by Bashir was undermined from the beginning by conflicting attitudes of senior officials in the cabinet and State Department, including long-time Sudan specialists in Obama's party and administration such as Susan Rice, who became U.S. Permanent Representative to the United Nations, as well as Congressman Donald Payne, who became chair of the House Foreign Affairs Subcommittee on Africa and Global Health.

On March 18, 2009, President Obama nominated retired Air Force major general Scott Gration as his special envoy for Sudan. Gration has been an advisor to Obama during his presidential campaign on a range of military and national security issues. Much of the debate on the new U.S. policy toward Sudan was centered around the style of the general in carrying out his new mission rather than the engagement policy itself. Engagement, as we have seen in previous chapters, was tried by former President Bush through Herman Cohen, Clinton through Congressman Harry Johnston, and George W. Bush through Andrew Natsios and Senator Danforth. Gration was thought by some to be well-suited to the role he had assumed. The son of a missionary, Gration spent most of his youth in what is now the Democratic Republic of the Congo and Kenya, where he learned to speak Swahili. That linguistic skill, it was claimed, would help personal interaction between the general and ordinary citizens in the region. Those who held that view were neither aware that Sudan, although part of East Africa, was not a Swahili-speaking country, nor that Gration's interlocutors in North and South Sudan, except for a limited number of them, spoke that language either. Apart from this cliché-ridden characterization of Sudan, Gration was reported to have spent two years as an instructor for Kenya's Air Force, which led some to assume that his military experience would give him legitimacy as a military man and might prove useful in negotiations with both rebels and military leaders. Nevertheless, Gration's pragmatic approach to conflict resolution was the reverse of that of human rights activists and Sudanese opposition leaders, whose agenda was to root out the NCP regime. As a result, Gration emerged as the most controversial U.S. presidential envoy.

The focus of much of the controversy surrounding Gration had been with regard to his analysis of the conflict in Darfur, especially his reticence to admit that genocide existed. In June 2009, he stated: "What we see [in Darfur] are remnants of genocide,"[79] a sentiment he shared with some observers. Gration's statements, which were based on his experience and personal observations in Darfur, implied that genocide was a matter of the past, if it had at all existed.

Gration's comments resulted in a backlash that exposed a deep disagreement on the Sudan question within the Obama administration. His statements, according to Journalist Josh Rogin, contradicted statements made by Susan Rice who repeatedly described the situation in Darfur as genocide. Rogin also wrote that "ABC News reported that Rice was 'furious'…when Gration said that Darfur was experiencing only the 'remnants of genocide,'" adding that the State Department rebutted Gration's statement with a confirmation that its "official position is that genocide is ongoing." Rogin went on to note that "Obama's approach to Sudan has been hobbled from the beginning by deep divisions between senior officials—especially Gration, the special envoy, and Rice, the U.N. ambassador—on how best to handle Khartoum…Gration is said to be big on carrots, while Rice preferred sticks." [80]

Sharing Rice's views was an advocacy community, including former U.S. government policy experts on Sudan such as Roger Winter; John Prendergast, cofounder of Enough Project; and Richard S. Williamson, former special envoy to Sudan and ambassador to the U.N Commission on Human Rights. Williamson, one of Gration's predecessors during the Bush administration, was merciless in his criticism of Obama's Sudan policy: "Now through a combination of northern [Sudanese] belligerence and the naïveté of U.S. President Barak Obama and his advisors, we are once again staring into the abyss as the administration's desperate appeal to Khartoum for forbearance in exchange for its removal from the state sponsors of terrorism list makes clear." [81]

Opposition to Gration's approach to the Sudanese government and the Darfur conflict grew following a September article in the *Washington Post* in which he was represented as being overly accommodating towards the Bashir regime. A *Washington Post* article by Stephanie McCrummen characterized U.S. diplomacy in Sudan as resting solely in Gration's hands and was highly critical that he was apparently "pushing toward normalized relations with the only country in the world led by a president indicted on war-crimes charges." [82] McCrummen also argued that such an approach was viewed by Gration's domestic critics as "dangerously, perhaps willfully, naïve." The article further drew attention to the negative reaction to Gration's willingness to engage the Bashir regime without regard to concerns among SPLM officials, Darfurian rebels, and northern opposition groups, especially on issues like elections, referendum, and democratization.

Most damaging to Gration was a direct quote attributed to him during his trip to Darfur. Talking about Sudanese stakeholders, he was reported to have said: "We've got to think about giving out cookies. Kids, countries—they react to gold stars, smiley faces, handshakes…" [83] Surely, little things please little minds, but for an emissary of the U.S. president to make light of an extant world crisis was outrageous. It was, therefore, natural that the quote was widely reported and presented Gration as minimizing the problems of a war-torn country to handshakes and distribution of cookies. To his U.S. critics, Gration was given the kiss of death when Ghazi Salahuddin, Bashir's advisor, praised him for trying to be evenhanded. The SPLM leaders, on the other side, treated Gration's approach as emboldening Bashir and making the final implementation of the CPA—in particular, preparations for the referendum—more difficult. The Darfur activist community responded to the *Washington Post* article with outrage. John Norris, executive director of the Enough Project, stated: "There still seems to be real reluctance to take concrete measures and impose tangible costs for Sudanese President al-Bashir's continued abuses…. In order to prevent a return to full-scale, national war, the U.S. must marshal more resources, exert more pressure, and hold all parties accountable."[84]

By this time it was clear that two camps had formed on U.S. Sudan policy. The first, led by Gration, was pragmatic, open to engagement, and favored a softer line toward Khartoum, including incentives and disincentives. The second inclined toward a tougher line on Khartoum. The latter group, which was mainly in Congress and within the cabinet represented by Susan Rice, preferred using pressure on the government in order to achieve a swift end to the Darfur conflict and ensure implementation the CPA. Alex de Waal, long an advocate of engaging Khartoum, supported the second group, arguing that a "tough line" would fail.[85] A journalist who interviewed Gration explained that the general's understanding of the strategy of engagement was a "process toward normalization of relations," which Gration argued was very different from normalization of relations itself. One of the journalist's talking to Gration hazarded to explain his tautology by saying: "Gration's approach to engaging Khartoum is to dangle the carrot (cookie?!) of normalization vaguely in the distant future."[86] The journalist concluded: "Gration is not nearly as naive about Khartoum as he is generally perceived to be. It's just a function of the fact that when doing diplomacy using a strategy of engagement, you can't talk publicly about all the misgivings you have about the regime you are trying to engage."[87]

Under pressure from the domestic Sudan advocacy groups and their congressional supporters, Gration was forced to back down from his statements on genocide. In a congressional hearing on July 29, 2009, in which the administration's new Sudan policy was reviewed in the context of the CPA implementation,[88] SPLM secretary general Pagan Amum Okiech participated and Donald M. Payne drew parallels to the Rwanda genocide and led a charge to get Gration to declare that the conflict in Darfur constituted an ongoing genocide.[89] The hearing also included statements from John Prendergast, a political analyst and human rights activist, Richard Williamson, and Roger Winter. Another hearing held on December 3, 2009, as an update on the situation in Darfur again included testimony by Scott Gration.[90] In his comments to the committee, Senator Sam Brownback claimed that the Bush administration, despite its efforts in Sudan, fell short of ending the "ongoing genocide" and that the U.S. government was "trying to apply nuance to genocide."[91] Congresswoman Barbara Lee added her comments, stating that "genocide should not be happening on our watch."[92] Senator Edward Royce maintained that the U.S. had joined other states who "sit by quietly and do nothing to ensure that sanctions work to protect Darfurians."[93] The purpose of the hearing was obvious: to twist

Gration's arm to admit that genocide, and not any other crime against humanity, was ongoing in Darfur.

In his testimony on December 3, 2009, Gration updated the committee on the administration's efforts on Sudan and explained, from his vantage point, the goals of the Sudan policy. He made a reference to "benchmarks", claiming that "we are trying to ensure that through the U.N. and through other mechanisms that we are able to see verifiable, irreversible changes on the ground."[94] When asked by Senator Brownback if President Bashir was responsible for genocide in Darfur, Gration initially evaded a direct answer by stating, "He was the president of the country during the time that genocide took place…his government was responsible for that and he was the leader of the government and therefore he would have been responsible."[95] When asked if he deals with individuals accused of genocide, he stated, "I have never met with President Bashir, and we don't have plans to meet with President Bashir."[96] He did say that he meets with other high-level NCP members because it was the only way to reach agreements, and that the U.S. government needed to continue to have engagement in order to save lives in Sudan.

Gration was repeatedly asked if he was dealing with a government that conducted an ongoing genocide in Sudan, to the point that he finally buckled under to his scrutineers and said, "That is correct." With such leading questions the hearing turned into an inquisition, rather than an investigative probe. The hearing was, in effect, both grotesque and revealing. It was grotesque because it made contacts between the envoy and Sudan government tantamount to a crime at a time when other U.S. diplomats and security operatives were in constant contact with officers of that pariah government. It was also revealing, since at no time was the envoy queried by the honorable members about the benchmarks for CPA implementation established by Washington itself at the Trilateral meeting held in June 2009, or about the ones Gration had established to ensure "verifiable, irreversible changes on the ground." If there had ever been a hunch that the topmost concern at that hearing was only to measure up to the demands of some Washington lobbyist than to respond to the must-haves of the Sudanese in Khartoum, Juba, and Al-Fashir, no more proof would be needed.

Gration was further subjected to another investigation at a meeting held off-the-record at the United States Institute of Peace on January 26, 2010. An open letter sent to President Obama in mid-February by 35 mostly smaller Sudan-related groups alleged that Gration declared in that meeting that the Sudanese government did not intentionally kill civilians in Darfur and that the U.S. government was planning to shift some $2 billion in funding from that region to South Sudan. The letter called for Gration's removal as envoy to Sudan. But, according to multiple sources, those groups were twisting Gration's words to make them seem more out-of-step with Obama's policy than they actually were. No transcript of the meeting exists, and only four of the thirty-five signatory groups in the letter to Obama actually had a representative in the meeting.

Nonetheless, the four asked for anonymity because all participants in the meeting had agreed to keep Gration's remarks off-the-record. However, there was a consensus that the letter to Obama mischaracterized much of what the special envoy had actually said. How can any noble cause be served through misrepresentation of facts? The facts about Darfur are so damning that they do not need embellishments. Only those with an agenda unrelated to the direct concern of Darfuris would resort to such mendacities.

Taking the above into consideration, the multiple goals of the U.S. policy in Sudan appeared to have been contradictory. In the first place, the United States sought to retain the cooperation of the government of Sudan in its wider global security agenda, or at least to minimize the damage and harm to the region that might issue from antagonizing the Sudanese government. The stability of the Sudanese state and its ongoing cooperation with U.S. agencies in counterterrorism efforts was essential to the U.S. regional security agenda. Also, given the primacy of its wider global political interests, the United States needed to maintain a relationship with the NCP led by Bashir while bypassing him in its dealings with Sudan, not because that would serve its national interests better, but only to please extremists in Washington who were baying for Bashir's blood such as pro-Israeli lobbyists. Any U.S. official who seemed to be crossing that red line was grilled by the media and Congress. On the face of it, what would have pleased those lobbyists most was not so much taking Bashir to the ICC for his "crimes against humanity," but molesting him for keeping company with Hamas, as it appeared from disclosures by WikiLeaks.[97]

This policy was not only contradictory; it had become messy to the extreme. The U.S. administration appeared to have realized that, short of the use of force, regime change in Sudan was not feasible and, thus, it ceased to be an option. Even the possibility of galvanizing the international community against the Khartoum regime, especially through the U.N. Security Council, became unfeasible in view of the frustration of U.S. initiatives by two of the council's Permanent Five: China and Russia. On the other hand, those who advocated engagement appeared to have believed that an aggressive policy would neither serve America's security interests in the region or worldwide, nor would it be wholeheartedly espoused at home in view of the experiences in Iraq and Afghanistan. The U.S. also sought to protect the CPA and to ensure that the rights guaranteed by that agreement to southern Sudan were preserved, in particular, the conduct of the referendum. A final aim was to put an end to the conflict in Darfur in order to improve regional security, resolve the humanitarian crisis, and appease domestic activists and humanitarian organizations.

Accordingly, much of the disagreement within the administration boiled down to debates over the relative balance between engagement and pressure. That mess up gave rise to an antithetical approach to the only punitive measure available to the United States against the NCP regime: keeping the country's name on the "terrorist list." As observed in early chapters, there were abundant reasons for including the name of Sudan on that list in the pre-9/11 period. However, with the repeated confirmation in reports to Congress that "bilateral [Sudan and United States] counterterrorism relationship remains solid," continued inclusion of Sudan on that list for non-terror-related issues became dubious.[98] The goal posts for those non-terror-related issues kept shifting. During the Bush era, the goal post was resolution of the Darfur conflict. The Obama administration changed the goal post to consummation of the CPA, especially the exercise by the people of South Sudan of the right to self-determination. Surprisingly, when President Bush added resolution of the Darfur conflict as a condition precedent to the removal of the Sudan from the list of infamy, then Senator Obama described that action as "reckless and cynical," adding in a latter statement that "no country should be removed from the list of state sponsors of terrorism for any reason other than the existence of verifiable proof that the government in question does not support terrorist organizations."[99]

Figure 4: President Bush accompanied by Andrew Natsios, presidential envoy to Sudan, receiving author in the White House during Salva Kiir visit (2007)

The conflict within the Obama administration over Sudan policy had its origins in former administrations. Like Gration, former U.S. envoy to Sudan Andrew Natsios, had endeavored to establish rapport with Khartoum, despite calls by religious and human rights groups for more aggressive action. According

488

to Julie Flint, while Natsios "acknowledged the need for some kind of process in Darfur, [he] prioritized North–South relations in the belief that 'once the CPA was signed, our job was to try to make it work—not undermine it.'" Flint said Natsios "believed that the worst of the killing was over in Darfur, but feared a new bloodbath in the South if the CPA collapsed."[100] According to Flint, "The language of encouragement adopted by Natsios provided a more constructive framework than the crude denunciation of some activist rhetoric."[101] Natsios, an affable and urbane diplomat, was careful not to stir much dust in his operations and, on that account, was able to establish good working relations with both parties. Yet, like Gration, Natsios was ultimately beset by divisions within the administration over the relative merits of engagement and confrontation, despite his efforts, which were blessed by Bush. The president, in April 2007, responded to the hawks in his administration and announced a plan for targeted economic sanctions against Sudan, a measure that undercut Natsios' credibility with the Sudanese government. Natsios resigned in December 2007.

As activists continued to insist that Gration was too inclined to give Khartoum the benefit of the doubt, pragmatists argued that forcing Gration's ouster in the critical final year of the interim period would spell disaster for the CPA and the prospects for a peaceful referendum.[102] On his blog, Alex de Waal decried the criticism against Scott Gration, arguing that Khartoum will only listen seriously to a promise or a threat from Washington, D.C., if senior members of the administration speak with one voice. "Any further attempts to undermine the Special Envoy will only have one outcome: it will damage the efforts to achieve a political settlement that can benefit the Sudanese people." He continued: "If the Special Envoy is hobbled by sniping then the best chances for political progress will be lost. Worse, if he were forced out, the most likely outcome would be six months of paralysis while a replacement were found (if anyone could be persuaded to take on this uniquely thankless job…)."[103]

After seven months of public acrimony, the U.S. administration finally agreed on a normalization of relations toward Sudan policy, which was announced by Secretary of State Hilary Clinton in October 2009.[104] The new policy defined U.S. strategic objectives in Sudan as cessation of conflict, implementation of the CPA [whatever that meant], and ensuring that Sudan does not become a safe haven for international terrorists. The announcement of the U.S.-Sudan policy clarified the U.S. position for first time in several years. Four key elements of the policy announced by the State Department's spokesperson were: engagement "with allies and with those with whom we disagree"; inclusivity in the sense of sustained and broad diplomatic interaction with not just the NCP, SPLM, and major Darfurian rebel groups, but also critical regional and international actors; and accountability—that is, rewarding parties who would create conditions that would foster concrete and sustainable improvements in the lives of Sudanese people and holding responsible those who would frustrate that process. This included frank dialogue with the government of Sudan about what needed to be accomplished, how the bilateral relationship could improve if conditions were transformed, and how the government would become even more isolated if conditions remained the same or worsened. Nevertheless, the issue of genocide loomed large in the debate.[105]

In view of the above, U.S. mediation efforts in Sudan became reactive, disjointed, and amenable to local American influences. Despite its threatened sticks and promised carrots to the protagonists, U.S. policy initiatives neither deterred the one nor enticed the other. In reality, U.S. presidential envoys tried hard to build bridges when, on one side, it was not clear to where the bridges would lead, and on the other side, it was very clear that the destination to which the bridge would lead was the last place they wished to travel.

NOTES

1   See Julie Flint and Alex de Waal, *Darfur: A Short History of a Long War* (London: Zed Books in association with International African Institute, 2005); Alex de Waal, "Who are the Darfurians? Arab and African Identities, Violence and External Engagement," *Contemporary Conflicts* (Social Science Research Council: December 10, 2004); Alex de Waal, ed., *War in Darfur and the Search for Peace* (Cambridge, MA: Global Equity Initiative, Harvard University, 2007); and Mahmood Mamdani, *Saviors and Survivors, Dar Fur, Politics and the War on Terror* (New York: Pantheon Books, 2009). Mamdani, who is originally from Uganda, taught in a number of African universities and is presently professor of government at the School of International and Public Affairs, Columbia University, New York.

2   The preamble to the protocol on power sharing provides: "Convinced that the successful implementation f this agreement shall provide a model for good governance in Sudan that shall help to create a solid basis to make unity of the country attractive and preserve peace." See: The Sudan People's Liberation Movement on Power Sharing, Naivasha, Kenya, May 26, 2005.

3   Article 72 of the Interim National Constitution identifies seven functions for the Government of National Unity. At its top are planning state policy and implementation of the CPA.

4   SLM is outgrowth of the first rebel movement which emerged on February 26, 2003 under the name of Darfur Liberation Front (DLF) led by Abdel Whid Muhammad Nour. Less than a month later and after meeting with John Garang in Asmara, Eritria Nour decided to change the name of the movement he was leading into Sudan Liberation Movement/Army (SLM/A). The idea was to underscore a national, not a regional, mission for the front.

5   Laurie Nathan, "The Making and Unmaking of the Darfur Peace Agreement," de Waal, ed., *War in Darfur and the Search for Peace*, 248.

6   *Zurga* is a descriptive term used by Arabiscised Darfurians of their co-citizens whose skin is darker and assumed to be of Arab pedigree.

7   Khalil Ibrahim, leader of the rebel Darfurian group Justice and Equality Movement (JEM), was the leader of the notorious NIF jihadists in southern

Sudan known as Dababeen. While the word "dababa" signifies military tank, the term "dabab" was a nickname given to young fighters who were assumed to face tanks with open chests.

8   The Abuja negotiations witnessed jostling for positions by Minni Minnawi and Abdel wahid Nour, the joint leaders of SLM/A. The discord between the two leaders led to a split between them along ethnic lines; Zaghawa behind Minnawi and Fur behind Nour.

9   The symposium was held at Addis Ababa University under the title "Darfur and the Crisis of Governance in Sudan," and later published as Salah M. Hassan and Carina Ray, eds., *Darfur and the Crisis of Governance in Sudan: A Critical Reader* (Ithaca, NY: Cornell University Press, 2009).

10   Arab tribes in Darfur comprise nomadic bedouins such as Rizeigat, Taaisha, Beni Halba, Maalia, Habaniya, etc., while non-Arab ethnic groups include, among others, Fur, Zaghawa, Bergu, Daju, Berti, Tunjur, Bagirma, Barnu, Kara, Masalit, Meidob, etc.

11   Atta El-Battahani, "Ideological Expansionist Movements Versus Historical Indigenous Rights in the Darfur Region of Sudan: From Actual Homicides to Potential Genocide," Hassan and Ray, eds., *Darfur and the Crisis of Governance in Sudan*, 52.

12   Mamdani, *Saviors and Survivors*, 256-7

13   Ibid., 256

14   The Murahaleen (people on the move) were a horsemen militia recruited by Sadig al-Mahdi's government in the mid-1980s to destabilize the SPLM. These masked death riders were known for raiding and torching villages, killing men, and taking women and children as war booty.

15   Abdullahi Osman El-Tom, "Too Black for the Arab-Islamic Project of Sudan," in Hassan and Ray, eds., *Darfur and the Crisis of Governance in Sudan*, 90-92.

16   "Tribes of Darfur, Memorandum No. 1 about Racial Sedition," December 18, 2003,
     http://www.darfurna.com/Darfur/Darfur/Alliance/Evidance/Tribes.htm

17   "UN Envoy Ordered to Leave Sudan," *BBC News*, October 22, 2006.

18   Ibid.

19   Supra note 8

20   Julie Flint, "Darfur's Armed Movements," in de Waal, ed., *War in Darfur and the Search for Peace*, 141.

21   Dawit Toga, "The African Union Mediation and the Abuja Peace Talks," in de Waal, ed., *War in Darfur and the Search for Peace*, 216.

22   Mamdani, *Saviors and Survivors*, 44–47.

23   A national inquiry commission chaired by former chief justice Dafa'allah Al-Haj Yousif and comprised, among others, of human rights lawyer Omer Shumeina, was formed by the president in 2004 to conduct an investigation on human rights abuses in Darfur.

24   The commission included Antonio Cassese (Italy) as chair and Mohamed Fayek (Egypt), Hina Jilani (Pakistan), Dumisa Ntsebeza (South Africa), and Theresa Striggner-Scott (Ghana).

25 Report of the International Commission of Inquiry on Darfur to the United Nations Security-General, prepared pursuant to Security Council Resolution 1564 of September 18, 2004, Geneva, January 25, 2005.

26 Julie Flint, *Rhetoric and Reality: The Failure to Resolve the Darfur Conflict* (Geneva: Small Arms Survey, January 2010), 34.

27 Ibid., 23.

28 "Darfur Rebels Agree to Truce with Sudan," Reuters (Khartoum), February 20, 2010. See also "A Peace Process Play-by-Play," Enough (Washington, DC: February 25, 2010).

29 Julie Flint, "Doha: A New Beginning or Another False Hope?" African Arguments, February 25, 2010.

30 Julie Flint, response to comment on "Doha: A New Beginning or Another False Hope? comment posted February 26, 2010, http://africanarguments.org/2010/02/25/doha-a-new-beginning/.

31 "Sudan: Rebel Groups May Sign Accord at Qatar," *Spero News,* March 1, 2010, http://www.speroforum.com/a/28154/Sudan-Rebel-groups-may-sign-accord-at-Qatar.

32 Tigani el-Sissi, "Absence of Political Will and Divisions within Darfur Armed Groups Frustrate Doha Talks," *Al Sharq* (Doha), September 11, 2010.

33 "Doha Round of Darfur Peace Talks To Conclude," Kuwait News Agency (Khartoum), December 29, 2010.

34 Ibid.

35 The government consistently accused the SPLM of harboring Darfurian rebels, as it continued to accuse Qaddafi of supporting JEM, though whispered. In later days President Museveni of Uganda became Khartoum's stalking horse.

36 "Joint Declaration Regarding Darfur Plebiscites," *Ajras Al-Hurriya* (Khartoum), April 3, 2011.

37 Ghazi Salahuddin, "Movements Are Not Concerned with the Plebiscite," *Al-Sudani* (Khartoum), April 5, 2011.

38 "JEM Suspends Participations in Doha Talks," *Al Ahdath* (Khartoum), April 6, 2011.

39 "Sudan Signs Darfur Deal with Splinter Rebel Group," Reuters (Doha), July 14, 2011.

40 "Darfur Rebel Leader Khalil Ibrahim Flees Libya," BBC News, September 12, 2011.

41 "Darfur Stakeholders Meeting Is an Important Step," interview with Princeton Lyman, *Al-Sahafa,* June 5, 2011.

42 "Darfur Forum on Invitation of US Administration," *Al-Sahafa,* August 14, 2011.

43 Ibid.

44 "Initiative for Debate to End Darfur Crisis,' *Al Tayyar,* August 12, 2011.

45 Ibid.

46 President Bush's speech to the UN, General Assembly, Guardian Tuesday 21 September 2004.http://www.guardian.co.uk/world2004/Sep/21/

47 Inside Colin Powell's Decision to Declare Genocide in Darfur, Rebecca Hamilton, the Atlantic. http://www.theatlantic.com/international/archive/2011/08/inside-colin-powell-decision-to-declare-genocide-in-darfur/243560/

48 Kurt Jonassohn and Karin Solveig Björnson, *Genocide and Gross Human Rights Violation in Comparative Perspectives* (New Brunswick, NJ: Transaction Publishers, 1998), 133–135.

49 Kenneth C. Randall, "Universal Jurisdiction under International Law," *Texas Law Review* (1988): 785–788.

50 John R Bolton, The Risks and weaknesses of The International Criminal Court from America's Perspective, Law and Contemporary Problems, Duke University, Vol. 64: No 1, winter 2001, 167-180, http://www.law.duke.edu/journals/64LCPBolton.

51 Tanya Elder, what you see before your eyes: documenting Raphael Lemkin's life by exploring his archival papers, 484 Journal of Genocide Research December (2005) 7(4) 469-499.

52 U.S. Genocide Convention Implementation of 1987 (the Proxmire Act), signed by President Reagan, November 4, 1988.

53 Genocide Accountability Act of 2007, 110th Cong., S. 888, 2007–2008, signed by the president December 21, 2007.

54 Henry Kissinger, "The Pitfalls of Universal Jurisdiction," *Foreign Affairs* (July/August 2001), 86.

55 In that case, the U.N. Security Council established the International Criminal Tribunal for Rwanda (ICTR) in November 1994 to review and pass judgment on the well documented cases of ethnic cleansing.

56 Wikipedia, Bosnian Genocide, http://en.wikipedia.org/wiki/Bosnian_genocide

57 UN Security Council, International Criminal Court Prosecutor tells Security Council Entire , Darfur Region Crime Scene: Sudan not cooperating on Arrest of two Indictees http://www.un.org/News/Press/docs/2008/sc9349.doc.htm.

58 "France Requests from Malawi to Arrest President al-Bashir," Newsessentials Blog, October 14, 2011, http://newsessentials.wordpress.com/2011/10/14/france-requests-from-malawi-arrest-president-al-bashir/.

59 The term refers to the five permanent members with veto power in the UN Security Council: China, France, Russia, United Kingdom and United States.

60 The African Union became the successor of the Organization of African Unity on July 9, 2002. All African states except Morocco became members.

61 "The Darfur Crisis: African Union's Effort," PBS Newshour, July 3, 2008.

62 In its resolution, the Security Council underscored the need for UNAMID "to make full use of its mandate and capabilities" to protect civilians and ensure unimpeded access to, and timely delivery of, humanitarian assistance."

63 In addition to Mbeki, the panel included General Abdulsalami Abubakar, former head of state and commander-in-chief in Nigeria; Pierre Buyoya, former president of Burundi; Ahmed Maher, former foreign minister of Egypt; Judge Florence Ndepele Mumba, reserve judge in courts in Cambodia for the prosecution of crimes against humanity, and before that judge of the appeals chamber for the U.N. International Criminal Tribunals for Yugoslavia and Rwanda; Kabir Abdulfatah Mohammed, former executive secretary of the Nigerian Petroleum Technology Development Fund; and Rakiya Omar, lawyer and renowned human rights activist.

64 *Darfur: The Quest for Peace, Justice and Reconciliation*, report of the African Union High-Level Panel on Darfur, October 2009.

493

65 Alex de Waal, "Reading the Responses to the AUPD Report," *African Arguments*, November 12, 2009, http://africanarguments.org/2009/11/12/reading-the-responses-to-the-aupd-report/.

66 Flint, response to comment on "Doha: A New Beginning or Another False Hope?," posted February 26, 2010. http://blogs.ssrc.org/sudan/2010/02/25/doha-a-new-beginning/

67 Ibid.

68 Sarah M.H Nouwen, "'Hybrid Courts': The Hybrid Category of a New Type of International Crimes Courts," *Utrecht Law Review* 2, issue 2 (December 2006).

69 "Darfur Prosecutor Pledges to Lift Immunities for Accused," *Al-Sahafa* (Khartoum), December 2010.

70 Supra note 64

71 "Bassolé Within the Firing Range of the AU," *Rai el Am* (Khartoum), April 12, 2011.

72 Justice Hayder Ahmed Daffalla was appointed as chair and judges Ali Ahmed Gashi and Mohamoud Abkam as court members.

73 Ruti Teitel, "Transitional Justice Genealogy," *Harvard Human Rights Journal* 16 (2003), 69-94.

74 M. Chérif Bassiouni, "Searching for Peace and Achieving Justice: The Need for Accountability," Law and Contemporary Problems 59, No. 4 (1997), 24.

75 "Sudan Orders Aid Agency Expulsions," CNN, March 4, 2009.

76 Mamdani, *Saviors and Survivors*, 29, 47 Mamdani, who is originally from Uganda, taught in a number of African universities and is presently professor of government at the School of International and Public Affairs, Columbia University, New York.

77 Olivier Degomme and Debarati Guha-Sapir, "Patterns of Mortality Rates in Darfur conflict," *The Lancet* 375, Issue 9711 (January 23, 2010), 294–300.

78 Susan E. Rice, Anthony Lake, and Donald M. Payne, "We Saved Europeans. Why Not Africans?" *Washington Post*, October 2, 2006.

79 Colum Lynch, "Sudan's 'Coordinated' Genocide in Darfur is over, US Envoy says," *Washington Post*, http://articles.washingtonpost.com/2009-06-18/world/36775973/sudanese-government-scott-gration-bashir

80 Josh Rogin, "'Stuck in the mud'—the Obama Administration's Civil War over Sudan," *Foreign Policy* (January 29, 2010).

81 Richard Williamson, "How Obama Betrayed Sudan," *Foreign Policy* (November 11, 2010).

82 Stephanie McCrummen, "U.S. Envoy's Outreach to Sudan Is Criticized as Naïve," *Washington Post* (El Fasher, Sudan), September 29, 2009.

83 Ibid.

84 Mary Beth Sheridan, "U.S. Envoy Gration Says Peace Accord Is in Peril, *Washington Post*, May 13, 2010.

85 Alex de Waal, "Why the U.S. Is Losing Influence in Sudan," African Arguments (December 23, 2009).

86 Rebecca Hamilton, "White House Defends Gration against Washington Post Article," posted September 29, 2009, http://bechamilton.com/?p=1386.

87 Ibid.

88 "Sudan: U.S. Policy and Implementation of the Comprehensive Peace Agreement, Hearing before the Subcommittee on Africa and Global Health of the Committee on Foreign Affairs, House of Representatives, 111th Cong., serial no. 111-71, July 29, 2009. Donald M. Payne (D-NJ), chair. Briefing by Mr. Pagan Amum Okiech, Secretary General, Sudan People's Liberation Movement. Attended by Roger P. Winter, John Prendergast, and Richard S. Williamson, among others.

89 Ibid., statement of Chairman Donald M. Payne, New Jersey, 2.

90 Sudan: A Review of the Administration's New Policy and A a Situation Update: Hearing before the Subcommittee on Africa and Global Health of the Committee on Foreign Affairs, House of Representatives, 111th Cong., serial no. 111-76, December 3, 2009. Donald M. Payne (D-NJ), was the current chair of the Subcommittee on Africa and Global Health. Witnesses included Major General Scott Gration, USAF, Retired, United States Special Envoy to Sudan; Randy Newcomb, Ph.D. President and Chief Executive Officer Humanity United; Mr. Enrico Carisch, Former Coordinator United Nations Panel of Experts on the Sudan; Mr. John Prendergast, Co-founder, Enough Project. For audio of the briefing: http://www.internationalrelations.house.gov/hearing_notice.asp?id=1139.

91 Ibid., statement of Senator Sam Brownback, California, 23.

92 *Sudan: A Review of the Administration's New Policy and a Situation Update,* statement of Congresswoman Barbara Lee, California, 8.

93 Ibid., statement of Senator Edward Royce, California, 10.

94 Supra note 89

95 Ibid.

96 Ibid.

97 A report dispatched to Washington on July 2008 by U.S. chargé d'affaires in Khartoum, Alberto Fernandez, claimed that the U.S. diplomat raised with presidential advisor, Mustafa Osman Ismail, the likelihood of Sudan's normalization of relations with Israel, with the insinuation that that move might help to remove Sudan from the list of states sponsoring terrorism.

98 Patrick Goodenough, "Obama Administration Links Sudan's Removal from Terror-Sponsor List to Non-Terror-Related Issue," February 8, 2011, CNS News, http://cnsnews.com/news/article/obama-administration-links-sudan-s-removal-terror-sponsor-list-non-terror-related-issue.

99 Ibid.

100 Flint, *Rhetoric and Reality,* 28.

101 Ibid., 29.

102 Josh Rogin, "Gration on Darfur: Inside a Meeting Gone Wrong," *Foreign Policy,* March 2, 2010. *The* open letter can be accessed at: http://savedarfurma.org/2010%200217%20Press%20release%20on%20letter%20to%20Obama.pdf.

103 Alex de Waal, "U.S. and Sudan: On the Virtue of Clarity," *African Arguments,* October 21, 2009, http://africanarguments.org/2009/10/21/u-s-and-sudan-on-the-virtue-of-clarity/.

104 "Sudan: A Critical Moment, A Comprehensive Approach," (Washington, DC: U.S. Department of State, October 19, 2009). See also "Clinton, Gration on the

Comprehensive Peace Agreement in Sudan," (Washington, DC: U.S. Department of State, January 8, 2010).

105 Ibid.

Conclusion

=============== ❖ ===============

We are all in the gutter, but some of us are looking at the stars.

Oscar Wilde,
Lady Windermere's Fan (Act III)

The Comprehensive Peace Agreement (CPA), in addition to putting an end to the destructive fury of war in South Sudan, had also constructed a highway that was to lead Sudan to permanent peace, sustainable development, and national unity in diversity. To achieve these ends, it envisioned the elimination of historical injustices, rationalization of the arthritic administration of the country, creation of new public institutions, and promulgation of national laws to ensure good governance. It was hoped that the interlocking dynamics of democracy, justice, and equitable development would tip the balance of probability in favor of faithful implementation of an agreement that would guarantee a level of peace and political stability Sudan had never enjoyed since independence. That proved not to be the case. From the second year of the interim period, the implementation of the agreement became tentative and fragmented. That, by no means, was the proper approach to the actualization of a compact that incorporated an unprecedented matrix of implementation with meticulously specified timelines, responsibilities, and goals.

In the previous chapters, a hopefully persuasive body of evidence was adduced to prove the above contention. In reality, both parties to the agreement and its guarantors did not treat CPA obligations as mandatory and legally binding commitments, but only as optional undertakings. As a result, numerous CPA obligations were either ignored by one party, or undervalued by the other. For example, while the Sudan People's Liberation Movement (SPLM) and CPA guarantors exhibited benign underestimation of, or unconcern for, cardinal obligations in the agreement, the National Congress

Party (NCP) virtually behaved as if it had not read the bold, let alone the fine, print in the agreement. Encouraged by the other side's perceived lack of concern, the NCP comfortably braved introducing into the CPA new terms (Abyei), changing timelines (elections and census), disregarding the creation of national institutions devised by the CPA to ensure that innovative practices or codes of conduct were not undermined by erstwhile bureaucracy (Human Rights and Lands Commissions), or emaciating other institutions (the Fiscal and Financial Allocation and Monitoring Commission and the Assessment and Evaluation Commission). By and large, the NCP was given the courage to completely mothball what was assumed to be the life-spark of the CPA: democratic transformation. The NCP had failed, or was reluctant, to recognize that the CPA meant what it said to such a degree that at every corner of the road it tried to put stumbling blocks, especially on matters that would have eased its monopolistic hold on power.

On the other hand, history of the SPLM's abdication of the fight for democratic transformation went back to the period immediately following Garang's demise, when a faction within its leadership colluded with the NCP to bulldoze the movement to go in reverse (Chapter Nine). When the SPLM succeeded in putting an end to that "nuisance," it was once again able to retrieve its steps and play a role with other parties in pushing forward the transformation agenda. Still, as the SPLM became exhausted by the NCP's dilatory tactics, especially with regard to conducting the referendum, the transformation trend lost momentum, either because of sheer weariness, or on account of the growing belief by some of its leaders that democratic transformation was not germane to the main cause of southern Sudan: separation. None of these leaders seemed to have sounded out why John Garang and his SPLM team had spent over two years after Machakos improving conditions that would transition Sudan from a one-party state to a multiparty democracy. They did not have the brave face at the time of negotiations to challenge their leader for "squandering" time on issues that were not cogent to South Sudan independence, if that was the main purpose of the negotiations.

Even though the CPA was concluded as a compact between two warring parties, it still had third-party beneficiaries: Sudanese political forces who were not signatories to it and regions that were suffering from historical injustices akin to those that had afflicted southern Sudan. As a result of Garang's dogged determination and his deep-seated commitment to achieving a just peace and unity, the negotiations, which were primarily begun to end war in one region of Sudan, turned out to be a peace agreement that would end more than one war in the country. So, it was not through divine revelation that all peace agreements that succeeded the CPA were modeled on it.[1] To Garang, the objective of ending all wars could not be achieved without transforming Sudan from a country dominated by one political group or ideology to one that would accommodate all political trends and transcend the perception of being a two-party deal. Indeed, were it not viewed by many third-party beneficiaries as a tool of national transformation that would progressively widen the margins of democracy, the CPA would not have been embraced by them.

In seeking to enlarge the margins of democracy within the parameters of the CPA, major northern political forces adopted a three-pronged strategy. That strategy comprised (i) waiting for the SPLM to deliver democratic transformation on a silver platter, or (ii) challenging that party to join them in an attempt to overthrow the government in Khartoum, mindless of the fact that the SPLM was part of that government, which had put an end to a war those parties had ignited and failed to extinguish, or (iii) continuing to moan over monopolization of power by two parties.

Evidence adduced in the book may have also revealed that opposition parties in North Sudan failed to liberate themselves from their historical prejudices and vanities, despite all the adversities they had gone through during nearly two decades of Bashir's autocratic governance. Their sight remained firmly fixed on the one thing that had preoccupied them since independence: struggle for power. One thing that Sudan's erstwhile ruling class refused to admit was that the country's unremitting instability had been basically due to its failure, since independence, to address the underlying causes of instability. Throughout the book the author has sketched a catalogue of blunders made, and opportunities missed, by the powers at the center. Despite evidence to the contrary, these powers continue to pretend, up to today, that they know better. But in politics leaders are judged by what they do, not by what they say, no matter how eloquently rendered. In an insightful report prepared for the United States Institute of Peace (USIP) on the occasion of the separation of South Sudan, authors Jon Temin, director of USIP's Sudan program, and Theodore Murphy, a Sudan consultant, convincingly demonstrated that "Sudan's decades of instability are, by and large, the product of internal dynamics and decisions, not misfortune or outside intervention."[2] The two researchers established that "successive Sudanese governments—including those preceding the current National Congress Party government—have failed to accommodate Sudan's considerable diversity."[3]

Having lost faith in the so-called national leadership, the people of Sudan in both rural areas and urban centers anticipated that the CPA would be a harbinger of a new era of participatory governance and justice for all. But halfway through the interim period, these groups became increasingly downhearted by the turn of events, and some had conjectured that John Garang's untimely departure from the scene was the reason why the CPA had gone off-target and the NCP was geared up to breathe new life into its old agenda. There may be some truth in that conjecture, since Garang has not only been the intellectual powerhouse behind the CPA, but also its persuasive salesman to both North and South Sudan. However, predicating the future of the CPA, indeed of the Sudan, on the energies of a mortal being shall be a sad commentary on our time. Without indulging in wishful thinking, forward-looking Sudanese still hope that the demise of Garang was only the death of a man, not the end of a lofty purpose.

Be that as it may, democratic transformation is a process that entails sustained struggle and should never be assumed to be a gift from anybody or a pie in the sky. It may be recalled that on the conclusion of the CPA negotiations, Garang told the media that the transformation envisaged by the agreement was a process, not an event. Processes demand strategies, programs of action, alignment of forces, and pertinent modus operandi to convert a situation from one form to another. This is as true in the sciences as it is in politics. In the first years of the interim period, the SPLM was on target when it prevailed upon the NCP, at the highest level, to come up with Republican Order 341 in December 2007 (Chapter Eight). In that order, timelines not exceeding mid-2008 were set for repeal of all laws inconsistent with the Interim National Constitution (INC), initiation of a national reconciliation process, and restriction of the abuse of power and extra-legal measures reportedly taken by the police and security services. Moreover, the order provided for steps to be taken to ensure total independence of the judiciary, as prescribed in the agreement and the constitution. With U.S. support, incorporation of democratic transformation as an agenda item in the Washington Trilateral meeting held on June 21, 2009 (Chapter Ten) was a continuation of the struggle for change. In its final document, the meeting set the end of 2009 as the date by which all Sudan laws that contradicted the constitution would be repealed. Alongside the two parties to the agreement and the host country, that meeting brought together representatives of the United Nations and all CPA observer nations.

In whatever way, those two processes became unfinished products when the SPLM, NCP, and sponsors of the Trilateral meeting failed to put the lid on the process they had initiated. The indifference shown by the SPLM and sponsors of the Washington talks to the NCP's heedless disregard to commitments it solemnly made on January 9, 2005, and reaffirmed in December 2007 and June 2009, had, without question, emboldened the NCP to violate the CPA without liability. This, in turn extenuated the CPA's ability to address the multifarious causes of conflict throughout Sudan. By establishing clear benchmarks that were to be religiously adhered to by the parties, the CPA created a cobweb of expectations. The most important of these expectations was transforming Sudan into a country that welcomed diversity and recognized that it would take all sorts to make a united Sudan. Sadly, that was not the way the parties to the agreement and its guarantors seemed to have viewed the process of democratic transformation. Every so often guarantors were on the lookout for an opportunity to rewrite the agreement, allegedly *faute de mieux*. Attempts to rewrite the agreement in

500

virtually all cases were impelled by the desire to appease the NCP. But, in reality, since January 9, 2005, when the parties and guarantors affixed their signatures to the CPA, it should have been clear to all and sundry that the *"mieux"* was exemplified in the CPA: an agreement reached after nearly three years of hard negotiations. The NCP's fudging of issues that were cardinal to comprehensive peace throughout the interim period was matched by that of the SPLM in the close of that period. Sailing under false colors, the SPLM tried its level best to worm its way out of moral commitments toward other Sudanese. Since its inception, the SPLM had been baptized with fire as a party committed to Sudan's unity. One of the SPLM's battle cries in its heyday was: "He who wants separation must fight for it." But on the eve of the referendum, not a few SPLM leaders reinvented themselves as heirs of the archseparatist of the 1960s, not of John Garang, the torchbearer of new Sudanism.

The euphoria the people of South Sudan manifested on July 9, 2011, as a result of being free to manage their own affairs, practice their diverse faiths and give worth to their distinctive cultures was not puzzling. What appeared to be puzzling was the perverse representation by some southern political elites, including some who often took pride in calling themselves New Sudanists, was that the referendum on self-determination was akin to that exercised by a colonized people to liberate themselves from colonial masters. That thinking had been premised on a reductionist concept that the SPLM had time and again denounced: that of an Arabo-Islamic North bringing to heel an African South. Even though there were a plenty of reasons to justify such a feeling among the southern Sudanese of the 1960s, those who still rated that view highly after the emergence of the SPLM should have been frozen in time. New Sudanists in both North and South Sudan were tutored to distinguish between people of the North and their ruling elites. Without belaboring the point, recognition of the right to self-determination to the people of South Sudan was reached by all Sudanese political forces in 1995 in Asmara (Chapter Seven), seven years before the conclusion of Machakos Protocol. In both cases (Asmara and Machakos) self-determination was envisaged as a political measure of last resort to give unity a last chance. That was why the SPLM Political Bureau and its chairman kept playing back the rhyme and rhythm of "Sudan on new basis" up to the last meeting of that body on August 13, 2010. However, the overwhelming surge toward secession was conclusive evidence that the power at the center had failed to make unity attractive, either because it reneged on contractual obligations built into the CPA or persisted in practices that made unity undesirable to southern Sudanese. When such practices are equally abominable to the majority of the people of the North, it becomes fruitless to assign blame to those people for conditions created by their rulers, which drove southern Sudanese to opt for secession, let alone depict them as exploiters of the South. Indeed, it was because of the SPLM's vision and foresight that Sudanese people, from Kassala in the East to Darfur in the West, joined hands with the Sudan People's Liberation Movement/Army (SPLM/A) in the struggle for change in Sudan. Regrettably, the born-again reductionists had neither lent an ear to President Mbeki's insightful remarks after the declaration of the results of the referendum (Chapter Ten), nor spared a thought to President Kiir's fine feelings revealed on the lowering of the Sudanese flag on independence day (Chapter Ten).

Regarding CPA third-party beneficiaries, they were either waiting for a free lunch where "there was no such thing as a free lunch"[4] or completely daunted by the NCP's political and security machines. With the trades unions domesticated, political parties divided and subdivided, and leaders of major national parties compromised, there was no serious popular action in favor of democratic transformation, save for valorous efforts by women and youth organizations, human rights activists, and a score of fearless academics and scribes in the print media. Even within the margin of freedom afforded to them by the CPA, major opposition parties failed to provide a serious challenge to the regime. That was either because of the vanity of their leaders (preoccupation with whom should come at the top) or their being ever ready to fall prey to NCP inducements. The performance of the parties in the April 2010 elections is a case in point (Chapter Eight). As a result, many political party activists who were disenchanted by the performance of their leaders voted with their feet and left the country; others either took to arms or established a toothless opposition in the diaspora.

Without a doubt, after the CPA the situation changed considerably from what it had been during the decade of the 1990s when panic and fright dominated life, and Big Brother was practically peeping through every keyhole. But the democratic transformation ushered in by the CPA was far from being realized despite the entrenchment of a Bill of Rights in the INC. In this regard, law enforcement agencies (police and security services) audaciously persisted in circumventing the Bill of Rights by turning their regulatory powers to prohibitive powers. The judiciary, on the other hand, rarely acted without fear or favor. The heavy media (radio and television) continued to be totally controlled by the ruling party, while the print media, of which the largest part was also party-controlled, were programmed not to blow the whistle when things went wrong.

As late as the last year of the interim period (2011), Mohammed Chande Othman, a U.N. human rights expert and chief justice of Tanzania, reported a list of human rights abuses that made a joke of Sudan's Bill of Rights. In his report to the U.N. Human Rights Council, Othman stated that the Sudan government had yet to review national laws to conform with the CPA, INC, and international human rights standards.[5] The expert added that "priority should be given to withdrawing enforcement powers, including arrest and detention by the national intelligence and security services, in line with the "information gathering and advisory role" envisioned for the services in the CPA and INC.[6] He also called for the establishment of the Human Rights Commission and ratification of remaining international instruments for the protection of human rights, including the Convention on the Elimination of All Forms of Discrimination Against Women and the Convention Against Torture and Other Cruel, Inhuman, and Degrading Treatment or Punishment. If this was the situation by the close of the interim period, it would be fairly concluded that the two and one-half years spent at Naivasha to improve on the transformative nature of the agreement was an exercise in futility. The Sudan government was obviously not delighted by Othman's judgment and, not relishing the tone and the tune of his report, it decided to shoot the piano player. Utterly unperturbed by the possibility of additional international opprobrium for human rights violations, the government persuaded the United Nations to end the expert's mission and reduce his role to that of a technical assistance in the human rights field. It did not take long for Othman to resign his job.

With South Sudan gone because of mistakes that were repeatedly committed from December 1955 up to 2005 by the ensemble of the northern ruling parties, as well as premeditated acts by the NCP throughout the interim period, Sudan's crises were far from over. Within the NCP and Sudan's traditional parties were groups who seemed to think that by July 9, 2011, they were home and dry and that the Republic of Sudan (or what had remained of it) was finally relieved from the schisms and discordances engendered by diversity. Nothing is further from truth. While South Sudan emerged as an independent state with a backbreaking load of liabilities and great possibilities, North Sudan was no less in a quandary, which could not be eluded through make-believe. Both states can turn their liabilities into assets if they rank their priorities right, manage their resources prudentially, and rise to the occasion.

In Chapters Ten and Eleven, the author outlined the challenges facing the Republic of South Sudan and enumerated, as impending dangers, the political exploitation of ethnic conflicts, awry prioritization in public expenditure, and increasing depravity in public life. While friends of the new republic continued to be worried about these phenomena, many of its ruling elite seemed neither to be worried nor embarrassed. Certainly, laws were passed and presidential cautionaries repeatedly issued, but to be fair to itself, the leadership had to be as good as its word. Actions speak louder than words. On the other hand, the NCP, to all appearances, had yet to recover from the shock of the separation of South Sudan. In reprisal, it seemed not to mind seeing the new government collapsing, if not expediting its collapse. This assumption was substantiated by a number of measures taken by the Sudan government against ordinary southern Sudanese citizens. These measures included expulsions *en masse* of law-abiding southern citizens from its territory, embargo of North-South trade, and termination of service contracts of southern Sudanese officials in the employ of the government, including university teachers, medical doctors, and hospital nurses. No matter how angry private individuals may allow themselves to become, men of state shall be counted upon not to let the sun go down on their anger. However, when all is said and done, both states have to learn how to live amicably together. For two countries sharing a 2,000-kilometer border and over 30 nomadic tribes seasonally crisscrossing that border, maintaining good neighborly relations is not a gesture of goodwill but a prerequisite of survival. The quibbling between the two states on economic issues that directly impinge on the lives of people on both sides of the border is nothing but bêtise, particularly when it is fueled by anger, on the one side, and desire to return like for like, on the other. If they fail to live amicably together, peace and stability in Sudan shall be transient and conflict wide-ranging. Propitiously, after months of haggling, the two governments reached an agreement on all outstanding issues on September 27, 2012. That agreement could not have been achieved without the decisive intervention of the United Nations Security Council, the African Union, and the innate abilities of the mediator, Thabo Mbeki. The framework agreement signed by Presidents Bashir and Salva Kiir comprised nine protocols, covering:

- The Cooperation Agreement between Sudan and South Sudan
- Oil Agreement between Sudan and South Sudan
- Agreement on Security Arrangements
- Agreements between Sudan and South Sudan on the Status of Nationals of the Other State and Related Matters.
- Agreement between Sudan and South Sudan on Post-Service Benefits
- Agreement on Trade between Sudan and South Sudan
- Agreement on Banking
- Agreement on Border Issues
- Agreement on Certain Economic Matters

In this situation the saying "better late than never" comes in handy. The only gap in the negotiations was leaving the Abyei issue in suspense, as it was referred to the African Union Peace and Security Council.

There is, nonetheless, a fringe within the Islamists that is smitten with the idea that the secession of South Sudan signified the end of the country's woes and would open the door wide for the inauguration of Sudan's Islamic Republic, or at least provide the Islamists with the opportunity to take the country back to the decade of the 1990s. If the experience of war in South Sudan had not been enough to prove the precariousness of this assumption, then the wars in Blue Nile (the citadel of the first Islamic kingdom in North-Central Sudan) and Darfur (the bastion of the first Islamic sultanate in western Sudan) should have. That fringe may also need to be reminded that the war in Darfur against the Islamist regime in Khartoum was not enkindled by

504

"ungodly" secularists, but by two firebrand Islamist leaders: Daoud Bolad and Khalil Ibrahim, who emerged from the belly of the National Islamic Front (NIF). Furthermore, the woes of the country shall be aggravated, not dissipated, as long as the center-periphery asymmetry continues and Khartoum's hegemony on the rest of the country endures, irrespective of who is at the helm. The concentration of authority in the national capital has not made it the fulcrum of power, but actually the epicenter of political and administrative inefficiency.

Apart from the hallucinations of that fringe, the Islamists in general seemed to believe that once the South was gone, they would be able to turn the country into a bed of roses. But if the roses they are promising the people of Sudan are similar to what the NCP has been rendering to them in the last two decades, then they and the country shall be in trouble. On its ascendancy to power, the NCP launched a civilizational project (*al mashru' al hadhary*) with a view to spreading the faith, leading the faithful in the path of righteousness, enabling the Sudanese people to wallow in bliss, and establishing a modern state imbued with the values of Islam. Much too often they claimed that they were also presenting to the world a model of governance heretofore unknown. There is nothing wrong with ambition, for every eel hopes to become a whale. Nonetheless, if the model of governance the NCP aspires to offer to the world is the same as the one Sudan has been burdened with since June 1989, then they shall, in fact, be offering a model that is damned with faint praise from the Sudanese themselves.

In spite of everything, the Islamist regime had pursued its goals with ruthless efficiency, supported by an array of well-trained cadres of whom some were tutored in the best universities of Europe and America, not in Iran or Afghanistan- That, for sure, was Dr Turabi's contribution to party politics, while other parties took as the gospel truth Robert Louis Stevenson's adage: "politics is perhaps the only profession for which no preparation is thought necessary."[7] In their two decades in office, the Islamists scored some important points in political and developmental fields that had put their northern opponents (the national political parties) in the shade. For one, they were the first party in office to recognize the right to self-determination for the people of South Sudan, even though that had come after 12 bloody years of jihad. They were also the first northern party to sign a peace agreement with South Sudan that enabled southern Sudanese to exercise that right (which led to secession), much as they had tried to writhe free of the agreement during the implementation period. That was a far cry from Sadig al Mahdi's position in 1987.[8] In the field of development, the NCP may also take pride in the development of the oil and mining sectors and the building of physical infrastructure. Repeatedly, northern political parties justified their underachievement in the economic development field (for they had nothing to say about their achievements in that of peace) by the fact that the Sudanese army never gave them a respite in which to rule. Between 1958–1989, there were three successful military coups, they say. That argument is not only flimsy, but also smacks of self-deception. In actuality, whenever the army seized power it was either under the guise of putting an end to war in South Sudan (1969 and 1989), or because it was galvanized by ideological political parties to capture power (communists and Nasserites in 1969, Islamists in 1989, and Baathists in a number of attempted coups during civilian rule). Furthermore, the army's meddling in politics was, in the first instance, a direct outcome of its entanglement by the parties in internal politics. That happened when civilian governments entrusted the army with putting an end to a civil war, which by its very nature, was an internal war fueled by economic, social, or cultural concerns. Failure to avert the escalation of conflict between 1955–1965, or put an end to it when it intensified between 1965–1972, was either due to the tunnel vision of post-independence rulers (at least insofar as war in the South was concerned), or to the absorption of the post-October 1964 governments in political horse-trading during the formation or reshuffle of governments. With that being their topmost priority, northern political parties had no time left for attending to effervescing conflicts in rural Sudan, including the South. In consequence, handling of the seething conflict in that region was left to the army. By that very act the army was politicized. The success of Nimeiri's government in 1972 and Bashir's in 2005 to reach a pacific settlement through negotiations, notwithstanding the unraveling of the agreement reached by the former and the mess up of the one concluded by the latter, proved that there was an alternative route to peace other than *a paxa Khartoumiana.*

The main function and primary duty of any army is to defend the country, its people, and its territory against external aggression—not to fight internal wars. Since the Sudanese army was not made up of mercenaries or partisan militias but of citizens entitled to formulate their own views on national matters, it followed that army officers and men were equally at liberty to express views on matters that had a bearing on war and peace. For example, the 1969 coup was preceded by an encounter between the acting minister of defense, Abdel Hamid Salih, and angry officers in Juba about the underequipment of the army by the government of the day. The minister was held hostage by the officers for a number of days. In the same way the confrontation between the army command and Prime Minister Sadiq al-Mahdi in 1988 paved the way for the NIF coup. Even though the army in that confrontation dabbled in few political issues, that was either because the issues they raised impinged on the war to which they were dragged by politicians, or they were goaded by leftist parties to raise those issues. Dissimilar to the Juba incident, army confrontation with the prime minister in 1987 was not only about equipping the army to fight the war better, but also about making peace based on al-Mirghani's initiative,[9] which al-Mahdi seemed to have been reluctant to implement (Chapter Two).

On the other hand, almost all ideological parties created coteries for them within the army as bridgeheads to power through the bullet. Those who engineered such coups emerged of late as champions of multiparty democracy, without any attempt on their part to exercise any degree of self-criticism. That is not meant to be an exercise in self-flagellation or conscience cleansing; it shall be an educative process, especially for new generations. None of these contemporaneous Sudanese democrats had planned coups in the decades of the 1970s and 1980s in order to install democracy; their objective was surely to emulate systems of rule initiated and sustained by their mentors in Cairo, Damascus, and Baghdad. More important, all military regimes from 1958 to 1989 were given a new lease in life from the very parties that were overthrown by the army.[10] That said, the place of any army in a democratic country is emphatically in the barracks, not in the piazza (street) or the palazzo (palace), as the Italians say. If men of the palazzo decided to dance with the tiger, then they should have no reason to wonder why their toes were being bitten during the dance. Northern Sudanese political parties, therefore, cannot absolve themselves from dragging the army into politics—the army that had allegedly not given them a respite to rule.

Whatever achievements the Islamists had scored in the political and developmental spheres came with heavy political, economic, and moral prices. To begin with, unlike all military coups Sudan had known before June 1989, the Islamists captured power mainly to recreate the whole state in their image. That was in stark contrast to Bashir's declaration upon launching his coup on June 30, 1989. In that declaration, Bashir chastised the party regime he had deposed mainly for (i) failure to ensure liberty, democracy, and national unity; (ii) inability to bring peace and inadequacy in equipping the armed forces to fight rebels; (iii) economic deterioration leading to soaring inflation figures and price hikes that drove citizens to the margins of hunger; (iv) collapse of health and education services; (v) spread of corruption, especially political corruption that led to expulsion of "honest civil servants" under the guise of "retirement for public interest," and (vi) collapse of public service institutions and programs as a result of the above, as well as recruitment of top civil servants on the basis of party allegiance, not merit. The wrongdoings enumerated by Bashir on June 30, 1989 were enough to make any party, or parties, unfit to rule. So what had the NIF done to rectify them?

Rather than straightening out the allegedly debilitated and depraved government it had deposed, the NIF, within its first year in office, had brazenly exceeded all limits on the exercise of power that Sudan had known. Treading in the steps of the worst despotic regimes, it began its "reformation" by totally monopolizing politics: banning all political parties, trades unions, and independent press. It then turned to the Sudanese army to mold it from a

507

professional, nonpartisan institution to an ideologized force for the first time in its history. In order to ensure full control of the army, it progressively retired all officers who were either not in good stead with the party or refused to be molded. It also disbanded the state security agency and replaced its operatives with Islamists. Eventually that agency was transformed into the cadre school of the NIF and the preparatory school from which future NIF ministers, governors, ambassadors, and heads of public corporations emerged. Likewise, the NIF took control of the nerve centers of economic life by laying its hands on banks—including the Central Bank—and reprivatizing the private sector, however improbable that might sound. In effect, all business enterprises that belonged to national entrepreneurs who did not belong, or were not close, to the Islamists were chased away from the marketplace by being denied financing, export licences, or other facilities. Even the judicial and civil services were not saved from purges and were eventually taken over at high and medium levels by Islamist cadres or fellow travelers. This ultimately led to the collapse of a merit-based administration. While the new regime thought to stabilize the South through brute force, it opted to control the North by a synthesis of intimidation, inducement, and terror. The purpose of this authoritarian monolithism was not only to dominate the country, but also to crush its people's spirit. However, as is the case with all absolutist regimes, totalitarianism soon proved to be the Achilles heel of the regime, as the absence of rule of law inevitably led to lawlessness. On the other hand, lack of transparency in governance bred corruption, while longevity in office made Islamist leaders arrogantly insensitive to those who did not share their vision or even to legitimate grievances expressed by ordinary citizens against commonplace administrative decisions. Sequentially, the arrogance of power obscured the regime's vision from distinguishing between what was appropriate and what was inappropriate in politics to the point that it became proficient at shooting itself in the foot, as if it had been coded to do so.

Unflustered by its mistakes, the regime every so often justified the most reckless action it had taken in the name of Allah. That included measures that were only meant to hide managerial shortcomings, conceal unseemly actions, or cover up business decisions that were far from being pure. As the Islamists doubled their efforts to turn the state into a lawless autocracy, they in inverse proportion abandoned Islamic ethos and standards of behavior they claimed were guiding them such as righteousness, respect of human worth, probity, and integrity. Coming from a political group that had turned politics into a morality play, that farce became too funny for words when some Islamists ventured, with forethought, to shield corrupt elements from being named and shamed through what was called *"fiqh al sutra"* (the jurisprudence of latency or disguise). Nothing of the sort is heard of in Islam or, indeed, in any respectable legal system. Cover-up in all legal systems is tantamount to conspiracy or complicity in crime. Thus, by paying lip service to values claimed to be embedded in the Quran and Islamic teachings, not only did the Islamists contravene universally acknowledged standards of probity in public life, but also disobeyed prescriptive words of God.

Although some Islamists had detected the country's descent down a slippery slope and raised the alarm bells, none of those who had been anchored in power were ready to abandon the claim of occupying the higher moral ground. As NCP government became overwhelmed with problems, especially after the separation of South Sudan, they scrambled to enfold opposition parties, especially the main sectarian parties—Umma and the Democratic Unionist Party (DUP)—which were subject to vilification by the NIF for two decades. The two parties, however, were sought by the NCP, not as effective partners in government but as a garnish to the regime. Apparently the two parties were not expecting otherwise. The NCP's approach to politics, and the sectarian leaders' response to it, revealed some characteristics that did not put any of them in a favorable light. In case of the NCP, it became obvious that even when in distress, it was still reticent to foreswear its absolutist approach to governance. As for the sectarian leaders, it became clear how low they were ready to stoop to accept the NCP's grudging thanks for their coming to its rescue. How ironical it was to see Sudan's two historical parties, who continued to draw support from a considerably large social base, allow themselves to play second fiddle to the very regime that had forced them out of power.

On December 4, 2011, President Bashir announced that DUP chairman, al-Mirghani agreed to join his government, while the Umma party chairman, al-Mahdi did so obliquely.[11] The sons of the two leaders were appointed as assistants to the president, a position that came immediately after that of the vice president. The decisions of the two leaders caused an uproar in their parties, especially among youth groups. Indeed, Bashir's announcement of his offer to the two religious leaders to join his party in government and the acceptance by the two of that offer came as a shock to the people of Sudan for more than one reason:

(i) It was beyond any reasonable man's comprehension why the Islamists would seek legitimization for, if not salvation of, their regime from sectarian leaders whom they had reviled and mercilessly traduced when they came to power in 1989.

(ii) Acceptance of undisguised alliance with the NCP by one sectarian leader (DUP) and the veiled one by the other (Umma) was shocking to the two parties rank and file as they saw the two leaders nominating their young sons to jobs for which they were not trained. No matter how prepared the sons were for other jobs, allowing them to steal the march to high offices in government from senior politicians in their parties cast a shadow over the democratic credentials of their fathers. Leaders who fail to practice democracy or respect hierarchy in their own parties cannot be credited with implanting democracy in the country.

(iii) Related to the above, the inadvertences by the sectarian leaders to the turmoil in the region from Egypt to Syria and Yemen over the tendency of party chiefs in these countries to make elevation to the highest office in the party or state a hereditary endowment[12] made people sparing of praise to those leaders.

(iv) By resuscitating the sectarian leaders as men with a foundational role in Sudanese national of politics in Sudan, the Islamists had conceded defeat of their plan to create a pattern of rule that transcended sectarian, ethnic, and partisan divides.

Without regrets for its derision of sectarianism in the past, the NCP made a revealing statement about the reasons that led it to embrace the sectarian parties. In a press interview, NCP spokesperson, Ibrahim Ghandour said "our invitation to al-Mirghani and al-Mahdi to join the government, despite our declared views on sectarianism, is not to be seen as a return to the days of the two Sayeds,[13] but is an endeavor by the NCP to create the largest national alliance in the history of Sudan."[14] That statement not only confirmed the failure of what the NCP claimed to be its last word on national identity, it also exposed the vacuity of its claim to represent all Sudan. Following the national elections of April 2010, the NCP asserted that it had garnered the support of two-thirds of the people of Sudan and persisted in saying so.

Regardless of all these unseemly practices, the Sudanese people were mostly jarred by their leaders' failure to present an alternative program that would address the complex of problems that besiege the country. If they had, that might have at least been a saving grace. Throughout their time in opposition, sectarian leaders kept reciting the wrongs the Islamist regime had committed. That was a redundant exercise because the people of Sudan knew from their own experience what had gone wrong in the country under the rule of the *Ingaz*. Despite the reasons it had given in 1989 for indicting the regime of the parties and, thus, justifying its removal from office, the *Ingaz* had not only emulated the misdeeds of that regime, but also outrivaled it in wrongdoing, which was an incredible feat. The sectarian leaders also did their utmost to reassure the Sudanese people that they were capable of presenting a better brand of Islam than the one offered by the Islamists, as if those who took to arms in different parts of the country, or the grumblings by school graduates who had been out of a job for years after graduation, were only manifestations of a doctrinal conflict with the regime. This approach to politics, in the eyes of many Sudanese, including some supporters of the sectarian parties, revealed the intellectual sterility of the leaders and their oblivion to problems that had troubled the Sudanese people for two decades.

Earlier in the book the author ventured to decipher the Islamist's strange addiction to power and propensity for the use of extreme force in response to even the least provocation. Extreme use of force by any despot or usurper of power is never a sign of strength but often signifies vulnerability and apprehensiveness. With the many political and economic wrongdoings it had committed, and the hundreds of corpses in the closets of some of its leaders, apprehensiveness by the NCP was understandable. Indeed, that apprehensiveness appeared to have already reached the level of pathological fear. However, if the Islamists are at all to continue having a niche in national politics, sensible elements within their ranks have to control regressive zealots among them who still believe that Sudan can be monopolized by one party. This is certainly undoable in this day and age, when all totalitarian regimes have collapsed or are tottering—and certainly not when the whole region is rising up to throw off the yoke of totalitarian, or any other ingrate regime that takes people for granted. Hence, in their efforts to chart the way forward for what they call Sudan's second republic (meaning by that what has remained of Sudan after the truncation of one-third of it), the Islamists may have to abandon few irrationalities:

(i) False belief that they can rule Sudan for evermore either because of an assumed omnipotence or of claimed legitimacy gained through elections. History annals are replete with stories on high-and-mighty regimes that had collapsed like houses of cards on the weight of their own mistakes. As for legitimacy gained through elections, everybody knew that those elections were dubious in the extreme, since it would have been very easy for any player who held four aces in his hand, irrespective of the way he obtained the cards, to win the game hands down. By the end of the day, regimes fall for exactly the reasons recited by Bashir on June 30, 1989, and not necessarily through military coups. So no matter how many battles such regimes won in their struggle for survival, they still never won the war.

(ii) Continuous intimidation of political adversaries in the name of Islam, and of which the Islamists seem to claim a monopoly, is counterproductive. In a country of believers like the Sudan, the regularity of such a claim is only commensurate to its absurdity. That is more so when, in practice, Islam became a hackneyed cliché rather than edifying rules that govern performance. Indeed, by portraying it as a religion that divides, not unites, people and sows hate, not love, among communities, the Islamists do serious disservice to that religion.

(iii) The Islamists' pretence that all shall be milk and honey in Sudan after secession of the South and the loss, under their watch, of one-third of the country and two-thirds of its oil revenue, boggles the mind. This attitude not only exhibits loose thinking, but also unveils a worrisome self-delusion. The Islamists (or at least a few of them) are too versed in the ways of the world to seriously believe in the viability of such autosuggestion. Making even a broad hint that Sudan is riding on the crest of the wave is the height of irresponsibility when the country is suffering from multiple adversities such as serious budget deficits, spiraling

511

inflation, soaring commodity prices, and very high levels of unemployment. As a result of all these adversities, the majority of the country's population is now caught in the poverty trap.

(iv) Playacting that the ship of state is not about to sink into a valley of darkness, even when danger signals are all over the place, is another symptom of self-deception, if not inexpedient escapism. To face such a serious situation. the Sudanese political and social forces, including the Islamists, have no choice other than pulling one and all so that the ship reaches safe shores.

(v) Belief that the successive victories scored by Islamist parties in North Africa shall give political Islam in Sudan a new lease in life is simply a phantasm, as the ascendancy of Islamist parties in these countries was achieved through the ballot in free and fair elections and on a level political ground for all competitors. In the world we live in, political power can only be sought, or kept, via this route.

(vi) Assumption by Sudanese Islamists that the rise to power through the ballot by their counterparts in some Arab countries (Egypt, Morocco and Tunisia), is the same as granting these powers a *carte blanche* to reshape the entire society to their image is a pipe dream. In this respect, the NCP shall serve itself and the country well by drawing from contemporary Egyptian experience. For example the Muslim Brothers party which was brought to power in 2012 by a reasonable majority (fifty two percent of the voters) in a free and fair election lost legitimacy only one year after that election. Attempt by the Muslim Brothers to reshape Egypt to their image and make of one religion (Islam) the only marker of national identity led to a popular revolt as never seen before in Egypt against the Brothers. That revolt led to the disfranchisement and outlawing of their party.

(vii) In any respectable system of rule—Islam included—when rulers err, they owe it to the people to admit their errors rather than cover them up. On coming to power, the Islamists had clear ideas of what they wanted to do. In the two decades that ensued, they pursued their ideas with intensity, scoring some successes and committing many blunders. But at no point in time did they see the need to recognize, let alone admit their liability for, these blunders. A regime that takes people—all people—for fools shall sooner or later be surprised. Even the average man in the street, with his native wit, would inevitably discover who the fool is.

(viii) Continuation by Islamists to pass themselves off as the puritanical sons of God, despite manifestations of vulgar nouveau richism by many of their cadres and their boon companions, must be a cause of embarrassment to the few unassuming Islamists who remained. Indeed, the false piety of leaders of a party that has become home to bloated plutocrats, self-indulgent party officers, and pseudobusinessmen who are making riches by ripping off the state, border on sacrilege when Islamists pretend that the Quran is their frame of life.

(ix) Lastly, the ruling Islamists may have to acknowledge, as they have done in the CPA, that the root cause of conflicts in Sudan is injustice. Without justice for all, things shall fall apart and the center shall not hold. For not

> only is justice the end in view for all those who struggle for the betterment
> of life, it is also a basic condition of humanity.

For all the above, the salvation of Sudan cannot by achieved through symbolic alliances with spent forces or the adoption of unemployable political self-seekers but by bringing together all stakeholders. If the NCP had belatedly discovered that conflict in one region, Darfur, could not be resolved without involving all Darfurian stakeholders, it would follow that the nation's crisis cannot be resolved otherwise.

In the decade of the 1970s a development commentator described Brazil as "the country of the future," adding "and it shall always be." By that statement the commentator meant that Brazil is a bountiful country endowed with plentiful human and natural resources to make it emerge as a leading country in South America. However, given the country's abiding misrule at the time, that expectation remained a vain hope. However, by the beginning of the third millennium, Brazil emerged as a world economic giant competing with first-league countries in the economic field. The Brazil of the last century was geographically, demographically, and climatologically the very same as the Brazil of this century. What had made the difference then? It is leadership. Needless to repeat that Sudan's leadership for two decades had failed because it was living in a virtual world in which it assigned to itself a role beyond its power or means: reinventing the Sudan in its image and enlightening the world on its virtuous governance. In the meantime, it made of preparing its own citizens for life everlasting a profession of faith. But whatever ideological prototype one adopts in politics, be it religious or secular, a nation's problems shall remain physical, not metaphysical.

Likewise, the author doesn't have to repeat that the national leadership that colonized the past had doubly failed; its failure has been exhibited in the disasters and blind stops it left in its trail, as well as in continuing, up to the present, to fight yesterday's wars. If anything, this is the ultimate evidence of its being frozen in an out-of-date matrix. Both are, therefore, to realize that politics is about the here and now and that citizens demand from their governors no less, and no more, than respect, acknowledgment of their self-esteem, satisfaction of basic needs, improvement of quality of life, and peace within their communities and with their neighbors.

Were it not so tragic, Sudan's history since independence would be nothing but a comedy of errors, with little comedy and errors beyond number. Although the agreement, signed on January 9, 2005, had comprehensively addressed all problems that had plagued the country and its people for 50 years, Sudan's past imperfect continued to haunt it. Unmistakably, Sudan's past isn't dead and behind. In fact, it isn't even past.[15] The way that the great achievement of the Comprehensive Peace Agreement was marred by willful transgressions, breaches of trust, unwitting errors, and betrayal of principles, without which there would have been no CPA, may be the greatest testimony to the credibility of this conclusion.

NOTES

1   Darfur Peace Agreement signed in Abuja in May 2006, Eastern Sudan Peace Agreement signed in Asmara on October 14, 2006, and Doha Peace Agreement on Darfur signed in Doha in July 2011.

2   Jon Temin and Theodore Murphy, *Toward a New Republic of Sudan*, (Washington, DC: United States Institute of Peace, June 2011), 2.

3   Ibid.

4   Title of a book by American economist, statistician, and Nobel Prize recipient Milton Friedman, *There's No Such Thing as a Free Lunch* (LaSalle, IL: Open Court, 1975).

5   United Nations Human Rights Council, 14th Session, agenda item 4, May 26, 2010. Report of the independent expert on the situation of human rights in Sudan. Mr Mohammed Chande Othman, http://www2.orchr.org/English/bodies/hrcouncil/docs/15session/A.HRC.15.CRP.len.pdf.

6   Ibid.

7   Robert Louis Stevenson, *Familiar Studies of Men and Books*, 175, Respectfully Quoted: A dictionary of Quotation, Bartleby.com, http://www.battleby.com/73/1427.html.

8   On the emergence of the Umma party after the general elections in 1987 as majority party, al Mahdi, the prime minister elect, met with Garang in Addis Ababa for eleven hours to explore avenues for resolution of Sudan's conflict. The main issue at the discussion between al Mahdi and Garang was the holding of a national peace conference. To participate in that conference Garang requested al Mahdi to repeal Nimeiri's shari'a laws which al Mahdi himself described as "only fit for the dust bin of history." When he was in the opposition Al Mahdi, probably wary of the National Islamic Front's reaction if he repealed these laws, refused to do so. The meeting closed by Garang saying to al Mahdi :"Brother Sadiq you have one of two choices, if you repeal the September laws you shall emerge as prime minister of the whole Sudan, and if you fail to do so you shall end up becoming the prime minister of Khartoum."

9   It may be recalled that al Mirghani, leader of the ruling Democratic Unionist Party concluded with Garang at Addis Ababa in November 1988 The Sudan Peace Initiative. That agreement was to prepare the ground for talks between the government in Khartoum once that government passed a law freezing the Shari'a laws enacted by President Nimeiri.

10 Al-Mirghani and al-Mahdi blessed Abboud's coup in a radio broadcast, while Ali Abdel Rahman and Mohamed Nurreldin—two bigwigs of the National Umma Party—pledged, among others, support to the Abboud regime. Sadiq al-Mahdi, on his part, broke rank with the Libya-based armed opposition against Nimeiri to make amends with him in July 1977, and on 25 November 1999 to make peace with Bashir following an agreement signed in Djibouti. In December 2011, al-Mirghani reached an agreement with Bashir to forgive and forget.

11 Al-Mahdi declined to join Bashir's government unless, and until, the regime changed its totalitarian nature. In this regard, he set certain conditions relating to civil rights and a common approach to the problems of Darfur, South Kordofan, and Blue Nile. Nevertheless, he acceded Bashir's request to appoint al-Mahdi's son, who was by then a colonel in the Sudan Armed Forces, to a high office in the state reportedly to be a conduit between his father and the president.

12 One of the reasons for the uprising in Egypt and Yemen was the perceived intentions of Presidents Hosni Mubarak and Ali Abdullah Saleh to prepare their sons to succeed them. On the other hand, Syrians had been grumbling about the conversion of republicanism in Syria into monarchism since the demise of President Hafiz al-Assad and the enthronement of his son as president.

13 Sayed Ali al Mirghani (leader of Khatmiya sect and patron of unionist political movements) and Sayed Abdel Rahman al Mahdi (leader of the Ansar sect and patron of the Umma party) dominated the political scene up the 1960s.

14 "Interview with Ibrahim Ghandour on NCP Invitation to al-Mirghani and al-Mahdi," *Al-Sudani*, December 7, 2011.

15 Loosely adapted from "The past is never dead. It's not even past," from William Faulkner, *Requiem for a Nun*, 80, Maria Gendron and Lisa Feldman Barrett, Reconstructing the Past: A century of Ideas About Emotion in Psychology, Emotion Review, Vol 1, No 4 (October 2009), Sage Publications http://www.affective-science.org/pubs/2009/gendron-barrett-2009.pdf

Postscript: Addiction to Failure and Allergy to Success

■■■■■■■■■■■■■■■❖■■■■■■■■■■■■■■■

This author elected to entitle an Arabic book he published in 1993 on the role of Sudan's political elite in cumulatively aggravating, rather than alleviating, Sudan's tales of woe as *Sudan's Political Elite and Addiction to Failure*. Throughout the first part of this book, as well as in the many treatises on Sudan's politics written by authors familiar with the country's history, this point had been made sufficiently clear. In effect, all problems that had given rise to war in southern Sudan and later to endless bloody conflicts in central Sudan (the Nuba Mountains) and western Sudan (Darfur) could have been politically resolved were it not for that elite's myopic and highhanded approach. Sudan's ruling elite at the time not only missed every opportunity for national reconciliation,[1] they also had the audacity to claim that they knew better. Be that as it may, our statement was adjudged by some Sudanese commentators to be overly damnatory as if the political blunders, managerial gaucherie, and economic downturns that had beset the country for the 49 years that ensued after Sudan's independence on January 1, 1956 to the conclusion of the CPA on January 9, 2005, were god-ordained.

The CPA signature was gladly received by Sudanese all over the country because they fairly believed that that agreement had given Sudan a new lease in life. It was also unsurprising that the CPA was hailed by Sudan's African neighbors as well as friends across the world. Those had reasonably conjectured that the largest country in Africa, with its agonies over, was at long last set to play the role it was destined by history and geography to play.

Without conflating causes with symptoms of Sudan's multiple crises, the success of the CPA was, to a large extent, due to its forthright approach to the underlying political, economic, social, and structural causes of these crises. Rather than settling for generalities, the agreement identified specific political, economic and managerial goals to be achieved within a specified time-frame. Such goals were wantonly missed by Sudanese peace negotiators in the past since issues relating to culture, religion or structural economic deprivation were deemed too thorny to touch. The CPA did not stop at defining goals but went on to draw a detailed road map to reach these goals and designed robust guarantees to ensure their implementation. In effect, one knows of no peace negotiations that had taken such long and exhaustive deliberations as those which took place in the Kenyan country side between Sudan's two warring parties or involved as many advisors, facilitators and mediators. But, when all is said and done what did the CPA achieve?

In a climate of concord and amity, the Sudanese negotiators reached consensus on principles and arrangements without which there would neither be peace, nor unity in Sudan. Those included:

- Recognition of Sudan's multiple diversities: ethnic, religious, cultural, and linguistic. Those principles were eventually encompassed in Article 1 (1) of the national constitution.[2]
- Acknowledgment of historical injustices reflected in the system of rule, apportionment of wealth and assignment of employment opportunities in the public sector.
- Promulgation, for the first time in Sudan's constitutional history, of a Bill of Rights grounded on the universal human rights declaration and international covenants governing those rights.
- Calling for the initiation of a process of national reconciliation and healing.
- Devolution of power and establishment of a decentralized system of rule.
- Granting Southern Sudanese full autonomy during the interim period to run the affairs of the region they occupy.
- Foundation of Sudan's national unity on upholding the above goals throughout the interim period and beyond.
- Granting the people of southern Sudan the right to self – determination by either choosing unity, if the above objectives were achieved and if not, exercising their right to secede. Evidently, the objectives enumerated above represented the value added that would entice the autonomous region in South Sudan to remain united with the north.[3]

Strange as it may sound, it was the Sudanese political elite in north and south Sudan—and nobody else—who frustrated the implementation of an agreement that represented the first serious attempt on nation–building in Sudan. Nation–building entails unifying people on the basis of citizenship, not native or regional particularities. It also requires homogenizing national cultures without vitiating any of them as well as molding different ethnic groups into one nation. In this respect, the NCP, by not honoring conditions that were carefully crafted in order to make voluntary unity possible, frustrated the attainment of that unity. In effect, the NCP demonstrated a remarkable level of recklessness in the manner with which it had treated the CPA, especially after Garang's demise. By all accounts, it seemed to believe that, irrespective of the terms of the agreement, it was at liberty to set its own terms and expect the other party to willingly follow suit.

Even when the other signatory party (SPLM) was forced to resort to take an extreme measure such as withdrawing from the national government in order to draw attention to serious breaches of the CPA, it was the SPLM, and not the wrongdoing NCP, which was scolded by the Khartoum media and a number of northern political commentators. Those critics presented the SPLM to the northern Sudanese public as an irresponsible party that wanted to be a government and an opposition party at the same time, as if breaches of cardinal clauses in the very agreement that gave the two parties legitimacy were inconsequential. This, to say the least, was nothing but a manifestation of bad faith, if not benightedness, on the part of these critics. What boggled the mind, however, was the fact that high on the list of issues raised by the SPLM when it withdrew from government were issues of national import and thus should have been of direct concern to the critics. These issues included initiation of the process of reconciliation and healing called for by the CPA, violations by the NCP government of freedoms also enshrined in the CPA and national constitution such as freedoms of expression and association, or measures pertaining to upholding the rule of law such as safeguarding independence of the judiciary and ensuring that law enforcement agencies did not act outside the terms of the constitution.

To add insult to injury, the NCP's attitude turned into vindictiveness bordering on racism when it appeared that the wind was blowing in favour of separation, not unity. The expulsion en masse of South Sudanese out of North Sudan, including those who were born in the north and neither opted for secession nor wished to return to the land of their ancestors, represented a serious violation of international law. However, the most glaring evidence of falling back on tribalism as a badge of identification was the enactment by the Sudan government of a new law governing issuing of national identity cards. Without holding that card no citizen would be entitled to services such as birth certificates, travel documents, or government employment. Appallingly, one of the requirements for being granted such identity card was tribal belonging to a North Sudan tribe. Accordingly, a Dinka, Shilluk, or Nuer who was born, raised, and permanently lived in north Sudan, shall not be entitled to that 'golden' card. Call this what you wish, but there is no way to disclaim the racial tinge in such action. Moreover, one cannot be stopped being filled with surprise when such narrow-minded identification of citizenship comes from a group that seeks to unify Muslims all over the world under one banner: the banner of Islam.

Little wonder, this unconcealed racial propensity had led to the emergence of a group—Forum for Peace—which is apparently supported and sustained by the NCP. The main purpose in life of that group became sowing hatred between northern and southern Sudanese. With a well-funded media organ, that group turned out to be a vehicle for calumniating southern Sudanese and habitually disparaging them and their culture. Not only was that behavior an affront to public decency in any civilized community, it was also repugnant to Sudan's own constitution.[4] Doubtless, there were few elements within the NCP who stood firm against this racist group, but the apparent impunity which that group enjoyed gave rise to doubting the commitment of NCP to principles embodied in the CPA, and protected by Sudan's constitution.

Regrettably, President Bashir himself gave an impetus to this trend. In a speech in Gadarif, Eastern Sudan following the South Sudan referendum, Bashir said that the referendum results should put an end to what he called *daghmassa* (mystification or illusive talk) about the true nature of Sudanese identity. Sudan, he said, "is from now on is only an Arabic and Islamic country" (Chapter Ten). Even if that statement was triggered by anger it was still inappropriate. But in Sudan's political theatre of the absurd Bashir continued to rule the country under a constitution to which he had given an oath of allegiance and which defined Sudan as a multi-racial, multi-lingual, and multi-ethnic country. Apart from spurning articles of Sudan's constitution, Bashir's statement also defied the principle on which the African Union is founded: recognition of the multiple diversities of the people of Africa. Nonetheless, Bashir was not alone in such double talk. Since the 1960s there had been a series of political leaders in north Sudan who seemed to believe that commitment to African unity was only reflected in garnished speeches in regional meeting or the fanfare of pan – African sports tournaments. Never ever, did it cross the minds of these leaders that such commitment should start with recognizing the Africa within Sudan. A multi–cultural country that does not recognize a component of its cultural diversity is one that is incapable of living with itself. Those who behave in this way can never be expected to sincerely tolerate living with their African neighborhood.

Aside from toleration, this attitude reflects a "great-sized monster of ingratitude"[5] toward Africa. Without African support there would have been no peace in Sudan. And without the solid stand behind President Bashir demonstrated by Africa since his indictment by ICC in 2008, things might have taken a turn for the worse. Equally, were it not for the perseverance of the African Union Peace and Security Council and its AUHIP, Sudan might have had more than one war at its hands. Up till this moment African mediators remain, with the patience of saints, on the ready to put out many unnecessary fires ignited by one Sudanese group against the other. Furthermore, for a political group that claims to be imbued with religious values, toleration of any racist inclination is but an anathema. Religions, Islam included, do not differentiate between people on the basis of color or ethnic origin. Needless to say, that with such unctuous behavior exhibited by northern Sudan's so-called God-fearing believers, it shall be much easier for the camel to go through the eye of the needle than for a made–up believer to enter Allah's Kingdom.

Concerning the northern political elite who claim to be in opposition of the Islamist regime and who never ceased claiming to be pace setters in the national political arena, they appear to be percipient of the inadequacies of which the southern Sudanese elite is accused, while remaining utterly oblivious to their own failures. One such failure is the remissness of these pace setters to bring pressure to bear on the NCP so as to realize the democratic transformation designed by that agreement and consecrated in the Interim National Constitution. This ineptness was made worse by the submission of the traditional political leaders in the North to the NCP's wiles. Save for shouting hackneyed catch phrases about the need for regime change, they in fact went a long way with the policies of that regime to divide and destroy. Eventually, they yielded to the regime's inducements even when it had become clear to every reasoning person that the regime was neither seeking political support, nor national reconciliation, but only subservience to its rule. The acceptance by the traditional leaders to be subservient to the very political party that had ousted them from power said more of the meekness of these leaders than of the adroitness of the coup plotters. By so doing not only did they alienate themselves from their social bases in rural Sudan, but also from Sudanese youth all over the country, And while the rural populace took up arms to make their voices heard, the Sudanese youth began to openly express in the social media their disdain of the country's seemingly imperishable leaders and set their hearts on political change akin to that achieved by their brothers and sisters in Egypt and Tunisia. In the meantime, the authors of the wrong–headed policy of appeasement are yet to realize that the policies they had pursued would end up creating a country divided into umpteen tribes, each with its own national flag and anthem.

The two traditional leaders (al Mahdi and al Mirghani), if not their minions, have been colonizing the political landscape in Sudan, more than any of their peers in Africa, Asia, Europe or South America. And though they had been soldiering on for half a century, at no point in time throughout this period had this Sudanese leadership the modesty to admit their responsibility for any of the troubles that had beset Sudan. Apparently, self-criticism is a term that does not exist in the political lexicon of leaders who believe that leadership is patrimonial, not earned through acumen, wisdom and self-denial. Their reluctance to incur blame for mistakes they had recurrently made only bred complacency and generated unconsciousness of political ethics. As well it exhibited serious lack of a sense of history, even though history, in part, is a cautionary tale.

Claiming that the political elite in South Sudan is free from blame shall not do justice to objectivity. Throughout Chapters Ten and Eleven

521

innumerable examples of that elite's mismanagement of affairs in South Sudan were retold. That mismanagement was partly due to inexperience, but a large part of it derived from the insatiable appetite of some elites to enrich themselves at the expense of the people they rule. Suffice it at this stage to highlight two counts on which the southern elite stands culpable. First is their giving short measure to clauses in the CPA that were not specifically relative to South Sudan but were, nonetheless central to the creation of a New Sudan. If there is any betrayal to Garang's vision that has been the one most hurting. For better or worse, Garang bequeathed on the Sudanese in the north and south a sense of dignity, self-respect, and above all great expectations. This seems to have frittered away after his demise.

However, the southern Sudanese elite's gravest sin is its failure to deliver to the people of South Sudan the dividends of peace. Those people did not go through the agony of war for three decades so as to have a national flag and anthem; they were, above all, yearning for what Garang's vision promised. This elite had been on the helm for seven years, and not only for the two post–independence years. That is a sufficiently long time to enable the governors of South Sudan to do one thing for their people: achieving food security. Southern Sudanese had been on the dole for three decades, not because they were incapable of feeding themselves, but because of unremitting wars. Nevertheless, South Sudan despite its bountiful land and abundant oil revenues was on the date of celebrating the second anniversary of its independence still dependent on imported food from neighboring countries and on food aid by international agencies. According to U.N. sources, 2.3 million people will need food assistance in this year (2013) while 3.2 million shall require other nutritional services.[6] In other words, 4.6 million of the country's population of 12 million are food insecure.[7] That dismal performance in achieving the most basic human need humiliates and shames a country that has the capacity to feed the whole of East Africa. It is in double measure shameful in a country whose founding father made of rural development the cornerstone of his development strategy and the leaders who succeeded him continued to gloat about "taking towns to rural areas," repeating John Garang's clarion call. Clearly, the successors, despite the gloating, are yet to internalize Garang's strategy. If they had ever done, they would not have allocated 5.2% of the national budget to agriculture while an estimated half of the budget was spent on government salaries and perks.[8] Moreover, according to the NGO Doctors Without Borders, eighty percent of healthcare in South Sudan was provided by external donors.[9] Not only that but also the pervasive corruption to which we have alluded in Chapter Eleven abided even at the time when the country was in dire straits as a result of the stoppage of oil flow in 2012. Regrettably, even in such a woeful economic situation a so-called cow-boy capitalism invaded the place aided by some politicians.[10]

On December 16, 2013, hell broke loose in Juba as a result of a political conflict within the top leadership of the SPLM. That conflict was initially triggered by President Salva Kiir's dismissal of his deputy, Riek Machar, from his position as vice president followed by that of the SPLM secretary general, Pagan Amom, from his party position. What appears to have made the hackles of SPLM leaders who aligned themselves with Machar rise was the integration within higher ranks of government of elements alleged to be former acolytes of the NCP leadership to replace SPLM/A cadres whose contribution to the struggle had been acclaimed. The president might have been prompted by a desire to widen the SPLM's base of support or ensure that his government was broadly-based. However, to disallow any misreading of his intentions, Salva Kiir did not take one necessary step expected from the SPLM leader: prior consultation with SPLM party organs on the decisions he was contemplating. The alignments that had taken place within the ranks of SPLM should, therefore, be viewed as symptom of political power-struggle. Regrettably, that political conflict mutated into an ethnic war.

All the same, a number of authors who analyzed the CPA came up with the conclusion that the agreement failed because it was flawed. In reality the responsibility for failure to implement cardinal elements of the agreement, resulted from serious shortcomings of the two countries elites: unfaithfulness to contractual obligations by one party, and selfishness as well as lethargy in moving towards fulfilling the main promise made the CPA, by the other.

As for CPA third party beneficiaries such as the northern opposition, their irresolution in the struggle to implement clauses in the agreement that would have led to democratic transformation, had immensely contributed to failures that could have been avoided. Ironically these same forces had settled at last for beseeching the domineering NCP to open up the political space for them so that they find place in that space, obviously on terms determined the NCP. Thus while the northern political elite in government and opposition, contributed jointly and severally in varying degrees to the deprivation of the people of Sudan of the unity, democracy and well–being heralded by the CPA, that of southern Sudan demonstrated painful imperfection in running the affairs of state and inability to live up to the values that had guided them for three decades of struggle. That elite which was baptized with fire and born and bred on the principle of power to the people had, with few exceptions, finished up mimicking the NCP's style of governance. So instead of having one country with two systems, Sudan ended up having two countries with one system.

Is it unkind, after all the above diagnosis of Sudanese politics in the pre- and post-CPA periods, to say that the recurrent tribulations in the two countries are not only a manifestation of addiction to failure by its political elite, but probably also evidence of its allergy to success?

NOTES

1 Chapter One of this book narrated how the ruling and opposition political elite had tricked southern Sudanese in 1956 on the issue of federation, in 1965 how they undermined the report of the Twelve-man Committee, and in 1983 how President Nimeiri unilaterally abrogated the Addis Ababa agreement after eleven years of peace in South Sudan. In 1986, Prime Minister al Mahdi missed a golden opportunity to reach a peace agreement with Garang by dilly-dallying on the abrogation of Nimeiri's shari'a laws.

2 "The Republic of Sudan is an independent, sovereign state. It is a democratic, decentralized, multi-cultural, multi-lingual, multi-racial, multi-ethnic and multi – religions country where such diversities co-exist."

3 "The people of southern Sudan shall either:
   a) Confirm unity of Sudan by voting to sustain the system of government established under the comprehensive peace Agreement and this constitution, or
   b) Vote for secession"

4 Article 4(b) of the Sudan Constitution states: "Religions, beliefs, traditions and custom are the source of moral strength and inspiration of the Sudanese people; (c) the cultural and social diversity of the Sudanese people is the foundation of national cohesion and shall not be used for causing division."

5 William Shakespeare, *Troilus and Cressida*, Act III scene iii.

6 Simon Tisdali, 'South Sudan: two years old but nothing to celebrate," *The Guardian*, July 4, 2013.

7 Ibid.

8 Ibid.

9 Simon Allison, "Was South Sudan a Mistake," *The Guardian*, January 8, 2014.

10 Farah Stockman, "Cow–boy capitalist rush into world's newest nation as locals struggle and politicians take a cut," *Boston Globe*, June 9, 2013.

Bibliography

■■■■■■■■■■■■■❖■■■■■■■■■■■■

Sudan Conflict

Books

Abdel-Rahim, Muddathir. *Imperialism and Nationalism in the Sudan: A Study in Constitutional and Political Development, 1899-1956.* Oxford Studies in African Affairs. Oxford: Clarendon Press, 1969.

Abdel Rahim, Mudathir. "Arabism, Africanism, and Self–Identification in Sudan." In *Sudan in Africa*, edited by Yusuf Fadl Hasan. Khartoum: Khartoum University Press, 1971.

Adar, Korwa G. and John G. "Sudan Peace Process Challenges and Future Prospects." Edited by Nyuot Yoh and Maloka Eddy. Africa Institute of South Africa, 2004.

Akol, Lam. *Southern Sudan Colonialism, Resistance and Autonomy.* Trenton, NJ: The Red Sea Press, 2007.

Akol, Lam. *SPLM/SPLA: Inside an African Revolution.* Khartoum University Press, 2001.

Alier, Abel. *Southern Sudan: Too Many Agreements Dishonoured.* Ithaca Press, 1990.

An-Na'im, Abdullahi Ahmed. "Constitutional Discourse and the Civil War in the Sudan." In *Civil War in the Sudan*, edited by Martin Daly and Ahmed alawd Sikainga. London: British Academic Press, 1993.

An-Na'im, Abdullahi Ahmed. "National Unity and the Diversity of Identities." In *The Search for Peace and Unity in the Sudan*, edited by Francis Deng and Prosser Gifford. Washington, DC: Wilson Center Press, 1987.

Beshir, Mohamed Omer. *The Southern Sudan: From Conflict to Peace.* London: C. Hurst and Company, 1974.

Beswick, Stephanie. *Sudan's Blood Memory.* University Of Rochester Press, 2004.

Deng, Lual A. *The Power of Creative Reasoning: The Ideas and Visions of John Garang.* Bloomington: iUniverse, 2013.

Deng, Francis Mading. *Sudan At The Brink: Self–Determination and National Unity.*" New York: Fordham University Press and The Institute for International Humanitarian Affairs, 2010.

Deng, Francis M., ed. *New Sudan in the Making.* Trenton: Red Sea Press, 2010.

Duffield, Mark R. *Global Governance and the New Wars: The Merging of Development and Security.* Zed Books, 2001.

Ghani, Ashraf and Clare Lockhart. *Fixing Failed States.* Oxford University Press, 2008.

Godana, Bonya Adhi. *Africa's Shared Water Resources: Legal and Institutional Aspects of the Nile, Niger and Senegal River Systems.* London: Frances, 1985.

Hasan, Yusuf Fadl, ed. *Sudan in Africa.* Khartoum: Khartoum University Press, 1971.

Iyob, Ruth and Khadiagala, Gilbert M. *Sudan: The Elusive Quest For Peace.* Lynne Rienner Publishers Inc., 2006.

James, Wendy. *War and Survival in Sudan's Frontierlands.* Oxford University Press, 2007.

Johnson, Douglas. *The Root Causes of Sudan's Civil Wars.* Oxford: James Currey, 2003.

Johnson, Hilde. *Waging Peace in Sudan.* Brighton: Academic Press, 2011.

Kaplan, Jeth. *Fixing Fragile States.* Hoover Institute of Policy Review, Stanford University, December 4, 2008.

Khalid, Mansour, ed. *Garang Speaks.* London: Kegan Paul International, 1987.

Khalid, Mansour, ed. *The Call for Democracy in Sudan.* Kegan Paul International, 1990.

Khalid, Mansour. *Nimeiri and the Revolution of Dis-May.* London: Kegan Paul International, 1985.

Khalid, Mansour. *The Government They Deserve: The Role of the Elite in Sudan's Political Evolution.* London: Kegan Paul International, 1990.

Khalid, Mansour. *War and Peace in Sudan: A Tale of Two Countries.* London: Kegan Paul International, 2003.

LeRiche, Matthew and Arnold Matthew. *South Sudan from Revolution to Independence.* London: C. Hurst & Co., 2012.

Lesch, Ann Mosely. *The Sudan: Contested National Identities.* Bloomington: Indiana University Press, 1998.

Mavrogordato, Jack. *Behind the Scenes: An Autobiography.* Tisbury: Elements Books, 1982.

Martin, Harriet. *Kings of Peace, Pawns of War: The Untold Story of Peace–Making.* London: The Centre for Humanitarian Dialogue, 2006.

Ministry of Foreign Affairs. *Peace and Unity in the Sudan: An African Achievement.* Khartoum University Press, 1973.

Natsios, Andrew. *Sudan, South Sudan, and Darfur: What Everyone Needs To Know.* Oxford University Press, 2012.

Niblock, Tim. *Class and Power in the Sudan.* London: Macmillan, 1996.

Nyaba, Peter Adwok. *The Politics of Liberation in South Sudan: An Insider's View.* Kampala: Fountain Publishers, 1997.

Roland Paris. *At War's End: Building Peace after Civil Conflict.* Cambridge University Press, 2004.

Reining, Conrad. *The Zande Scheme.* Evanston: Northwestern University Press, 1966.

Shanmugaratnam, N., ed. *Between War & Peace in Sudan and Sri Lanka.* Oxford: James Currey, 2008.

Sikaianga, Ahmed Alawad. "Some Comments on Militias in the Contemporary Sudan." In *Civil War in the Sudan,* edited by M.W. Daly and Ahmed Alawad Sikainga. London: British Academic Press, 1993.

Taha, Faisal A. *The Sudan Ethiopian Boundaries Dispute.* Abu Dhabi Printing and Publishing, 1983.

Terje, Tredt. *The River Nile in the Age of the British: Political Ecology and the Quest for Economic Power.* The American University in Cairo Press (published by arrangement with I.B. Tauris and Co. Ltd.), 2004.

Toynbee, Arnold Joseph. *Between Niger and Nile.* Oxford University Press, 1965.

Waihenya, Waithaka. *The Mediator: General Lazaro Sumbeiywo and the Southern Sudan Peace Process.* Nairobi: Kenway Publications, 2006.

Woodward, Peter. *Sudan 1898 – 1989: The Unstable State.* Boulder: Lynne Rienner, 1990.

John Young, John. *The Fate of Sudan: The Origins and Consequences of A Flawed Peace Process.* London: Zed Books Ltd., 2012.

Zartman, I. William. *Ripe for Resolution: Conflict and Intervention in Africa.* Oxford University Press, 2012.

Documents, Articles, and Reports

Adar, Korwa G. "New Regionalism and Conflict Resolution: The Case of IGAD in Sudan." *African Journal on Conflict Resolution* (2) (2000a): 39-66.

Addis Ababa Peace Agreement 1972. http://www.madin-gaweil.com/addis-ababa-peace-agreement-1972.htm.

Affendi, Abdelwahab el. "The Impasse in the IGAD Peace Process for Sudan: The Limits of Regional Peacemaking?" *African Affairs,* Vol. 100, No. 401 (October 2001): 581-599.

Affendi, Abdelwahab el. "Discovering the South: Sudanese Dilemmas for Islam in Africa." *African Affairs,* Vol. 89 (July 1990): 37-389.

Ahmed, Abdel Ghaffar M., ed. "Tribal Elite: A base for social stratification in the Sudan." Economic and Social Research Council, National Council for Research, Khartoum (1976).

Arnold, Matthew and Matthew Le Riche. "Neither 'joint' nor 'integrated': The Joint Integrated Units and the Future of the CPA." Geneva: Sudan Human Security Baseline Assessment, Small Arms Survey (2008).

Arnold, Matthew B. and Chris Alden. "'This Gun Is Our Food': Disarming the White Army Militias of South Sudan." Conflict, Security and Development 7 (2007): 361–385

Batthani, Atta. "A Complex Web: Politics and Conflict in Sudan." In Peace by Piece, Addressing Sudan's Conflicts. Edited by Mark Simmons and Peter Dixon. Conciliation Resources, Accord, Issue 18 (2006): 10-13.

Cape Town University. "Stabilizing Sudan: Domestic, Sub Regional and Extra–Regional." Centre for Conflict Resolution (August 2011).

Carter Center. "Preliminary Statement on the Final stages of Sudan's Electoral Process" (17 March, 2010).

Carter Center." Report on Widespread Irregularities in Sudan's Vote Tabulation" (10 May, 2010).

Carter Center. "Preliminary Statement of the Election Observation Mission in Sudan Presidential, Gubernatorial, and Legislative Elections" (17 April, 2010).

Carter Center. "Urging Political Parties and Blue Nile Popular Consultation Commission to Ensure Genuine Dialogue on Key Issues in Blue NILE State." Khartoum (21 March, 2011).

"Communique." Sudan People's Liberation Movement. SPLM Interim Political Bureau Meeting No. 2, Juba (October 4–11, 2007).

Craven, Mathew. "The Problem of State Succession and Identity of States under International Law." European Journal of International Law 9 (1998).

Danforth, John C. (US Special Envoy to Sudan). "Report to the President of the United States on the outlook for peace in Sudan." US Department of State, Washington DC (2002).

Deng, Luka Biong. "The Sudan Comprehensive Peace Agreement: A Framework for Sustainable Peace and Democratic Transformation of Sudan." Statement to United States Congress Subcommittee on Africa and Global Health, The House Committee on Foreign Affairs (18 June 2007) http://www.sudantribune.com.

Deng, Francis and Morrison, J. Stephen. "US Policy to End Sudan's War." Report of the CSIS Task Force on US – Sudan Policy, John Hopkins University, Center for Strategic and International Studies, Washington DC (2001).

Final report of the Panel of Experts relating to sanctions in the Sudan as requested by the Security Council in paragraph 2 of resolution 1665 (2006)
http://www.un.org/ga/search/view_doc.asp?symbol=S/2006/795

Garfield, Richard. "Violence and Victimization after Civilian Disarmament: The Case of Jonglei." Geneva: Small Arms Survey, Graduate Institute of International Studies (2007).

General literature on Abyei: Abyei Area Boundaries, Map 1, Abyei Boundary Commission Report, at http://www.gurtong.net/Forum/tabid/81/forumid/107/threadid/42852/scope/posts/Default.aspx

Human Rights Watch/Africa, 'Behind the Red Line: Political Repression in Sudan' (USA, Human Rights Watch/Africa, 1996), http://www.un.org/ga/search/view_doc.asp?symbol=S/2006/795

IGAD Secretariat. "Ownership of Land and Natural Resources." Land Commission Draft Framework. (15 October 2003) Naivasha, Kenya, http://www.splmtoday.com/Draftframework.html.

International Crisis Group. "Sudan's Best Chance for Peace: How Not to Lose It." *Africa Report* No. 52, Nairobi / Brussels (17 September 2002).

International Crisis Group. "Sudan Endgame." Africa Report No. 65, Nairobi/ Brussels (25 June 2003).

International Crisis Group. "Nakuru Protocol, draft framework for resolution of outstanding issues arising out of the elaborations of the Machakos Protocol."(July 2003).

International Crisis Group. "Towards an Incomplete Peace." *Africa Report* No.73. Nairobi /Brussels (11 December 2003).

International Crisis Group. "The Khartoum –SPLM Agreement: Sudan's Uncertain Peace." *Africa Report* No.96, Nairobi/Brussels.

International Crisis Group. "Sudan's Comprehensive Peace Agreement: The Long Road Ahead." *Africa Report* No.106, Nairobi/Brussels (31 Mar 2006).

International Crisis Group. "Dialogue or Destruction? Organizing for Peace as the War in Sudan Escalates." *Africa Report* No.48, Nairobi/Brussels (27 June 2006).

International Crisis Group. "A Strategy for Comprehensive Peace in Sudan." *Africa Report* No. 130, Nairobi/Brussels (26 Jul 2007).

International Crisis Group. "Sudan's Comprehensive Peace Agreement: Beyond the Crisis." *Africa Report* No. 106, Nairobi/Brussels (March 13, 2008).

Johnson, Douglas H. "The Abyei Protocol Demystified." *Sudan Tribune*, December 10, 2007.

Johnson, Douglas H. "Why Abyei Matters: The Breaking Point of Sudan's Comprehensive Peace Agreement?" *African Affairs* 107 (2007): 1–19.

Juba Declaration on Unity and Integration between the Sudan People's Liberation Movement/Army (SPLM/A) and the South Sudan Defence Forces (SSDF), January 8, 2006.

Land Tenure Study in Southern Sudan: Key Findings and Recommendations for Southern Sudan Land Policy. Washington, DC: United States Agency for International Development, 2010.

Lyman, Princeton. "A Comprehensive Assessment: Toward US Policy in Sudan." Testimony before the House of Representatives, Sub-Committee on Africa, Global Health and Human Rights, Washington DC, October 4, 2011.

Mamdani, Mahmood. "South Sudan and the African Experience: The Quest for a New Political Order." 20 May, 2011, https://indypendent.org/2011/05/20/south-sudan-and-african-experience-quest-new-political-order.

Mbeki, Thabo (AUHIP chairman). "Remarks," at the Ceremony to Announce the Final Results of the South Sudan Referendum, Khartoum, 7 February 2011.

Muggah, Robert. "Reflections on Disarmament, Demobilisation and Reintegration in Sudan." *Humanitarian Exchange Magazine* 33, April 2006.

Muggah, Robert. "Stabilizing Fragile States and Humanitarian Space." In *Ending Wars, Consolidating Peace: Economic Perspectives*, Mats Berdal and Achim Wennammann. London: International Institute for Strategic Studies, 2011.

Nantulya, Paul. "The Machakos Protocol and Prospects for Peace in Sudan." *Accord*, Issue 4 (2003): 11-12.

Petterson, Donald, Kassahun Berhanu, Shadrack B. O. Gtto, Douglas H. Johnson, and Godfrey Muriuki. *Abyei Boundaries Commission Report.* IGAD, www.sudanarchive.net.

Prunier, Gerard. "Oil and war in Sudan." *Les Cahiers de l'IFRA*, No. 21 (2001):123-128

Rotberg, Robert. *Failed States in a World of Terror.* Council of Foreign Relations, Washington, DC, July – August 2002.

Rottenburg, Richard, Guma Kuna Koney, and Enrico Ille. "The Genesis of Recurring Wars in Sudan." *Rethinking the Violent Conflicts in the Nuba Mountains / South Kordofan.* University of Halle, October 2011.

Salahuddin, Ghazi. "Post –Secession Sudan: Challenges and Opportunities." Lecture at School of Oriental and African Studies, London, 17 December, 2011.

Salman, Salman M. A. "Water Resources in the Sudan: Past Experiences and Future Trends." *African Yearbook of International Law*, 16 (2010).

Salmon, Jago. *A Paramilitary Revolution: The Popular Defence Forces.* Geneva: Small Arms Survey, Graduate Institute of International Studies, 2007.

Schomerus, Mareike. *The Lord's Resistance Army in Sudan: A History and Overview.* Geneva: Small Arms Survey, Graduate Institute of International Studies, 2007.

Schomerus, Mareike and Tim Allen. "South Sudan At Odds With Itself: Dynamic of Conflict and Predicaments Of Peace." London School of Economics and Political Science, London, 2010.

Simmons, Mark and Peter Dixon, eds. "Peace by Piece: Addressing Sudan's Conflicts." London: Conciliation Resources, 2006.

"The Southern Front Reopens." *Africa Confidential* 47 (December 15, 2006).

"SPLM Withdraws from Sudan National Unity Government." *Sudan Tribune* (Khartoum), October 11, 2007.

SPLM Manifesto, SPLM Secretariat Torit, 31 July, 1983.

SPLM Strategic Framework for War-to-Peace Transition. New Site, Kapoeta County: SPLM Economic Commission, 2004.

SPLM/SPLA Torit Resolutions. SPLM/SPLA Political High Command, Torit, Equatoria, September 12, 1991.

Sudan Country Analysis Brief, Washington, DC: U.S. Energy Information Administration, 2010.

Sudan Joint Assessment Mission. "Conflict Analysis Guidelines," Domenico Polloni, Senior Policy Advisor – United Nations, Khartoum / Nairobi JAM Conflict Advisor – North / South. www.unmis.org, accessed 23 July, 2005.

Temin, John and Theodore Murphy. "Towards a New Republic of Sudan." Washington, DC, United States Institute of Peace, 2011.

Thomas, Edward. "Sudan, Against the Gathering Storm." Chatham House, Royal Institute of International Affairs, London, 2009.

Tothill, J. D. "An experiment in the social emergence of indigenous races in remote places." Memorandum in Ministry of Agriculture, Khartoum, File 2-1, Vol. 1, 1943.

United Nations Sudan Sanctions Committee. "Report of the Panel of Experts" (October 2006).

"Sudan Framework for Sustained Peace, Development and Poverty Eradication." The World Bank, United Nations, and International Monetary Fund, Staff Assessment of Progress, February 15, 2006.

UNHCHR. "Access to Justice for victims of sexual violence." Report of UN High Commissioner for Human Rights, 29 July 2005.

"The UN Strongly Condemns the Killing of an Indian Peacekeeper in Southern Sudan," United Nations Mission in Sudan Press Release, Khartoum, Juba, January 27, 2007.

Vergee, Aly. "Unfinished Business, State Elections in South Kordofan: Briefing for the Rift Valley Institute." March 31, 2011.

Vuni, Isaac. "30 Killed in Sudan's Eastern Equatoria after Ugandan LRA Attacks." Sudan Tribune (Kapoeta), January 16, 2007.

Darfur

Aegis Trust. "Darfur – Management of a Genocidal Crisis" (November 2004) Amnesty International. "Darfur – Rape as a Weapon of War: Sexual Violence and its Consequences" (19 July 2004).

Austin, Greg and Ben Koppelman. *Darfur and Genocide: Mechanisms for Rapid Response, an End to Impunity.* London: Foreign Policy Centre, 2004.

Bolton, John R. "The Risks and Weaknesses of the International Criminal Court from America's Perspective." *Law and Contemporary Problem* 167 (Winter 2011)

Burr, J. Millard and Robert O. Collins. *Darfur: The Long Road to Disaster.* Princeton: Markus Weiner, 2006.

"Darfur Documents Confirm Government Policy of Militia Support." Human Rights Watch (2004).

De Waal, Alex. *Islamism and its Enemies in the Horn of Africa.* London: Indiana University Press, 2004.

De Waal, Alex. *Famine That Kills: Darfur, Sudan, 1984-1985.* Oxford: Clarendon, 1989.

De Waal, Alex. "Counter-insurgency on the cheap." London Review of Books, 5 August, 2004.

De Waal, Alex. "Who are the Darfurians? Arab and African Identities, Violence and External Engagement." *African Affairs* 104 (2005): 181-206.

De Waal, Alex. "Briefing: Darfur, Sudan – prospects for peace." *African Affairs* 104 (2005): 127-36.

De Waal, Alex, ed. *War in Darfur and the Search for Peace.* Global Equity Initiative/Justice Africa, 2007.

El - Battahani, Atta. "Ideological Expansionist Movements versus Historical Indigenous Rights in the Darfur Region of Sudan." In *Darfur and the crisis of Governance in Sudan,* edited by Hassan and Ray, 52.

Eltom, Abdullahi. "Darfur: Inside the Crisis." *Democracy Now,* September 5, 2006. http://www.democracynow.org,accessed

Flint, Julie, Leslie Lefkow, and Jemera Rone. "Darfur Destroyed: Ethnic Cleansing by Government Militia Forces in Western Sudan." *Human Rights Watch* 16 (2004).

Flint, Julie and Alex de Waal. *Darfur: A Short History of a Long War.* London: Zed Books, 2005.

Foreign Policy Committee. "Darfur and Genocide: Mechanisms for Rapid Response – and End to Impunity," August 2004.

Grono, Nick. "Briefing–Darfur: The International Community's Failure to Protect," *African Affairs* 105 (2006): 621–32.

Haggar, Ali. "The Origins and Organization of the Janjawiid in Darfur." In *War in Darfur and the Search for Peace*, edited by Alex de Waal. Cambridge, Mass: Harvard University Press, 2007

Harir, Sharif. "Arab belt versus African belt: ethnic and political strife in Darfur and cultural and regional factors." In Sudan: Short Cut to Decay, edited by Sharif Harir and Terje Tvedt. Uppsala, 1997, 144-85.

Hassan, Salah and Ray, Carina E., eds. *Darfur and the Crisis of Governance in Sudan: A Critical Reader.* Ithaca: Cornell University Press, 2009.

Human Rights Watch. "Darfur in Flames – Atrocities in West Sudan," (2 April, 2004).

Human Rights Watch. "Darfur Destroyed: Ethnic Cleansing by Government Militia Forces in Sudan," (May 2004).

Human Rights Watch. "Darfur documents confirm government policy of militia support," (July 2004).

International Crisis Group. "Darfur Rising: Sudan's New Crisis." *Africa Report* No. 76, Nairobi/Brussels, (25 March, 2004). www.crisisgroup.org.

International Crisis Group. "Peace in Northern Uganda?," *African Report* No. 41, Nairobi/Brussels (13 September, 2006).

International Crisis Group. "Getting the UN into Darfur." *Africa Report* No. 43, Nairobi/Brussels (12 October, 2006).

International Crisis Group. "Darfur's New Security Reality." *Africa Report* No. 134, Nairobi/Brussels (26 November, 2007).

International Crisis Group. "Sudan: Destroying Ethnic Identity." Vol. III, Issue XV (December 10, 1991).

International Crisis Group. "Sudan's Southern Kordofan Problem: The Next Darfur?" *Africa Report* 145 (21 October, 2008).

Johnson, Douglas. "Peace, Genocide and Crimes Against Humanity in Sudan." In *Violence, Political Culture and Development in Africa*, edited by P. Kaarsholm. Oxford: James Currey, 2005.

Kasfir, N. "Sudan's Darfur: is it genocide?" *Current History* 104, 682 (2005): 195-202.

Lefkow, Leslie and Jemera Rone. "Darfur in Flames: Atrocities in Western Sudan." *Human Rights Watch* 16 (2004).

Mamdani, Mahmood. *Saviors and Survivors: Darfur, Politics, and the War on Terror.* New York: Pantheon Books, 2009.

Mans, Ulrich. "Sudan: the new war in Darfur." *African Affairs* 103 (2004): 291-94.

Marchal, Roland. "Le soudan d'un conflit a l'autre." *Les Etudes de CERI* (Sept 2004): 107-8.

O'Fahey, R.S." Does Darfur have a Future in Sudan?" *Fletcher Forum of World Affairs*, 30, 1 (2006).

Prunier, Gerard. *Darfur: The Ambiguous Genocide*. London: Cornell University Press, 2005.

Slim, Hugo. "Dithering over Darfur? A Preliminary Review of the International Response." *International Affairs* 80 (2004): 811–28.

Smith, James and Ben Walker. *Darfur: Management of a Genocidal Crisis*. Retford, UK: Aegis Publishing House, 2004.

Totten, S. and Markusen, E. "The US Government Darfur Genocide investigation." Journal of Genocide Research, 7, 2 (2005): 279-90.

UNHCHR. "Situation of Human Rights in Darfur Region of Sudan." Report of the UN High Commissioner for Human Rights and follow-up to the World Conference on Human Rights, 7 May, 2004.

United Nations. "Report of the International Commission of Inquiry on Darfur to the United Nations Secretary – General, Pursuant to Security Council Resolution 1564 of 18 September 2004," New York, 2005.

United Nations. "Report of the International Commission of Inquiry on Darfur to the UN Secretary General," Geneva, 26 June, 2005.

Vehnamaki, M. "Darfur Scorched: Looming Genocide in Western Sudan." *Journal of Genocide Research*, 8, 1 (2006): 51-82.

General Literature on Oil

Alden, Chris. *China in Africa: Partner, Competitor, or Hegemon?* London, New York: Zed Books, 2007.

Alden, Christopher, Daniel Large, and Ricardo Soares de Oliveira. *China Returns to Africa: A Rising Power and a Continent Embrace*. London: C. Hurst Publishers, 2008.

Ballentine, Karen and Heiko Nitzschke. *Profiting from Peace: Managing the Resource Dimensions of Civil War*. Boulder, CO: Lynne Rienner Publications, 2005.

Batruch, Christine. "Oil and Conflict: Lundin Petroleum's Experience in Sudan." In *Business and Security: Public-Private Sector Relationships in a New Security Environment*, edited by A.J.K. Bailes and I. Frommelt, 148–60. Oxford: Oxford University Press, 2004.

"China Lends Sudan USD 3.6 Million, USD 1.2 Million Aid." *Sudan Tribune* (Khartoum), July 5, 2005.

Global Witness. "Fuelling Mistrust, The Need for Transparency in Sudan's Oil Industry," London, 2009.

Goodan, Peter S. "China Invests Heavily in Sudan's Oil Industry: Beijing Supplies Arms Used on Villagers." *Washington Post* (Leal, Sudan), December 23, 2004.

Gary, Ian and Terry Lynn Karl. Bottom of the Barrel: Africa's Oil Boom and the Poor. Baltimore, MD: Catholic Relief Services, 2003.

"Oil Shares Worry Investors, but Should They?" *Wall Street Journal*, April 9, 2003. http://online.wsj.com/article/SB1049851123174880000.html

"Ottawa Aids Firm in Genocide Case/Talisman Sued in U.S. over Sudan Role/Washington Asked to Intervene in Court." *Toronto Star*, July 6, 2005.

Patey, Luke Anthony. *A Complex Reality: The Strategic Behaviour of Multinational Oil Corporations and the New Wars in Sudan.* Copenhagen: Danish Institute for International Studies, 2006.

Sherman, Jake. *Private Sector Actors in Zones of Conflict: Research Challenges and Policy Responses.* New York: Fafo Institute for Applied Social Science Programme for International Cooperation and Conflict Resolution and the International Peace Academy, 2001.

Stiansen, Endre. "GOS Revenue, Oil and the Cost of the War." Paper presented at *Money Makes the War Go Round? The EU and Transforming the Economy of War in Sudan*, Brussels, June 12–13, 2002.

"Sudan's New Oil Wealth Still a Source of Conflict." *Sudan Tribune* (Lankien, South Sudan), January 11, 2006.

Swanson, Philip. *Fuelling Conflict: The Oil Industry and Armed Conflict.* New York: Fafo Institute for Applied Social Science, 2002.

"Talisman Marks End of Era with Completion of Sudan Sale." *Oil and Gas Journal* 101 (2003).

Total. "History of Total's Presence in Sudan." 2009 http://sudan.total.com/fichiers/mediaLibrary/SOUDAN/publicati ons/PDF_du_site_Total_au_Soudan_VA.pdf

Wu, Kang and Shair Ling Han. "Chinese Companies Pursue Oil and Gas Assets." *Oil and Gas Journal* 111 (2005).

Vesely, Milan. "Sudan Oil Fuels the Conflict." *African Business*, June 1, 2001.

Yunus, Kamarul. "Malaysian Firms to Gain from Sudan Peace." *Sudan Tribune* (Kuala Lumpur, Malaysia), January 13, 2005.

Index

■ ■ ■ ■ ■ ■ ■ ■ ■ ■ ■ ■ ■ ❖ ■ ■ ■ ■ ■ ■ ■ ■ ■ ■ ■ ■ ■

T